Handbook of Identity and Research

Seth J. Schwartz · Koen Luyckx ·
Vivian L. Vignoles

Editors

Handbook of Identity Theory and Research

Volume 2
Domains and Categories

Editors
Seth J. Schwartz
Department of Epidemiology
  and Public Health
Leonard M. Miller School of Medicine
University of Miami
1425 N.W. 10th Avenue, Suite 321
Miami, Florida 33136, USA
sschwartz@med.miami.edu

Koen Luyckx
Department of Psychology
Catholic University of Leuven
Tiensestraat 102
3000 Leuven
Belgium
koen.luyckx@psy.kuleuven.be

Vivian L. Vignoles
School of Psychology
University of Sussex
Falmer, Brighton BN1 9QH
UK
v.l.vignoles@sussex.ac.uk

Printed in 2 volumes
ISBN 978-1-4419-7987-2 (hardcover)   ISBN 978-1-4419-7988-9 (eBook)
ISBN 978-1-4614-5102-0 (softcover)
DOI 10.1007/978-1-4419-7988-9
Springer New York Heidelberg Dordrecht London

Library of Congress Control Number: 2011921352

Springer is part of Springer Science+Business Media (www.springer.com)

For my maternal grandparents, Larry and Alvina Joseph, who were so important to me as a child; and for my wife, Lisa, and my daughters, Angelica and Alexia, who are so important to me now.

Seth J. Schwartz

For my parents, my wife Els, and my children Guust and Frida.

Koen Luyckx

For Claudia, Luca, and Marta Vignoles, with all my love and gratitude for their patience with my identity work.

Vivian L. Vignoles

Preface

There is a story behind this book. I will tell it from a first-person perspective, because it starts – and ends – with a promise I made to my mentor many years ago. The story helps to place the book into context, as well as to detail the sequence of "happy accidents" that occurred along the way and helped to bring the book through to completion.

The story starts back in 1995, when I was a graduate student under the tutelage of the late Dr. Richard (Dick) Dunham, Professor of Psychology at Florida State University. Dick told me one day that he had an idea that he was really excited about, and he just couldn't wait to tell me what it was. We were riding in his car with the convertible top down on a warm spring day when he said, "Let's write a book – a grand book about identity!" I looked at him in amazement, and then we shook hands and I promised him that we would work together to create the book.

For a couple of years, we talked about the book, and all the people we wanted to write chapters. We even held a retreat with some prospective co-editors, but Dick's declining health – and my move to Miami to pursue my doctoral degree at Florida International University – made it virtually impossible to pull the book together. Dick retired in the summer of 1998 and moved to San Diego, California, and his health continued to worsen until his death in April 2002.

For years after Dick retired, I put the book out of my mind. I finished my doctoral degree, got married, started my first assistant professorship, and became a father. Then, in the summer of 2007, I had an e-mail conversation with someone working in a completely different subfield of identity from the one I was working in. Through this exchange, I discovered how vast and fragmented the identity literature is. Consequently, the exchange reawakened the book and the promise I made to Dick Dunham.

A few months later, in late December 2007, I had a flash of inspiration. It was time to put together a "grand book" of identity that would bring together the various "identity literatures" in one place for the very first time. I ran home, sat down at my computer, and put together a table of contents. I came up with a list of about 15 chapters and a "wish list" of authors for them. At this point, however, I had no idea who would be willing to publish such a book.

Meanwhile, my Belgian colleague Koen Luyckx, with whom I had been collaborating for about 3 years, had graciously invited me to co-chair a symposium that he had put together for the biennial meeting of the Society for

Research on Adolescence, which would be held in Chicago in early March 2008. On February 28, 2008, I received an e-mail from Judy Jones, a senior book editor at Springer, saying that she had spotted our symposium in the conference program book and wanted to explore whether a book could be created out of the presentations in our symposium. Sure, I'll meet with her, I thought. I'll see what she thinks of the "grand book" idea.

I met Judy for lunch on March 6, 2008, and I brought my laptop computer with the table of contents that I had written in December. Before she could start asking me about the symposium, I opened the computer and showed Judy the table of contents. She thought for a minute or two and then erupted with enthusiasm. "This is a great idea!" she told me. "This is definitely something we'd be interested in publishing." She told me that she would send me a proposal form, and that I should get started identifying chapter authors. "But you're going to need help," Judy advised. "This project is too big for you to do by yourself."

When I returned home from the conference, Judy e-mailed me the book proposal form, and I completed it immediately. I started thinking of anyone and everyone I knew who was prominent in any subfield of identity – people who were colleagues as well as those whose work I had read and cited in the past. I set to work e-mailing these people and inviting them to contribute chapters. Almost everyone said yes. The book was starting to come together!

It occurred to me shortly thereafter that Judy would never have contacted me had it not been for Koen's generosity in inviting me to co-chair his symposium, so I decided to invite him to co-edit the book with me. Koen was an emerging scholar in the personal identity literature, and he had a number of colleagues and contacts in Europe who were working on identity. He would be a valuable addition to the editorship. He took a few days to think about it, and then he agreed. He recruited some of his colleagues and other people whose work he knew to write chapters, and by this time we were up to about 25 chapters. But something was missing. Koen and I knew a little about the social-psychological side of identity theory and research, but we knew that we didn't know enough. We needed a third co-editor to cover those areas of identity and, after consulting with some people, Viv Vignoles was recommended as a potential co-editor.

Koen and I put together an e-mail to Viv, explaining how the book project had come about and what we were looking for in a third co-editor. Like Koen, Viv took a few days to think about it and then, after exchanging a few e-mails, Viv was aboard, and our editorial team was complete. As luck would have it, not only was Viv well-versed in the social-psychological perspectives that we had sought to cover, but he also argued for including several perspectives from the self-concept literature, and he introduced Koen and me to some sociological and discursive perspectives that previously we had hardly been aware of. We realized that the field of Identity Studies was even bigger (and more disconnected) than we had thought! And Viv was the perfect person to complete our editorial team. Once more, things seemed to be moving into place naturally, almost as though the process was being guided by an invisible hand.

Viv proceeded to suggest a reorganization of our table of contents, as well as a number of new chapters that should be included. The table of contents quickly increased from 25 chapters to 40. As Koen and I had done earlier, Viv invited prominent scholars to write chapters, and the large majority of them accepted the invitation. Koen, Viv, and I marveled among ourselves how this book was coming together, and that so many people, many of whom were major names and leaders in their respective fields, were willing to contribute chapters to this book that we were editing. Even though all three of us were still at a fairly junior level within the academic profession, chapter authors appeared to sense that we were putting together something very timely and important. By June, we had commitments for almost all of the chapters on the list.

Chapters started coming in by the early fall of 2008, and we knew we had our work cut out for us. For each chapter, one of us was designated as the editor, and another of us acted as a reviewer. The "editor" was responsible for securing one or more outside reviewers for the chapter, such that each chapter would be reviewed by at least two people. In some cases, these reviewers were authors of other chapters. One of our goals was to integrate and build bridges among these various perspectives, so having contributors review each other's chapters seemed like a logical way to facilitate this. In other cases, people who were outside the book – many of whom we did not know personally, and from many different academic disciplines – contributed their time and expertise to improve the chapters. We thank and appreciate every one of them for the time and expertise that they contributed to the book.

One of Dick's original objectives for the book, and one that we emphasized strongly, was the need to facilitate integration among the various perspectives on identity. As we discuss in much more detail in the introductory chapter, many of the subfields of identity operate almost in isolation, such that often they are hardly aware of one another's existence. One of the purposes of this "grand book," then, was to build bridges among areas of the Identity Studies literature that otherwise would have remained separate and unconnected. In our in-text comments on each of the chapters, Koen, Viv, and I suggested key places where other chapters – especially chapters from alternative schools of thought – could be cross-referenced. Chapter authors were generally grateful for these suggestions, and many of them asked us to send them copies of the chapters we were asking them to cross-reference. Even within the writing and editing process, our goal to facilitate integration within the identity literature was beginning to be accomplished.

Our deadline to submit the book to Springer was the end of August 2010. Koen, Viv, and I continued reviewing and re-reviewing chapters until the very end of that month. The last chapter was accepted on the morning of August 31st, and we submitted the completed manuscript to Springer at 11:54 pm US Eastern time that night – exactly 6 min before the deadline. Dick Dunham's dream had become a reality. The "grand book" on identity had been finished.

I have many people to thank for helping to make this book a reality. I am extremely grateful to Koen and Viv for co-editing this book with me and for believing in the promise of facilitating integration among the many sub-fields of identity. Judy was prophetic when she advised me that I could never have done this alone. Even with three of us working together, it took a huge amount of work to bring this project to completion. I could not have asked for two more dedicated, enthusiastic, hardworking, and absolutely brilliant co-editors. I thank them both from the bottom of my heart.

Koen, Viv, and I also owe Judy a huge debt of gratitude. She gave the original go-ahead for the handbook, and she supported us every step of the way. She was there to answer all of our questions and to reassure us when we needed it. We are very grateful.

The three of us also wish to acknowledge Garth Haller at Springer for guiding the book through the copy-editing, typesetting, proof correction, and publishing process. We thank him for all his help.

Most of all, I want to thank Dick Dunham for discovering me as a 19-year-old college student, for pushing me until I finally started to realize my potential, and for teaching me so much about the world (both academically and in general). It is an honor and a pleasure to have stewarded his dream to reality, and I am humbled that I was the one that he trusted enough to leave it with.

Miami, Florida, USA   Seth J. Schwartz
September 2, 2010

Contents

Volume 2   Domains and Categories

About the Editors

Seth J. Schwartz is associate professor in the Department of Epidemiology and Public Health at the University of Miami Leonard M. Miller School of Medicine in the United States. He received his master's degree in family and child sciences from Florida State University and his PhD in developmental psychology from Florida International University. His research focuses on identity, broadly defined, including both personal and cultural identity; on acculturation, ethnicity, and cultural adaptation; on parenting and parent–adolescent relationships; and the effects of identity and family processes on positive and negative adolescent and young adult psychosocial and health outcomes.

Koen Luyckx is assistant research professor in the Department of Psychology at the Catholic University of Leuven in Belgium. He received his master's degree in psychology and his PhD in developmental psychology from the Catholic University of Leuven. His primary research interests are personal identity processes; the transition to adulthood; parenting, parent–adolescent conflict, and parent–adolescent relationships; psychosocial adaptation to being afflicted with a chronic illness; coping; burn-out and engagement at the workplace; and long-term development of psychosocial indices and interdependencies across childhood and adolescence.

Vivian L. Vignoles is senior lecturer in the School of Psychology at the University of Sussex in the United Kingdom. He received his first degree in sociology and psychology from the University of Bristol and his PhD in social psychology from the University of Surrey. His primary research interests are in self and identity processes and cross-cultural psychology, especially the interplay of cultural, contextual, and motivational influences on identity construction, as well as combining qualitative and quantitative methodologies, and developing a better understanding of the relationship between individual and social representation processes.

Contributors

Jeffrey Jensen Arnett Department of Psychology, Clark University, Worcester, MA, USA, arnett@jeffreyarnett.com

Michael Bamberg Department of Psychology, Clark University, Worcester, MA, USA, mbamberg@clarku.edu

Verónica Benet-Martínez ICREA & Universitat Pompeu Fabra, Barcelona, Spain, veronbm@mail.ucr.edu

Peter L. Benson Search Institute, Minneapolis, MN, USA, peterb@search-institute.org

Michael D. Berzonsky Department of Psychology, State University of New York, Cortland, NY, USA, michael.berzonsky@cortland.edu

Wim Beyers Department of Developmental, Personality and Social Psychology, Ghent University, Ghent, Belgium, wim.beyers@ugent.be

Helen Boucher Bates College, Lewiston, ME, USA, hboucher@bates.edu

Ian Burkitt Department of Social Sciences and Humanities, University of Bradford, Bradford, UK, i.burkitt@bradford.ac.uk

Kay Bussey Department of Psychology, Macquarie University, Sydney, NSW, Australia, kay.bussey@mq.edu.au

Molly R. Butterworth Department of Psychology, University of Utah, Salt Lake City, UT, USA, molly.butterworth@psych.utah.edu

Gustavo Carlo Department of Psychology, University of Nebraska, Lincoln, NE, USA, gcarlo@unl.edu

Serena Chen Department of Psychology, University of California, Berkeley, CA, USA, serchen@berkeley.edu

Lisa M. Diamond Department of Psychology, University of Utah, Salt Lake City, UT, USA, diamond@psych.utah.edu

Frank R. Dillon Robert Stempel College of Public Health and Social Work, Florida International University, Miami, FL, USA, fdillon@fiu.edu

Helga Dittmar School of Psychology, University of Sussex, Falmer, Brighton, UK, h.e.dittmar@sussex.ac.uk

Anna De Fina Italian Department, Georgetown University, Washington, DC, USA, definaa@georgetown.edu

Naomi Ellemers Social Psychology of Organisations, Leiden University, Leiden, The Netherlands, ellemers@fsw.leidenuniv.nl

Jochen E. Gebauer Department of Psychology, Humboldt University of Berlin, Berlin, Germany, mail@jochengebauer.info

Luc Goossens Department of Psychology, Catholic University of Leuven, Leuven, Belgium, luc.goossens@psy.kuleuven.be

Eva G.T. Green Faculty of Social and Political Sciences, University of Lausanne, Lausanne, Switzerland, eva.green@unil.ch

Aiden P. Gregg School of Psychology, University of Southampton, Southampton, UK, a.gregg@soton.ac.uk

Harold D. Grotevant Department of Psychology, College of Natural Sciences, University of Massachusetts, Amherst, MA, USA, hgroteva@psych.umass.edu

Sam A. Hardy Department of Psychology, Brigham Young University, Provo, UT, USA, sam_hardy@byu.edu

Daniel Hart Center for Children and Childhood Studies, Rutgers University, Camden, NJ, USA, daniel.hart@rutgers.edu

S. Alexander Haslam School of Psychology, University of Exeter, Exeter, UK, a.haslam@exeter.ac.uk

Whitney L. Heppner Department of Health Disparities Research (Unit 1440), University of Texas M. D. Anderson Cancer Center, Houston, TX, USA, whithepp@gmail.com

Steven Hitlin Department of Sociology, University of Iowa, Iowa City, IA, USA, steven-hitlin@uiowa.edu

Que-Lam Huynh Department of Psychology, San Diego State University, San Diego, CA, USA, huynh.quelam@gmail.com

Leah James School of Social Work, University of Michigan, Ann Arbor, MI, USA, leahej@umich.edu

Lene Arnett Jensen Department of Psychology, Clark University, Worcester, MA, USA, ljensen@clarku.edu

Michael H. Kernis (deceased) Department of Psychology, University of Georgia, Athens, GA, USA

Lynn Von Korff Department of Family Social Science, University of Minnesota, St. Paul, MN, USA, vonko002@umn.edu

Michael W. Kraus Department of Psychology, University of California, Berkeley, CA, USA, mwkraus@gmail.com

Jane Kroger Psychology Department, University of Tromsø, Tromsø, Norway, jane.kroger@uit.no

Laurent Licata Social Psychology Unit, UniversitéLibre de Bruxelles, Bruxelles, Belgium, licata@ulb.ac.be

Koen Luyckx Department of Psychology, Catholic University of Leuven, Leuven, Belgium, koen.luyckx@psy.kuleuven.be

Douglas A. MacDonald Department of Psychology, College of Liberal Arts and Education, University of Detroit Mercy, Detroit, MI, USA, macdonda@udmercy.edu

Claudia Manzi Athenaeum Center for Family Studies and Research, Catholic University of Milan, Milano, Italy, claudia.manzi@unicatt.it

James E. Marcia Department of Psychology, Simon Fraser University, Burnaby, BC, Canada, marcia@sfu.ca

Dan P. McAdams Department of Human Development and Social Policy, Northwestern University, Evanston, IL, USA, dmca@northwestern.edu

Jessica McKenzie Department of Psychology, Clark University, Worcester, MA, USA, jemckenzie@clarku.edu

Lies Missotten Department of Psychology, Catholic University of Leuven, Leuven, Belgium, lies.missotten@psy.kuleuven.be

Bonnie Moradi Department of Psychology, University of Florida, Gainesville, FL, USA, moradib@ufl.edu

David Moshman Department of Educational Psychology, University of Nebraska, Lincoln, NE, USA, dmoshman1@unl.edu

Angela-MinhTu D. Nguyen Department of Psychology, University of California, Riverside, CA, USA, angela-minhtu.nguyen@email.ucr.edu

Daphna Oyserman Department of Psychology, School of Social Work, Institute for Social Research, University of Michigan, Ann Arbor, MI, USA, daphna.oyserman@umich.edu

Seth T. Pardo Department of Human Development, Cornell University, Ithaca, NY, USA, seth.pardo@gmail.com

Cameron Richardson Department of Human Development, University of Maryland, College Park, MD, USA, crichar1@umd.edu

Eugene C. Roehlkepartain Search Institute, Minneapolis, MN, USA, gener@search-institute.org

Margarita Sanchez-Mazas Faculty of Psychology and Educational Sciences, Geneva University, Geneva, Switzerland, margarita.sanchez-mazas@unige.ch

Ritch C. Savin-Williams Department of Human Development, Cornell University, Ithaca, NY, USA, rsw36@cornell.edu

Eugenia Scabini Athenaeum Centre for Family Studies and Research, Catholic University of Milan, Milano, Italy, eugenia.scabini@unicatt.it

Peter C. Scales Search Institute, Minneapolis, MN, USA, scalespc@search-institute.org

Deborah Schiffrin Department of Linguistics, Georgetown University, Washington, DC, USA, schiffrd@georgetown.edu

Deborah J. Schildkraut Department of Political Science, Packard Hall, Tufts University, Medford, MA, USA, deborah.schildkraut@tufts.edu

Seth J. Schwartz Department of Epidemiology and Public Health, Leonard M. Miller School of Medicine, University of Miami, Miami, FL, USA, sschwartz@med.miami.edu

Constantine Sedikides School of Psychology, University of Southampton, Southampton, UK, cs2@soton.ac.uk

Richard T. Serpe Department of Sociology, Kent State University, Kent, OH, USA, rserpe@kent.edu

Vladimir B. Skorikov Department of Psychology, University of Hawaii, Hilo, HI, USA, skorikov@hawaii.edu

Peter B. Smith School of Psychology, University of Sussex, Falmer, Brighton, UK, p.smith@sussex.ac.uk

Bart Soenens Department of Developmental, Personality, and Social Psychology, Ghent University, Gent, Belgium, bart.soenens@ugent.be

Russell Spears School of Psychology, Cardiff University, Cardiff, UK, spearsr@cardiff.ac.uk

Alex Stepick Department of Global and Sociocultural Studies, Florida International University, Miami, FL, USA, stepick@fiu.edu

Carol Dutton Stepick Research Center on Social and Economic Policy, Florida International University, Miami, FL, USA, stepick@fiu.edu

Sheldon Stryker Department of Sociology, Indiana University, Bloomington, IN, USA, strykers@indiana.edu

Adriana J. Umaña-Taylor School of Social and Family Dynamics, Program in Family and Human Development, Arizona State University, Tempe, AZ, USA, adriana.umana-taylor@asu.edu

Jennifer B. Unger Institute for Health Promotion and Disease Prevention Research, University of Southern California Keck School of Medicine, Alhambra, CA, USA, unger@usc.edu

Patricia Vanderkooy Department of Global and Sociocultural Studies, Florida International University, Miami, FL, USA, tricia.vanderkooy@gmail.com

Maarten Vansteenkiste Department of Developmental, Personality, and Social Psychology, Ghent University, Gent, Belgium, maarten.vansteenkiste@ugent.be

Vivian L. Vignoles School of Psychology, University of Sussex, Falmer, Brighton, UK, v.l.vignoles@sussex.ac.uk

Fred W. Vondracek Department of Human Development and Family Studies, Pennsylvania State University, University Park, PA, USA, fwv@psu.edu

Alan S. Waterman Department of Psychology, The College of New Jersey, Ewing, NJ, USA, water@tcnj.edu

Britt Wilkenfeld Department of Human Development, University of Maryland, College Park, MD, USA, britt_wilkenfeld@dpsk12.org

Roger L. Worthington Department of Educational, School and Counseling Psychology, University of Missouri, Columbia, MO, USA, worthington@missouri.edu

Part IV
Moral and Spiritual Domains

Moral Identity

Sam A. Hardy and Gustavo Carlo

Abstract

Moral identity is a construct at the intersection of moral development and identity formation. It is thought to be a source of moral motivation linking moral reasoning (our judgments about whether certain actions are right or wrong) to behavior. In other words, people with a stronger sense of moral identity will be more likely to do what they know is right, and more likely to show enduring moral commitments. In this chapter, we first discuss several conceptualizations of moral identity. Some scholars conceptualize moral identity as a trait-like tendency to view morality as central to one's explicit sense of identity. Others argue that underlying moral identity is a network of cognitively accessible moral schemas which aid in the processing of social information in moral situations. Second, we review moral exemplar studies, narrative studies, correlational studies, and experimental studies linking moral identity to moral action and enduring moral commitments. Third, we discuss the development of moral identity. Although most work suggests that moral identity primarily emerges in adolescence and young adulthood, we also point to some earlier foundations. Lastly, we note some skepticism regarding the moral identity concept, and outline directions for future research.

What is at the root of heroic moral acts and lifelong moral commitment? During World War II, potentially hundreds of thousands of people not of the Jewish faith helped Jews hide and survive ethnic cleansing under Nazi occupation, putting themselves and their families at risk. Other individuals, such as Mahatma Gandhi, Mother Teresa, and Bishop Desmond Tutu, are world-renowned for their persistent and far-reaching dedication to moral causes. Furthermore, millions throughout the world live praiseworthy lives of moral integrity, often in the face of great opposition. How are we to understand such commitment to morality? Can identity theory and research help us in this regard?

Most work on morality over the past half century has stemmed from Kohlberg's (1969) Cognitive Developmental Theory, which emphasized moral reasoning—defined as the capacity to make judgments about whether certain actions are right or wrong. But, several factors have

S.A. Hardy (✉)
Department of Psychology, Brigham Young University, Provo, UT, USA
e-mail: sam_hardy@byu.edu

led to greater interest in the role of identity in morality. First, moral reasoning is only a modest predictor of moral action (Blasi, 1980). Second, highly moral people do not have unusually sophisticated moral reasoning capacities (Colby & Damon, 1992). Hence, scholars such as Blasi (1980, 1983), Rest (1983), and even Kohlberg himself (Kohlberg & Candee, 1984), saw the need to identify moderators and mediators of links between moral reasoning and moral action. *Moral identity*, one such construct, capitalizes on identity theory and research to improve our understanding of moral motivation and commitment. In this chapter, we (1) outline various conceptions of moral identity; (2) identify psychological and behavioral outcomes of moral identity; and (3) discuss the processes and predictors of moral identity formation.

Conceptualizing Moral Identity

Defining moral identity is a formidable task, as the construct intersects two rich and highly abstract literatures: identity and morality. Generally, moral identity involves the importance or salience of morality to a person's identity. However, there are diverse perspectives on the details of what this means. Most approaches to moral identity can be classified as *character perspectives* or *social cognitive perspectives* (Lapsley, 2008; Monin & Jordan, 2009; Shao, Aquino, & Freeman, 2008). This distinction roughly aligns with the two disciplines of personality psychology: trait approaches and social cognitive approaches (Lapsley & Hill, 2009).

Character Perspectives

Approaches classified as character or "personological" perspectives are those that describe moral identity as a trait-like individual difference in the degree to which morality is central to one's identity and unified with one's personal values and goals. A great starting point for this approach to moral identity is the work of Augusto Blasi

(1983, 1984, 1995, 2004a). He drew attention to the potential gap between moral understanding and moral action, and argued that moral identity may help bridge that gap (Walker, 2004).

Blasi's Self Model: Blasi's (1983) Self Model of links between moral judgment and action has three components. First, before leading to moral action, a moral judgment may pass through a *judgment of responsibility*, such that an action is not only seen as moral, but as necessary for the individual—as his or her responsibility (cf. Kohlberg & Candee, 1984). Second, the criteria for judgments of responsibility often stem from the structure of the self. More specifically, what Blasi called *moral identity* reflects individual differences in the extent to which being moral is central or essential to one's sense of self. The third component of the Self Model is *self-consistency*, the natural human tendency to want to live consistently with one's sense of self. When a person's self is centered on moral concerns, this inclination serves as a key moral motivation. In summary, Blasi postulated that moral judgments might more reliably predict moral behavior if they are filtered through responsibility judgments based on moral identity, and propelled into action via the tendency toward self-consistency (for discussions of the Self Model, see Frimer & Walker, 2008; Hardy & Carlo, 2005; Walker, 2004).

Underlying Blasi's Self Model are his ideas about the structure of identity (Blasi, 1993, 2004b; Blasi & Glodis, 1995), based heavily on Erikson's (1968) notion of identity and Loevinger's (1976) work on ego development. Blasi argues that people differ both in terms of the issues around which they base their identities (identity contents—the things that make up one's identity) and the way they subjectively experience their identity (identity structure—the organization, maturity, and phenomenological experience of one's identity; others have made similar distinctions—see Berzonsky, Chapter 3, this volume; Oyserman & James, Chapter 6, this volume; Soenens & Vansteenkiste, Chapter 17, this volume). As subjective identity matures, the sense of self becomes based more on internal, psychological identity contents (e.g., values and goals) than external identity contents (e.g., physical characteristics, relationships, and behavior; see Damon & Hart, 1988). The self also becomes more organized and unified, with hierarchical organization of identity contents such that some are chosen as more central and essential than others (see Stryker & Serpe, Chapter 10, this volume; Vignoles, Chapter 18, this volume). Additionally, there is an increased sense of agency over one's self, such that the identity contents one cares most about are actively appropriated into the core self (similar to the notion of self-regulation or internalization in Self-Determination Theory; Soenens & Vansteenkiste, Chapter 17, this volume). Hence, with mature subjective identity there is a greater desire for self-consistency—fidelity with one's core self is seen as a necessity and self-inconsistency elicits intense negative affect (see Schlenker, Miller, & Johnson, 2009; Stryker & Serpe, Chapter 10, this volume; Vignoles, Chapter 18, this volume; Waterman, Chapter 16, this volume).

For Blasi, then, the structure of identity provides the key mechanism by which identity can serve as a source of motivation for moral action. For some people, morality is not simply about what is right or wrong, it is self-defining. Such individuals have identity contents which are moral (e.g., moral principles). However, even among individuals with moral identity contents, there is variability in how these contents are experienced. In other words, links between moral identity contents and moral action might be moderated by subjective identity maturity. More specifically, when individuals with mature subjective identity appropriate moral identity contents, the heightened sense of agency, self-consistency, and commitment to actualize one's core self can act as a powerful source of moral motivation. This has not been empirically tested.

Moral identity as unity between self and moral goals: Congruent with Blasi's ideas, Anne Colby and William Damon (1992) focused on moral identity as the unity of the moral and self systems. In their qualitative study of individuals known for exemplary moral commitments (i.e., moral exemplars), they found that such people experienced a unity between self and morality such that their own personal interests and desires were synonymous with their sense of what was morally right. In other words, moral exemplars "seamlessly integrate their commitments with their personal concerns, so that the fulfillment of one implies the fulfillment of the other" (Colby & Damon, 1992, p. 300). Perhaps moral commitments for such individuals are personally expressive, or what Waterman (Chapter 16, this volume) calls "eudaimonistic."

Such integration of personal and moral goals can serve as a powerful source of moral motivation and commitment (Colby & Damon, 1992; Frimer & Walker, 2009). Moral commitments are not seen as a sacrifice requiring self-denial because the self is defined with a moral center. Rather, moral exemplars would be denying the self only by failing to follow their moral sense. They do not perceive a dilemma or choice involved regarding their exemplary moral commitments; they are simply doing what they must do (see also Monroe, 2001). This enables them to act with certainty and spontaneity, with little fear, doubt, or hesitation.

Moral identity as altruistic personality: Some see moral identity as at the heart of, or nearly synonymous with an "altruistic personality" (Carlo, PytlikZillig, Roesch, & Dienstbier, 2009; Staub, 2005). The altruistic personality is a set of other-oriented tendencies or traits, such as empathy, social responsibility, and moral reasoning, which motivate prosocial behaviors and mitigate antisocial behaviors (whether deliberately or automatically; for reviews, see Carlo et al., 2009; Dovidio, Piliavin, Shroeder, & Penner, 2006). Care exemplars are individuals known for such altruistic personalities (Colby & Damon, 1992; Oliner & Oliner, 1988; Walker & Frimer, 2007). Driving or unifying the other-oriented tendencies of such individuals is a personal investment in helping others—indeed a sense of moral or altruistic identity.

Narrative moral identity: There is growing interest in narrative approaches to identity, which see a person's life story as a key component of identity (McAdams, Chapter 5, this volume). While some are skeptical of the usefulness of narrative approaches for understanding moral identity (Blasi, 2004a), others are quite intrigued (Frimer & Walker, 2009; McAdams, 2009; Pratt, Arnold, & Lawford, 2009). Pratt and colleagues argue that the essence of moral identity may be the extent to which moral values and moral themes are integrally woven throughout the fabric of our self-narratives. Studies of moral exemplars seem to echo the importance of such morally laden narratives to moral functioning (Colby & Damon, 1992).

Social Cognitive Perspectives

In recent years a number of scholars have attempted to draw on social cognitive theory to better understand moral identity (Cervone & Tripathi, 2009; Lapsley & Hill, 2009). Social cognitive theorists view personality as a dynamic system of cognitive–affective processes that interact with situational influences (Bandura, 1986; Mischel, 1968). Thus, these approaches attempt to find social cognitive mechanisms that underlie moral functioning.

Moral identity as chronically accessible moral schemas: Schemas are knowledge structures in the mind that can represent various aspects of ourselves, our relationships, and our experiences. Schemas that are more cognitively accessible are more readily activated for use in processing social information (Higgins, 1999). Moral identity may entail moral schemas being chronically accessible for interpreting and responding to social situations (Gibbs, 2009; Lapsley & Lasky, 2001; Lapsley & Narvaez, 2004; Narvaez, Lapsley, Hagele, & Lasky, 2006). Moral schemas seen by individuals as important to their sense of identity may also be those that are chronically accessible (Lapsley & Narvaez, 2004). This notion received some empirical validation recently (Aquino, Freeman, Reed, Lim, & Felps, 2009), and is in line with work on attitudes suggesting that importance and accessibility are moderators of attitude–behavior relations, with importance generally preceding accessibility (Ajzen & Fishbein, 2005).

Accessibility of moral schemas enables automaticity in moral responding and what might be seen as *moral expertise* (Narvaez & Lapsley, 2005). In other words, accessibility of moral schemas allows individuals to be more sensitive to moral aspects of situations, and to interpret and respond to those situations more quickly in light of their moral commitments. Moral exemplars may be experts in morality as others are experts at chess or piano. The high level of certainty and the lack of hesitancy that characterize their moral actions may be due to rich networks of accessible moral schemas (Lapsley & Narvaez, 2004; Narvaez & Lapsley, 2005).

Moral identity as a self-important social identity: One moral schema that may be most relevant to moral identity is an individual's conception of what it means to be a moral person (Aquino & Reed, 2002; Hitlin, Chapter 20, this volume; Stets & Carter, 2006). Social psychologists suggest we have different social identities for the various groups to which we belong (*group-based identities*), the roles we participate in (*role-based identities*), and the kind of people we want to portray ourselves as to others (*person identities*; Stets & Carter, 2006; see also Spears, Chapter 9, this volume; Stryker & Serpe, Chapter 10, this volume). These social identities are organized into a social self-schema, with some being more important to the self than others. Moral identity might be considered a potential "person" social identity organized around traits characteristic of a moral person. Two facets of this are the contents making up a person's moral identity (the traits he or she uses to describe a moral person) and the centrality of that moral identity to his or her self (Aquino & Freeman, 2009; Aquino & Reed, 2002; Stets & Carter, 2006). The more a person's moral identity is central to the self, the larger role it will play in behaviors and commitments (Stets, Carter, Harrod, Cerven, & Abrutyn, 2008). However, situational factors can influence the degree to which the moral identity is activated (Aquino & Freeman, 2009; Aquino et al., 2009; Monin & Jordan, 2009).

Moral identity as commitment to moral social roles: Some see moral identity as the degree to which moral actions and social roles are important to the self (Hart Atkins, & Frod, 1999; Kurtines, Mayock, Pollard, Lanza, & Carlo, 1991). In other words, rather than seeing moral identity as a "person" social identity (as above), they see it as one or more "role-based" social identities regarding the actions and roles most salient to us. In line with this, Hart and colleagues (Hart, 2005) use volunteer service as a marker or proxy for moral identity. Similarly, in their study of blood donors Piliavin and Callero (1991) used the centrality of the "blood donor" role to the self as an indicator of an "altruistic identity."

Moral identity as moral self-representations in autobiographical memory: The self is often seen as the organization of mental representations of self stored in autobiographical memory (Kihlstrom, Beer, & Klein, 2003). These self-representations, which include information about time, place, and role, are stored in memory aided by emotion. Thus, part of having a moral identity may involve self-representations being infused with moral meaning through moral emotions, and being stored and organized in one's autobiographical memory to create a moral self-narrative (Damasio, 1994; Lapsley, 2008; Reimer, 2003; Reimer & Wade-Stein, 2004). Anticipated consequences of possible actions are evaluated based on emotions associated with this moral self-narrative regarding similar situations and outcomes in the past. Thus, "somatic markers" or physiological correlates of moral emotion guide decision-making by providing moral intuitions that point toward and motivate moral actions.

Moral identity as a moral ideal self: Possible selves, like the desired or ideal self and the dreaded or feared self, are self-schemas that motivate future behaviors (Oyserman & James, Chapter 6, this volume). The desired self is a representation of the self one ideally wants to become in the future, and thus acts as a goal pulling the individual in a certain direction. The dreaded self, on the other hand, is the type of person one wants to avoid becoming. Part of having a moral identity might be the degree to which one's desired self is moral (and perhaps one's dreaded self is immoral). In this way, having a moral identity entails a commitment to being and becoming

what one sees as a moral person. However, little empirical work has examined this possibility.

Alternative Perspectives

Moral identity from an identity status paradigm: Much of the theory and research on identity formation may enrich understanding of moral identity. First, work stemming from Erikson's (1968) ideas sees identity formation as involving exploration and commitment. For example, from the identity statuses paradigm (Kroger & Marcia, Chapter 2, this volume), a person who has not made moral commitments might be in identity diffusion. An individual who dogmatically accepts moral principles taught by his or her parents or religion might fall under foreclosure. However, as individuals seek to personally validate moral principles through reflection and real-world experience (i.e., acting on moral principles and observing the consequences), they are in identity moratorium. Once they appropriate certain moral principles and commitments as their own, and see them as self-defining, they have reached identity achievement.

One of the primary domains of identity commitments the identity status paradigm has emphasized is ideological commitment. Although the measures have focused on commitments to religious and political views, and career choice, it seems this also encompasses moral principles. In this sense, a person with a strong moral identity might be one who has critically reflected on (i.e., explored) various moral principles and then made commitments to those moral principles seen as most important and self-defining.

One extension of the identity status paradigm further refines commitment and exploration to allow greater attention to processes rather than states of identity (Luyckx, Schwartz, Goossens, Beyers, & Missotten, Chapter 4, this volume). As part of this, they differentiate making commitments from further identification with those commitments. As people experiment with and elaborate on moral commitments they have made, those commitments deepen. This might explain the unity between personal and moral goals experienced by moral exemplars (Colby & Damon, 1992).

A second extension of the identity status paradigm, the *identity styles* model, focuses on three approaches to processing identity-relevant information: informational, normative, and diffuse-avoidant (see Berzonsky, Chapter 3, this volume). People with an informational orientation deliberately grapple with various "moral" principles and commitments to determine which should define them. On the other hand, normative-oriented individuals automatically adopt whatever moral principles and commitments seem consistent with norms held by people they care about. Lastly, diffuse-avoidant orientated people procrastinate thoughts of moral principles and commitments, and are driven more by situational factors. In short, the identity styles differ in the extent to which they may facilitate the processes of moral identity formation.

Moral identity from a relational perspective: Although there are a number of uses of the term "relational" (for review, see Chen et al., Chapter 7, this volume), what we are proposing here is a "strong relationality," where one's identity is not merely influenced by relationships but partially constituted by them (Slife, 2004). According to this approach, rather than being "self-contained objects" (Slife, 2004, p. 160) that internalize abstractions (e.g., moral values) from the outside, we are a "nexus of relationships" (Slife, 2004, p. 166), and are engaged in practices that are embedded in particular contexts (with the context construed broadly to include not only the immediate context, but also the historical context, for example). Thus, relationships are more fundamental to our experience and our nature than abstractions.

In terms of identity, a "relationist identity allows for individual uniqueness, but it does so through a distinct nexus of relationships rather than a distinct set of beliefs and values" (Slife, 2004, p. 166). Similarly, morality is not fundamentally about abstract universal moral principles that we must learn to apply to specific situations; rather, it is about context-dependent truths that we must learn to be sensitive to and respond to (Slife & Richardson, 2008). Further,

identity is unavoidably moral (i.e., there is no such thing as an amoral identity) in that morality is inherently a part of our world, and our identity is the framework from which we view and relate to the world (Taylor, 1989). Thus, a person with a moral identity is not a self-contained individual who appropriates moral principles into his or her sense of self, and carries a stable and explicit moral identity around with him or her. Rather, a person with a moral identity is one whose framework (i.e., identity) is aligned with the moral truths of his or her particular relational context, and who is committed to living truthfully to that framework (Williams & Olson, 2008). Additionally, a person with a moral identity values relationships to others and the community, and uses such relationships as moral compasses.

Potential Integrations

Work to compare and contrast these perspectives is nascent, so it is still unclear to what extent they are compatible, and if not, which best captures the phenomena of moral identity. From social cognitive perspectives, underlying the moral identity described by character perspectives is a network of moral schemas (Aquino & Freeman, 2009; Lapsley & Narvaez, 2004; Shao et al., 2008). In other words, moral issues that may be explicitly important to a person's identity are likely undergirded by cognitively accessible moral schemas. However, some worry this unnecessarily reduces moral identity to cognitive representations, thus not fully capturing or perhaps even allowing for the intentional and agentic nature of the self (Blasi, 2001; Campbell, Christopher, & Bickhard, 2002).

Another fundamental difference between the perspectives is the extent to which moral identity is seen as stable or variable across situations. Whereas the character perspectives see moral identity as a more stable and trait-like individual difference, social cognitive perspectives see it as more fluid, or "moment to moment," and situated in and influenced by the context (Aquino & Freeman, 2009; Lapsley & Narvaez, 2004; Monin & Jordan, 2009). Moral schemas which underlie moral identity must be activated in the situation for use in information processing. From a social cognitive perspective one possible integration is that what is relatively stable is the self-centrality or self-importance and chronic accessibility of moral schemas, but situational cues influence the likelihood that these schemas will be activated (Aquino et al., 2009). However, given that character perspectives generally question the presence or utility of schemas, this integration may not work for them (see Blasi, 2001).

In short, while some efforts at integration are being made, particularly among social cognitive scholars, it is unclear yet how much mileage will come from these resolutions. At the heart of the issue are fundamental differences in assumptions about the nature of morality and the self that may prevent satisfactory integration of these perspectives. For instance, from a relational perspective, moral identity is not even contained within the individual, but actually partially constituted by the context (Slife, 2004).

Linking Moral Identity to Moral Action

Moral identity may be an important source of moral motivation; in fact, some argue that it may be the best predictor of moral commitment and moral actions (Damon & Hart, 1992). The exact mechanisms involved depend on how moral identity is conceptualized. Such mechanisms might include self-consistency (e.g., Blasi, 2004a), autobiographical memory (e.g., Reimer, 2003), goals (e.g., Colby & Damon, 1992), and moral schemas (e.g., Narvaez & Lapsley, 2005). These mechanisms are in line with more general ideas about identity as a motivator of action (e.g., McAdams, Chapter 5, this volume.; Oyserman & James, Chapter 6, this volume; Soenens & Vansteenkiste, Chapter 17, this volume; Stryker & Serpe, Chapter 10, this volume; Vignoles, Chapter 18, this volume). Although few mechanisms of moral identity have been systematically examined, empirical work has fairly consistently found moderately strong links between moral identity and moral action. Four types of studies provide information about outcomes of

moral identity: moral exemplar studies, narrative studies, correlational studies, and experimental studies. While some of these studies take a character approach (e.g., Colby & Damon, 1992; Hart & Fegley, 1995), others are from a social cognitive orientation (e.g., Aquino, Reed, Thau, & Freeman, 2007; Stets & Carter, 2006). Across perspectives, findings consistently link moral identity to morally relevant outcomes.

Moral Exemplar Studies

In these studies, exemplary moral individuals are identified through a nomination process and studied in detail using qualitative and quantitative methods, and, in some cases, moral exemplars are compared to a control group of non-exemplars. In one in-depth qualitative study, adult moral exemplars expressed almost complete integration of their self and moral goals (i.e., what they personally desired was in line with what they knew was right), such that morality was central to their identity; this strong moral identity seemed at the heart of their extensive lifelong moral commitments (Colby & Damon, 1992). In multi-method studies of adolescent morality, moral exemplars more frequently described themselves using moral trait terms and moral goals than comparison adolescents, incorporated their ideal selves into their actual selves more so than did comparison youth (Hart & Fegley, 1995; Reimer & Wade-Stein, 2004), and showed greater overlap between their descriptions of their actions and their personal goals (Reimer, Goudelock, & Walker, 2009). So, moral exemplars define themselves more in terms of moral traits, moral goals, and personal ideals than others, and see greater integrity between such self-important goals and their own actions.

Narrative Studies

Recently, some have used a narrative approach to better understand moral identity. As part of narrative interviews in two different studies, Pratt and colleagues (Pratt et al., 2009) asked participants (adolescents and young adults) to tell various types of life stories. These stories were each rated for salience of moral identity, as indicated by things such as concern for the needs and rights of others. In one study, moral identity was cross-sectionally related to generative concern (a person's desires, commitments, and actions directed toward making a difference in the world), and in the other study it longitudinally predicted generative concern and community service several years later.

Frimer and Walker (2009) used structured interviews to collect self-understanding narratives, and then coded them for values orientations based on Schwartz's (1992) circumplex model of universal values. The centrality of morality to identity was indexed as the degree to which communal (universalism and benevolence) and agentic (power and achievement) value orientations co-occurred in the same "chunks" of a self-narrative rather than in different portions of the narrative. In other words, this co-occurrence of communal and agentic value orientations suggests reconciliation of self-oriented and moral or other-oriented goals. Degree of moral centrality predicted self-report and behavioral measures of moral behavior.

Correlational Studies

One of the primary challenges of studying moral identity is that it is difficult to adequately measure such a rich construct. The only survey measure that has been extensively evaluated for reliability and validity is a 10-item, self-report scale designed by Aquino and Reed (2002). This measure involves (1) presenting participants with a list of nine moral traits, (2) asking them to visualize a person with those traits (their self or someone else) and how that person would think, feel, and act, and (3) having them rate statements such as, "It would make me feel good to be a person who has these characteristics." The prompt to imagine someone with a certain set of moral traits is thought to activate the person's moral identity schema (their image of what it means to be a moral person), then the items allow them to rate

their agreement with 10 statements pertaining to that schema. Based on the properties of identity outlined by Erikson (1968), two 5-item subscales were identified: symbolization and internalization. Symbolization is the extent to which people see themselves as outwardly displaying a moral social identity to the world, whereas internalization is the relative centrality of a moral social identity in their overall self-schema.

Generally, internalization is more strongly related to morally relevant behavior than symbolization. Perhaps internalization is more autonomous or self-regulated whereas symbolization is more focused on self-presentation. Among adults, both internalization and symbolization positively predicted self-report volunteerism (Aquino & Reed, 2002). However, among adolescents, only internalization predicted actual donation behavior. In another series of studies, internalization but not symbolization predicted various moral responses to out-group members: felt moral obligation toward out-group members, willingness to extend love and status to strangers, perceived worthiness of relief efforts for out-group members, willingness to donate money to relief efforts for out-group members, and willingness to forgive out-group members of violence (Reed & Aquino, 2003). More recently, those higher on moral disengagement (the tendency to rationalize immoral action in a way that maintains one's sense of moral integrity) were less likely to think that the best response to the perpetrators of the 9/11 attack on the World Trade Center would be to kill them (versus forgiving, helping, imprisoning, or fining them; Aquino et al., 2007). This effect was moderated by the internalization aspect of moral identity such that those higher in internalization were less likely to rationalize killing the perpetrators (cf. Moshman, Chapter 39, this volume). Lastly, among adolescents, internalization and symbolization related positively to felt moral obligation to out-group members, and negatively to social dominance orientation (preference for group inequality; Hardy, Bhattacharjee, Aquino, & Reed, 2010).

Another research group conducted an interesting study looking at the independent and interactive effects of moral judgment and moral identity (assessed using Aquino and Reed's measure) on moral action (Reynolds & Ceranic, 2007). They hypothesized that when social consensus is high regarding a moral issue, moral identity is more likely to predict behavior independent of moral judgment, but, when social consensus is low, moral identity and moral judgment will interact in predicting behavior. Specifically, in situations of low consensus, stronger moral identity and greater preference for consequentialism (i.e., focus on consequences as basis for morality) will lead to consequentialist behaviors, whereas stronger moral identity paired with an affinity for formalism (i.e., focus on obligation to moral principles as basis for morality) will result in more formalistic moral action. They found partial support for these hypotheses, with findings generally more robust for internalization than symbolization. In terms of direct effects of moral identity, neither dimension related to cheating or responses to business-related ethical dilemmas, internalization negatively predicted self-reported unethical business behaviors (symbolization was positively related), and symbolization (but not internalization) was linked to self-reported charitable giving. Again, perhaps symbolization is partially about self-presentation—that is, wanting to look good to others. A number of the proposed interactions with moral judgment were also found, particularly for internalization.

In addition to Aquino and Reed's (2002) moral identity scale, the other most common way to quantitatively assess moral identity has been to have people rate the importance of various moral and non-moral values to their sense of self (e.g., Barriga, Morrison, Liau, & Gibbs, 2001; Hardy, 2006; Pratt, Hunsberger, Pancer, & Alisat, 2003). Moral identity scores are then typically computed by subtracting the mean of the ratings for non-moral values from the mean of the moral values. There is no standard scale (rather, each study has used slightly different instructions, response options, and values), and minimal work has been done to validate these measures. In general, studies using such measures have reported links between moral identity and morally relevant action and emotions:

moral identity negatively predicted teens' antisocial behaviors (Barriga et al., 2001), positively predicted teens' community involvement activities (Pratt et al., 2003), and positively predicted young adults' prosocial behaviors (Hardy, 2006).

Another quantitative measurement approach in developmental and social psychology entails the administration of a set of personality measures conceptually associated with moral behaviors (Carlo et al., 2009; Dovidio et al., 2006; Staub, 2005). Several studies yield evidence that a composite of altruistic or prosocial personality measures reliably predict a range of prosocial behaviors, including long-term volunteerism, assisting someone who is suffering, and willingness to risk one's own life rather than put others at risk. For example, Carlo, Eisenberg, Troyer, Switzer, and Speer (1991) showed that a composite of altruistic personality measures was associated with selflessly motivated helping (relieving a stranger's suffering when given a chance to escape easily from the situation) but not egoistically motivated helping. Based on this approach, Penner and his colleagues (Penner, Fritzche, Craiger, & Freifeld, 1995) developed a standardized measure of a "prosocial personality" (which includes measures of sympathy, perspective taking, social responsibility, ascription of responsibility, prosocial behaviors) and several studies demonstrate the reliability and validity of this measure (see Dovidio et al., 2006).

In sociological social psychology, Jan Stets and colleagues (2006; Stets et al., 2008) have used a social identity approach similar to that of Aquino and Reed (2002) to examine outcomes of moral identity. They assessed the extent to which people had a social identity characterized by moral traits (i.e., whether they see themselves as moral), and then the salience of that moral identity (i.e., its importance relative to other social identities). In one study, participants were asked to recall a number of moral situations they have been in, and then report the action they took and how they felt afterward (Stets & Carter, 2006). Moral identity predicted the likelihood to report moral responses to the moral situations. Further, when people reported having not taken the moral action, moral identity predicted the extent of negative emotions felt (e.g., guilt). In a second study, moral identity (but not moral identity salience) predicted likelihood of moral actions—but neither predicted moral emotion in response to moral or immoral actions (Stets et al., 2008). Perhaps this lack of findings for moral identity salience is due to limitations of the measure, which involved having participants report how they would identify themselves to another person when meeting for the first time by choosing from a list of descriptors (e.g., friend, student, and moral person). It is unclear how many people who have a salient moral identity would actually choose "moral person" as their primary descriptor in an initial encounter.

Lastly, Perugini and Leone (2009) looked at the role of explicit and implicit moral identity in predicting deliberative and spontaneous moral action. Explicit moral identity was assessed using self-reports of moral personality characteristics (e.g., honesty), and implicit moral identity using an implicit associations test (IAT) with moral–immoral as the target category and me–others as the paired category. Deliberative moral action was measured as responses to moral dilemmas. Spontaneous moral action was assessed using a behavioral measure where individuals were "accidentally" compensated two lottery tickets rather than one for participation in the study, and the experimenter observed whether or not they returned the "extra" ticket. Explicit moral identity predicted deliberative moral actions while implicit moral identity predicted spontaneous moral actions, in line with dual processing models suggesting somewhat independent explicit and implicit processing linking attitudes and behaviors (Wilson, Lindsey, & Schooler, 2000).

Experimental Studies

Only a few studies provide experimental tests of moral identity. In one such study, Aquino and colleagues (2007) sought to understand how moral identity and moral disengagement might influence affective responses to prisoner abuse. They primed moral identity by having participant

write brief stories about themselves using certain trait terms, with one group being given the nine moral trait terms from Aquino and Reed's (2002) moral identity measure, and the other group given positive but non-moral traits (e.g., happy). Participants also completed a measure of moral disengagement and, following reading a news article about abuse of Iraqi prisoners by US troops, completed a measure of current negative affect. While the moral identity prime did not directly predict negative affect, there was an interaction with moral disengagement. In the non-prime condition those higher on moral disengagement experienced less negative affect in response to the abuse story; there was no such relation in the prime condition. Priming moral identity thus reduced the effectiveness of moral disengagement.

In a more recent set of four studies, Aquino and colleagues (2009) elucidated the role of situations in links between moral identity and action. In the first study, priming moral identity predicted intention to act morally; however, this effect was stronger in people for whom moral identity was less central to their self (as measured by the internalization scale from their self-report moral identity measure). Furthermore, the link between moral identity centrality and moral action intentions was mediated by the chronic accessibility of the moral identity self-schema. So, when being a moral person is important to one's identity, moral schemas are more chronically accessible and, thus, priming is less necessary.

Conversely, in a second study, situational factors that elicited self-interest motives decreased the accessibility of the moral identity schema and thus increased intentions to lie—but the effect of self-interest on accessibility was greater for those with high moral identity centrality. The third study showed that magnitude of financial incentives for performance predicted likelihood of lying in a business negotiation for those higher on moral identity centrality, but not for those lower on centrality. This shows that the beneficial effects of moral identity can be overridden by competing situational pressures.

The fourth study combined many elements of these prior studies. To start, some participants received a moral identity prime, and others did not. Then, in groups of five, participants were involved in a decision task that pitted self-interest against the interests of the group. The task involved a series of 20 decisions. Over time they were given feedback (manipulated by the researchers) suggesting that the others in their group were making self-interested decisions—providing an increasing situational pressure against moral action. The outcome variable was the number of times the participants made cooperative decisions that benefited the group. Initially (early in the sequence of decisions), those high on moral identity cooperated the same regardless of experimental condition, whereas those low on moral identity cooperated more in the moral identity prime condition than the control condition. However, this pattern changed over time as participants received feedback about others acting self-interestedly. By the end of the experiment, for those high on moral identity centrality, the prime condition showed greater cooperation; but, for those low on moral identity centrality there were no differences between the prime and control conditions. So, initially (in the absence of strong self-interest motives) the prime best helped those low on moral identity to cooperate; however, in the face of temptations to defect, the prime helped those with high moral identity stay true to their commitments. In sum, the centrality and accessibility of the moral identity self-schema, and interactions among them, are important in predicting moral action.

Moral Identity Formation

If moral identity is an important component of moral functioning, an understanding of how it develops will be theoretically and practically useful. Each approach to conceptualizing moral identity leads to different ideas about the processes and predictors of moral identity formation. Although relevant theory and research has thus far stemmed largely from character perspectives, developmental work from social cognitive perspectives is emerging.

Moral Identity Formation from Character Perspectives

From character perspectives moral identity formation involves the merging of moral and identity development, rather than a unique developmental system (e.g., Bergman, 2004; Damon, 1984; Hart, 2005). In fact, it may be that morality and identity are two facets of the same developmental system (Davidson & Youniss, 1991). The developmental paths are so congruent that some view moral identity as the goal of both moral and identity development (Blasi, 1993; Damon & Hart, 1992; Erikson, 1968; Moshman, 2005). Thus, although maturity of moral understanding is important in its own right, integration with identity may yield greater motivation and commitment. Moreover, although identity can be grounded on any identity contents, it may be ideal for identity to be based on morality, which enables better relationships with self and others.

Although much of the talk about moral identity formation focuses on adolescence, there is some evidence for the presence of early precursors or forms of moral identity in childhood (see Thompson, 2009). For instance, as children comply with parental demands or rules, they begin to see themselves as "good" boys or girls (Kochanska, 2002). Preschoolers with this moral component to their sense of self are more likely to endorse statements describing themselves as individuals who feel badly about doing the wrong thing, apologize and try to make amends for their own wrongdoing, and are concerned about others' wrongdoing. Furthermore, the affective bases of moral identity (e.g., empathy, guilt, shame) emerge early in life (Hoffman, 2000; Kochanska, 2002), and their integration with moral ideals and with one's sense of self are fundamental to moral identity formation. Thus, it seems that certain aspects of a moral sense of self can be identified in childhood, although no work has specifically linked these early childhood processes to adolescent moral identity.

Throughout childhood and adolescence, developments in moral understanding and identity pave the way for further integration of the moral and self systems. Moral understanding development involves a shift toward interpersonal and ideological thinking about moral issues (Lapsley, 1996; Moshman, 2005). Thus, compared to children, adolescents are more sensitive to the expectations, attitudes, and needs of others, and feel a greater responsibility to others. Additionally, morality for adolescents is more principled in nature, and less focused on external factors like punishment and reciprocity, which are more characteristic of childhood morality. The move toward a morality based on ideology and social responsibility primes the moral system for integration with identity.

Maturation in the identity system involves at least two major shifts that open up the way for integration with morality (Damon, 1984; Damon & Hart, 1992). First, in early adolescence the self becomes understood more from a social personality perspective, emphasizing interactions with others (Damon & Hart, 1988). Many facets of social interaction that can characterize self-understanding at this stage are morally relevant—such as being kind, thoughtful, and generous. Second, during late adolescence, the self becomes more ideologically defined, such as being based on one's moral principles, religious beliefs, or political views (Damon & Hart, 1988). In other words, adolescents construct an ideological theory of themselves that likely includes moral dimensions. Thus, as identity becomes more social and ideological in nature, it is primed for integration with morality.

The integration of morality and self during adolescence and beyond is also enabled by the growing sense of agency and responsibility. Although children have a rudimentary understanding of right and wrong, they feel less responsible for doing what is right than adolescents (e.g., children often anticipate feeling good following transgressions; Nunner-Winkler, 2007). This disconnect of morality from the self may be partly due to an immature sense of agency. Without mature agency, there is less awareness that one can appropriate certain identity contents (e.g., moral principles) as central to one's sense of identity, and distance oneself from other less desirable identity contents (e.g., negative

personal characteristics; Blasi, 2001). Thus, children feel less accountable, less ownership over their actions and identities, and less concern for self-consistency. Instead, children are primarily externally regulated, driven more by impulses or desires, external consequences, and the perceptions of others, than by internal moral standards (Blasi, 2001; cf. Soenens & Vansteenkiste, Chapter 17, this volume). Thus, although early precursors of moral identity are evident in children, it is clear there is still room to grow (Thompson, 2009).

Empirical studies from character perspectives indicate that moral identity formation is associated with certain individual characteristics and developmental contexts, as well as opportunities for moral action (see Hart, 2005). In terms of individual characteristics, academic achievement was a positive predictor while internalizing (e.g., withdrawing and feeling worthless) was a negative predictor of moral identity (as assessed by participation in community service) 2 years later (Hart et al., 1999). Additionally, young adult moral exemplars in social organizations were higher than comparisons on trait agreeableness, and more advanced in moral reasoning, faith development, adult attachment, and identity formation (Matsuba & Walker, 2004). Similarly, Canadian recipients of awards for bravery or altruism differed from comparisons on a number of aspects of their life narratives, including greater salience of themes of personal agency (e.g., self-mastery), connection to others (including childhood attachments to caregivers), positive emotions (e.g., hope and optimism), and overcoming and learning from adversity (Walker & Frimer, 2007). Thus, certain personality characteristics may better enable moral identity formation.

In terms of developmental contexts, religious involvement and effective parenting are predictive of moral identity. Hart and Atkins (2004) found that youth involved in community service (their moral identity proxy) tended to be more religious. Regarding parenting, parental involvement (Hart et al., 1999), parental demandingness (Pratt et al., 2003), and overall family support

(Hart, Atkins, & Ford, 1998) were longitudinal predictors of moral identity. Inductive discipline, which helps children appreciate the consequences of their actions to self and others, is related to the internalization of moral values (Hoffman, 2000). Similarly, parental warmth was positively linked to the greater internalization of moral values into the self (Hardy, Padilla-Walker, & Carlo, 2008).

Colby and Damon's (1992) qualitative moral exemplar study also revealed compelling insights regarding the role of social relationships on moral identity formation. Many of their moral exemplars, when asked to look back on their life paths, noted how both positive and negative relationships had a salient impact on their moral commitments. For instance, parents and other role models provided scaffolding for moral identity formation by channeling or persuading them toward valuing certain values and goals. Even in adulthood, interactions with family and peers which often challenged their worldviews resulted in gradual transformations of their values and goals. On the other hand, interactions with others who held opposing views also led exemplars to transform, articulate, and strengthen their values and goals throughout life. Thus, moral identity formation can occur through social interactions over the life course.

The integration of morality and identity can also be encouraged by providing opportunities for learning and acting on moral principles—such as community service and other prosocial actions. From a character perspective, acting on moral principles is one way individuals learn to value such principles and see themselves as capable of making a difference in the world (Hart, 2005). For example, Youniss and Yate's (1997) ethnographic study of youth volunteering at a soup kitchen as part of a high school social justice class showed that such experiences can transform moral identity in youth. Similarly, two longitudinal studies have shown community involvement (i.e., political involvement, community service, and kindness toward others; Pratt et al., 2003) and involvement in clubs and teams (Hart et al., 1999) to be predictive of moral identity 2 years later.

Social Cognitive Perspectives on Moral Identity Formation

Moral identity formation from social cognitive perspectives hinges on the building of rich networks of chronically accessible moral schemas (Lapsley & Narvaez, 2004). Moral schemas include prototypes, such as one's mental image of what it means to be a moral person, action scripts or event representations for specific morally relevant behaviors, and possible selves. Compared to adolescents, children likely have fewer moral schemas, and those they have may be less elaborate and less accessible for information processing. Thus, they are less able to promptly and appropriately respond to moral situations. In other words, if moral maturity is seen as a form of expertise (Narvaez & Lapsley, 2005), most children are novices.

Little is known about the development of moral prototypes because most work has focused on adults (e.g., Walker & Pitts, 1998). However, a recent study of adolescents provides some evidence for developmental trends in that older teens may have more nuanced descriptions of moral personhood than younger teens (Hardy, Walker, Skalski, Olsen, & Basinger, in press). Further, work on other prototypes (e.g., images of adolescents who drink alcohol) has demonstrated a potential role for the socialization or modeling of prototypes, particularly by parents (Gerrard, Gibbons, Zhao, Russell, & Reis-Bergan, 1999). So, at any given phase of development a person's mental image of what it means to be a moral person seems contingent on cognitive maturity (e.g., language and abstract thought) and social learning.

In addition to the content and structure of moral prototypes (Hardy et al., in press), there is individual variability in the degree to which prototypes are important to the self and cognitively accessible (Aquino et al., 2009). In other words, individuals differ in the extent to which their image of what it means to be a moral person is an important social identity for them (Aquino & Reed, 2002; Stets & Carter, 2006), and this importance should then lead to greater cognitive accessibility for information processing (Bizer &

Kroznick, 2001). As with other social cognitions such as attitudes and values (Grolnick, Deci, & Ryan, 1997), the importance of the moral prototypes to the self can be facilitated or hindered by contexts such as the family environment (Hardy et al., 2010).

While some scholars see moral prototypes as fundamental to moral identity formation (Aquino & Reed, 2002; Stets & Carter, 2006), for others the schemas most critical to moral identity are mental representations of moral actions (Lapsley & Narvaez, 2004; Reimer, 2003). Scripts or event representations of moral actions develop through social experiences children have (e.g., helping someone who is hurt or volunteering at a homeless shelter; Lapsley & Narvaez, 2004). Event representations of enacted or observed moral actions form behavioral scripts in autobiographical memory that make engaging in those behaviors more automatic, and the self-evaluative and moral affect linked to these schemas pull individuals toward or away from similar behaviors in the future (Reimer, 2003). These processes can be facilitated by personal reflection and dialogue with caregivers and others about the meaning of the experiences (Lapsley & Hill, 2009; Lapsley & Narvaez, 2004; Narvaez & Lapsley, 2005; Thompson, 2009).

Lastly, beginning in adolescence individuals also form self-schemas related to the type of person they fear becoming (i.e., feared or dreaded self) and the type of person they want to be (i.e., ideal, desired, or hoped-for self; Markus & Nurius, 1986; Oyserman & James, Chapter 6, this volume). When activated, these *possible selves* serve as goal states that individuals want to move toward or away from. Thus, part of moral identity formation from a social cognitive perspective may involve the construction of possible selves laden with moral meaning or comprised of moral dimensions. For example, there may be individual differences in the amount of overlap between one's mental image of a moral person and one's mental image of the type of person he or she wants to become. This may be one way in which the degree to which morality is integrated into a person's self-system can provide moral motivation.

Models of Moral Identity Formation

A few scholars have proposed models of moral identity formation (Bergman, 2004; Damon, 2000; Hart, 2005). While Bergman and Damon's models likely would be classified under character perspectives, Hart's model may have elements of both character and social cognitive perspectives. All three try to map out processes involved with the integration of morality and identity (Hart's model is the most elaborated and researched and thus will be discussed in more detail here). Hart (2005) includes individual and contextual predictors at two different layers of proximity to moral identity. The more distal layer includes enduring personality characteristics (e.g., empathy) and social structures (e.g., family) that are the background or foundation of child and adolescent development. These factors show considerable stability over time, are relatively resistant to change, and are largely outside of the person's volitional control. The more proximal layer includes factors that more directly influence moral identity formation and ultimately constitute moral identity. These include moral judgments and attitudes, self-understanding and identity commitments, and opportunities for moral action. Such factors are more malleable and are under individual control. Personality and social structures influence moral identity formation primarily through these mediating factors. Additionally, relations between moral identity and the mediating factors (i.e., moral cognitions, self and identity, and opportunity) are reciprocal.

Conclusion

This chapter reviewed theory and research on conceptions of moral identity, outcomes of moral identity, and the processes and predictors of moral identity formation. So, what do we know about moral identity? First, we know that although moral identity entails a unity or integration of a person's sense of identity and morality, there are diverse ways to describe and account for this (Lapsley, 2008; Monin & Jordan, 2009; Shao et al., 2008). Second, we know that moral identity is associated with a range of moral emotions and actions—this has been demonstrated using diverse methodologies, including experimental design. Third, we know that situational factors can moderate links between moral identity and moral action. Fourth, we have some limited knowledge of potential mechanisms by which moral identity leads to action, such as self-consistency and chronically accessible moral schemas. Fifth, we know that moral identity formation involves some sort of integration of identity formation and moral development processes, although it is still unclear whether these processes are ever distinct. Sixth, we have identified a number of predictors of moral identity, including parenting, religion, personality, moral reasoning, identity status, and involvement in moral and prosocial action, among others.

Skepticism of Moral Identity

Although the research reported above seems promising, moral identity is not without its skeptics. Most criticism of the concept has emerged from social domain theorists (Nucci, 2004; Turiel, 2002). To them, the discrepancy between moral judgment and moral action is not of critical importance. Rather, in a given situation there are multiple judgments at work—moral (i.e., obligatory notions of justice and rights), conventional (i.e., norm-based, socially prescribed issues), prudential (i.e., issues of safety), and personal (i.e., arbitrary notions of one's preferences), and it is the coordination of these judgments that matters most. Thus, they are hesitant to include other personality variables that may unnecessarily complicate morality.

While a more extensive response to Nucci's critique is available elsewhere (Bergman, 2004), we will note a few of our observations here. We appreciate the attention social domain theorists grant to the complexities of thought and behavior in real situations, but they do not sufficiently account for individual differences in labeling certain actions as moral. Further, it is unclear what leads individuals to prioritize a moral judgment over other sorts of judgments. Perhaps those with

a stronger sense of moral identity are more likely to emphasize congruence with moral judgments over conventional, prudential, and personal judgments. Put differently, while the primary focus of social domain theory is to understand the parameters of the moral domain of judgments and actions, moral identity can be viewed as a means to link moral judgments to moral conduct.

Despite this skepticism, we argue that moral identity is an important area of theory and research. First, research on moral identity offers an efficient way to integrate the moral psychology and identity literatures. Second, moral identity demonstrates one way in which self-concept is relevant to, and may motivate, social outcomes. Third, a moral identity framework can integrate and broaden much of the existing work on moral development, which has tended to focus narrowly on single dimensions of morality. Fourth, a moral identity approach brings to the forefront motivational processes that may hold critical clues for understanding moral commitment. Finally, moral identity may lead to promising innovations in moral education, given the potential role of bridging the moral judgment–moral action gap.

Future Directions

Thus far, much understanding has been gained from the research on moral identity but there are important challenges and gaps for future research. First, much more measurement development is needed. Moral identity is generally assessed with self-report surveys (e.g., Hardy et al., 2010), or indirectly, as moral exemplarity (i.e., identifying someone who is a highly moral person; e.g., Matsuba & Walker, 2004) or involvement in community service (e.g., Hart et al., 1999). Surveys may only tap a small part of what it means to have a moral identity, and indirect approaches assume that people who volunteer or are morally exemplary have a moral identity. An exception is the interview measure of moral identity recently developed by Frimer and Walker (2009), which may provide a richer assessment technique. Second, more sophisticated study designs are needed to better infer cause and effect relations. For example, most studies are either cross-sectional (e.g., Hardy et al., 2010) or include at most two occasions of measurement (e.g., Pratt et al., 2003), limiting the ability to examine development. And third, our knowledge on moral identity is still rather scant. In particular, we know little about cultural differences in moral identity, the neurological bases for moral identity, the degree to which moral identity is stable across situations and time, the processes by which moral identity develops, the mechanisms by which moral identity leads to action, and the interplay of moral cognitions (e.g., moral reasoning) and emotions (e.g., empathy, guilt) in moral identity. Perhaps most importantly, little has been done to compare and contrast, or seek to integrate, the various approaches to moral identity. As theory and research on moral identity continues to progress, we are eager to see what emerges.

Acknowledgments We are indebted to Augusto Blasi, Darcia Narvaez, Lawrence Walker, the editors, and an anonymous reviewer for their feedback on earlier drafts of this manuscript. Additionally, we appreciate Ryan Funk and Michael Williams for help with editing.

References

Ajzen, I., & Fishbein, M. (2005). The influence of attitudes on behavior. In D. Albarracin, B. T. Johnson, & M. P. Zanna (Eds.), *The handbook of attitudes* (pp. 173–221). Mahwah, NJ: Erlbaum.

Aquino, K., & Freeman, D. (2009). Moral identity in business situations: A social cognitive framework for understanding moral functioning. In D. Narvaez & D. Lapsley (Eds.), *Personality, identity, and character: Explorations in moral psychology* (pp. 375–395). New York: Cambridge University Press.

Aquino, K., Freeman, D., Reed, A., II., Lim, V. K. G., & Felps, W. (2009). Testing a social cognitive model of moral behavior: The interactive influence of situations and moral identity centrality. *Journal of Personality and Social Psychology, 97,* 123–141.

Aquino, K., & Reed, A., II. (2002). The self-importance of moral identity. *Journal of Personality and Social Psychology, 83,* 1423–1440.

Aquino, K., Reed, A., II, Thau, S., & Freeman, D. (2007). A grotesque and dark beauty: How moral identity and mechanisms of moral disengagement influence cognitive and emotional reactions to war. *Journal of Experimental Social Psychology, 43,* 385–392.

Bandura, A. (1986). *Social foundations of thought and action.* Englewood Cliffs, NJ: Prentice Hall.

Barriga, A. Q., Morrison, E. M., Liau, A. K., & Gibbs, J. C. (2001). Moral cognition: Explaining the gender difference in antisocial behavior. *Merrill-Palmer Quarterly, 47,* 532–562.

Bergman, R. (2004). Identity as motivation: Toward a theory of the moral self. In D. K. Lapsley & D. Narvaez (Eds.), *Moral development, self, and identity* (pp. 21–46). Mahwah, NJ: Erlbaum.

Bizer, G. Y., & Kroznick, J. A. (2001). Exploring the structure of strength-related attitude features: The relation between attitude importance and attitude accessibility. *Journal of Personality and Social Psychology, 81,* 566–586.

Blasi, A. (1980). Bridging moral cognition and moral action: A critical review of the literature. *Psychological Bulletin, 88,* 1–45.

Blasi, A. (1983). Moral cognition and moral action: A theoretical perspective. *Developmental Review, 3,* 178–210.

Blasi, A. (1984). Moral identity: Its role in moral functioning. In W. M. Kurtines & J. L. Gewirtz (Eds.), *Morality, moral behavior, and moral development* (pp. 129–139). New York: Wiley-Interscience.

Blasi, A. (1993). The development of identity: Some implications for moral functioning. In G. G. Noam, T. E. Wren, G. Nunner-Winkler, & W. Edelstein (Eds.), *Studies in contemporary German social thought* (pp. 99–122). Cambridge, MA: The MIT Press.

Blasi, A. (1995). Moral understanding and the moral personality: The process of moral integration. In W. M. Kurtines & J. L. Gewirtz (Eds.), *Moral development: An introduction* (pp. 229–253). Needham Heights, MA: Allyn and Bacon.

Blasi, A. (2001). Moral motivation and society: Internalization and the development of the self. In G. Dux & F. Welz (Eds.), *Moral und Recht im Diskurs der Moderne. Zur Legitimation gesellschaftlicher Ordnung* (pp. 313–329). Opladen: Leske and Budrich.

Blasi, A. (2004a). Moral functioning: Moral understanding and personality. In D. K. Lapsley & D. Narvaez (Eds.), *Moral development, self, and identity* (pp. 189–212). Mahwah, NJ: Erlbaum.

Blasi, A. (2004b). Neither personality nor cognition: An alternative approach to the nature of the self. In C. Lightfoot, C. Lalonde, & M. Chandler (Eds.), *Changing conceptions of psychological life* (pp. 3–25). Mahwah, NJ: Erlbaum.

Blasi, A., & Glodis, K. A. (1995). The development of identity: A critical analysis from the perspective of the self as subject. *Developmental Review, 15,* 404–433.

Campbell, R. L., Christopher, J. C., & Bickhard, M. H. (2002). Self and values: An interactivist foundation for moral development. *Theory & Psychology, 12,* 795–823.

Carlo, G., Eisenberg, N., Troyer, D., Switzer, G., & Speer, A. L. (1991). The altruistic personality: In what contexts is it apparent? *Journal of Personality and Social Psychology, 61,* 450–458.

Carlo, G., PytlikZillig, L. M., Roesch, S. C., & Dienstbier, R. A. (2009). The elusive altruist: The psychological study of the altruistic personality. In D. Narvaez & D. Lapsley (Eds.), *Personality, identity, and character: Explorations in moral psychology* (pp. 271–294). New York: Cambridge University Press.

Cervone, D., & Tripathi, R. (2009). The moral functioning of the person as a whole: On moral psychology and personality science. In D. Narvaez & D. Lapsley (Eds.), *Personality, identity, and character: Explorations in moral psychology* (pp. 30–51). New York: Cambridge University Press.

Colby, A., & Damon, W. (1992). *Some do care: Contemporary lives of moral commitment*. New York: Free Press.

Damasio, A. (1994). *Descartes error: Emotion, reason, and the human brain*. New York: Putnam.

Damon, W. (1984). Self-understanding and moral development from childhood to adolescence. In W. M. Kurtines & J. L. Gewirtz (Eds.), *Morality, moral behavior, and moral development* (pp. 109–127). New York: Wiley.

Damon, W. (2000). Setting the stage for development of wisdom: Self-understanding and moral identity during adolescence. In W. S. Brown (Ed.), *Understanding wisdom: Sources, science, and society* (pp. 339–360). Philadelphia: Templeton Foundation Press.

Damon, W., & Hart, D. (1988). *Self-understanding in childhood and adolescence*. New York: Cambridge University Press.

Damon, W., & Hart, D. (1992). Self-understanding and its role in social and moral development. In M. H. Bornstein & M. E. Lamb (Eds.), *Developmental psychology: An advanced textbook* (3rd ed., pp. 421–464). Hillsdale, NJ: Erlbaum.

Davidson, P., & Youniss, J. (1991). Which comes first, morality or identity? In W. Kurtines & J. Gewirtz (Eds.), *Handbook of moral behavior and development* (Vol. 2, pp. 105–121). Hillsdale, NJ: Erlbaum.

Dovidio, J. F., Piliavin, J. A., Schroeder, D. A., & Penner, L. A. (2006). *The social psychology of prosocial behavior*. Mahwah, NJ: Erlbaum.

Erikson, E. H. (1968). *Identity: Youth and crisis*. Oxford: Norton & Co.

Frimer, J. A., & Walker, L. J. (2008). Towards a new paradigm of moral personhood. *Journal of Moral Education, 37*, 333–356.

Frimer, J. A., & Walker, L. J. (2009). Reconciling the self and morality: An empirical model of moral centrality development. *Developmental Psychology, 45*, 1669–1681.

Gerrard, M., Gibbons, F. X., Zhao, L., Russell, D. W., & Reis-Bergan, M. (1999). The effect of peers' alcohol consumption on parental influence: A cognitive mediation model. *Journal of Studies on Alcohol, Supplement, 13*, 32–44.

Gibbs, J. C. (2009). *Moral development and reality: Beyond the theories of Kohlberg and Hoffman* (2nd ed.). Needham Heights, MA: Allyn & Bacon.

Grolnick, W. S., Deci, E. L., & Ryan, R. M. (1997). Internalization within the family: The self-determination theory perspective. In J. E. Grusec & L. Kuczynski (Eds.), *Parenting and children's internalization of values: A handbook of contemporary theory* (pp. 135–161). Hoboken, NJ: Wiley.

Hardy, S. A. (2006). Identity, reasoning, and emotion: An empirical comparison of three sources of moral motivation. *Motivation and Emotion, 30*, 207–215.

Hardy, S. A., Bhattacharjee, A., Aquino, K., & Reed, A., Jr. (2010). Moral identity and psychological distance: The case of adolescent parental socialization. *Journal of Adolescence, 33*, 111–123.

Hardy, S. A., & Carlo, G. (2005). Identity as a source of moral motivation. *Human Development, 48*, 232–256.

Hardy, S. A., Padilla-Walker, L. M., & Carlo, G. (2008). Parenting dimensions and adolescents' internalization of moral values. *Journal of Moral Education, 37*, 205–223.

Hardy, S. A., Walker, L. J., Skalski, J., Olsen, J. A., & Basinger, J. C. (in press). Adolescent naturalistic conceptions of morality. *Social Development*.

Hart, D. (2005). The development of moral identity. In G. Carlo & C. P. Edwards (Eds.), *Nebraska Symposium on Motivation: Moral development through the lifespan: Theory, research, and application* (pp. 165–196). Lincoln, NE: University of Nebraska Press.

Hart, D., & Atkins, R. (2004). Religious participation and the development of moral identity in adolescence. In T. A. Thorkildsen & H. J. Walberg (Eds.), *Nurturing morality* (pp. 157–172). New York: Kluwer Academic/Plenum.

Hart, D., Atkins, R., & Ford, D. (1998). Urban America as a context for the development of moral identity in adolescence. *Journal of Social Issues, 54*, 513–530.

Hart, D., Atkins, R., & Ford, D. (1999). Family influences on the formation of moral identity in adolescence: Longitudinal analyses. *Journal of Moral Education, 28*, 375–386.

Hart, D., & Fegley, S. (1995). Prosocial behavior and caring in adolescence: Relations to self-understanding and social judgment. *Child Development, 66*, 1346–1359.

Higgins, E. T. (1999). Persons or situations: Unique explanatory principles or variability in general principles? In D. Cervone & Y. Shoda (Eds.), *The coherence of personality: Social-cognitive bases of consistency, variability, and organization* (pp. 61–93). New York: Guilford Press.

Hoffman, M. L. (2000). *Empathy and moral development: Implications for caring and justice*. New York: Cambridge University Press.

Kihlstrom, J. F., Beer, J. S., & Klein, S. B. (2003). Self and identity as memory. In M. R. Leary & J. P. Tangney (Eds.), *Handbook of self and identity* (pp. 68–90). New York: Guilford Press.

Kochanska, G. (2002). Committed compliance, moral self, and internalization: A mediational model. *Developmental Psychology, 38*, 339–351.

Kohlberg, L. (1969). Stage and sequence: The cognitive developmental approach to socialization. In D. A. Goslin (Ed.), *Handbook of socialization theory and research* (pp. 347–480). Chicago: Rand McNally.

Kohlberg, L., & Candee, D. (1984). The relationship of moral judgment to moral action. In W. M. Kurtines & J. L. Gewirtz (Eds.), *Morality, moral behavior, and moral development* (pp. 53–73). New York: Wiley-Interscience.

Kurtines, W. M., Mayock, E., Pollard, S. R., Lanza, T., & Carlo, G. (1991). Social and moral development from the perspective of psychosocial theory. In W. M. Kurtines & J. L. Gewirtz (Eds.), *Handbook of moral behavior and development* (Vol. 1, pp. 303–333). Hillsdale, NJ: Erlbaum.

Lapsley, D. K. (1996). *Moral psychology*. Boulder, CO: Westview Press.

Lapsley, D. K. (2008). Moral self-identity as the aim of education. In L. P. Nucci & D. Narvaez (Eds.), *Handbook of moral and character education* (pp. 30–52). New York: Routledge.

Lapsley, D. K., & Hill, P. L. (2009). The development of the moral personality. In D. Narvaez & D. Lapsley (Eds.), *Personality, identity, and character: Explorations in moral psychology* (pp. 185–213). New York: Cambridge University Press.

Lapsley, D. K., & Lasky, B. (2001). Prototypic moral character. *Identity, 1,* 345–363.

Lapsley, D. K., & Narvaez, D. (2004). A social-cognitive approach to the moral personality. In *Moral development, self, and identity* (pp. 189–212). Mahwah, NJ: Erlbaum.

Loevinger, J. (1976). *Ego development: Conceptions and theories*. San Francisco: Jossey-Bass.

Markus, H., & Nurius, P. (1986). Possible selves. *American Psychologist, 41,* 954–969.

Matsuba, M. K., & Walker, L. J. (2004). Extraordinary moral commitment: Young adults involved in social organizations. *Journal of Personality, 72,* 413–436.

McAdams, D. P. (2009). The moral personality. In D. Narvaez & D. Lapsley (Eds.), *Personality, identity, and character: Explorations in moral psychology* (pp. 11–29). New York: Cambridge University Press.

Mischel, W. (1968). *Personality and assessment*. New York: Wiley.

Monin, B., & Jordan, A. H. (2009). The dynamic moral self: A social psychological perspective. In D. Narvaez & D. Lapsley (Eds.), *Personality, identity, and character: Explorations in moral psychology* (pp. 341–354). New York: Cambridge University Press.

Monroe, K. R. (2001). Morality and a sense of self: The importance of identity and categorization for moral action. *American Journal of Political Science, 45,* 491–507.

Moshman, D. (2005). *Adolescent psychological development: Rationality, morality, and identity* (2nd ed.). Mahwah, NJ: Erlbaum.

Narvaez, D., & Lapsley, D. K. (2005). The psychological foundations of everyday morality and moral expertise.

In D. K. Lapsley & F. C. Power (Eds.), *Character psychology and character education* (pp. 140–165). Notre Dame, IN: University of Notre Dame Press.

Narvaez, D., Lapsley, D. K., Hagele, S., & Lasky, B. (2006). Moral chronicity and social information processing: Tests of a social cognitive approach to moral personality. *Journal of Research in Personality, 40,* 966–985.

Nucci, L. (2004). Reflections on the moral self construct. In D. K. Lapsley & D. Narvaez (Eds.), *Moral development, self, and identity* (pp. 111–132). Mahwah, NJ: Erlbaum.

Nunner-Winkler, G. (2007). Development of moral motivation from early childhood to early adulthood. *Journal of Moral Education, 36,* 399–414.

Oliner, S. P., & Oliner, P. M. (1988). *The altruistic personality: Rescuers of Jews in Nazi Europe*. New York: The Free Press.

Penner, L. A., Fritzche, B. A., Craiger, J. P., & Freifeld, T. S. (1995). Measuring the prosocial personality. In J. Butcher & C. D. Spielberger (Eds.), *Advances in personality assessment* (Vol. 10, pp. 147–163). Hillsdale, NJ: Erlbaum.

Perugini, M., & Leone, L. (2009). Implicit self-concept and moral action. *Journal of Research in Personality, 43,* 747–754.

Piliavin, J. A., & Callero, P. L. (1991). *Giving blood: The development of altruistic identity*. Baltimore: The Johns Hopkins University Press.

Pratt, M. W., Arnold, M. L., & Lawford, H. (2009). Growing towards care: A narrative approach to prosocial moral identity and generativity of personality in emerging adulthood. In D. Narvaez & D. K. Lapsley (Eds.), *Personality, identity, and character: Explorations in moral psychology* (pp. 295–315). New York: Cambridge University Press.

Pratt, M. W., Hunsberger, B., Pancer, S. M., & Alisat, S. (2003). A longitudinal analysis of personal values socialization: Correlates of a moral self-ideal in late adolescence. *Social Development, 12,* 563–585.

Reed, A., II, & Aquino, K. F. (2003). Moral identity and the expanding circle of moral regard toward outgroups. *Journal of Personality and Social Psychology, 84,* 1270–1286.

Reimer, K. (2003). Committed to caring: Transformation in adolescent moral identity. *Applied Developmental Science, 7,* 129–137.

Reimer, K., Dewitt Goudelock, B. M., & Walker, L. J. (2009). Developing conceptions of moral maturity: Traits and identity in adolescent personality. *Journal of Positive Psychology, 4,* 372–388.

Reimer, K., & Wade-Stein, D. (2004). Moral identity in adolescence: Self and other in semantic space. *Identity, 4,* 229–249.

Rest, J. R. (1983). Morality. In P. Mussen, J. Flavell, & E. Markman (Eds.), *Handbook of child psychology: Cognitive development* (Vol. 3, pp. 556–628). New York: Wiley.

Reynolds, S. J., & Ceranic, T. L. (2007). The effects of moral judgment and moral identity on moral behavior: An empirical examination of the moral individual. *Journal of Applied Psychology, 92*, 1610–1624.

Schlenker, B. R., Miller, M. L., & Johnson, R. M. (2009). Moral identity, integrity, and personality responsibility. In D. Narvaez & D. Lapsley (Eds.), *Personality, identity, and character: Explorations in moral psychology* (pp. 316–340). New York: Cambridge University Press.

Schwartz, S. H. (1992). Universals in the content and structure of values: Theoretical advances and empirical tests in 20 countries. *Advances in Experimental Social Psychology, 25*, 1–65.

Shao, R., Aquino, K., & Freeman, D. (2008). Beyond moral reasoning: A review of moral identity research and its implications for business ethics. *Business Ethics Quarterly, 18*, 513–540.

Slife, B. D. (2004). Taking practice seriously: Toward a relational ontology. *Journal of Theoretical and Philosophical Psychology, 24*, 155–178.

Slife, B. D., & Richardson, F. C. (2008). Problematic ontological underpinnings of positive psychology: A strong relational alternative. *Theory & Psychology, 18*, 699–723.

Staub, E. (2005). The roots of goodness: The fulfillment of basic human needs and the development of caring, helping and nonagression, inclusive caring, moral courage, active bystandership, and altruism born of suffering. In G. Carlo & C. P. Edwards (Eds.), *Moral motivation through the lifespan* (Vol. 51, pp. 33–72). Lincoln, NE: University of Nebraska Press.

Stets, J. E., & Carter, M. J. (2006). The moral identity: A principle level identity. In K. A. McClelland & T. J. Fararo (Eds.), *Purpose, meaning, and action: Control system theories in sociology* (pp. 293–316). New York: Palgrave MacMillan.

Stets, J. E., Carter, M. J., Harrod, M. M., Cerven, C., & Abrutyn, S. (2008). The moral identity, status, moral education, and the normative order. In D. T. Robinson & J. Clay-Warner (Eds.), *Social structure and emotion* (pp. 227–249). Boston: Elsevier.

Taylor, C. (1989). *Sources of the self: The making of the modern identity.* Cambridge, MA: Harvard University Press.

Thompson, R. A. (2009). Early foundations: Conscience and the development of moral character. In D. Narvaez & D. Lapsley (Eds.), *Personality, identity, and character: Explorations in moral psychology* (pp. 159–184). New York: Cambridge University Press.

Turiel, E. (2002). *The culture of morality: Social development, context, and conflict.* New York: Cambridge University Press.

Walker, L. J. (2004). Gus in the gap: Bridging the judgment-action gap in moral functioning. In D. K. Lapsley & D. Narvaez (Eds.), *Moral development, self, and identity* (pp. 1–20). Mahwah, NJ: Erlbaum.

Walker, L. J., & Frimer, J. A. (2007). Moral personality of brave and caring exemplars. *Journal of Personality and Social Psychology, 93*, 845–860.

Walker, L. J., & Pitts, R. C. (1998). Naturalistic conceptions of moral maturity. *Developmental Psychology, 34*, 403–419.

Williams, R. N., & Olson, T. D. (2008, November). *Moral reasoning in the context of ethical obligation: Recasting the starting point for moral education.* Paper presented at the meeting for the Association for Moral Education, South Bend, Indiana.

Wilson, T. D., Lindsey, S., & Schooler, T. Y. (2000). A model of dual attitudes. *Psychological Review, 107*, 101–126.

Youniss, J., & Yates, M. (1997). *Community service and social responsibility in youth.* Chicago: University of Chicago Press.

Values, Personal Identity, and the Moral Self

Steven Hitlin

Abstract

This chapter outlines a theoretical backdrop for incorporating research on human values into the study of the self. The chapter takes a sociological, interactional perspective suggesting that socially shaped patterns can be empirically determined underlying the supposedly idiosyncratic notion of "personal identity." Human beings anchor their sense of self across situations within feelings of right and wrong and the importance they place on various abstract, desirable goals. Values allow the study of this aspect of personal identity and allow bridges to be built with the long-standing sociological literature on the relationship of social structure and individuals' values. I illustrate how this focus on the moral dimension of values operates at two well-established levels of the self – cognition and emotion – and sets the stage for the broad development of a theory of the moral actor over time.

In the range of sociological assumptions about human nature, scholars rarely focus on the moral dimension of social actors. This aspect of personhood has been at the root of philosophical discussion for millennia and is important in many areas of psychological thought. However, current theories of the self have not paid adequate attention to the self's moral aspects, despite early work by James (1892), Mead (1934), and others that explicitly called attention to the moral dimensions of social action. Advances in the understanding of values, long dormant but recently undergoing a partial resurgence, anchor the growing understanding of the moral self (see Hardy & Carlo, Chapter 19, this volume). Individuals' value structures represent moral intuitions about prohibited and desired behaviors that are only sometimes able to be articulated (e.g., Rokeach, 1973). Incorporating values into the self provides a mechanism through which consistency and inconsistency in social action are plausible and predictable, actors' internal experiences are linked to social structure, and cognitive and emotional dimensions are integrated within one's overall sense of self.

Values represent empirically accessible mechanisms that frame actors' moral intuitions and narrative self-constructions in terms of the actors themselves as moral beings. Values represent a powerful mechanism through which one's

S. Hitlin (✉)
Department of Sociology, University of Iowa, Iowa City, IA, USA
e-mail: steven-hitlin@uiowa.edu

S.J. Schwartz et al. (eds.), *Handbook of Identity Theory and Research*,
DOI 10.1007/978-1-4419-7988-9_20, © Springer Science+Business Media, LLC 2011

location in the social environment becomes internalized, whereby demonstrated commonalities in social outlooks based on social position or group identity shape the self (see Hitlin & Piliavin, 2004). That social structures are enacted and recreated through individual action is widely understood, but with a few exceptions (e.g., Blasi, 1984) the moral dimension of this activity has been neglected compared to piecemeal aspects of the self like self-esteem and self-efficacy, what Tesser, Crepaz, Beach, Cornell, and Collins (2000) refer to as the self-zoo. Individuals develop an intuitive, reflexively accessible sense of noble and ignoble goals that judge, evaluate, and legitimate behavior within situations or upon reflection afterward. Over time, we construct patterned understandings of ourselves as existing within moral frameworks that constrain desirable action. Values form a core of the self, become instantiated through intuitions and self-narratives, and frame actors' interpretations, judgments, and action.

This chapter posits a sociological perspective on the core psychological issue of morality. Sociology, once the driving discipline for the study of values (see Spates, 1983; Wuthnow, 2008), currently is characterized by a surprising shortage of exploration about morality (Calhoun, 1991; Holstein & Gubrium, 2000; Smith, 2003). Values, viewed as an internalized representation of cultural moral ideals, may differ across societies but do so within a bounded range shaped by evolutionarily necessary aspects that stem from life in surviving social groups (Schwartz, 1992). Understood sociologically, a sense of personal identity anchored in values captures internalized representations of social affiliation, location, or group membership. This chapter reincorporates morality into notions of identity by tracing the contours of a sociologically sensitive model of the self's moral core – that is, personal identity. This perspective offers at least two important contributions to the study of the moral aspects of identity. First, compared to the typical focus on altruism, values offer the possibility of a broader understanding of what is considered moral. Second, values have been extensively linked to individuals' social–structural position

and group membership, suggesting that values are a core mechanism through which social positions become internalized. For example, social class, coupled with one's occupational type, shapes the values parents teach to their children (e.g., Kohn, 1959; Kohn & Schooler, 1983). Thus, this approach links identity to social structure through the development of personal values.

In this chapter, I defend the proposition – certainly accepted in philosophical work, if less commonly in social psychological theories – that personal identity is intrinsically moral. Additionally, it is a concept that bridges two understandings of identity, what I summarize elsewhere as "ego" versus "social" (Hitlin & Lancianese, 2008). The "ego" dimension draws on traditionally psychological scholars, such as Erikson (1968) and Piaget (1960), and captures a sense of coherence across life experiences (see also Côté, 1997; Kroger & Marcia, Chapter 2, this volume); the "social" dimension is based on either roles or social commonalities among members of groups (see Serpe & Stryker, Chapter 10, this volume; Spears, Chapter 9, this volume). Synthesizing these two dimensions of identity through the concept of values offers the empirical possibility of studying the self's moral dimension. After explaining the utility of values for studying the moral self, I illustrate how this focus on the moral dimension of self at two well-established levels of the self – cognition and emotion – allows for the broad development of a theory of the moral actor over time.

The Problem: The Current Amoral Conception of the Social Actor

A sociological understanding of the self largely traces back to the work of George Herbert Mead (1934, 1938), who is lesser known for an admittedly brief focus on the ways in which moral values become implicated within social interaction. This strand is also found in Weber's (1922/1978) concern with individuals providing action with meaning. Within his typology of action, Weber highlighted "value-rational" actions, indicating that such actions make sense to actors given the moral principle they are pursuing; suicide bombers are acting morally from a particular perspective. This concern with the moral dimension of social actors and social action has largely faded from current sociological theorizing (Smith, 2003), though it remains active in one notable research tradition in psychology (see Hardy & Carlo, Chapter 19, this volume).

Whereas "ego" identity scholars – who tend to be psychologists – focus on inner sameness and continuity within the individual (see Kroger & Marcia, Chapter 2, this volume), the sociological equivalent is rooted in the notion of the self. "Self" is a generalized term often employed without carefully delineated referents (Katzko, 2003), yet is ubiquitous in sociological theorizing. The self, as employed in these theoretical traditions, is the internalized, subjective-yet-agentic link between individuals and social environments (see Joas, 2000). It represents an important mechanism through which social positions become internalized and translated into situated behavior. The self is a socially constructed product of symbolic actors interacting within social environments (see Stryker & Serpe, Chapter 10, this volume)[1] and allows for a sense of agentic control that can be absent from personality-based models of behavior. As decades of data demonstrate, supposedly stable personality attributes are not able to explain empirical evidence for vast intra-individual variation in behaviors across situations and over the life course (Mischel, 2004). Sociologists are often left, however, with a peculiar conception of the individual as a holder of separate social and role identities and rarely as a cohesive person (Hewitt, 1989); sociology is rarely concerned with the Eriksonian notion of continuity across roles. Sociologists have not spent enough time theorizing "how people shape their doings in each given situation to have meaning as they move among situations" (Katz, 1999, p. 324).[2] Put differently, with the exception of the tradition of symbolic interactionism proffered by Blumer (1969) and his adherents, sociological models tend to be less concerned with individual variation and initiation of action than with their overwhelmingly structurally patterned regularities as observed in behavior over time.

The term "identity" is often employed as a placeholder for other social processes (Brubaker & Cooper, 2000), and the use of this term to mean so many different things makes cross-disciplinary dialogue quite difficult. Some authors in the "ego" identity tradition, notably Erikson (1968), discuss moral concerns as constituting a portion of people's reported sense of coherence (e.g., Dunkel, 2005), but this conception finds its clearest articulation in the work of the philosopher Charles Taylor (1988). As I will try to show throughout the present chapter, values offer the opportunity for future empirical work to refine these theoretical claims in light of the vast research literature (summarized below). Actors' moral senses are frameworks for evaluation of self and others, and offer a cohesive cognitive–emotional core that allows for both consistency *and* situationally influenced variation in social action across the life course.

Other scholars focus on a "moral identity" construct (see Hardy & Carlo, Chapter 19, this volume; Stets & Carter, 2006), but there are reasons to prefer a notion of the moral self based in values rather than in "moral identity." The concept of moral identity defines morality along conventional, prosocial lines (emphasizing qualities such as honesty, conscientiousness, and altruism). This approach is imbued with cultural presuppositions that distract one from the exploration of the *range* of moral motivations. In the "moral identity" approach, people who are motivated by, for instance, self-interest or hedonism are considered "un-"moral. But reifying a single brand of morality, no matter how common, precludes the possibility that some people orient themselves toward unconventional moral codes that comprise significant aspects of their self-concept and that guide their resulting behavior. For instance, an individual who is strongly focused on achievement – and who "steps over others" to reach the top – might view his or her actions as quite moral, though he or she would not score well on traditional measures of moral identity. By focusing on "the" moral identity, we overlook the conflicting goals and values that social actors face.

The Value of Values

Human beings make moral judgments, differentiating between behaviors that "ought" (or "ought not") to occur. A moral judgment is more fundamental than simply labeling something "good" or "bad"; it carries an implication of what the world and its inhabitants should be like. Morality is a broad concept, one that constitutes the "inhibitive" and "proactive" elements of moral agency (Bandura, 1999). Early on in socialization, we acquire a basic sense that cer tain actions are taboo or forbidden. Alternatively, we can discuss morality as focused on something laudable, such as the virtues debated by philosophers. Although a society's set of prohibitions is likely circumscribed, the list of proactive goals is broad and ranges from concrete to abstract goals (e.g., peace, justice, self-fulfillment, or tradition) that overlap and even contradict. Values – "conceptions of the desirable" (in Parsons's (1937) term) – represent the proactive aspect of the moral agent, namely those ideals that she or he views as most worthwhile to pursue.

Values refer to variably important goals that transcend situations and that act as guiding principles for people's (or other social entities; Schwartz, 1994) decisions and behavior. Values represent orientations toward solving the problems that social groups necessarily face, such as individual autonomy, preserving the social fabric, and managing relations with the natural and social worlds (Schwartz, 2004b). Values refer and relate to many different domains (such as work and family), attitudes, ideologies, and belief systems (Maio, Olson, Bernard, & Luke, 2003; Rohan, 2000). Scholarly interest in values appears to have undergone something of a resurgence (for overviews, see Hitlin & Piliavin, 2004; Karp, 2000; Maio et al., 2003; Marini, 2000; Rohan, 2000; Schwartz, 2004a; Wuthnow, 2008).

Schwartz has studied values around the world and consistently found that people in over 70 nations (Schwartz, 2004b) recognize the following 10 values, each defined in terms of the motivational goal that underlies it (Schwartz & Bilsky, 1987, 1990). The primary content of a value is the type of goal or motivational concern it expresses, and these goals map quite nicely onto notions of morally laudable behaviors and outcomes.

Achievement: competitive personal success
Hedonism: self-centered sensual gratification
Stimulation: risk taking and adventure
Self-direction: autonomous thought and action
Universalism: tolerance and concern for welfare of all others
Benevolence: welfare for those with whom one is in frequent contact
Conformity: self-restraint, subordinating one's inclinations to others' expectations
Tradition: traditional and religious activities
Security: stability, safety, and harmony of society, relationships, and self
Power: status and prestige; control people and resources

One other value that Schwartz terms "spirituality" is inconsistently located across samples, and thus is omitted from his basic scheme. These values can be arrayed in a circular fashion, whereby values that are adjacent to each other (power and achievement) share aspects and reflect opposite goals compared with others in the circle (e.g., conformity is the opposite of hedonism). This general array has been supported by different methodological approaches (for details, see Kasser & Ryan, 1996; Oishi, Schimmack, Diener, & Suh, 1998; Pakizeh, Gebauer, & Maio, 2007). Because of its cross-cultural support and psychological depth, I will draw on this conceptual approach toward values for my argument, rather than drawing from other influential approaches (e.g., Hechter, Ranger-Moore, Jasso, & Horne, 1999; Inglehart & Baker, 2000; Rokeach, 1973).[3]

Values are best understood as organized components that mutually constrain each other (Hodges & Geyer, 2006); values are, in a theoretical sense, a zero-sum game, with larger focus on one dimension suggesting a resultantly less important focus on their opposites. Values' universal recognition stems from the commonalities of human social interaction across different contexts and cultures (Schwartz & Bilsky, 1987, 1990). For example, every social group needs to cooperate, develop a minimal amount of trust, and deal with other necessary aspects of collective survival. Particular cultures may prioritize the values differently, but the list of values is cross-culturally consistent. Moreover, values are not the sole determinants of behavior. Values exist at the global, ideological level and thus represent distal causal forces affecting individual action to the extent an individual has internalized those values (Eyal et al., 2009; Schwartz, 1996). They are more abstract (Howard, 1995; Rokeach, 1973) and durable (Konty & Dunham, 1997) than are attitudes and thus are even more distally related to action (see also Maio & Olson, 2000).

Values situate us in moral space. They are cognitive–emotional frameworks underlying self-perception and social interaction. Values have stable (but not fixed) properties that allow conceptualization of the self as unified yet situationally enacted, with space for change across the life course. Values are symbolic tools that reinforce our experiences of coherence across social and group identities as well as across social situations. Importantly, values are empirically measurable, leading to the potential to empirically investigate the moral self.

Values also involve a cognitive component (Rokeach, 1973), but as William James (1892) points out, we do not experience values as cold, cognitive imperatives. Values include strong motivational affect because of their perceived importance. Values operate dynamically through action (Joas, 2000) and represent an important influence on behavior within and across situations (e.g., Blankenship & Wegener, 2008). Their emotional, intuitive aspect – stemming from the fundamental perception of self-evident "rightness" – becomes important in understanding the place of values within the self.

The accumulated scholarship on values, and on moral development more broadly, posits both universal elements of, and culture-specific variation in, their development and exercise. The self has similar universal and culture-specific properties (e.g., Markus & Kitayama, 1991; Triandis, 1995), suggesting ways to merge literatures on the self and values. Scholars have suggested the importance of values for the self (Gecas,

2000; Kasser, 2002; Rohan, 2000; Smith, 1991; Turner, 1968), but these implications have not been extensively theorized nor empirically studied. Put differently, although there is cultural variation in the symbolic content from which people derive their sense of self, there are also universal aspects of personhood. Reflexivity, the ability for a social actor to view herself as others see her, is a fundamental, universal property of the self (Callero, 2003; Mead, 1934; Wiley, 1994). The self as the seat of individual agency not only is limited to a modern, Western conception of self but stems from the fundamentally social nature of human actors. Three trans-cultural human experiences form the basis for selfhood (Baumeister, 1999): (a) reflexive consciousness, (b) interpersonal being (member of groups and relationships), and (c) self as executive functioning agent (making choices).

Personal Identity and the Self

The concept of personal identity (Deaux, 1992; Hewitt, 1989; Hitlin, 2003) becomes the anchor for a synthesis of self and values. In contrast to social identities, personal identity comprises those supposedly idiosyncratic aspects of an individual's experiences, temperament, and development. For instance, there are many similarities between two people occupying the role of "student." But they differ in their sense of personal identity – the history, experiences, orientations, and behavioral intentions that characterize them like no other individuals.

One's personal identity is experienced as constitutive of one's sense of self. To change an aspect of one's history or core orientations is to fundamentally change the person; it is something different than changing a hairstyle or sports team allegiance. Were I to value something different, to suddenly find something immoral that I previously believed was moral, I would experience a fundamental shift in my sense of who I "really" am. Personal identity is intertwined with a sense of authenticity (see Heppner & Kernis, Chapter 15, this volume; Soenens & Vansteenkiste, Chapter 17, this volume; Waterman, Chapter 16, this volume), which is a primary motivational aspect of the self (Gecas, 1986, 1991). Experiences of authenticity, which are intensively real and personal, are socially shaped (e.g., Turner, 1976). We feel a range of emotions, reactions, and perceive social feedback as a consequence of our behavior. Translating into classic debates about the essentialist versus constructivist self, I adopt a constructivist position, anchoring those constructions within social groups, institutions, and cultures more than might be typical in many psychological circles. Given that these experiences are anchored in values, however, there are likely biological elements (e.g., Bilsky & Schwartz, 1994) that interact with social–structural forces (and constraints). The key issue is that these feelings are constructed over the course of one's life based on one's interactions, and those interactions are socially shaped and patterned. Even though these are socially constructed, they feel like universal truths (Joas, 2000).

From a sociological perspective, these feelings are developed by and constructed within social commitments, the basis of the "social" identity approach. People feel inauthentic if they fail to live up to important social commitments; a teacher who fails to instruct students well, or a father whose children become disciplinary problems, is far from agnostic about shortcomings of performing their roles. However, people do not dispassionately analyze such violations as simple mistakes; rather we feel that we have committed significant violations to ourselves and others. The accompanying negative emotions (see Tangney, Steuwig, & Mashek, 2007) signify disturbed moral valences and the enactment or violation of important self-meanings (Blasi, 1999). These moral reactions, anchored in our emotions, constitute our sense of personal identity. Moral outlooks are experienced as constitutive of who one is both as an individual and as a member of a community. As I endeavor to demonstrate, cross-culturally recognized values form the basis for individual moral orientations (Nisan, 1984; Schwartz, 2004a); values are derived socially but are experienced personally.

Personal identity organizes the orientations and experiences that constitute each individual as a unique entity. It is the internal barometer from which patterned senses of right, wrong, and the desirable are developed. Personal identity suggests the possibility – an important Western belief – of an enduring, patterned, cross-situational moral orientation, an essential self that exists outside of situations. It signifies nonconscious intuitions that provide feedback about the moral propriety of actual or imagined interactions and behaviors. Moral intuitions involve "the sudden appearance in consciousness, or at the fringe of consciousness, of an evaluative feeling (like–dislike, good–bad) about the character or actions of a person, without any conscious awareness of having gone through steps of search, weighing evidence, or inferring a conclusion" (Haidt & Bjorklund, 2008, p. 188). Personal identity involves what MacIntyre (1981) refers to as "continuities of each individual's history" that lead to a sense of integration that is vital for understanding people as moral agents over time. Personal identity is an umbrella term for pre-reflective patterns of habit and intuitions that are based in fundamental proactive and prohibitive moral orientations. Actions are a mixture of personal dispositions and situational influences, but there are patterns in how we judge people and situations. Some individuals are more predisposed to "see" situations as calling for benevolent action, whereas others are more likely to interpret the world through a window of self-interestedness (e.g., Simpson & Willer, 2008). Rather than appealing to vague intuitions, placing values at the center of personal identity offers the opportunity to anchor these perceptions within a sociological understanding of the self, based on extensive literatures about how social class, occupation, family, and other aspects of context influence individual values (see Hitlin & Piliavin, 2004).

Moral situations are inherently ambiguous; otherwise, behavioral scripts would be obvious (Walker, 2000). However, scholars suggest that what might be ambiguous to an outsider seems straightforward for those who are moral exemplars (Colby & Damon, 1992). This suggests that, contrary to purely situationist accounts of human behavior (e.g., Kelley et al., 2003), individual perceptions matter. The argument advanced here is that a portion of these perceptions involves individual values, shaped by cultural values, that contribute to explaining why different people attend to different aspects of their social environments. These principles – of which values are theoretically and empirically at the core – operate as cognitive–emotional filters for incoming information. We cognitively notice "facts" that fit with our precognitions, and we are motivated (in part) to verify our view of ourselves (Gregg, Sedikides, & Gebauer, Chapter 14, this volume; Swann, 1983). These frameworks are not deterministic of future action; people innovate and shift habits throughout the life course. But our personal identity, anchored in values, dictates what "facts" we observe or what arguments seem persuasive in moral situations. These informational assumptions (Turiel, 2002) shape judgment and action, both when time allows for deliberation and when sudden responses are necessitated (Berzonsky, Chapter 3, this volume). An advantage of viewing personal identity through the lens of values is that values consist of both emotional and cognitive components. Interaction is typically not guided by fully articulated thoughts, but rather by vague notions and internal sensations. These moral intuitions are anchored in cross-situationally stable value structures, which themselves are anchored in social networks, communities, and a wider culture. We can ask people to report their abstract values apart from situational context, as the Schwartz empirical method does, which leads to a trans-situational sense of personal identity removed from context. Our sense of right and wrong exists apart from and outside of concrete situations that may test those senses. The empirically interesting questions, however, revolve around which aspects of personal identity are implicated in different situations. To what extent, we might ask, does an individual's strong valuing of benevolence (caring about others) shape actions across contexts where demonstrating such caring might be difficult?

Blasi (1984) suggests that moral judgment is largely a cognitive process motivated by a desire for self-consistency (see also Schwalbe, 1991). If we see ourselves in a particular way, actions that fail to live up to that self-definition will lead to uncomfortable feelings of inconsistency. This is part of the story, but it also represents an overly cognitive version of models of the self and action. The place of moral intuition also involves one's self; we want our intuitions and cognitions to match our view of ourselves as moral beings. When a social object (e.g., an action, an issue, or a person's behavior) strikes us as morally wrong or laudable, we feel something deeper than a simple cognitive evaluation, something experienced as more central to ourselves. Erikson's (1968) work notably focused on the complex interrelation of social life, concrete situations, internal feelings, and a sense of personal continuity. But I am positing a firmer internal barometer of personal identity – based on relatively stable values – across situations than Erikson did (see Stevens, 2008). From my perspective, it is not the case that one has more or less a sense of personal identity, as Erikson postulated (Kroger, 2000; see Kroger & Marcia, Chapter 2, this volume), but that this sense of identity can be anchored in different values. This leads to another set of empirical questions – the extent to which some people might hold no strong values, and as such are relatively less motivated by particular social outcomes. The thesis advanced here proposes that all people have some values that are important and thus that it makes little sense to say a given person has a "stronger" personal identity than do others. Someone else may more strongly be focused on hedonistic goals than I am, but I in turn may value universalistic ends. This differs from the sense that someone else might be "more" of a Yankees fan than I am, in theory, but these questions require empirical investigation.

Personal identity is thus a combination of personality factors and self-reflected understandings that circumscribe potential action. When a social situation becomes odd or problematic, we do not simply try to maximize utility; as decades of sociological work in the tradition of Erving Goffman (e.g., 1959) suggest, we attempt to "repair" situations based on the identities we are claiming in that context. Interactional claims and biographical histories are linked with our moral intuitions that discriminate among various behavioral choices as feeling "like us" or not. We may act in a manner distinct from our typical activity, but later on discuss how we "weren't ourselves." Values and moral intuitions form the referent for adjudications between actions that "are" and "are not" ourselves (see Turner, 1976 on a related point). Values serve as important emotional *and* cognitive referents about what is a "real" sense of self, and they are linked to and shaped by important social identities. Most of the time, our situated self is circumscribed enough, both by social–structural pressures and by individual biography, that our subjective sense of proper behavior is relatively straightforward. It is precisely in situations of role ambiguity, where it is not clear what action is proscribed by the relevant social identity, where we see the importance of our moral horizons (see Hitlin & Elder, 2007); when situated identities do not suffice, we fall back on our value-based personal identity to adjudicate between better and worse behavioral options.

Personal Identity, Moral Horizons, and Narrative Self-understanding

This moral core is self-reflexively accessible through examining intuitive emotional reactions. To communicate such experiences, however, we translate them – to ourselves and others – into narratives. These narratives are the articulation of core emotional experiences of aligning oneself with valued principles (see McAdams, Chapter 5, this volume). This moral sense remains consistent across social and role identities and serves as the barometer that individuals use to guide situated behavior. We have a variety of legitimating discourses available to justify actions (Bandura, 1991; Rokeach, 1973; Swidler, 2001), but these discourses are not randomly chosen. Core intuitions tap into beliefs and feelings about the world, and often become narrated only after the fact – in a pragmatic fashion – when we reflect

upon our actions. Reflected feedback becomes appropriated to ourselves and forms the basis for moral feelings (e.g., pride or shame). If we ask people to describe their personal identity, they will present a narrative based on feelings, roles, group memberships, and cultural discourses. This version – or any point-in-time version – of the self involves what Wegner (2002) refers to the self as a "public relations agent," convincing others (and ourselves) of a plausible coherence through narrative (see also Bamberg, Schiffrin, & De Fina, Chapter 8, this volume; Lewis, 1997). We make up a story about how our actions, across a variety of situations, fit together, forming what John Dewey (1922) suggested was a "useful fiction" of ourselves. Contrary to many "essentialist" perspectives, from the perspective I am advocating here, personal identity is not a "thing" but rather a loop of thought, feeling, intention, and memory (Dennett, 2003). Morality is, I have been arguing, at the core of this loop, the filter through which our moral horizons comprise an apparently stable, though actually flexible, sense of self. We need stances on moral issues and principles to develop a sense of personal integrity (e.g., Honneth, 2005).

McAdams (Chapter 5, this volume) offers a psychologically sensitive model linking narrative to these various thoughts, feelings, and identities based on social commitments and group identification (see also McAdams, 1995, 2001). Narrative operates on top of what McAdams terms "basic traits" and "characteristic adaptations" (goals, values, beliefs, and life concerns). McAdams stresses that a personal narrative is necessary to understand ourselves across time; we tell stories about where we are, where we have been, and how the past and the present relate to where we are going. These stories are not simply self-generated but draw from the various cultural plots and understandings that are available to us (e.g., Somers & Gibson, 1994).

Personal identity, our sense of who we are and are not, is not a fixed entity. Feelings, intuitions, and emotions may not always neatly line up with beliefs, goals, and ideals. However, in constructing narratives, we can create an illusion of linearity and coherence across the disparate experiences, situations, and roles that make up a human life. We edit, omit, and reconstruct events to create such a narrative that allows us to seamlessly take today's self and link it to yesterday's self.[4] These narratives frame, reflect, and reciprocally shape the self's moral vantage point, what Charles Taylor (1989) refers to as moral horizons (see also Holstein & Gubrium, 2000). The moral aspect of personal identity, anchored in values, frames the intuitions we have and the narratives we create about these intuitions.

Taylor's "horizon" metaphor is instructive. He describes "identity" in the Eriksonian sense of the word (elsewhere Taylor uses the term "self" in its broader social science understanding), as the portion of self without which the world would not be intelligible. Our identity commitments, Taylor suggests, provide frameworks "within which they can determine where they stand on questions of what is good, or worthwhile, or admirable, or of value (1994, pp. 27–28). It makes no sense to talk about a person without understanding those goals and values through which she or he makes sense of her or his life (Smith, 2003), what Damasio (1999) refers to as a "continuity of reference." Taylor's work, while not fully sociological, builds to a more-than-cognitive view of the self by focusing on the importance of moral horizons (Calhoun, 1991).

Values serve as primary horizons for shaping individuals' sense of self. Over time, consistencies in moral outlook shape feeling, perception, and action within interactions and act as cognitive–emotional signposts for novel situations. Certain lines of action feel "right" and are experienced as genuine expressions of our self. When situationally plausible, we engage in actions that reflect our values. Over time, repeated observations of actions and consequences contribute to a narrative self-understanding that, in turn, frames future situations. This core sense is not re-constituted from scratch in each situation; rather, it acts spontaneously but not randomly. Situational pressures may dampen one's ability to act in line with core values, yet these values still serve as internal barometers, horizons, or instantaneous referents through which we orient ourselves to situations;

we feel "real" when we discuss our values with others (Pronin, Fleming, & Steffel, 2008). Moral horizons constitute primary frames by which selves obtain coherence.

Values are realized in moments of self-formation (Joas, 2000). They shape the evaluative standards through which we situate ourselves in moral space and reflexively evaluate ourselves, our actions, and others. Values are what Taylor (1994) calls "hypergoods," meta-analytical schemata for adjudicating about social reality, the ways we decide which of two "good" things may be best. For example, I may like ice cream and being fit. Hypergoods help us figure out which good is most personally pressing, though situations may make one or the other momentarily salient (Ainslie, 2001). It makes no sense to discuss personal identity without understanding these evaluative structures, fundamentally social but experienced as a vital part of the self. Values imbue objects with positive or negative valences and, as such, determine (or at least weight) decisions made within action (e.g., Feather, 1992).

Mechanisms of the Moral Aspects of Personal Identity

We can start to refine potential mechanisms through which personal values influence situated behavior and narrative self-understandings that, in turn, influence self-construction over the life course. Although values are typically measured as ideals, people experience them physiologically (e.g., Batson, Engel, & Fridell, 1999); neurologists suggest that values anchor the experience of oneself as a distinct entity (Damasio, 1999). The primary nature of a morally orienting self suggests a predisposition for the very act of valuing, a property found in children (e.g., Kagan, 1994 [1984]), and thus something that – like the notion of the self – appears as characteristic of our species.

Developmentally, the internalization of moral standards becomes more and more reflected in an individual's notion of self (e.g., Kohlberg, 1981). In children, morality and the self begin as two separate conceptual systems, but these two developmental domains become increasingly interrelated during adolescence (Keller & Edelstein, 1993). Younger children are especially sensitive to the opinions of others, but typically by age 10, children understand and make use of abstract principles like justice and equality. By adolescence, they accept more responsibility for others' welfare and begin to assemble personal theories of morality, though they often hold too rigidly to these theories with limited recognition of nuance. By adulthood, these personal moral systems are assimilated into the person's sense of self (Damon, 1984).

Research supporting the social intuitionist model (SIM) (Haidt, 2001) demonstrates that moral reactions occur much more quickly than can be explained through cognitive processing; only after experiencing a moral intuition do we search for cognitive rationalizations that can support that judgment. We have immediate reactions to the rightness, wrongness, or general desirability of objects and actions. The SIM focuses on instantaneous moral judgments and ways in which these core reactions can, given the right social circumstances, shift over time (Haidt & Joseph, 2004). Moral reasoning and judgment do not shift solely based on logic or self-reflection (though philosophers might argue otherwise), but rather social engagement, dialogue, and potentially peer pressure. The notion of moral intuitions has received neurological support (Damasio, 1999; Greene & Haidt, 2002) and fits with anthropological suggestions that "gut" moral feelings are similar to the way primates demonstrate empathy (de Waal, 1996, 2005). A strength of incorporating the SIM is its focus on the social aspect of changes in intuitions over time. Our moral intuitions are constitutive of who we are, but as personal identity changes over time, so too can these intuitions. Empirical evidence supports the idea that shifts in moral intuitions occur through important others' attempts to persuade us (Haidt, 2003). These attempts operate not only at a cognitive level – the way in which some psychologists argue that morality develops (e.g., Colby & Kohlberg, 1984; Kohlberg & Candee, 1984; Kohlberg, 1981;

Nunner-Winkler, 1993) – but also through sheer social pressures.

"Moral exemplars," individuals who exhibit extremely prosocial behaviors (Colby & Damon, 1995; Damon & Hart, 1992), inform this discussion. People selected as having highly developed moral (prosocial) senses (e.g., American Civil Rights pioneers, those who opposed the Nazis) report that their actions in moral situations felt obligatory; they did not suggest they had deliberated over their laudable behaviors. Both their interpretations and their intuitions contributed to their behaving in ways that we consider moral. Some people, based on their internal moral horizons, are predisposed to interpret and react to situations along prosocial lines (e.g., Monroe & Epperson, 1994). Such individuals receive moral "credit" from others for actions that they, themselves, felt were obligatory. These individuals report broader concern for the welfare of others than is typical (Colby & Damon, 1995). We might expect that they would score high on universalistic values. When moral concerns are invoked, action is not seen as optional; self-horizons are cognitively and intuitively felt as obligatory.

This conception addresses issues regarding situations that do not align neatly with prior expectations. Social identities circumscribe routine behavior (see Serpe & Stryker, Chapter 10, this volume), but some situations require novel reactions or choices. Roles may conflict, multiple life options may be ahead of us, and we may face situations where multiple value systems are relevant. Such choices are rarely straightforward and often engage conflicting values (Turiel, 2002), and this is a basic part of social life (Berlin, 1990). Morality involves deciding among various moral demands, not just the extent to which we privilege prosocial behaviors and ideals. By incorporating a notion of values as part of a cross-culturally recognizable, socially derived system of possible moral preferences, we create a fuller picture of social life. In America's abortion debate, for example, personal freedom – a core American value – is at the root of both sides' framings; the issue is which person's autonomy, mother or unborn child, takes precedence. The debate is not about the value itself but rather about the informational assumptions that dovetail with actors' moral intuitions about the rightness or wrongness of each side of the debate or about whose needs are more important. The analytical question becomes answering how people decide from among competing values alongside their interpretive habits, beliefs, and informational assumptions.

Conclusion

Ancient thinkers privileged morality as humanity's distinguishing feature (Kagan, 2004). Social scientists (with notable exceptions, discussed here) have largely moved away from Durkheim's goal of a sociology of morality (but see Hitlin & Vaisey, 2010). Perspectives and empirical tools useful for this enterprise are scattered across social science disciplines, and integrating them would be of great help in constructing a sociology of morality. This chapter offers an attempt in this direction, to allow analysis of actors' moral dimension based on a proper understanding of the place of values within personal identity. Individuals' values form moral self-horizons, framed by moral intuitions and informational assumptions. These horizons contribute to a sense of having a core self and shift the focus toward understanding individuals' achieved sense of coherence (echoed in McAdams' work in Chapter 5, this volume).

Values constitute a vital aspect of the core of the self from which people agentically assemble and structure important social identities to create the "useful fiction" of a coherent self. There are pre-reflective consistencies in the frameworks through which we define situations that lead to consistencies in behavior and intuitive responses across situations. Of course, members of a society are differentially able to select themselves into situations that will allow them to develop (and will allow others to ascribe to them) various social identities. These social groupings have patterned influences on value formation and thus individuals' moral frameworks. Some of what we mean by "working class," or "Hispanic," certainly has

to do with shared horizons of interpretation and understanding of their positions in social space (e.g., Waters, 1990).

Morality has its abstract aspects, the things philosophers and legal scholars debate, but to realize values in any meaningful way, action is required (Joas, 1985; Mead, 1932). Over time, we create coherent self-narratives from culturally available symbolic material. This implicates our personal identity, which is – at its core – a moral entity, framed by values providing cognitive–emotional horizons through which we understand and evaluate ourselves and others (see also Archer, 2000). A pragmatically informed model of the self posits values as the anchor for personal identity as well as the ongoing, habitual responses incorporated into one's moral character. This character develops as we enact social roles, within and across situations.

Embedded within this chapter is a wider call for the study of morality to go beyond a focus on conventionally prosocial behavior to explore structural patterns in moral codes and their appropriation into the self. The inherent prosocial bias of the term "moral" limits exploration. Virtues like truthfulness and modesty are not universally privileged, nor do most ethical systems advocate blind adherence to these virtues. We have a great deal to learn about moral development within societies, including patterned variation across groups within that society. Future work on identity should focus on these patterns and processes. We can learn more about social preconditions that socially structured relationships have on moral development, as well as how these processes may be culturally and historically variable (Calhoun, 1991). We should explore how, when, and under what circumstances do individuals and social groups identify with certain values over others.

Finally, moral aspirations are never fully attainable. They signify goals that humans consistently struggle to achieve (Calhoun, 1994). These struggles, and the ideals that motivate them, are largely the essence of the human condition. The study of values offers the possibility of beginning to systematize the links between self and society, social role and group membership, and the variety of potentially competing moral ideals that people face in their lives.

Notes

1. This is a cursory overview of the literature on the self. For further reviews, see Callero (2003) and Owens (2003).
2. Let me note, following Kohn (1989), that these criticisms of sociological approaches do not exempt psychological approaches from their own lack of focus on core human concerns, like obscuring issues of social structure, power, ethnicity, and other influences on personal identity.
3. See any of the Schwartz citations for details on empirical measurement.
4. The editors of the handbook suggest that scholars like Erikson or Marcia are looking at the self from a "macro" point of view, theorizing a unification that is more complicated the closer one looks, much as objects look solid until viewed through a microscope whereby they are clearly not solid at all.

References

Ainslie, G. (2001). *The breakdown of will*. Cambridge: Cambridge University Press.

Archer, M. S. (2000). *Being human: The problem of agency*. Cambridge: Cambridge University Press.

Bandura, A. (1991). Social cognitive theory of moral thought and action. In W. M. Kurtines & J. L. Gewirtz (Eds.), *Handbook of moral behavior and development* (pp. 45–103). Hillsdale, NJ: Lawrence Erlbaum.

Bandura, A. (1999). Moral disengagement in the perpetration of inhumanities. *Personality and Social Psychology Review, 3,* 193–209.

Batson, C. D., Engel, C. L., & Fridell, S. R. (1999). Value judgements: Testing the somatic-marker hypothesis using false physiological feedback. *Personality and Social Psychology Bulletin, 25,* 1021–1032.

Baumeister, R. F. (1999). The nature and structure of the self: An overview. In R. F. Baumeister (Ed.), *The self in social psychology* (pp. 1–20). Philadelphia: Taylor & Francis.

Berlin, I. (1990). *The crooked timber of humanity*. Princeton, NJ: Princeton University Press.

Blankenship, K. L., & Wegener, D. T. (2008). Opening the mind to close it: Considering a message in light of important values increases message processing and later resistance to change. *Journal of Personality and Social Psychology, 94,* 169–213.

Blasi, A. (1984). Moral identity: Its role in moral functioning. In W. M. Kurtines & J. L. Gewirtz (Eds.), *Morality, moral behavior, and moral development* (pp. 128–139). New York: Wiley.

Blasi, A. (1999). Emotions and moral concerns. *Journal for the Theory of Social Behaviour, 29,* 1–19.

Blumer, H. (1969). *Symbolic interactionism: Perspective and method*. Englewood Cliffs, NJ: Prentice Hall.

Brubaker, R., & Cooper, F. (2000). Beyond "identity". *Theory and Society, 29,* 1–47.

Calhoun, C. (1991). Morality, identity, and historical explanation: Charles Taylor on the sources of the self. *Sociological Theory, 9,* 232–263.

Calhoun, C. (1994). Social theory and the politics of identity. In C. Calhoun (Ed.), *Social theory and the politics of identity* (pp. 9–36). Malden, MA: Blackwell.

Callero, P. L. (2003). The sociology of the self. *Annual Review of Sociology, 29,* 115–133.

Colby, A., & Damon, W. (1992). *Some do care: Contemporary lives of moral commitment*. New York: The Free Press.

Colby, A., & Damon, W. (1995). The development of extraordinary moral commitment. In M. Killen & D. Hart (Eds.), *Morality in everyday life: Developmental perspectives* (pp. 342–370). Cambridge: Cambridge University Press.

Colby, A., & Kohlberg, L. (1984). Invariant sequence and internal consistency in moral judgment stages. In W. M. Kurtines & J. L. Gewirtz (Eds.), *Morality, moral behavior, and moral development* (pp. 41–51). New York: Wiley.

Cote, J. E. (1997). An empirical test of the identity capital model. *Journal of Adolescence, 20,* 577–597.

Damasio, A. (1999). *The feeling of what happens*. San Diego, CA: Harcourt.

Damon, W. (1984). Self-understanding and moral development from childhood to adolescence. In W. M. Kurtines & J. L. Gewirtz (Eds.), *Morality, moral behavior, and moral development* (pp. 109–127). New York: Wiley.

Damon, W., & Hart, D. (1992). Self-Understanding and its role in social and moral development. In M. H. Bornstein & M. E. Lamb (Eds.), *Developmental psychology: An advanced textbook* (pp. 421–464). Hillsdale, NJ: Lawrence Erlbaum Associates.

Deaux, K. (1992). Personalizing identity and socializing self. In G. Breakwell (Ed.), *Social psychology of identity and the self concept* (pp. 9–33). London: Academic Press.

Dennett, D. C. (2003). *Freedom evolves*. New York: Viking.

de Waal, F. (1996). *Good natured: The origins of right and wrong in humans and other animals.* Cambridge, MA: Harvard University Press.

de Waal, F. (2005). Morality and the social instincts: Continuity with the other primates. *Tanner Lectures on Human Values, 25,* 1–40.

Dewey, J. (1922). *Human nature and conduct.* New York: Henry Holt and Co.

Dunkel, C. S. (2005). The relation between self-continuity and measures of identity. *Identity: An International Journal of Theory and Research, 5,* 21–34.

Erikson, E. H. (1968). *Identity, youth, and crisis.* New York: W. W. Norton.

Eyal, T., Sagristano, M. D., Trope, Y., Liberman, N., & Chaiken, S. (2009). When values matter: Expressing values in behavioral intentions for the near vs. distant future. *Journal of Experimental Social Psychology, 45,* 35–43.

Feather, N. T. (1992). Values, valences, expectations, and actions. *Journal of Social Issues, 48,* 109–124.

Gecas, V. (1986). The motivational significance of self-concept for socialization theory. In E. J. Lawler (Ed.), *Advances in group processes* (pp. 131–156). Greenwich, CT: JAI Press.

Gecas, V. (1991). The self-concept as a basis for a theory of motivation. In J. A. Howard & P. L. Callero (Eds.), *The self-society dynamic: Cognition, emotion, and action* (pp. 171–187). New York: Cambridge University Press.

Gecas, V. (2000). Value identities, self-motives, and social movements. In S. Stryker, T. J. Owens, & R. W. White (Eds.), *Self, identity, and social movements* (pp. 93–109). Minneapolis, MN: University of Minnesota Press.

Goffman, E. (1959). *The presentation of self in everyday life.* Garden City, NY: Doubleday.

Goffman, E. (1983). The interaction order. *American Sociological Review, 48,* 1–17.

Greene, J., & Haidt, J. (2002). How (and where) does moral judgment work? *Trends in Cognitive Sciences, 6,* 517–523.

Haidt, J. (2001). The emotional dog and its rational tail: A social intuitionist approach to moral judgment. *Psychological Review, 108,* 814–834.

Haidt, J. (2003). The emotional dog does learn new tricks (a reply to Pizarro and Bloom). *Psychological Review, 110,* 197–198.

Haidt, J., & Bjorklund, F. (2008). Social Intuitionists answer six questions about moral psychology. In W. Sinnott-Armstrong (Ed.), *Moral psychology* (pp. 181–217). Cambridge, MA: MIT Press.

Haidt, J., & Joseph, C. (2004). Intuitive ethics: How innately prepared intuitions generate culturally variable virtues. *Daedalus, 133,* 55–66.

Hechter, M., Ranger-Moore, J., Jasso, G., & Horne, C. (1999). Do values matter? An analysis of advance directives for medical treatment. *European Sociological Review, 15,* 405–430.

Hewitt, J. P. (1989). *Dilemmas of the American self.* Philadelphia, PA: Temple University Press.

Hitlin, S. (2003). Values as the core of personal identity: Drawing links between two theories of the self. *Social Psychology Quarterly, 66*(2), 118–137.

Hitlin, S. (2008). *Moral selves, evil selves: The social psychology of conscience.* New York: Palgrave Macmillan.

Hitlin, S., & Elder, G. H., Jr. (2007). Agency: An empirical model of an abstract concept. In R. Macmillan (Ed.), *Advances in life course research: Constructing adulthood: agency and subjectivity in adolescence and adulthood* (pp. 33–67). Amsterdam: Elsevier/JAI Press.

Hitlin, S., & Lancianese, D. (2008). Identity. In D. Carr (Ed.), *Encyclopedia of life course and human development* (pp. 249–252). Florence, KY: Thomson.

Hitlin, S., & Piliavin, J. A. (2004). Values: A review of recent research and theory. *Annual Review of Sociology, 30,* 359–393.

Hitlin, S., & Vaisey, S. (2010). *Handbook of the sociology of morality.* New York: Springer.

Hodges, B. H., & Geyer, A. L. (2006). A nonconformist account of the Asch experiments: Values, pragmatics, and moral dilemmas. *Personality and Social Psychology Review, 10,* 2–19.

Holstein, J. A., & Gubrium, J. F. (2000). *The self we live by: Narrative identity in a postmodern world.* New York: Oxford University Press.

Honneth, A. (2005). Between Aristotle and Kant – sketch of a morality of recognition. In W. Edelstein & G. Nunner-Winkler (Eds.), *Morality in context* (pp. 41–56). Amsterdam: Elsevier.

Howard, J. A. (1995). Social cognition. In K. Cook, G. A. Fine, & J. S. House (Eds.), *Sociological perspectives on social psychology* (pp. 90–117). Boston: Allyn and Bacon.

Inglehart, R., & Baker, W. E. (2000). Modernization, cultural change, and the persistence of traditional values. *American Sociological Review, 65,* 19–51.

James, W. (1892). *The self.* Cleveland, OH: World Publishing.

Joas, H. (1985). *G. H. Mead: A contemporary re-examination of his thought.* Cambridge, MA: MIT Press.

Joas, H. (2000). *The genesis of values.* Cambridge: Polity Press.

Kagan, J. (1994). *The nature of the child.* New York: HarperCollins.

Kagan, J. (2004). The uniquely human in human nature. *Daedalus, 133,* 77–88.

Karp, D. R. (2000). Values: Theory and research. In E. F. Borgotta & R. J. V. Montgomery (Eds.), *Encyclopedia of sociology* (pp. 3212–3227). New York: Macmillan Reference.

Kasser, T. (2002). Sketches for a self-determination theory of values. In E. L. Deci & R. M. Ryan (Eds.), *Handbook of self-determination research* (pp. 123–140). Rochester, NY: University of Rochester Press.

Kasser, T., & Ryan, R. M. (1996). Further examining the American dream: Differential correlates of intrinsic and extrinsic goals. *Personality and Social Psychology Bulletin, 22*, 280–297.

Katz, J. (1999). *How emotions work*. Chicago: University of Chicago Press.

Katzko, M. W. (2003). Unity versus multiplicity: A conceptual analysis of the term "self" and its use in personality theories. *Journal of Personality, 71*, 83–114.

Keller, M., & Edelstein, W. (1993). The development of the moral self from childhood to adolescence. In T. E. Wren & G. G. Noam (Eds.), *The moral self* (pp. 310–336). Cambridge, MA: MIT Press.

Kelley, H. H., Holmes, J. G., Kerr, N. L., Reis, H. T., Rusbult, C. E., & Van Lange, P. A. M. (2003). *An atlas of interpersonal situations*. New York: Cambridge University Press.

Kohlberg, L. (1981). *The philosophy of moral development: Moral stages and the idea of justice (Vol. 1)*. New York: Harper & Row.

Kohlberg, L., & Candee, D. (1984). The relationship of moral judgement to moral action. In W. M. Kurtines & J. L. Gewirtz (Eds.), *Morality, moral behavior, and moral development* (pp. 52–74). New York: Wiley.

Kohn, M. L. (1959). Social class and parental values. *American Journal of Sociology, 64*, 213–228.

Kohn, M. L. (1989). Social structure and personality: A quintessentially sociological approach to social psychology. *Social Forces, 68*(1), 26–33.

Kohn, M., & Schooler, C. (1983). *Work and personality: An inquiry into the impact of social stratification*. Norwood, NJ: Ablex.

Konty, M. A., & Dunham, C. C. (1997). Differences in value and attitude change over the life course. *Sociological Spectrum, 17*, 177–197.

Kroger, J. (2000). Ego identity status research in the new millennium. *International Journal of Behavioral Development, 24*, 145–148.

Lewis, M. (1997). *Altering fate: Why the past does not predict the future*. New York: Guilford Press.

MacIntyre, A. C. (1981). *After virtue: A study in moral theory*. London: Duckworth.

Maio, G. R., & Olson, J. M. (2000). What is a "value-expressive" attitude? In G. R. Maio & J. M. Olson (Eds.), *Why we evaluate: Functions of attitudes* (pp. 249–269). Mahwah, NJ: Lawrence Erlbaum Associates.

Maio, G. R., Olson, J. M., Bernard, M. M., & Luke, M. A. (2003). Ideologies, values, attitudes, and behavior. In J. DeLamater (Ed.), *Handbook of social psychology* (pp. 283–308). New York: Plenum.

Marini, M. M. (2000). Social values and norms. In E. F. Borgatta & R. J. V. Montgomery (Eds.), *Encyclopedia of sociology*. New York: Macmillan.

Markus, H., & Kitayama, S. (1991). Culture and the self: Implications for cognition, emotion, and motivation. *Psychological Review, 98*, 224–253.

McAdams, D. P. (1995). What do we know when we know a person? *Journal of Personality, 63*, 365–396.

McAdams, D. P. (2001). The psychology of life stories. *Review of General Psychology, 5*, 100–122.

Mead, G. H. (1932). *The philosophy of the present*. Chicago: Open Court Publishing.

Mead, G. H. (1934). *Mind, self, and society from the standpoint of a social behaviorist*. Chicago: University of Chicago Press.

Mead, G. H. (1938). *The philosophy of the act*. Chicago: University of Chicago Press.

Mischel, W. (2004). Toward an integrative science of the person. *Annual Review of Psychology, 55*, 1–22.

Monroe, K. R., & Epperson, C. (1994). "But what else could I do?" Choice, identity, and a cognitive-perceptual theory of ethical political behavior. *Political Psychology, 15*, 201–226.

Nisan, M. (1984). Content and structure in moral judgment: An integrative view. In W. M. Kurtines & J. L. Gewirtz (Eds.), *Morality, moral behavior, and moral development* (pp. 208–224). New York: Wiley.

Nunner-Winkler, G. (1993). The growth of moral motivation. In G. G. Noam & T. E. Wren (Eds.), *The moral self* (pp. 269–291). New Baskerville, CT: MIT Press.

Oishi, S., Schimmack, U., Diener, E., & Suh, E. M. (1998). The measurement of values and individualism–collectivism. *Personality and Social Psychology Bulletin, 24*, 1177–1189.

Owens, T. J. (2003). Self and identity. In J. DeLamater (Ed.), *Handbook of social psychology* (pp. 205–232). New York: Kluwer.

Pakizeh, A., Gebauer, J. E., & Maio, G. R. (2007). Basic human values: Inter-value structure in memory. *Journal of Experimental Social Psychology, 43*, 458–465.

Parsons, T. (1937). *The structure of social action a study in social theory with special reference to a group of recent European writers*. New York: McGraw-Hill.

Piaget, J. (1960). *The moral judgment of the child*. New York: Free Press.

Pronin, E., Fleming, J. J., & Steffel, M. (2008). Value revelations: Disclosure is in the eye of the beholder. *Journal of Personality and Social Psychology, 95*, 795–809.

Rohan, M. J. (2000). A rose by any name? The values construct. *Personality and Social Psychology Review, 4*, 255–277.

Rokeach, M. (1973). *The nature of human values*. New York: Free Press.

Schwalbe, M. L. (1991). Social structure and the moral self. In J. A. Howard & P. L. Callero (Eds.), *The self-society dynamic: Cognition, emotion, and action* (pp. 281–303). New York: Cambridge.

Schwartz, S. H. (1992). Universals in the content and structure of values: Theoretical advances and empirical tests in 20 countries. In M. P. Zanna (Ed.), *Advances in experimental social psychology* (pp. 1–65). San Diego, CA: Academic Press.

Schwartz, S. H. (1994). Are there universal aspects in the structure and content of human values? *Journal of Social Issues, 50*, 19–45.

Schwartz, S. H. (1996). Value priorities and behavior: Applying a theory of integrated values systems. In C. Seligman, J. M. Olson, & M. P. Zanna (Eds.), *The Ontario symposium: The psychology of values* (pp. 1–24). Mahwah, NJ: Lawrence Erlbaum Associates.

Schwartz, S. H. (2004a). Basic human values: Their content and structure across cultures. In A. Tamayo & J. Porto (Eds.), *Valores e trabalho [Values and work].* Brasilia: Editora Universidade de Brasilia.

Schwartz, S. H. (2004b). Mapping and interpreting cultural differences around the world. In H. Vinken, J. Soeters, & P. Ester (Eds.), *Comparing cultures: Dimensions of culture in a comparative perspective.* Leiden: Brill.

Schwartz, S. H., & Bilsky, W. (1987). Toward a psychological structure of human values. *Journal of Personality and Social Psychology, 53*, 550–562.

Schwartz, S. H., & Bilsky, W. (1990). Toward a psychological structure of human values: Extensions and cross-cultural replications. *Journal of Personality and Social Psychology, 58*, 878–891.

Simpson, B., & Willer, R. (2008). Altruism and indirect reciprocity: The interaction of person and situation in prosocial behavior. *Social Psychology Quarterly, 71*(1), 37–52.

Smith, M. B. (1991). *Values, self, and society: Toward a humanist social psychology.* New Brunswick, NJ: Transaction Publishers.

Smith, C. (2003). *Moral, believing animals: Human personhood and culture.* New York: Oxford University Press.

Somers, M., & Gibson, G. (1994). Reclaiming the epistemological "other": Narrative and the social construction of identity. In C. Calhoun (Ed.), *Social theory and the politics of identity* (pp. 35–99). Oxford: Blackwell.

Spates, J. L. (1983). The sociology of values. *Annual Review of Sociology, 9*, 27–49.

Stets, J. E., & Carter, M. J. (2006). The moral identity: A principle level identity. In K. McClelland & T. J. Fararo (Eds.), *Purpose, meaning, and action: Control system theories in sociology.* New York: Palgrave Macmillan.

Stevens, R. (2008). *Erik Erikson: Shaper of identity.* New York: Palgrave Macmillan.

Swann, W. B., Jr. (1983). Self-verification: Bringing social reality into harmony with the self. In J. M. Suls &

A. G. Greenwald (Eds.), *Social psychological perspectives on the self* (pp. 33–66). Hillsdale, NJ: Lawrence Erlbaum Associates.

Swidler, A. (2001). *Talk of love: How culture matters.* Chicago: University of Chicago Press.

Tangney, J. P., Stuewig, J., & Mashek, D. J. (2007). Moral emotions and moral behavior. *Annual Review of Psychology, 58*, 345–372.

Taylor, C. (1988). The moral topography of the self. In S. B. Messer, L. A. Saas, & R. L. Woolfolk (Eds.), *Hermeneutics and psychological theory* (pp. 298–320). New Brunswick, NJ: Rutgers University Press.

Taylor, C. (1989). *Sources of the self: The making of the modern identity.* Cambridge, MA: Harvard University Press.

Taylor, C. (1994). Reply to commentators. *Philosophy and Phenomenological Research, 54*, 203–213.

Tesser, A., Crepaz, N., Beach, S. R. H., Cornell, D., & Collins, J. C. (2000). Confluence of self-esteem regulation mechanisms: On integrating the self-zoo. *Personality and Social Psychology Bulletin, 26*, 1476–1489.

Triandis, H. (1995). *Individualism and collectivism.* Boulder, CO: Westview Press.

Turiel, E. (2002). *The culture of morality: Social development, context, and conflict.* New York: Cambridge University Press.

Turner, R. H. (1968). Self-conception in social interaction. In K. J. Gergen & C. Gordon (Eds.), *The self in social interaction* (pp. 93–106). New York: Wiley.

Turner, R. H. (1976). The real self: From institution to impulse. *American Journal of Sociology, 84*, 1–23.

Walker, J. S. (2000). Choosing biases, using power, and practicing resistance: Moral development in a world without certainty. *Human Development, 43*, 135–156.

Waters, M. C. (1990). *Ethnic options: Choosing identities in America.* Berkeley, CA: University of California Press.

Weber, M. (1978). *Economy and society an outline of interpretive sociology.* Berkeley, CA: University of California Press.

Wegner, D. M. (2002). *The illusion of conscious will.* Cambridge, MA: MIT Press.

Wiley, N. (1994). The politics of identity in American history. In C. Calhoun (Ed.), *Social theory and the politics of identity* (pp. 130–149). Cambridge, MA: Blackwell.

Wuthnow, R. (2008). The sociological study of values. *Sociological Forum, 23*, 333–343.

Douglas A. MacDonald

Abstract

Interest in spirituality, and its relation and relevance to identity as per the theories of Erikson and Marcia, has been on the increase in recent years. While the available studies suggest that spirituality has import for identity development, the literature is somewhat limited due to problems with conceptualization and measurement of spirituality. This chapter attempts to address this problem by introducing readers to the empirically derived five-dimensional model of spirituality developed by MacDonald (2000). After overviewing MacDonald's measurement model and some of its supporting research, attention is then given to the creation of a new biopsychosocial model of spirituality that integrates all five major components of the construct and explicates how they relate to, and are affected by, spiritual identity development. To foster scientific study, the chapter ends with a proposal for a three-dimensional model of spiritual identity which identifies biosocial factors influencing the emergence of spiritual identity.

Although spirituality and identity are intimately linked in the spiritual and religious literature (e.g., see Byrom, 1990; Cleary, 1989; Suzuki, 1957; Suzuki, Fromm, & DeMartino, 1960; Wilber, 1980), scientific investigation into their relation and relevance to each other has not garnered much attention until fairly recently (e.g., Chae, Kelly, Brown, & Bolden, 2004; Lerner, Roeser, & Phelps, 2008; Poll & Smith, 2003; Templeton & Eccles, 2006; Zinder, 2007). This is not to say that the topic has been ignored by psychologists or other social scientists; ideas regarding the relation of identity to spirituality and religion can be found in the work of many seminal thinkers and researchers (e.g., Allport, 1955; Jung, 1967, 1969; Maslow, 1970, 1971). However, with only a few exceptions, virtually none of these earlier efforts have resulted in any systematic study on the topic.

When one examines the current literature, it quickly becomes apparent that Erik Erikson's (1980) lifespan psychosocial theory and Marcia's (1966) model of identity status have come

D.A. MacDonald (✉)
Department of Psychology, College of Liberal Arts and Education, University of Detroit Mercy, Detroit, MI, USA
e-mail: macdonda@udmercy.edu

S.J. Schwartz et al. (eds.), *Handbook of Identity Theory and Research*,
DOI 10.1007/978-1-4419-7988-9_21, © Springer Science+Business Media, LLC 2011

to serve as the dominant conceptual frameworks for studying spirituality and identity (e.g., Hunsberger, Pratt, & Pancer, 2001; Marcia, 1993; Markstrom, 1999; Tisdell, 2002; Kroger & Marcia, Chapter 2, this volume). This comes as no surprise given that these theories have been the primary catalysts for much research and theoretical work on identity development in general. And, akin to other areas of identity research, these theories seem to hold potential for illuminating the role of spirituality in identity formation.

For instance, using an adaptation of Marcia's (1966) identity status model (see Kroger & Marcia, Chapter 2, this volume), Kiesling, Sorell, Montgomery, and Colwell (2006) studied role salience (i.e., the importance of spirituality to one's sense of identity) and role flexibility (i.e., the extent to which consideration has been given to changing one's sense of spiritual identity) in a sample of 28 adults identified as being spiritually devout. Using a detailed interview protocol, Kiesling et al., obtained information about the motivational, emotional, and behavioral aspects of a variety of social roles related to different aspects of identity, including spiritual identity. In their study, spiritual identity was defined as "a role-related aspect of an individual's overall sense of ego identity" (p. 1270) that is concerned with questions regarding the meaning and ultimate purpose of existence.

Content analysis of their interview data resulted in the identification of three main themes, which were labeled salience/meaning (i.e., centrality and meaning of spiritual identity in relation to a person's overall identity), influence/investment (i.e., the extent to which people's motivational and affective states relate to and influence their commitment to their sense of spiritual identity), and reflectiveness/continuity and change (i.e., whether or not people reflect upon their spiritual identity and perceive it as remaining the same or changing over time). Participants were then categorized into three of the four identity statuses within Marcia's (1966) model – foreclosed, moratorium, and achieved; 11 participants were assigned to the foreclosed group, 4 were placed in moratorium, and 13 in achievement.

None of the participants were categorized as identity diffused with respect to their spiritual identity. Applying the themes to each of the identity categories, Kiesling et al. (2006) found several important points of difference across the groups.

For instance, they observed that individuals in the foreclosed group viewed spiritual identity as inherited and a part of childhood, and that these individuals tend to rely on authority and family to define this aspect of their identity. Those in the moratorium group, alternatively, did not rely on authority to define truth. Moreover, unlike the foreclosed participants who were motivated to have a secure relationship with a higher power, individuals in identity moratorium were motivated to develop spiritual identity due to its perceived psychological benefit and/or in response to intellectual and ethical considerations. Those in the achieved group tended to see spiritual identity as a choice and demonstrated the highest level of motivation and affective intensity. In contrast to foreclosed individuals who were not able to imagine the implications of abandoning their spiritual identity, those within the achieved status were able to anticipate the consequences of losing this aspect of their personal identity. Finally, for both the foreclosed and achieved groups, spiritual identity was perceived as having a marked impact on daily behavior and perceptions of self-worth, whereas the spiritual identity of individuals in moratorium seemed to exert a less consistent impact on daily behavior and ratings of self-worth.

Based on their results, Kiesling et al. (2006) concluded that spiritual identity is an important part of ego identity in adults. More specifically, they state that (a) spirituality appears to nurture a sense of connection either with a higher power, with a spiritual community, or with highly valued aspects of self, (b) interactions with significant others have a notable effect on how spirituality is used for meaning-making, (c) efforts to engender positive traits (e.g., compassion) and to deemphasize negative traits (e.g., greed) influence the construction of spiritual identity, (d) intentional effort is required to develop and foster spiritual identity, and (e) spiritual identity seems to show patterns of change and consistency in a way comparable to other aspects of identity.

In contrast to Kiesling et al. (2006), who framed their study and their conceptualization of spiritual identity exclusively in terms of identity status theory, Poll and Smith (2003) attempted to approach the topic in a more integrative fashion. Starting with the ideas of William James (1890, 1902), they drew from Eriksonian psychosocial theory, other psychodynamic theories, and from cognitive, narrative, and systems perspectives to arrive at their own model of spiritual identity development.

Borrowing from the theistic assumptions of Richards and Bergin (1997), which include belief in the existence of God and of a soul, Poll and Smith used their integrated theory to define spiritual identity as "an individual's belief that she or he is an eternal being and connected to God" (p. 129). They maintain that the primary mechanism responsible for the emergence of spiritual identity is the interaction of spiritual experiences, which occur throughout the lifespan, with intentional efforts on the part of the person to incorporate and integrate such experiences into a constructed sense of self. Poll and Smith further assert that the development of spiritual identity is not necessarily linear; though spiritual development can and does occur in early life, it is possible for spiritual identity to emerge in adulthood through what they refer to as a "second birth" or rebirth. They also contend that the extent to which spiritual identity can affect functioning and well-being is a result of the match or congruence between a person's experiences and behavior and her/his perception of God.

Within this framework, Poll and Smith propose a four-stage lifespan model of spiritual identity development, which begins with the stage called Pre-awareness. During this stage, individuals do not have any conscious awareness of themselves as eternal beings in relationship to God. Further, they do not tend to think of themselves in spiritual terms, regardless of whether or not they have had spiritual experiences. In the second stage, called Awakening, a period of crisis, conflict, and/or learning prompts

individuals to begin thinking of themselves as spiritual beings. The quality of this awareness, however, is viewed as fragmented, inconsistent, and generally situation-specific (e.g., a person only thinks of God when involved in a crisis). During Recognition, the third stage, recollections of earlier spiritual experiences are compared to the experiences arising during the Awakening phase, and the individual begins to generalize across situations and starts to develop a more stable sense of spiritual identity. However, the salience and importance of this emerging spiritual sense of self is still not fully expressed. Rather, other aspects of identity will typically be given more weight and attention (e.g., those based on various social roles and relationships). Lastly, in the fourth stage, called Integration, Poll and Smith indicate that spiritual experiences become fused with one's self-concept. This, in turn, results in the emergence of a lasting and coherent sense of spiritual identity. In this phase, spirituality comes to occupy a core place in a person's overall sense of identity.

In addition to these two studies, which are discussed to illustrate the potential of identity theory for developing our understanding of spiritual identity, a number of additional studies have been published and further shed light on the role of spirituality in identity formation in different populations, such as women, adolescents, and various ethnic groups (e.g., Fukuyama & Sevig, 2002; Paranjpe, 1998). In terms of ethnicity, research suggests that compared to white Americans, African Americans appear to consider spirituality to be more of a core component of their self-concepts and ethnic identities (Chae et al., 2004; Markstrom, 1999; Zinder, 2007). For adolescents, evidence indicates that spirituality and religion are not only important to their overall sense of identity, but that spirituality and religion seem to be associated to a range of positive outcomes (Juang & Syed, 2008).

Problems with Current Spirituality Research

Although the current work on spiritual identity appears promising, research involving spirituality as a whole is characterized by a pervasive and persistent shortcoming – namely, the problem of adequately defining what spirituality is in the first place. As noted by myself and others (e.g., MacDonald, 2000; MacDonald & Friedman, 2002; Zinnbauer et al., 1997; Roehlkepartain, Benson, & Scales, Chapter 22, this volume), there is a considerable degree of divergence in how spirituality is conceptualized, both as a general domain of functioning and as a component of other aspects of human functioning (e.g., spiritual well-being, spiritual intelligence, spiritual identity). These inconsistencies, in turn, introduce ambiguity in the meaning of research findings and, by extension, have a markedly negative impact on the generation of a cumulative body of scientific knowledge. In fact, the murkiness and inconsistencies in its definition are so pervasive that it has led some investigators to suggest that spirituality should be abandoned as a scientific construct altogether (e.g., Hoge, 1996; Koenig, 2008).

Take, for instance, the definitions of spiritual identity advanced by Kiesling et al. (2006) and Poll and Smith (2003). Although it may be argued that both of these research groups developed their definitions based upon the assumption that spirituality and religion are different but related (a view that has become increasingly accepted among religion and spirituality researchers over the past 10 years; see Hill et al., 2000; MacDonald & Friedman, 2001), it is apparent that they are not defining spiritual identity in the same way. For Kiesling et al., it is defined in a manner that treats spirituality as a unidimensional and psychologized concept within which spiritual identity is reduced to a social role with ostensible existential overtones (e.g., they define it primarily in terms of meaning-making). In essence, it could be contended that they "fit" their definition of spirituality to the theory of identity they were using. Slife, Hope, and Nebeker (1999) have criticized much of the available research on the grounds that conceptions of spirituality and associated constructs like spiritual identity are often modified to accommodate specific scientific interests without due consideration being given

to the broader and substantive philosophy-of-science issues that encompass spirituality studies (e.g., can the transcendent or God truly be studied scientifically?).

Poll and Smith, on the other hand, appear to adopt a somewhat more sophisticated definition of spirituality, differentiating spiritual experience from spiritual beliefs and identity and proposing a mechanism through which they interact. Their multicomponent approach to spiritual identity is more in line with trends seen in the development of conceptual and measurement models where spirituality is defined in multidimensional terms (MacDonald & Friedman, 2002). Unfortunately, their utilization of Judeo-Christian concepts in their definition of spiritual identity raises issues not only about whether or not spirituality can be genuinely and meaningfully construed as different from religion, but also whether or not theological concepts have a place within science (Helminiak, 2008; Slife et al., 1999). Notwithstanding such philosophy of science considerations, by adopting a clearly Judeo-Christian set of assumptions about the existence and nature of God and the soul, Poll and Smith may be seen as limiting their theory to sociocultural contexts and populations for which the Judeo-Christian worldview is the predominant way of understanding spirituality. That is, their model may not apply as well to people from differing religious and spiritual traditions.

A Taxonomic Model of Spirituality

Undoubtedly, there are numerous challenges to studying spirituality scientifically, including, but certainly not limited to, the determination of whether or not it is (a) the same or different from religion, (b) capable of being operationalized with theistic or theological concepts (e.g., divine, sacred, transcendent, God) in a manner that is consistent with the assumptions and methods of naturalistic science (Helminiak, 2008; Hill et al., 2000; MacDonald, 2009; Slife et al., 1999), and (c) best viewed as a wholly positive domain of human functioning (as opposed to one that has both health-promoting and health-compromising expressions; Grof & Grof, 1990; Hunt, Dougan, Grant, & House, 2002; MacDonald, 2009; MacDonald & Friedman, 2002). However, despite such challenges, there has been some movement toward the development of measurement models that permit productive theory construction and empirical research. One of the more promising ones is a five-dimensional model that I proposed over a decade ago (MacDonald, 1997, 2000).

Recognizing the need for a comprehensive framework for organizing the burgeoning literature on spirituality, and borrowing from the empirical methodologies used in devising taxonomic models of personality (e.g., the Five Factor model of personality; Costa & McCrae, 1992, 1995), I created a multidimensional descriptive model based upon a series of conjoint factor analyses involving a total of 19 different extant measures of spirituality and related constructs. At the same time, I constructed a self-report instrument, called the Expressions of Spirituality Inventory (ESI), to assess the five factors that were found across the multiple-factor analyses. Descriptions of each dimension, along with sample items from the ESI, can be found in Table 21.1.

As reported in MacDonald (1997, 2000), each of the dimensions comprising the model have been shown to be factorially robust (e.g., they were observed to emerge in factor analyses across measures and samples), and despite some significant inter-correlations among them, each was found to be conceptually unique. Evidence for uniqueness was obtained through factor analyses of ESI items and through the finding of differential patterns of correlations between the ESI dimension scores and measures of conceptually related constructs. For instance, out of the five dimensions, ESI Religiousness tends to produce the strongest correlations (magnitudes ranging from 0.50s to 0.80s) with measures of explicitly religious constructs (e.g., intrinsic religious orientation, religious faith, personal piety). ESI Cognitive Orientation toward Spirituality has tended to correlate highest to non-religious measures of spirituality (e.g., r= 0.70 has been found between this dimension and the trait

of Self-Transcendence within the seven-factor model of Temperament and Character developed by Cloninger, Svrakic, & Przybeck, 1993). The ESI Experiential/Phenomenological Dimension has been found with be most strongly associated to measures of spiritual, mystical, and peak experiences. ESI Paranormal Beliefs has been shown to consistently and strongly correlate to measures of belief in supernatural phenomena and abilities. Finally, ESI Existential Well-Being has been observed to be most strongly and significantly associated with explicit measures of existential and well-being constructs and strongly but negatively correlated with measures of psychological distress and dysfunction (e.g., Kassab & MacDonald, 2010; MacDonald, 2000; MacDonald & Holland, 2002a, 2002b, 2002c, 2003). In the initial psychometric examination of the ESI, it was found that scores on the various dimensions demonstrate satisfactory inter-item reliability and generally good discriminant, convergent, factorial, and criterion validity. Of particular importance were analyses showing that the ESI does not appear to be unduly confounded by institutionalized religion: whereas scores from three of the five dimensions (all but Paranormal Beliefs and Existential Well-Being) were observed to be significantly higher for people reporting membership in an organized religion as compared to those who did not report an affiliation, there were no meaningful or consistent differences found across religious affiliation groupings (MacDonald, 2000). Further, in a work in progress (MacDonald et al., 2010), the ESI has been found to demonstrate satisfactory factorial validity across cultures, languages, and faith systems as observed in preliminary confirmatory factor analyses done with samples drawn from the United States, Poland, Slovakia, Uganda, India, Korea, and Japan.

The ESI, and the dimensional model that it operationalizes, may be viewed as a significant step forward for spirituality studies for at least three reasons. First, it embodies one of the most inclusive and comprehensive descriptions of spirituality currently available in the literature. In fact, in a manner similar to the Five Factor Model of personality (Costa & McCrae, 1995), it may

Table 21.1 Description of the ESI dimensions

ESI Dimension	Example of item content
Cognitive orientation toward spirituality (COS)	
Non-religious beliefs, attitudes, and perceptions about the reality, nature, and importance of spirituality to day-to-day personal functioning and well-being	Spirituality is an essential part of human existence I am a spiritual person
Experiential/Phenomenological dimension (EPD)	
Experiences considered to be spiritual in nature. Includes experiences labeled mystical, religious, transpersonal, peak, and transcendent as well as core phenomenological descriptive features associated with such experiences	I have had an experience during which the nature of reality became apparent to me I have had an experience in which I seemed to transcend space and time
Existential well-being (EWB)	
Sense of meaning and purpose and perception of self as efficacious and able to handle the inherent challenges of existence	I am not comfortable with myself (−) I seldom feel tense about things
Paranormal beliefs (PAR)	
Beliefs regarding the existence of paranormal phenomena including ESP. Also includes belief in witchcraft and spiritualism (i.e., ghosts)	It is possible to communicate with the dead Dreams can sometimes be used to predict the future
Religiousness (REL)	
Expression of spirituality through genuine religious belief, practice, and lifestyle (e.g., prayer, meditation, attendance of religious services). Akin to the concept of intrinsic religious orientation	I believe that God or a higher power is responsible for my existence I practice some form of prayer

Note: (−) means item is negatively phrased.

be viewed as a taxonomy of spirituality; it identifies and describes several of the core components of spirituality as a domain of human functioning. Of the measures that MacDonald (1997, 2000) factor analyzed, none were found to contribute to all five dimensions, including some instruments that were themselves explicitly constructed to be comprehensive multidimensional measures (e.g., Spiritual Orientation Inventory from Elkins, Hedstrom, Hughes, Leaf, & Saunders, 1988; and the Spirituality Assessment Scale from Howden, 1992). The ESI therefore represents an important advance over previously available measures of spirituality.

As a side note, though the inclusion of Paranormal Beliefs may appear problematic, as I have argued elsewhere (MacDonald, 1997, 2000), practically all religious and spiritual systems, both Eastern and Western, accommodate belief

in the emergence of unusual abilities (e.g., miracles, mind reading, levitation, precognition) as a product of advanced spiritual development. Consequently, I reasoned that it was important to have Paranormal Beliefs represented in the model. Also, the inclusion of Religiousness in the model may cause some confusion, especially for those unfamiliar with research and theory in the psychology of religion. In particular, some may view its inclusion as suggesting that religion in its totality is treated as a part of spirituality. Such a perception would be inaccurate. Within my model, Religiousness relates specifically to what is better known as intrinsic religious orientation, a construct concerning involvement in, and commitment to, religious beliefs and practices simply for their own sake rather than extrinsic religiosity (i.e., involvement in religion for personal or social gain; see

Allport & Ross, 1967). Finally, some questions may be raised with regard to Existential Well-Being. Examination of the description of the dimension and sample item content as provided in Table 21.1 suggests that it might be better viewed in terms of general well-being and not as something specific to spirituality. This was something with which I struggled when initially developing the model. For example, in MacDonald (1997), Existential Well-Being was also labeled Positive Self-Appraisal, and extensive discussion was given to its appropriateness for inclusion as part of the construct domain of spirituality. However, despite its appearance as an index of general well-being, based upon the factor analytic findings as well as the correlations between measures explicitly designed to measure existential and spiritual well-being, I concluded that such a dimension appears to be embedded in a significant number of existing measures of spirituality. As such, if my factor model were to embody all major components of spirituality as found in available assessment instruments, then Existential Well-Being would need to remain in the model. Consequently, concerns about the inclusion of existential well-being, or any other well-being construct (e.g., religious well-being, spiritual-well-being), in the domain of spirituality need to extend beyond the ESI and my model to the broader spirituality measurement literature (see Koenig, 2008, for a discussion of the problems related to the potential confound of well-being with spirituality).

Second, the model has been utilized with a fair degree of success as a framework for organizing available empirical research on the relation of spirituality to health and well-being. When reviewing the health research from the perspective of my model, MacDonald and Friedman (2002) suggested that different patterns of relations emerge depending on how spirituality is conceptualized. In particular, some dimensions show reasonably consistent positive associations to health (e.g., Cognitive Orientation toward Spirituality, Religiousness, Existential Well-Being), whereas others show mixed to negative associations (e.g., Experiential/Phenomenological Dimension and

Paranormal Beliefs). Studies using the ESI itself have generally replicated this differential directionality of associations to health and pathology across the dimensions (e.g., MacDonald & Holland, 2002a, 2002b, 2002c, 2003).

Third, and of perhaps greatest relevance to this chapter, the model explicitly incorporated item content related to spiritual identity (defined in general terms as the extent to which a person sees spirituality contributing to his/her sense of self or self-concept), when developing the ESI and found that this item content substantively contributed to the model. In particular, when the ESI items were factor analyzed, items concerning spiritual identity were found to consistently and strongly load on Cognitive Orientation toward Spirituality (COS), a dimension that relates to beliefs, attitudes, and perceptions regarding the meaning and relevance of spirituality to one's life and personal functioning (e.g., lifestyle choices, coping with stressors, and problem-solving). By extension, empirical findings involving COS may be seen as generally applicable to studies on spiritual identity. Incidentally, COS has been found to be highly correlated with measures of religiousness (including ESI Religiousness), and to some measures of religious well-being and moderately correlated with measures of spiritual experience (including the ESI Experiential/Phenomenological Dimension; MacDonald, 2000).

Using the Taxonomic Model of Spirituality to Generate a Directional Model of Spirituality and Spiritual Identity

Though my taxonomic model appears to serve as a good framework for delineating the content domain of spirituality, it may be criticized on the grounds that it is atheoretical and merely descriptive. Consequently, although it may be useful for identifying patterns of empirical relationship between spirituality and various aspects of functioning, the model does not really provide a theoretical basis for explaining any such relationships. For this model to be of maximum utility, the dimensions need to be theoretically contextualized so that their relations to functioning can be explained. Fortunately, the available literature seems to provide some guidance in this regard. In fact, it appears that the dimensions can be organized into a directional biopsychosocial model.

Spiritual experiences, represented as the Experiential/Phenomenological Dimension in my model, have been found in both clinical and non-clinical populations to have stable neuroanatomical correlates in the frontal, temporal, and parietal lobes through both electroencephalography (EEG) and more sophisticated brain-imaging techniques such as positron emission tomography (PET), single photon emission computed tomography (SPECT), and functional magnetic resonance imaging (fMRI) (Beauregard & O'Leary, 2007; Newberg, D'Aquili, & Rause, 2001; Persinger, 1984). The reliability of these findings has led some investigators to conjecture that not only are our nervous systems hardwired to create spiritual experiences, but that these experiences are naturally occurring phenomena that are accessible to investigation through scientific methodologies (e.g., Beauregard & O'Leary, 2007; Newberg et al., 2001).

As a logical extension of this perspective, it may be argued that spiritual experiences are part of our innate developmental potential and can be understood as potent causal agents in the expression of spirituality as manifested in other forms, including spiritual identity. It is important to emphasize that spiritual experiences, while themselves being an aspect of spirituality, may or may not result in the development of a spiritual identity or lead to the emergence of spiritual or religious beliefs and practices as reflected in the other dimensions of my model. As noted by Poll and Smith (2003), whose theory of spiritual identity development attributes a similar causal function to spiritual experiences, the extent to which spiritual experiences result in a sense of spiritual identity depends on whether or not the experiences are viewed as being of a spiritual nature rather than reflective of problems in functioning (such as a psychotic disorder; see Clarke, 2001).

In contrast, the Religiousness dimension appears to be more cogently linked to socialization processes concerning spirituality (see Roehlkepartain, Benson, & Scales, Chapter 22, this volume, for additional perspectives on socialization influences). That is, religion in general appears to be best viewed as a social vehicle through which we learn language, concepts, and practices that not only facilitate an understanding of spirituality in general (including spiritual experiences), but also contribute to the further unfolding of spirituality in an experiential way (e.g., by learning meditation, a practitioner may volitionally induce spiritual experiences). Of course, it should be kept in mind that participation in, and socialization by, religious institutions alone may not be sufficient to activate spiritual experiences and to contribute to the emergence of other expressions of spirituality (Grof & Grof, 1990). Nevertheless, taken together, it appears reasonable to view Religiousness and the Experiential/Phenomenological Dimension as important, discrete, but related components of spirituality that embody biological (nature) and socialization (learning, nurture) mechanisms. These mechanisms, in turn, interact and lead to the emergence of other aspects of spirituality, most notably those expressions involving beliefs, identity, and behavior (MacDonald, 2000).

Directing attention to the dimensions of COS and Paranormal Beliefs, respectively, it appears that these two dimensions are similar in that they primarily concern beliefs and attitudes rather than experiences, behaviors, or practices. In the case of COS, the beliefs relate to the existence and importance of spirituality to life and daily functioning, whereas for Paranormal Beliefs, the beliefs center upon the assumption that human beings have the ability to engage in activities (e.g., such as predicting the future, moving objects with one's mind, or reincarnation) that do not conform to the usual processes, mechanisms, and rules of cause-and-effect subscribed to by science. Although some elements of COS involve ways in which an individual may incorporate spirituality into his/her own personal choices and behaviors (e.g., the ESI contains such items as "I am more aware of my lifestyle choices because of my spirituality" and "I consider the spiritual consequences of a choice when making a decision"; also see Table 21.1), it is also comprised of general beliefs about the relevance and significance of spirituality without reference to the person's own functioning (e.g., consider such ESI items as "Spirituality gives life focus and direction" and "A spiritual life has many rewards"). Paranormal Beliefs are similar to these latter COS items; it does not relate to an individual's belief that he or she specifically can perform unusual acts that defy conventional understanding about reality. Instead, it concerns beliefs that people in general are capable of such acts (see Table 21.1 for sample ESI items).

In light of the content of these two dimensions of spirituality, one may contend that both COS and Paranormal Beliefs reflect internalized cognitive schema (i.e., mental representations or structures that organize information and shape perceptual processes). These schema, in turn, may be viewed as contributing to ego states and operations (e.g., they causally influence how people perceive, and ascribe meaning to experience of self and others as well as how people adapt and cope with stressors) (Hine, 1997), including one's sense of identity. It is noteworthy that when I (MacDonald, 1997, 2000) examined the inter-correlations among the ESI dimensions, COS was found to be strongly associated with Religiousness and moderately correlated with the Experiential/Phenomenological Dimension (EPD), and Paranormal Beliefs was moderately correlated to the EPD. This suggests that both EPD and Religiousness may be seen as core causal components of spirituality that contribute to the manifestation of spirituality in terms of beliefs, attitudes, and perception of one's identity.

Lastly, there is Existential Well-being (EWB). This fifth dimension differs from all others in that its content exclusively relates to perceptions of one's own functioning (see Table 21.1 for sample items from the ESI). More specifically, EWB seems to encompass evaluative perceptions concerning the degree to which individuals see themselves as coping and adapting

adequately to stressors and life events. Also unlike the other aspects of spirituality, EWB has been found to be minimally associated with any other ESI dimension (MacDonald, 2000; Migdal, 2007).

When these characterizations of the ESI dimensions are considered collectively, it appears possible to organize them to create a directional model of spirituality comprised of three levels. The first level is comprised of Religiousness and the Experiential/ Phenomenological Dimension and may be seen as representing the core biosocial mechanisms that influence the development of mental structures and associated ego functions and perceptual processes. These resulting structures, functions, and processes, in turn, make up the second level of spirituality that is operationalized in terms of COS and Paranormal Beliefs. The third level, consisting of EWB, relates to expressions of spirituality as manifested in appraisals of one's own functioning and sense of satisfaction with one's perceived competencies and ability to live effectively (e.g., having a sense of meaning and purpose and felt control over one's life).

Whereas both Religiousness and the Experiential/Phenomenological Dimension have direct effects on Cognitive Orientation toward Spirituality and Paranormal Beliefs in my proposed directional model, Existential Well-being presents a challenge; While it seems to be embedded in many extant definitions and measures of spirituality and, as I stated above, may be seen as a component of spirituality (albeit a controversial one; see MacDonald, 1997 and Koenig, 2008 for extended discussions of this issue), within my research, it has been found to be minimally correlated with the other ESI dimensions. If there is no empirical association between EWB and other major expressions of spirituality, then it seems difficult to justify a model that proposes a direct connection. However, under the assumption that EWB is a legitimate dimension of spirituality, it seems that an argument can be made for incorporating EWB into the overall model by viewing it as an indirect product of other components of spirituality operating through personality and social influences shown in the literature to have relevance to spirituality. Included among such influences are social support, optimism, extraversion, emotional stability, locus of control, and ego boundary permeability.

Social support and optimism are mentioned because of studies that show them to have a moderating influence on the relation of spirituality to adjustment (Haber, Jacob, & Spangler, 2007; Salsman, Brown, Brechting, & Carlson, 2005; Weber & Cummings, 2003; Yakushko, 2005). Extraversion and emotional stability (the inverse of neuroticism), as represented in Five Factor Model of Personality (Costa & McCrae, 1992) have been found in empirical studies to associate to EWB as well as other dimensions of spirituality (e.g., the Experiential/Phenomenological Dimension) (MacDonald, 2000; MacDonald & Holland, 2003).

Though lacking explicit support in the literature, locus of control is included on rational grounds. In particular, it seems that the extent to which a person adopts an internal locus of control may be linked to both his/her internalized sense of spirituality and to the extent to which he/she feels capable of effectively addressing existential issues of life (e.g., finding meaning and purpose, coping with death). Unpublished empirical findings that I have obtained (MacDonald & Kassab, 2010) support this line of reasoning – external locus of control is significantly negatively correlated with EWB, Cognitive Orientation toward Spirituality, and Religiousness.

Finally, ego permeability is included to accommodate ways in which ego boundaries (i.e., psychological boundaries that demarcate self from not-self) function and impact how people experience themselves. Ego permeability may be seen as the quality of one's ego boundaries, and relates to the extent to which these boundaries permit information and psychological material from the environment and/or different parts of the mind (e.g., the unconscious) to move in and out of conscious awareness. Although many concepts have been advanced in the literature over the past six decades that

relate to ego permeability including regression-in-the-service-of-the-ego, ego permissiveness, openness-to-experience, and transliminality (e.g., see MacDonald, Holland, & Holland, 2005), little attention has been given to such concepts in theory and research on both identity and spirituality. Extant research indicates that ego permeability is positively related to higher levels of spiritual experiences and to both positive and negative states of functioning (Hartmann, 1991; Houran, Thalbourne, & Lange, 2003; Hunt et al., 2002; MacDonald et al., 2005; Thalbourne & Delin, 1994). In the context of my directional model, ego permeability can be seen as influencing both the frequency and intensity of spiritual experiences, and a person's awareness of beliefs and attitudes (i.e., personal mental schema) contributing to one's sense of identity. In turn, the heightened access to these experiences and one's core beliefs about self play out in how a person evaluates himself/herself in terms of EWB (e.g., people who view themselves as inherently spiritual beings by virtue of spiritual experiences and awareness of their beliefs about their sense of personal identity are more likely to base judgements about themselves and their quality of life on such beliefs).

Although spirituality defined in terms of the four ESI dimensions of Religiousness, Experiential/Phenomenological Dimension, Cognitive Orientation toward Spirituality, and Paranormal Beliefs is proposed here as indirectly effecting levels of Existential Well-being through these social and personality variables, it is important to note that the relation of all five ESI dimensions to each other may be further influenced by demographic characteristics. Research suggests that the manner in which spirituality is expressed may vary as a function of age and ethnicity. For instance, in terms of age, Heintz and Baruss (2001) used the ESI to compare a sample of people in late life (mean age = 72.6 years) to the sample used to develop the ESI (mean age = 21.0 years) and found that the older sample scored significantly higher on ESI Cognitive Orientation toward Spirituality, Religiousness, and EWB, and significantly lower on Paranormal Beliefs. No significant differences were found on the

Experiential/Phenomenological Dimension. In regard to ethnicity, evidence suggests that African Americans tend to demonstrate a stronger identification with spirituality than whites (Chae et al., 2004; Zinder, 2007). Considering these findings, it appears that age and ethnicity may be treated as potential moderating variables (i.e., age and ethnicity may differentially affect how the ESI dimensions relate to each other). Additional studies need to be done to establish if the relation of the four ESI dimensions to EWB in fact varies across both age and cultural groups.

The inclusion of EWB in the model can also be substantiated in another way. As argued by Poll and Smith (2003), and as postulated by identity theories (e.g., Eriksonian psychosocial theory), crises, conflict, and/or challenges that arise due to development through the lifespan can serve as catalysts for self-reflection and psychological change. Within the context of spirituality, such crises have been described by some clinicians and scholars in terms of a "spiritual emergency" (e.g., Grof & Grof, 1990). Since EWB involves appraisal of one's functioning, it could be reasoned that lower levels of EWB may be associated with problems in functioning that are consistent with experiencing difficulties in coping with such crises. If this is accurate, then it may be that lower levels of EWB could prompt a review and revision of beliefs and values (i.e., mental schema as found in COS and Paranormal Beliefs) that, in turn, contribute to a positive change in self-appraisal manifested in higher EWB. Stated in another and more direct manner, personal crises may result in lower perceived happiness, which leads one to look inward and to turn to one's sense of spirituality as a way of finding a resolution to the crisis. This then results in greater development of one's spirituality that fosters a heightened sense of meaning and purpose in life and higher levels of personal happiness. When levels of EWB are high, it would be expected that a person would not feel compelled to engage himself/herself in a process of examination of one's identity and spirituality, given that there is already a perceived sense of personal happiness.

In support of this possibility, research has shown that higher levels of EWB may be associated with "positive illusions" (or positive self-serving bias in self-perception; see Taylor & Brown, 1988), as reflected in the finding of significant positive correlations between EWB and scores on measures of self-deceptive enhancement and social desirability (MacDonald, 1997, 2000). Positive illusions have been noted as contributing to tendencies to be less self-aware and to engage in less critical self-examination. At the same time, they are linked with higher levels of reported well-being (Huber & MacDonald, 2010). Thus, lower levels of EWB could influence other aspects of spirituality and could be shown with a path leading from EWB back to COS.

Specific Application of the Model to Spiritual Identity The directional model discussed thus far represents an effort to fully integrate and explicate possible causal relations among the broad dimensions of spirituality that make up my taxonomy (MacDonald, 1997, 2000). However, as noted earlier, spiritual identity seems to be most relevant to one dimension, COS. Given the location of COS in the full model, it appears possible to provide a more parsimonious directional model that applies to spiritual identity. Specifically, Religiousness and the Experiential/Phenomenological Dimension serve as the social and biological causal factors that exert both direct and indirect effects on the formation and maintenance of spiritual identity as manifested in COS. For the Experiential/Phenomenological Dimension, the frequency and intensity of spiritual experiences, and their impact on spiritual identity, is partly the result of ego permeability such that people with more permissive ego boundaries will be more likely to report greater numbers of spiritual experiences and to have a sense of spiritual identity. For Religiousness, in addition to the direct effects of the doctrine and practices of a faith system on spiritual identity, the extent to which these components are internalized and maintained is influenced by social support variables including family and community values, beliefs, and lifestyle practices. Psychosocial theories of development assert that the degree to which one's personal experiences, values/beliefs, and behaviors are perceived as consistent with those social groups and/or institutions to which a person belongs helps to define and reinforce one's sense of identity and one's roles and place within those groups and institutions. This line of reasoning would seem to apply to the development of spiritual identity.

Conclusion

Even though spiritual identity has become the focus of increasing research efforts, available theory and research does not provide a very coherent picture of what spiritual identity is and how it relates to the broader literature on spirituality. The directional model of spirituality and spiritual identity presented in this chapter represents an effort toward utilizing a state-of-the-art taxonomic model of spirituality (MacDonald, 1997, 2000) to organize our understanding as to how the various aspects of spirituality work together, both directly and indirectly, in shaping spiritual identity. A particular strength of the model is that it readily lends itself to empirical investigation – all concepts included can be measured through existing paper-and-pencil tests. At the same time, the model is consistent with conventional identity theory and allows for the application of multiple theoretical approaches to the study of spiritual identity without excluding any important components of spirituality. It is my hope that researchers interested in spiritual identity are able to use the ideas presented here to further investigation into this emerging area of empirical study in a manner which does justice to the complexity of spirituality as a unique domain of human functioning.

Acknowledgments The author would like to thank Dr. Harris Friedman, Dr. Catherine Tsagarakis, Nore Gjolaj, Jacek Brewczynski, the editors, and the anonymous reviewer for their helpful comments on earlier versions of this chapter.

References

Allport, G. W. (1955). *Becoming: Basic considerations for a psychology of personality*. New Haven, CT: Yale University Press.

Allport, G. W., & Ross, M. (1967). Personal religious orientation and prejudice. *Journal of Personality and Social Psychology, 5*, 432–443.

Beauregard, M., & O'Leary, D. (2007). *The spiritual brain: A neuroscientist's case for the existence of the soul*. New York: Harper Collins.

Byrom, T. (Trans.) (1990). *The heart of awareness: A translation of the Ashtavakra Gita*. Boston: Shambhala Press.

Chae, M. H., Kelly, D. B., Brown, C. F., & Bolden, M. A. (2004). Relationship of ethnic identity and spiritual development: An exploratory study. *Counseling and Values, 49*, 15–26.

Clarke, I. (Ed.). (2001). *Psychosis and spirituality: Exploring the new frontier*. London: Whurr Publishers.

Cleary, T. (1989). *Zen Essence: The science of freedom*. Boston: Shambhala Press.

Cloninger, C. R., Svrakic, D. M., & Przybeck, T. R. (1993). A psychobiological model of temperament and character. *Archives of General Psychiatry, 50*, 975–990.

Costa, P. T., Jr., & McCrae, R. R. (1992). *Revised NEO Personality inventory (NEO-PI-R) and NEO five-factor inventory (NEO-FFI) professional manual*. Odessa, FL: Psychological Assessment Resources.

Costa, P. T., Jr., & McCrae, R. R. (1995). Solid ground in the wetlands of personality: A reply to Block. *Psychological Bulletin, 117*(2), 216–220.

Elkins, D. N., Hedstrom, L. J., Hughes, L. L., Leaf, J. A., & Saunders, C. (1988). Toward phenomenological spirituality: Definition, description, and measurement. *Journal of Humanistic Psychology, 28*(4), 5–18.

Erikson, E. H. (1980). *Identity and the life cycle*. New York: Norton.

Fukuyama, M. A., & Sevig, T. (2002). Spirituality in counseling across cultures. In P. Pedersen, J. Draguns, W. Lonner, & J. Trimble (Eds.), *Counseling across cultures* (5th ed., pp. 273–295). Thousand Oaks, CA: Sage.

Grof, C., & Grof, S. (1990). *The stormy search for the self*. Los Angeles: Jeremy Tarcher Press.

Haber, J. R., Jacob, T., & Spangler, D. J. C. (2007). Dimensions of religion/spirituality and relevance to health research. *International Journal for the Psychology of Religion, 17*(4), 265–288.

Hartmann, E. (1991). *Boundaries of the mind*. New York: Basic Books.

Heintz, L. M., & Baruss, I. (2001). Spirituality in late adulthood. *Psychological Reports, 88*(3), 651–654.

Helminiak, D. A. (2008). Confounding the divine and the spiritual: Challenges to a psychology of spirituality. *Pastoral Psychology, 57*(3–4), 161–182.

Hill, P. C., Pargament, K. I., Hood, R. W., Jr., McCullough, M. E., Swyers, J. P., Larson, D. B., et al. (2000). Conceptualizing religion and spirituality: Points of commonality, points of departure. *Journal for the Theory of Social Behaviour, 30*(1), 51–77.

Hine, J. (1997). Mind structure and ego states. *Transactional Analysis Journal, 27*(4), 278–289.

Hoge, D. R. (1996). Religion in America: The demographics of belief and affiliation. In E. P. Shafranske (Ed.), *Religion and the clinical practice of psychology* (pp. 21–41). Washington, DC: American Psychological Association.

Houran, J., Thalbourne, M. A., & Lange, R. (2003). Methodological note: Erratum and comment on the use of the Revised Transliminality scale. *Consciousness and Cognition, 12*(1), 140–144.

Howden, J. W.. (1992). *Development and psychometric characteristics of the Spirituality Assessment Scale* (Doctoral Dissertation, Texas Women's University).

Huber, J. T., & MacDonald, D. A.. (2010). An investigation of the relations between altruism, empathy, and spirituality. Manuscript submitted for publication.

Hunsberger, B., Pratt, M., & Pancer, S. M. (2001). Adolescent identity formation: Religious exploration and commitment. *Identity: An International Journal of Theory and Research, 1*, 365–386.

Hunt, H., Dougan, S., Grant, K., & House, M. (2002). Growth enhancing versus dissociative states of consciousness: A questionnaire study. *Journal of Humanistic Psychology, 42*, 90–106.

James, W. (1890). *The principles of psychology (Vol. 1)*. New York: Holt and Company.

James, W. (1902). *The varieties of religious experience: A study of human nature*. New York: The Modern Library.

Juang, L., & Syed, M. (2008). Ethnic identity and spirituality. In R. M. Lerner, R. W. Roeser, & E. Phelps (Eds.), *Positive youth development and spirituality: From theory to research* (pp. 262–284). West Conshohocken, PA: Templeton Foundation Press.

Jung, C. G. (1967). *Collected works. Symbols of transformation (Vol. 5)*. Princeton, NJ: Princeton University Press.

Jung, C. G. (1969). *Collected works. Psychology and religion (1928-1954) (Vol. 11)*. Princeton, NJ: Princeton University Press.

Kassab, V. A., & MacDonald, D. A. (2010). Examination of the psychometric properties of the Spiritual Fitness Assessment. *Journal of Religion and Health*. Retrieved electronically January 25, 2010. DOI 10.1007/s10943=010-9325–z.

Kiesling, C., Sorell, G. T., Montgomery, M. J., & Colwell, R. K. (2006). Identity and spirituality: A psychosocial exploration of the sense of spiritual self. *Developmental Psychology, 42*, 1269–1277.

Koenig, H. G. (2008). Concerns about measuring spirituality in research. *Journal of Nervous and Mental Disease, 196*, 349–355.

Lerner, R. M., Roeser, R. W., & Phelps, E. (Eds.). (2008). *Positive youth development and spirituality: From theory to research*. West Conshohocken, PA: Templeton Foundation Press.

MacDonald, D. A. (1997). *The development of a comprehensive factor analytically derived model of spirituality and its relationship to psychological functioning* (Doctoral Dissertation, University of Windsor, Windsor, Ontario, Canada).

MacDonald, D. A. (2000). Spirituality: Description, measurement and relation to the Five Factor Model of personality. *Journal of Personality, 68*, 153–197.

MacDonald, D. A. (2009). Identity and spirituality: Conventional and transpersonal perspectives. *International Journal of Transpersonal Studies, 28*, 86–106.

MacDonald, D. A., & Friedman, H. L. (2001). The scientific study of spirituality: Philosophical and methodological considerations. *Biofeedback Newsmagazine, 29*(3), 19–21.

MacDonald, D. A., & Friedman, H. L. (2002). Assessment of humanistic, transpersonal, and spiritual constructs: State of the Science. *Journal of Humanistic Psychology, 42*(4), 102–125.

MacDonald, D. A., Friedman, H. L., Brewczynski, J., Holland, D., Gubrij, Z., Kumar, S. K. K., et al. (2010). Spirituality across cultures and languages. Manuscript in preparation.

MacDonald, D. A., & Holland, D. (2002a). Examination of the psychometric properties of the Temperament and Character Inventory Self-Transcendence Dimension. *Personality and Individual Differences, 32*, 1013–1027.

MacDonald, D. A., & Holland, D. (2002b). Spirituality and boredom proneness. *Personality and Individual Differences, 32*, 1113–1119.

MacDonald, D. A., & Holland, D. (2002c). Spirituality and self-reported complex-partial epileptic-like signs. *Psychological Reports, 91*, 785–792.

MacDonald, D. A., & Holland, D. (2003). Spirituality and the MMPI-2. *Journal of Clinical Psychology, 59*, 399–410.

MacDonald, D. A., Holland, C. J., & Holland, D. (2005). Musings on the psychological meaning of openness. *Australian Gestalt Journal, 8*, 67–70.

MacDonald, D. A., & Kassab, V. A.. (2010). [Correlations between the Rotter Internal-External Locus of Control Scale and the Expressions of Spirituality Inventory]. Unpublished raw data.

Marcia, J. E. (1966). Development and validation of ego-identity status. *Journal of Personality and Social Psychology, 3*, 551–558.

Marcia, J. E. (1993). The ego identity status approach to ego identity. In J. E. Marcia, A. S. Waterman, D. R. Matteson, S. L. Archer, & J. L. Orlofski (Eds.)., *Ego identity: A handbook for psychological research* (pp. 3–41). New York: Springer.

Markstrom, C. (1999). Religious involvement and adolescent psychosocial development. *Journal of Adolescence, 22*, 205–221.

Maslow, A. H. (1970). *Religions, values, and peak experiences*. New York: Viking Press.

Maslow, A. H. (1971). *The farther reaches of human nature*. New York: Penguin.

Migdal, L. (2007). *The structure of existential well-being and its relation to other well-being constructs*. Unpublished Doctoral Dissertation. University of Detroit Mercy, Detroit, MI.

Newberg, A., D'Aquili, E., & Rause, V. (2001). *Why god won't go away: Brain science and the biology of belief*. New York: Ballantine Books.

Paranjpe, A. C. (1998). *Self and identity in modern psychology and Indian thought*. New York: Plenum Press.

Persinger, M. A. (1984). Striking EEG profiles from single episodes of glossolalia and Transcendental Meditation. *Perceptual and Motor Skills, 58*, 127–133.

Poll, J. B., & Smith, T. B. (2003). The spiritual self: Toward a conceptualization of spiritual identity development. *Journal of Psychology and Theology, 31*(2), 129–142.

Richards, P. S., & Bergin, A. E. (1997). *A spiritual strategy for counseling and psychotherapy*. Washington, DC: American Psychological Association.

Salsman, J. M., Brown, T. L., Brechting, E. H., & Carlson, C. R. (2005). The link between religion and spirituality and psychological adjustment: The mediating role of optimism and social support. *Personality and Social Psychology Bulletin, 31*, 522–535.

Slife, B. D., Hope, C., & Nebeker, R. S. (1999). Examining the relationship between religious spirituality and psychological science. *Journal of Humanistic Psychology, 39*(2), 51–85.

Suzuki, D. T. (1957). *Mysticism, Christian and Buddhist*. New York: Perennial Library.

Suzuki, D. T., Fromm, E., & DeMartino, R. (1960). *Zen Buddhism and psychoanalysis*. New York: Harper.

Taylor, S. E., & Brown, J. D. (1988). Illusion and well-being: A social psychological perspective on mental health. *Psychological Bulletin, 103*(2), 193–210.

Templeton, J. L., & Eccles, J. S. (2006). The relation between spiritual development and identity processes. In E. C. Roehlkepartain, P. E. King, L. Wagener, & P. Benson (Eds.), *The handbook of spiritual development in childhood and adolescence* (pp. 252–265). Thousand Oaks, CA: Sage.

Thalbourne, M. A., & Delin, P. S. (1994). A common thread underlying belief in the paranormal, creative personality, mystical experience, and psychopathology. *Journal of Parapsychology, 58*(1), 3–38.

Tisdell, E. J. (2002). Spiritual development and cultural context in the lives of women adult educators for social change. *Journal of Adult Development, 9*, 127–140.

Weber, L. J., & Cummings, A. L. (2003). Relationships among spirituality, social support, and childhood maltreatment in university students. *Counseling and Values, 47*(2), 82–95.

Wilber, K. (1980). *The Atman project: A transpersonal view of human development*. Wheaton, IL: Theosophical Publishing House.

Yakushko, O. (2005). Influence of social support, existential well-being, and stress over sexual orientation on self-esteem of gay, lesbian, and bisexual individuals. *International Journal for the Advancement of Counselling, 27*(1), 131–143.

Zinder, J. R.. (2007). Spiritual identity, spiritual self-labeling, and health in African American and White undergraduates. *Dissertation Abstracts International: Section B: The Sciences and Engineering, 67*(7-B), 4148.

Zinnbauer, B. J., Pargament, K. I., Cole, B., Rye, M. S., Butter, E. M., Belavich, T. G., et al. (1997). Religion and spirituality: Unfuzzying the fuzzy. *Journal for the Scientific Study of Religion, 36*, 549–564.

Spiritual Identity: Contextual Perspectives

22

Eugene C. Roehlkepartain, Peter L. Benson, and Peter C. Scales

Abstract

Examining how spirit develops as part of identity development can deepen our understanding of how meaning, purpose, connectedness, and authentic living contribute to human thriving – and what happens when they go awry. However, research in this field has been limited by a conflation of "religion" and "spirituality" both theoretically and empirically, limited data on spirituality outside of Western contexts or Judeo-Christian religious traditions, and an emphasis on individual development with little regard to interaction with developmental systems, ecologies, or contexts. By examining the intersection of spiritual development, identity development, and ecological approaches to human development, this chapter proposes integrating more robust understandings of spiritual development into current approaches to adolescent identity formation while also deepening theoretical approaches to spiritual development by grounding them in ecological contexts, including family; peers and mentors; school; youth organizations; religious communities; and the natural world. It draws on preliminary findings from a study of 7,200 youth aged 12–25 in eight countries that suggest that this integration may be fruitful for future research.

Some of the most exquisite and important phenomena of human life are also among the most difficult to investigate in the behavioral sciences. Among these are the following: (a) how persons explore the mysteries of the self and of the universe; (b) the capacity to apprehend beauty and benevolence; (c) the experiences of awe and wonder; (d) the inclination to seek community and connectedness; and (e) the capacity for persons to find joy, purpose, and hope in life. These phenomena themselves, and the processes that energize and guide them, are fundamental to what it means to be human.

Religion, in its many historical and contemporary manifestations, has informed these phenomena, but it is not synonymous with them (MacDonald, Chapter 21, this volume). These are manifestations of spirit (from the Latin *spiritus*, meaning breath). Spirit – or how one finds and

E.C. Roehlkepartain (✉)
Search Institute, Minneapolis, MN, USA
e-mail: gener@search-institute.org

S.J. Schwartz et al. (eds.), *Handbook of Identity Theory and Research*,
DOI 10.1007/978-1-4419-7988-9_22, © Springer Science+Business Media, LLC 2011

expresses one's breath or life energy – is central to understanding humanness (Johnson, 2008). By examining how spirit develops and flourishes (or goes awry), we have the potential to tap the deep resources of meaning, purpose, connectedness, and authentic living that are embedded in what we call spiritual development.

There appears to be a growing international interest in the science of spiritual development among children and adolescents, bolstered in part by the emerging research suggesting that spirituality and spiritual development play important roles in human development and thriving. However, most current research on adolescent spiritual development has been constrained by critical limitations (see Roehlkepartain, King, Wagener, & Benson, 2006). These include the following: (a) conflating "religion" and "spirituality"; (b) limited data regarding spirituality among young people outside of Western contexts or Judeo-Christian religious traditions; (c) a preponderance of research that focuses on individual development with little regard to interaction with developmental systems or ecologies; and (d) conducting research with limited measures and without robust undergirding theoretical frameworks or foundations (Benson, 2006; Rew & Wong, 2006; MacDonald, Chapter 21, this volume).

This chapter seeks to address these limitations by examining the intersection of three concepts: spiritual development, identity development, and ecological approaches to human development. In doing so, we seek to make a theoretical case for both integrating more robust understandings of spiritual development into current approaches to adolescent identity formation and deepening theoretical approaches to spiritual development by grounding them in ecological approaches. Throughout the chapter, we offer findings with multi-country samples of adolescents that suggest that this integration may be fruitful for future research.

Definitional Issues in Spiritual Development

A major challenge is that, despite a number of helpful explorations (e.g., Hill & Pargament,

2003; Hill et al., 2000; MacDonald, 2000; Slater, Hall, & Edwards, 2001; Zinnbauer et al., 1997), there is little consensus on the boundaries or dimensions of the domain of spiritual development (or spirituality and other related terms). In the social sciences, spirituality was historically viewed as a dimension of religious experience (James, 1902). However, as Wulff (1997) suggests, the meaning of religion has evolved to focus more on the institutional, beliefs, and rituals and practices, with spirituality being increasingly seen as referring to experiential or subjective phenomena (see MacDonald, Chapter 21, this volume for a thorough exploration of the definitional issues).

Rather than focusing on beliefs, experiences, and practices (the typical approach to defining "spirituality"), we seek to identify and measure core processes in human development that can best be described as spiritual *development*. Drawing on Coles (1990) and Rizzuto (1979), and other scholars, this approach hypothesizes that spiritual development is a human wellspring out of which emerges the pursuit of meaning, connectedness to others and to the sacred, purpose in life, and contributions to society. Each and all of these functions can be informed and shaped by religious – and other – systems of ideas, practices, and cultural narratives. In addition, these core processes are integrally linked with identity development.

Several operating hypotheses have guided our work to date, including the following: (a) spiritual development is an intrinsic part of being human. It includes processes that are manifested in many diverse ways among individuals, cultures, traditions, and historical periods. (b) Spiritual development involves both an inward journey (inner experiences and/or connections to the infinite or unseen) and an outward journey (being expressed in daily activities, relationships, and actions). In this sense, it involves complex interactions between contextual variables and individual developmental processes. (c) Spiritual development is a dynamic, nonlinear process that varies across individual and cultural differences. (d) Although spiritual development is a unique stream of human development, it cannot be separated from other aspects of development, such as physical, emotional, and cognitive development. And (e) spiritual development can be conceptually distinguished from religious development or formation, though the two are integrally linked in the lived experiences of many (though not all) people, traditions, and cultures (see MacDonald, Chapter 21, this volume).

Several of these assumptions or hypotheses merit further explication. First, it is important to unpack the relationship between spiritual development and religion. We propose that spiritual development can occur with or without explicit religious beliefs, practices, or community (also see Saucier & Skrzypińska, 2006). However, many people utilize or access religion as a guiding narrative and normative community for their spiritual development. When this occurs, one's spiritual development can be closely aligned with one's religious beliefs, identity, and worldview. However, one can develop spiritually without religious institutions, beliefs, or practices. Furthermore, the broader ecology of community, relationships, and social norms also shapes spiritual development. Thus, these two phenomena are related and overlapping, but they may also be different.

Another important framing of our approach to spiritual development has been to cast it as a component of optimal development, which is also called thriving (Benson & Scales, 2009) or flourishing (Keyes & Haidt, 2003). Often associated with positive psychology (Seligman & Csikszentmihalyi, 2000; Snyder & Lopez, 2005), this strength-based approach counterbalances an overemphasis in the social sciences on pathologies and deficits with a focus on identifying and nourishing human capacities, such as life satisfaction, hope, generosity, connectedness, self-regulation, and prosocial orientation. Within the field of identity theory and development, this approach particularly resonates with Waterman's (1993; Chapter 16, this volume) emphasis on personal expressiveness (*eudaimonia*).

This is not to say, however, that all spiritual commitments, beliefs, practices, and experiences are positive and life giving. As suggested by the inclusion of religious and spiritual problem in the *Diagnostic and Statistical Manual of Mental Disorders* (DSM-IV-TR) (American Psychiatric Association, 2000), certain forms of spiritual beliefs, practices, and experiences can distort reality or cause harm to self or others. These harmful effects can include narcissism, conflict-ridden or authoritarian spiritual practices, denial of reality, spiritual delusions, or terrorism (Hill et al., 2000; Wagener & Malony, 2006). Others have focused on meditative, mystical, paranormal experiences (such as precognition or communicating with the spirit world), psychedelic-induced trances (including using psychoactive drugs such as opiates or LSD), or other unusual consciousness events that can cause physical and psychological harm [which Grof & Grof (1989) describe as "spiritual emergences or emergency"].

Though we emphasize the positive potential of spiritual development, the social sciences through most of the twentieth century either ignored this domain of life or attended only to eclectic issues, including pathological expressions (MacDonald, 2000). So rather than minimizing the potential for pathology, we seek to articulate underlying developmental processes of *normal* spiritual development, which may be shaped, either positively or negatively, through a wide range of influences, beliefs, and practices.

Toward a New Framework of Adolescent Spiritual Development

In many respects, the scientific study of spiritual development is not new. Since the late 1800s, scholars such as William James, G. Stanley Hall, J. H. Leuba, Edwin Starbuck, Max Weber, and Emile Durkheim have examined the role of religion (and, more recently, spirituality) in human development and society. However, for a variety of reasons, it was marginalized in social sciences through much of the twentieth century (see Davie, 2003; Paloutzian, 1996).

An important movement in reclaiming spirituality in the social sciences was transpersonal psychology, which emerged in the 1960s. This network emphasized on integrating Eastern and Western thought and studying mystical and metaphysical experiences (e.g., Hartelius, Caplan, & Rardin, 2007). Though he no longer associates with transpersonal psychology, Wilber's (e.g., 2000) integrated theory of development has been particularly influential, though it is rarely cited in mainstream developmental and psychological studies.

In addition, a number of recent contributions in developmental sciences have advanced the literature on child and adolescent spiritual development. For example, for the first time since it began publication in 1946, the *Handbook of Child Psychology* includes a chapter on spiritual development in its sixth edition (Oser, Scarlett, & Bucher, 2006). That same year, Sage released the first *Handbook of Spiritual Development in Childhood and Adolescence* (Roehlkepartain et al., 2006) and the *Encyclopedia of Religious and Spiritual Development in Childhood and Adolescence* (Dowling & Scarlett, 2006).

In 2006, Search Institute launched the Center for Spiritual Development in Childhood and Adolescence to develop grounded theory and systematic research aimed at explicating an understanding of spiritual development as an integral component of human development, particularly during childhood and adolescence. To begin these theory-building efforts, we conducted extensive focus groups with youth, parents, and youth workers in 13 countries (Kimball, Mannes, & Hackel, 2009) and engaged an international network of 119 scientific, theological/philosophical, and practice advisors in a Web-based consensus-building process around the processes of spiritual development (Roehlkepartain, 2009). Using a Web-based adaptation of the Delphi Technique (Dalkey, 1969), advisors ranked potential dimensions of spiritual development to identify those that they believed were most important. This process yielded the broad, if preliminary, outlines of a theoretical framework shown in Table 22.1.

Though this process did not result in a consensus definition of spiritual development, one definitional approach that generated significant support was that *spiritual development is a constant, ongoing, and dynamic interplay between one's inward journey and one's outward journey*. In other words, spiritual development presses us to look outward to connect or embed our lives with all of life, while also compelling us to look inward to accept or discover our potential to grow, learn, contribute, and matter (Soenens & Vansteenkiste, Chapter 17, this volume; Waterman, Chapter 16, this volume). This approach, then, may suggest that "spirit" is an intrinsic capacity that propels young people to link their discovery of self and the world in pursuit of a flourishing life.

This framework shares many features of other multi-dimensional models of spirituality, including MacDonald's (Chapter 21, this volume) work. The unique contribution of the proposed theoretical model lies in (a) its focus on adolescence; (a) its grounding in qualitative data from youth in multiple contexts and cultures; (c) the engagement of experts from multiple disciplines, contexts, and traditions in developing this shared conceptual approach; and (d) a focus on core developmental processes, rather than spiritual beliefs, practices, or experiences (all of which interactively influence and give expression to these core processes in a bidirectional interplay). In other words, the core developmental processes dynamically interact with the beliefs, practices, relationships, and contexts in which the young person is embedded, with each influencing the other (Benson, Roehlkepartain, & Scales, in press; Benson & Scales, 2009; Lerner, Roeser, & Phelps, 2008).

These emphases make the approach we outline below somewhat distinct. As the field matures and additional testing of various models and approaches is completed in diverse cultures and contexts with diverse populations, we would anticipate that the most robust elements of various models will emerge. In the meantime, we propose the need for ongoing exploration by different scholars, with each seeking to be clear about the underlying assumptions and theories behind a particular approach. Such a discovery process offers great potential to enrich the field's overall understanding of this dimension of human development.

Table 22.1 Theoretical framework of dynamics of spiritual development

Awareness or awakening – Developing an awareness of one's inherent strength as well as developing an awareness of the beauty and majesty of the universe. This involves both (a) awareness of one's inherent strengths and capacities (self-awareness) and (b) awareness of the world, including awareness of the beauty and majesty of the universe, often experienced through the awe and wonder that draws one to see self in as part of something larger (Shiota, Keltner, & Mossman, 2007). Dimensions include the following:

- Accepting, seeking, creating, or experiencing a reason for being or a sense of meaning and purpose
- Being present to oneself, others, the world, and/or one's sense of transcendent reality
- Forming a worldview regarding major life questions, such as the purpose of existence, life and death, and the existence or the non-existence of the divine or God
- Living in awareness of something beyond the immediacy of everyday life
- Experiencing enlightenment, awakening, liberation, salvation, or other experiences of transcendence or deepening
- Accepting or discovering one's potential to grow, contribute, and matter

Interconnecting and belonging – Developing the perspective that life is interconnected and interdependent, and seeking, accepting, or experiencing significance in relationships to and interdependence with others, the world, or one's sense of the transcendent (often including an understanding of God or a higher power). This may include the following:

- Experiencing a sense of empathy, responsibility, and/or love for others, for humanity, and for the world
- Finding significance in relationships to others, the world, or one's sense of the transcendent
- Finding, accepting, or creating deeper significance and meaning in everyday experiences and relationships
- Linking oneself to narratives, communities, mentors, beliefs, traditions, and/or practices that remain significant over time

Living a life of strength – Developing a life orientation grounded in hope, purpose, and gratitude so that one authentically expresses one's identity, passions, values, and creativity through relationships, activities, and/or practices. This may include the following:

- Engaging in relationships, activities, and/or practices that shape bonds with oneself, family, community, humanity, the world, and/or that which one believes to be transcendent
- Living out one's beliefs, values, and commitments in daily life
- Experiencing or cultivating hope, meaning, or resilience in the midst of hardship, conflict, confusion, or suffering
- Living out an orientation to life in response to that which one perceives to be worthy of dedication and/or veneration
- Attending to spiritual questions, challenges, and struggles
- Expressing one's essence, passions, value, and creativity in the world as a way of showing veneration or expressing one's sense of transcendence

Findings from Recent Global Research

The framework of core spiritual developmental processes outlined in Table 22.1 (above) provided the conceptual foundation for a survey instrument that we, our colleagues, and our research partners administered to more than 7,200 youth (ages 12–25) in eight countries in 2008 (Australia, Canada, Cameroon, India, Thailand, Ukraine, the United Kingdom, and the United States). Though this field test involved convenience samples in only a few nations (and thus might not be generalizable beyond those samples), it involves a culturally and religiously diverse sample of young people, allowing for preliminary insights into patterns of spiritual development in their lives (Roehlkepartain, Benson, Scales, Kimball, & King, 2008).

We have begun using this data set to test the theory of core spiritual developmental processes posited through our consensus-building process and grounded in findings from focus groups with youth (Kimball et al., 2009). We explore several hypotheses: (a) there are core developmental processes or tasks that are salient across traditions and cultures (including the eight nations and five self-reported religious affiliations in our sample: Buddhist, Christian, Hindu, Muslim, and agnostic/atheist/none); (b) young people's experiences of these processes correlate with positive developmental outcomes; (c) these processes explain variance in youth outcomes over and above young people's self-reported religiousness; and (d) these processes tend to become more integrated as young people age.

We began our analyses using items associated with the major constructs identified through the consensus-building process with advisors described above and shown in Table 22.1. We then conceptually and theoretically divided the concept of "awareness" into two constructs (self and world). This yielded four measures that approximate the terrain of spiritual development that grew out of the consensus-building process with international advisors (shown in Table 22.1): awareness or awakening: self; awareness or awakening: world; interconnecting and belonging; and living a life of strength. Several of our initial hypotheses have been supported by preliminary analyses. However, ongoing analyses are needed to either confirm or challenge the first hypothesis (regarding the salience of these spiritual developmental processes across all eight countries as well as the diverse religious traditions in the sample).

Evidence supporting the second hypothesis (b) is clearer (and consistent with previous research): young people reporting higher levels of various components of spiritual development consistently report lower levels of high-risk behaviors and higher levels of academic success, physical and psychosocial health, and civic engagement. Indeed, the results of 85% of analyses testing the effect of spiritual developmental processes on developmental outcomes were in the hypothesized direction. These patterns generalized across the samples in the eight countries and across religious affiliations. Furthermore, youth who most successfully integrated the four dimensions of spirituality proposed here (as evidenced by scoring high on all four) exhibit relative strength on this same range of outcomes.

Third, as hypothesized (c), the integration of these four processes described above can occur without active engagement with religious and spiritual traditions. After controlling for gender, age, and religious engagement, the four dimensions of spiritual development significantly explain variance on each of the indicators of thriving, health, and risk behaviors included in the study. This suggests that these four processes of spiritual development – both individually and collectively – have explanatory value over and above religious engagement and belief. Indeed, about 20% of the aggregated sample reported high levels of the four dimensions of spiritual development but were not affiliated with organized religion.

Fourth (hypothesis d), healthy development, we would argue, moves in the direction of integration (see Soenens & Vansteenkiste, Chapter 17, this volume), with the four core processes of spiritual development becoming increasingly interrelated. One proximal test of this is to examine whether the percentage of youth who demonstrate this integration (evidenced by higher scores on all four dimensions) increases with age. This hypothesis is supported when comparing youth ages 12–14, 15–17, 18–21, and 22–25 who score high on all four of the processes (see Table 22.2).

Although this was a cross-sectional study, and so *developmental* processes can only be inferred, integration becomes stronger with each advance in age, suggesting promising grounds for further investigation with longitudinal samples. In addition, we recognize that this is only one way to show "integration," and one theoretically could have high scores without these dimensions/processes being integrated or interacting with each other. It is also true that "integration" might not even require a "high" score on each process, because developmental systems theory would suggest that the optimal level of each of these processes would vary with the individual and her or his relation to context. Thus, high levels of interconnectedness and living a life of strength might be necessary for optimal spiritual development in one specific person–context system, but a high level of cognitive awareness of self might not be.

Table 22.2 Youth scoring high on four spiritual developmental processes, by age

Age of respondent	High score on all four processes (%)
12–14	16
15–17	18
18–21	21
22–25	27

In another case, connectedness and a life of strength might be impossible without a high level of self and world awareness. In both cases, though, person–context systems are "integrated" in a way that effectively promotes growth. So, further analyses are needed to shed light on the nature of the relations among these processes, both variable-centered analyses that illuminate group averages and person-centered analyses that uncover the diverse meanings of the descriptor, "integrated."

The core spiritual developmental processes on which the above analyses are focused provide a starting point for theoretically exploring the person–context interactions underlying spiritual development. How are these processes shaped by family, peer groups, mentors, religious communities, and their narratives; the mass media; music; art; and the social norms that permeate and potentially connect multiple socializing systems? What happens when these processes are shaped primarily by harmful or misanthropic forces? Or how is healthy development augmented when young people's own sense of agency and vocation is positively nurtured and reinforced by life-affirming people and places? With these kinds of questions in mind, we now turn to a theoretical exploration of some of the contexts in young people's "spiritual ecologies." These potentially link with the growing theoretical and empirical literature that embeds identity development within a dynamic ecological context.

Person–Context Dynamics in Spiritual Development

Three persistent critiques of current theory and research on spiritual development (which echo discussions related to identity development) are (a) that they too often reflect an individualistic, Western worldview that focuses narrowly on the self and self-fulfillment; (b) that they presume that a spiritual tradition or identity is "inherited," rather than being actively shaped by the person as agent of her or his own development; and (c) that they describe linear, predictable pathways that do not account for the dynamic processes of spiritual formation or the interplay of persons and their contexts. The theoretical framework described above begins to address this question. In addition, a number of identity development theories further illuminate the dynamic interplay between individuals and their environments.

Spiritual Development as Relational, Socially Embedded Processes

The individualistic focus of many conceptualizations of spirituality reflects what Markus and Kitayama (1991) describe as the "self-ways" dominant in English-speaking, Western societies. This bias "has obscured attention to the powerful ways in which religion and spirituality guide and influence relational life" (Mattis & Jagers, 2001, p. 520; also see Mattis, Ahluwalia, Cowie, & Kirkland-Harris, 2006; Templeton & Eccles, 2006).

In contrast, most contemporary theorists agree that identity formation occurs through countless interactions between persons and their physical and social environments (e.g., Bosma & Kunnen, 2001). This understanding draws on ecological–developmental approaches, such as ecological systems theory (Bronfenbrenner, 1979), developmental systems theory (Ford & Lerner, 1992; Lerner, Lerner, De Stefanis, & Apfel, 2001), co-constructionist perspectives on identity development (Berman, Schwartz, Kurtines, & Berman, 2001), and identity capital (Côté, 1996), or other current theoretical approaches. Similarly, a growing number of approaches to spiritual-ity and spiritual development (e.g., Hay & Nye, 1998; Ho, 1995; Nicolas & DeSilva, 2008) are consistent with these perspectives.

Baltes and Baltes (1990) offer a key theoret-ical approach to understanding the interaction between the person and the world, one that is relevant to spiritual development. Called "selective optimization with compensation," this theory holds that persons select, from among a range of potential resources, a subset that can help them to reach their own personal goals. This process of selection involves both one's preferences *and* the availability of options within one's social ecology. Compensation emphasizes the ways in which one adapts to maintain func-tioning in the face of losses or barriers that limit options. Similarly, self-determination theory (Ryan & Deci, 2000; Soenens & Vansteenkiste, Chapter 17, this volume) describes how social conditions impact whether people become actively engaged and proactive or passive and alienated.

Although these theories were not focused explicitly on spiritual development, the princi-ples apply, particularly when efforts are made to optimize broader environments in which spiri-tual development can flourish. For example, per-sons, communities, and contexts that seek to nurture spiritual development may or may not be "in sync" developmentally with adolescents. Furthermore, both adolescents and the contexts in which they function must adapt to changing sociocultural dynamics, including the increased diversity of religious and spiritual beliefs, prac-tices, and narratives.

Young People as Active Agents in Their Own Spiritual Development

To say that spiritual development is embedded in relationships and through the dynamic interplay of person and context in no way minimizes the active role that young people play as agents of their own development. Indeed, personal agency is foundational to identity (and spiritual) formation (Schwartz, Côté, & Arnett, 2005).

How personal agency is manifested informs how we understand the processes of spiritual development.

Numerous identity theorists have conceptu-alized identity development as involving both active and passive processes (Blos, 1979; Erikson, 1968). For example, Marcia (1966, 1980) argued that adolescents form identity passively by accepting the roles and self-images provided by others (foreclosure). Blos (1979) described passive identity formation as resisting making choices about identity (dif-fusion). Active identity develops based on a searching process and is associated with self-assurance, self-certainty, and a sense of mas-tery (Adams, Gullotta, & Montemayor, 1992). Luyckx, Goossens, and Soenens (2006) have advanced our understanding of identity devel-opment by identifying four structural dimen-sions of identity formation: commitment mak-ing, identification with commitment, exploration in depth, and exploration in breadth that inte-grate identity formation and identity evaluation and embed them in a developmental context (see Luyckx, Schwartz, Goossens, Beyers, & Missotten, Chapter 4, this volume).

In addition, Waterman's (1993, Chapter 16, this volume) focus on personal expressiveness (*eudaimonia*) offers important possibilities for enriching how theories of spiritual develop-ment approach active personal agency. Waterman summarizes the goals of identity formation as discovery of personal potential, choosing pur-poses in living, and finding opportunities to live out that purpose. This structure resonates with our theoretical framework that links self-awareness and other awareness with living a life of strength. Similarly, Benson and Scales (2009) have described the theory and measurement of *thriving* in adolescence as involving the iden-tification and nurturing of one's deep personal interests or "sparks" (akin to our awareness pro-cess, or Waterman's discovery of personal poten-tial), the support received from others to pursue them (our interdependence/aconnection process), and the contribution one makes to others and to society through the pursuit of one's sparks (part of the process of living a life of strength and purpose). One of the strongest thriving markers for both middle- and high-school students was their affirmation of a transcendent force and the importance of their spirituality in affecting daily actions. Thus, this conceptualization of thriving explicitly connects aspects of identity development with aspects of spiritual development.

Several researchers have focused on religious identity processes (not specifically spiritual development), finding that individuals tend to proceed toward achievement during emerging adulthood (Meeus, Iedema, Helsen, & Vollebergh, 1999), particularly if they have an intrinsic religious orientation (DeHaan & Schulenberg, 1997). Sanders (1998) found that college students with a diffused religious identity (low commitment and low exploration) reported lower levels of faith maturity than did those with a religious identity characterized by moratorium, foreclosure, or achievement. Those reporting achievement (high commitment and high exploration) were most likely to be engaged in service to humanity.

We would anticipate that similar patterns would be evident when examining dynamics of spiritual development as distinct from religious identity. In focus groups with 171 adolescents (ages 12–19) in 13 countries, participants often reported that they are rarely encouraged to engage in active spiritual exploration; rather, they are typically expected to adopt the religious beliefs, practices, and worldviews of their families and traditions (Kimball et al., 2009), with "commitment" to a particular worldview or religious tradition and "discovery" of one's own path and worldview being perceived as competing, rather than complementary, goals.

Spiritual Development as Dynamic, Nonlinear Processes

Finally, these multiple, interacting influences and variables challenge understandings of spiritual development that build on linear or stage theories. Meeus et al. (1999) note that unidirectional interpretations of identity development that move from lower to higher statuses are

inadequate. A similar critique has challenged approaches to spiritual development that focus on stages of development (Fowler, 1981) or progressive/maturational models of spiritual development (Scarlett, 2006). Theory and research on spiritual development is less advanced, however, in articulating the possible pathways and patterns of development through adolescence. We anticipate that trajectories could parallel the stable, regressive, progressive, and fluctuating patterns of identity formation that van Hoof (1999) identified and that Meeus and colleagues (2010) demonstrated in a five-wave longitudinal study of ages 12–20.

Exploring the Ecologies of Spiritual Development

Young people interact with multiple ecological resources, influences, and contexts as they shape their own personal and collective (or social or group) spiritual identities. Individuals actively or passively exercise their personal agency in shaping, and being shaped by, the people and places around them, with those closest to them likely having the greatest influence. In this section, we introduce a range of illustrative contexts, resources, and influences that young people selectively optimize for their own development, beginning with interpersonal contexts (e.g., families, peers) and social–structural contexts (e.g., institutions, culture, and place).

Family

Family (including parents, siblings, grandparents, and other extended family) is a primary context for spiritual development (Boyatzis, Dollahite, & Marks, 2006; Dollahite, Marks, & Goodman, 2004; Mahoney, Pargament, Tarakeshwar, & Swank, 2001). In Search Institute's exploratory study of spiritual development in eight countries (described above), young people surveyed were most likely to point toward family when asked to identify who helps them most in their spiritual life. In total, when forced to select the single most significant influence, 44% of the youth surveyed selected this option, compared to just 14% of youth who indicated that their religious institution (church, synagogue, mosque, temple, or other religious or spiritual place) helped them the most (Roehlkepartain et al., 2008).

Through parental modeling, rituals, narratives, conversations, and other family practices and dynamics, the family plays a vital role not only in the direction, formative interactions, rituals, and practices that shape spiritual development and identity but also in socializing adolescents to seek out (or not to seek out) other resources, relationships, and opportunities that will further affect the adolescent's development. These may include the kinds of activities in which he or she participates and the people with whom the young person spends time.

The centrality of the family is particularly salient in a relational, ecological approach to spiritual development. Indeed, Black (2004) noted that, in the Hindu and Buddhist traditions (as well as others), "self" is defined as a part of a family, not primarily as an individual person who is influenced by family. Thus, individual autonomy, valued more in the West, carries less weight than does an internalized sense of interconnectedness and following family traditions, teachings, and guidelines (also see Smith, Chapter 11, this volume, on cross-cultural perspectives).

Boyatzis et al. (2006) adopt a sociocultural approach to families and spiritual development, moving beyond "transmission" models that focus only on parental influence on their children's spiritual (and religious) development. Shifting to bidirectional, transactional models changes one's assumptions about power dynamics in families as well as the place of the child within the family. For example, Boyatzis and Janicki (2003) found that children initiated half of all family conversations related to religion. This shift also reflects an important emphasis on the adolescent's agency in actively shaping spiritual identity, both of the self and the family.

Another vital dynamic in the family's role in spiritual development is generativity (Boyatzis et al., 2006; Scabini & Manzi, Chapter 23, this volume). "Generative spirituality is a transcendent connection with the next generation that flows from and encourages convictions of abiding care for that generation" (Boyatzis et al., 2006, p. 304). These scholars point to three aspects of generative spirituality for families: a shared spiritual paradigm, shared spiritual practices, and a shared spiritual community. As a result, although generativity does not necessarily involve spirituality, it can nonetheless transmit spiritual attitudes and orientations.

Recent research has also begun to emphasize the role of the extended family in spiritual and religious development. For example, a three-generational longitudinal study in the United States found that grandparents, independent of the influence of parents, influence their grandchildren's religious beliefs and practices into young adulthood, suggesting that grandparents serve as independent and joint agents of *religious* socialization (Bengtson, Copen, Putney, & Silverstein, 2009). Whether and how extended family shapes *spiritual* development remains untested, but theoretically important.

Peers and Mentors

Extending beyond the family, young people are embedded in a broader web of relationships and interactions that also are integral to spiritual development. Though there is a long history of (and strong theoretical rationale for) recognizing the role of non-family adults and peers in shaping spiritual development, research examining these relationships has been scant. Schwartz, Bukowski, and Aoki (2006) examined the multiple ways in which peers, mentors, and spiritual leaders can complement (or compensate for) family interactions in shaping spiritual development and suggested that these relationships may be not only transactional but also transformational, with friendship enriching spiritual development and spirituality strengthening friendships. For example, having friends and mentors who both model and verbally share their spirituality has been found to strengthen young people's own spiritual commitments (Schwartz et al., 2006). From the other direction, many of the expressions of a spiritual life and commitment (e.g., joy, compassion, empathy, care, justice) can enrich and deepen friendships, even when the content of those friendships is not explicitly spiritual.

Community-Based Socializing Institutions

Beyond the interpersonal relationships in families and with mentors and peers, a variety of socializing institutions are also important contexts that interact with young people's spiritual lives. Each of these, alone or in combination, potentially informs spiritual developmental processes through norms and rituals, the relationships that form between the young person and the people in these social institutions, the narratives and belief systems that are present, the physical space and aesthetics, and other factors. We introduce several of these contexts as illustrative, recognizing that there are others and that the most salient institutions vary by culture, tradition, context, and young person.

Schools. The role of schools in spiritual development is a matter of considerable debate and varies considerably across different societies and nations. For example, Letendre and Akiba (2001) found that Japanese teachers were much more likely than US teachers to say that students' spiritual development impacted their academic abilities. In fact, US teachers rated it as having the least impact, whereas Japanese teachers rated it as having a relatively strong impact. The authors attributed this difference to a cultural norm in Japan where spirituality permeates the culture as a whole, whereas in the United States, mandates regarding separation of church and state are perceived as precluding addressing spiritual issues in schools.

Much of the research and practice related to schools and spiritual development has occurred in Europe, particularly the United Kingdom, where education in spirituality has become part of law (Minney, 1991). Within this environment, Meehan (2002) reviewed a variety of educational practices that likely create conducive environments for spiritual development (as a core part of

human development) without promoting a sectarian religious agenda. These include an emphasis on quality relationships, encouraging youth to ask and pursue questions, promoting imagination and creativity, and offering silence and reflection. He also highlights a number of places where spiritual development can be explicitly integrated into the school curriculum, including arts, mathematics, language arts, and science. If we understand spiritual development as involving young people's sense of themselves and their place in the world, their sense of meaning, purpose, and contribution, their curiosity and quest for understanding the world around them, their sense of connectedness to others and to the universe, then it becomes more self-evident how schools affect, either positively or negatively, the spiritual journey.

Youth development organizations. In many contexts, young people have opportunities to participate in sports, arts, outdoor education, camping, leadership development, service clubs, and other programs and organizations focused on providing positive opportunities and relationships for youth outside of school. Many of these organizations recognize the importance of holistic development, and they may even have mandates to nurture young people to grow in body, mind, and spirit. But with few exceptions, they struggle with how to address the spiritual dimension of development, particularly if they seek to engage young people from a wide variety of religious and cultural traditions (Garza, Artman, Roehlkepartain, Garst, & Bialeschki, 2007). Among the challenges is the lack of clear guidelines, understanding of lines of authority, or consensus on appropriate practices to guide whether and how to acknowledge or attend to young people's spiritual development (Green, 2008; Pittman, Garza, Yohalem, & Artman, 2008).

In addition, Green (2008) argues that the emphasis on measurement and behavioral outcomes for youth programs undermines their strength in nurturing development, character, and values. She writes, "Classic youth work is voluntary and predicated on the principle that the young person is in control and has the resources or can get the resources he or she needs, and the role of the youth worker is to facilitate this process" (p. 64).

Engaging in young people's spiritual development has the potential to reclaim a central role in youth development programs and practices in attending to deeper issues of character and identity. This engagement could take many forms, depending on the nature and purpose of the program. At a basic level, it might involve equipping youth workers to be open to and supportive of young people's spiritual questions and journey without imposing their own beliefs on the young people. It could also involve creating time, places, and opportunities in which young people can reflect on and nurture the core spiritual developmental processes of awareness, interdependence/connecting, and living a life of strength and purpose. This may include, for example, opportunities to engage in social action and reflecting on these experiences in light of their spiritual paths. Most important, however, may be to create contexts in which youth find their own voice and are active agents in shaping their experiences in partnership with the adult allies.

Religious communities. In some senses, religious congregations (churches, mosques, synagogues, temples, ashrams, and others) are the institutions in many societies with a specific and unique commitment to nurturing the spiritual life, albeit within a particular narrative, ideology, and community of practice. Thus, they represent a crucible for exploring the dynamic interplay of numerous processes in spiritual development (Roehlkepartain & Patel, 2006).

A number of studies have documented the contributions of religious institutions to identity formation, religious development, spiritual development, and other life outcomes. King and Furrow (2004) explored religious communities as sources of social capital, which involves interpersonal, associational, and cultural social ties and resources that are embedded in particular contexts. King and Furrow found that much of the relationship between religious commitment and moral outcomes is mediated through the amount of social capital present in religious institutions (also see King, 2003; Smith & Denton, 2006; Wagener, Furrow, & King, 2003). A national

study of US adults identified part of the mechanism for this role of social capital. Adults who more frequently attended religious services were much more likely than those who attended infrequently or never to rate a variety of ways of engaging with young people (e.g., having meaningful conversations with them, talking about personal values and religious beliefs, offering guidance on decision making) as important, and also to say that the adults they knew engaged with youth in these ways. That is, religiously involved adults felt more personal and social motivation to engage with other people's children in a number of ways that help shape the youths' identities (Scales et al., 2003). Thus, young people who participate in religious communities have access to the structural, relational, and cognitive dimensions of social capital that is embedded in religious institutions, which, in turn, contributes to their moral development.

Similarly, other researchers in the United States have found that involvement in religious institutions uniquely contributes to identity development when compared to involvement in other youth activities such as sports, arts, or service to others. For example, 66% of youth who described their experiences in faith-based activities endorsed the item "This activity got me thinking about who I am," compared with 33% of students who described their experiences in the other organized activities (Larson, Hansen, & Moneta, 2006) (The sample was divided based on self-reported levels of engagement, and respondents focused their responses on particular activities, even if they are involved in several).

These studies each point to the potential of religious communities to contribute to the development of spiritual identity, potentially offering their members a sense of connectedness to each other and something beyond themselves, a shared narrative and worldview, and a role model and expectations for how one lives one's life. The question remains, of course, about the extent to which religious communities actually fulfill this potential for young people, particularly in light of declining youth participation in religious contexts in many parts of the world. In addition, much less is known about how specific beliefs and practices within a particular religious context (such as extreme authoritarianism) may undermine or misdirect healthy spiritual development.

Physical Place and the Natural World

Though it is often overlooked as a resource and shaping context, physical place appears to be particularly salient in young people's spiritual development. Search Institute's international survey found being outside and in nature to be a primary place where many young people say they nurture their spiritual lives (Roehlkepartain et al., 2008) – a much more common response than being in a religious community. Other research has shown that youth consider camping to be a spiritual experience, whether or not the camp is religiously affiliated (Henderson & Bialeschki, 2008). These findings resonate with Sheldrake's (2001) case for "place" as a factor in identity development. He writes, "The concept of 'place' refers not simply to geographical location but also to a dialectical relationship between environment and human narrative. 'Place' is any space that has the capacity to be remembered and to evoke what is most precious" (p. 43).

Of course, the notion of a sacred connection to earth, water, and animal life has a rich history in many indigenous cultures (Abrams, 1997), and specific places take on spiritual significance in every community, whether it is called "spiritual" or not. Weil (1977), a philosopher, wrote, "To be rooted [firmly established and having a sense of belonging] is perhaps the most important and least recognized need of the human soul" (p. 41). Giving young people access to such places (particularly in settings where the streets are unsafe or unwelcoming) becomes an important resource for young people's spiritual development.

Shared Myths and Narratives

The myths and narratives that shape life and meaning making involve a lifelong creative process in which persons actively create (whether consciously or not) a story, using source material that can come from many institutions, places, and relationships (McAdams, 1993, Chapter 5, this volume). For some, this source material includes the myths, narratives, sacred texts, symbols, and worldview of their religious tradition. For others, political and philosophical narratives are most formative. Often, these narratives live in the music, art, rituals, and stories told by elders, and in the crucible of relationships.

Culture, Ethnicity, and Globalization

Individuals potentially participate in, learn from, respond to, and integrate multiple cultures. There may be national culture and cultures of identity and religious cultures, each providing scripts and norms shaping the spiritual developmental process. Culture informs inherited texts, narratives, stories, language, symbols, rituals, and norms that shape identity – and are central in spiritual development.

Taking multiple cultures seriously has great potential to strengthen the theory and research on spiritual development by challenging both the assumption that worldview and practice are essentially the same (and presumed to be like one's own experience) and, on the other hand, avoiding approaching other worldviews as either "exotic curiosities" or antidotes to the "spiritual emptiness" (Ho, 1995, p. 115) they may experience within their inherited tradition or culture. For example, Mattis et al. (2006) challenge the widespread enlightenment assumption that assumes a separation between sacred and secular domains of life, noting that, for many cultural groups, religion and spirituality are perceived as inextricably bound and interwoven with each other and with the whole culture.

Taking these cultural differences seriously both enriches and challenges our assumptions about spiritual development. Gottlieb (2006) illustrates this potential through her anthropological examination of the place of the spirit in the Beng culture of Ivory Coast in West Africa. Gottlieb describes a society where children are viewed as closer to the spirit world because of the cultural assumption of reincarnation. Rather than being an abstract concept, this worldview permeates their respect for children, how adults interact with children, and virtually all areas of community and family life. Other similarly rich examinations of particular people, times, and places will enrich the field as scholars broaden our understanding of spiritual development in its many manifestations.

Beyond the issues of examining specific and diverse cultures as a way of enriching our understanding of spiritual development, scholars have begun turning their attention to globalization and its potential impact on identity (Arnett, 2002; Jensen, Arnett, & McKenzie, Chapter 13, this volume). Globalization provides a broader array of influences, narratives, and relationships from which young people draw in shaping their identities and spiritual paths. Arnett (2002) argues that many people now develop bicultural identities (also see Huynh, Nguyen, & Benet-Martínez, Chapter 35, this volume) that include a local identity and an identity linked to the global culture. Jensen (2003) views this globalization as presenting both opportunities and challenges for identity formation, as young people seek to integrate diverse, sometimes conflicting, beliefs and behaviors from different socializing influences. At the same time, they have the opportunity to develop new skills and attitudes that equip them to function effectively in a multicultural world. A solution to this challenge may lie in what Erlich (2000) called "ethical neopluralism," which consists of "a healthy mix of wide moral consensus and tolerance for diversity of ethical positions within that consensus" (p. 304). This could involve synthesizing a worldview from various belief systems, or it could stimulate deeper exploration of one's own tradition or philosophy, prompted by genuine engagement with other perspectives (e.g., Avest, 2009; Patel, 2007).

Significant Life Events and Changes

Finally, spiritual development is shaped by a wide range of personal, historical, and cultural events. Elder's (1999) life-course theory reminds us that specific times and places shape the content, patterns, and directions of people's lives. Furthermore, different people experience historical change in different ways, which uniquely shapes their developmental trajectory and life course.

Thus, age-related developmental tasks inform goals and priorities and what one chooses to select and to optimize. In addition, life events – some representing the tragic side of life and some representing its generous and healing side – can have a powerful impact on a person's spiritual pathways. In this sense, Antonovsky's (1991) concept of sense of coherence has important implications for the intersection of spiritual and identity development. This theory sheds light on how individuals comprehend and manage internal and external stimuli, and how they make meaning from those experiences. How young people begin to understand themselves and their place and purpose in the world based on what happens around them and to them is central to their spiritual identity formation. These issues also lie at the heart of how humans develop a coherent worldview that helps them manage stress and contributes to their overall health and well-being.

Conclusion

Though the underlying dynamics of spiritual development have been part of the human experience for millennia, the social sciences are in their infancy in seeking to understand the developmental processes underlying spiritual identity formation in adolescence, particularly within a global context. Much of what is known is limited to particular disciplines, contexts, or traditions. Developing a multi-disciplinary and global field of inquiry and network of scholars remains an important challenge for the field.

Emerging theory and research continue to underscore the salience and power of this dimension of human identity development in the lives of young people, their families, and their communities. By grappling with this understudied dimension of human identity, we enrich our understanding of what it means to be human and the conditions under which young people – and the families, communities, and cultures in which they are embedded – can flourish.

Acknowledgments The writing of this chapter, and the research behind it, was supported by the John Templeton Foundation, Philadelphia, Pennsylvania, USA.

References

Abrams, D. (1997). *The spell of the sensuous: Perception and language in a more-than-human world*. New York: Random House.

Adams, G. R., Gullotta, T. P., & Montemayor, R. (Eds.). (1992). *Adolescent identity formation*. Newbury Park, CA: Sage.

American Psychiatric Association (2000). *Diagnostic and statistical manual of mental disorders* (4th ed.) (DSM-IV-TR). Arlington, VA: American Psychiatric Publishing.

Antonovsky, A. (1991). The structural sources of salutogenic strengths. In C. L. Cooper & R. Payne (Eds.), *Personality and stress: Individual differences in the stress process* (pp. 67–104). New York: Wiley.

Arnett, J. J. (2002). The psychology of globalization. *American Psychologist, 57*(10), 774–783.

Avest, K. (2009). Dutch children and their "God": The development of the "God" concept among indigenous and immigrant children in the Netherlands. *British Journal of Religious Education, 31*(3), 251–262.

Baltes, P. B., & Baltes, M. M. (1990). Psychological perspectives on successful aging: The model of selective optimization with compensation. In P. B. Baltes & M. M. Baltes (Eds.), *Successful aging: Perspectives from the behavioral sciences* (pp. 1–34). New York: Cambridge University Press.

Bengtson, V. L., Copen, C. E., Putney, N. M., & Silverstein, M. (2009). A longitudinal study of the intergenerational transmission of religion. *International Sociology, 24*(3), 325–345.

Benson, P. L. (2006). The science of child and adolescent spiritual development: Definitional, theoretical, and field-building challenges. In E. C. Roehlkepartain, P. E. King, L. M. Wagener, & P. L. Benson (Eds.), *The handbook of spiritual development* (pp. 484–497). Thousand Oaks, CA: Sage.

Benson, P. L., Roehlkepartain, E. C., & Scales, P. C. (in press). Spirituality and positive youth development. In L. Miller (Ed.), *The Oxford handbook of psychology of spirituality and consciousness*. New York: Oxford University Press.

Benson, P. L., & Scales, P. C. (2009). The definition and preliminary measurement of thriving in adolescence. *Journal of Positive Psychology, 4*, 85–104.

Berman, A. M., Schwartz, S. J., Kurtines, W. M., & Berman, S. L. (2001). The process of exploration in identity formation: The role of style and competence. *Journal of Adolescence, 24*, 513–528.

Black, N. (2004). Hindu and Buddhist children, adolescents, and families. *Child and Adolescent Psychiatric Clinics of North America, 13*, 201–220.

Blos, P. (1979). *The adolescent passage*. New York: International Universities Press.

Bosma, H. A., & Kunnen, E. S. (2001). Determinants and mechanisms in ego identity development: A review and synthesis. *Developmental Review, 21*, 39–66.

Boyatzis, C. J., Dollahite, D. C., & Marks, L. D. (2006). The family as a context for religious and spiritual development in children and youth. In E. C. Roehlkepartain, P. E. King, L. M. Wagener, & P. L. Benson (Eds.), *The handbook of spiritual development in childhood and adolescence* (pp. 297–309). Thousand Oaks, CA: Sage.

Boyatzis, C. J. & Janicki, D. L. (2003). Parent–child communication about religion: Survey and diary data on unilateral transmission and bi-directional reciprocity styles. *Review of Religious Research, 44*, 252–270.

Bronfenbrenner, U. (1979). *The ecology of human development*. Cambridge, MA: Harvard University Press.

Coles, R. (1990). *The spiritual life of children*. Boston: Houghton Mifflin.

Côté, J. E. (1996). Sociological perspectives on identity formation: The culture–identity link and identity capital. *Journal of Adolescence, 19*, 417–428.

Dalkey, N. C. (1969). *The Delphi method: An experimental study of group opinion*. Santa Monica, CA: Rand.

Davie, G. (2003). The evolution of the sociology of religion: Theme and variations. In M. Dillon (Ed.), *Handbook of the sociology of religion* (pp. 61–75). Cambridge, UK: Cambridge University Press.

DeHaan, L. G., & Schulenberg, J. (1997). The covariation of religion and politics during the transition to young adulthood: Challenging global identity assumptions. *Journal of Adolescence, 20*, 537–552.

Dollahite, D. C., Marks, L. D., & Goodman, M. (2004). Families and religious beliefs, practices, and communities: Linkages in a diverse and dynamic cultural context. In M. J. Coleman & L. H. Ganong (Eds.), *The handbook of contemporary families: Considering the past, contemplating the future* (pp. 411–431). Thousand Oaks, CA: Sage.

Dowling, E. M. & Scarlett, W. G. (2006). *Encyclopedia of religious and spiritual development in childhood and adolescence*. Thousand Oaks, CA: Sage.

Elder, G. H. (1999). *Children of the great depression: Social change in life experience* (25th anniversary ed.). Boulder, CO: Westview Press.

Erikson, E. H. (1968). *Identity: Youth and crisis*. New York: Norton.

Erlich, P. (2000). *Human natures: Genes, cultures, and the human prospect*. New York: Penguin.

Ford, D. H., & Lerner, R. M. (1992). *Developmental systems theory: An integrative approach*. Thousand Oaks, CA: Sage.

Fowler, J. W. (1981). *Stages of faith*. New York: HarperCollins.

Garza, P., Artman, S., Roehlkepartain, E. C., Garst, B. A., & Bialeschki, M. D. (2007). *Is there common ground? An exploratory study of the interests and needs of community-based and faith-based youth workers*. Washington, DC: National Collaboration for Youth; and Minneapolis: Search Institute.

Gottlieb, A. (2006). Non-Western approaches to spiritual development among infants and young children: A case study from West Africa. In E. C. Roehlkepartain, P. E. King, L. M. Wagener, & P. L. Benson (Eds.), *The handbook of spiritual development in childhood and adolescence* (pp. 150–162). Thousand Oaks, CA: Sage.

Green, M. (2008). Putting spiritual development of young people on the map: An English perspective. In P. L. Benson, E. C. Roehlkepartain, & K. L. Hong (Eds.), *New directions for youth development* (Vol. 118, pp. 59–72). San Francisco: Jossey-Bass.

Grof, S., & Grof, C. E. (Eds.). (1989). *Spiritual emergency: When personal transformation becomes a crisis*. Los Angeles: Tarcher.

Hartelius, G., Caplan, M., & Rardin, M. A. (2007). Transpersonal psychology: Defining the past, divining the future. *Humanist Psychologist, 35*(2), 135–160.

Hay, D., & Nye, R. (1998). *The spirit of the child*. London: Fount.

Henderson, K. A., & Bialeschki, M. D. (2008). Spiritual development and camp experiences. In P. L. Benson, E. C. Roehlkepartain, & K. L. Hong (Eds.), *New directions for youth development* (Vol. 118, pp. 107–110). San Francisco: Jossey-Bass.

Hill, P. C., & Pargament, K. I. (2003). Advances in the conceptualization and measurement of religion and spirituality: Implications for physical and mental health research. *American Psychologist, 58*, 64–74.

Hill, P. C., Pargament, K. I., Hood, R. W., McCullough, M. E., Swyers, J. P., Larson, D. B., et al. (2000). Conceptualizing religion and spirituality: Points of commonality, points of departure. *Journal for the Theory of Social Behaviour, 30*, 52–77.

Ho, D. Y. F. (1995). Selfhood and identity in Confucianism, Taoism, Buddhism, and Hinduism: Contrasts with the West. *Journal for the Theory of Social Behaviour, 25*(2), 115–139.

James, W. (1902/1958). *The varieties of religious experience: A study in human nature*. New York: New American Library.

Jensen, L. A. (2003). Coming of age in a multicultural world: Globalization and adolescent cultural identity formation. *Applied Developmental Science, 7*(3), 189–196.

Johnson, C. (2008). The spirit of spiritual development. In R. M. Lerner, R. W. Roeser, & E. Phelps (Eds.), *Positive youth development and spirituality: From theory to research* (pp. 25–41). West Conshohocken, PA: Templeton Foundation Press.

Keyes, C. L. M., & Haidt, J. (Eds.). (2003). *Flourishing: Positive psychology and the life well-lived*. Washington, DC: American Psychological Association.

Kimball, E. M., Mannes, M., & Hackel, A. (2009). Voices of global youth on spirituality and spiritual development: Preliminary findings from a grounded theory study. In M. de Souza, L. J. Francis, J. O'Higgins-Norman, & D. Scott (Eds.), *International handbook of education for spirituality, care, and wellbeing* (pp. 329–348). Dordrecht: Springer.

King, P. E. (2003). Religion and identity: The role of ideological, social, and spiritual contexts. *Applied Developmental Science, 7*(3), 197–204.

King, P. E., & Furrow, J. L. (2004). Religion as a resource for positive youth development: Religion, social capital, and moral outcomes. *Developmental Psychology, 40*(5), 703–713.

Larson, R., Hansen, D., & Moneta, G. (2006). Differing profiles of developmental experiences across types of organized youth activities. *Developmental Psychology, 42*, 849–863.

Lerner, R. M., Lerner, J. V., De Stefanis, I., & Apfel, A. (2001). Understanding developmental systems in adolescence: Implications for methodological strategies, data analytic approaches, and training. *Journal of Adolescent Research, 16*, 9–27.

Lerner, R. M., Roeser, R. W., & Phelps, E. (Eds.). (2008). *Positive youth development and spirituality: From theory to research*. West Conshohocken, PA: Templeton Foundation Press.

Letendre, G., & Akiba, M. (2001). Teacher beliefs about adolescent development: Cultural and organizational impacts on Japanese and US middle school teachers' beliefs. *Compare: A Journal of Comparative Education, 31*(2), 187–203.

Luyckx, K., Goossens, L., & Soenens, B. (2006). A developmental contextual perspective on identity construction in emerging adulthood: Change dynamics in commitment formation and commitment evaluation. *Developmental Psychology, 42*, 366–380.

MacDonald, D. A. (2000). Spirituality: Description, measurement, and relation to the five factor model of personality. *Journal of Personality, 68*, 157–197.

Mahoney, A., Pargament, K. I., Tarakeshwar, N., & Swank, A. B. (2001). Religion in the home in the 1980s and 1990s: A meta-analytic review and conceptual analysis of links between religion, marriage, and parenting. *Journal of Family Psychology, 15*, 539–596.

Marcia, J. E. (1966). Development and validation of ego identity status. *Journal of Personality and Social Psychology, 3*, 551–558.

Marcia, J. E. (1980). Identity in adolescence. In J. Andelson (Ed.), *Handbook of adolescent psychology* (pp. 159–187). New York: Wiley.

Markus, H., & Kitayama, S. (1991). Culture and the self: Implications for cognition, emotion, and motivation. *Psychological Review, 98*, 224–253.

Mattis, J. S., Ahluwalia, M. K., Cowie, S. E., & Kirkland-Harris, A. M. (2006). Ethnicity, culture, and spiritual development. In E. C. Roehlkepartain, P. E. King, L. M. Wagener, & P. L. Benson (Eds.), *The handbook of spiritual development in childhood and adolescence* (pp. 97–309). Thousand Oaks, CA: Sage.

Mattis, J. S., & Jagers, R. J. (2001). A relational framework for the study of religiosity and spirituality in the lives of African Americans. *Journal of Community Psychology, 29*, 519–539.

McAdams, D. P. (1993). *The stories we live by: Personal myths and the making of the self*. New York: Guilford.

Meehan, C. (2002). Promoting spiritual development in the curriculum. *Pastoral Care in Education, 20*(1), 16–24.

Meeus, W., Iedema, J., Helsen, M., & Vollebergh, W. (1999). Patterns of adolescent identity development: Review of literature and longitudinal analysis. *Developmental Review, 19*, 419–461.

Meeus, W., van de Schoot, R., Keijsers, L., Schwartz, S., & Branje, S. (2010). On the progression and stability of adolescent identity formation: A five-wave longitudinal study in early-to-middle and middle-to-late adolescence. *Child Development, 81*(5), 1565–1581.

Minney, R. (1991). What is spirituality in an educational context? *British Journal of Educational Studies, 39*(4), 386–397.

Nicolas, G., & DeSilva, A. M. (2008). Application of the ecological model: Spirituality research with ethnically diverse youths. In R. M. Lerner, R. W. Roeser, & E. Phelps (Eds.), *Positive youth development and spirituality: From theory to research* (pp. 305–321). West Conshohocken, PA: Templeton Foundation Press.

Oser, F. K., Scarlett, W. G., & Bucher, A. (2006). Religious and spiritual development throughout the life span. In W. Damon & R. M. Lerner (Eds.), *Handbook of child psychology* (Vol. 1, 6th ed., pp. 942–998). Theoretical models of human development. Hoboken, NJ: Wiley.

Paloutzian, R. F. (1996). *Invitation to the psychology of religion* (2nd ed.). Needham Heights, MA: Allyn & Bacon.

Patel, E. (2007). *Acts of faith: The story of an American Muslim, the struggle for the soul of a generation*. Boston: Beacon Press.

Pittman, K., Garza, P., Yohalem, N., & Artman, S. (2008). Addressing spiritual development in youth development programs and practices: Opportunities and challenges. In P. L. Benson, E. C. Roehlkepartain, & K. L. Hong (Eds.), *New directions for youth development* (Vol. 118, pp. 29–44). San Francisco: Jossey-Bass.

Rew, L. & Wong, Y. J. (2006). A systematic review of associations among religiosity/spirituality and adolescent health attitudes and behaviors. *Journal of Adolescent Health, 38*, 433–442.

Rizzuto, A. -M. (1979). *The birth of the living God: A psychoanalytic study*. Chicago: University of Chicago Press.

Roehlkepartain, E. C. (2009). Toward a consensus on dimensions of spiritual development. Manuscript in preparation.

Roehlkepartain, E. C., Benson, P. L., Scales, P. C., Kimball, L., & King, P. E. (2008). *With their own voices: A global exploration of how today's young people experience and think about spiritual development*. Minneapolis, MN: Search Institute.

Roehlkepartain, E. C., King, P. E., Wagener, L. M., & Benson, P. L. (2006). *The handbook of spiritual development in childhood and adolescence*. Thousand Oaks, CA: Sage.

Roehlkepartain, E. C., & Patel, E. (2006). Congregations: Unexamined crucibles for spiritual development. In E. C. Roehlkepartain, P. E. King, L. M. Wagener, & P. L. Benson (Eds.), *The handbook of spiritual development in childhood and adolescence* (pp. 324–336). Thousand Oaks, CA: Sage.

Ryan, R. M., & Deci, E. L. (2000). Self-determination theory and the facilitation of intrinsic motivation, social development, and well-being. *American Psychologist, 55*, 68–78.

Sanders, J. L. (1998). Religious ego identity and its relationship to faith maturity. *Journal of Psychology, 132*, 653–658.

Saucier, G., & Skrzypińska, K. (2006). Spiritual but not religious? Evidence for two independent dispositions. *Journal of Personality, 74*, 1257–1292.

Scales, P. C., Benson, P. L., Mannes, M., Hintz, N. R., Roehlkepartain, E. C., & Sullivan, T. K. (2003). *Other people's kids: Social expectations and American adults' involvement with children and adolescents*. New York: Kluwer Academic/Plenum.

Scarlett, W. G. (2006). Toward a developmental analysis of religious and spiritual development. In E. C. Roehlkepartain, P. E. King, L. M. Wagener, & P. L. Benson (Eds.), *The handbook of spiritual development in childhood and adolescence* (pp. 21–33). Thousand Oaks, CA: Sage.

Schwartz, K. D., Bukowski, W. M., & Aoki, W. T. (2006). Mentors, friends, and gurus: Peer and nonparent influences on spiritual development. In E. C. Roehlkepartain, P. E. King, L. M. Wagener, & P. L. Benson (Eds.), *The handbook of spiritual development in childhood and adolescence* (pp. 310–323). Thousand Oaks, CA: Sage.

Schwartz, S. J., Côté, J. E., & Arnett, J. J. (2005). Identity and agency in emerging adulthood: Two developmental routes in the individualization process. *Youth and Society, 37*, 201–229.

Seligman, M. E. P., & Csikszentmihalyi, M. (2000). Positive psychology: An introduction. *American Psychologist, 55*, 5–14.

Sheldrake, P. (2001). Human identity and the particularity of place. *Spiritus, 1*, 43–64.

Shiota, M. N., Keltner, D., & Mossman, A. (2007). The nature of awe: Elicitors, appraisals, and effects on self-concept. *Cognition and Emotion, 21*, 944–963.

Slater, W., Hall, T. W., & Edwards, K. J. (2001). Measuring religion and spirituality: Where are we and where are we going? *Journal of Psychology and Theology, 29*, 4–21.

Smith, C. & Denton, M. L. (2006). *Soul searching: The religious and spiritual lives of American teenagers*. New York: Oxford University Press.

Snyder, C. R., & Lopez, S. J. (Eds.). (2005). *Handbook of positive psychology*. New York: Oxford University Press.

Templeton, J. L., & Eccles, J. S. (2006). The relation between spiritual development and identity process. In E. C. Roehlkepartain, P. E. King, L. M. Wagener, & P. L. Benson (Eds.), *The handbook of spiritual development in childhood and adolescence* (pp. 252–265). Thousand Oaks, CA: Sage.

van Hoof, A. (1999). The identity status field re-reviewed: An update of unresolved and neglected issues with a view on some alternative approaches. *Developmental Review, 19*, 497–565.

Wagener, L., Furrow, J. L., King, P. E., et al. (2003). Religious involvement and developmental resources in youth. *Review of Religious Research, 44*, 271–284.

Wagener, L. M., & Malony, H. N. (2006). Spiritual and religious pathology in childhood and adolescence. In E. C. Roehlkepartain, P. E. King, L. M. Wagener, & P. L. Benson (Eds.), *The handbook of spiritual development in childhood and adolescence* (pp. 137–149). Thousand Oaks, CA: Sage.

Waterman, A. S. (1993). Two conceptions of happiness: Contrasts of personal expressiveness (eudaimonia) and hedonic enjoyment. *Journal of Personality and Social Psychology, 64*(4), 678–691.

Weil, S. (1977). *The need for roots* (A. Willis, Trans.). London: Routledge.

Wilber, K. (2000). *Integral psychology: Consciousness, spirit, psychology, therapy*. Boston: Shambhala.

Wulff, D. M. (1997). *Psychology of religion: Classic and contemporary* (2nd ed.). New York: John Wiley & Sons.

Zinnbauer, B. J., Pargament, K. I., Cole, B., Rye, M. S., Butter, E. M., Belavich, T. G., et al. (1997). Religion and spirituality: Unfuzzying the fuzzy. *Journal for the Scientific Study of Religion, 36*, 549–564.

Part V
Family, Gender, and Sexuality

Family Processes and Identity

Eugenia Scabini and Claudia Manzi

Abstract

Family is a unique relationship context that influences the contents and processes of identity. The identity of individuals emerges, at least in part, from being members of a family. Moreover, the family context influences not only the development of one's personal identity as a family member but also other aspects of personal identity. Family is not a neutral environment for identity development. On the contrary, it deeply affects the individual process, starting during adolescence, that leads to the development of one's identity (Grotevant & Cooper, 1986). In this chapter, first we briefly review the main theories that have tried to outline a definition of family, from which we have derived our own definition. Second, we analyze the concept of family identity. We address the topic of family identity at three different levels: (1) at the group level, which is the specific identity of the family as a group; (2) at the couple subsystem level, since the couple has its own identity and, thus, its own set of potentials to be pursued; (3) at the individual subsystem level, which is the component of individual identity that comes from being part of a specific family group. Finally, we aim to describe family members' identity processes and how they are affected by the family system and in particular by the process of mutual differentiation.

Family bonds are important in all human societies. The relational context of family is uniquely important in the study of identity processes: interdisciplinary perspectives have documented the preeminent role that family plays in the acquisition of social understanding, caregiving, health, and well-being. In this chapter, we attempt to demonstrate that the family is a unique relationship context that influences the contents and processes of identity. The family has been studied from different theoretical perspectives such as sociology, anthropology, and psychology. The goal of our approach is to integrate these three

E. Scabini (✉)
Athenaeum Centre for Family Studies and Research,
Catholic University of Milan, Milano, Italy
e-mail: eugenia.scabini@unicatt.it

S.J. Schwartz et al. (eds.), *Handbook of Identity Theory and Research*,
DOI 10.1007/978-1-4419-7988-9_23, © Springer Science+Business Media, LLC 2011

different points of view into an original perspective called the relational–symbolic model (Cigoli & Scabini, 2006).

The aim of this chapter is threefold: first, we delineate the defining features of the family as a system and as the most important naturally occurring group in society. Thus, we will briefly review the main theories that have tried to delineate the definition of family and from which we have derived our own definition of family. In the second part of the chapter, we analyze the concept of family identity at three different levels: at the level of the family as a group, at the dyadic level of couple relationships, and at the level of individual family members. Finally, we aim to describe family members' identity processes and how they are affected by the family system. We will also focus on the reciprocal influences between the family system and family members' identities.

Defining Features of the Family

Theoretical Roots: Family as a Unit, Group, and System

The family is a highly complex social organism that mirrors and actively interacts with its social and cultural context. It has, therefore, assumed various forms, as documented by both historical research (Laslett & Wall, 1972) and cross-cultural comparisons of families from different cultural backgrounds (Georgas, Berry, van dc Vijvcr, Kagitcibasi, & Poortinga, 2006). As a result of its multifaceted nature, it is difficult to identify what are the "basic characteristics" of the family (i.e., the invariant aspects that operate across different family forms).

During the first few decades of the twentieth century, sociologists first identified the defining features of the family as a unity of interacting personalities (e.g., Burgess, 1926; Cooley, 1909). But it was a psychologist, Kurt Lewin, who, through his new conceptualization of the group, supplied the conceptual categories for making the family a subject of study in the social sciences.

Lewin (1951) defined the group as a "dynamic whole." The term *whole* means that it is different from the sum of its members, or parts: more specifically, the group, and therefore the family, has definite properties of its own, which differ from the properties of its parts or from the sum of its parts. The term *dynamic* underlines the fact that what is most important is not the similarity of group members, but rather their interdependence with and connectedness to one another.

Field theory, as developed by Lewin, makes it possible to view the relational properties of a group in terms of the relationship between the parts and the whole. The family is a well-organized group with a high degree of unity. Its members play different roles within the whole, that is, the family. Hence, social psychology, especially in its focus on group memberships and intergroup relations (see, e.g., Haslam & Ellemers, Chapter 30, this volume; Spears, Chapter 9, this volume), can inform the study of the family. In fact, for many years, the family was presented as the most significant example of a small natural group (Levine & Moreland, 2006).

After Lewin, interest in groups as real social entities waned in favor of studies of ad hoc artificial groups (e.g., Asch, 1956; Moscovici & Zavalloni, 1969; Tajfel, Billig, Bundy, & Flament, 1971). Consequently, family scholars showed increasing dissatisfaction with the concept of the family as a small group, and started to highlight the differences between the family and other types of groups. The greatest differences were attributed to two elements: *function* and *temporal dimension*. Whereas the function of groups, especially work groups, is their efficiency and productivity, the role of the family is in the development of its members, and in the development of the family as an entity unto itself. With regard to the temporal dimension, it has been observed that most other small social groups generally have a limited lifetime, whereas the family—by definition—has a past, a present, and a future (Klein & White, 1996; Olson, Russell, & Sprenkle, 1983).

The second important perspective which has played a crucial role in family literature, together with field theory, is family systems theory (e.g., Bateson, 1973; Bowen, 1966; Haley, 1976; Minuchin, 1974). Family systems theory has been a reference point for both researchers and family therapists, and has been continually updated and revised over the years. In the beginning, this approach also linked basic family characteristics to concepts of unity, interaction, and relationship (e.g., von Bertalanffy, 1968). In fact, this theory has attempted to balance the idea of (a) family as a whole with its own irreducible features, with (b) the fact that, at the same time, the family exists only when its components interact with each other.

Family components have been conceived in terms of subsystems: for example, the married couple is a subsystem, as is the sibling system. Moreover, each individual is seen as a subsystem in her/his own right, because s/he is a family member with a certain degree of autonomy, but still interdependent with other members and with the functioning of the family system. Within the family, the various subsystems interact, thereby influencing and shaping the family system as a whole. We will see in the next section how being part of these systems, and being part of a specific subsystem, inform one's individual identity.

The concept of systems, analogous to Lewin's field concept, highlights the properties of the whole and represents an important epistemological revolution. This concept has been used in a general sense, concentrating on identifying the basic family patterns of interaction (Beavers & Voeller, 1983; Olson et al., 1983) and focusing mainly on what is happening here and now, but failing to consider family history and the influence of the sociocultural context in which the family is embedded. Only since the 1990s has this issue received major attention, for example, in Bronfenbrenner's (1989) Ecological Systems Theory, McGoldrick and colleagues' family life-cycle model (McGoldrick & Carter, 2003), and the relational–symbolic model by Scabini and Cigoli (2000 and Cigoli & Scabini, 2006).

In sum, both field theory and systems theory have contributed to making the family an object of study in psychology and sociology, even if these theories have not been able to identify properly the characteristics that make the family a specific system and a specific group, different from other systems and groups with whom it interacts and with its own features and functions.

The Organizational/Relational Principle

The last few decades have witnessed the emergence of a more complex view of family, and the definition of family has been more clearly delineated. As stated by Klein and White (1996), in order to develop a theory about how families work, one must first define what family is and must identify the distinguishing features of the family. In particular, the relational–symbolic model (Cigoli & Scabini, 2006) delineates the distinctive characteristics both of the family as a system and of its subsystems, taking into account the meanings that different cultures ascribe to these characteristics. To introduce our perspective on family, we will use the concepts of organization and relationship, and then we will provide our specific view of family.

The term "organization," as used by Sroufe and Fleeson (1988), refers to the fact that the family is an organized system with an internal hierarchy that permeates its relationships—and, in particular, its intergenerational relationships—and that interacts purposively with the socio-cultural context. Specifically, the family system organizes *primary relationships*. In the next paragraphs, we explain what we mean by relationship and what we mean by primary.

A family *relationship* binds people together over time, even without their being aware; it refers to what has been established (and continues to be agreed), implicitly or explicitly, with regard to values, meanings, rituals, and the assignment of roles. In this vein, the concept of relationship is on a higher level from that of interaction. As a necessary starting point, we can define *interaction* as the ordinary exchange between family members and examine the communication exchange that occurs between them in the present (here and now) (Haley, 1973; Eisler,

Dare, & Szmukler, 1988). However, family relationships cannot be reduced to a mere sequence of observable, reciprocal measurable interactions. The relational level comprises meanings that transcend those that emerge from interaction (Hinde, 1997; Szapocznik, Rio, Hervis, Mitrani, Kurtines, & Faraci, 1991).

The distinguishing characteristic of family relationships is that they are *primary*. Following Cooley (1909) we define the family as a primary group because it is "fundamental in forming the social nature and ideals of the individual" (p. 25). Specifically, we argue that family relationships can be understood as primary in two ways:

a. Family relationships cut across basic divisions of humankind, such as gender and generational differences, and they give rise to future generations that are essential for the survival of society. Following this reasoning, we focus here on nuclear and extended versions of the heterosexual family with biological children, which are the most widespread family forms across countries. We acknowledge that this definition of the family is controversial at the present time and that different types of close relationships do not fit in this definition, but we wish to make our definition clear so that the reader is better able to follow the ideas we present in this chapter. Alternative family forms are examined in other chapters of this volume (e.g., Grotevant & Von Korff, Chapter 24, this volume; Savin-Williams, Chapter 28, this volume).

b. Family membership imposes strong constraints on individual development. One can escape from a role within the family, but not from family membership. For example, children have no choice about being born into a family and to their parents. Family members may *act* as if they were not bonded to one another, as if they were outside the family group—for example, they can sever their relationships because of conflicts, or decide not to keep in touch with other members of the family—but even when they act as if family relationships are optional, "they do so to the detriment of their own sense of identity" (Walsh, 2003, p. 377).

In sum, building from these concepts of organization and relationship, we define the family as an organization of primary relationships that connects and binds together different genders and different generations to give rise to a new generation. The connection between generations includes both parent–child relationships and relationships between family lineages, both paternal and maternal (i.e., family history). In fact, our perspective outlines the intergenerational side of relationships, which means that we take into consideration the role of different generations in order to understand current patterns of family functioning.

Another particular feature of our perspective is the attention to specific dynamics of exchange between the family and its cultural context. From our perspective, this pattern of exchange is defined not only in terms of person–context reciprocal influence, but also in terms of transmission between generations. We state, in fact, that there is a deep connection between the exchange between generations in a family and the exchange between generations in society. A good example is the transition to adulthood in southern Europe. In this transition the exchange between family generations takes a protective form, reflected in a prolonged cohabitation of young adults with their parents. This pattern compensates for the negative exchange between generations in societies characterized by injustice and unfairness. In fact, over the past decades, the welfare states of these countries have supported the active generation, now adult or elderly, yet they are no longer able to do the same for the younger generation that is about to cross the threshold of adulthood (Cigoli & Scabini, 2006).

The Family Identity

Having clarified the definition of family, we shall now illustrate what we mean by family identity. Our definition of identity here is close to Waterman's (Chapter 16, this volume) concept of "daimon" or true self. Thus, with the term family identity we refer to the family's true nature, to the family's potentialities, the realization of which represents the best fulfillment it is capable of. In other words, when we refer to family identity we talk about the patterns of those dimensions that differentiate the family from other important entities and constitute its unique set of potentials and represent its deep nature.

We will address the topic of family identity at three different levels:

1. at the group level, that is, the specific identity of the family as a group;
2. at the couple subsystem level, in fact, each family subsystem, and especially the couple, has its own identity and, thus, its set of potentials to be pursued;
3. at the individual subsystem level, that is, the component of individual identity that comes from being part of a specific family group.

We will explain each of these concepts related to family identity in the following paragraphs.

Family Identity as a Group: The Symbolic Dimension and the Caring Principle

Earlier in this chapter, we clarified our definition of family, focusing our attention on the structural characteristics of the family. However, to speak of family identity, we have to refer not only to the structural features of its bonds but also to the symbolic qualities of these bonds. By symbolic qualities, we refer to those aspects of the family bond that make this bond properly human and that, if respected within a particular family, make the family function well. In fact, depending on whether the family achieves its symbolic potentials, it may produce positive or negative individual outcomes. For example, if family relationships are warm and supportive, family members are likely to display positive psychosocial and health outcomes (e.g., Feaster & Szapocznik, 2002; Passmore, Fogarty, Bourke, & Baker-Evans, 2005). However, chaotic or distant relationships between or among family members are related to distress, substance use, and poor health (Dishion, Capaldi, & Yoerger, 1999; Stouthamer-Loeber, Wei, Homish, & Loeber, 2002).

Research in family psychology underscores the symbolic qualities of the family bond in terms of intimacy (Cordova, Gee, & Warren, 2005; Feeney, Noller, & Ward, 1998; Moss & Schwebel, 1993), emotional support (Burleson & Mortenson, 2003; Cutrona, 1996; Lawrence et al., 2008), satisfaction (Bradbury, Fincham, & Beach, 2000), and empathy (Losoya & Eisenberg, 2001; Soenens, Duriez, Vansteenkiste, & Goossens, 2007). Other aspects that are receiving increased attention are commitment (Bradbury, Karney, Iafrate, & Donato, 2010; Iafrate, Donato, & Bertoni, 2010), family obligation (Freeberg & Stein, 1996; Fuligni, Alvarez, Bachman, & Ruble, 2005; Stein, 2009), filial responsibility (Dellmann-Jenkins & Brittain, 2003; Kuperminc, Jurkovic, & Casey, 2009), and family values (Barni, 2009; Grusec, Goodnow, & Kuczynski, 2000).

From our perspective, these constructs seem to reflect two different, but not opposing, dimensions of the family bond: the emotional–affective dimension and ethical–legal dimension.[1] When one or both of these dimensions of the family bond is absent, it produces high levels of distress in family members. Hence, the quality of family relationships is determined by the degree of co-presence of those affective and ethical characteristics that converge in what we call the principle of caring: caring for the other person and for the relationship. The emotional–affective side of the bond is rooted in the presence of trust–hope, and the ethical side in justice–loyalty (Jurkovic, 1998).

Erikson (1968, 1982) viewed trust and hope as properties of the developing person that are supported by the family in its fostering of personal growth (Meltzer & Harris, 1983). Within the study of close relationships, trust has become increasingly important in recent decades (Borawski, Ievers-Landis, Lovegreen, & Trapl, 2003; Crocetti, Rubini, & Meuss, 2008; Kerr, Stattin, & Trost, 1999).

The importance of justice and loyalty in family relationships is a key concept in the intergenerational and contextual approach introduced by Boszormenyi-Nagy and Spark (1973). These authors see family as a system of credit–debit and obligations that cross generations like invisible threads making up a family's connective tissue.

In the relational–symbolic model, *both* the affective *and* ethical dimensions of family relationships are considered important; the family bond rests on a foundation of trust and hope, and develops if it respects justice, loyalty, and obligation. Every culture expresses the affective and ethical aspects of the family bond in its own way and may attribute greater value to one rather than another. In many Western cultures, we have shifted from a strong focus on ethical–legal aspects to a point where affective–emotional aspects are considered decidedly more important, and so we find this characteristic in all family relationships (Levine, Sato, Hashimoto, & Verma, 1995). However, both the affective and ethical components are important (e.g., Finley & Schwartz, 2006). In brief, the family fulfills its identity if it can keep its affective and ethical bonds (both of which are essential parts of the caring principle) alive: that is, if it respects its symbolic qualities.

It is worth noting that it may be especially valuable to study family identity at the group level during transition periods (e.g., transition to parenthood, transition to adulthood), which test and reveal the strengths and weaknesses of family bonds. As stated by Cowan and Cowan (2003), the study of transitional periods provides important opportunities for family researchers and clinicians because, on the one hand, they function as "natural experiments" to test hypotheses on family relationships, and, on the other hand, they can be "opportune moments to consider preventive interventions that could be helpful in moving families closer to adaptive positions" (p. 430). The transition periods within a family are also crucial moments for identity redefinition.

Family Subsystem Identity: The Couple Identity

We have focused until now on the identity of the family as a group. Now we consider a specific subsystem identity, namely couple identity. From the point of view of family systems theory, the couple is a subsystem and so, when a couple is formed, properties of the new couple bond change and are different from the sum of the individual partners' identities. This has been highlighted in Acitelli's and colleagues' work, where it is clear that the marital bond produces a new form of identity (Acitelli, Rogers, & Knee, 1999). From this perspective, couple identity involves the extent to which the relationship itself is seen as an entity (rather than seeing only two individuals). Hence, partners in close relationships incorporate into their self-concepts the connection between the self and the other, i.e., their relationship (Badr, Acitelli, & Carmack Taylor, 2007). Similar to what happens in group identification (Brewer, 2007), individuals engaged in an important (intimate) relationship develop a sense of "we-ness." Note that the couple identity, as an aspect of individual identity, changes with major life transitions and assumes different features at different stages of life (e.g., marriage, childbirth, etc.).

Another consequence of being involved in a couple relationship is that the individual tends to include the other's attributes and the relationship in their mental representation of self. Agnew, Arriaga, and Wilson (2008) maintain that, as one's commitment to a relationship develops, cognitive structures representing the self become restructured. People start to perceive themselves less as individuals and more as part of a pluralistic self-and-partner collective, and they develop a couple-oriented identity. According to the self-expansion model (Aron & Aron, 1986; Aron, Aron, Tudor, & Nelson, 1991), in close relationships a process of inclusion of the other within the self occurs; the self expands to include the other's characteristics such as resources, perspectives, and identities (Aron et al., 2004; cf. Chen, Boucher, & Kraus, Chapter 7, this volume). This mental representation of the self-in-relationship is referred to as *cognitive interdependence*.

However, our perspective adds another aspect to the couple's identity. The couple's new identity is not only a result of the encounter between two personalities, but also an encounter between two family histories. From this point of view, in order to create a true identity, the couple must be able to differentiate itself from the families of origin; to do so, it must have a certain autonomy in exercising its function and a certain amount of decisional power (e.g., Bowen, 1978; Cowan & Cowan, 2005).

Autonomy and decisional power vary greatly among cultures both within the marital relationship and in the relationship of the couple with the families of origin. For example, in many Islamic cultures, marriages are arranged rather than chosen, and the power balance between the two spouses seems unequal, with the woman being subordinated to her husband (Jen'nan Ghazal, 2004; Zaidi & Shuraydi, 2002). Moreover in these cultures, and in Hindu and Confucian cultures, the marital couple has little autonomy and little decisional power vis-à-vis the families of origin—and this was once true of Western cultures as well. In most contemporary Western cultures, on the other hand, power within a couple is equal (the two spouses have equal rights and obligations), and the couple is seen as autonomous and separate from the families of origin (Georgas et al., 2006). Nonetheless, the family of origin does exercise its influence. In fact, several theoretical approaches have provided insight into how some family-of-origin characteristics may shape the way partners enter their adult romantic relationships, and several models have provided evidence of the effects of family of origin on the offspring's couple relationship (Bryant & Conger, 2002; Busby, Gardner, & Taniguchi, 2005; Mallinckrodt, 2000; Sabatelli & Bartle-Haring, 2003).

Relationships with the family of origin become even more significant when the marital couple becomes a parental couple. In particular, as a parental couple it becomes "a linear bridge" between family generations (Hill, 1970), and carries out the function of mediator between generations (Cigoli & Scabini, 2006). In particular, a couple is mediator between its children and its parents (Brambilla, Manzi, & Regalia, 2010). Such mediation is influenced by the specific contexts in which the couple lives and works. In sum, a couple's identity is fulfilled when the couple has succeeded in building a sense of weness in connection with previous family history, through a process of personal re-elaboration of the positive and negative carried over from the family of origin.

Individual Identity Within the Family

Vignoles, Regalia, Manzi, Golledge, and Scabini (2006) define identity as the subjective concept of oneself as a person. Starting from this definition, we can state that individual identity within the family refers to aspects of self related to (1) belonging to a specific family and (2) the specific identity role played within different family subsystems, e.g., couple relationship, sibling relationship, and parent–child relationship.

With respect to the first concept, family identity at the individual level may be seen as a particular social identity and implies the perception of one's family as an ingroup (Banker & Gaertner, 1998) and the sense of identification with this group (Soliz & Harwood, 2006). The family, in fact, is inherently a shared ingroup for all members and can be considered as "generally the most salient ingroup category in the lives of individuals" (Lay et al., 1998, p. 434). We have to remember that being part of one's family group is very different than many other group memberships. As we have already stated, family membership cannot be psychologically cancelled. This means that individual identity always involves being part of one's family, even if individuals choose to disassociate from it.

The concept of family social identity has been used recently to study the intergroup relationship within the family context. In fact, even if family members share a common family identity, they also possess identities signifying intergroup boundaries within the family (Harwood, Soliz, & Lin, 2006). Such intergroup boundaries may be superseded when family identity (i.e., a common ingroup) is salient (Gaertner & Dovidio, 2000). Soliz and Harwood (2006), for example, have studied the intergroup relationship between different generations (youth and elder) within the family context.

Regarding the role identities that individuals play within family subsystems, we should also highlight that family identity is an intricate mix of many interdependent relationships. So, being a sister, a wife, a mother, and a daughter are not role identities independent of each other. For example, one's identity as a parent may be linked both to one's identity as a partner and also to one's identity as a son/daughter. Thus, parents are also "offspring" of the preceding generation (the grandparents), and their identities are also affected by their own parental and filial relationships, within an intergenerational chain (Cigoli & Scabini, 2006).

Among the different types of relations and roles that a person may serve within his/her life, the most important is the filial relation. Everyone is a son or a daughter, even if they may not become a partner or a parent. The term "filial" involves both the relationship between offspring and each individual parent (mother and father), and the relationship between maternal and paternal lineages. We can assert, therefore, that the "psychic field" of the filial relation is much wider than the dual space created by the relationship between parents and offspring: it is at least a trigenerational system (McGoldrick & Carter, 2003) or, more simply, a multigenerational system (Cigoli & Scabini, 2006). In fact, the family system shows a sort of intergenerational continuity; functional and dysfunctional patterns tend to be repeated across generations, even if not in a deterministic way.

According to Cowan and Cowan (2005), four types of theoretical explanations of intergenerational continuity dominate the current scene. First, some of the repetition of relationship patterns across generations seems to be affected by genetic and other biological mechanisms (Caspi et al., 2002; Plomin, 1994). Second, psychoanalytic formulations propose that both the child's identification with the same-sex parent and the internalization of that parent's superego (i.e., the ethical principles of the parent) provide guidelines for what constitutes appropriate behavior in family relationships (Fraiberg, 1975; Freud, 1922). Third, attachment theory assumes that adults have developed "working models" of parent–child relationships based on experiences with key attachment figures in their families of origin (Bowlby, 1988; Van Ijzendoorn, 1992). These working models lead to the repetition of secure or insecure patterns of attachment in the next generation. Fourth, social learning theorists (Bandura, 1977; Patterson, 1975) offer an explanation of intergenerational transmission on the basis that children learn patterns of family behavior by observing adults interacting with others and noting which behaviors are reinforced or punished, that they tend to repeat when they form their own families.

Each of these explanations of intergenerational transmission assumes that the parent–child relationship influences individual identity because it determines the individual's access to family heritage (at different levels: genes, unconscious contents, relational schemas, behaviors).

Our specific perspective is that individuals develop a filial identity through a personal internalization of the family heritage, which leads the individual to gain a special and unique place in the family history. If the child does not achieve a personal re-elaboration of the family values and heritage, this may end in two possible negative outcomes. On the one hand, he/she may interrupt the intergenerational transmission by refusing the family heritage a priori; on the other hand, he/she may simply incorporate the parental standards into his/her self-system without any personal re-elaboration.

Zentner and Renaud (2007) outlined that the task of building identity within the family involves three main component processes: family transposition (what the parents want to transmit to their children), filial accurate perception (the extent to which the child receives the message that the parent intended to transmit), and individual re-elaboration (the extent to which the child reconsiders the patterns from her/his family of origin). In the next section, we will see that, from our perspective, the re-elaboration process is not reducible to cognitive elaboration, but deals with the affective and ethic symbolic dimensions of the family.

Building Identity in the Family Context: Individuation and Differentiation Processes

We have now discussed the defining features of the family and the meaning of family identity at the family group level and at the family subsystem level (both dyads and individuals). We have seen that both dyad and individual identities emerge, at least in part, from being members of a family and that this implies a process of internalization of family heritage. But not only is the family identity developed within the family context; we could say, in fact, that the whole subsystem identity, for example the couple identity, is developed mainly within the family context. In other words, the family context influences the development of not just one's personal identity as a family member, but also other aspects of personal identity, such as, for example, one's professional identity. Family is not a neutral environment in which identity development takes place. In contrast, it deeply affects the individual process, starting during adolescence, that leads to the development of one's identity (Grotevant & Cooper, 1986).

Scholars interested in the topic of how identity develops within the family context have focused their attention mainly on the individuation process—whereby young people begin to explore (or discover) who they might become. The classic theories of Blos (1967) and Kroger (1985), rooted in psychoanalytic theory, define the individuation process in terms of separation—stating that adolescents must separate from their parents in order to develop an identity. These theories assume that the adolescent must adopt a "rebellious" position in order to individuate. Other authors stress instead the stable connection between adolescents and their parents as providing the optimal context for individuation (see Grotevant & Cooper, 1986; Youniss & Smollar, 1985). Recently, Meeus, Iedema, Maassen, and Engels (2005) empirically supported this second perspective. In this vein, the individuation process has been redefined as a task of gaining autonomy while maintaining relatedness to parents (Kruse & Walper, 2008).

In the family literature, the process of individuation has been viewed from a systemic perspective. According to this approach, we should distinguish the individuation process from the differentiation process. The former is located at the individual level, whereas the latter is located at the family system level and regulates distance between family members (i.e., the degree the family system allows the individuation process of its members) (Sabatelli & Mazor, 1985).

Many authors agree that, to understand identity development within the family context, the individuation process and the differentiation process have to be considered together, as a systemic co-construction process (e.g., Buhl, 2008). In order to understand how individual family members define their identities within the family context, we must keep in mind the interdependence that characterizes the family. Thus, not only individuals, but the whole family system is involved in the process of identity subsystem definition. This is why, in the symbolic–relational perspective, we more appropriately use the term mutual differentiation. In the next section, we will analyze what we mean by this process.

The Mutual Differentiation Process

Mutual differentiation is the dialectic process of individuals and families freeing themselves from each other, *but* still remaining emotionally related. It is a relational process that deals with the ethical and affective symbolic properties of the family system. We use the term *mutual* because, as family subsystems and the overall family system grow together, the process of the family subsystem's identity development involves both the family system and the family subsystems, and their relations. Thus, it is not just the individual or the family dyads that have to individuate from the family, but the family must also permit and encourage this process (see also Stierlin, 1974). We also use the term *differentiation* because, for the family and its subsystems to function adequately, they should satisfy the basic human needs of relatedness, autonomy, and distinctiveness. These needs have been conceptualized in many theories to be related to the definition of adult identity.

The *relatedness need* refers to the "desire to feel connected with others" (Ryan & Deci, 2000) and the need to maintain or enhance feelings of closeness to, or acceptance by, other people, whether in dyadic relationships or within ingroups (Baumeister & Leary, 1995). This need has been identified as a fundamental human motivation (e.g., Deci & Ryan, 2000). The relatedness motive has been included in several theories of identity motivation (Brewer, 1991; Leary & Baumeister, 2000; Snyder & Fromkin, 1980). Bauer and McAdams (2000) propose that the need for relatedness, together with autonomy and competence needs, point individuals toward an well-defined identity structure.

Within the family, the need to belong is satisfied by the presence of strong family bonds, which include feelings and behaviors such as emotional closeness, support, nurturance, and so on. This is the dimension that we call *family cohesion*, the sense of closeness, intimacy and belonging shared within the family, which represents the expression of the emotional–affective pole of family relations. Low levels of family cohesion are labeled *family disengagement* (e.g., Anderson & Sabatelli, 1992; Olson, 1982).

The autonomy need has been defined within self-determination theory by its primary etymological meaning of self-governance, or rule by the self (e.g., Ryan & Deci, 2006). Autonomy is considered a basic psychological need (along with relatedness and competence), and its effects on individual functioning have been shown to be pervasive (Ryan & Deci, 2006). In relation to identity development, it has been shown that those who are autonomy-oriented organize their behavioral regulation by taking elective interest in possibilities and choices (see Soenens & Vansteenkiste, Chapter 17, this volume).

Finally, the *distinctiveness need* pushes toward the establishment and maintenance of a sense of differentiation from others (Vignoles, Chryssochoou, & Breakwell, 2000) and of uniqueness (Snyder & Fromkin, 1980). Vignoles et al. (2000) define this need as the *motive* that pushes toward the establishment and maintenance of a sense of differentiation from others. The distinctiveness dimension deals with the basic human need of developing a unique identity. Culture may determine (in part) the sources from which the distinctiveness need may be fulfilled, but some form of distinctiveness

is logically necessary in order to develop a meaningful sense of self (Codol, 1981), and hence the motive is theorized to be universal (see Vignoles, Chapter 18, this volume).

In the family literature, qualities of the family system that satisfy or threaten both the basic human needs of distinctiveness and autonomy fall under a common umbrella (multidimensional) construct, called *family enmeshment.* Family enmeshment is defined as a particular *characteristic* of the family bond, reflecting the extent to which family members' interpersonal boundaries are violated or respected in the family context. In particular, Scabini (1985) has emphasized the importance of considering interpersonal boundaries within the family. This kind of boundary reflects the amount of respect for the psychological individuality of each person in the family: when an individual's boundaries are not respected, his or her ability to feel, develop opinions, and make decisions within the family is negatively impacted. Family enmeshment is related to the ethical pole of family relations because it is strongly linked with the absence of a sense of justice, recognition, and respect for individual identity (see Barber et al., 2008).

Figure 23.1 shows the relational–symbolic perspective on the mutual differentiation process.

Cohesion and Enmeshment in the Family Literature

There is substantial disagreement among family scholars about the nature of the relationship between the two domains of family cohesion and family enmeshment. Or, in other words, whether these constructs form a single dimension (where family enmeshment represents extremely high levels of cohesion) or two separate ones (low versus high family cohesion, and low versus high family enmeshment).

In Olson's circumplex model, family cohesion and family enmeshment are seen as aspects of a single dimension, assuming that a high level of cohesion constitutes a lack of family differentiation or, in other words, family enmeshment

Fig. 23.1 Mutual
differentiation process:
identity is the outcome of the
relationship between
individual and family system
on the dimensions of
belonging and distinctiveness

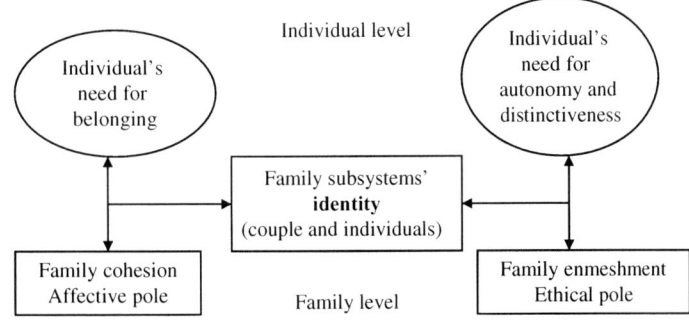

(e.g., Minuchin, 1974; Olson, 1982). These theorists propose a curvilinear relationship between
cohesion and optimal family functioning: intermediate levels of cohesion are considered most
adaptive, whereas both high and low extremes
(often referred to as enmeshment and disengagement, respectively) are thought to be maladaptive. On the other hand, many scholars have
argued that the one-dimensional model leads to
an unclear and partial view of individual and
family processes, and that the optimal situation is where a combination of *both* closeness
and respect for autonomy and distinctiveness is
achieved for individuals and for families (e.g.,
Green & Werner, 1996).

Thus, the one-dimensional model, with family
enmeshment at one end and family cohesion
at the other, has been criticized in the family
literature. Starting from previous theories of the
family system and the concepts of boundaries
and enmeshment, Green and Werner (1996)
criticized the assumption that enmeshment
(lack of self–other differentiation) and disengagement (which is supposed to involve too
much self–other differentiation, that is, too
much individuation) represent opposing ends of
the same continuum. Their theoretical model
views the cohesion–enmeshment domain of
family functioning as entailing not a single
dimension but rather two independent orthogonal
dimensions: intrusiveness (blurring or violation of boundaries) and closeness–caregiving
(relationship-enhancing behaviors such as
warmth and nurturance). Thus, from this perspective, higher levels of relatedness and low
levels of intrusiveness are adaptive in the family

context—but a family can be highly cohesive
and can promote individual autonomy.

Empirical studies have tended to refute the
one-dimensional model (e.g., Barber & Buehler,
1996; Manzi, Vignoles, Regalia, & Scabini,
2006). Hence, authors have begun to disentangle concepts of cohesion (at individual or family
level) and enmeshment (at individual or family
level), both theoretically and empirically (e.g.,
Gavazzi, 1993; Green & Werner, 1996). Recently,
some authors have stated that a better compre-
hension of the relationship between these two
dimensions of the family functioning may be
gained through a better understanding of the
multidimensionality of the construct of family
enmeshment. In fact, this construct is an umbrella
term for a variety of parenting practices and family processes. Some of these aspects may be in
opposition with family cohesion, others may not
be. In the following section we address this issue
and present two studies in which different dimensions of family enmeshment have been analyzed empirically. One of these studies has also
addressed how culture impacts these different
dimensions.

In fact, there is a substantial agreement in the
literature that culture affects the meaning and
the relationship between these poles (Kagitçibasi,
2005; Trommsdorff, 2005). As we have seen,
however, there is still confusion about the definition of these dimensions and about the way
to interpret the impact of culture on them. What
is the human experience of relatedness? What
is the human experience of differentiating? Are
these universal human experiences, or not? The
answers to these questions are very important

in understanding the process of building identity within the family.

The Multidimensional Model of Family Enmeshment

Few studies have tested empirically the multidimensionality of family enmeshment. Soenens, Vansteenkiste, et al. (2007) provide evidence for the distinction between the dimension of promotion of volitional functioning and promotion of independence in a sample of Belgian students. *Promotion of volitional functioning* within the family context (Grolnick, Ryan, & Deci, 1991) as opposed to conditional regard (e.g., Assor, Roth, & Deci, 2004) refers to the degree to which parents allow their children to make *autonomous decisions* about their lives or, the opposite, the degree to which they are manipulative and intrusive. This dimension of parenting is related to the individual need for autonomy (as theorized in self-determination theory: see Soenens & Vansteenkiste, Chapter 17, this volume), and interferes with the individual's decision-making process. An example item to measure this construct is: "My mother/father allows me to decide things for myself" or "My mother/father insists upon doing things her/his way (reverse coded)."

The construct of *promotion of independence* in the family context, as conceptualized by Silk, Morris, Kanaya, and Steinberg (2003), involves the degree to which families promote distinctiveness, or, the opposite, intrude on the cognitive sphere of its members by imposing contents, values, and worldviews. The promotion of the *independence* dimension may be related to the individual's cognitive boundaries, that is, whether and how others interfere with individual self-representation. An example item to measure this construct is: "My mother/father emphasizes that it is important to get my ideas across even if others don't like it" or "My mother/father pushes me to think independently." In their study, Soenens and colleagues found that perceived promotion of volitional functioning uniquely predicted adjustment, whereas perceived promotion of independence did not. Volitional

functioning therefore represents autonomous and self-directed thinking, whereas independence does not necessarily do the same.

Starting from these findings, Manzi, Regalia, Soenens, Fincham, and Scabini (2011) conducted a cross-cultural study to disentangle four different dimensions of family enmeshment taken from different authors in the literature: promotion of volitional functioning, promotion of independence, family separation, and psychological control. They also explored how culture affected the relationship between these dimensions, and between these dimensions and individual well-being.

The first two dimensions—promotion of independence and promotion of volitional functioning—were the same as in Soenens and colleagues' (2007) study. The construct of *family separation* was taken from Bloom (1985) and measures the degree to which the family promotes physical separation between its members: in other words, the degree to which the family allows individual members to pass time on their own and to organize their time independently. The *separation* dimension deals with individual *physical and temporal boundaries*, that is, if and how others interfere in the individual organization of personal time and space. Its opposite is proximity. An example item to measure this construct is: "Family members find it hard to get away form each other."

Finally, *family psychological control* (Barber, 1996) deals with the family's respect for the worth of each individual family member. In this case, the sense of identity is deeply affected, and the individual develops a negative sense of self.[2] Individuals with a negative sense of the self are not able to perceive their own self as positive and distinct from important others, and they are also characterized by high levels of emotional interactivity with important others (Green & Werner, 1996). An example item to measure this construct is: "My mother/father brings up past mistakes when she/he criticizes me."[3]

The study was conducted in four different countries: Italy and Belgium, two Western European countries with differing family cultures; as well as the United States and China.

Participants were first-year university students. Results suggest an interesting pattern. In all four countries, participants' perceptions clearly differentiated among the four constructs of promotion of volitional functioning, promotion of independence, separation and psychological control within the family context, providing empirical evidence for the theoretical disentanglement of these dimensions of family differentiation. As expected, results also indicated that culture moderated the relationships among these dimensions. To better understand these patterns, Manzi and colleagues also explored how these four dimensions were related to depression (see Fig. 23.2).

Manzi et al. found that parental psychological control was the most important and positive predictor of individual depression in all four countries. In fact, this dimension was the only direct predictor of depression in all four countries. Moreover, in all four countries, there was a significant indirect effect of promotion of volitional functioning, through family psychological control, on depression. For Belgian, American, and Italian participants, promotion of independence also had a significant indirect effect on depression, again mediated by psychological control, but this was not the case in the Chinese sample. Finally, only for the Belgian and North American samples did family separation have a negative indirect impact on depression. For Chinese participants, family separation was unrelated to depression, whereas for Italians, family separation was indirectly but positively related to depression.

In summary, this study suggests that we can meaningfully disentangle four dimensions of family enmeshment: family separation, family promotion of independence, family promotion of volitional functioning, and family psychological control. Moreover, culture may impact the ways in which these dimensions are interpreted and interrelated across cultures. In particular, family psychological control (negatively) and family promotion of volitional functioning (positively) seem to be "universally" valued and equally important for the individual and for his/her well-being. Family promotion of independence seems to be important for individuals in Western countries but not in the Chinese context. This result is consistent with the assumption that Eastern societies promote a less independent self-construal (Markus & Kitayama, 1991). Finally, family separation seems to be valued as an indicator of family distinctiveness only in Belgium and the United States—the two most individualistic countries in the sample. For Chinese and Italians, however, separation from the family may not be perceived as a positive indicator of family functioning. On the contrary, especially

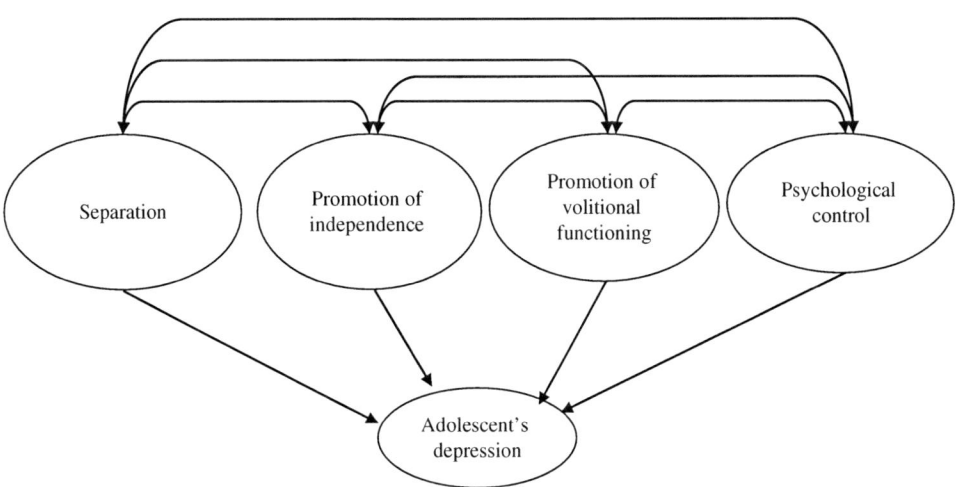

Fig. 23.2 Model tested by Manzi et al. (2011)

in Italian culture, it could be perceived as problematic.

Building Couple Identity Within the Family Context

Before concluding this final section on how family may affect identity development, we would like to direct attention to an insufficiently studied field of research: how the couple subsystem defines its identity in the context of the partners' families of origin. Earlier, we noted that the new couple has to develop its own identity within the family context. The mutual differentiation process is typically linked to the individual identity development during adolescence, but it could also easily be applied to the couple subsystem. Cigoli and Scabini (2006) argue that couple functioning, similar to individual functioning, involves an individuation process. As the adolescent develops his/her identity within the family, building clear individual boundaries, the same happens for the couple, which must differentiate itself from each partner's family of origin and must build clear and well-defined identity boundaries.

Until now, little effort has been made to explore empirically the process of couple identity formation and how the family of origin may affect this process. An exception is a recent study by Manzi, Parise, Iafrate, and Vignoles (2010). In this study, it was proposed that family enmeshment may affect the process of partners including each other into their sense of self. The longitudinal study, conducted in a sample of more that 350 couples, showed interesting results. First, for both women and men, higher levels of enmeshment with the family of origin were predictive of lower levels of "inclusion of the partner into the self" (after Aron & Aron, 1986). That is, coming from a family with high levels of enmeshment may pose a barrier to a couple's functioning and, in particular, to the development of a couple identity. A second interesting result was that each partner's level of family enmeshment was predictive of both partners' couple satisfaction. In other words, high levels of family enmeshment

for the male partner also predicted lower couple satisfaction in the female partner, and vice versa.

Results of this study clearly show that, similar to what occurs for individual identity, family of origin may affect the couple's identity development. Moreover, it outlines not only the importance of intergenerational relations, but also the strong interdependence between the two lineages when a new couple is created (Sabatelli & Bartle-Haring, 2003).

Conclusions

In this chapter, we have addressed the topic of identity and family processes. Our starting point was to show that family is a particular group and that it has a specific identity as a group. We referred to the relational–symbolic model developed by Cigoli and Scabini (2006) to delineate the defining features of the family and the concept of family identity at the individual, couple, and group levels. We have also stressed how the identities of family subsystems (individuals and dyads) are built within the family through the mutual differentiation process. In this process, both the family system and the family subsystem interconnect to satisfy the basic human needs to belong, to be autonomous, and to be distinct, which are all essential for identity development (cf. Adams & Marshall, 1996).

At the intervention level, we could say that what we have so far seen theoretically is also relevant for systemic–relational clinical practice. The goal of this kind of intervention is to help the family and family subsystems build clear and defined boundaries in order to provide a clear sense of identity among family members (Bowen, 1978). Such intervention programs are usually preventive in nature and are especially useful in dealing with family transitions (see Cowan & Cowan, 2005). Most of these training programs have been developed to help families increase their relational skills linked to couple and parent–child bonds such as conflict management, communication, and intimacy (see Bodenmann & Shantinah, 2004; Olson & Olson, 1999; Patterson & Forgatch, 1987;

Webster-Stratton, 1981). These programs may indirectly promote a better-defined sense of identity within the family. Only a few efforts, however, have been devoted to the redefinition of identity after the most important family life-cycle transitions. A good example in such an intervention is the "Becoming a Family Project" developed by Cowan and Cowan (1992), which represents the first training program for the transition to parenthood. The title itself directs particular attention to the link between family processes and the psychological birth of a new family member. In this project, aspects of identity are treated as emerging issues in order to understand and manage the transition to parenthood (see also Manzi, Vignoles, & Regalia, 2010, regarding the study of identity change after family transition).

In conclusion, we would like to stress once more the importance of the ways in which culture affects the relationship between family dynamics and identity development. We believe that, within the family context, it is meaningful to search for universal characteristics but that culture affects how these are displayed and how they develop. This is particularly important for those who want to research or promote family processes and identity development in a multicultural society and for those who are looking for tools to guide and intervene.

showed that people with negative self-views embrace negative rather than positive partners, this for the desire of self-stability. However, the theory leaves unclear why a person may develop a negative rather than a positive self-view in the first place. Here, we suggest that a negative sense of self can result from negative family patterns and, in particular, an intrusive and controlling relationship with parents.

3. In the family psychology literature, there is an ongoing debate on how the construct of psychological control is related to the construct of promotion of volitional functioning. Recently, Soenens, Vansteenkiste, and Sierens (2009) proposed to consider promotion of volitional functioning as the opposite end of psychological control—in other words, they stated that parents promoting autonomy necessarily do not enact controlling and manipulative behaviors. Here, following Barber's conceptualization of the psychological control construct (Barber, 2002; Barber et al., 2008), we consider promotion of volitional functioning and psychological control as two different, even if related constructs. They are related because both pertain to the dimension of family differentiation. They are different because psychological control affects the child's sense of self, whereas promotion of volitional functioning is related to the child's capacity to make autonomous choices.

Notes

1. Other scholars have proposed similar, but not identical, categorizations of family-relational components (see, for example, Finley & Schwartz, 2004).
2. Note that within social psychology literature on identity, self-verification theory (Swann, Chang-Schneider, & Angulo, 2007) has focused its attention on the positive and negative sense of self. Specifically in the famous Mr. Nice and Mr. Nasty study, positive and negative sense of self were studied in relation to close relationships. The study

References

Acitelli, L. K., Rogers, S., & Knee, C. R. (1999). The role of the identity in the link between relationship thinking and relationship satisfaction. *Journal of Social and Personal Relationships*, *16*, 591–619.

Adams, G. R., & Marshall, S. K. (1996). A developmental social psychology of identity: Understanding the person in context. *Journal of Adolescence*, *19*, 1–14.

Agnew, C. R. Arriaga, X. B., & Wilson, J. E. (2008). Committed to what? Using the bases of relational commitment model to understand continuity and change in social relationships. In J. P. Forgas & J. Fitness (Eds.), *Social relationships: Cognitive, affective, and motivational processes. The Sydney symposium on social psychology*. New York: Psychology Press.

Anderson, S., & Sabatelli, R. (1992). The differentiation in the family system scale (DIFS). *The American Journal of Family Therapy, 1*, 77–88.

Aron, A., & Aron, E N. (1986). *Love and the expansion of self: Understanding attraction and satisfaction.* New York: Hemisphere.

Aron, A., Aron, E. N., Tudor, M., & Nelson, G. (1991). Close relationships as including other in the self. *Journal of Personality and Social Psychology, 60,* 241–253.

Aron, A., McLaughlin-Volpe, T., Mashek, D., Lewandowski, G., Wright, S. C., & Aron, E. N. (2004). Including close others in the self. *European Review of Social Psychology, 15,* 101–132.

Asch, S. E. (1956). Studies of independence and conformity: A minority of one against a unanimous majority. *Psychological Monographs, 70,* Whole no. 416.

Assor, A., Roth, G., & Deci, E. L. (2004). The emotional costs of parents' conditional regard: A self-determination theory analysis. *Journal of Personality, 72,* 47–89.

Badr, H., Acitelli, L. K., & Carmack Taylor, C. L. (2007). Does couple identity mediate the stress experienced by caregiving spouses? *Psychology and Health, 22,* 211–229.

Bandura, A. (1977). *Social learning theory.* New York: General Learning Press.

Banker, B. S., & Gaertner, S. L. (1998). Achieving stepfamily harmony: An intergroup-relations approach. *Journal of Family Psychology, 12,* 310–325.

Barber, B. K. (1996). Parental psychological control: Revisiting a neglected construct. *Child Development, 67,* 3296–3319.

Barber, B. K. (Ed.). (2002). *Intrusive parenting: How psychological control affects children and adolescents.* Washington, DC: American Psychological Association.

Barber, B. K., & Buehler, C. (1996). Family cohesion and enmeshment: Different constructs, different effects. *Journal of Marriage and the Family, 58,* 433–441.

Barber, B. K., Olsen, J. A., Xia, M., McNeely, C. M., Bose, K., Kritiyapichatkul, C., Krauskopf, D. R., & Ward, C. L. (2008, May). *Examining the essence of parental psychological control: Exploring parental disrespect.* Paper presented at the European Association for Research on Adolescence, Torino, Italy.

Barni, D. (2009). *Trasmettere valori. Tre generazioni familiari a confronto* [Transmitting values: Comparing three generations of family members]. Milan: Unicopli.

Bateson, G. (1973). *Steps to an ecology of mind.* London: Paladin.

Bauer, J. J., & McAdams, D. P. (2000). Competence, relatedness, and autonomy in life stories. *Psychological Inquiry, 11,* 276–279.

Baumeister, R. F., & Leary, M. R. (1995). The need to belong: Desire for interpersonal attachments as a fundamental human motivation. *Psychological Bulletin, 117,* 497–529.

Beavers, W. R., & Voeller, M. N. (1983). Family models: Comparing and contrasting the Olson circumplex model with the Beavers systems model. *Family Process, 22,* 85–97.

Bloom, B. L. (1985). A factor analysis of self-report measures of family functioning. *Family Process, 24,* 225–239.

Blos, P. (1967). The second individuation process of adolescence. *Psychoanalytic Study of the Child, 22,* 162–186.

Bodenmann, G., & Shantinah, S. D. (2004). The couples coping enhancement training (CCET): A new approach to prevention of marital distress based upon stress and coping. *Family Relations, 53,* 477–484.

Borawski, E. A., Ievers-Landis, C. E., Lovegreen, L. D., & Trapl, B. A. (2003). Parental monitoring, negotiated unsupervised time, and parental trust: The role of perceived parenting practices in adolescent health risk behaviors. *Journal of Adolescent Health, 33,* 60–70.

Boszormenyi-Nagy, I., & Spark, G. (1973). *Invisible loyalties: Reciprocity in intergenerational family therapy.* New York: Harper & Row.

Bowen, M. (1966). The use of family theory in clinical practice. *Comprehensive Psychiatry, 7,* 345–374.

Bowen, M. (1978). *Family treatment in clinical practice.* New York: Jason Aronson.

Bowlby J. (1988). *A secure base: Clinical applications of attachment theory.* London: Routledge.

Bradbury, T. N., Fincham, F. D., & Beach, S. R. (2000). Research on the nature and determinants of marital satisfaction: A decade in review. *Journal of Marriage and the Family, 62,* 964–980.

Bradbury, T. N., Karney, B., Iafrate, R., e Donato, S. (2010). Building better intimate relationships: Advances in linking basic research and preventive interventions. In V. Cigoli e M. L. Gennari (a cura di), *Close relationships and community psychology: An international perspective* (pp. 224–240). Milano: Franco Angeli.

Brambilla, M., Manzi, C., & Regalia, C. (2010). Near is my shirt, but nearer is my skin: Exploring intergenerational relations, identity processes, and well-being of second-generation adolescents in Italy. Manuscript submitted for publication.

Brewer, M. B. (1991). The social self: On being the same and different at the same time. *Personality and Social Psychology Bulletin, 17,* 475–482.

Brewer, M. B. (2007). The importance of being we: Human nature and intergroup relations. *American Psychologist, 62,* 728–738.

Bronfenbrenner, U. (1989). Ecological systems theory. In R. Vasta (Ed.), *Annals of child development* (Vol. 6, pp. 187–249). Greenwich, CT: JAI Press.

Bryant, C. M. & Conger, R. D. (2002). An intergenerational model of romantic relationship development. In A. L. Vangelisti, H. T. Reiss, & M. A. Fitzpatrick (Eds.), *Stability and change in relationships.* New York: Cambridge University Press.

Buhl, H. M. (2008). Development of a model describing individuated adult child-parent relationships.

International Journal of Behavioral Development, 32, 381–389.

Burgess, E. (1926). The Family as a unit of interacting personalities. *Family, 7,* 3–9.

Burleson, B., & Mortenson, S. (2003). Explaining cultural differences in evaluations of emotional support behaviors: Exploring the mediating influences of value systems and interaction goals. *Communication Research, 30,* 113–146.

Busby, D. M., Gardner, B. C., & Taniguchi, N. (2005). The family of origin parachute model: Landing safely in adult romantic relationships. *Family Relations, 54,* 254–264.

Caspi, A., McClay, J., Moffitt, T., Mill, J., Martin, J., Craig, I. W., et al. (2002). Role of genotype in the cycle of violence in maltreated children. *Science, 297,* 851–854.

Cigoli, V., & Scabini, E. (2006). *Family identity: Ties, symbols, and transitions.* Mahwah, NJ: Lawrence Erlbaum Associates.

Codol, J. P. (1981). A cognitive approach to the feeling of identity. *Social Science Information/Information sur les Sciences Sociales, 20,* 111–136.

Cooley, C. (1909). *Social organization: A study of the larger mind.* New York: Charles Scribner.

Cordova, J. V., Gee, C. B., & Warren, L. Z. (2005). Emotional skillfulness in marriage: Intimacy as a mediator of the relationship between emotional skillfulness and marital satisfaction. *Journal of Social and Clinical Psychology, 24,* 218–235.

Cowan, C. P., & Cowan, PA. (2003). Normative family transitions, normal family process, and healthy child development. In F. Walsh (Ed.), *Normal family processes: Growing diversity and complexity* (3rd ed., pp. 424–459). New York: Guilford Press.

Cowan, C. P., & Cowan, P. A. (2005). Two central roles for couple relationships: Breaking negative intergenerational patterns and enhancing children's adaptation. *Sexual and Relationship Therapy, 20,* 275–288.

Cowan, P. A., & Cowan, C. P. (1992). *When partners become parents.* New York: Basic Books.

Crocetti, E., Rubini, M., & Meuss, W. (2008). Capturing the dynamics of identity formation in various ethnic groups: Development and validation of a three-dimensional model. *Journal of Adolescence, 31,* 207–222.

Cutrona, C. (1996). *Social support in couples.* Thousand Oaks, CA: Sage.

Deci, E. L., & Ryan, R. M. (2000). The "what" and "why" of goal pursuits: Human needs and the self-determination of behavior. *Psychological Inquiry, 11,* 227–268.

Dellmann-Jenkins, M., & Brittain, L. (2003). Young adults' attitudes toward filial responsibility and actual assistance to elderly family members. *Journal of Applied Gerontology, 22,* 214–229.

Dishion, T. J., Capaldi, D. M., & Yoerger, K. (1999). Middle childhood antecedents to progression in male adolescent substance use: An ecological analysis of risk and protection. *Journal of Adolescent Research, 14,* 175–206.

Eisler, I., Dare, C., & Szmukler, G. I. (1988). What's happened to family interaction research? An historical account and a family systems viewpoint. *Journal of Marital and Family Therapy, 14,* 45–65.

Erikson, E. H. (1968). *Identity: Youth and crisis.* New York: Norton.

Erikson, E. H. (1982). *The life cycle completed.* New York: Norton.

Feaster, D., & Szapocznik, J. (2002). Interdependence of stress processes among African American family members: Influence of HIV serostatus and a new infant. *Psychology and Health, 17,* 339–363.

Feeney, J. A., Noller, P., & Ward, C. (1998). *Marital satisfaction and spousal interaction in satisfaction in close relationships.* New York: Guilford.

Finley, G. E., & Schwartz, S. (2004). The father involvement and nurturant fathering scales: Retrospective Measures for adolescent and adult children. *Educational and Psychological Measurement, 64,* 143–164.

Finley, G. E., & Schwartz, S. J. (2006). Parsons and Bales revisited: Young adult children's characterization of the fathering role. *Psychology of Men and Masculinity, 7,* 42–55.

Fraiberg, S. (1975). The development of human attachments in infants blind from birth. *Merrill-Palmer Quarterly, 21,* 315–334.

Freeberg, A. L., & Stein, C. H. (1996). Felt obligation towards parents in Mexican-American and Anglo-American young adults. *Journal of Social and Personal Relationships, 13,* 457–471.

Freud, S. (1922). *A general introduction to psychoanalysis.* New York: Boni and Liveright.

Fuligni, A. J., Alvarez, J. M., Bachman, M., & Ruble, D. N. (2005). Family obligation and the academic motivation of young children from immigrant families. In C. R. Cooper, C. García Coll, T. Bartko, H. Davis, & C. Chatman (Eds.), *Hills of gold: Rethinking diversity and contexts as resources for children's developmental pathways.* Mahwah, NJ: Lawrence Erlbaum Associates.

Gaertner, S. L., & Dovidio, J. F. (2000). *Reducing intergroup bias: The common ingroup identity model.* Philadelphia, PA: Psychology Press.

Gavazzi, S. M. (1993). The relation between family differentiation levels in families with adolescents and the severity of presenting problems. *Family Relations, 42,* 463–468.

Georgas, J., Berry, J. W., van de Vijver, F. J. R., Kagitcibasi, C., Poortinga, Y. H. (2006). *Families across cultures: A 30-nation psychological study.* Cambridge, UK: Cambridge University Press.

Green, R. J., & Werner, P. D. (1996). Intrusiveness and closeness-caregiving: Rethinking the concept of family enmeshment. *Family Process, 35,* 115–136.

Grolnick, W. S, Ryan, R. M., & Deci, E. L. (1991). The inner resources for school achievement: Motivational mediators of children's perceptions of their parents. *Journal of Educational Psychology, 83*, 508–517.

Grotevant, H. D., & Cooper, C. R. (1986). Individuation in family relationships: A perspective on individual differences in the development of identity and role-taking skill in adolescence. *Human Development, 29*, 82–100.

Grusec, J. E., Goodnow, J. J. & Kuczynski, L. (2000). New directions in analyses of parenting contributions to children's acquisition of values. *Child Development, 71*, 205–211.

Haley, J. (1973). *Uncommon therapy: The psychiatric techniques of Milton Erickson.* New York: Norton.

Haley, J. (1976). *Problem solving therapy.* San Francisco: Jossey-Bass.

Harwood, J., Soliz, J., & Lin, M. C. (2006). Communication accommodation theory: An intergroup approach to family relationships. In D. O. Braithwaite & L. A. Baxter (Eds.), *Engaging theories in family communication: Multiple perspectives.* Thousand Oaks, CA: Sage.

Hill, R. (1970). *Family development in three generations.* Cambridge, UK: Schenkman.

Hinde, R. A. (1997). *Relationships: A dialectical perspective.* London: Psychology Press.

Iafrate, R., Donato, S., Bertoni, A. (2010). Knowing and promoting the couple bond: Research findings and suggestions for preventive interventions. *INTAMS review, Journal for the Study of Marriage & Spirituality, 16*(1), 65–82.

Jen'nan Ghazal R. (2004). Family, religion, and work among Arab American women. *Journal of Marriage and Family, 66*, 1042–1050.

Jurkovic, G. J. (1998). *Lost childhoods. The plight of the parentified child.* New York: Brunner/Mazel.

Kagitçibasi, C. (2005). Autonomy and relatedness in cultural context: Implications for self and family. *Journal of Cross-Cultural Psychology, 36*, 403–422.

Kerr, M., Stattin, H., & Trost, K. (1999). To know you is to trust you: Parents' trust is rooted in child disclosure of information. *Journal of Adolescence, 22*, 737–752.

Klein, D. M., & White, J. M. (1996). *Family theories: An introduction.* Thousand Oaks, CA: Sage.

Kroger, J. (1985). Separation–individuation and ego identity status in New Zealand university students. *Journal of Youth and Adolescence, 14*, 133–147.

Kruse, J., & Walper, S. (2008). Types of individuation in relation to parents: Predictors and outcomes. *International Journal of Behavioral Development, 32*, 390–400.

Kuperminc, G. P., Jurkovic, G. J., & Casey, S. (2009). Relation of filial responsibility to the personal and social adjustment of Latino adolescents from immigrant families. *Journal of Family Psychology, 23*, 14–22.

Laslett, P., & Wall, R. (Eds.). (1972). *Household and family in past time.* Cambridge, UK: Cambridge University Press.

Lawrence, E., Bunde, M., Barry, R. A., Brock, R. L. Sullivan, K. T., Pasch, L., White, G. A., Dowd, C. E.,

& Adams, E. E. (2008). Partner support and marital satisfaction: Support amount, adequacy, provision and solicitation. *Personal Relationships, 15*, 445–463.

Lay, C., Fairlie, P., Jackson, S., Ricci, T., Eisenberg, J., Sato, T., et al. (1998). Domain-specific allocentrism/idiocentrism: A measure of family connectedness. *Journal of Cross-Cultural Psychology, 29*, 434–460.

Leary, M. R., & Baumeister, R. F. (2000). The nature and function of self-esteem: Sociometer theory. In M. P. Zanna (Ed.), *Advances in experimental social psychology* (Vol. 32). San Diego, CA: Academic Press.

Levine, J. M., & Moreland, R. L. (Eds.). (2006). *Small groups.* New York: Psychology Press.

Levine, R., Sato, S., Hashimoto, T., & Verma, J. (1995). Love and marriage in eleven cultures. *Journal of Cross-Cultural Psychology, 26*, 554–571.

Lewin, K. (1951). In D. Cartwright (Ed.), *Field theory in social science; selected theoretical papers.* New York: Harper & Row.

Losoya, S. H., & Eisenberg, N. (2001). In J. A. Hall & F. J. Bernieri (Eds.), *Affective empathy.* Mahwah, NJ: Lawrence Erlbaum Associates Publishers.

Mallinckrodt, B. (2000). Attachment, social competencies, social support, and interpersonal process in psychotherapy. *Psychotherapy Research, 10*, 239–266.

Manzi, C., Parise, M., Iafrate, R., & Vignoles, V. L. (2010, January). Self-enhancement and couple relationships: Predictors and consequences of positive illusions. Poster presented at the 11th annual meeting of the Society for Personality and Social Psychology, Las Vegas, NV, USA.

Manzi, C., Regalia, C., Soenens, B., Fincham, D. F., & Scabini, E. (2011). *Disentangling different dimensions of intrusive parenting.* Manuscript submitted for publication, Catholic University of Milan, Italy.

Manzi, C., Vignoles, V. L., & Regalia, C. (2010). Accommodating a new identity: Possible selves, identity change and well-being across two life-transitions. *European Journal of Social Psychology, 40*, 970–984.

Manzi, C., Vignoles, V. L., Regalia, C., & Scabini, E. (2006). Cohesion and enmeshment revisited: Differentiation, identity, and well-being in two European cultures. *Journal of Marriage and Family, 68*, 673–689.

Markus, H., & Kitayama, S. (1991). Culture and the self: Implications for cognition, emotion, and motivation. *Psychological Review, 98*, 224–253.

McGoldrick, M., & Carter, B. (2003). The Family Life Cycle. In F. Walsh (Ed.), *Normal family processes.* New York: Guilford.

Meeus, W., Iedema, J., Maassen, G. & Engels, R. (2005). Separation–individuation revisited: On the interplay of parent–adolescent relations, identity and emotional adjustment in adolescence. *Journal of Adolescence, 28*, 89–106.

Meltzer, D., & Harris, M. (1983). *Il ruolo educativo della familia* [The educational role of the family]. Torino: C.S.T.

Minuchin, S. (1974). *Families and family therapy.* Cambridge, MA: Harvard University Press.

Moscovici, S., & Zavalloni, M. (1969). The group as a polarizer of attitudes. *Journal of Personality and Social Psychology, 12,* 125–135.

Moss, B. F., & Schwebel, A. I. (1993). Marriage and romantic relationships: Defining intimacy in romantic relationships. *Family Relations, 42,* 31–37.

Olson, D. H. (1982). Circumplex model of marital and family system. In F. Walsh (Ed.), *Normal family processes.* New York: Guilford.

Olson, D. H., & Olson, A. K. (1983). Circumplex model of marital and family systems VI: Theoretical update. *Family Process, 22,* 69–84.

Olson, D. H., Russell, C. R., & Sprenkle, D. H. (1999). PREPARE/ENRICH Program: Version 2000. In R. Berger & M. T. Hannah (Eds.), *Preventive approaches in couple therapy* (pp. 196–216). Philadelphia: Brunner/Mazel.

Passmore, N. L., Fogarty, G. J., Bourke, C. J. & Baker-Evans, S. F. (2005). Parental bonding and identity style as correlates of self-esteem among adult adoptees and nonadoptees. *Family Relations, 54,* 523–534.

Patterson, G. R. (1975). *Families: Applications of social learning to family life* (revised ed.). Champaign, IL: Research Press.

Patterson, G. R., & Forgatch, M. S. (1987). *Parents and adolescents: Living together.* Eugene, OR: Castalia.

Plomin, R. (1994). *Genetics and experience: The interplay between nature and nurture.* Thousand Oaks, CA: Sage Publications.

Ryan, R. M., & Deci, E. L. (2000). Intrinsic and extrinsic motivations: Classic definitions and new directions. *Contemporary Educational Psychology, 25,* 54–67.

Ryan, R. M., & Deci, E. L. (2006). Self-regulation and the problem of human autonomy: Does psychology need choice, self-determination, and will? *Journal of Personality, 74,* 1557–1585.

Sabatelli, R. M., & Bartle-Haring, S. E. (2003). Family of origin experiences and adjustment in married couples. *Journal of Marriage and Family, 65,* 159–169.

Sabatelli, R. M., & Mazor, A. (1985). Differentiation, individuation, and identity formation: The integration of family systems and individual development. *Adolescence, 20,* 619–633.

Scabini, E. (1985). *L'organizzazione famiglia tra crisi e sviluppo* [The family organization between crisis and development]. Milano: Franco Angeli.

Scabini, E., & Cigoli, V. (2000). *Il famigliare. Legami, simboli e transizioni* [The family core. Bonds, symbols and transitions]. Milano: Raffaello Cortina.

Silk, J. S., Morris, A. S., Kanaya, T., & Steinberg, L. (2003). Psychological control and autonomy granting: Opposite ends of a continuum or distinct constructs? *Journal of Research on Adolescence, 13,* 113–128.

Snyder, C. R., & Fromkin H. L. (1980). *Uniqueness: The human pursuit of difference.* New York: Plenum Press.

Soenens, B., Duriez, B., Vansteenkiste, M., & Goossens, L. (2007). The intergenerational transmission of empathy-related responding in adolescence: The role of maternal support. *Personality and Social Psychology Bulletin, 33,* 299–311.

Soenens, B., Vansteenkiste, M., Lens, W., Luyckx, K., Goossens, L., Beyers, W., & Ryan, R. M. (2007). Conceptualizing parental autonomy support: Adolescent perceptions of promotion of independence versus promotion of volitional functioning. *Developmental Psychology, 43,* 633–646.

Soenens, B., Vansteenkiste, M., & Sierens, E. (2009). How are parental psychological control and autonomy-support related? A cluster-analytic approach. *Journal of Marriage and Family, 71,* 187–202.

Soliz, J., & Harwood, J. (2006). Shared family identity, age salience and intergroup contact: Investigation of the grandparent-grandchild relationship. *Communication Monographs, 73,* 87–107.

Sroufe, L. A., & Fleeson, J. (1988). The coherence of family relationships. In R. A. Hinde & J. Stevenson-Hinde (Eds.), *Relationships within families: Mutual influences.* Oxford, UK: Oxford University Press.

Stein, C. H. (2009). I owe it to them: Understanding felt obligation towards parents in adulthood. In K. Shifren (Ed.), *How caregiving affects development: Psychological implications for child, adolescent and adult caregivers.* Washington, DC: American Psychological Association.

Stierlin, C. H. (1974). *Separating parents and adolescents.* New York: Quadrangle.

Stouthamer-Loeber, M., Wei, E., Homish, D., & Loeber, R. (2002). Which family and demographic factors are related to both maltreatment and persistent serious juvenile delinquency? *Children's Services: Social Policy, Research, and Practice, 5,* 261–272.

Swann, W. B., Jr. Chang-Schneider, C., & Angulo, S. (2007). Self-verification in relationships as an adaptive process. In J. Wood, A. Tesser, & J. Holmes (Eds.), *Self and Relationships.* New York: Psychology Press.

Szapocznik, J., Rio, A. T., Hervis, O. E., Mitrani, V. B., Kurtines, W. M., & Faraci, A. M. (1991). Assessing change in family functioning as a result of treatment: The structural family systems rating scale (SFSR). *Journal of Marital and Family Therapy, 17*(3), 295–310.

Tajfel, H., Billig, M. G., Bundy, R. P., & Flament, C. (1971). Social categorization and intergroup behaviour. *European Journal of Social Psychology, 1,* 149–177.

Trommsdorff, G. (2005). Parent-child relations over the lifespan: A cross-cultural perspective. In K. H. Rubin & O. B. Chung (Eds.), *Parenting beliefs, behaviors, and parent-child relations: A cross-cultural perspective* (pp. 143–183). New York: Psychology Press.

Van IJzendoorn, M. H. (1992). Intergenerational transmission of parenting: A review of studies in nonclinical populations. *Developmental Review, 12,* 76–99.

Vignoles, V. L., Chryssochoou, X., & Breakwell, G. M. (2000). The distinctiveness principle: Identity, meaning and the bounds of cultural relativity. *Personality and Social Psychology Review, 4,* 337–354.

Vignoles, V. L., Regalia, C., Manzi, C., Golledge, J., Scabini, E. (2006). Beyond self-esteem: Towards an integrated model of motivated identity construction. *Journal of Personality and Social Psychology, 90,* 308–333.

Von Bertalanffy, L. (1968). *General system theory: Foundations, development, applications.* New York: George Braziller.

Walsh, F. (Ed.). (2003). *Normal family processes.* New York: Guilford.

Webster-Stratton, C. (1981). Modification of mothers' behaviors and attitudes through videotape modeling group discussion. *Behavior Therapy, 12,* 634–642.

Youniss, J., & Smollar, J. (1985). *Adolescent relations with mother, fathers, and friends.* Chicago: University of Chicago Press.

Zaidi, A. U., Shuraydi, M. (2002). Perceptions of arranged marriages by young Pakistani Muslim women living in a western society. *Journal of Comparative Family Studies, 33,* 495–514.

Zentner, M., & Renaud, O. (2007). Origins of adolescents' ideal self: An intergenerational perspective. *Journal of Personality and Social Psychology, 92,* 357–375.

Adoptive Identity

Harold D. Grotevant and Lynn Von Korff

Abstract

Adoptive identity addresses these questions: "Who am I as an adopted person?" and "What does being adopted mean to me, and how does this fit into my understanding of my self, relationships, family, and culture?" The process of identity construction is observed in adoptive identity exploration, as adopted persons reflect on the meaning of adoption in their lives, take active steps to gather information that will enhance this understanding, and construct a meaningful narrative. A highly developed narrative is internally consistent, reflects multiple points of view, and has been developed through a process of exploration and reflection. Despite the increasing popular interest in adoptive identity, relevant theories and supportive research are still emerging. This chapter begins with an overview of the four worlds of adoption: domestic infant adoption, domestic adoption from the public child welfare system, international adoption, and kinship adoption. Knowledge of commonalities and differences across these types of adoption is critical for understanding adoptive identity. Next follows a discussion of the family, community, and societal contexts in which adoptive identity development occurs. The chapter then turns to identity theory. Our approach is grounded in Eriksonian and narrative theories, and incorporates recent theoretical work by Von Korff (2008) on the role of affect in adoptive identity. Finally, several promising approaches to identity intervention are discussed in the context of cautions, because the path toward adoptive identity is not linear and may extend well into adulthood. The chapter concludes with a discussion of future prospects in adoptive identity theory and research.

For many adopted persons, the question of identity is interwoven with specific questions about one's lineage, such as "Who are my biological parents?" "Where was I born?" "What were my earliest days like?" and "What is my genetic heritage?" All of us, adopted or not, learn about

H.D. Grotevant (✉)
Department of Psychology, College of Natural Sciences,
University of Massachusetts, Amherst, MA, USA
e-mail: hgroteva@psych.umass.edu

S.J. Schwartz et al. (eds.), *Handbook of Identity Theory and Research*,
DOI 10.1007/978-1-4419-7988-9_24, © Springer Science+Business Media, LLC 2011

our origins through stories told to us by family members (Bohanek, Marin, Fivush, & Duke, 2006). For adopted persons, family stories are often missing information about them because the information is unavailable or has been withheld. Thus, it should not be a surprise that much of the literature (e.g., popular, memoir, clinical) on identity and adoption is about missing information – such as unknown origins or relatives, or unknown or unknowable health or genetic history. However, identity refers to more than the amount of information one has; it is the story that one constructs with that information.

Adoptive identity addresses these questions: "Who am I as an adopted person?" and "What does being adopted mean to me, and how does this fit into my understanding of my self, relationships, family, and culture?" A narrative approach to adoptive identity development focuses on meaning-making (Grotevant, 1993, 1997; Grotevant, Dunbar, Kohler, & Esau, 2000; Von Korff, 2008; Bamberg, DeFina, & Schiffrin, Chapter 8, this volume; McAdams, Chapter 5, this volume). How is an adoptee's narrative socially constructed, and how does that narrative help the person know where he or she fits into the world?

The process of meaning-making is observed in adoptive identity exploration, as adopted persons reflect on the meaning of adoption in their lives, take active steps to gather information that will enhance this understanding, and construct a meaningful narrative. The quality of the narrative is reflected in its coherence (Polkinghorne, 1988; McAdams, Chapter 5, this volume). A highly developed narrative is internally consistent, reflects multiple points of view, and has been developed through a process of exploration and reflection (Dunbar & Grotevant, 2004; Von Korff, 2008). Despite the increasing popular interest in adoptive identity, relevant theories and supportive research are still emerging. This chapter begins with an overview of the four worlds of adoption: domestic infant adoption, domestic adoption from the public child welfare system, international adoption, and kinship adoption. Knowledge of commonalities and differences across these different types of adoption is critical for understanding adoptive identity. Next, we discuss the family, community, and societal contexts in which adoptive identity development occurs. The chapter then turns to identity theory. Our approach is grounded in Eriksonian and narrative theories and incorporates recent theoretical work by Von Korff (2008) on the role of affect in adoptive identity. Finally, we present perspectives on identity intervention and discuss several promising approaches and cautions. The chapter concludes with a discussion of future prospects in adoptive identity theory and research.

Diverse Worlds of Adoption: Backdrop to Understanding Identity Development

In North America and Western Europe, the term "adoption" is used to describe very different circumstances: the infant voluntarily placed by her unmarried birth parents so that she would have greater economic and educational advantages than they felt they could provide; the teenager who was removed from his parents' home by social services because of sexual abuse, subsequently placed in foster care, and then declared eligible by the courts for permanent adoption; the child orphaned as a result of the AIDS epidemic in Africa, moved to an institution, and subsequently adopted by a family in the United States; and the teenager whose parents divorced and married other people, and whose stepfather legally adopted her. What these children have in common is that the rights and responsibilities of their birth parents were legally terminated and transferred to others who will raise them. But adopted persons bring with them different amounts of knowledge about their birth families, as well as widely divergent experiences that serve as building blocks as they go about constructing their adoptive identities.

In short, adoption as a family form is intimately connected to circumstances of culture, history, economics, and ideology. Thus, understanding adoptive identity requires a working knowledge of the different worlds of adoption, because the worlds differ by characteristics of the child and of the adoptive parents (e.g., age, health, gender, country of origin); differences between the child and the adoptive parents (e.g., racial, ethnic, or personality differences); reasons for the child's placement (e.g., poverty, voluntary or involuntary removal of the child from the birthparents' home, parental death, parental divorce); and characteristics of the intermediary creating the adoptive placement (e.g., private (non-governmental) agency, public child welfare service). Understanding these differences among types of adoption, and among individual adoptees, provides an important backdrop for the study of adoptive identity.

Four distinctive types of adoption predominate in North America and Western Europe today: domestic adoption of infants, domestic adoption from the public child welfare system, international adoption, and kinship adoption. The following sketches of the four worlds of adoption highlight the different identity challenges that await adopted persons in each of these situations.

Domestic Adoption of Infants

Infants are placed for adoption within their countries of origin for a number of reasons, but most commonly because the child's birth parents feel that they cannot provide the kind of home they would want for their child. Such parents might be young, still in school, or in occupations that would not provide the resources needed to raise a child. Others might not be in a committed relationship and might want their child to be raised in a two-parent home. Still other birth mothers might find themselves pregnant as a result of rape or incest, and may neither be willing to raise their child nor to terminate the pregnancy. Placements of these types are frequently termed "voluntary," because the birth parent(s) make the decision to place the child for adoption. Infant placements still occur within the United States but are rare in Western Europe, where the social safety net provides economic resources that make it more feasible for single parents to raise children.

The past few decades have seen a shift in infant placements toward arrangements characterized by openness, or contact between the child's adoptive family and birth relatives. Advocates of open adoption typically cite the facilitation of identity development as one of the advantages of this arrangement. Closed adoptions, in which children had no identifying information about their birth relatives, created a variety of identity-relevant concerns for children who grew up in that system. Clinical literature (e.g., Riley & Meeks, 2006) and memoirs (e.g., Lifton, 1975) have highlighted the struggles that many adopted persons felt because they knew nothing of their origins in a society that is heavily oriented toward biological ties (e.g., Wegar, 1997) and the importance of genetics in health (e.g., Finkler, Skrzynia, & Evans, 2003). The most common identity-relevant issues in domestic infant adoption include "searching" (a broad concept referring to activities that range from searching for information about relatives to searching for the relatives themselves) and forging an identity as a member of two families.

Domestic Adoption from the Public Child Welfare System

Unlike the situation where birth parents make an adoption plan for their child, children are sometimes removed from their homes by the child welfare system because the parents are judged to be unfit due to abuse and/or neglect. In the United States, a system of concurrent planning is used, in which there are attempts to assist the child's family (e.g., through drug treatment, job assistance, counseling) so that he or she can return home. If these attempts are unsuccessful, parental rights are terminated and the child becomes available for adoption. These children may live in one or many more foster homes between being removed from their families and placed for adoption (McRoy, Lynch, Chanmugam, Madden, & Ayers-Lopez, 2009). This world of adoption evokes its own set of identity issues: Where does the child fit? Who are his or her parents? How does one develop a clear sense of self when being moved from one foster family to another, changing schools and neighborhoods each time? How does a child maintain contact with birth relatives who are not considered harmful to the child, such as siblings or grandparents (e.g., Neil, 2004)? How does this contact contribute to the child's emerging sense of identity? How does the child reconcile his or her relationship with abusive or neglectful parents whose rights have been terminated?

International Adoption

Humanitarian efforts to find homes for children in orphanages following World War II and the Korean War set the stage for the broader practice of contemporary international (also referred to as intercountry or transnational) adoption (Selman, 2009). A different set of identity-related concerns emerges for these children. How do they make meaning of the fact that they look different than their adoptive parents? How do they understand their connection to adoptive and birth families who do not share a common language, set of cultural practices, or national heritage? How does a young adult make meaning of the ethical issues surrounding international adoption, such as economic disparities or social policies that persuade women to place their babies for adoption? A growing number of internationally adopted children are searching for birth relatives or information about them (e.g., Tieman, van der Ende, & Verhulst, 2008). How does one do this across cultural divides and norms that may bring shame or even danger to a child's birth parents?

Kinship Adoption

Many children whose biological parents cannot parent them are raised informally by relatives or are legally adopted by kin such as grandparents or stepparents. In the case of stepparent adoption, the child may continue to live with one biological parent, and so many of the identity questions that characterize the other worlds of adoption take different forms. Identity questions may arise around the child's relations to the parent(s) whose rights were terminated, either voluntarily or involuntarily. What does it mean to a teenage girl when her biological father allows someone else to adopt her? What does it mean to a child, adopted by his stepfather, to have a new last name and a new set of relatives?

This brief venture into the four different worlds of adoption has highlighted the context-sensitivity of adoptive identity. It also underscores the need to look beyond the word "adoption" to understand the adopted person's unique family circumstances.

Family and Broader Contexts of Adoptive Identity Development

Family Contexts

Family environments set the stage for adolescent identity formation, shaping children through a process of mutual influence (Erikson, 1963, 1968, 1980). As children reach adolescence, they redefine their relationships with their parents or guardians. Adolescents begin to develop autonomy with respect to these relationships; they leave childhood behind, modifying old commitments and forming new ones in the realms of school, work, relationships, and ideology (Cooper, 1999; Grotevant, 1998; Grotevant & Cooper, 1998).

Adoptive identity is also negotiated and enacted in relational contexts within families. The early socialization process for adopted children usually engages the child with a family adoption story or narrative (Brodzinsky, Lang, & Smith, 1995). The story, which typically contains information about birth parents and circumstances surrounding adoption, communicates the "facts" that the adoptive parents wish to disclose at that time, as well as subtle positive or negative cues about the child's birth parents and their circumstances. All of the features of the story are likely to influence the child's developing narrative. In the early years, the family serves as a source of interpretation for the child through stories, artifacts (photos, gifts, etc.), songs, written material, and social affiliations. The family narrative is influenced by adoption professionals' advice to parents about what should be told, how much, and when (Wrobel, Kohler, Grotevant, & McRoy, 2003). The family's comfort with acknowledging that adoptive parenting is inherently different from biological parenting (e.g., Kirk, 1981), and their comfort with discussing adoption, also serve as part of the context.

Adopted children and adolescents may come to reconsider their received family narrative over time in several ways. With the development of abstract reasoning, they may begin to reflect on the complex legal, societal, relational, and sexual meanings involved in adoption (Brodzinsky, Singer, & Braff, 1984). Missing information, such as the identities of birth parents or reasons for the adoptive placement, may raise questions about the family narrative. If a child had not been told about the adoption or about important aspects of the adoption, discovering these details could lead to questions about why it was necessary to keep this information secret. Further, secrets about important personal information, and the misleading family narratives associated with such secrets, may undermine a child's sense of self and family belonging (Brown-Smith, 1998) and, in some cases, may be experienced as traumatic (e.g., Fisher, 1973; Morgan, 2008). Even when children are raised to believe that adoption is a valid way to build a family, uninformed comments from others about adoption may challenge this view or prompt questions about why the family's narrative differs from that of others. As adolescents consider these issues and reframe their family adoption narrative, they begin to integrate adoptive identity into their larger sense of self (Grotevant, 1997).

Adoption often becomes "visible" within families because of real or perceived differences in physical appearance, abilities, or personality. Within biologically related families, similarities and differences are frequently attributed to heredity; if there is no one in the immediate family whom the child resembles, the similarity may be attributed to an extended family member. In adoptive families, parent–child similarities and differences are obviously not due to heredity. When nothing is known about the child's birth parents, attributions are sometimes still made to hypothesized characteristics of birth family members: "Your mother must have had hair just like that" (see Perry, 2006). Differences tend to be more visible in families with children adopted transracially or transnationally.

How families deal with difference plays an important role in adoptive identity development. Kaye (1990) examined discourse processes in families considered "high distinguishing" (i.e., emphasizing the difference between adoptive and biological status) and "low distinguishing" (minimizing the difference between the two). Examining transcripts of family discussions, Kaye asked whether the adolescent's freedom to express views about adoption that were different from his or her parents' views might be related to the adoptee's identity formation. He found that both emphasizing and minimizing differences were associated with family problems and with low adolescent self-esteem, and that both discourse styles may have negative consequences for identity development. When differences were acknowledged without being emphasized, adolescents' real experiences of difference were validated, while their connection to the adoptive family was simultaneously underscored.

Community and Societal Contexts

Adoptive identity cannot be understood without placing it in the context of societal attitudes toward kinship. Social scientists such as Schneider (1980) and Wegar (1997) have argued that Western societies base kinship ties primarily, if not exclusively, on blood relations. When biological relationships are emphasized, adopted persons are put in a problematic position, because their familial ties are grounded in social, rather than biological, relations (Leon, 2002).

The boundaries between adoptive and biological parenthood are being blurred as an increasing number of infant adoptions are open from the beginning. In open adoptions, birth mothers may choose the parents who adopt their child, and the adoptive parents may be present at the birth. Even if the parties do not plan extensive contact after the placement, they have met and they know how to contact each other. There is no pretense of the child's "passing" as a biological child of the adoptive parents. Participation in such arrangements implies that adoptive parents are aware that their family's boundaries extend beyond the household to an adoptive kinship network, consisting of the adopted child, adoptive family members, and birth family members. In fact, some adoptive parents have found that open adoption enhanced their role as parents, giving them opportunities to talk directly with their children about their origins, medical histories, and birth relatives (Von Korff, Grotevant, Koh, & Samek, 2010).

Although all family relationships present opportunities for secrets and conflicts to occur, the nature of open adoptions reduces the likelihood of secrets related to the circumstances of adoption, because the relevant parties are known to each other. Even though there may be fewer secrets about biology or heritage in open adoptions, this does not mean that all of the children's questions are answered. An open adoption does not reduce the questioning that accompanies adolescence. In fact, we have found that all adopted children are curious about their birth families, but that children in arrangements with different degrees of openness are curious about different things (Wrobel & Dillon, 2009). For example, children in confidential adoptions may wonder who their birth parents are and what they look like, whereas children in open adoptions may wonder when their birth parents will visit next and whether their birth parents will share details about their birth and placement.

Adopting children across racial or national lines makes families bicultural or multicultural, although some families embrace this transformation more than others. The racial and cultural composition of the family's community will determine whether their status is a source of visible difference or not. Depending on the community context, adopted children may experience a range of reactions, from open arms to teasing or denigration. The "fit" of the adoptive

family with its community context will have an impact on the identity development of its children (McGinnis, 2009). For example, Cheri Register, an American parent of two daughters adopted from Korea, wrote a book about her experience with family-community fit titled *Are Those Kids Really Yours?* (Register, 1991). The title echoed the many encounters she had had with strangers in the grocery store, airport, and neighborhood. It speaks to the issue of self-in-context, and not only the child's identity but also the identity of the whole family (Suter, 2008). Lee (2003) has underscored the salience of this dilemma, labeling it the "transracial adoption paradox." For children adopted by White parents across racial or ethnic lines, the child or adolescent may be viewed by the larger society as an ethnic minority or a person of color. However, they may be perceived by some (and perhaps by themselves) as members of the majority culture, because they were adopted into a White family and grew up in that context.

These sometimes contradictory experiences can affect the way in which identity development proceeds for adolescents and young adults. More specifically, in a recent study of Korean adoptees, Shiao and Tuan (2008) found that ethnic identity exploration during early adulthood was contingent on adoptees' freedom from family responsibilities and personal problems, proximity to opportunities for exploration, belief that their "racial visibility" placed limits on their acceptance by others, and openness to interacting with other Asians.

Even when children adopted transracially or internationally are accepted in their communities, they may encounter challenges to their emerging sense of identity when they move into different contexts. For example, a Korean child adopted into a predominantly White, rural community may have access to status and acceptance associated with the "white privilege" (McIntosh, 1988) of his or her adoptive parents (i.e., the transracial adoption paradox; Lee, 2003). However, if the child attends college in a large multicultural urban area, others may respond socially in ways that challenge his or her identity (Meier, 1999). All of a sudden, he or she may be regarded as a "person of color," a label discordant with his or her self-view. Through social interactions, adopted adolescents may begin to identify or align themselves with their biological parents' racial or ethnic groups, but may find they do not fit in because they do not know the language or cultural values. Adolescents may also seek out adoption-related groups and affiliation with the "adoption community" when they move into contexts where their adoptive status or family and community membership is questioned. The availability of numerous adoption-related websites, blogs, and Internet chat rooms has made it possible for adolescents to participate in this exploration separately from their family, even before they leave home.

If the child was adopted transracially or internationally, is there a community of similar individuals with whom the child (and perhaps the family) can identify and interact? The availability of the community itself is only one piece of the puzzle; the child and parents must be interested in interacting with the community, and the community itself must be welcoming. For example, in regions where there is a high concentration of families who have adopted from Korea, there are Korean culture camps offered in the summer, often organized by adoptive parents or adoption agencies. Although many children benefit from them and love to attend, other children want nothing to do with them. Similarly, members of the child's ethnic community may not be interested in interacting with the adopted child, who is different from them as well as from his or her adoptive parents (Meier, 1998). This experience of non-acceptance also influences identity development.

Adoptive Identity Theory: A New Synthesis

Eriksonian Foundations

Identity versus role confusion is the fifth stage in Erikson's epigenetic theory of psychosocial development (Erikson, 1963, 1968, 1980; Kroger & Marcia, Chapter 2, this volume). This life stage, which coincides with adolescence and the transition to adulthood, represents the period when youth experience major neurological, emotional, and cognitive changes, while also being called upon to explore and make decisions about education and career, ideology, and interpersonal relationships. Theory holds that a coherent and meaningful sense of identity, formed in concert with one's social and cultural environment, is central to healthy psychological adjustment during this developmental stage and beyond (see also Berzonsky, Chapter 3, this volume; Luyckx, Schwartz, Goossens, Beyers, & Missotten, Chapter 4, this volume; Waterman, Chapter 16, this volume).

Erikson's theory of development is epigenetic: the central themes of each developmental stage – trust versus mistrust, autonomy versus shame, initiative versus guilt, and so on – influence current and subsequent developmental stages (Erikson, 1968). Additionally, themes central to each stage are revisited throughout the life cycle. Thus, identity development is a lifelong process, occurring at the intersection between the individual and his or her social context (Erikson, 1980; Graafsma, Bosma, Grotevant, & deLevita, 1994).

Erikson's theory of development is also psychosocial. The challenges involved in each developmental stage arise from the interaction of individual development (physiological, cognitive, emotional) and societal demands and expectations. In contemporary Western societies, adolescence and emerging adulthood represent the time of life during which youth are expected to move forward toward occupational futures (as they make decisions about educational paths and economic self-sufficiency), toward becoming responsible citizens (through developing political and value stances), and toward becoming mature relationship partners (as they consider decisions about family formation; Arnett, 2000).

Identity development is dynamic and complex because each of these identity domains (e.g., occupational, political, relational) has its own developmental course (Bosma, 1985; Grotevant, 1987), and each waxes and wanes in importance over time (Goossens, 2001; Meeus, 1996). Most of the domains studied by identity researchers well into the 1990s concerned aspects of identity over which adolescents have some degree of choice, such as occupation, religion, political values, and views of themselves in relationships (see Kroger & Marcia, Chapter 2, this volume). More recently, there has been interest in understanding assigned identities, where the individual has little or no choice about a particular identity domain, such as gender, ethnicity, sexual orientation, or adoptive status (Grotevant, 1992; see also Bussey, Chapter 25, this volume; Savin-Williams, Chapter 28, this volume; Umaña-Taylor, Chapter 33, this volume). What is important, then, is not the choice about whether to take on this identity – but rather, the need to determine, "What does this identity mean to me?"

Adoptive Identity Development: A Narrative Approach

Because adoptive status is assigned rather than chosen, adoptive identity development involves "coming to terms" with adoption in the context of the family and culture into which one has been adopted (Grotevant, 1997). As reviewed at the beginning of this chapter, adoptive identity addresses these questions: "Who am I as an adopted person?" "What does being adopted mean to me?" and "How does this fit into my understanding of my self, relationships, family, and culture?" The overall process of identity development may be more complex for adopted than non-adopted persons, because this additional layer of issues requires consideration.

Like other aspects of identity, adoptive identity development is stimulated during adolescence by factors internal and external to the developing person. Cognitive (e.g., hypothetical reasoning) and biological changes (leading to sexual interest and activity) evoke curiosity in adopted individuals about their origins and the implications that their past might have for their future (Wrobel & Dillon, 2009). Thus, adolescence is a normative time for adoptive identity exploration. However, individuals' evolving

sense of self continues to interact with contextual challenges across the life course, making adoptive identity development a lifelong task. For example, a serious illness may raise new questions if the adopted person does not have medical history information about one or both birth parents and the death of one's adoptive parents may lead to pursuit of birth relatives.

We take a narrative approach toward adoptive identity development (Grotevant, 1993, 1997; Grotevant et al., 2000; Von Korff, 2008). Narrative psychology focuses on meaning-making (McAdams, Chapter 5, this volume). How is one's narrative socially constructed, and how does that narrative help the person know where he or she fits into the world? The process of meaning-making is evident in adoptive identity exploration, as adopted persons reflect on the meaning and impact of adoption on their lives, take active steps to gather information that will enhance that understanding, and construct a meaningful narrative. Thus, exploration is the "work" of identity. A number of psychological and contextual factors influence adolescents' propensity to explore, while cognitive and affective outcomes of exploration also influence future orientation toward exploration and help to reshape one's identity narrative (Grotevant, 1987).

Emotion and Narrative Adoptive Identity Development

As we have emphasized, narrative identity is constructed as young people tell unique stories about the self, stories that create and communicate a sense of meaning to the self and to others (McAdams, Chapter 5, this volume). Von Korff (2008) built on seminal ideas in narrative identity research (Bosma & Kunnen, 2001; Bruner, 1990; Singer, 2004) by proposing links between research and theory on emotion and the interactive family processes that are at the heart of the construction of narrative identity. A fundamental premise of this model is that identity forms over time as parents facilitate social interactions that are *emotionally meaningful* to their children.

Adoption provides an ideal context to examine this model for two reasons. First, openness arrangements – the different levels of contact taking place between adoptive and birth family members – offer a rich and powerful source of variation in family context because of the dramatically different amounts of information shared and types of contact experienced across families. These diverse openness arrangements present different relational contexts in which adoptive identity development occurs. Second, contact between children's adoptive and birth relatives provides an emotionally vivid and meaningful form of social interaction for adoptees. Young people who have been adopted experience a range of emotions during contact with birth family members. In our research, adolescents who had met their birthmothers reported feeling pleasure, happiness, or contentment (27%); anxiety or apprehension (24%); and joy, elation, or extreme happiness (14%) after the meetings (Grotevant et al., 2007).

Emotional experiences are critical to narrative identity formation because they lead to conversation sharing. People who experience emotions generally tell the story of their experiences to others, repeatedly, sharing them most often with family members (Rimé, 1995, 2007). Given the large range and number of emotions associated with contact with birth family members, contact should involve a relatively greater number of opportunities for adopted persons to participate in meaningful adoption-related storytelling about the self with their adoptive family members during childhood and adolescence. Adoption-related conversation between adoptees and their family members, particularly adoptive parents, is proposed to be a key factor in the process of adoptive identity formation. Identity research holds that conversational sharing plays a role in narrative identity formation by providing young people with opportunities to reconstruct past events (McLean, Pasupathi, & Pals, 2007; Polkinghorne, 1988). During conversation, people rehearse, recall, and invent information consistent with their understanding and neglect or forget information that is inconsistent with it (Pasupathi, 2001; Riessman, 1993). Conversations about adoption between adoptive parents and adopted children, sparked by emotions, are likely to be particularly important during adolescence – the period when autobiographical reasoning develops (Habermas & Bluck, 2000) in concert with narrative identity (McAdams, 1985).

Characteristics associated with parent–child adoption-related conversations, such as elaboration and frequency, should be associated with the level of coherence in adoptive identity narratives. Qualities in parent–child (Fivush, 2001; Reese, 2002) and peer-to-peer conversation have been shown to help children construct self-stories, playing a role in processes linked to the development of autobiographical reasoning (Pasupathi & Hoyt, 2009; Pasupathi, Stallworth, & Murdoch, 1998) and self-concept (Pasupathi, Alderman, & Shaw, 2007). In addition, the way in which young people interpret and give meaning to their emotional experiences and the way they label their emotions (e.g., joy, anxiety, elation, apprehension) changes as they share, reshape, and reinterpret them in conversation with parents and others (Bellelli et al., 1995). Thus, emotional expression serves as a means of organizing identity narratives, and of conveying meaning to the self and others (Haviland & Kahlbaugh, 2004).

From Identity Theory to Measurement

Erikson's theory of development, including his definition of identity, not only draws heavily from psychoanalytic theory, but also includes eco-systemic and anthropological elements. Erikson wisely revised his theory in response to social change, personal experience, and ideas from the biological sciences and the humanities – incorporating what he learned from Lewin, Benedict, and Bateson; and by observing family interactions in the laboratory, in the homes of his clients, and in non-European cultures, such as the Sioux and Yurok Indian Tribes. Erikson's work serves as a springboard for several interrelated lines of identity research. Some identity researchers draw primarily from Erikson's psychodynamic framework (Marcia, 2001), others primarily from his sociological or anthropological framework (Côté

& Levine, 2002), while others, including our own, draw from his developmental life span or narrative framework (Dunbar & Grotevant, 2004; Grotevant, 1987, 1993; McAdams, 2001; Von Korff, 2008).

Our views about adoptive identity development have been worked out in the context of our Minnesota/Texas Adoption Research Project (MTARP), a longitudinal study of adoptive kinship networks varying in degree of contact between adoptive and birth family members (see Grotevant & McRoy, 1998; Grotevant, Perry, & McRoy, 2005). Our approach to the measurement of adoptive identity is linked tightly to our theoretical foundations in developmental and narrative psychology. Because adoptive identity may include many different aspects of the adoptive experience that differ across respondents, we assess adoptive identity through a broad-ranging interview. The entire adoptive identity interview is used as the basis for coding three key indicators of narrative adoptive identity: identity exploration, which represents the process of identity development; and internal consistency and flexibility, which represent narrative coherence (Von Korff, Grotevant, & Friese, 2007). These indicators were drawn from two earlier-developed systems: the narrative coding system of the Family Narrative Consortium (Fiese et al., 1999) and the coding system for assessing identity exploration (Grotevant & Cooper, 1981). Latent profile analysis (M*plus* version 5.1, Muthén & Muthén, 2008) was used to confirm that these three indicators form one underlying latent construct representing "narrative adoptive identity." Results were consistent for sample data collected during two salient developmental periods, middle adolescence and emerging adulthood (Von Korff & Grotevant, 2007).

Depth of adoptive identity exploration refers to the degree to which participants reflect on the meaning of adoption or of being adopted, or are actively engaged in a process of gathering information or decision-making about what adoption means in their life. Specifically, exploration includes contrasting how one thought about something in the past in comparison to the present; contrasting one's own role, ideas, thoughts, or actions with those of others;

reflecting on the meaning or implications of adoption or being adopted; gathering information on any aspect of adoption or being adopted; and describing the process of making a decision about, experimenting with, or questioning an issue related to adoption or being adopted. An example of one contrast statement is, "She [birthmother] is a lot like me in an astonishing amount of ways. It's funny because I believed that your environment had more to do with your behavior than genetics, but looking at my birthmother and our similarities, I really rethink that particular argument."[1]

A narrative is highly *internally consistent* when it includes examples that support personal theories or themes, as well as synthesizing statements that pull the narrative together. An example of an emerging adult's personal theme is, "It is important to recognize distinctions between adoptive and biological parents," and an example of one statement that supports this personal theme is, "... don't be threatened if your child wants to find his/her biological parents. They may be naturally curious and they aren't looking to replace you." A narrative lacks internal consistency when it has few or no examples, lacks synthesizing statements, or includes contradictions that are unexplained or unrecognized (Fiese et al., 1999).

Flexibility refers to the degree to which participants view issues as others might see them. Participants with flexible narratives consider the complex nature of issues and relationships, such as, "Yeah, there was, you know, just growing up, I've kind of tried to put it all behind me and realize that, yeah, he's [birth father] made his mistakes. He's got his own demons." Inflexible narratives adhere rigidly to a story-line and consider relationships only from the person's own vantage point.

Adoptive Identity Interventions

Adoption educators, clinicians, and researchers have suggested a number of approaches to intervention with adopted persons. Some are preventive in nature, whereas others are therapeutic. This section provides a brief overview of several approaches. We begin, however, with some general orienting statements about working with adopted persons.

Our own research has demonstrated that there are highly varied identity narratives among adoptees, even within gender and age groups (e.g., Dunbar & Grotevant, 2004; Von Korff, 2008). Consequently, those who work with adopted persons should guard against a "one-size-fits-all" approach, assuming that adoption is equally salient to all adoptees or that all experience the same feelings with equal intensity. Likewise, it should make us cautious about rushing to intervene as if we knew what was optimal for adoptees, because the path toward adoptive identity is not linear and may extend well into adulthood.

Differences in the salience of adoptive identity, in comparison to other identity domains, may be linked to interest in activities such as exploring adoption-related careers (e.g., social worker) and viewing adoption as linked to one's religion (e.g., It was God's will that I was adopted by this particular family). Searching for birth relatives may be perceived as a necessary activity for some adolescents to feel "complete," but it may be seen as irrelevant to others. Although it may be useful to connect some internationally adopted youth with organized cultural resources such as culture camps or homeland tours, some may not be comfortable with these activities. Because there is no single course for adoptive identity development, the design of interventions must take into account adolescents' individual characteristics and goals, as well as the specific family and community resources available to them. In addition, those working with adoptees should be aware of the different levels of background information available to their clients as a function of their type of adoption (e.g., international versus domestic; open versus closed) and the degree to which adoption is discussed openly within their family. Specific suggestions for working with adopted children and adolescents in school settings may be found in Wrobel, Hendrickson, and Grotevant (2006).

When adopted persons experience challenges in adoptive identity development, it is typically because they perceive a lack of complete and accurate information about themselves, especially about their placement and foster care histories prior to adoption, their birth parents, their health histories, their genetic backgrounds, and the reasons they were placed for adoption. Availability of this information varies by type of adoption. Persons adopted domestically as infants have the potential for having or obtaining the most information. As more domestic adoptions involve contact with birth relatives, the amount of information shared will increase. However, some states in the United States still have closed records, and many adults adopted between the 1930s and 1980s have little or no information about their backgrounds. Children placed through the child welfare system face a different set of identity challenges. Depending on their age when they were removed from their birth families, children may still remember their birth parents, siblings, and other relatives. Some children have been in many foster homes, but may lose information about prior placements each time they move. For children adopted internationally, information will vary by country of origin. Children who were abandoned will have no information; those raised by foster parents or well-run children's homes may have quite a bit.

Despite adoptees' lack of information, there appear to be alternative pathways to adoptive identity formation. Consistent with Von Korff's (2008) theory of emotion and narrative adoptive identity formation, contact with birth relatives may be only one of many forms of meaningful adoption-related social interactions available to help young people develop coherent and meaningful narrative adoptive identity. Through the efforts of their adoptive parents, young people may also have friendships with people whose cultural background is similar to theirs, associations with cultural institutions, and ties to post-adoption support services offered by agencies. These activities may lead to increased opportunities for adoptees to engage in meaningful adoption-related conversation with others, enhancing their ability to explore and reflect on adoptive identity. Future research should examine the many ways in which adoptees and adoptive parents integrate different types of adoption-related social interactions that enhance narrative adoptive identity formation into their daily family lives.

A straightforward intervention that deals with the lack of background information is preparation of a "lifebook" for each adopted child. Lifebooks contain documents, photos, notes, greeting cards, school awards, report cards, art work, and other memorabilia that will help children know and keep more of their histories. Ideally, the lifebook would be started at the child's birth and then kept up by social workers, foster parents, and adoptive parents throughout the child's life. The lifebook would accompany the child from one placement to the next, no matter how many placements there might be. Although there may always be open questions for adoptees, this straightforward preventive or promotive intervention could contribute significantly to adoptive identity development (e.g., Backhaus, 1984) by providing adoptees with an account of their personal history. Because narrative adoptive identity is co-constructed between the adopted person and the individuals in their lives who matter to them, lifebooks will likely be most beneficial when combined with opportunities to converse with significant others about the meaning and significance of their experiences.

Social-construction and narrative approaches to identity have also highlighted the therapeutic value of writing. In a series of experimental studies, Pennebaker (1997) showed that writing about emotion-laden topics can produce beneficial changes in immune function, heart rate, distress, and a range of other physical and psychological outcomes. The adoption field is known for its many memoirs, documentaries, blogs, and other forms of personal expression. The writers and artists themselves acknowledge the benefits that they gain from their work. For example, in a blog titled "Bijou's Odyssey – Not Quite There Yet," [http://bijousodyssey.wordpress.com], the author is quite clear about the personal benefits of writing: (a) free therapy – "This blog is an outlet: the public can choose to read it or not, I can choose to discard useless comments"; (b) enlightenment – "I somehow feel I have the responsibility to work toward change in the adoption realm";

and (c) support – "The written word of blogging adoptees and parents who relinquished children continue to keep me going through the perplexity of search, reunion etc. It is nice to know I'm not the only people-pleasing, diplomatic reject-ee out there."

Pasupathi (2001) proposed a model linking the social construction of one's personal past to healthy adult development. She posited that conversational recounting with other people contributes to the social construction of autobiographical memory. She stated that "the social construction of the past in conversation opens the door for maintaining stability in one's identity or incorporating change" (p. 661). Further, she noted that reminiscence therapy for older adults is based on the assumption that recall and integration of past experiences contribute to successful aging. Research by Taft and Nehrke (1990) has shown that reminiscence and structured life review can contribute to the achievement of ego integrity in older adults. Systematic research exploring links between interventions such as writing and reminiscence with adoptive identity development for adolescents and young adults would be very timely.

Taken together, the work on therapeutic writing, narrative identity processing, and conversational recounting supports the use of techniques such as journaling, blogging, writing, talk therapy, open discussions with family and friends, and engagement with support groups as potential identity interventions for adoptees. Controlled studies are needed to establish the specific benefits experienced by those involved in adoption. Nevertheless, anecdotal accounts are strong, and the existing research is suggestive enough that such research would be worth conducting.

Finally, some interventions are specific to certain populations of adoptees. Between 1948 and 2006, over 400,000 children were brought to the United States for adoption from other countries (Selman, 2009). Many of these children were adopted by White parents across cultural and racial lines. In the early days of international adoption, the primary concern of parents was for the child's health and safety. As Western countries have gained more experience with international adoption, and as concerns about cultural identity have become more salient, parents have sought different ways of helping their children retain or develop some sense of the culture of their home country. Some parents have acknowledged that the act of adopting a child from another culture necessarily makes their family multicultural, opening up the need for the family to engage the child's cultural community in terms of contact with friends, experience with the food and language of the child's culture, and acquaintance with the child's cultural history (e.g., Carstens & Julia, 2000; Hanigan Scroggs & Heitfield, 2001; Huh & Reid, 2000).

In recent years, groups of adoptive parents have banded together to provide culturally relevant interventions for their children, such as culture camps and homeland tours. Culture camps typically bring together a number of children from the same culture, along with their families, for a concentrated period of time, to experience being with children who look like each other, eat foods from their culture, learn about cultural customs, and learn the language. There is some evidence that culture camps can improve children's sense of ethnic identity (e.g., Huh & Reid, 2000). However, adoptive parents report that some children are much more interested than others in activities such as culture camps and homeland tours.

As the population of international adoptees becomes older, many are turning to each other for ongoing support and opportunities to engage in identity work. In the past decade, adult Korean adoptees have formed informal and formal associations across the world and have organized periodic "gatherings" (McGinnis, 2009). The first was held in 1999 in Washington, DC, and hosted nearly 400 adults adopted between 1955 and 1985, with the explicit purpose of creating an opportunity for these pioneers in intercountry adoption to share their experiences (Freundlich & Lieberthal, 2000). Subsequent gatherings have grown larger and have met around the world. They have the obvious advantage of providing many opportunities for ongoing social construction of identity, both in structured workshops and in informal socialization with

peers. Since then, a number of organizations have been created by adults adopted from China, India, the Philippines, and Vietnam (to name a few), for the purpose of creating community and sharing experiences. These pioneers of intercountry adoption are also providing new information on those factors that may be helpful in forming healthy adoptive and ethnic identities (McGinnis, 2009).

Future Prospects and Directions

The story of identity development in adoptees begins with innate curiosity, is nurtured in family communication about adoption, and proceeds in rounds of exploration and consolidation that are driven by many factors, including the barriers and facilitators encountered along the way (Grotevant, 1987; Wrobel & Dillon, 2009). As we emphasized in our introduction, adopted persons have different amounts of knowledge and widely divergent experiences that serve as building blocks helping them construct and reconstruct their adoptive identities. Future research may reveal that understanding these differences in experiences among adoptees is critical to the study of adoptive identity.

For example, contrast two experiences drawn from the four worlds of adoption. Children placed for adoption at an early age benefit from hearing stories about their early adoption experiences, which can help shape their adoption narratives. Nevertheless, these children may lack specific information about their birth families and their pre-placement origin. On the other hand, children living with a succession of foster families may know the identity of birth family members, but lack specific information about their life experiences and, even after adoption, may not have access to adults who know and can tell stories of their early experiences, making it more difficult for these children to shape their sense of identity based on their past experience. Adoptive identity presents as a fascinating and challenging domain, because content varies from person to person while cultural and historical shifts in thinking about adoption strongly influence what people feel is appropriate to know or want to know.

Thus, although our understanding of adoptive identity has progressed over the past decade, this area is ripe for future development. As is true for many other areas of identity scholarship, new and better measures are needed. We developed a set of rating scales for coding adoptive identity narratives (Von Korff et al., 2007), but work remains in comparing this measure to other existing identity measures.

Further research is also needed in several other areas. First, we need further understanding of the role of family processes in adoptive identity development. Current work on family communication and the barriers and facilitators affecting curiosity and information seeking (e.g., Wrobel & Dillon, 2009; Wrobel, Grotevant, & Von Korff, 2009) in adoptees is very promising. Second, more research is needed at the intersection of adoptive and ethnic identities. Particularly for persons adopted across national or cultural lines, the issues of adoption and ethnicity are often difficult to separate. First person accounts often deal with the two issues as a package, and further theorizing about their intersection would be useful (e.g., Koh, 2008). Third, more research is needed to understand how adoptive identity development evolves over the life span. The middle adult years, often characterized by a reordering of priorities and goals in line with one's life purpose and meaning, may be a rich period in which to examine how adopted adults revisit or explore for the first time aspects of their adoptive identity. Finally, research could beneficially test the effectiveness of some of the interventions discussed above. At present, there is little systematic evidence about how such interventions work or when interventions would be warranted, especially given the differing experience of adoptees across the four worlds of adoption. We still have much to learn about the fascinating process of adoptive identity development and its nonlinear and lifelong nature.

Acknowledgments The authors gratefully acknowledge the adoptive parents, adopted adolescents, and birth mothers who participated in the longitudinal Minnesota-Texas Adoption Research Project and who have contributed significantly to our understanding of adoptive identity. Funding for the Minnesota-Texas Adoption Research Project has come from the National Institute of Child Health and Human Development (R01-HD-049859), National Science Foundation (BCS-0443590), William T. Grant Foundation (7146), Minnesota Agricultural Experiment Station, Office of Population Affairs of the US Department of Health and Human Services, and the Hogg Foundation for Mental Health. During the preparation of this chapter, both authors were supported by funds from the Rudd Family Foundation Chair in Psychology at the University of Massachusetts Amherst. Thanks also to Holly Grant, Bibiana Koh, Hollee McGinnis, Danila Musante, Di Samek, and Susan Krauss Whitbourne, who provided comments on the first draft of this chapter.

Note

1. Quotations are taken from identity interviews from the Minnesota-Texas Adoption Research Project, but are de-identified in order to ensure confidentiality.

References

Arnett, J. J. (2000). Emerging adulthood: A theory of development from the late teens through the twenties. *American Psychologist, 55*(5), 469–480.

Backhaus, K. A. (1984). Life books: Tool for working with children in placement. *Social Work, 29*, 551–554.

Bellelli, G. (1995). Knowing and labeling emotions: The role of sharing. In J. A. Russell, et al. (Eds.), *Everyday conceptions of emotions* (pp. 491–503). Dordrecht: Kluwer.

Bijou (2007, February, 19). Another ungrateful bastard. Message posted to http://bijousodyssey. wordpress.com/

Bohanek, J. G., Marin, K. A., Fivush, R., & Duke, M. P. (2006). Family narrative interaction and children's sense of self. *Family Process, 4*, 39–54.

Bosma, H. A. (1985) *Identity development in adolescence: Coping with commitments.* Unpublished doctoral dissertation, State University, Groningen, the Netherlands.

Bosma, H. A., & Kunnen, E. S. (2001). *Identity and emotion: Development through self-organization.* Cambridge, UK: Cambridge University Press.

Brodzinsky, D. M., Lang, R., & Smith, D. W. (1995). Parenting adopted children. In M. Bornstein (Ed.), *Handbook of parenting: Vol. 3. Status and social conditions of parenting* (pp. 209–232). Mahwah, NJ: Erlbaum.

Brodzinsky, D. M., Singer, L. M., & Braff, A. M. (1984). Children's understanding of adoption. *Child Development, 55*, 869–878.

Brown-Smith, N. (1998). Family secrets. *Journal of Family Issues, 19*, 20–42.

Bruner, J. (1990). *Acts of meaning.* Cambridge, MA: Harvard University Press.

Carp, E. W. (2004). *Adoption politics: Bastard Nation and Ballot Initiative 58.* Lawrence, KS: University Press of Kansas.

Carstens, C., & Julia, M. (2000). Ethnoracial awareness in intercountry adoption: US experiences. *International Social Work, 43*, 61–73.

Cooper, C. R. (1999). Multiple selves, multiple worlds: Cultural perspectives on individuality and connectedness in adolescent development. In A. Masten (Ed.), *Cultural processes in child development: Minnesota Symposium on Child Development* (pp. 25–57). Hillsdale, NJ: Erlbaum.

Côté, J. E., & Levine, C. G. (2002). *Identity formation, agency, and culture: A social psychological synthesis.* Mahwah, NJ: Erlbaum.

Dunbar, N., & Grotevant, H. D. (2004). Adoption narratives: The construction of adoptive identity during adolescence. In M. W. Pratt & B. H. Fiese (Eds.), *Family stories and the life course: Across time and generations* (pp. 135–162). Mahwah, NJ: Erlbaum.

Erikson, E. H. (1950/1963). *Childhood & society.* New York: W.W. Norton & Company.

Erikson, E. H. (1968). *Identity youth and crisis.* New York: W.W. Norton & Company.

Erikson, E. H. (1959, 1980). *Identity and the life cycle.* New York: W.W. Norton & Company.

Fiese, B. H., Sameroff, A. J., Grotevant, H. D., Wamboldt, F. S., Dickstein, S., & Fravel, D. L. (1999). The stories that families tell: Narrative coherence, narrative interaction, and relationship beliefs. *Monographs of the Society for Research in Child Development, 64*(2), Serial No. 257.

Finkler, K., Skrzynia, C., & Evans, J. P. (2003). The new genetics and consequences for family, kinship, medicine and medical genetics. *Social Science and Medicine, 57*, 403–412.

Fisher, F. (1973). *In search of Anna Fisher.* New York: Ballantine Books.

Fivush, R. (2001). Owning experience: The development of subjective perspective in autobiographical memory. In C. Moore & K. Lemmon (Eds.), *The self in time: Developmental perspectives* (pp. 35–52). Hillsdale, NJ: Erlbaum.

Freundlich, M., & Lieberthal, J. K. (2000). *The gathering of the first generation of adult Korean adoptees: Adoptees' perceptions of international adoption.* New York: Evan B. Donaldson Adoption Institute.

Goossens, L. (2001). Global versus domain-specific statuses in identity research: A comparison of two self-report measures. *Journal of Adolescence, 24*, 681–699.

Graafsma, T. L. G., Bosma, H. A., Grotevant, H. D., & deLevita, D. J. (1994). Identity and development: An interdisciplinary view. In H. A. Bosma, T. L. G. Graafsma, H. D. Grotevant, & D. J. deLevita (Eds.), *Identity and development: An interdisciplinary approach* (pp. 159–174). Thousand Oaks, CA: Sage.

Grotevant, H. D. (1987). Toward a process model of identity formation. *Journal of Adolescent Research, 2*, 203–222.

Grotevant, H. D. (1992). Assigned and chosen identity components: A process perspective on their integration. In G. R. Adams, R. Montemayor, & T. Gulotta (Eds.), *Advances in adolescent development* (Vol. 4, pp. 73–90). Newbury Park, CA: Sage.

Grotevant, H. D. (1993). The integrative nature of identity: Bringing the soloists to sing in the choir. In J. Kroger (Ed.), *Discussions on ego identity* (pp. 121–146). Hillsdale, NJ: Erlbaum.

Grotevant, H. D. (1997). Coming to terms with adoption: The construction of identity from adolescence into adulthood. *Adoption Quarterly, 1*, 3–27.

Grotevant, H. D. (1998). Adolescent development in family contexts. In W. Damon (Series Editor) & N. Eisenberg (Volume Editor), *Handbook of child psychology; Vol. 3: Social, emotional, and personality development* (5th ed.) (pp. 1097–1149). New York: Wiley.

Grotevant, H. D., & Cooper, C. R. (1981). Assessing adolescent identity in the areas of occupation, religion, politics, friendships, dating, and sex roles: Manual for administration and coding of the interview. *JSAS Catalog of Selected Documents in Psychology, 11*, 52 (MS. No. 2295).

Grotevant, H. D., & Cooper, C. R. (1998). Individuality and connectedness in adolescent development: Review and prospects for research on identity, relationships, and context. In E. Skoe & A. von der Lippe (Eds.), *Personality development in adolescence: A cross national and life span perspective* (pp. 3–37). London: Routledge.

Grotevant, H. D., Dunbar, N., Kohler, J., & Esau, A. M. L. (2000). Adoptive identity: How contexts within and beyond the family shape developmental pathways. *Family Relations, 49*, 379–387.

Grotevant, H. D., & McRoy, R. G. (1998). *Openness in adoption: Exploring family connections.* Thousand Oaks, CA: Sage.

Grotevant, H. D., Perry, Y., & McRoy, R. G. (2005). Openness in adoption: Outcomes for adolescents within their adoptive kinship networks. In D. Brodzinsky & J. Palacios (Eds.), *Psychological issues in adoption: Research and practice* (pp. 167–186). Westport, CT: Praeger.

Grotevant, H. D., Wrobel, G. M., Von Korff, L., Skinner, B., Newell, J., Friese, S., et al. (2007). Many faces of openness in adoption: Perspectives of adopted adolescents and their parents. *Adoption Quarterly, 10*(3–4), 79–101.

Habermas, T., & Bluck, S. (2000). Getting a life: The emergence of the life story in adolescence. *Psychological Bulletin, 126*, 748–769.

Hanigan Scroggs, P., & Heitfield, H. (2001). International adopters and their children: Birth culture ties. *Gender Issues, 19*, 3–30.

Haviland, J. M., & Kahlbaugh, P. (2004). Emotion and identity. In M. Lewis & J. M. Haviland-Jones (Eds.), *Handbook of emotions* (pp. 293–305). New York: Guilford.

Huh, N. S., & Reid, W. J. (2000). Intercountry, transracial adoption and ethnic identity: A Korean example. *International Social Work, 43*, 75–87.

Kaye, K. (1990). Acknowledgment or rejection of differences?. In D. M. Brodzinsky & M. D. Schechter (Eds.), *The psychology of adoption* (pp. 121–143). New York: Oxford University Press.

Kirk, D. H. (1981). *Adoptive kinship: A modern institution in need of reform*. Toronto, ON: Butterworth.

Koh, B. (2008, October). *Adoptive identity in adolescence: A conceptual process model*. Paper presented at Identity and the Adopted Teen: Surviving the Crucible of Adolescence, New York.

Lee, R. M. (2003). The transracial adoption paradox: History, research, and counseling implications of cultural socialization. *The Counseling Psychologist, 31*, 711–744.

Leon, I. G. (2002). Adoption losses; Naturally occurring or socially constructed. *Child Development, 73*, 652–663.

Lifton, B. J. (1975). *Twice born: Memoirs of an adopted daughter*. New York: Penguin.

Marcia, J. E. (2001). A commentary on Seth Schwartz's review of identity theory and research. *Identity, 1*, 59–76.

McAdams, D. P. (1985). *Power, intimacy, and the life story: Personological inquiries into identity*. New York: Guilford.

McAdams, D. P. (2001). The psychology of life stories. *Review of General Psychology, 5*, 100–122.

McGinnis, H. (2009). *Beyond culture camp: Promoting healthy identity formation in adoption*. New York: Evan B. Donaldson Adoption Institute.

McIntosh, P. (1988). White privilege: Unpacking the invisible backpack. http://www.uakron.edu/centers/conflict/docs/whitepriv.pdf

McLean, K. C., Pasupathi, M., & Pals, J. L. (2007). Selves creating stories creating selves: A process model of narrative self-development. *Personality and Social Psychology Review, 11*, 262–278.

McRoy, R. G., Lynch, C. J., Chanmugam, A., Madden, E., & Ayers-Lopez, S. (2009). Children from care CAN be adopted. In G. M. Wrobel & E. Neil (Eds.), *International advances in adoption research for practice* (pp. 97–118). Chichester, UK: Wiley-Blackwell.

Meeus, W. (1996). Studies on identity development in adolescence: An overview of research and some new data. *Journal of Youth and Adolescence, 25*, 569–598.

Meier, D. I. (1998). *Loss and reclaimed lives: Cultural identity and place in Korean American inter-country adoptees*. Unpublished doctoral dissertation. Department of Geography, University of Minnesota, Minneapolis, MN.

Meier, D. I. (1999). Cultural identity and place in adult Korean-American intercountry adoptees. *Adoption Quarterly, 3*(1), 15–48.

Morgan, R. (2008). *Late discovery: Identity shift and recovery*. Manuscript posted to "Are You Adopted? Are You Sure?" http://www.latediscovery.org/blog/

Muthén, B., & Muthén, L. (1998–2009). *Mplus version 5.1*. Los Angeles: Muthén & Muthén.

Neil, E. (2004). The "Contact after Adoption" study: Indirect contact and adoptive parents' communication about adoption. In E. Neil & D. Howe (Eds.), *Contact in adoption and permanent foster care: Research, theory and practice* (pp. 46–64). London: British Association for Adoption and Fostering.

Pals, J. L. (2006). The narrative identity processing of difficult life experiences: Pathways of personality development and positive self-transformation in adulthood. *Journal of Personality, 74*, 2–31.

Pasupathi, M. (2001). The social construction of the personal past and its implications for adult development. *Psychological Bulletin, 127*, 651–672.

Pasupathi, M., Alderman, K., & Shaw, D. (2007). Talking the talk: Collaborative remembering and self-perceived expertise. *Discourse Processes, 43*, 55–77.

Pasupathi, M., & Hoyt, T. (2009). The development of narrative identity in late adolescence and emergent adulthood: The continued importance of listeners. *Developmental Psychology, 45*, 558–574.

Pasupathi, M., Stallworth, L. M., & Murdoch, K. (1998). How what we tell becomes what we know: Listener effects on speakers' longterm memory for events. *Discourse Processes, 26*, 1–25.

Pennebaker, J. W. (1997). Writing about emotional experiences as a therapeutic process. *Psychological Science, 8*, 162–166.

Perry, Y. V. (2006). *Comparing: A grounded theory of adoptive mothers' lay beliefs about genetics*. Unpublished doctoral dissertation, University of Minnesota, St. Paul, MN.

Polkinghorne, D. (1988). *Narrative knowing and the human sciences*. Albany, NY: SUNY Press.

Reese, E. (2002). Social factors in the development of autobiographical memory: The state of the art. *Social Development, 11*, 124–142.

Register, C. (1991). *Are those kids really yours? American families with children adopted from other countries*. New York: Free Press.

Riessman, C. K. (1993). *Narrative analysis*. Thousand Oaks, CA: Sage.

Riley, D., & Meeks, J. (2006). *Beneath the mask: Understanding adopted teens*. Baltimore: C.A.S.E. Publishers.

Rimé, B. (1995). The social sharing of emotional experience as a source for the social knowledge of emotion. In J. A. Russell, J. M. Fernandez-Dols, A. S. R. Manstead, & J. C. Wellenkamp (Eds.), *Everyday conceptions of emotions. An introduction to the psychology, anthropology, and linguistics of emotion* (pp. 475–489). Dordrecht: Kluwer.

Rimé, B. (2007). Interpersonal emotional regulation. In J. Gross (Ed.), *Handbook of emotional regulation* (pp. 466–485). New York: Guilford.

Schneider, D. M. (1980). *American kinship: A cultural account*. Chicago: University of Chicago Press.

Selman, P. (2009). From Bucharest to Beijing: Changes in countries sending children for international adoption 1990 to 2006. In G. M. Wrobel & E. Neil (Eds.), *International advances in adoption research for practice* (pp. 41–70). Chichester, UK: Wiley-Blackwell.

Shiao, J. L., & Tuan, M. H. (2008). Korean adoptees and the social context of ethnic exploration. *American Journal of Sociology, 113*, 1023–1066.

Singer, J. A. (2004). Narrative identity and meaning making across the adult lifespan: An introduction. *Journal of Personality, 72*, 437–459.

Suter, E. A. (2008). Discursive negotiation of family identity: A study of U.S. families with adopted children from China. *Journal of Family Communication, 8*, 126–147.

Taft, L. B., & Nehrke, M. F. (1990). Reminiscence, life review, and ego integrity in nursing home residents. *International Journal of Aging and Human Development, 30*, 189–196.

Tieman, W., van der Ende, J., & Verhulst, F. C. (2008). Young adult international adoptees' search for birth parents. *Journal of Family Psychology, 22*, 678–687.

Von Korff, L. (2008). *Pathways to narrative adoptive identity formation in adolescence and emerging adulthood*. Unpublished doctoral dissertation, University of Minnesota, St. Paul, MN.

Von Korff, L., & Grotevant, H. D. (2007). [Latent profile analysis: Adolescent & emerging adult narrative adoptive identity] Unpublished raw data.

Von Korff, L., Grotevant, H. D., & Friese, S. (2007). *Manual for coding narrative adoptive identity in emerging adulthood*. Minnesota/Texas Adoption Research Project. St. Paul, MN: University of Minnesota.

Von Korff, L., Grotevant, H. D., Koh, B. D., & Samek, D. (2010). Adoptive mothers: Identity agents on the pathway to adoptive identity formation [Special Issue]. *Identity: An International Journal of Theory and Research, 10*, 122–137.

Wegar, K. (1997). *Adoption, identity, and kinship: The debate over sealed records*. New Haven, CT: Yale University Press.

Wrobel, G. M., & Dillon, K. (2009). Adopted adolescents: Who and what are they curious about?. In G. M. Wrobel & E. Neil (Eds.), *International advances in adoption research for practice* (pp. 217–244). Chichester, UK: Wiley-Blackwell.

Wrobel, G. M., Grotevant, H. D., & Von Korff, L. (2009, April). *Curiosity about birthparents in emerging adulthood: Context, motivation and behavior*. In K. Freeark & K. L. Rosenblum (chairs), Adoptive families: Processes that promote well-being and family connections. Symposium presented at the meeting of the Society for Research in Child Development, Denver, CO.

Wrobel, G. M., Hendrickson, Z., & Grotevant, H. D. (2006). Adoption. In G. G. Bear & K. M. Minke (Eds.), *Children's needs III: Development, prevention, and intervention* (pp. 675–688). Bethesda, MD: National Association of School Psychologists.

Wrobel, G. M., Kohler, J. K., Grotevant, H. D., & McRoy, R. G. (2003). The Family Adoption Communication (FAC) Model: Identifying pathways of adoption-related communication. *Adoption Quarterly, 7*(2), 53–84.

Gender Identity Development

Kay Bussey

Abstract

Gender features strongly in most societies and is a significant aspect of self-definition for most people. Following a brief description of views on gender identity from the perspectives of humanistic social science, sociology, and psychology, this chapter provides an analysis of gender identity development from the perspective of social cognitive theory. Social cognitive theory describes how gender conceptions are developed and transformed across the life span. Through a combination of personal and sociostructural factors, people construct self-conceptions of gender, which influence gender-related conduct through the motivational and self-regulatory processes associated with gender identity. A broad range of social influences including parents, peers, the media, and other social systems contribute to the development of gender conceptions and to the self-regulatory processes linked to them. However, people are not simply products of the varying social systems that impinge on them. Rather, it is shown that people contribute to transforming their gender conceptions and bringing about social change. Gender roles are changing through people's actions which affect the social subsystems that influence the development and transformation of gender identity.

Gender is fundamental to the organization of society. From the moment of birth, children's gender is an important aspect of their lives in that it influences how parents treat them, the names they are given, and how they are dressed. As children age, other adults and peers interact differently with children depending on their gender (Bussey & Bandura, 1999; Leaper & Friedman, 2007; Raley & Bianchi, 2006). The educational system and the media further contribute to this differentiation (Buchmann, DiPrete, & McDaniel, 2008; Gill, 2007). From these gendered experiences, gender stereotypes are learned and gender identity develops and transforms over the life course.

The view of gender identity presented in this chapter is based on social cognitive theory where gender identity is viewed as part of a person's

K. Bussey (✉)
Department of Psychology, Macquarie University, Sydney, NSW, Australia
e-mail: kay.bussey@mq.edu.au

S.J. Schwartz et al. (eds.), *Handbook of Identity Theory and Research*, DOI 10.1007/978-1-4419-7988-9_25, © Springer Science+Business Media, LLC 2011 broader concept of his or her personal identity (Bussey & Bandura, 1999). From this perspective, identity formation is not fixed at any point in time, but rather it is an ongoing process that transforms over the life course. Before presenting an analysis of gender identity development based on this theoretical perspective, a brief analysis of the major alternative approaches to gender identity is provided. Following this, the key tenets of social cognitive theory are presented. It is shown that a significant part of the self-conception that people develop relates to their gender. Importantly, gender identity is not just a personal matter, but there is a social aspect as well. The social influences that contribute to the development and maintenance of gender identity are considered. Finally, as gender roles are undergoing extensive change, the implications for gender identity are discussed.

Theoretical Perspectives

Before briefly examining the different theoretical perspectives, a comment about the terminology adopted in this chapter is warranted. There has been extensive discussion about the use of the terms "sex" and "gender" (Deaux, 1993; Segal, 2010; West & Zimmerman, 1987). Sex has typically been used when referring to biologically based differences between males and females and gender when referring to socially influenced differences. It is increasingly apparent, however, that such a clear-cut distinction is not supported by the evidence. Many of the differences between men and women are the product of both biological and social factors. Also, it has been shown that even differences which manifest early in development and which are often assumed to be biologically determined (e.g., spatial ability) can be modified through experience and training (Barnett & Rivers, 2004; Conner, Schackman, & Serbin, 1978). Therefore, in this chapter, the more inclusive term, gender, is used without any assumption as to whether differences between males and females are solely attributable to biological or social factors. Further, it will become apparent from the ensuing discussion

of the different theoretical approaches to gender identity that there is no commonly agreed definition of gender identity.

There are several major theoretical approaches to the conceptualization of gender identity. Some focus on the individual characteristics of the person, whereas others focus on social roles and social structures. Some approaches only consider the acquisition of gender identity during the early childhood years, whereas others focus mainly on adulthood. After presenting these approaches, a comprehensive social cognitive theory model of gender identity will be presented which spans the life course, taking into account both personal and social factors.

Humanistic Social Science and Sociological Perspectives

There has been considerable discussion within the humanistic social science disciplines about gender identity, or masculinities and femininities as it is sometimes described in this literature (Connell, 1995; Schrock & Schwalbe, 2009; Segal, 2010). Scholars from these disciplines, however, do not speak with a united voice. For some, gender differences are the product of a gendered division of labor and sociostructural practices that support status and power differences. In West and Zimmerman's (1987) view of "doing gender," gender differences are a result of what one does, not what one is. It is posited that gender differences are predicated on the differing power relations between the genders rather than on nat ural preordained differences. The social arrangements that support these gender differences—for example, occupational stratification and segregation with women mainly assuming lower status positions—are seen as legitimating natural explanations for these differences. This is quite a departure from earlier accounts in which masculinity and femininity were viewed as complementary. Rather than unequal power relations between men and women, the division of labor was believed to give rise to this complementarity, particularly in the family, where the husband-father adopted the instrumental role and the wife-mother adopted the expressive role (Parsons & Bales, 1955).

Feminist scholars have long debated gender differences and gender identity. Most cultural feminists focus on empowering women by valuing their positive qualities such as nurturing, caring, and cooperation (Worrell, 1996). Many radical feminists support this stance, but also posit that a change in societal structures, particularly in the patriarchal family, is needed to reduce the major source of domination and oppression (Shelton & Agger, 1993). Increasingly, however, research demonstrating gender similarities is at odds with a strict mapping of masculinity to males and femininity to females. In addition to the similarities between men and women, there are great differences among men and among women, depending on their socioeconomic status, ethnicity, and education. Acknowledging this, gender theorists recognize the diversity within masculine and feminine identities while questioning the biological underpinnings of gender differences. Butler takes these views further in her claim that: "There is no gender identity behind the expressions of gender; that identity is performatively constituted by the very 'expressions' that are said to be its results" (Butler, 1990, p. 25). It is argued that not all people of the same-gender category are alike. By simply categorizing people on the basis of gender, it is all too easy to legitimize the link between gender and biological sex.

Psychological Perspectives

In contrast with the humanistic focus on debating how gender identities should be conceptualized and how they are embedded in societal structures, psychological perspectives have tended to focus more on the processes by which individuals relate to whichever conceptions of gender are prevailing in their social contexts—including how individuals come to see themselves in gender-differentiated ways and adopt gender-differentiated behaviors in the first place. In Kohlberg's (1966) developmental theory, gender identity is ascribed a key role in the gender development process. This approach to gender identity centers on children's learning to gender-label themselves and others, and understanding that this aspect of the self persists over time and across different situations. Kohlberg's theory posits that gender constancy, which is the understanding that gender identity is stable and does not change over time and in different situations, provides the motivation to engage in gender-stereotypic behavior. As most children acquire gender constancy understanding between the ages of 5 and 7 years, Kohlberg's perspective assumes there is little or no variability in gender identity beyond this age. However, if this fixed gender identity is the major motivator guiding enactment of gendered behavior, it is difficult to account for the variation in such behavior adopted by older children and adults. Further, evidence for the role of gender constancy in the enactment of gendered behaviors and preferences in the first few years of life is lacking. In fact, children develop preferences for and behave in ways similar to their own gender well before they have achieved gender constancy (Bussey & Bandura, 1999; Ruble, Martin, & Berenbaum, 2006).

Also focusing on the childhood years is Martin and Halverson's (1981) gender schema theory approach. Gender identity in this theory refers to children labeling themselves and others as a boy or a girl. This approach posits that gender labeling enables children to develop schemas that are then used to motivate them to engage in similar activities and pursuits to those of their gender (Martin, Ruble, & Szkrybalo, 2002). To attain cognitive consistency, children are motivated to behave in ways compatible with gender stereotypes. This theory can more ably account for the variability in the adoption of gender roles as the content and reliance on gender schemas varies across children and contexts. In this approach, gender schemas are accorded most significance in guiding behavior, and although gender identity may guide the development of gender schemas, it does not seem to play as strong a role in subsequent gender development.

In another version of gender schema theory (Bem, 1981), greater emphasis is accorded to individual variability in the reliance on gender schemas rather than on factors associated with how they are developed. In this approach, gender identity refers to a person's masculinity or femininity as measured by self-descriptive personality traits. Traits regarded as masculine include instrumental characteristics such as independence and dominance and those regarded as feminine include characteristics such as nurturance and being sensitive to the needs of others. People are designated as gender schematic if they score high on one scale (either masculinity or femininity) and low on the other. Although instrumentality and expressivity are differentially related to men and women in that men typically score higher than women on instrumentality and women typically score higher than men on expressivity, Spence (1984; Spence & Buckner, 1995) has questioned whether instrumentality and expressivity measure masculinity and femininity, respectively. Spence along with others contends that masculinity and femininity are difficult to define while noting that lay people's conceptions of these terms extend beyond a consideration of personality traits (Deaux & Lewis, 1984; Helgeson, 1994; Spence & Buckner, 1995). In studies involving lay people, gender differences in social roles, occupations, physical appearance, interests, and biological characteristics are all deemed part of masculinity and femininity. It therefore seems that Bem's measure is more an assessment of self-perceived gender-related personality attributes than a measure of masculinity and femininity or gender identity.

Other approaches, developed with adults, have focused on identification with social categories. Social identity theory (Tajfel & Turner, 1979; see Spears, Chapter 9, this volume) posits that assignment to a group, even on an arbitrary basis, produces allegiance to the group. People's perceptions of in-group similarities and out-group differences serve to promote in-group identification and favoritism. In the sphere of gender relations, there is considerable support for these processes with adults and some support for them with children. Powlishta (1995) found that boys and girls rated themselves as more similar to others of their gender and that girls showed higher

levels of in-group favoritism than did boys. On the other hand, Parish and Bryant (1978) found that adolescent boys favored the other gender more than they favored their own gender.

Self-categorization theory (Turner, Hogg, Oakes, Reicher, & Wetherell, 1987) developed from the social identity theory approach similarly proposes that in-group similarities are highlighted and differences from the out-group are maximized. However, self-categorization theory adopts a more dynamic approach by positing that self-categorization is situation-dependent. For example, when age is salient, children are expected to self-categorize as children rather than as adults; when gender is salient, children are expected to self-categorize as either boys or girls. Consistent with this approach, Grace, David, and Ryan (2008) showed that children emulated models of the same gender when gender was made salient, and that they emulated models of the same age when age was made salient. This approach invests considerable power in the situation to guide individuals' preferences and behavior. Typically, however, people do not adopt all of the characteristics of the group with whom they identify. From the self-categorization perspective, it is unclear how people decide which aspects of the identified group they will adopt.

Other approaches have emphasized the multidimensionality of identification with a group, such as with ethnicity, race, or gender. In the approach taken by Ashmore, Deaux, and McLaughlin-Volpe (2004), for example, collective identity rather than social identity is used to emphasize an individual's identification with a particular group. Apart from believing that one shares membership with others in a group or category, this approach is also predicated on the notion that cognitive beliefs are jointly held by members of a group. Ashmore et al. (2004) specified a number of elements of collective identification: self-categorization, evaluation, importance, attachment, sense of independence, social embeddedness, behavioral involvement, and content and meaning. Although this is a comprehensive approach which draws on many different theories of identity, there is no consensus on the common elements associated with any collective identity. Additionally, this approach is not informative about developmental processes and how and under what circumstances identities may transform. It is a static appraisal of a person's current endorsement of the elements that are believed to comprise collective identification.

In keeping with a multidimensional approach to gender identity, Egan and Perry (2001) showed empirically that various components of gender identity—knowledge of one's gender, gender compatibility (self-perceptions of gender typicality and feeling contented with one's gender), felt pressure (feeling pressured from others to conform to gender stereotypes), and intergroup bias (believing that one's own gender is superior to the other)—were not strongly related to each other. This approach shares some similarity with the multidimensional approach of Ashmore et al. (2004) in that children rated their self-perceptions on a variety of dimensions. For example, the gender typicality dimension refers to children's perceived similarity to those of their own gender. Children's score on this dimension was one of the stronger indicators of their psychological adjustment. Children who believed they were more similar to their own gender fared better on a number of adjustment indices. This finding has been replicated cross-culturally in Mainland China (Yu & Xie, 2010). This multidimensional approach of Egan and Perry, despite being tested with children, pays little attention to the developmental antecedents of gender identity.

Although a thorough evaluation of these different approaches to gender identity is beyond the scope of this chapter, it is clear from the analysis of the developmental theories that more attention needs to be given to gender identity beyond the early childhood years. It is also evident that greater consideration of developmental processes is required from the social identity and self-categorization approaches. Further, Ashmore et al. (2004) also noted that it is important for the multidimensional approach to consider the variability of gender identity across time and situation. Global ratings of each of the elements of the collective category, such as gender typicality, provide little indication of their importance in different contexts. At the other end of the spectrum, although the humanistic social science and sociological approaches provide important insights into the sociostructural influences on gender identity, they focus less on the personal determinants of gender identity.

Social Cognitive Theory

From the social cognitive theory perspective, identity formation is an important aspect of human development, as it plays a central role in human agency (Bandura, 2008). People develop conceptions of themselves from their experiences, including transactions with others, and their self-reflections. Gender identity is seen as one of the most pervasive and enduring aspects of personal and social identity. From the moment of birth, interactions with others are influenced by gender. Therefore, it is hardly surprising that gender identity has an important influence on self-conceptions and life courses. Gender identity, like other aspects of identity, is not just an intrapsychic matter (see Vignoles, Schwartz, & Luyckx, Chapter 1, this volume). Social factors contribute to the way people are treated and how they respond. Gender is an important determinant of social interaction in most societies, although its influence is stronger in some societies than in others (Whiting & Edwards, 1988). The stronger its influence, the more people develop goals and aspirations based on gender and regulate their behavior according to their gender.

From this viewpoint, gender identity is part of the broader conception of the self, which in turn represents a central feature of human functioning. Moreover, gender identity development is not simply understood as an unfolding of biological dictates, nor is it under the exclusive influence of environmental forces. Rather, it is posited that individuals direct their life paths through their capacity for forethought and cognitive self-regulation. They not only choose their life course, but they *create* environments to attain their life goals within the existing sociostructural opportunities and constraints. Individuals actively construct their identity during their early years and continue to develop and transform their identity across their life span.

The social cognitive view differs from most developmental theories in which gender identity has been primarily associated with children's knowledge of their biological sex (Powlishta, Sen, Serbin, Poulin-Dubois, & Eichstedt, 2001). Most of these theories have taken a biologically deterministic view by assuming that, once self-labeling as a boy or a girl occurs, children's understanding of gender links the biological and the psychological. It is postulated that "children's recognition of their biological sex is almost invariably accompanied by the development of what has been called gender identity, a basic existential sense and acceptance of themselves as male or female" (Spence & Buckner, 1995, p. 115).

In social cognitive theory it is posited that, although one's biological sex is fixed from birth, gender identity does not follow a linear and predictable age-related pattern based on biological assignation and age-related cognitions linked to one's biological sex. Gender identity is viewed as multifaceted rather than as monolithic; it varies across individuals and across the life span within a given individual. Gender identity develops not only from self-knowledge of one's biological sex, but also from an interplay between personal and social factors. The physical differentiation between the genders is amplified in most cultures by gender-differentiated dress and activities and the associated gender-differentiated social consequences (Whiting & Edwards, 1988). This differentiation heightens gender distinctions and contributes to the important role of gender in the construction of one's identity.

Gender identity involves the self-representation of a gendered self, mediated by self-regulatory processes. Gender identity is informed by knowledge of one's biological sex and of the beliefs associated with gender, how one is perceived and treated by others depending on one's gender, and an understanding of the collective basis of gender. The self-regulatory processes associated

with gender enable people to regulate their behavior in different contexts. The agentic self-representation of gender includes personal standards related to gender, the appraisal of one's capabilities based on one's gender, long-term goals and aspirations based on gender, positive and negative outcome expectations for life choices based on gender, and the actual and perceived environmental constraints and opportunities.

From this view, gender identity involves much more than simply acquiring knowledge about one's own gender and about the other gender at an early age. Rather, from the social cognitive theory perspective, gender identity is conceptualized as an ongoing process that may change across the life span and as societal views about gender change. What it means to be highly identified with one's gender varies across the life span. Also, while two people may equally identify with their gender, the pattern of gender-related behaviors they display may be quite different.

In the agentic social cognitive view, individuals develop their gender identity from personal and social influences. These influences interact bi-directionally in a model of reciprocal interaction affecting, as well as being affected by, gender-related conduct. In the model of triadic reciprocal causation (Bandura, 1986; Bussey & Bandura, 1999), *personal*, *behavioral*, and *environmental* factors operate as interacting determinants influencing each other bi-directionally. The *personal* contribution includes biological proclivities, self-conceptions, goals, behavioral and judgmental standards, and self-regulatory processes associated with gender identity; the *environmental* contribution refers to the broad array of social influences such as parental and peer influences, the media, educational and occupational systems that are encountered daily and that impact on gender identity; *behavior* refers to activity patterns that are gender-related. In this model of triadic causation there is no fixed pattern of reciprocal interaction. Personal factors, for example, can influence the environment just by their physical presence. A person's gender is sufficient to influence others' interaction with her/him and the opportunities s/he is afforded in life. The contribution of each of the components depends on the activities, situations, sociostructural constraints, and opportunities involved. When societal conditions dictate strong adherence to gender roles, there is little leeway for personal factors, such as gender identity, to influence choice of activities and lifestyle. The relative strength of each of the components of the triadic model is expected to vary over time, across situational circumstances (e.g., cultural contexts), and across activity domains.

Currently, particularly in Western countries, gender roles are undergoing significant change (Segal, 2010; Twenge, 1997). Men are becoming increasingly involved in the care of young children, from pushing strollers to changing diapers, something that was a rarity a few decades ago. Young girls are eschewing dolls in favor of electronic games and women are heading up multinational corporations and assuming high political office in greater numbers. The social changes underway are transforming the fixed, traditional notions of masculinity and femininity grounded in a rigid conception of gender roles. Although gender differentiation remains important in most societies, the expression of gender roles has changed remarkably over the past several decades. Amidst such changing gender roles, the influence of gender identity in daily life varies depending on the context and on the significance of gender identity in a person's life.

In the following sections, an analysis of the development of gender identity and its regulation is presented. Once children are knowledgeable of their own and others' gender, gender identity is shown to regulate gender-related activities through three main sociocognitive processes: outcome expectations related to gendered conduct, self-evaluative standards, and self-efficacy beliefs. As will be shown later, three modes of social influence—modeling, enactive experience, and direct tuition—affect the development of not only gender conceptions and competencies but also the three major sociocognitive regulators of gendered conduct.

Acquiring and Understanding of Gender Conceptions

Before infants can demonstrate awareness of their own gender, they gain considerable knowledge about gender and begin to display traditional gender-related preferences. Adults treat infants quite differently based on their gender (Leaper, 2002). These gendered transactions experienced by the infant provide the setting for the emergence of gender identity.

During the first year, infants can discriminate between male and female faces (Cornell, 1974; Fagan & Singer, 1979; Leinbach & Fagot, 1993) and between male and female voices (Miller, 1983; Miller, Younger, & Morse, 1982). They also show the emergence of intermodal gender knowledge, that is, infants are able to associate male and female faces with male and female voices, respectively (Poulin-Dubois, Serbin, Kenyon, & Derbyshire, 1994).

In the second year, children begin to show a preference for activities and objects stereotypically related to their gender (Caldera, Huston, & O'Brien, 1989; O'Brien & Huston, 1985; Roopnarine, 1986). Starting from about 18 months, both boys and girls look longer at gender-stereotypical objects associated with their own gender than at objects stereotypically associated with the other gender (Serbin, Poulin-Dubois, Colburne, Sen, & Eichstedt, 2001).

By 3 years of age, most children have some awareness of gender stereotypes (Kuhn, Nash, & Brucken, 1978; Serbin, Poulin-Dubois, & Eichstedt, 2002; Weinraub et al., 1984). Poulin-Dubois, Serbin, Eichstedt, Sen, and Beissel (2002) found that girls demonstrated stereotype knowledge earlier than did boys. In particular, by 24 months girls were aware of the association between gender-stereotypical household activities and the gender of the person who characteristically performs such activities. Boys, however, did not demonstrate such knowledge until 31 months—and then only for male stereotyped activities.

Although infants can discriminate between the two sexes during the first year and by the second year show gender-stereotypic preferences in that they look more at objects linked to their own than the other gender, it seems unlikely that knowledge of gender stereotypes is guiding their gender preferences. In the study by Serbin et al. (2001), both boys and girls of 18 months preferred to look at activities associated with their own gender. However, only girls of 18 and 24 months formed associations between a person's gender category and gender-stereotypical objects. That is, after seeing a male-related object, they looked more at the male than at the female face and after seeing a female-related object they looked more at the female than at the male face. Boys even as old as 24 months did not show any evidence of associating gender categories and gender-stereotypical objects, even though they preferred to look at objects associated with their own gender. This suggests that the preference for same-gender-stereotypical objects is more the result of parents providing their infants with same-gender-stereotypical toys and encouraging their use than this preference being guided by infants' cognitive categorization of the gender association of the preferred object. Parents respond approvingly toward their children when they engage in same-gender-stereotypical activities and disapprovingly when they engage in activities stereotypically related to the other gender (Caldera et al., 1989; Fagot, Leinbach, & O'Boyle, 1992; Leaper & Friedman, 2007). There is also stronger disapproval by parents of cross-gendered conduct by boys than by girls (Sandnabba & Ahlberg, 1999). This is mirrored by boys' stronger preference for same-gender activities than is evident for girls (Blakemore, LaRue, & Olejnik, 1979). This asymmetry in children's gender preferences is more consistent with an asymmetry in social influences than with an asymmetry in gender knowledge. The social pressures for gender conformity are stronger for boys than they are for girls; however, girls are more knowledgeable of the gender association of the activities than are boys (Serbin et al., 2002).

Thus, as argued by Bussey and Bandura (1999), children choose activities associated with gender stereotypes before they have a conception of their own gender or are even knowledgeable about the gender stereotypes. Once they have developed a conception of their own gender, however, they are increasingly able to self-regulate their behavior on this basis. It is shown in the following section that the emergence of gender identity is a gradual process and that there is no automatic link between gender identity and the enactment of gender-related activities. Rather, in the social cognitive agentic view of gender identity, gender-related conduct is initially regulated by anticipated outcomes of how significant others are expected to react to varying displays of gendered conduct. During the course of development, regulatory control increasingly shifts to self-regulatory control—guided by conceptions of one's capability to engage in the activity (self-efficacy) and self-reactions to one's gendered conduct.

The Development of Gender Identity and Its Regulatory Control

It takes time for children to develop knowledge of their gender. As described above, children gain considerable gender-related knowledge before this occurs. They prefer activities that are associated with their gender and they develop substantial knowledge of gender stereotypes. Of course, children's ability to label their own gender and that of others is of great importance in the process of developing gender identity.

The emergence of gender identity begins once infants are able to recognize themselves. This happens at about 18 months (Lewis & Brooks-Gunn, 1979). The acquisition of language skills further heightens the salience of gender. Children first develop knowledge of gender labels for adults before they develop them for children. At 18 months, when girls but not boys, heard the word "man" they looked longer at a photograph of a man than of a woman and when they heard the word "lady," they looked longer at a photograph of a woman than of a man. Although boys and girls of this age looked longer at a boy face when they heard the word "boy," they did not look longer at a girl's face when they heard the word "girl" (Poulin-Dubois, Serbin, & Derbyshire, 1998). Leinbach and Fagot (1986) found that by 24 months, most children could discriminate the gender labels for boys and girls by pointing to appropriate photographs.

Most research on gender labeling has assessed children's gender labeling of others or used a composite assessment of their gender labeling of self and other without differentiating between the two types of labeling (Kohlberg, 1966; Ruble et al., 2006). In a study of the emergence of gender labeling, Zosuls et al. (2009) assessed children's self and other gender labeling from mothers' diaries of their child's language development. They found that a small percentage of children, mainly girls, self-labeled their gender by 21 months. However, children showed some evidence of gendered play at 17 months—before they had demonstrated gender self-labeling. In Thompson's (1975) classic study of the emergence of gender understanding, the focus was not just on self-labeling, but also on children's ability to categorize themselves on the basis of gender by sorting and labeling their own and others' photographs. Most children between 24 and 26 months did not consistently sort their own photograph on the basis of gender, although they were able to associate gender-stereotypic activities with pictures of males and females. Thus, children's knowledge of gender stereotypes was more advanced than their gender self-categorization. By 36 months, most children could label others' gender, self-categorize their own gender, and were aware of gender-role stereotypes. However, knowledge of gender stereotypes was unrelated to children's ability to classify their own gender category.

From the social cognitive theory perspective, gender identity involves more than learning to gender-label self and others. It is part of the broader emerging conception of self that occurs during the first 2 years of life (Bandura, 2008). During these years, infants develop a personal sense of agency through enabling strategies provided particularly by parents. Through intentional guidance and the provision of tasks that allow infants to produce effects through actions and to master tasks on their own, infants develop a sense of personhood. As we will see later, children's gender is one of the most important influences on the way parents treat them. Thus, the construction of gender identity is not just a personal process, but also a social process involving not only parents but a range of social influences including the media, peers, teachers, and others. In the early years, however, parental influence is paramount. Parents highlight their son's and daughter's names and treat them as distinct persons; they also verbally label their child's gender and link activities with that gender. Not only do parents contribute to their children learning about their gender, but they underscore its importance in the child's life.

The broadening understanding of gender from the personal to the collective basis provides children with a social connection to other members of their gender. By their third year, children begin to form into groups with children of their own gender (Maccoby, 1998). Increasingly, over the childhood years, gender segregation characterizes children's groups and is an important arena in which children acquire gender-related skills and concepts. The marked gender segregation that occurs in peer interactions underscores the emphasis placed on gender in most societies. The more time that children spend in gender-segregated peer interaction, the more gender-typed they become, and the more they anticipate positive social outcomes for gender-stereotypic conduct (Martin & Fabes, 2001).

Further testimony to children's understanding of the collective aspects of their gender is their belief that other members of their gender share certain attributes and have similar preferences as their own and experience the same consequences for the same gender-related behavior as they do (Bauer & Coyne, 1997; Gelman, Collman, & Maccoby, 1986). From about 3 years of age, children begin to realize that they are treated in similar ways to others of their gender (Bussey & Bandura, 1992). By observing how others respond to members of their own gender, children are able to anticipate how others would respond to them. Children soon realize that the same outcomes are likely to happen to them as have happened to other members of their gender for performing the same behavior (Bussey & Bandura, 1984).

The increasing gender segregation that typically occurs over the middle-school years serves to highlight further the likely outcomes for particular behaviors associated with one's gender. As noted by Bigler, Brown, and Markell (2001), for a social category to take on personal importance for children, it needs to be both perceptually salient and functionally significant. Gender, as we have seen, is not only a perceptually salient category but is also associated with important social consequences. Indeed, the social consequences associated with gender are pervasive (see Bussey & Bandura, 1999). Hence, it is not surprising that gender is viewed as one of the more enduring and central categorizations that people make (Deaux & Stewart, 2001).

Gender categories, however, are not monolithic entities; not all females are the same and not all males are the same. Although the realization of the collective basis of gender is important, there is variability in the extent to which individuals are similar to others of their gender. There are not two distinct human groups of males and females with no overlapping characteristics. The actual differences between the genders in many areas of functioning are small and have been diminishing over the past two decades (Hyde, Lindberg, Linn, Ellis, & Williams, 2008). In fact, the degree of overlap between the genders in their cognitive, social, and psychological functioning is almost as great as the variability between the groups (Barnett & Rivers, 2004). For example, although on average men marginally outperform women on quantitative tasks, in fact, many women score higher than men and many men score lower than women on these tasks. The commonality in many of the behaviors performed by males and females becomes increasingly evident to children as they age and are exposed to varying social experiences. They realize that the categories of male and female are not fixed entities such that all males behave in one way and all females behave in another way. Not all girls or boys look the same; they vary in physical appearance such as hair color, skin color, height, and many other personal characteristics such as whether they are funny or aggressive. Children learn that there is wide variation

among those who are categorized as the same gender.

For some children, belonging to a gender category will take on more significance than for other children. From the social cognitive theory perspective, gender is not expected to be as central to the identity of some children as it is for others. The centrality of children's gender identity will depend on the extent to which they anticipate approval from others and anticipate feelings of pride for behaving in ways similar to those of their gender, and on the extent to which they believe they are capable of undertaking activities performed by others of their gender, all of which may vary in different contexts. This is different from other approaches where people make global ratings of the centrality of a collective category, such as gender, for themselves, without reference to specific contexts (Ashmore et al., 2004).

Therefore, despite most people's awareness of their gender, there is considerable variation in the extent to which their gender is central to their identity and in the extent to which they behave in gendered ways. Children and adults do not adopt all aspects of behavior associated with their gender category. Apart from the differentiation across individuals at a given point in time, there is also variation within individuals across the life course (Priess, Lindberg, & Hyde, 2009). This variation is due, in part, to the extent to which people exercise self-regulatory processes associated with gender identity, their gender-related goals, and the different social contexts that they choose and those in which they find themselves.

From the social cognitive theory perspective, variation in the influence of gender identity on gendered conduct is linked to the exercise of personal influence operating through self-regulatory processes. People develop self-standards for conduct along gender lines, they appraise their capabilities for different pursuits depending on the gender-relatedness of the pursuit, and they anticipate positive and negative outcomes for courses of action depending on the gender linkage of the behavior. Of course, the gender linkage of various pursuits and activities varies at different historical times and in different cultures. For example, in most Western societies women are regarded as more emotionally expressive than men. However, in Iran, a Middle Eastern culture, the reverse is true: men are regarded as more emotionally expressive than women (Epstein, 1997). As already stated, once children begin to self-regulate their gendered conduct, this is initially based on anticipated social sanctions, but later it is increasingly based on anticipated self-sanctions and self-efficacy beliefs. By bringing to bear such contextually informed sociocognitive processes the expression of gender identity varies for different people in different situations. The more that these processes are engaged, the greater the extent to which gender identity is expected to influence gender-related conduct.

Self-Regulation Based on Gender

Gender-related social sanctions. In most societies, gender-differentiated behavior is heavily socially sanctioned. Males and females are treated differently when they perform the same activities. Consequently, early in the course of development, children begin to anticipate social outcomes, such as approval and disapproval, for performing certain activities depending on their gender (Bussey & Bandura, 1992). These anticipatory outcomes are constructed from the evaluative social outcomes such as praise and criticism that they experience, from what they are told about the likely outcomes, and from observing the outcomes that others receive from parents, peers, and the media. Parents, for example, emphasize the importance of the gender category by explicitly stating the anticipated consequences based on gender, "Don't do that. Other people will laugh because it is for girls."

Children's development of anticipated outcomes is further broadened once they know their gender and that of others and realize that they share similar outcomes for the same behavior with other members of their gender and different outcomes from those received by the other gender. Children learn that the same activity performed by a girl may lead to approval but disapproval if it is performed by a boy.

Social consequences not only convey information about the likely outcomes of courses of action, but they provide the motivational incentives for choosing particular courses of action (Bandura, 1986; Bussey & Bandura, 1999). Such anticipatory outcomes provide the motivation to enact gendered conduct. In particular, when children realize that they belong to a larger social group of same-gendered people and that there are pervasive consequences linked to gender, their gender takes on special significance. Consequently, the more that children experience social consequences for gender-related conduct, the more likely that their gender will influence the extent to which they anticipate social outcomes such as approval and praise for gender-related conduct. This is more the case for boys, as fathers are especially likely to inform their sons of the anticipated outcomes of their behavior based on their gender (Raag & Rackliff, 1998) and children sanction boys more than girls for engaging in activities associated with the other gender (Blakemore, 2003). The more differentiation there is between the genders within a given context or society, the more the social consequences for activities and pursuits differ by gender and the more likely that gender identity provides the basis for the regulation of conduct and activities.

Gender self-sanctions. During the course of development, children's gendered conduct increasingly becomes regulated by self-sanctions, based on personal standards (Bussey & Bandura, 1992). However, although self-sanctions take on increasing significance, social sanctions remain important regulators across the life span. Once personal standards are developed, they provide the guidance for gender-related conduct; anticipatory self-sanctions, such as self-approval and self-criticism, provide the motivation. That is, anticipatory self-sanctions motivate the alignment of one's conduct with one's standards. Anticipation of self-approval for same-gender-related activities and anticipatory self-criticism for other-gender-related activities keep one's gendered conduct in line with personal standards.

Although most children are raised in traditional families and societies, in a world of changing gender roles, there is greater possibility for variation in the self-regulation of gender-related conduct. For some individuals, gender has less influence on the development of their self-conceptions than it has for others. Among those individuals for whom gender identity is central, self-regulatory processes are more pervasively embedded in the gender domain. From the social cognitive theory perspective, self-regulation involves three main components: self-monitoring, self-judgment of behavior based on personal standards, and self-evaluation (Bandura, 1986; Bussey & Bandura, 1999).

Self-monitoring is the first step in the exercise of self-influence. As children become aware of the considerable social significance associated with gender, they increasingly monitor their behavior on this basis (Serbin & Sprafkin, 1986). As we will see, the social significance of gender is conveyed by multiple social influences including parents, peers, and the media. Because boys are more heavily sanctioned than girls for not conforming to gender-stereotypic conduct, they are more likely than girls to monitor their behavior on the basis of gender. Boys have an added incentive to monitor their behavior on the basis of gender, because within most societies, males are accorded higher power and status than females (Bussey & Bandura, 1999).

Although self-monitoring sets the stage for the self-regulation of gender-related conduct, by itself self-monitoring provides little basis for self-evaluation. It is through self-judgments of one's behavior on the basis of one's personal standards for gender-related conduct that self-sanctions guide conduct. When people measure up to their standards, they react with self-approval, and when they violate their standards, they react with self-censure (Bandura, 2008). Indeed, acting in accord with gendered personal standards promotes well-being and positive self-appraisal (Witt & Wood, 2010).

Through varied social experiences, children develop their own gender-linked standards. Because of the wide range of potential social experiences, there is considerable diversity in the gender-related standards that children assume for themselves. As reviewed later in this chapter, these gender-related standards are informed by social sources such as parents, peers, and the media.

Individuals are able to self-regulate the extent to which their own behavior conforms to gender stereotypes. Among those individuals for whom gender is central to their identity, self-monitoring, personal standards, and self-sanctions are likely to be more strongly linked to gender. Such people are more likely to monitor their own behavior on the basis of its gender-relatedness, and if they have developed personal standards that value gender-related conduct, they will anticipate greater self-worth for behaving similarly to others of their gender. Importantly, societal gender roles are not static; they change and people are more or less likely to modify their gender standards depending on the value they ascribe to the changing gender roles.

Regulatory self-efficacy beliefs. One of the core concepts in the agentic regulation of human functioning is self-efficacy (Bandura, 1997). During the course of development, children develop beliefs about their ability to perform gender-related conduct. Self-efficacy refers to people's beliefs about their ability to think and act in specific ways and at certain levels of attainment. For people to exercise agency over their lives, they need to believe in their capabilities to achieve certain goals and to act in specific ways. Without such beliefs, people are unlikely to have any intentional influence over their life course. Therefore, self-efficacy beliefs are central sociocognitive regulators of gendered conduct (Bussey & Bandura, 1999). Unless individuals believe they are able to engage in a particular activity, they are unlikely to attempt it or develop the skills that will lead to eventual mastery of the activity.

The importance of self-efficacy for affecting human functioning across the life span and across a diverse array of human functioning has been verified through meta-analyses (Moritz, Feltz, Fahrbach, & Mack, 2000; Multon, Brown, & Lent, 1991; Stajkovic & Luthans, 1998). Self-efficacy has also been shown to play a major role in the gender domain. For example, gender differences in self-efficacy beliefs have been obtained for emotional well-being. Bandura, Pastorelli, Barbaranelli, and Caprara (1999) showed that low social self-efficacy is a stronger contributor to depression in girls than in boys. Gender differences in perceived self-efficacy are abundant in the achievement domain (Bandura, Barbaranelli, Caprara, & Pastorelli, 2001; Eccles, Freedman-Doan, Frome, Jacobs, & Yoon, 2000; Eccles & Wigfield, 2002; Leaper & Friedman, 2007). These effects have far-reaching implications in educational and occupational settings.

Gender plays a significant role in the development of self-efficacy beliefs. People construct beliefs by synthesizing information from four sources: mastery experiences (successful activity performance), vicarious experiences (modeling), social persuasion (encouragement about one's capabilities), and physiological and emotional states (Bandura, 1997). The way in which this information is synthesized is influenced, to a greater or lesser degree, by gender (Bussey & Bandura, 1999). In the following paragraphs, each of these four sources is discussed in more detail.

The first source of influence is through mastery experiences. These experiences are considered the most effective means for developing personal efficacy (Bandura, 1997). During the course of development, children are provided with considerable opportunities to master activities associated with their own gender. Parents routinely provide children with activities and experiences that are stereotypically associated with their gender (Leaper, 2002). Children therefore typically develop greater proficiencies at activities that are stereotypically associated with their own than the other gender. Success at same-gender-typed tasks and failure at other-gender-typed tasks serves to verify the importance of one's gender in the self-appraisal of one's capabilities. Unless children are encouraged to master activities associated with the other gender, they will not only fail to develop skills associated with those tasks, but they will likely attribute their poor performance to their gender. Children and adults are usually less likely to persevere and develop the skills and competencies associated with tasks typically performed by the other gender.

Further, self-efficacy beliefs are influenced by the way in which one's performance is appraised by others and oneself. The same level of performance can be appraised as a success by one student and as a failure by another (Lopez, Lent, Brown, & Gore, 1997). Similarly, boys and girls may appraise their performance differently when performing the same activity depending on its gender association. For example, in the achievement domain, although girls in elementary school typically outperform boys in science (Britner & Pajares, 2001), girls develop lower self-efficacy beliefs for science and math than do boys. In turn, the lower math self-efficacy beliefs of female undergraduates in comparison with male undergraduates may explain their poorer math performance (Pajares & Miller, 1994). It is therefore apparent that gender self-conceptions play an important part in self-conceptions of ability. Peer groups that are highly gender-segregated provide an important arena for further mastery of activities associated with one's own gender. These experiences all serve to promote the development of self-efficacy beliefs associated with one's gender.

The next most effective means for developing self-efficacy beliefs is through vicarious experiences, particularly social modeling. The greater the similarity between the model and the observer, the greater the likelihood that the observer's self-efficacy will increase through watching the model succeed. Gender is an important basis of similarity between model and observer. For example, in one study, women were more likely to raise their physical self-efficacy beliefs and muscular endurance when they saw a female rather than a male model display physical stamina (Gould & Weiss, 1981). Female scientists who observed their mothers engage in technological activities reported that this influenced their self-efficacy beliefs for engaging in scientific pursuits (Zeldin & Pajares, 2000). Through seeing others of one's gender master certain activities, observers develop beliefs about their own capabilities. Observers are more likely to boost their efficacy for performing tasks, even those linked to the other gender, if they observe members of their own gender perform well at them. However, there is little opportunity to see such models in highly gender-segregated societies, where there is strong demarcation between the activities performed by men and those performed by women. Under such circumstances, self-efficacy beliefs are more likely to be based on one's gender than on one's ability.

Social persuasion is the third means for influencing self-efficacy beliefs. Parents often actively encourage children to engage in activities that are congruent with their gender by stating that it is an activity that most children of their gender are able to perform. Social persuasion can also undermine efficacy. For example, when girls' poor performance on math tasks is ascribed to their gender, their beliefs in their efficacy to perform well on math tasks are likely to be lowered (Dweck, 2002).

The final source of self-efficacy beliefs is physiological states such as anxiety, stress, and mood. Students' confidence is more likely to be boosted when they experience, or anticipate experiencing, less stress and anxiety when they perform a particular activity. This is important because negative mood states and anxiety can interfere with performance, thereby lowering self-efficacy beliefs. A certain degree of arousal can be beneficial in the performance of complex tasks and activities, however, it is the interpretation of the physiological states that can be debilitating or enhancing. Girls in elementary school typically reported higher levels of anxiety about their performance in science classes than did boys (Britner & Pajares, 2006). In such situations girls are prone to perceive anxiety as reflecting their lack of competence at science. However, by highlighting other females who are accomplished in this sphere and providing mentoring for girls, teachers can help to alleviate the negative impact of anxiety on girls' self-efficacy beliefs thereby maintaining their performance in science and other "male" subjects.

When gender is a significant aspect of identity, self-efficacy beliefs are strongly influenced by gender. Women who strongly identify with the stereotypic female role hold lower self-efficacy beliefs for succeeding at male-dominated occupations than those who are less identified with

this role (Matsui, Ikeda, & Ohnishi, 1989). In situations where the female gender stereotype was made salient, high- and low-gender-identified women did not differ in their self-efficacy beliefs for being successful in feminine-typed occupations. However, when the female gender-stereotype was not made salient, the more weakly gender-identified women reported lower self-efficacy beliefs for successfully performing in feminine-typed occupations than did more highly gender-identified women (Oswald, 2008). In general, the more that people's self-conceptions are based on their gender, the greater the difference in their self-efficacy beliefs for successfully performing those activities stereotypically associated with their own than with the other gender. Whereas for people whose self-conceptions are less based on their gender, there is little difference in their self-efficacy beliefs for engaging in same or other gender activities (Matsui et al., 1989).

Social Influences on the Development of Gender Identity

Many social influences including parents, peers, and the media work in concert to emphasize the importance of gender. All these influences contribute to the development of gender identity and the sociocognitive motivators associated with gender identity through the three major modes of social influence: modeling, enactive experience, and direct tuition. These same sources of influence operate across the life span and provide different information that is relevant at different times in the life course and as social conditions change.

Modeling. Modeling of gender roles is pervasive in most societies. It provides information about expected conduct based on gender and serves to highlight the importance of gender in various activities. Gender roles are modeled by parents, peers, and teachers in children's immediate environment as well as by more distal models portrayed on television, in movies, in books, and on the internet. According to social cognitive theory, people do not simply emulate models' behavior in its entirety. Rather, from this view, four processes govern the selective emulation of models: attentional processes, retention processes, production processes, and motivational processes (Bandura, 1986). People pay attention to different models and to different aspects of modeled behavior, they selectively commit the modeled behavior to memory, their capacity to emulate modeled behavior varies, and their enactment of the modeled activity depends on anticipated social and self-sanctions and self-efficacy beliefs associated with enacting it.

In most societies there is a marked differentiation in the activities modeled by males and females. The more highly gender-segregated the society, the more males and females display different behaviors (Maccoby, 1998; Munroe & Romney, 2006; Whiting & Edwards, 1988). Models therefore provide important information about gender-differentiated behavior. Although boys and girls observe both genders, because of the social sanctions associated with gender-related conduct, they often choose to pay more attention to models of their own gender. Indeed, as noted earlier, from a young age, children prefer to attend to same-gender models than to other-gender models (Bussey & Bandura, 1984). However, because there is typically more enforcement of gender conformity for boys than for girls, boys pay more attention to same-gender models than do girls (Slaby & Frey, 1975).

Apart from attending to models, people need to rehearse the information observed and commit it to memory. The more society is gender-differentiated and the more one is motivated to conform to stereotypic gender roles, the more one is likely to think about and rehearse modeled behavior associated with one's own gender and the more one is likely also to develop the necessary skills and competencies to reproduce the modeled activity. However, simply having the ability to enact behavior displayed by others does not mean that this will be carried out, unless one is motivated to do so.

The fourth process governing modeled behavior encompasses motivational processes. People are motivated to emulate behaviors that produce valued outcomes. In most societies conformity to stereotypic gender roles is valued. The more that one sees others of one's gender receiving favorable outcomes for the enactment of certain behaviors and unfavorable outcomes for the enactment of others, the more gender becomes an important determinant of which models to emulate. People also use the model's gender as a guide for developing their self-efficacy beliefs. As discussed earlier, for example, women are more likely to increase their self-efficacy beliefs for lifting weights if they see other women lift comparable weights (Gould & Weiss, 1981).

It is apparent that modeling of gender-differentiated conduct plays an important role in highlighting the significance of one's gender. This is particularly so when highly differentiated conduct displayed by male and female models is accompanied by differentiated social approval and disapproval. These displays not only convey information about gender stereotypes, but they also strengthen the importance of gender identity, further contributing to acquiring gender stereotypes and being influenced by them. Of course, just as modeling can promote the status quo in relation to gender-differentiated conduct and can strengthen the importance of gender identity, models can also serve as a vehicle of social change. Successful collective action by the less powerful to reduce inequitable social practices has been effectively used by campaigners of social change. In one such instance, women in India fought for the rights of their daughters to be educated after listening to a radio serial drama in which the cultural norms associated with girls' education were challenged (Bandura, 2006).

Enactive experience. Through children's enactment of various types of gender-linked conduct, they learn to abstract that there are social sanctions tied to gender-related conduct. A girl learns, for example, that if she performs the same behavior as performed by most girls, this typically meets with social approval and acceptance. However, if she performs the same behavior that most boys perform, this typically meets with censure and disapproval. Through abstracting and synthesizing the various evaluative reactions to gender-related behavior, children begin to realize the significance of the gender of the person performing the behavior. This influences whether they believe that their similar performances will meet with approval or disapproval. The more that sanctioning of behavior is based on gender, the more that self-regulatory processes related to gender are used to guide behavior. Therefore, in those societies, and for those individuals, where social sanctions are pervasively based on gender, gender identity is more likely to influence the enactment of a wide range of activities.

Direct tuition. Direct tuition is an important mode of social influence that affects developing gender conceptions. Children are informed about the associations between activities and gender. Early in a child's life, parents direct their children to select certain activities on the basis of the activity's gender linkage, for example, "No, that's not for you, it's a boys' toy." There is widespread social consensus about the gender associations of activities, books, and movies and this information is often directly conveyed to people throughout their lives. Such gender demarcation serves to further highlight the significance of gender and gender identity.

These three modes of social influence, modeling, enactive experience, and direct tuition are used by parents, peers, and the media to guide gender identity development. From these influences, children not only learn to label their gender and that of others, but they also begin to regulate their gendered conduct on the basis of their gender identity.

Parental influences. Parents convey information to their children about their gender that contributes to the formation of their gender identity using all three modes of social influence discussed above. Typically, this occurs in a highly gendered context created by parents. Before they even begin to interact with their young infant, parents often have structured their child's life in a highly gendered way. The infant's room is furnished, clothes are purchased, and the infant named according to the infant's gender (Etaugh & Liss, 1992; Pomerleau, Bolduc, Malcuit, & Cossette, 1990). As the child ages, parents continue to provide play activities that are associated with their gender (Leaper & Friedman, 2007).

Apart from the gender-differentiated structures that parents put in place for their young, mothers and fathers typically model different activities (Kujawski & Bower, 1993; Langlois, Ritter, Roggman, & Vaughn, 1991; Serbin et al., 2002). This serves to highlight the differences between the two genders. By 24 months, infants have begun to appreciate the highly gender-differentiated conduct of most mothers and fathers (Serbin et al., 2002).

Parents' evaluative reactions to children's conduct are also highly gender differentiating. Those parents who espouse stereotypic gender values encourage gender-related activities in their children (Blakemore, 1998; Fagot et al., 1992; Katz, 1996; Weisner & Wilson-Mitchell, 1990). The asymmetry between the genders is further evident here too, in that boys are more strongly sanctioned for cross-gendered conduct than are girls, and fathers more strongly enforce gender-stereotypic conduct in their sons than in their daughters (Bussey & Bandura, 1999; Kane, 2006; Leaper, 2002; Raley & Bianchi, 2006). For children, and particularly for boys, gender is used as a basis for parental socialization practices. Although children in the early years may not see a link between their gender identity and the activities they select, parents certainly do. It is not surprising that children develop this knowledge early on, particularly when growing up in gender-stereotypic families.

Parents exert a strong influence on children's development of gender conceptions by directly instructing their children in gender labeling. They label the child's gender and practice this self-labeling with them. They also label the gender of others. Gender labeling takes on more prominence in gender-typed families than in egalitarian ones (Fagot et al., 1992; Stennes, Burch, Sen, & Bauer, 2005). Parents also use the child's gender to direct their conduct. Parents instruct their children on the appropriateness of specific activities depending on their gender, for example, "that's not a boy's toy" or "boys don't cry" (Leaper, 2002). This instruction is stronger for boys than for girls and stronger from fathers than from mothers (see Leaper & Friedman, 2007) and characterizes the gender asymmetry in the broader society.

As children age, parents provide subtle messages to their children about their capabilities based on gender. Parents' beliefs about their children's competencies are as much influenced by their gender as by their actual competencies in academic and sporting domains (Fredricks & Eccles, 2002). Parents tend to underestimate their daughters' sporting and math competencies while overestimating them for their sons. The longitudinal research of Eccles and her colleagues (Eccles et al., 2000) shows that, over time, girls' self-conceptions of their math ability decline to match their parents' expectations. This decline in girls' beliefs in their self-competence has far-reaching effects on their choice of college majors and occupational choices. In this way, girls' gender identity impacts their future career choices by diminishing their self-efficacy beliefs associated with math- and science-related occupations. Boys too develop self-conceptions of their ability based on their gender. They are less likely than girls to enter the highly feminized caring (e.g., nursing) and teaching occupations (Watt, 2010).

It is noteworthy that girls' gender identity does not always lead to lower self-efficacy beliefs for math and science. In families where children are encouraged to excel in non-gender-stereotypic subjects, self-efficacy beliefs are less likely to be undermined and the attendant effects on course selection and occupational choice are unaffected. In egalitarian families, girls are more likely to do well at science and math than in more stereotypic families (Updegraff, McHale, & Crouter, 1996). Zeldin and Pajares (2000) found that the encouragement that women scientists received from their parents was important in shaping and maintaining their self-efficacy in male-dominated domains. Such experiences helped women mobilize the necessary confidence to face and overcome academic and social obstacles. One father encouraged his daughter to pursue a career in engineering, "He was very good at math and always encouraged me in math and science, and I thought I could do anything the boys could do" (pp. 227–228). Another father encouraged his daughter's perseverance with math, "we would

work through the problems together, and he really emphasized that it just takes practice. You just practice and pretty soon you start to see a pattern" (p. 228).

Peer influences. As we have already seen, one of the hallmarks of middle childhood is the extensive gender segregation that occurs in the peer group. This provides a fertile arena in which to learn about the importance of gender and the activities that are associated with each gender. The more time that children spend interacting with same-gender peers, the more gender-typed they become (Martin & Fabes, 2001). They emulate same-gender peers, are directed to conform to gender-stereotypical activities, and are positively evaluated when they do conform (Bussey & Perry, 1982; Leaper & Friedman, 2007; Martin & Fabes, 2001).

The influence of gender on children's social relationships contributes to the development and maintenance of gender identity. From as early as 30 months, children's playmates are increasingly of the same gender as themselves. Gender-segregated play begins at this time and increases during the middle childhood years (Leaper, 1994; Maccoby, 2002). This segregation makes gender even more salient as boys and girls seek to differentiate themselves from each other in conformity with societal expectations. The two genders differ on the basis of dress, names, and activities. It is not surprising that gender differences flourish in this gender-segregated culture that emerges early in children's development (Maccoby, 1998). The difference between genders is highly salient and not conforming to conduct consistent with one's gender carries severe repercussions, especially for boys (Blakemore, 2003; Martin, 1989; Thorne, 1993). Play in same-gender groups further heightens the relevance of one's gender in everyday interaction. Typically, in such same-gender groups, children learn gender-typed play patterns and develop skills and competencies and self-efficacy beliefs associated with such conduct.

Despite the substantial evidence showing that interaction with peers contributes to learning and enacting traditional gender roles and highlights the differences between the genders, children can also subvert this process by selecting their own peer groups to master activities of their choice. Women scientists who have successfully navigated male-dominated science and technological careers have provided interesting insights into their peer-group experiences (Zeldin & Pajares, 2000). They highlighted the importance of forming peer subgroups at school that supported their scientific and technological interests. These girls self-selected into groups such as the math or the chemistry club to associate with and receive support from girls with similar interests. This course of action enabled girls who like math and science to avoid the typical negative reactions from girls who do not like science (Breakwell, Vignoles, & Robertson, 2003). One woman who pursued a math-related career described her experience with her chosen peer group in the following way, "Well, in high school, my friends were a little bit more the high achiever types, and we all went through the math classes together. Some of my good friends were in math" (Zeldin & Pajares, 2000, p. 232). By creating their own peer-group environments, these girls were able to develop their self-efficacy and competence in male-dominated fields within a supportive and encouraging environment.

Media influences. The media is not gender-neutral. In the previous century, females were underrepresented in most forms of media including television, radio, books, and movies. In the current electronic era, this underrepresentation continues, despite the greater range of media content available on the internet (Leaper & Friedman, 2007; Signorielli, 2001; Signorielli & Bacue, 1999). Although more recently there has been some increase in female representation on television and a decrease in the portrayal of gender-role stereotypes, males and females largely continue to be portrayed in gender-stereotypic ways, particularly in their dress styles, occupations, and personality characteristics. There is a focus on young, slim women and muscular men (Signorielli & Bacue, 1999), and women more than men are portrayed as engaging in domestic duties and as sex objects (Coltrane & Messineo, 2000).

The gender of child actors in television advertisements is highlighted by their gender-differentiated activities so that some activities are designated "for boys" and others "for girls." Boys demonstrate their preference for action-oriented and aggressive activities and girls demonstrate their preference for nurturant activities directed toward dolls and fashion and beauty products (Signorielli, 2001). Boys' activities are directed toward sports, future occupations, and activities away from the home, whereas girls are still directed toward domestic activities and self-grooming. Perhaps the most gender-differentiated area in the media is sports. Male athletes are far more likely than female athletes to receive media coverage both on and off the field. In fact, some studies report that as little of 10% of sports coverage is devoted to female athletes (Koivula, 1999). Males are portrayed as aggressive, dominant, and powerful. These representations further contribute to gender differentiation and highlight the significance of gender in the sports arena.

In recent years, greater gender equity in the representation of characters in children's books has been achieved. However, females are still underrepresented as main characters and in illustrations, and children are still presented in gender-stereotypic roles (Diekman & Murnen, 2004; Gooden & Gooden, 2001). Teenage books for girls focus on relationships and body image rather than cultivating activities and interests that build skills and competencies (Malkin, Wornian, & Chrisler, 1999). Females are significantly underrepresented in music and video games, and if they are depicted, they are often portrayed as sex objects (Sommers-Flanagan, Sommers-Flanagan, & Davis, 1993).

The pervasiveness of gender differentiation in the media highlights the social significance of gender. Greater television viewing is typically associated with greater exposure to stereotypic gender behavior and with the subsequent development of more gender-stereotypic conceptions (Anderson, Huston, Schmitt, Linebarger, & Wright, 2001; Davies, Spencer, Quinn, & Gerhardstein, 2002; Morgan & Shananhan, 1997; Ward, 2003). Davies et al. (2002) showed that after watching gender-stereotypic television commercials women performed more poorly on a math test than women who watched counter-stereotypic commercials. It was further shown that this effect was particularly strong among women who thought about women in more gender-stereotypical ways. After viewing gender-stereotypical commercials, women were also less interested in pursuing future careers such as engineering and computer science that were reliant on proficiency in math. This underscores the earlier discussion showing that watching the performances of similar others is a potent source for informing beliefs about one's competence. Thus, the media's depiction of males and females engaging in gender-stereotypic behavior increases the salience of gender and influences people's beliefs about others' reactions, their own reactions, and self-efficacy beliefs for conduct based on their gender.

The continuing underrepresentation of women and their depiction in less powerful and authoritative roles than men does not provide support or incentives for women to master activities beyond stereotypic gender roles or to master activities that are highly valued by society. Despite the recent rhetoric of "girl power," the media continues to highlight the sexuality and physical appearance of women and girls rather than their competencies and achievements (Gill, 2007). Boys are more likely to spend time playing computer games, watching sports, and highly aggressive action programs, whereas girls spend more time watching relationship-focused programs (Lemish, Liebes, & Seidmann, 2001; Subrahmanyam, Kraut, Greenfield, & Gross, 2001). Further, it has been shown that the more central gender is to one's self-concept, the more likely one will seek out highly gender-stereotypic media—this further contributes to gender self-conceptions and the regulation of behavior along gender lines. Conversely, those for whom gender is a less pervasive influence on their self-conceptions may seek to watch less stereotypic media content (Ochman, 1996; Thompson & Zerbinos, 1997; Ward & Friedman, 2006). Although not as readily available through the mass media, there are pockets of the media that present more gender-equitable content. The internet, for example, provides access to such content worldwide. This enables people to transcend their immediate environment and discover more gender-equitable media depictions that present a wider range of possibilities unrestricted by stereotypic conceptions of gender.

Transforming Gender Identity

It is evident from the foregoing discussion that gender identity is not fixed at any one point in time. According to some developmental theories of gender identity, once developed there is little variation in gender identity across the life course. However, it is argued here that gender identity varies across the life course. The influence of gender identity is exercised through the sociocognitive motivators of social sanctions, self-sanctions, and self-efficacy beliefs linked to gender. Personal change is effected through changes to the sociocognitive motivators, as a result of reflecting on and evaluating the relevance of experience and changing sociostructural arrangements in society.

As children mature cognitively and expand their social experiences, not only do they begin to realize that the two genders are treated differently, but they also begin to understand that there are power and status differences between males and females (Katz, 1996). This differential value accorded the two genders is apparent to children as young as 5 years of age, and it is more apparent to girls than it is to boys (Brown & Bigler, 2004). It is therefore evident that, from an early age, children begin to reflect on their experiences of belonging to a particular gender and the positive and negative discrimination associated with it.

Not all people accept the restrictions imposed by their gender. As noted earlier, from the social cognitive theory perspective, people can create or choose their own environments. For example, women who wish to achieve in math and science subjects may seek peer groups and mentors who are supportive of such endeavors (Zeldin & Pajares, 2000). In such environments, individuals develop their competencies and self-efficacy beliefs and personal standards for activities that would not be encouraged elsewhere.

At a broader level, history is replete with examples of those with less power and social advantage taking collective action to remedy their situation. Drawing on their collective gender identity, women have been able to build their collective self-efficacy beliefs to mobilize actions to change social structures and thus bring about greater gender equality. Collective self-efficacy is of particular importance in the gender domain, because gender is a collective as well as a social category. Collective efficacy relating to gender identity refers to individuals' beliefs in their ability to work together with other members of their gender to achieve specific goals (Bandura, 1997). It operates similarly to personal efficacy in that it influences the amount of effort people expend in performing a task, how much they persevere when confronted with difficulties, and their vulnerability to discouragement. However, the focus of analysis is beliefs about the group rather than about the individual.

Collective efficacy has been shown to influence performance outcomes across a range of domains (see Fernandez-Ballesteros, Diez-Nicolas, Caprara, Barbaranelli, & Bandura, 2002). In this context, the collective action of women has led to permanent changes in laws and policies relating to gender discrimination. For example, early in the twentieth century the suffragettes mobilized collectively to gain the vote for women. Later, the Women's Movement of the 1960s sought further to reduce discrimination. Women demanded access to education, increased work opportunities, and reproductive freedom, and they challenged the normalcy of domestic violence and women's unpaid labor in the domestic sphere (Biaggio, 2000).

Gender roles continue to change. By the 1980s the restrictiveness of masculinity was being questioned as "Men's Studies" came into prominence (Segal, 2010). Increasingly, men are broadening their self-conceptions (in terms of toughness, independence, assertiveness), pursuits, and interests beyond those that are stereotypically associated with men (Segal, 2010). Men have also increased their involvement in childcare and

homemaking (Giele & Holst, 2004). Although many of the activities that fathers undertake with their children are more instrumental (discipline, protecting, monitoring schoolwork) than expressive (caregiving, emotional development, spiritual development), some fathers are involved in more expressive forms of fathering; both types of involvement are perceived as nurturant by fathers and their children (Finley & Schwartz, 2004, 2006). Women's circumstances have changed too. There now are numerous female heads of state, and there are many women serving in public life. Women are not only active in the political domain, but they also occupy influential roles in universities, on boards of large businesses, and in the medical field. They now participate in most occupations, including the military. The marked gender segregation of the workforce characteristic of previous centuries is easing. Young girls can aspire to high political office and find suitable role models to inform their aspirations. The changing nature of work from the hunter-gatherer days that required strong physical capabilities has meant that women face fewer barriers in their occupational choice (Wood & Eagly, 2002). The reduction of gender differences in abilities has further enabled some blurring of the demarcation of occupational choice based on gender. However, there still remains substantial gender discrimination.

Participation in sports provides an example of how legislative changes as well as changing societal views affect the gender association of activities and the ensuing linkage of gender identity with such participation. Sporting participation for most of the twentieth century has been the province of men. However, in the United States, since the 1972 enactment of Title IX of the US Civil Rights Act, there has been a dramatic increase in high school girls' participation in sport. It has jumped from 1 in 27 to 1 in 2.5, while boys' participation rate has remained at 1 in 2 (Women's Sports Foundation, 2007). Most of the sports have been played in gender-segregated groups. However, this segregation is starting to weaken, particularly in younger age groups. Still, many parents believe that sons are more competent than their daughters at sports (Fredricks & Eccles, 2002), and the media focuses on professional male athletes and often condones their aggressive and dominant behavior (Tenenbaum, Stewart, Singer, & Duda, 1996). Males continue to draw their popularity and prestige from sports, whereas this is much less true for girls (Suitor & Reavis, 1995). In male sporting groups teammates strongly enforce the enactment of masculine gender stereotypes of aggression and drinking (Olrich, 1996). Although the impediment to women's sports participation was attenuated through the removal of structural barriers to their participation by Title IX, it takes time for other social influences such as parents, peers, and the media to value and encourage such participation. The greater the participation of women in sports and the less that sports participation is gender-segregated, the weaker is the link between gender identity and sports participation. This is not because children's knowledge of their gender has changed. Rather, once girls are encouraged to the same extent as boys to participate in sports, they feel pride in their sporting achievements, and hold high self-efficacy beliefs for such conduct and gender identity is less likely to be a determining influence on sports participation.

How does this blurring of gender roles impact gender identity? As reviewed in this chapter, the perceptual salience of the gender category is important for gender identity formation. To maintain a category (such as gender) such that it is an important aspect of one's identity, the category must have functional significance. As gender segregation and gender differentiation attenuate and the genders are treated more equally, gender identity would be expected to play a less pervasive role in most people's lives. This does not mean that a person's gender is not of importance; rather, it need not dictate every aspect of a person's life. Once gender is less pervasively tied to activities, a person's gender may be less of a major determinant of how others respond to them, how they respond to themselves, and the skills and competencies and self-efficacy beliefs that they develop across a wide variety of domains.

Biological sex is a defining characteristic as are other characteristics such as eye color. Eye color, however, is not a collective category that carries the same social significance as gender. Historically, biological differences between the genders were important as women spent a large part of their adult life having and rearing children while men were involved in activities outside the home that often required considerable physical strength. Scientific advances enabling women to control their reproduction have meant that women do not need to be solely responsible for raising children and keeping house. The changing circumstances of women have seen them develop skills and competencies equivalent to those developed by men (Barnett & Rivers, 2004). Although there are more men than women in technology and science, women are increasingly nominated for Nobel Prizes. Moreover, we are at a point in time when neuroscience research is showing the malleability of the human brain. Even if there are differences between male and female infants' brains, it is increasingly possible that developing skills associated with the other gender will attenuate differences in brain functioning between the genders. These possibilities challenge earlier essentialist positions that argue for a strong biological contribution to gender differences. Regardless of their "biological predisposition," increasing numbers of men are expressing nurturance and engaging in more caregiving activities with their children than has occurred in the past. Once nurturance is appreciated for its human value rather than being more associated with one gender than the other, there will be less social restraint from expressing nurturance independent of one's gender.

Conclusion

It has been argued in this chapter that gender is a collective category in which social influences build on biological differences between the genders to heighten gender differentiation. It was shown that people are treated differently depending on their gender by the various social subsystems they encounter across the life span. Within these contexts there is considerable variability in people's self-development and the gender identity they assume for themselves. Although people's knowledge of their gender rarely changes across the life course, the relative influence of their gender identity on their overall functioning depends on the prevailing social conditions and their engagement of self-regulation processes related to gender. In cultural contexts where gender equity is valued and legally sanctioned, people have considerably more leeway in the extent to which gender influences their identity and life course. In other cultural contexts, where women have few rights, there is little choice about the pervasive influence of gender on women's identity and life course. However, even within the most restrictive social conditions, it is possible for an undervalued group such as women to mobilize collective resources to challenge the status quo so that they can exercise greater agency over their identity and life course.

Acknowledgments I wish to thank Albert Bandura for his extensive comments on an earlier draft of this chapter.

References

Anderson, D. R., Huston, A. C., Schmitt, K. L., Linebarger, D. L., & Wright, J. C. (2001). Early childhood television viewing and adolescent behavior: The recontact study. *Monographs of the Society for Research in Child Development, 66* (1, Serial No. 264), 1–147.

Ashmore, R. D., Deaux, K., & McLaughlin-Volpe, T. (2004). An organizing framework for collective identity: Articulation and significance of multidimensionality. *Psychological Bulletin, 130*, 80–114.

Bandura, A. (1986). *Social foundations of thought and action: A social cognitive theory*. Englewood Cliffs, NJ: Prentice Hall.

Bandura, A. (1997). *Self-efficacy: The exercise of control*. New York: Freeman.

Bandura, A. (2006). On integrating social cognitive and social diffusion theories. In A. Singhal & J. W. Dearing (Eds.), *Communication of innovations: A journey with Ev Rogers* (pp. 111–135). New Delhi: Sage.

Bandura, A. (2008). Toward an agentic theory of the self. In H. W. Marsh, R. G. Craven, & D. M. McInerney (Eds.), *Self-processes, learning, and enabling human potential* (pp. 15–49). Charlotte, NC: Information Age Publishing.

Bandura, A., Barbaranelli, C., Caprara, G. V., & Pastorelli, C. (2001). Self-efficacy beliefs as shapers of children's aspirations and career trajectories. *Child Development, 72*, 187–206.

Bandura, A., Pastorelli, C., Barbaranelli, C., & Caprara, G. V. (1999). Self-efficacy pathways to depression. *Journal of Personality and Social Psychology, 76*, 258–269.

Barnett, R., & Rivers, C. (2004). *Same difference: How gender myths are hurting our relationships, our children, and our jobs*. New York: Basic Books.

Bauer, P. J., & Coyne, M. J. (1997). When the name says it all: Preschoolers' recognition and use of the gendered nature of common proper names. *Social Development, 6*, 271–291.

Bem, S. L. (1981). Gender schema theory: A cognitive account of sex typing. *Psychological Review, 88*, 354–364.

Biaggio, M. (2000). History of the contemporary women's movement. In M. Biaggio & M. Herson (Eds.), *Issues in the psychology of women* (pp. 3–14). New York: Kluwer Academic/Plenum Publishers.

Bigler, R. S., Brown, C. S., & Markell, M. (2001). When groups are not created equal: Effects of group status on the formation of intergroup attitudes in children. *Child Development, 72*, 1151–1162.

Blakemore, J. E. O. (1998). The influence of gender and parental attitudes on preschool children's interest in babies: Observations in natural settings. *Sex Roles, 38*, 73–95.

Blakemore, J. E. O. (2003). Children's beliefs about violating gender norms: Boys shouldn't look like girls and girls shouldn't act like boys. *Sex Roles, 48*, 411–419.

Blakemore, J. E. O., LaRue, A. A., & Olejnik, A. B. (1979). Sex-appropriate toy preferences and the ability to conceptualize toys as sex-role related. *Developmental Psychology, 15*, 339–340.

Breakwell, G. M., Vignoles, V. L., & Robertson, T. (2003). Stereotypes and crossed-category evaluations: The case of gender and science education. *British Journal of Psychology, 94*, 437–455.

Britner, S. L., & Pajares, F. (2001). Self-efficacy beliefs, motivation, race, and gender in middle school science. *Journal of Women and Minorities in Science and Engineering, 7*, 271–285.

Britner, S. L., & Pajares, F. (2006). Sources of science self-efficacy beliefs of middle school students. *Journal of Research in Science Teaching, 43*, 485–499.

Brown, C. S., & Bigler, R. S. (2004). Children's perceptions of gender discrimination. *Developmental Psychology, 40*, 714–726.

Buchmann, C., DiPrete, T. A., & McDaniel, A. (2008). Gender inequalities in education. *Annual Review of Sociology, 34*, 319–337.

Bussey, K., & Bandura, A. (1984). Influence of gender constancy and social power on sex-linked modeling. *Journal of Personality and Social Psychology, 47*, 1292–1302.

Bussey, K., & Bandura, A. (1992). Self-regulatory mechanisms governing gender development. *Child Development, 63*, 1236–1250.

Bussey, K., & Bandura, A. (1999). Social cognitive theory of gender development and differentiation. *Psychological Review, 106*, 676–713.

Bussey, K., & Perry, D. G. (1982). Same-sex imitation: Lie avoidance of cross-sex models or the acceptance of same-sex models? *Sex Roles, 8*, 773–794.

Butler, J. (1990). *Gender trouble: Feminism and the subversion of identity*. New York: Routledge.

Caldera, Y. M., Huston, A. C., & O'Brien, M. (1989). Social interactions and play patterns of parents and toddlers with feminine, masculine and neutral toys. *Child Development, 60*, 70–76.

Coltrane, S., & Messineo, M. (2000). The perpetuation of subtle prejudice: Race and gender imagery in 1990s television advertising. *Sex Roles, 42*, 363–389.

Connell, R. W. (1995). *Masculinities*. Sydney: Allen & Unwin.

Conner, J. M., Schackman, M., & Serbin, L. A. (1978). Sex-related differences in response to practice on a visual-spatial test and generalization to a related test. *Child Development, 49*, 24–29.

Cornell, E. H. (1974). Infants' discrimination of photographs of faces following redundant presentations. *Journal of Experimental Child Psychology, 18*, 98–106.

Davies, P. G., Spencer, S. J., Quinn, D. M., & Gerhardstein, R. (2002). Consuming images: How television commercials that elicit stereotype threat can restrain women academically and professionally. *Personality and Social Psychology Bulletin, 28*, 1615–1628.

Deaux, K. (1993). Commentary: Sorry, wrong number— A reply to Gentile's call (Special section: Sex or gender?). *Psychological Science, 4*, 125–126.

Deaux, K., & Lewis, L. L. (1984). Structure of gender stereotypes: Interrelationships among components and gender label. *Journal of Personality and Social Psychology, 46*, 991–1004.

Deaux, K., & Stewart, A. J. (2001). Framing gendered identities. In R. K. Unger (Ed.), *Handbook of the psychology of women and gender* (pp. 84–97). New York: Wiley.

Diekman, A. B., & Murnen, S. K. (2004). Learning to be little women and little men: The inequitable gender equality of nonsexist children's literature. *Sex Roles, 50*, 373–385.

Dweck, C. S. (2002). Beliefs that make smart people dumb. In R. J. Sternberg (Ed.), *Why smart people can be so stupid* (pp. 24–41). New Haven, CT: Yale University Press.

Eccles, J. S., Freedman-Doan, C., Frome, P., Jacobs, J., & Yoon, K. S. (2000). Gender-role socialization in the family: A longitudinal approach. In T. Eckes & H. Trautner (Eds.), *The developmental social psychology of gender* (pp. 333–360). Mahwah, NJ: Lawrence Erlbaum.

Eccles, J. S., & Wigfield, A. (2002). Motivational beliefs, values, and goals. *Annual Review of Psychology, 53*, 109–132.

Egan, S. K., & Perry, D. G. (2001). Gender identity: A multidimensional analysis with implications for psychosocial adjustment. *Developmental Psychology, 37*, 451–463.

Epstein, C. F. (1997). The multiple realities of sameness and difference: Ideology and practice. *Journal of Social Issues, 53*, 259–278.

Etaugh, C., & Liss, M. B. (1992). Home, school, and playroom: Training grounds for adult gender roles. *Sex Roles, 26*, 129–147.

Fagan, J. F., & Singer, L. T. (1979). The role of simple feature differences in infants' recognition of faces. *Infant Behavior and Development, 2*, 39–45.

Fagot, B. I., Leinbach, M. D., & O'Boyle, C. (1992). Gender labeling, gender stereotyping, and parenting behaviors. *Developmental Psychology, 28*, 225–230.

Fernandez-Ballesteros, R., Diez-Nicolas, J., Caprara, G. V., Barbaranelli, C., & Bandura, A. (2002). Determinants and structural relation of personal efficacy to collective efficacy. *Applied Psychology: An International Review, 51*, 107–125.

Finley, G. E., & Schwartz, S. J. (2004). The father involvement and nurturant fathering scales: Retrospective measures for adolescent and adult children. *Educational and Psychological Measurement, 64*, 143–164.

Finley, G. E., & Schwartz, S. J. (2006). Parsons and Bales revisited: Young adult children's characterization of the fathering role. *Psychology of Men & Masculinity, 7*, 42–55.

Fredricks, J. A., & Eccles, J. S. (2002). Children's competence and value beliefs from childhood through adolescence: Growth trajectories in two male-sex-typed domains. *Developmental Psychology, 38*, 519–533.

Gelman, S., Collman, P., & Maccoby, E. (1986). Inferring properties from categories versus inferring categories from properties: The case of gender. *Child Development, 57*, 396–404.

Giele, J. Z., & Holst, E. (2004). New life patterns and changing gender roles. *Advances in Life Course Research, 8*, 3–22.

Gill, R. (2007). *Gender and the media*. Cambridge: Polity Press.

Gooden, A. M., & Gooden, M. A. (2001). Gender representation in notable children's picture books: 1995–1999. *Sex Roles, 45*, 89–101.

Gould, D., & Weiss, M. (1981). Effect of model similarity and model self-talk on self-efficacy in muscular endurance. *Journal of Sport Psychology, 3*, 17–29.

Grace, D. M., David, B. J., & Ryan, M. K. (2008). Investigating preschoolers' categorical thinking about gender through imitation, attention, and the use of self-categories. *Child Development, 79*, 1928–1941.

Helgeson, V. S. (1994). Relation of agency and communion to well-being: Evidence and potential explanations. *Psychological Bulletin, 116*, 412–428.

Hyde, J. S., Lindberg, S. M., Linn, M. C., Ellis, A., & Williams, C. (2008). Gender similarities characterize math performance. *Science, 321*, 494–495.

Kane, E. W. (2006). "No way my boys are going to be like that!" parents' responses to children's gender nonconformity. *Gender & Society, 20,* 149–176.

Katz, P. A. (1996). Raising feminists. *Psychology of Women Quarterly, 20,* 323–340.

Kohlberg, L. (1966). A cognitive-developmental analysis of children's sex-role concepts and attitudes. In E. E. Maccoby (Ed.), *The development of sex differences* (pp. 82–173). Stanford, CA: Stanford University Press.

Koivula, N. (1999). Gender stereotyping in televised media sport coverage. *Sex Roles, 41,* 589–604.

Kuhn, D., Nash, S. C., & Brucken, L. (1978). Sex role concepts of two- and three-year-olds. *Child Development, 49,* 445–451.

Kujawski, J. H., & Bower, T. G. R. (1993). Same-sex preferential looking during infancy as a function of abstract representation. *British Journal of Developmental Psychology, 11,* 201–209.

Langlois, J. H., Ritter, J. M., Roggman, L. A., & Vaughn, L. S. (1991). Facial diversity and infant preferences for attractive faces. *Developmental Psychology, 27,* 79–84.

Leaper, C. (1994). Exploring the consequences of gender segregation on social relationships. In C. Leaper (Ed.), *Childhood gender segregation: Causes and consequences* (New Directions for Child Development, No. 65, pp. 67–86). San Francisco: Jossey-Bass.

Leaper, C. (2002). Parenting girls and boys. In M. H. Bornstein (Ed.), *Handbook of parenting: Children and parenting* (Vol. 1, 2nd ed., pp. 189–225). Mahwah, NJ: Erlbaum.

Leaper, C., & Friedman, C. K. (2007). The socialization of gender. In J. E. Grusec & P. D. Hastings (Eds.), *Handbook of socialization: Theory and research* (pp. 561–587). New York: Guilford Press.

Leinbach, M. D., & Fagot, B. I. (1986). Acquisition of gender labels: A test for toddlers. *Sex Roles, 15,* 655–666.

Leinbach, M. D., & Fagot, B. I. (1993). Categorical habituation to male and female faces: Gender schematic processing in infancy. *Infant Behavior and Development, 16,* 317–332.

Lemish, D., Liebes, T., & Seidmann, V. (2001). Gendered media meanings and uses. In S. Livingstone & M. Bovill (Eds.), *Children and their changing media environment* (pp. 263–282). Mahwah, NJ: Erlbaum.

Lewis, M., & Brooks-Gunn, J. (1979). *Social cognition and the acquisition of self.* New York: Plenum.

Lopez, F. G., Lent, R. W., Brown, S. D., & Gore, P. A. (1997). Role of social-cognitive expectations in high school students' mathematics-related interest and performance. *Journal of Counseling Psychology, 44,* 44–52.

Maccoby, E. E. (1998). *The two sexes: Growing up apart, coming together.* Cambridge, MA: Harvard University Press.

Maccoby, E. E. (2002). Gender and group processes: A developmental perspective. *Current Directions in Psychological Sciences, 11,* 54–58.

Malkin, A. R., Wornian, K., & Chrisler, J. C. (1999). Women and weight: Gendered messages on magazine covers. *Sex Roles, 40,* 647–655.

Martin, C. L. (1989). Children's use of gender-related information in making social judgments. *Developmental Psychology, 25,* 80–88.

Martin, C. L., & Fabes, R. A. (2001). The stability and consequences of young children's same-sex peer interactions. *Developmental Psychology, 37,* 431–446.

Martin, C. L., & Halverson, C. F. (1981). A schematic processing model of sex typing and stereotyping in children. *Child Development, 52,* 1119–1134.

Martin, C. L., Ruble, D. N., & Szkrybalo, J. (2002). Cognitive theories of early gender development. *Psychological Bulletin, 128,* 903–933.

Matsui, T., Ikeda, H., & Ohnishi, R. (1989). Relations of sex-typed socializations to career self-efficacy expectations of college students. *Journal of Vocational Behavior, 35,* 1–16.

Miller, C. L. (1983). Developmental changes in male/female voice classification by infants. *Infant Behavior and Development, 6,* 313–330.

Miller, C. L., Younger, B. A., & Morse, P. A. (1982). The categorization of male and female voices in infancy. *Infant Behavior and Development, 5,* 143–159.

Morgan, M., & Shananhan, J. (1997). Two decades of cultivation research: An appraisal and meta-analysis. In B. R. Burleson (Ed.), *Communication yearbook* (Vol. 20, pp. 1–46). Thousand Oaks, CA: Sage.

Moritz, S. E., Feltz, D. L., Fahrbach, K. R., & Mack, D. E. (2000). The Relation of self-efficacy measures to sport performance: A meta-analytic review. *Research Quarterly for Exercise and Sport, 71,* 280–294.

Multon, K. D., Brown, S. D., & Lent, R. W. (1991). Relation of self-efficacy beliefs to academic outcomes: A meta-analytic investigation. *Journal of Counseling Psychology, 38,* 30–38.

Munroe, R. L., & Romney, A. K. (2006). Gender and age differences in same-sex aggregation and social behavior—A four-culture study. *Journal of Cross Cultural Psychology, 37,* 3–19.

O'Brien, M. H., & Huston, A. C. (1985). Development of sex-typed play behavior in toddlers. *Developmental Psychology, 21,* 866–871.

Ochman, J. M. (1996). The effects of nongender-role stereotyped, same-sex role models in storybooks on the self-esteem of children in grade three. *Sex Roles, 35,* 711–735.

Olrich, T. W. (1996). The role of sport in the gender identity development of the adolescent male. *Dissertation Abstracts international: Humanities and Social Sciences, 56,* 4320.

Oswald, D. L. (2008). Gender stereotypes and women's reports of liking and ability in traditionally masculine and feminine occupations. *Psychology of Women Quarterly, 32,* 196–203.

Pajares, F., & Miller, D. (1994). Role of self-efficacy and self-concept beliefs in mathematical problem solving: A path analysis. *Journal of Educational Psychology, 86,* 193–203.

Parish, T. S., & Bryant, W. T. (1978). Mapping sex group stereotypes of elementary and high school students. *Sex Roles, 4,* 135–140.

Parsons, T., & Bales, R. F. (1955). *Family, socialization and interaction process.* Glencoe, IL: Free Press.

Pomerleau, A., Bolduc, D., Malcuit, G., & Cossette, L. (1990). Pink or blue: Environmental gender stereotypes in the first two years of life. *Sex Roles, 22,* 359–367.

Poulin-Dubois, D., Serbin, L. A., & Derbyshire, A. (1998). Toddlers' intermodal and verbal knowledge. *Merrill-Palmer Quarterly, 44,* 339–354.

Poulin-Dubois, D., Serbin, L. A., Eichstedt, J. A., Sen, M. G., & Beissel, C. F. (2002). Men don't put on make-up: Toddlers' knowledge of the gender stereotyping of household activities. *Social Development, 11,* 166–181.

Poulin-Dubois, D., Serbin, L. A., Kenyon, B., & Derbyshire, A. (1994). Infants' intermodal knowledge about gender. *Developmental Psychology, 30,* 436–442.

Powlishta, K. K. (1995). Intergroup processes in childhood: Social categorization and sex role development. *Developmental Psychology, 31,* 781–788.

Powlishta, K. K., Sen, M. G., Serbin, L. A., Poulin-Dubois, D., & Eichstedt, J. A. (2001). From infancy through middle childhood: The role of cognitive and social factors in becoming gendered. In R. K. Unger (Ed.), *Handbook of the psychology of women and gender* (pp. 116–132). New York: Wiley.

Priess, H. A., Lindberg, S. M., & Hyde, J. S. (2009). Adolescent gender-role identity and mental health: Gender intensification revisited. *Child Development, 80,* 1531–1544.

Raag, T., & Rackliff, C. L. (1998). Preschoolers' awareness of social expectations of gender: Relationships to toy choices. *Sex Roles, 38,* 685–700.

Raley, S., & Bianchi, S. (2006). Sons, daughters, and family processes: Does gender of children matter? *Annual Review of Sociology, 32,* 401–421.

Roopnarine, J. L. (1986). Mothers' and fathers' behaviors toward the toy play of their infant sons and daughters. *Sex Roles, 14,* 59–68.

Ruble, D. N., Martin, C. L., & Berenbaum, S. (2006). Gender development. In W. Damon & R. M. Lerner (Eds.), *Handbook of child psychology: Social, emotional and personality development* (Vol. 3, 6th ed., pp. 858–932). New York: Wiley.

Sandnabba, N. K., & Ahlberg, C. (1999). Parents' attitudes and expectations about children's cross-gender behavior. *Sex Roles, 40,* 249–264.

Schrock, D., & Schwalbe, M. (2009). Men, masculinity, and manhood acts. *Annual Review of Sociology, 35,* 277–295.

Segal, L. (2010). Genders: Deconstructed, reconstructed, still on the move. In M. Wetherell & D. T. Mohanty (Eds.), *The Sage handbook of identities* (pp. 321–338). Los Angeles: Sage.

Serbin, L. A., Poulin-Dubois, D., Colburne, K. A., Sen, M. G., & Eichstedt, J. A. (2001). Gender stereotyping in infancy: Visual preferences for and knowledge of gender-stereotyped toys in the second year. *International Journal of Behavioral Development, 25,* 7–15.

Serbin, L. A., Poulin-Dubois, D., & Eichstedt, J. A. (2002). Infants' response to gender-inconsistent events. *Journal of Infancy, 3,* 531–542.

Serbin, L. A., & Sprafkin, C. (1986). The salience of gender and the process of sex-typing in three- to seven-year-old children. *Child Development, 57,* 1188–1199.

Shelton, B. A., & Agger, B. (1993). Shotgun wedding, unhappy marriage, non-fault divorce? Rethinking the feminism-Marxism relationship. In P. England (Ed.), *Theory on Gender/Feminism on Theory.* New York: Aldine De Gruyter.

Signorielli, N. (2001). Television's gender role images and contribution to stereotyping: Past, present, future. In D. Singer & J. Singer (Eds.), *Handbook of children and the media* (pp. 341–358). Thousand Oaks, CA: Sage.

Signorielli, N., & Bacue, A. (1999). Recognition and respect: A content analysis of prime-time television characters across 3 decades. *Sex Roles, 40,* 527–544.

Slaby, R. G., & Frey, K. S. (1975). Development of gender constancy and selective attention to same-sex models. *Child Development, 52,* 849–856.

Sommers-Flanagan, R., Sommers-Flanagan, J., & Davis, B. (1993). What's happening on music television? A gender role content analysis. *Sex Roles, 28,* 745–753.

Spence, J. T. (1984). Gender identity and its implications for concepts of masculinity and femininity. In T. B. Sonderegger (Ed.), *Nebraska Symposium on Motivation: Psychology and gender* (Vol. 32, pp. 59–96). Lincoln, NE: University of Nebraska Press.

Spence, J. T., & Buckner, C. (1995). Masculinity and femininity: Defining the undefinable. In P. J. Kalbfleisch & M. J. Cody (Eds.), *Gender, power, and communication in human relationships* (pp. 105–138). Hillsdale, NJ: Lawrence Erlbaum Associates.

Stajkovic, A. D., & Luthans, F. (1998). Self-efficacy and work-related performance: A meta-analysis. *Psychological Bulletin, 124,* 240–261.

Stennes, L. M., Burch, M. M., Sen, M. G., & Bauer, P. J. (2005). A longitudinal study of gendered vocabulary and communicative action in young children. *Developmental Psychology, 41,* 75–88.

Subrahmanyam, K., Kraut, R., Greenfield, P., & Gross, E. (2001). New forms of electronic media: The impact of interactive games and the internet on cognition, socialization, and behavior. In D. Singer & J. Singer (Eds.), *Handbook of children and the media* (pp. 73–99). Thousand Oaks, CA: Sage.

Suitor, J. J., & Reavis, R. (1995). Football, fast cars, and cheerleading: Adolescent gender norms, 1978–1989. *Adolescence*, *30*, 265–272.

Tajfel, H., & Turner, J. (1979). An integrative theory of intergroup conflict. In W. Austin & S. Wochel (Eds.), *The social psychology of intergroup relations* (pp. 33–47). Monterey, CA: Brooks/Cole.

Tenenbaum, G., Stewart, E., Singer, R. N., & Duda, J. (1996). Aggression and violence in sport: An ISSP position stand. *International Journal of Sport Psychology*, *27*, 229–236.

Thompson, S. K. (1975). Gender labels and early sex role development. *Child Development*, *46*, 339–347.

Thompson, T. L., & Zerbinos, E. (1997). Television cartoons: Do children notice it's a boy's world. *Sex Roles*, *37*, 415–432.

Thorne, B. (1993). *Gender play: Girls and boys in school*. New Brunswick, NJ: Rutgers University Press.

Turner, J. C., Hogg, M. A., Oakes, P. J., Reicher, S. D., & Wetherell, M. S. (1987). *Rediscovering the social group: A self-categorization theory*. Oxford, UK: Blackwell.

Twenge, J. M. (1997). Attitudes towards women, 1970–1995: A meta-analysis. *Psychology of Women Quarterly*, *21*, 35–51.

Updegraff, K. A., McHale, S. M., & Crouter, A. C. (1996). Egalitarian and traditional families: What do they mean for girls' and boys' achievement in math and science? *Journal of Youth and Adolescence*, *25*, 73–88.

Ward, L. M. (2003). Understanding the role of entertainment media in the sexual socialization of American youth: A review of empirical research. *Developmental Review*, *23*, 347–388.

Ward, L. M., & Friedman, K. (2006). Using TV as a guide: Associations between television viewing and adolescents' sexual attitudes and behavior. *Journal of Research on Adolescence*, *16*, 133–156.

Watt, H. M. G. (2010). Gender and occupational choice. In J. Chrisler & D. M. McCreary (Eds.), *Handbook of gender research in psychology* (Vol. 2, pp. 379–400). New York: Springer.

Weinraub, M., Clemens, L. P., Sockloff, A., Ethridge, T., Gracely, E., & Meyers, B. (1984). The development of sex role stereotypes in the third year: Relationship to gender labeling, identity, sex-typed toy preference, and family characteristics. *Child Development*, *55*, 1493–1503.

Weisner, T. S., & Wilson-Mitchell, J. E. (1990). Nonconventional family life-styles and sex typing in 6-year-olds. *Child Development*, *61*, 1915–1933.

West, C., & Zimmerman, D. (1987). Doing gender. *Gender & Society*, *1*, 125–151.

Whiting, B. B., & Edwards, C. P. (1988). *Children of different worlds: The formation of social behavior*. Cambridge, MA: Harvard University Press.

Witt, M. G., & Wood, W. (2010). Self-regulation of gendered behavior in everyday life. *Sex Roles*, *62*, 635–646.

Women's Sports Foundation. (2007). *Women's sports and fitness facts and statistics*. Retrieved August 26, 2010, from http://www.womenssportsfoundation.org/binary-data/WSF_ARTICLE/pdf_file/28.pdf

Wood, W., & Eagly, A. H. (2002). A cross-cultural analysis of the behavior of women and men: Implications for the origins of sex differences. *Psychological Bulletin*, *128*, 699–727.

Worrell, J. (1996). Feminist identity in a gendered world. In J. C. Chrisler, C. Golden, & P. D. Rozee (Eds.), *Lectures on the psychology of women*. New York: McGraw-Hill.

Yu, L., & Xie, D. (2010). Multidimensional gender identity and psychological adjustment in middle childhood: A study in China. *Sex Roles*, *62*, 100–113.

Zeldin, A. L., & Pajares, F. (2000). Against the odds: Self-efficacy beliefs of women in mathematical, scientific, and technological careers. *American Educational Research Journal*, *37*, 215–246.

Zosuls, K. M., Ruble, D. N., Tamis-LeMonda, C. S., Shrout, P. E., Bornstein, M. H., & Greulich, F. K. (2009). The acquisition of gender labels in infancy: Implications for gender-typed play. *Developmental Psychology*, *45*, 688–701.

Transgender Experience and Identity

Lisa M. Diamond, Seth T. Pardo, and Molly R. Butterworth

Abstract

In this chapter, we review and critique how conventional models of gender and sexual identity development have represented the experiences of transgender individuals, and we argue for an expanded model of transgender identity development which can accommodate the diversity of their lived realities. *Transgender* is a broad category typically used to denote any individual whose gender identity or presentation either violates conventional conceptualizations of "male" or "female" or mixes different aspects of male and female role and identity. Despite increasing social scientific acknowledgment and investigation of transgender experience, most contemporary perspectives presume that the primary identity dilemma for transgender individuals is a conflict between one's psychological gender and one's biological sex, such that the normative and healthy endpoint of transgender identity development is the achievement of a stable, integrated, unambiguous identification as 100% male or 100% female, often achieved via some form of physical transformation aimed at bringing one's psychological gender and one's physical gender presentation into alignment. Yet there is increasing evidence that such dichotomous models of gender fail to accommodate the true complexity and diversity of transgender experience. Hence, in this chapter we argue for broader, more flexible models of gender identity development among transgender individuals which can accommodate the fact that for some of these individuals, identity development will have a linear trajectory leading to a singular outcome, whereas for others, identity development may be a recursive process that accommodates multiple and shifting identity states over time. We explore the implications of such an expanded model of identity development for clinical practice and intervention with transgender individuals.

By the age of 3 or 4, most children have developed a clear sense of gender identity – that is, an enduring sense of themselves as male or female – which persists throughout their lifespan. Yet for transgender individuals, this is not the case.

L.M. Diamond (✉)
Department of Psychology, University of Utah, Salt Lake City, UT, USA
e-mail: diamond@psych.utah.edu

S.J. Schwartz et al. (eds.), *Handbook of Identity Theory and Research*,
DOI 10.1007/978-1-4419-7988-9_26, © Springer Science+Business Media, LLC 2011

Transgender is a broad category typically used to denote any individual whose gender-related identification or external gender presentation conflicts in some way with their birth sex, and who therefore violates conventional standards of unequivocal "male" or "female" identity and behavior. The very fact that the present volume includes a chapter on transgender identity signifies the enormous changes that have occurred in psychological research on gender identity and its development and expression. In recent years, empirical research on the experiences of children, adolescents, and adults who violate conventional norms for gender-typical behavior, or who are consciously questioning their gender identity, has increased dramatically (Bockting & Coleman, 2007; Denny, Leli, & Drescher, 2004; Grossman & D'Augelli, 2006; Halberstam, 2005; S. Hines, 2007; Johnson, 2007; Lev, 2004; Mallon & DeCrescenzo, 2006; Seil, 2004; Wren, 2002).

Nonetheless, contemporary views of gender-transgressive individuals tend to interpret their experiences through a rigid and dichotomous model of gender which presumes that the primary identity dilemma for transgender individuals is a conflict between one's psychological gender and one's biological sex. To be sure, this is quite commonly the case for *transsexual* individuals, who typically report feeling that they are "trapped in the wrong body" and who seek to bring their psychological sense of gender and their physical sex into alignment through a combination of physical transformation (via clothes, makeup, demeanor, hormones, or surgery) and a formal change in legal status. Yet, although transsexualism might be the most widely known form of transgender experience (among both psychologists and laypeople alike), it is certainly not the only one. In fact, the word and concept "transgender" came into use specifically because many individuals with more complex and ambiguous experiences of gender identity – for example, individuals who feel that they are *both* male and female, or *neither* – were poorly described by models of transsexualism. Moreover, individuals with new forms of gender blending and bending continue to stretch

the range and variety of identities that fit under the transgender umbrella.

Hence, our goal in this chapter is to provide an introduction to the diversity of transgender experience, review previous research on the development of transgender identity, and argue for broad, dynamic, and flexible models of transgender identity. Such flexibility is critical if such models will successfully accommodate all forms of transgender expression, from individuals who seek to change their gender expression, either permanently or temporarily, to those who seek to blend their gender expression, to those who seek altogether novel forms of context-dependent gender identity and presentation. Specifically, we maintain that identity models organized around *the process of change and transition itself*, rather than the presumed goal of achieving a stable and socially intelligible "new gender," will be more successful in describing the diverse experiences of transgender individuals and in guiding future research on their healthy development and self-actualization.

Sex and Gender: Concepts Defined

Academic psychology continues to use the terms sex and gender relatively interchangeably (M. Hines, 2004; Schaefer & Wheeler, 1995), yet the two terms are semantically distinct. *Sex* is most often used to describe one's status as male or female (Deaux, 1993; Ruble, Martin, & Berenbaum, 2006), determined biologically via sex chromosomes and assessed at birth by the appearance of external genitalia (which generally suffices, except for rare disorders of sexual differentiation in which there may be disjunctures between chromosomal sex and genital morphology). In contrast, *gender* refers to the trait characteristics and behaviors culturally associated with one's sex (Fausto-Sterling, 2000; M. Hines, 2004). Gender also refers to a person's subjective judgments and inferences about sex including stereotypes, roles, presentation, and expressions of masculinity and femininity (Deaux, 1993; Ruble et al., 2006). Gender *identity* represents a person's sense of self as a boy/man or a girl/woman. As such, it carries an expected set of role behaviors, attitudes, dress style, and appearance. Gender identity is implicitly presumed to develop in a manner that corresponds directly with biological sex, such that boys develop male identities and girls develop female identities (Money & Ehrhardt, 1972; Zucker & Bradley, 1995).

Before proceeding, it bears noting that this overall framework relies on a central assumption – that sex is a "natural category" individuals are *born* with, whereas gender represents the cultural meanings attached to that category – which has come under fire over the years. Queer theorists such as Butler (1990) have criticized this framework for reifying the distinction between biology (sex) and culture (gender), for naturalizing categorical distinctions between "male" and "female" bodies and biology, and for obscuring the manner in which social discourse constructs and creates *sex* in the same way that it creates *gender*. Fausto-Sterling (1993), similarly, has argued that the notion of "two and only two" sexes is a cultural rather than a "natural" phenomenon, and that we might just as well posit five biological "sexes," based on the surprisingly high number of children born with ambiguous or mixed genitalia. We will revisit critiques of the sex/gender binary later on; for now, we employ it for the sake of clarity and consistency, while noting its shortcomings.

Developmental research on gender identity typically focuses on the age and the processes by which children develop understanding in three major domains: categorical sex differences (Ruble et al., 2007), self-awareness and constancy of biological sex (Kohlberg, 1966), and gender-congruent role behaviors (Bem, 1983). Research suggests that consistent labeling of men and women as "male" or "female" occurs by age three, and that stability in one's own self-labeling as male or female occurs between age 3 and 5, although there continue to be conflicting findings on the specific timing of the latter milestone (Maccoby, 1990; Ruble et al., 2007; for a more extensive review of research on normative gender identity, see Bussey, Chapter 25, this volume).

Children and adults who fail to develop a stable, psychological sense of gender that corresponds with their biological sex, and who meet certain cross-gender behavioral traits, may be diagnosed with *gender identity disorder (GID)* (American Psychiatric Association, 2000; Carroll, Gilroy, & Ryan, 2002; Levine et al., 1999). According to the most recent version of the Diagnostic and Statistical Manual of Mental Disorders (DSM-IV), GID is characterized by "a strong and persistent cross-gender identification" (Criteria A), by a "persistent discomfort with [one's biological] sex or a sense of inappropriateness in the gender role of that sex" (Criteria B), "not concurrent with a physical intersex condition" (Criteria C), and by "clinically significant distress" (American Psychiatric Association, 2000, p. 581). Cross-gender identification may also be demonstrated by preferences for gender nonconforming roles in fantasy play, for wearing the clothing of the opposite sex, and/or the desire to engage in activities associated with the opposite sex (such as standing to urinate among girls and sitting to urinate among boys).

Often, though not always, a child with GID will spontaneously state, sometimes as early as 2 or 3 years of age, that his/her true gender identity does not match his/her biological sex (Strong, Singh, & Randall, 2000; Zucker & Bradley, 1995). The DSM-IV revised its definition of GID diagnosis to distinguish childhood manifestations from adolescent and adult manifestation, while still acknowledging that GID may persist across the life course (American Psychiatric Association, 2000; Zucker, 2005a). Although not all adolescents and adults who meet the clinical criteria for GID consider themselves transsexual, it is safe to say that the vast majority of self-identified transsexuals meet the clinical criteria for GID. The clinical criteria carry substantial weight, because the American medical community polices access to hormonal treatment and sex reassignment surgery fairly rigidly, restricting it to transsexual adults who meet the strict criteria for GID or gender dysphoria (Denny et al., 2004; Seil, 2004), such as early appearing and persistent gender confusion, intense and consistent motivation to be the opposite sex (and not simply to periodically dress as the opposite-sex, as is characteristic of transvestitism), intense discomfort or dislike of one's body, and persistence of these subjective experiences in the face of directed attempts at "retraining" (Bockting, Knudson, & Goldberg, 2007; Devor, 2004; Docter & Fleming, 2001; Lippa, 2001; Schaefer & Wheeler, 1995). Notably, transsexual individuals meeting these clinical criteria typically report markedly improved psychological outcomes after undergoing surgical transitions, reporting higher levels of self-esteem and more positive body images (Wolfradt & Neumann, 2001).

In contrast, the vast range of transgender-identified individuals who claim that they are "both" or "neither" male/female, or who adopt complex constellations of male/female identification and presentation, are not considered by the medical community to be appropriate candidates for sex reassignment. In fact, many such individuals do not seek complete sex reassignment at all, preferring instead to modify selected parts of their body (such as breasts or facial hair) or to forgo physical change altogether and focus on modifications in their social status and legal standing (Bilodeau, 2005; Lev, 2004). This is consistent with the fact that such individuals typically reject the notion that they are simply "trapped in the wrong body" and hence do not view a wholesale substitution of one gender identification for the other as a personal goal or as a potential solution to any experiences of distress or discomfort they might face. It is this group of gender-fluid individuals that poses a fundamental dilemma to our attempts to develop broad-based models of transgender identity development.

From Transgender Experience to Transgender Identity

Transsexualism yields fairly straightforward suppositions and predictions regarding normative identity development: whereas the average boy or girl seeks and achieves a clear, consistent, and enduring sense of gender identity between the ages of 2 and 5, the transsexual individual must revisit this process repeatedly in the context of his/her gender transformation. Transsexual identity development, then, may not entail the development of a *transsexual* identity at all, but movement *through* a transsexual or transgender identity to a new identity as unequivocally male or female (Bockting & Coleman, 2007; Wilson, 2002). The highest form of success, within this context, is to "pass": to accomplish such a complete change in gender status that the individual's history of questioning and confusion is replaced by – or more accurately, transformed into – a lived authenticity. Many transsexuals wish *not* to be thought of as "a woman who used to be a man," or "a man who used to be a woman," but simply a "woman" or a "man," with the body and legal status to match (e.g., Girchick, 2008; Wilson, 2002). Of course, this is not uniformly the case. Some transsexuals maintain a strong connection to the transsexual community even after completing a full gender change, and some maintain identity labels (such as "transman" or "transwoman") that acknowledge their history of gender transition.

Decisions about whether to embrace or "move beyond" one's history of gender transition might be moderated by developmental status. An increasing number of individuals are self-identifying as transgender and seeking sex reassignment at earlier ages (Zucker, Bradley, Owen-Anderson, Kibblewhite, & Cantor, 2008). Some of these youth adopt intermediate identities such as "tranny boys," suggesting that they perceive mixed, fluid, and ambiguous gender presentations as potentially stable identity outcomes. Little is currently known about the full range of factors which influence transsexual youths' and adults' motives to embrace an enduring identification as "trans" – even after completing a full gender transition – or to view such identities as temporary stepping stones along the route to a normative "female" or "male" identity. This is clearly a priority for future research.

As noted earlier, perhaps the most important development in research on gender over the past 20 years has been the realization that the transsexual trajectory is not the only form of transgender experience, and may not even be the modal one (Devor, 2004; Ekins & King, 1999; Gagné, Tewksbury, & McGaughey, 1997; Halberstam, 2005). Rather, similar to the aforementioned case of "tranny boys," an increasing number of transgender individuals have come to adopt and embrace fluid, shifting, and ambiguous gender identifications, which seek to combine attributes of masculinity and femininity rather than to "switch" from one gender identity to the other. For example, Gagné et al. (1997) charted multiple identifications in their diverse sample of transgender participants, all of whom were born male. In addition to transsexuals (i.e., those who desired to permanently adopt unequivocally female identities), their sample included preoperative transsexuals (who hoped to pursue sex reassignment surgery in the future, but had not yet done so), nonoperative transsexuals (who lived socially as women and made use of hormones and breast augmentation to feminize their appearance, but had no plans to pursue full-blown sex-reassignment surgery), radical transgenderists (who maintained a masculine gender identity but cross-dressed in a conscious attempt to explore feminine aspects of their personality and challenge traditional binary notions of gender), and ambigenderists and "third-gender" individuals (who lived alternately as men and women or consciously combined masculine and feminine characteristics, emphasizing the degree to which their bodies and self-concepts occupied a spectrum of female and male characteristics).

Similarly, consider the experience of several transwomen interviewed by Girchick (2008), all of whom challenged the notion that transgender individuals sought to resolve any discrepancy between an internal and external sense of gender (typically through sex-reassignment surgery), and who instead gave voice to an empowering embrace of gender ambiguity or fluidity, and a rejection of dichotomous models of sex and gender.

Because I am so openly gender-variant and fluid, I reserve the right to express the truth of that "in the moment".... I believe in "shape shifting" with truth.... Is the goal to get from A to B or is the goal to remain open to fluidity? That's the key. So, it's not so much that surgery will necessary limit your expression, it's the mindset that goes with your need for surgery. Because most folks who want surgery think they're only going from A to B, and that is a limiting mindset (p. 70).

I feel like there's tremendous pressure to have an external appearance and body that are consistent with the internal identity... I have spent much of my life desperately wishing I had a male body. But I'm starting to feel comfortable with the apparent contradictions between my female body and my male presentation. This contradiction is part of my strength and my identity (p. 71).

I think when you're born one and cross over to the other side, so to speak, you're really neither.... And I think a lot of us feel like we are lying, and then we are forced to lie, and ugh. It's like they get you coming and going and there's no way you can in good conscience mark M or F, 'cause neither applies. Or both apply (p. 74).

The terminology contemporarily used by transgender individuals is also notably diverse, including (but not limited to) gender blender, gender bender, gender outlaw, gender queer, drag king/queen, trans, transgender(ist), and queer (Carroll et al., 2002; Ekins & King, 1999). Such individuals pose a fundamental challenge to binary notions of gender by persistently violating or collapsing the border between masculine and feminine appearance and self-concept. Queer theorists have tended to embrace such "gender outlaws" (Bornstein, 1994), heralding their opposition to the hegemonic notion that there are, and should be, "two and only two" genders (Fausto-Sterling, 1993; Feinberg, 1996; Roen, 2002).

Psychologists, however, have taken a more mixed and ambivalent approach to these diverse forms of transgender (reviewed in Mallon & DeCrescenzo, 2006), especially when adopted by adolescents. Is it healthy to claim a permanently liminal form of gender identity? How can we speak of "transgender identity development" if no single identity "goal" can be identified, or if the stated goal involves a wholesale deconstruction of the notion of a fixed and stable self? After all, as early as 1987, the Diagnostic and Statistical Manual of Mental Disorders (DSM-III) recognized a lack of coherent identity as a risk factor for poor mental health outcomes (American Psychiatric Association, 1987)? How do transpeople conceptualize their gender identities, and negotiate the constancy of their biological sex with a conflicting gender identity schema?

There is scant empirical data available on such questions. In contrast to the extensive body of research on conventional gender identity development (Kohlberg et al., 1974; Ruble et al., 2006, 2007; Bussey, Chapter 25, this volume), little research focuses on the developmental processes or the structure and properties of transgender identities in nonclinical populations (Gagné et al., 1997; Mason-Schrock, 1996), and almost no longitudinal studies have been conducted on this topic. Rather, the majority of research on transgender populations focuses on their experiences of discrimination, limited access to health care, physical health challenges, conflicting surgical outcomes, and mental health concerns (Devor, 2004; Lev, 2004; Zucker & Bradley, 1995). Furthermore, most of the existing empirical research on gender nonconformity and transgender individuals has focused on gender atypical *males*, usually in childhood (American Psychiatric Association, 2000; Zucker, 2005b; Zucker & Bradley, 1995). In contrast, there is a dearth of empirical research on normative or resilient developmental outcomes among gender nonconforming and transgender natal females (Zucker, 2005b).

Existing Models of Transgender Identity

Nonetheless, some scholars have attempted to articulate coherent models of transgender and/or transsexual identity development. Perhaps most notable among these attempts is Devor's (2004) 14-stage developmental model, which outlines a progression from early confusion and persistent attempts at social comparisons to gradual self-acceptance, identity synthesis, and pride. For example, in stage one, abiding anxiety characterizes the individual's distinct discomfort with his/her biological sex and his/her preference for cross-gender activities and companionship. Later, during a first identity comparison stage, the individual compares his/her assigned birth-sex with his/her preferred gender roles, and if discrepant,

begins actively seeking out and experimenting with alternative gender expressions and identities. The fourth stage is gender identity discovery, during which he/she accidentally or intentionally learns about the existence of transsexualism and becomes aware that this phenomenon "fits" his/her own sense of identity. After seeking more information about transsexualism, the person begins a second identity comparison stage characterized by disidentification with the birth-sex and reidentification as "transsexed" or as "transgender." Eventually (and often after a notable delay) the individual accepts his/her transsexual identity and discloses it to others. The fact that Devor's model is specific to transsexualism, rather than the full range of transgender experience, can be seen in the fact that the final stages of the model specifically involve planning, saving money for, and undertaking complete sex reassignment, after which the individual experiences a final sense of integration between mind and body and a resulting experience of self-acceptance and pride.

Importantly, Devor's theoretical model has not been empirically validated (Pardo, 2009). Hence, it is unknown whether the majority of transsexuals follow such a linear progression. Certainly, the linear stage models of lesbian-gay-bisexual identity development on which Devor's model is based have been roundly critiqued and arguably discredited over the years, as empirical research has shown that the process of adopting a sexual-minority identity is often characterized by abrupt, nonlinear, and recursive processes of identity exploration, negotiation, and renegotiation (Diamond, 2005a, 2005b, 2007, 2008; Golden, 1987). Based on such findings, it is plausible that transsexual identity development, too, is complex, dynamic, and nonlinear. Devor's model may only apply to the subset of transgender individuals with clear-cut gender dysphoria, for whom the "discovery" of a mismatch between their psychological sex and their physical body represents a critical turning point.

In acknowledgment of these weaknesses, Devor (2004) actually delivers a stern set of cautions against overgeneralizing his model, noting that "It cannot possibly apply to all individuals," that "some people may *never* experience some of the stages," and "that others will move through them in different orders, at different rates, or perhaps not at all" (pp. 43–44). With so many caveats, one may reasonably wonder, "What, then, is the point of a model at all?" Yet although we must remain circumspect about the specific form, order, sequencing, and generalizability of certain transgender developmental pathways, this does not mean that the identification of such pathways is either impossible or inappropriate. The fact that so many transgender-identified individuals report early questioning of their gender identity, often as young as age 10, followed by adoption of a trans-identity around puberty and subsequent disclosure of this identity to others (Grossman & D'Augelli, 2006), suggests that the investigation of potential developmental sequences of transgender experience is a plausible and worthwhile goal that may shed light on the nature, etiology, and general trajectory of transgender experience. In particular, it might help to clarify the extent and source of variability in this experience. For example, are differences between *transsexual* adults (who report a notable disjuncture between their psychological and physical gender) and *transgender* adults (who report mixed gender identifications, or who reject all gender identifications) reflected in their early developmental trajectories? Might such developmental differences shed light on the etiology of their distinct experiences?

The conceptual model developed by Denny et al. (2004) attempts to deemphasize the rigid gender binary that characterizes conventional models of gender identity development, and instead presumes the existence of parallel gender continuums inclusive of male and female dimensions. According to this model, individuals can strongly identify with both male and female dimensions, or with neither (Denny et al., 2004). In addition, rather than positing a single modal developmental pathway, it posits the existence of multiple, individualized trajectories. In this respect, the model is similar to Savin-Williams' *differential developmental trajectories* approach to the development of sexual identity (Savin-Williams, 2005; Chapter 28, this

volume). Savin-Williams' differential developmental approach acknowledges that there may be common experiences and developmental milestones which characterize sexual minorities, but nonetheless emphasizes within-group variability in developmental pathways. Hence, rather than seeking one common developmental trajectory, this approach seeks to identify and understand the *multiple* possible trajectories within the sexual-minority population, and to identify the factors which cause trajectories to converge or diverge at different developmental stages.

Debating the Role of the Gender Binary

This differential developmental trajectories approach would appear to be particularly appropriate to modeling the multiplicity of transgender experiences. Importantly, however, this multiplicity should not be interpreted as utterly arbitrary, representing a limitless undoing of all possible positions and forms (Nataf, 1996). Rather, research suggests that there are certain common elements that bridge otherwise diverse transgender experiences, and these common elements deserve careful attention by identity theorists. In particular, we can speak of a general divide between individuals (such as transsexuals) whose experiences revolve around and reinforce a gender binary by seeking the physical presentations of gender that correspond to their psychological sense of gender, and those whose experience of transgender straddles, rejects, or collapses that binary. Similar to Gagné et al. (1997), Ekins and King (1999) have attempted to systematically chart these different manifestations of transgender experience, differentiating between four different types of narratives commonly recounted by transgender individuals: Narratives of *migration*, *oscillation*, *negation* (or "erasing"), and *transcendence*.

In their framework, migration narratives are those recounted by transsexuals, who emphasize the process of "crossing over" permanently from one gender to another, and who speak of finding a "home" in the desired gender. For these individuals, the transition is permanent and unequivocal. In contrast, transgender individuals with oscillation narratives describe repeated movement back and forth across gender boundaries. They might view one gender identification as "truer" than another, but they do not plan to adopt a permanent gender presentation on either side of the "gender divide." Rather, oscillation transgenderists consider the very process of moving back and forth across the border to be meaningful in and of itself. Importantly, Ekins and King emphasized that this process of moving back and forth across the gender binary did not challenge or dismantle the binary; rather, it functioned to *reinforce* its meaning and rigidity on a cultural level. This is because it is the very *difference* between the male and female "sides" of the border that provides the energy, dynamism, and motivation underlying "border crossing."

In sharp contrast to these two groups, transgender individuals with negation or transcendence narratives pose a more direct challenge to binary notions of gender. As described by Ekins and King, negation narratives speak of erasing or undoing gender – not only the signs and indicators of one's "born" biological sex, but of *all* clear-cut markers and indicators of gender, through selectively adding or eliminating gender-related attributes in a manner that deliberately creates an ambiguous gender presentation. Ekins and King argue that negation narratives actually resemble the growing number of science fiction fantasy stories, which posit futuristic worlds "beyond" gender.

Finally, there are transcendence narratives, which are similar to negation narratives in their attempt to undo and subvert gender, but which have a more explicitly political aim. Bornstein's *Gender Outlaw* (1994) might be considered the paradigmatic expression of this form. In these narratives, the negation and undoing of gender polarities is not simply a personal decision, written on the body and acted out in behavior, but it is explicitly undertaken with the aim of dismantling the hegemonic power of gender dichotomies on a social and cultural level. In transcendence narratives, personal attempts to "ungender" oneself are fundamentally and inextricably linked

with larger political struggles in which the entire social bases of gender-related practices and politics are questioned. As Stone (1991) argued, such transmen and transwomen who reject society's insistence on "passing," and instead allow their ambiguous bodies to be "read" in their complex and unsettling ambiguity, "fragment and reconstitute the elements of gender in new and unexpected geometries" (p. 296).

The Personal, the Political, and the Theoretical

The divide between modes of transgender experience that seek to substitute one gender for the other, those that mesh the two genders into an androgynous new whole, and those which seek to dismantle dichotomous notions of gender altogether has become a contentious area of debate among psychological and social theorists of gender. To be sure, this distinction – and the attendant debates – has important implications for theorizing about transgender identity. In particular, as articulated by S. Hines (2006), there appears to be an inherent contradiction between approaches to transgender identity which seek to destabilize the notion of a singular and stable gender identity, and approaches which straightforwardly advocate the substitution of an old, "false" identity with the new, "correct" one. The former approach has been ardently championed by theorists questioning the "naturalness" of sex (most notably Butler, 1990, and Fausto-Sterling, 1993, as noted earlier), and who seek to expose the socially constructed nature of femaleness and maleness altogether. Yet others have cautioned against universalizing this particular interpretation of transgender, which runs the risk of dismissing and invalidating the lived experiences of transsexuals who hold a more conventional sense of authentic gendered selves, and who seek a stable, fixed identity as "male" or "female" (S. Hines, 2006; Namaste, 1996; Prosser, 1998).

The difference between these two types of transgender experience – one operating within conventional gender constructs and one actively resisting them – is sharply manifested in their respective interpretations of *change and transition.* Both camps are relevant for highlighting elements of transgender identity development. Transsexuals who seek a fixed "home" in one gender or the other (Prosser, 1998; Wilson, 2002) typically view their own trajectory of gender reidentification and authentication as having a defined end, a point in time when the personal gender transformation will be complete. As noted by Wilson (2002), for such individuals the completion of their transformation may entail a withdrawal from the very transgender social and support groups that may have initially proved helpful, since the very identity of "transgender" may cease to hold personal relevance once the new "male" or "female" identity has been successfully adopted. In fact, the former "transgender" identity may be explicitly cast off as a painful reminder of the former false self (see also Brown & Rounsely, 2003).

Yet for transgender individuals who seek to dismantle fixed notions of gender, the process of questioning and transformation may prove to be ever present, with no definitive beginning or end. Furthermore, the transitional process *itself* may change over time. As S. Hines (2006) indicated, "the relationship between gender identity and presentation shifts and evolves *through transition*" (p. 60, emphasis added) such that the degree of "fit" between a certain psychological sense of gender and a particular physical presentation may be quite different 2 years into a transition than it was at the outset. This exemplifies the degree to which no single identity goal is sought. Rather, the overarching aim is to continually seek and approximate a particular form of psychological and physical gender coherence that is, in essence, a moving target.

For these individuals, the journey is itself the outcome. As Kogan (2009) argues in a lucid critique of the recent *legal* history of transgender experience and status, we might best consider all transgender individuals – and for that matter, all "normative" men and women as well – to be undertaking a lifelong "sex/gender journey" (similar to Denny et al., 2004 notion of individualized gender trajectories). In this journey, individuals seek their own particular manifestation of "maleness" or "femaleness," never quite achieving the archetype of "Man" or "Woman" heralded by society, but instead coming to approximate it in different ways at different points during the life course, and sometimes explicitly seeking to manifest or reject *both* archetypes.

Placing Change at the Center: Dynamical Systems Theory

Perhaps the most successful approach to theorizing transgender identity development might be one which places change and transition at the center of analysis, and which views identity "outcomes" as states which are continually constructed and reconstructed over time, rather than achieved with a certain finality. The closest approximation to such an approach, with respect to theory, comes from *dynamical systems theory.* We do not want to imply that this particular strain of theory can "fix" all of the aforementioned weaknesses of existing models of transgender identity development. Rather, we want to highlight dynamical systems theory for the creative and generative possibilities that it offers for future model building.

Dynamical systems models seek to explain how complex patterns emerge, stabilize, change, and restabilize over time. Over the past decade social scientists have increasingly applied this approach to complex human phenomena (for early, seminal examples, see Fogel & Thelen, 1987; Thelen, Kelso, & Fogel, 1987; Thelen & Smith, 1994) to better represent how dynamic interchanges between individuals and their environments give rise to novel forms of thought and behavior. Thus far, dynamical systems approaches have made notable contributions to our understanding of motor development (Kelso, 1997; Turvey, 1990), cognition (Thelen & Smith, 1994), perception (Gilden, 1991), emotion (Fogel, Nwokah, Dedo, & Messinger, 1992; Fogel & Thelen, 1987; Izard, Ackerman, Schoff, & Fine, 2000), personality (Lewis, 2000; Read & Miller, 2002), language (Christman, 2002; Elman, 1995), children's play (Steenbeek &

van Geert, 2005), coping (Lewis, Zimmerman, Hollenstein, & Lamey, 2004), antisocial behavior (Granic & Patterson, 2006), and – most appropriate for this discussion – gender development (Fausto-Sterling, 2000).

Dynamical systems models belong to a larger family of theoretical perspectives seeking to replace deterministic models of social-behavioral phenomena with approaches that emphasize dynamic person–environment interactions occurring over time. Other examples of this approach include general systems theory, developmental systems theory, ecological perspectives, contextualism, transactionalism, and holistic-interactionism (reviewed in Granic, 2005). At their core these approaches all emphasize transformative, bidirectional, changing interactions among endogenous factors (such as genes, hormones, skills, capacities, thoughts, and feelings) and exogenous factors (such as relationships, experiences, cultural norms, family history, etc.,). According to dynamical systems theory, interactions among these elements can actually *create* novel psychological and behavioral phenomena during periods of fundamental reorganization in the overall system, denoted "phase shifts" (Granic, 2005). Phase shifts occur when certain parameters governing the system – or certain relationships *among* parameters – start to vary outside of certain critical thresholds (Fogel & Thelen, 1987). As a result, existing patterns of thought and behavior break down and new patterns take their place.

This process, denoted *self-organization*, is defined as the spontaneous development of order within a complex system (Kelso, 1997). A closely related concept is *emergence*, defined as the coming-into-being of altogether novel behaviors or experiences through dynamic, unpredictable interactions between different elements in the system. As reviewed by Fogel (2006), researchers and theorists have increasingly come to view emergence and transformation as fundamental processes of psychological change, encompassing not only qualitative shifts in subjective experience, but also processes of cognitive discovery and creativity (for example Gottlieb, 1992; Nelson, 1997; Overton, 2002; Tronick et al., 1998).

This would appear to be directly relevant to transgender experience and development. From this perspective, the fundamental task for transgender identity development is not simply to discover, acknowledge, and reveal a deeply hidden "true self," but rather to *create* one's "true self" through a process of self-reflection, perspective-shifting, and (for some) physical transformation (compare to emerging views on the relationship between self-construction and self-discovery in personal identity, as elucidated by Waterman, Chapter 16, this volume and Soenens & Vansteenkiste, Chapter 17, this volume). The new sense of authentic identity which emerges is, in the end, altogether new. It was *not* "in there all along," simply waiting to be released. It is, rather, a hard-fought achievement, a truly novel creation forged out of the individual's entire history of gender experience *and* his/her creative explorations of new forms of gendered self-expression. This perspective actually shares much with Lev's (2004) model of "transgender emergence," which emphasizes the transgender individual's *active engagement* with processes of self-reflection aimed at instantiating a new sense of identity authenticity. One strength of this approach is its necessarily broad timeframe – the process of identity transition and transformation is necessarily open, and potentially recursive, revisited repeatedly as the individual occupies different contexts and seeks to integrate new traits and characteristics into his/her emerging sense of self. Another strength of this approach is the active and autonomous role granted to the transgender individual. The specific nature and character of the authentic identity is *in one's own hands* – not dictated by social norms, therapists, or medical standards. Hence, "mixed" forms of gender presentation which might be deemed "incomplete" from the perspective of developmental models based on transsexualism, are instead authentic and viable identity outcomes. The application of dynamical systems theory to transgender identity and development is one of the most provocative and interesting directions for future research.

Intersections with Sexuality

Another important element which requires more systematic integration into future models of transgender identity development concerns the complex interplay between gender identity and sexual identity and orientation. Historically, it was presumed that the link between gender identity and sexual identity/orientation was fairly straightforward: being attracted to women was a fundamental component of being a man, and being attracted to men was a fundamental component of being a woman (Block, 1909; Forel, 1908; Krafft-Ebing, 1882). According to this logic, men who were attracted to men were not *completely* male; they possessed, instead, some degree of essential femininity. The same logic, in reverse, applied to women who were attracted to women. This conflation between same-sex desire and "gender reversal" (such that gay men are necessarily feminine and lesbians necessarily masculine) has been vigorously critiqued over the years by researchers studying the development and expression of same-sex sexuality (Gottschalk, 2003; Hegarty, 2009; Paul, 1993; Rottnek, 1999). In the context of transgender, this model would appear to suggest that *all* transgender individuals are fundamentally gay, lesbian, or bisexual *before* modifying their original gender presentation (i.e., those born with female bodies are attracted to women, and those born with male bodies are attracted to men), and fundamentally heterosexual afterwards (because by switching their own gender identity, they have transformed a same-sex attraction into an other-sex attraction). Yet this simplistic model of the links between gender identity and sexual orientation simply does not fit the empirical data. Research has documented incredible diversity in transgender individuals' experiences of same-sex and other-sex desire, both before and after modifying their gender identities and presentations (Hines, 2007). Some male-to-female transsexuals seek female sexual partners and identify as lesbians; others seek male partners and identify as heterosexual women (Chivers & Bailey, 2000). Some biologically female transgender individuals

identify as butch (i.e., highly masculine) lesbians and continue to participate actively in the lesbian community, whereas others take on identities as men and seek heterosexual female partners; yet others pursue sexual relations with both men and women. This diversity is possible because gender identity and sexual identity, despite conventional assumptions to the contrary, are fundamentally distinct constructs, such that variability in one dimension does not neatly map onto the other (Devor, 1997; Lawrence, 2004).

At the same time, this does not mean that gender and sexuality are altogether unrelated. For some individuals, these two forms of identity reciprocally inform and influence one another, such that one's experience of "femaleness" and "maleness" is interbraided with one's subjective understanding, experience, and interpretation of sexual desire for female and male partners. Correspondingly, experiences of "same-sex" and "other-sex" desire and behavior are often embedded within the social and interpersonal context of gender presentation – after all, the very designation of a particular desire or behavior as "same sex" or "other sex" requires a stable appraisal of the gender status of everyone involved. Hence, although gender identity and sexual identity are separate phenomena, their relationship is dynamic and reciprocal, informed by an individual's personal sense of gender *and* his/her appraisal of the gender of social partners. It is not surprising, then, that individuals who begin to explore multiplicity and fluidity with respect to their gender identity often become progressively more aware of multiplicity and fluidity in their erotic attractions as well. S. Hines (2007), for example, noted that just as gender is an inherently relational phenomenon, actively negotiated through interactions with other (gendered) individuals, so too is sexuality, and especially for individuals who have questioned, modified, or rejected their natal sex. For these individuals, their subjective experience and understanding of desire necessarily change as their own relationship to their body, their identity, *and* the bodies and identities of their intimate partners changes.

An example of this dynamic interplay between fluidity in gender and fluidity in sexuality is provided by "Mark," a participant in Diamond's (2008) longitudinal study of sexual identity development. Mark was born with a female body, and grew up with a conventional female gender identity. He had been aware of sexual attractions to women since adolescence, and during his early twenties he identified as lesbian. Yet over the years, he began to question his gender identity, and eventually adopted a male gender presentation. Surprisingly, he found that as he delved deeper into the masculine sides of his personality, and took on an increasingly masculine role in self-presentation and interpersonal interaction, he became unexpectedly attracted *to men* (although his attractions to women did not diminish). As Mark described, "It was odd; guys would flirt with me, and I would be like, "Hey, I don't mind that. That doesn't turn me off or make me angry or whatever. Because it used to really annoy me, and it doesn't anymore." (Diamond, 2008, p. 196). Mark connected his own reconstituted experiences of desire for men with his changed appraisal of men's social location with respect to his own: he noted that it was the traditional male-female heterosexual dynamic that he had always found distasteful. Now that he identified as Mark, his desires for men – and his interpersonal and sexual interactions with them – no longer inhabited the conventional male-female heterosexual dynamic, and this shift opened up new erotic possibilities. Mark also described changes in the *types* of men he found attractive after taking on a masculine gender presentation, and these changes were intriguingly related to issues of power and social location. As Mark became "more male" himself, he became increasingly attracted to openly gay men. Hence, although he was still biologically female, and the objects of his desire were male, he experienced these desires (and the resulting erotic dynamic) as fundamentally *homosexual* rather than heterosexual, reflecting a "gay male" side of himself. Perhaps because this form of desire permitted him to maintain more control than is typically afforded heterosexual women in their interactions with men, Mark felt much more comfortable with his attractions to – and relationships with – men than had been the case when he was a teenage

girl. His experiences clearly indicate that the critical "trigger" for Mark's sexual desires was never, in fact, a stable, trait-like degree of femininity or masculinity in another person, but instead a particular interpersonal dialectic regarding gender and social relations.

Such experiences highlight the value of attending to the complex, mutual, dynamic influences between gender identity and sexual identity, and their embeddedness in specific social locations. In modeling multiple trajectories of transgender identity development, we must take care to treat the degree of interdependence between gender identity and sexual identity/desire as an open question, and one which might vary dramatically across different individuals, and also across different stages of the lifespan. Charting these forms of variation, and exploring their implications for long-term self-esteem and well-being among transgender youth and adults, is a key direction for future research.

Mental Health Implications of Transgender Identity

We have considered a multiplicity of identity outcomes and trajectories. Now, what are their implications for mental health? For example, is it "healthier" to transition to a fixed gender identity which conforms to conventional boundaries separating "male" and "female," or to seek a liminal, fluid, transgender identity which collapses and deconstructs those categories? To answer this question, we must consider the major threats to psychological health among transgender men and women.

Research reliably indicates that social stigmatization – manifested in some cases by outright physical victimization – poses the preeminent threat to transgender individuals' mental and physical health. These findings concord with the *minority stress* model of sexual-minority health (Meyer, 2003), which specifies that sexual minorities' acute exposure to environmental stressors such as verbal or physical abuse, institutional discrimination, interpersonal harassment, and general social marginalization confers cumulative psychological stress. This stress, in turn, negatively affects both mental and physical well-being.

Institutional reports, popular media, and biographical accounts document an abundance of gender prejudice and gender-based violence perpetrated against transgender individuals (Brown & Rounsely, 2003; Feinberg, 1996, 2006). A recurring survey conducted by the National Coalition of Anti-Violence Programs (NCAVP) of bias-motivated violence against gender and sexual minorities has found that hate crimes against gender-nonconforming adolescents and adults accounted for one-fifth of all documented murders (National Coalition of Anti-Violence Programs, 1999, 2007). A recent survey of 515 trans-identified people (392 male-to-female, 123 female-to-male; Clements-Nolle, Marx, & Katz, 2006), reported that 28% of the respondents had been in an alcohol or drug treatment program, 62% had experienced gender discrimination, 83% had experienced gender-related, verbal discrimination, 59% had experienced sexual assault (rape), and 32% had reported attempted suicide. Among the sample's youth (< 25 years of age), nearly half had attempted suicide as a result of gender-based victimization.

It should be no surprise that other recent empirical investigations suggest that gender-nonconforming adolescents are particularly vulnerable to environmental stressors. Brown and Rounsely (1996), for example, found that gender-nonconforming adolescents routinely experienced taunting, teasing, and bullying at school. Sausa (2005) reported that nearly all the gender-nonconforming adolescents in his study recalled school-based verbal and physical harassment, which left three-quarters of them feeling unsafe. They felt singled out or traumatized several times a day, including during gym class, at school events, or when using single-sex restrooms. In yet another study (D'Augelli, Pilkington, & Hershberger, 2002), lesbian, gay, and bisexual youth confirmed that peers verbally harassed and physically abused their gender-nonconforming peers more frequently than themselves.

Even youths who escape victimization in school must contend with heightened psychosocial stress in their daily lives. In addition to the normative stressors associated with adolescent social and psychological development, gender-nonconforming adolescents often struggle with an increasing awareness that their *psychological* sense of self does not neatly correspond to their body. The physical changes brought about by puberty only heighten this discrepancy, potentially escalating a youth's potential sense of internal alienation and confusion. Youths may be unable to articulate to others *why* they feel different, and hence frequently report feeling isolated, depressed, hopeless, or utterly invisible to friends and family (Swann & Herbert, 1999). From a symbolic interactionist perspective (Serpe & Stryker, Chapter 10, this volume), it might be viewed as inevitable that a youth's gender nonconformity influences his psychological well-being, given that the social stigma attached to gender nonconformity necessarily alters – sometimes profoundly – the nature of such a youth's social interchanges with strangers as well as friends and family. Hence, to the extent that psychological well-being is fundamentally embedded in social relations, the altered social relations of gender-nonconforming youths create notable strains for their psychological development.

Left unchecked, the accumulation of stressors at home, at school, and at work may provoke sustained feelings of shame, alienation, and inadequacy among gender-nonconforming youths. To cope with these feelings, youths may display a range of externalizing problems, including running away from home, dropping out of school, abusing substances, or self-harm (D'Augelli, Hershberger, & Pilkington, 2001; Sausa, 2005). Others may seek to modify their bodies to achieve a greater sense of comfort and personal authenticity. For example, some transgender adolescents with particularly pronounced cross-gender identifications have reported self-injecting silicone or steroids to create a more feminine or masculine appearance in accordance with their gender identity. Klein (1999) suggested that restricted access to carefully monitored and orchestrated gender transitions can result in increased risk-taking behavior including self-mutilation, substance abuse, prostitution, and exposure to HIV.

In the context of these risks and stressors, what conclusions might we draw about different trajectories of transgender identity development? One likely possibility is that during the adolescent years, it may be difficult – or impossible – to tell whether a particular youth is "headed" for one trajectory or another. Although some adolescents may self-identify as transsexual at fairly early ages, expressing clear desires to permanently change their gender, it is important to remember that such youths may perceive that this is the *only* outcome of gender questioning. The possibility of adopting a more fluid, liminal sense of gender may have never occurred to many youths; in addition, they are unlikely to have any visible models of such forms of gender fluidity. Hence, their ability to craft a meaningful autobiographical narrative (see McAdams, Chapter 5, this volume) which contains – and makes sense of – their conflicting and changing experiences of masculinity and femininity is impaired. Given this limitation, the healthiest identity trajectory for transgender adolescents may be one which makes no presumptions about desirable outcomes, and sets no timetables for resolution, but instead remains open to multiple possibilities over potentially long periods of time. Youths need time, support, information, and autonomy as they grapple with their own sense of gendered selfhood and seek a comfortable and personally authentic constellation of female-typed, male-typed, and gender-neutral traits. *Changes* in this constellation – at the level of cognition as well as appearance, and occurring during adolescence as well as adulthood – may be part and parcel of the identity development process.

One thing, however, is abundantly clear. Neither transgender youths nor adults can embark on this process without a basic sense of safety. As long as transgender individuals are forced to navigate their school and family worlds with an ever-present, debilitating fear of stigmatization, ostracization, humiliation, and physical violence, they cannot be expected to achieve a healthy

sense of self-determination, whether such self-determination involves switching their gender identity or making peace with a lasting sense of gender fluidity.

With respect to transgender youth, it is evident that supportive adults play a key role in facilitating resilience and positive development (Garofalo, Deleon, Osmer, Doll, & Harper, 2006; Grossman & D'Augelli, 2006; Mallon & DeCrescenzo, 2006). Decades of research on resilience, conducted with mainstream as well as at-risk populations, has shown that adults can strengthen youth by teaching them how to respond positively to adversity (Bernard, 2006). With respect to transgender youth in particular, adults may require special education and awareness. For example, learning the preferred name and pronoun usage of a transgender youth is critical to gaining their trust and supporting their own developmental pathway. Similarly, ensuring and maintaining confidentiality is critical for demonstrating to transgender youth that their safety will not be compromised, given the risks that these youths typically face for discrimination and violence. Finally, research on resilience (Bernard, 2006) also indicates that young people flourish when they know that adults believe and nurture their capacity to succeed. Accordingly, it is important to encourage transgender and gender-nonconforming youth to be visible and proud leaders and role models for others just like them.

Conclusion

In this chapter we have reviewed the literature on the documented diversity of transgender experience, as well as previous research on the development of transgender identity. In contrast to the theoretical identity models based on sexuality research which prioritize stable, uniform endpoints, we have argued for new, flexible models that conceptualize transgender identity development as a dynamic, highly individualized process, which may be undertaken multiple times over the lifespan, and for which the *journey* is as important as the outcome. We make a call for new lines of empirical research using this approach to explore the full range of trajectories of transgender identity development. Identity models organized around the process of change and *transition itself*, rather than those which prescribe a limited range of "healthy" outcomes, will be most successful in elucidating the individual and contextual factors which promote mental and physical well-being among transgender youths and adults, and which support their self-actualization.

In many ways, the state of flux and transformation that currently characterizes research on identity development among transgender populations resembles similar transformations that took place within the field of sexual identity research regarding acknowledgment and validation of bisexuality. With a few notable exceptions (Blumstein & Schwartz, 1977; Paul, 1985; Shuster, 1987), early investigations of sexual identity development focused exclusively on lesbian and gay individuals, not even mentioning bisexuals in the title (reviewed in Diamond, 2008). Yet both researchers and laypeople persistently questioned whether bisexuality represented a "true" and stable identity or whether it was best construed as a transitional phase that individuals traversed on the way to their "true" homosexuality (Rust, 2000, 2001). Overall, this battle has been largely resolved, and most researchers now consider bisexuality to be a stable identity in and of itself with its own distinctive phenomenology and developmental trajectory (Rust, 2002; Weinberg, Williams, & Pryor, 1994). However, the long-fought battle for such legitimacy exemplifies the degree to which psychologists have difficulty reconciling the notion that a healthy identity might, in fact, be characterized by a fundamental *liminality* in sexual and gender expression.

We now face a similar crossroads with respect to transgender identity development. Whereas previous research on transgender populations has presumed that the fundamental identity "project" was to unilaterally switch from one gender to the other, and has focused primarily on their psychological deficits and challenges, it is now time to acknowledge the complexity of the transgender population and to explore how the multiple meanings that transgender individuals attach to their shifting gender identities may positively influence their identity development and their overall well-being. Toward this end, we must work systematically to develop and test models which allow for a multiple continuum framework that allows for simultaneous parallel continuums for biological sex (more to less female and more to less male), gender identity (man to not-man and woman to not-woman), and gender expression (more to less masculine and more to less feminine) (Doorn, Poortinga, & Verschoor, 1994; Girchick, 2008). As Devor argued (2004), "each of us has a deep need to be witnessed by others for whom we are" (p. 46). By respecting and scientifically investigating the full range of transgender experiences and transgender developmental trajectories, identity theorists can play a critical part in this witnessing.

References

American Psychiatric Association. (1987). *Diagnostic and statistical manual of mental disorders* (3rd ed., revised). Washington, DC: American Psychiatric Association.

American Psychiatric Association (2000). *Diagnostic and statistical manual of mental disorders* (4th ed.). Washington, DC: American Psychiatric Association.

Bem, S. L. (1983). Gender schema theory and its implications for child development: Raising gender-aschematic children in a gender-schematic society. *Signs, 8*, 598–616.

Bernard, B. (2006). The foundations of the resiliency paradigm. In N. Henderson (Ed.), *Resiliency in action: Practical ideas for overcoming risks and building strengths in youth, families, and communities* (pp. 3–7). Ojai, CA: Resiliency in Action.

Bilodeau, B. (2005). Beyond the gender binary: A case study of two transgender students at a Midwestern research university. *Journal of Gay and Lesbian Issues in Education, 3*, 29–44.

Block, I. (1909). *The sexual life of our time*. London: Heinemann.

Blumstein, P., & Schwartz, P. (1977). Bisexuality: Some social psychological issues. *Journal of Social Issues, 33*, 30–45.

Bockting, W. O., & Coleman, E. (2007). Developmental stages of the transgender coming-out process: Towards an integrated identity. In A. E. Eyler & S. Monstrey (Eds.), *Principles of transgender medicine and surgery* (pp. 185–210). New York: Haworth Press.

Bockting, W. O., Knudson, G., & Goldberg, J. M. (2007). Counseling and mental health care for transgender adults and loved ones. *International Journal of Transgenderism, 9,* 35–82.

Bornstein, K. (1994). *Gender outlaw: Men, women, and the rest of us.* New York: Routledge.

Brown, M., & Rounsely, C. (2003). *True selves: Understanding transsexualism – For families, friends, coworkers, and helping professionals.* San Francisco: Jossey-Bass.

Brown, M. L., & Rounsely, C. A. (1996). *True selves: Understanding transsexualism-for families, friends, co-workers, and helping professionals.* San Francisco: Jossey-Bass.

Butler, J. P. (1990). *Gender trouble: Feminism and the subversion of identity.* London: Routledge.

Carroll, L., Gilroy, P. J., & Ryan, J. (2002). Counseling trangendered, transsexual, and gender-variant clients. *Journal of Counseling & Development, 80,* 131–138.

Chivers, M. L., & Bailey, J. M. (2000). Sexual orientation of female-to-male transsexuals: A comparison of homosexual and nonhomosexual types. *Archives of Sexual Behavior, 29,* 259–278.

Christman, S. S. (2002). Dynamic systems theory: Application to language development and acquired aphasia. In R. G. Daniloff (Ed.), *Connectionist approaches to clinical problems in speech and language: Therapeutic and scientific applications* (pp. 111–146). Mahwah, New Jersey: Lawrence Erlbaum Associates, Publishers.

Clements-Nolle, K., Marx, R., & Katz, M. (2006). Attempted suicide among transgender persons: The influence of gender-based discrimination and victimization. *Journal of Homosexuality, 51,* 53–69.

D'Augelli, A. R., Hershberger, S. L., & Pilkington, N. W. (2001). Suicidality patterns and sexual orientation-related factors among lesbian, gay, and bisexual youths. *Suicide and Life-Threatening Behavior, 31,* 250–264.

D'Augelli, A. R., Pilkington, N. W., & Hershberger, S. L. (2002). Incidence and mental health impact of sexual orientation victimization of lesbian, gay, and bisexual youths in high school. *School Psychology Quarterly, 17,* 148–167.

Deaux, K. (1993). Commentary: Sorry, wrong number: A reply to Gentile's call. *Psychological Science, 4,* 125–126.

Denny, D., Leli, U., & Drescher, J. (2004). Changing models of transsexualism. In U. Leli & J. Drescher (Eds.), *Transgender subjectivities: A clinician's guide* (pp. 25–40). New York: Haworth Press.

Devor, H. (1997). *FTM: Female-to-male transsexuals in society.* Bloomington, IN: Indiana University Press.

Devor, A. H. (2004). Witnessing and mirroring: A fourteen stage model of transsexual identity formation. *Journal of Gay & Lesbian Psychotherapy, 8,* 41–67.

Diamond, L. M. (2005a). A new view of lesbian subtypes: Stable vs. fluid identity trajectories over an 8-year period. *Psychology of Women Quarterly, 29,* 119–128.

Diamond, L. M. (2005b). What we got wrong about sexual identity development: Unexpected findings from a longitudinal study of young women. In A. Omoto & H. Kurtzman (Eds.), *Sexual orientation and mental health: Examining identity and development in lesbian, gay, and bisexual people* (pp. 73–94). Washington, DC: American Psychological Association Press.

Diamond, L. M. (2007). A dynamical systems approach to female same-sex sexuality. *Perspectives on Psychological Science, 2,* 142–161.

Diamond, L. M. (2008). *Sexual fluidity: Understanding women's love and desire.* Cambridge, MA: Harvard University Press.

Docter, R. F., & Fleming, J. S. (2001). Measures of transgender behavior. *Archives of Sexual Behavior, 30,* 255–271.

Doorn, C. D., Poortinga, J., & Verschoor, A. M. (1994). Cross-gender identity in transvestites and male transsexuals. *Archives of Sexual Behavior, 23,* 185–217.

Ekins, R., & King, D. (1999). Towards a sociology of transgendered bodies. *The Sociological Review, 47,* 580–602.

Elman, J. L. (1995). Language as a dynamical system. In R. F. Port & T. van Gelder (Eds.), *Mind as motion: Explorations in the dynamics of cognition* (pp. 195–225). Cambridge, MA: The MIT Press.

Fausto-Sterling, A. (1993, March/April). The five sexes: Why male and female are not enough. *The Sciences,* 20–24.

Fausto-Sterling, A. (2000). *Sexing the body: Gender politics and the construction of sexuality.* New York: Basic Books.

Feinberg, L. (1996). *Transgender warriors: Making history from Joan of Arc to Dennis Rodman.* Boston: Beacon Press.

Feinberg, L. (2006). *Drag king dreams.* New York: Carroll & Graff.

Fogel, A. (2006). Dynamic systems research on interindividual communication: The transformation of meaning-making. *Journal of Developmental Processes, 1,* 7–30.

Fogel, A., Nwokah, E., Dedo, J. Y., & Messinger, D. (1992). Social process theory of emotion: A dynamic systems approach. *Social Development, 1,* 122–142.

Fogel, A., & Thelen, E. (1987). Development of early expressive and communicative action: Reinterpreting the evidence from a dynamic systems perspective. *Developmental Psychology, 23,* 747–761.

Forel, A. (1908). *The sexual question: A scientific, psychological, hygienic and sociological study* (C. F. Marshall, Trans.). New York: Physicians & Surgeons Book Company.

Gagné, P., Tewksbury, R., & McGaughey, D. (1997). Coming out and crossing over: Identity formation and proclamation in a transgender community. *Gender & Society, 11*, 478–508.

Garofalo, R., Deleon, J., Osmer, E., Doll, M., & Harper, G. W. (2006). Overlooked, misunderstood and at-risk: Exploring the lives and HIV risk of ethnic minority male-to-female transgender youth. *Journal of Adolescent Health, 38*, 230–236.

Gilden, D. L. (1991). On the origins of dynamical awareness. *Psychological Review, 98*, 554–568.

Girchick, L. B. (2008). *Transgender voices: Beyond women and men.* London: University Press of New England.

Golden, C. (1987). Diversity and variability in women's sexual identities. In Boston Lesbian Psychologies Collective (Ed.), *Lesbian psychologies: Explorations and challenges* (pp. 19–34). Urbana: University of Illinois Press.

Gottlieb, G. (1992). *Individual development and evolution: The genesis of novel behavior.* New York: Oxford University Press.

Gottschalk, L. (2003). Same-sex sexuality and childhood gender non-conformity: A spurious connection. *Journal of Gender Studies, 12*, 35–50.

Granic, I. (2005). Timing is everything: Developmental psychopathology from a dynamic systems perspective. *Developmental Review, 25*, 386–407.

Granic, I., & Patterson, G. R. (2006). Toward a comprehensive model of antisocial development: A dynamic systems approach. *Psychological Review, 113*, 101–131.

Grossman, A. H., & D'Augelli, A. R. (2006). Transgender youth: Invisible and vulnerable. *Journal of Homosexuality, 51*, 111–128.

Halberstam, J. (2005). *In a queer time and place: Transgender bodies, subcultural lives.* New York: NYU Press.

Hegarty, P. (2009). Toward an LGBT-informed paradigm for children who break gender norms: Comment on Drummond et al. (2008) and Rieger et al. (2008). *Developmental Psychology, 45*, 895–900.

Hines, M. (2004). *Brain gender.* New York: Oxford University Press.

Hines, S. (2006). What's the difference? Bringing particularity to queer studies of transgender. *Journal of Gender Studies, 15*, 49–66.

Hines, S. (2007). *Transforming gender: Transgender practice of identity, intimacy, and care.* Bristol: The Policy Press.

Izard, C. E., Ackerman, B. P., Schoff, K. M., & Fine, S. E. (2000). Self-organization of discrete emotions, emotion patterns, and emotion-cognition relations. In M. D. Lewis & I. Granic (Eds.), *Emotion, development, and self-organization: Dynamic systems approaches to emotional development* (pp. 15–36). New York: Cambridge University Press.

Johnson, K. (2007). Transsexualism: Diagnostic dilemmas, transgender politics and the future of transgender care. In V. Clark & E. Peel (Eds.), *Out in psychology: Lesbian, gay, bisexual, trans and queer perspectives* (pp. 445–464). New York: Wiley.

Kelso, J. A. S. (1997). *Dynamic patterns: The self-organization of brain and behavior.* New York: The MIT Press.

Klein, R. (1999). Group work practice with transgendered male to female sex workers. *Journal of Gay and Lesbian Social Services, 10*, 95–109.

Kogan, T. (2009). *Attacking law's binary vision of sex: The sex/gender journey and the "in-between" body.* Manuscript under review.

Kohlberg, L. (1966). Moral education in the schools: A developmental view. *School Review, 74*, 1–30.

Kohlberg, L., Ullian, D. Z., Friedman, R. C., Richart, R. M., Vande Wiele, R. L., & Stern, L. O. (1974). Stages in the development of psychosexual concepts and attitudes. In *Sex differences in behavior.* Oxford, UK: Wiley.

Krafft-Ebing, R. (1882). *Psychopathia sexualis* (M. E. Wedneck, Trans.). New York: Putnams.

Lawrence, A. A. (2004). Autogynephilia: A paraphilic model of gender identity disorder. *Journal of Gay & Lesbian Psychotherapy, 8*, 69–87.

Lev, A. I. (2004). *Transgender emergence: Therapeutic guidelines for working with gender-variant people and their families.* Binghamton, NY: Haworth Clinical Practice Press.

Levine, S. B., Brown, G. R., Coleman, E., Cohen-Kettenis, P. T., Hage, J. J., Van Maasdam, J., et al. (1999). The standards of care for gender identity disorders. *Journal of Psychology & Human Sexuality, 11*, 1–34.

Lewis, M. D. (2000). The promise of dynamic systems approaches for an integrated account of human development. *Child Development, 71*, 36–43.

Lewis, M. D., Zimmerman, S., Hollenstein, T., & Lamey, A. V. (2004). Reorganization in coping behavior at $1\frac{1}{2}$ years: Dynamic systems and normative change. *Developmental Science, 7*, 56–73.

Lippa, R. (2001). On deconstructing and reconstructing masculinity-femininity. *Journal of Research in Personality, 35*, 168–207.

Maccoby, E. (1990). Gender and relationships: A developmental account. *American Psychologist, 45*, 513–520.

Mallon, G. P., & DeCrescenzo, T. (2006). Transgender children and youth: A child welfare practice perspective. *Child Welfare Journal, 85*, 215–241.

Mason-Schrock, D. (1996). Transsexuals' narrative construction of the 'true self.'. *Social Psychology Quarterly, 59*, 176–192.

Meyer, I. H. (2003). Prejudice, social stress, and mental health in lesbian, gay, and bisexual populations: Conceptual issues and research evidence. *Psychological Bulletin, 129*, 674–697.

Money, J., & Ehrhardt, A. A. (1972). *Man and woman, boy and girl: The differentiation and dimorphism of gender identity from conception to maturity.* Baltimore: Johns Hopkins University Press.

Namaste, V. K. (1996). Tragic misreadings: Query theory's erasure of transgender subjectivity. In B. Beemyn & M. Eliason (Eds.), *Queer studies: A lesbian, gay, bisexual and transgender anthology* (pp. 183–203). New York: NYU Press.

Nataf, Z. (1996). *Lesbians talk transgender*. London: Scarlet Press.

National Coalition of Anti-Violence Programs. (1999). *Anti-lesbian, gay, transgender, and bisexual violence in 1999: A report of the National Coalition of Anti-Violence Programs*. Retrieved June 1, 2008, from www.ncavp.org/publications/NationalPubs.aspx

National Coalition of Anti-Violence Programs. (2007). *Anti-lesbian, gay, transgender, and bisexual violence in 2007: A report of the National Coalition of Anti-Violence Programs*. Retrieved June 1, 2008, from www.ncavp.org/publications/NationalPubs.aspx

Nelson, K. (1997). Cognitive change as collaborative construction. In E. Amsel & K. A. Renninger (Eds.), *Change and development: Issues of theory, method, and application* (pp. 99–115). Mahway, NJ: Lawrence Erlbaum Associates.

Overton, W. F. (2002). Understanding, explanation, and reductionism: Finding a cure for Cartesian anxiety. In T. Brown & L. Smith (Eds.), *Reductionism and the development of knowledge* (pp. 29–51). Mahway, NJ: Lawrence Erlbaum Associates.

Pardo, S. T. (2009). *An exploratory study of identity conceptualization and development in a sample of gender nonconforming biological females*. Unpublished Master's Thesis. Cornell University, Ithaca, NY.

Paul, J. P. (1985). Bisexuality: Reassessing our paradigms of sexuality. In F. Klein & T. Wolf (Eds.), *Two lives to lead: Bisexuality in men and women* (pp. 21–34). New York: Harrington Park Press.

Paul, J. P. (1993). Childhood cross-gender behavior and adult homosexuality: The resurgence of biological models of sexuality. In J. P. DeCecco & J. P. Elia (Eds.), *If you seduce a straight person, can you make them gay?* (pp. 41–54). New York: Harrington Park Press.

Prosser, J. (1998). *Second skins: The body narratives of transsexuality*. New York: Columbia University Press.

Read, S. J., & Miller, L. C. (2002). Virtual personalities: A neural network model of personality. *Personality and Social Psychology Review, 6,* 357–369.

Roen, K. (2002). 'Either/or' and 'both/neither': Discursive tensions in transgender politics. *Signs, 27,* 501–522.

Rottnek, M. (Ed.) (1999). *Sissies and tomboys: Gender nonconformity and homosexual childhood*. New York: New York University Press.

Ruble, D. N., Martin, C. L., & Berenbaum, S. A. (2006). Gender development. In N. Eisenberg, W. Damon, & R. M. Lerner (Eds.), *Handbook of child psychology, social, emotional, and personality development (Vol. 3, 6th ed.*, pp. 858–932). Hoboken, NJ: Wiley.

Ruble, D. N., Taylor, L. J., Cyphers, L., Greulich, F. K., Lurye, L. E., & Shrout, P. E. (2007). The role of gender constancy in early gender development. *Child Development, 78,* 1121–1136.

Rust, P. C. R. (2000). Academic literature on situational homosexuality in the 1960s and 1970s. In P. C. R. Rust (Ed.), *Bisexuality in the United States: A reader and guide to the literature* (pp. 221–249). New York: Columbia University Press.

Rust, P. C. R. (2001). Two many and not enough: The meanings of bisexual identities. *Journal of Bisexuality, 1,* 31–68.

Rust, P. C. R. (2002). Bisexuality: The state of the union. *Annual Review of Sex Research, 13,* 180–240.

Sausa, L. A. (2005). Translating research into practice: Trans youth recommendations for improving school systems. *Gay and Lesbian Issues in Education, 3,* 15–28.

Savin-Williams, R. C. (2005). *The new gay teenager*. Cambridge, MA: Harvard University Press.

Schaefer, L. C., & Wheeler, C. C. (1995). Harry Benjamin's first ten cases (1938–1953): A clinical historical note. *Archives of Sexual Behavior, 24,* 73–93.

Seil, D. (2004). The diagnosis and treatment of transgendered patients. In U. Leli & J. Drescher (Eds.), *Transgender subjectivities: A clinician's guide* (pp. 99–116). New York: Haworth Press.

Shuster, R. (1987). Sexuality as a continuum: The bisexual identity. In Boston Lesbian Psychologies Collective (Ed.), *Lesbian Psychologies* (pp. 56–71). Urbana, IL: University of Illinois Press.

Steenbeek, H., & van Geert, P. (2005). A dynamic systems model of dyadic interaction during play of two children. *European Journal of Developmental Psychology, 2,* 105–145.

Stone, S. (1991). The "Empire" strikes back: A posttranssexual manifesto. In K. Straub & J. Epstein (Eds.), *Body guards: The cultural politics of gender ambiguity* (pp. 280–304). New York: Routledge.

Strong, S. M., Singh, D., & Randall, P. K. (2000). Childhood gender nonconformity and body dissatisfaction in gay and heterosexual men. *Sex Roles, 43,* 427–439.

Swann, S., & Herbert, S. E. (1999). Ethical issues in the mental health treatment of gender dysphoric adolescents. *Journal of Gay & Lesbian Social Services: Issues in Practice, Policy & Research, 10,* 19–34.

Thelen, E., Kelso, J. A. S., & Fogel, A. (1987). Self-organizing systems and infant motor development. *Developmental Review, 7,* 39–65.

Thelen, E., & Smith, L. B. (1994). *A dynamic systems approach to the development of cognition and action*. Cambridge, MA: MIT Press.

Tronick, E. Z., Brushweiller-Stern, N., Harrison, A. M., Lyons-Ruth, K., Morgan, A. C., Nahum, J. P., et al. (1998). Dyadically expanded states of consciousness and the process of therapeutic change. *Infant Mental Health Journal, 19,* 290–299.

Turvey, M. T. (1990). Coordination. *American Psychologist, 45,* 938–953.

Weinberg, M. S., Williams, C. J., & Pryor, D. W. (1994). *Dual attraction: Understanding bisexuality*. New York: Oxford University Press.

Wilson, M. (2002). 'I am the Prince of pain, for I am a princess in the brain': Liminal transgender identities, narratives and the elimination of ambiguities. *Sexualities*, *5*, 425–448.

Wolfradt, U., & Neumann, K. (2001). Depersonalization, self-esteem and body image in male-to-female transsexuals compared to male and female controls. *Archives of Sexual Behavior*, *30*, 301–310.

Wren, B. (2002). 'I can accept my child is transsexual but if I ever see him in a dress I'll hit him': Dilemmas in parenting a transgendered adolescent. *Clinical Child Psychology and Psychiatry*, *7*, 377–397.

Zucker, K. J. (2005a). Gender identity disorder in children and adolescents. *Annual Review of Clinical Psychology*, *1*, 467–492.

Zucker, K. J. (2005b). Measurement of psychosexual differentiation. *Archives of Sexual Behavior*, *34*, 375–388.

Zucker, K. J., & Bradley, S. J. (1995). *Gender identity disorder and psychosexual problems in children and adolescents*. New York: The Guilford Press.

Zucker, K. J., Bradley, S. J., Owen-Anderson, A., Kibblewhite, S. J., & Cantor, J. M. (2008). Is gender identity disorder in adolescents coming out of the closet? *Journal of Sex & Marital Therapy*, *34*, 287–290.

Sexual Identity as a Universal Process

27

Frank R. Dillon, Roger L. Worthington, and Bonnie Moradi

Abstract

This chapter summarizes advances in current theoretical and empirical literature on sexual identity development. It proposes a model of sexual identity that offers a more global (i.e., non-sexual identity group specific) perspective in comparison to existing sexual identity group-specific sexual identity models. Attention to commonalities in sexual identity development across sexual identity subgroups can offer a more global perspective that captures shared experiences of sexual identity development as well as differences between subgroups. The proposed unifying model of sexual identity development incorporates what has been learned from years of theory and research concerning sexuality, LGB and heterosexual identity development, attitudes toward sexual minority individuals, and the meaning of ordinate and subordinate group membership. The model describes the intersection of various contextual factors that influence the individual and social processes underlying sexual identity development. The unifying model is innovative in its applicability across sexual orientation identities, as well as its inclusion of a wide range of dimensions of sexual identity and possible developmental trajectories. The chapter concludes with a discussion of preliminary research findings that inform the unifying model and that have implications for future research. We hope this model allows researchers, educators, and practitioners to develop interventions and conduct investigations on broader questions about human sexuality without being constrained to gay–straight dichotomies of sexual orientation and the related methodological limitations that have characterized sexual identity theory and research in the past.

Identity consists of a stable sense of one's goals, beliefs, values, and life roles (Erikson, 1950; Marcia, 1987). It includes, but is not limited to, gender, race, ethnicity, social class, spirituality, and sexuality. *Identity development* is a dynamic process of assessing and exploring one's identity,

F.R. Dillon (✉)
Robert Stempel College of Public Health and Social Work, Florida International University, Miami, FL, USA
e-mail: fdillon@fiu.edu

S.J. Schwartz et al. (eds.), *Handbook of Identity Theory and Research*,
DOI 10.1007/978-1-4419-7988-9_27, © Springer Science+Business Media, LLC 2011

and making commitments to an integrated set of identity elements (Marcia, 1987). Identity formation was originally conceived as a focal task of adolescence (Erikson, 1950), but the concept has more recently been applied throughout the lifespan (see Kroger & Marcia, Chapter 2, this volume).

In this chapter, we focus on sexual identity development. During the past two decades, there have been numerous theoretical and empirical advances in understanding sexual identity development as applied to individuals identified as lesbian, gay, bisexual, and heterosexual (e.g., Diamond & Savin-Williams, 2000; Eliason, 1995; Fassinger & Miller, 1996; McCarn & Fassinger, 1996; Savin-Williams & Diamond, 2000; Worthington, Savoy, Dillon, & Vernaglia, 2002; see Savin-Williams, Chapter 28, this volume). Within these advances, conceptual models and measurements of sexual identity development were designed for specific sexual identity subgroups (e.g., lesbians, gay men, heterosexuals). It is important to note, however, that only limited progress has been achieved in the construction of models and measures for bisexual or heterosexual individuals (see Diamond, Pardo, & Butterworth, Chapter 26, this volume; Savin-Williams, Chapter 28, this volume).

Sexual identity subgroup models and measures serve an important role in elucidating identity experiences and processes that are unique to each subgroup. Attention to commonalities in sexual identity development across sexual identity subgroups can offer a global perspective that captures shared experiences of sexual identity development as well as differences between subgroups. Thus, group-specific and universal models of sexual identity development can be viewed as having complementary strengths and limitations in that aspects of sexual identity development that are uniquely salient to specific groups are the focus of group-specific models, and aspects that are shared across groups are the focus of universal models. The need for both group-specific and universal foci also parallels greater societal acceptance of diversity in sexual identity groups (e.g., Yang, 2000).

The purpose of this chapter is to describe current theoretical and empirical literature on sexual identity development, and to arrive at a proposed model of sexual identity that offers a global (i.e., non-group specific) perspective. This proposed model can offer a complementary perspective to existing group-specific (i.e., gay and lesbian, bisexual, and heterosexual) sexual identity models and is not intended to replace such models. In the subsequent sections, we (a) review and evaluate prominent literature and concepts concerning sexual identity development within specific sexual identity subgroups, (b) introduce a unifying model of sexual identity development that can be applied across sexual identity subgroups, and (c) discuss preliminary findings from recent research that can inform the unifying model and that may have implications for future research.

Sexual Orientation, Sexual Orientation Identity, and Sexual Identity

A number of scholars have argued that sexual *identity* would be more reliably assessed, and validly represented, if it were disentangled from sexual *orientation* (e.g., Chung & Katayama, 1996; Drescher, 1998a, 1998b; Drescher, Stein, & Byne, 2005; Rust, 2003; Stein, 1999; Worthington et al., 2002). Our conceptualization of *sexual orientation* refers to an individual's patterns of sexual, romantic, and affectional arousal and desire for other persons based on those persons' gender and sex characteristics [American Psychological Association (APA) Task Force on Appropriate Therapeutic Responses to Sexual Orientation, 2009]. Sexual orientation is linked with individual physiological drives that are beyond conscious choice and that involve strong emotional feelings (e.g., falling in love). *Sexual orientation identity* is what we term the individual's conscious acknowledgment and internalization of sexual orientation. Sexual orientation identity is thought to be linked with relational and other interpersonal factors that can shape an individual's community, social supports, role models, friendships, and partner(s) (e.g., APA Task Force on Appropriate Therapeutic Responses to Sexual Orientation, 2009; APA, 2003). We conceptualize sexual orientation identity as subsuming sexual orientation, with the former construct reflecting a conscious acknowledgment of the latter construct. Thus, to simplify our discussion, we use the term *sexual orientation identity* throughout the chapter to refer to these overlapping concepts in a single phrase. It is worth noting that Savin-Williams (Chapter 28, this volume) uses the phrase *sexual identity label* to represent what we term sexual orientation identity. Savin-Williams prefers *label* over *identity* because the former is terminologically distinct from sexual identity and because *label* captures his intent to use the term as a group descriptor. We use the term sexual orientation *identity* to be explicit about this concept as a conscious acknowledgment of identity and to locate it within the broader construct of sexual identity.

We conceptualize sexual orientation identity as one of many dimensions of *sexual identity.* We consider other dimensions of sexual identity that are commonly attributed to sexual orientation identity (sexual behavior with men and/or women; social affiliations with lesbian, gay, bisexual (LGB) individuals, and/or heterosexual individuals and communities; emotional attachment preferences for men and/or women; gender role and identity; Klein, Sepekoff, & Wolf, 1985) as correlates of sexual orientation identity, but not sole characteristics of sexual orientation identity. These elements are part of sexual identity as a larger construct. We view sexual identity as also including other dimensions of human sexuality (e.g., sexual needs, sexual values, modes of sexual expression, preferred characteristics of sexual partners, preferred sexual activities and behaviors) as well as group membership identity (e.g., a sexual orientation identity, or considering oneself as a member of sexuality-related social groups) and attitudes toward sexual minority individuals. These concepts and their roles in sexual identity development are elaborated upon in the chapter.

Measuring Sexual Identity

Content analyses of research on sexual diversity in psychology have indicated that the most common method of assessing what we term the *sexual orientation identity* (others term sexual orientation or sexual orientation label) of participants is to request self-identification as gay, lesbian, bisexual, heterosexual, or some variation on these types of categories (Buhrke, Ben-Ezra, Hurley, & Ruprecht, 1992; Clark & Serovich, 1997; Huang et al., 2009; Phillips, Ingram, Smith, & Mindes, 2003). This method provides categorical self-identification. These categories are typically used as a global proxy for the cognitive, behavioral, emotional, and physiological bases underlying sexual identity. However, a substantial body of research has suggested a variety of ways in which self-identified heterosexual, gay, and lesbian individuals might exhibit bisexual behavior or attractions without categorically identifying as bisexual (e.g., Diamond, 2000, 2003a, 2008; Diamond & Savin-Williams, 2000; Worthington & Reynolds, 2009). This is further complicated by the substantial number of individuals who report predominantly other-sex sexual feelings and behaviors, who also have experiences of same-sex attraction or behavior, but who do not identify as gay, lesbian, or bisexual (Diamond, 2008; McConaghy, Buhrich, & Silove, 1994; Worthington & Reynolds, 2009; see Savin-Williams, Chapter 28, this volume). A universal model of sexual identity may advance the current state of research and measurement by addressing limitations and constraints inherent in categorization of sexual orientation, feelings, and behaviors.

Both categorical and more continuous conceptualizations of sexual orientation identity have evolved over the last 60 years since Kinsey and his colleagues (Kinsey, Pomeroy, & Martin, 1948; Kinsey, Pomeroy, Martin, & Gebhard, 1953) first published their classic works on sexual *behavior* of males and females. Kinsey et al. used a seven-category taxonomic system in which "0" corresponded to "*exclusively heterosexual*" and "6" corresponded to "*exclusively homosexual*." It is noteworthy that, although the scale is intended to index sexual behavior, it is often used as a measure of sexual orientation identity. A number of scholars have criticized the Kinsey Scale (e.g., Masters & Johnson, 1979; Sell, Wells, & Wypij, 1995; Shively & DeCecco, 1977) because it presents same- and other-sex sexual behavior as opposites along a single continuum. Specifically, in Kinsey's binary model, increasing desire for one sex represents reduced desire for the other sex, which in reality may not always be the case. In contrast, other theorists have suggested that same-sex and other-sex attractions and desires may coexist relatively independently and may not be mutually exclusive (Diamond, 2003b, 2008; Sell et al., 1995; Shively & DeCecco, 1977; Storms, 1980; Worthington & Reynolds, 2009). In multi-dimensional models of sexual orientation identity, the intensity of an individual's desire for or arousal toward other-sex individuals can be rated separately from the intensity of that individual's desire for or arousal toward same-sex individuals, and this allows for a more nuanced understanding of sexual diversity (Worthington & Reynolds, 2009).

In understanding measurement issues related to sexual identity, readers are cautioned to recognize that inconsistent terms, methods, and concepts have plagued the sexual orientation and sexual identity literatures. As noted earlier, scholars often inappropriately presume interchangeability of terms (e.g., sexual orientation, sexual identity). The field also operationalizes key sexual identity variables in inconsistent ways (e.g., categorical self-identification, use of a continuous self-identification scale such as a Kinsey-type scale, and physiological measures). The sexual orientation and identity literature also does not typically account for historical shifts across time in both popular and scholarly conceptualizations of variables tied to human sexuality, especially self-ascriptions related to sexual orientation identity (e.g., gay, lesbian, bisexual, queer, heterosexual, metrosexual, bicurious, heteroflexible, pansexual, polyamorous, trans-amorous, uncertain, disidentified, ex-gay, ex–ex-gay). Therefore, much of this literature is difficult to interpret— especially when comparing findings across time,

samples, and investigators (Meyer & Wilson, 2009; Moradi, Mohr, Worthington, & Fassinger, 2009). In one attempt to reconcile incompatible definitions and conceptualizations of variables related to sexual orientation, Tolman and Diamond (2001) have suggested that sexual orientation can be conceptualized as having inherent biological determinants (essentialism) as well as being strongly influenced by and given meaning through socio-cultural forces (constructionism). That is, rather than understanding sexual orientation from either a social constructionist or an essentialist paradigm, the integration of aspects from both perspectives may better reflect the multi-dimensionality and dynamics of human sexual orientation.

Tolman and Diamond's clarification of the nature of sexual orientation as having *both* essentialist *and* constructionist components is consistent with the distinctions among sexual orientation, sexual orientation identity, and sexual identity as proposed in this chapter and in Worthington et al. (2002). Modern scholarship examining the stability of sexual orientation also seems to support our conceptualizations of sexual orientation, sexual orientation identity, and sexual identity (e.g., Diamond, 2003a; Horowitz & Newcomb, 2001; Rosario, Schrimshaw, Hunter, & Braun, 2006, see Savin-Williams, Chapter 28, this volume). Specifically, some dimensions of sexual identity, such as relationships, emotions, behaviors, values, group affiliation, and norms, appear to be relatively fluid; by contrast, sexual orientation [i.e., an individual's patterns of sexual, romantic, and affectional arousal and desire for other persons based on those persons' gender and sex characteristics (APA Task Force on Appropriate Therapeutic Responses to Sexual Orientation, 2009)] has been suggested to be stable for a majority of people across the lifespan (Bell, Weinberg, & Hammersmith, 1981; Ellis & Ames, 1987; Haldeman, 1991; Money, 1987). Our distinctions among sexual orientation, sexual orientation identity, and sexual identity attempt to capture and acknowledge both fluid and stable aspects of sexual identity. These distinctions are also consistent with the aforementioned constructionist and essentialist distinction.

As the reader may have noticed, the stability of sexual orientation is supported by some earlier empirical studies (e.g., Haldeman, 1991, 1994) but is questioned by more recent empirical studies (Kinnish, Strassberg, & Turner, 2005; Savin-Williams, Chapter 28, this volume). New empirical data concerning sexual fluidity could reflect a greater acceptance of sexual minority individuals in society in comparison to 20 years ago (Savin-Williams, 2005, Chapter 28, this volume). That is, more people may be acknowledging sexual minority orientations (i.e., "coming out") because of a more accepting societal climate. Yet, it is not clear from existing research whether sexual orientation is more variable across time for some individuals and not for others, or whether individuals may be relatively more or less open to *experiencing* and *acknowledging* variations in sexual arousal and desire at different points in their personal development. That is, *experiencing* arousal may be different than *acknowledging* arousal, which may vary across contexts and relationships. For instance, Diamond's (2003a, 2003b, 2008) research on women and same-sex attractions indicates that many women's acknowledged identities vary as contexts, relationships, and behaviors change, but that their overall levels of sexual desire and attraction generally do not change.

Sexual Orientation Identity Development

Models of sexual identity *development* may provide an additional perspective regarding the nature and variety of sexual orientation identities over time. In her groundbreaking work, Cass (1979) set the foundation for much of the theory building and exploratory research on the sexual identity of gay men and lesbians (e.g., Troiden, 1988, 1993). In this work, Cass described a multistage process from confusion to identity synthesis where the individual addresses the impact of stigma while passing through milestones of identity awareness and formation. This work has been more recently considered descriptive of the *coming out process* for sexual minority individuals rather than as a model of identity development (e.g., McCarn & Fassinger, 1996). That is, the model may only consider one aspect of sexual identity development—acceptance and disclosure of one's sexual orientation identity as gay or lesbian.

Although they are too numerous to fully review here, there has been a proliferation of models intended to describe lesbian and gay identity development. Readers are referred to Reynolds and Hanjorgiris (2000) and Savin-Williams (2005, Chapter 28, this volume) for a thorough review and critique of existing models. These critiques note that past gay and lesbian identity development models have often neglected individual differences in race, ethnicity, age, and socioeconomic class (Savin-Williams, 2005, this volume). Savin-Williams (Chapter 28, this volume) also discusses the previously noted problems of the *gay–straight binary* inherent in many of these models (see also Moradi, Mohr, et al., 2009, for more on this discussion). Specifically, these models meet their intended aim to delineate identity development for specific groups but are limited in their generalizability to other identities (e.g., bisexuality, heterosexuality) and to description of sexual identity development *across* groups.

Building on existing sexual minority identity formation models, Fassinger and colleagues (Fassinger & Miller, 1996; McCarn & Fassinger, 1996) produced arguably the most sophisticated models of lesbian and gay identity development. Their models include four phases of sexual identity development (awareness, exploration, deepening/commitment, and internalization/synthesis). The Fassinger et al. models are distinct in its conceptualization of phases of both individual and group membership identity. Within the awareness phase, at the individual level, one recognizes being different, and at the group level, one acknowledges that there are different possible sexual orientations. This recognition and acknowledgement leads to the next phase, exploration, wherein exploration of same-sex attractions occurs at the individual level and exploration of one's position in the lesbian and gay community begins at the group level. Through this exploration, the deepening/commitment phase occurs—the crystallization of a gay or lesbian sexual identity at the individual level and personal involvement in the lesbian and gay community at the group level. The final phase is internalization/synthesis. Within this final stage, a gay or lesbian identity is integrated into one's general self-concept at the individual level and across contexts (e.g., home, work, neighborhood) at the group level. Importantly, the individual and group phases do not necessarily occur in parallel fashion, and an individual could experience concordant or nonconcordant phases of individual and group identity. For instance, a person could commit to a lesbian or gay identity at the individual level (e.g., have a same sex partner), but still be at an earlier stage at the group level (i.e., not have identified self to others as lesbian or gay, not engaged in lesbian and gay community). Two quantitative measures of lesbian and gay identity development have been developed to assess each status of the models: the Gay Identity Scale (Fassinger, 1997) and the Lesbian Identity Scale (Fassinger & McCarn, 1997).

Although the Fassinger and Miller (1996) and McCarn and Fassinger (1996) models are a clear advance over earlier lesbian and gay identity models, there are some limitations in the Fassinger models that require attention. In particular, one must identify as gay or lesbian to complete the instruments associated with the models. As a result, research using these instruments is likely to sample only from participants who identify as gay or lesbian and who are in the deepening/commitment or internalization/synthesis statuses of sexual identity development (see Savin-Williams, Chapter 28, this volume).

We contend that some of the limitations of past sexual identity development models can be addressed through a unifying, generalizable sexual identity development theory and accompanying instrumentation. For instance, a sexual identity development measure that does not categorize participants into sexual orientation identity categories (or ask participants to do so) at recruitment has the advantage of capturing participation from gay, lesbian, bisexual, or other participants who, on the basis of sexual orientation identity or commitment to sexual identity, might not otherwise volunteer for research exclusively related to lesbian, gay, and bisexual (LGB) identities (see Worthington, Navarro, Savoy, & Hampton, 2008). A universal model of sexual identity is also applicable to heterosexual individuals, who may not go through the stages identified by Fassinger and colleagues. Thus, a more global conceptualization of sexual identity broadens the scope of measurement and can improve empirical investigations of sexual identity.

Bisexual identity. Although there may be some overlap in the experiences of the coming out process and identity development for lesbians, gay men, and bisexual men and women, bisexuality has been identified as a unique and often misunderstood phenomenon (Klein, 1993). Kinsey et al. (1948) long ago advanced the notion that bisexuality was much more common than previously expected. In their seminal research on bisexuality, Weinberg, Williams, and Pryor (1994) suggested that "becoming bisexual involves the rejection of not one but two recognized categories of sexual identity" (p. 26). They described a stagewise model of bisexual identity development that includes initial confusion, finding and applying the label, settling into the identity, and continued uncertainty. They emphasize that a substantial amount of bisexual identity development involves confusion, exploration, and uncertainty. Nevertheless, although larger proportions of their bisexual research participants expressed ongoing and past uncertainty about self-identification compared to heterosexuals, lesbians, and gay men, the vast majority of bisexuals expressed comfort and certainty with their bisexual identity.

Similar to Weinrich and Klein (2003) and to the differential developmental trajectories framework posited by Savin-Williams (Chapter 28, this volume), empirical studies by Weinberg et al. (1994) have highlighted within-group differences among bisexuals by identifying several different "types" of bisexuality, including the pure, mid, heterosexual leaning, homosexual leaning, and varied types. This research demonstrates several important aspects of bisexuality that counteract stereotypes: (a) bisexuality is a unique and legitimate identity; (b) substantial external pressures to conform to the gay–straight dichotomy may result in considerable confusion, exploration, and uncertainty; and (c) there are important within-group differences among bisexual individuals that have critical influences on sexual identity development (see also Worthington & Reynolds, 2009).

Heterosexual identity. Heterosexual identity development is a relatively new and understudied area of sexual identity theory and research (Ellis & Mitchell, 2000). One of the first studies of heterosexual identity applied Marcia's identity development theory (see Kroger & Marcia, Chapter 2, this volume) within an exploratory qualitative investigation of how undergraduate students' heterosexual sexual identities formed (Eliason, 1995; see Savin-Williams, Chapter 28, this volume). Although the study was conducted with a small number of participants ($n = 26$), Eliason determined that the largest proportion of her participants exhibited identity *foreclosure*. Another large percentage of students were categorized in identity *diffusion*, primarily because they expressed confusion about the definition of sexual identity. Eliason found gender differences among the small number of participants who were categorized as identity *achieved*. Whereas the men appeared to commit to heterosexuality based primarily on a rejection of gay identity, the women appeared to be more open to other alternatives at a later point. Similarly, all participants categorized as identity *moratorium* were women, with no men categorized into this status.

Sullivan (1998) applied concepts commonly associated with racial identity development (i.e., Hardiman & Jackson, 1992) to the identity development process of both LGB and heterosexual college students. She described the development of heterosexual identities within five stepwise stages (*naïveté, acceptance, resistance, redefinition,* and *internalization*) shaped by an atmosphere of homophobia and heterosexism. No research, to our knowledge, has examined the validity of the Sullivan model. Potential questions for future empirical research concerning

the Sullivan model include the following: what developmental events lead a heterosexual person to examine her or his sexual identity with an appreciation of sexual minorities in society (the *resistance* stage)? And how might heterosexual persons be distributed across these categories?

Mohr (2002) introduced a model of adult heterosexual identity in an effort to conceptualize heterosexual therapists' barriers to and facilitators of effective practice with LGB clients. Like the Sullivan model, no empirical studies to our knowledge have examined the Mohr model. Nevertheless, it potentially contributes to our limited theoretical base concerning heterosexual identity. Mohr argues that therapists' ineffective practice with LGB clients can be understood as a manifestation of efforts by therapists to develop, maintain, and express heterosexual identities in ways that contribute to a positive and coherent sense of self, although these efforts are detrimental to the therapy process. Mohr's model describes heterosexual identity as a result of the interaction between individuals' sexual orientation schemas or *working models* and their core motivations to fulfill basic needs for social acceptance and psychological consistency. This entirely theoretical model also describes the importance of social context (e.g., work, home, community) and multiple identities (e.g., race, ethnicity, gender) in processes related to heterosexual identity.

Another model of heterosexual identity development was advanced by Worthington et al. (2002), who built on the earlier work of McCarn and Fassinger (1996). A unique feature of this model relative to the previously described models is that it includes sexual orientation as one component of heterosexual individuals' broader sexual identity. This heterosexual identity development model is the foundation for the unifying model proposed later in the present chapter. In the Worthington et al. (2002) heterosexual identity model, sexual orientation identity was conceptualized as one of six dimensions of the larger construct of individual sexual identity: (a) *perceived sexual needs*, (b) *preferred sexual activities*, (c) *preferred characteristics of sexual partners*, (d) *sexual values*, (e) *recognition and identification of sexual orientation*, and (f) *preferred modes of sexual expression*. Multiple interrelated biopsychosocial factors (e.g., biological, microsocial, gender, cultural, religious, and systemic) were posited as influencing an individual's progression through five heterosexual identity development statuses. Although a complete presentation of the heterosexual identity model is beyond the scope of this chapter, we briefly review the original tenets below because they also represent theorized determinants of sexual identity development in the unifying sexual identity model proposed later in the chapter.

Biological determinants of sexual identity were considered in the heterosexual model because many biological influences (e.g., amino acids, hormonal variations, genetic familiality, molecular genetics, prenatal sex hormones, prenatal maternal stress, functional cerebral asymmetry, neuroanatomical sex differences, sibling sex ratio and birth order, temperament, and physical attractiveness) have been proposed to influence sexual identity. Although these biological factors are posited to operate, empirical evidence supporting their role is limited (Zucker & Bradley, 1995). In addition to biological factors, microsocial influences (Bronfenbrenner, 1977) stemming from one's immediate relationships with family, peers, coworkers, neighbors, and others also were included in the initial model because gender roles, sexual knowledge, sexual attitudes/values, and some sexual behaviors are often learned within microsocial contexts (e.g., peer group, classmates, family). In addition, heterosexual identity was conceptualized as dependent and concomitant to gender identity development processes because a person's biological sex triggers a range of social norms for gender characteristics and behaviors, including sexual identity. For instance, as soon as a newborn baby enters the world, her or his biological sex is emphasized (e.g., through the colors of her/his bedroom and her/his clothes and toys). In turn, gender characteristics based on societal and cultural norms (often stereotypically masculine and feminine) are attributed to the individual (Gilbert & Scher, 1999). The individual then internalizes societal constructions of gender

and acts according to these internalized norms in her or his interpersonal interactions (West & Zimmerman, 1987). An important way in which one internalizes societal constructions of gender and acts according to these internalized norms is through enacting a heterosexual identity. That is, gender role prescriptions for women include being sexually oriented toward men and gender role prescriptions for men include being sexually oriented toward women. Related to this notion is evidence that heterosexual self-presentation is an important societal norm for masculinity (Mahalik et al., 2003; Parent & Moradi, 2009), and aspects of sexual identity such as sexual fidelity and relational orientation are important societal norms for femininity (Mahalik et al., 2005; Parent & Moradi, 2010). Furthermore, gender role traditionality is fairly consistently correlated with prejudicial attitudes toward nonheterosexual groups (e.g., Goodman & Moradi, 2008).

Cultural context was also theorized as a critical influence on heterosexual identity development. Contexts such as family (see Scabini & Manzi, Chapter 23, this volume), community, cultural norms, and oppression may facilitate or inhibit an individual's affectional preferences and sexual behaviors, thereby affecting her or his sexual identity development. Furthermore, because many religions regulate sexual behavior among their members and instruct specific values and moral convictions regarding sexuality, religious orientation is theorized to shape sexual identity development, particularly the statuses of sexual identity exploration and commitment. Related research demonstrates that sexual values are associated with religious orientation (Davidson, Darling, & Norton, 1995; Robinson & Calhoun, 1982; Tozer & Hayes, 2004) and that homonegativity correlates with religiosity (e.g., Herek & Capitanio, 1996; Johnson, Brems, & Alford-Keating, 1997; Worthington, Dillon, & Becker-Schutte, 2005). Finally, because systemic homonegativity, sexual prejudice, and privilege are so pervasive at both macro- and micro-levels of society (Levitt et al., 2009; Rostosky, Riggle, Horne, & Miller, 2009), these forces are hypothesized to influence sexual identity development.

We describe these influences more specifically in the next sections of the chapter.

Although the McCarn and Fassinger (1996) model aims to describe the sexual identity development process of sexual minority individuals, and whereas the Worthington et al. (2002) model intends to describe this process for heterosexual individuals, these two conceptual models contain quite similar features. They propose similar processes of identity development (e.g., both models reflect the processes of *exploration*, *commitment*, and *synthesis/integration*), consider individual as well as group identity, and account for multiple dimensions of—and influences on—sexual identity development. Bieschke (2002) suggested that the Worthington et al. model may serve as a unifying model of sexual identity development. Accordingly, the next section of this chapter presents a new unifying model of sexual identity development. This newer model represents an updated version of the Worthington et al. (2002) model and attempts to integrate research on correlates of sexual identity and theories of lesbian, gay, bisexual, and heterosexual identity development into one inclusive working model.

A Unifying Model of Sexual Identity Development

We define *sexual identity development* as the individual and social processes by which persons acknowledge and define their sexual needs, values, sexual orientation, preferences for sexual activities, modes of sexual expression, and characteristics of sexual partners. We add to this definition the assumption that sexual identity development entails an understanding (implicit or explicit) of one's membership in either a privileged dominant group (heterosexual) or a marginalized, minority group (gay, lesbian, or bisexual identity), with a corresponding set of attitudes, beliefs, and values with respect to members of other sexual identity groups.

Similar to the Worthington et al. (2002) heterosexual identity model and McCarn and Fassinger (1996) lesbian and gay identity development model, the unifying model proposed here describes two parallel, reciprocal developmental determinants: (a) an individual sexual identity development process and (b) a social identity process (see Fig. 27.1). These two processes are

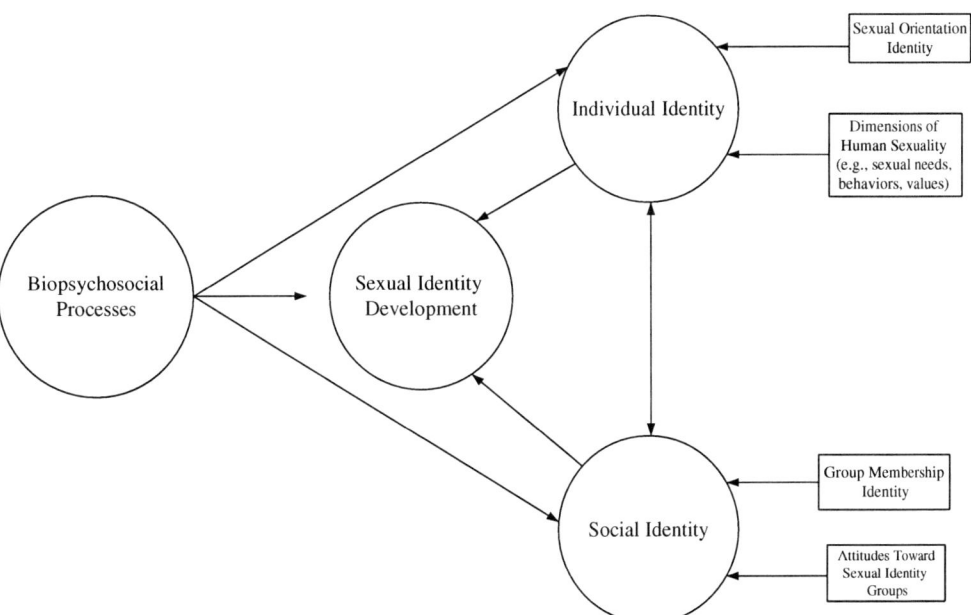

Fig. 27.1 Determinants of sexual identity development

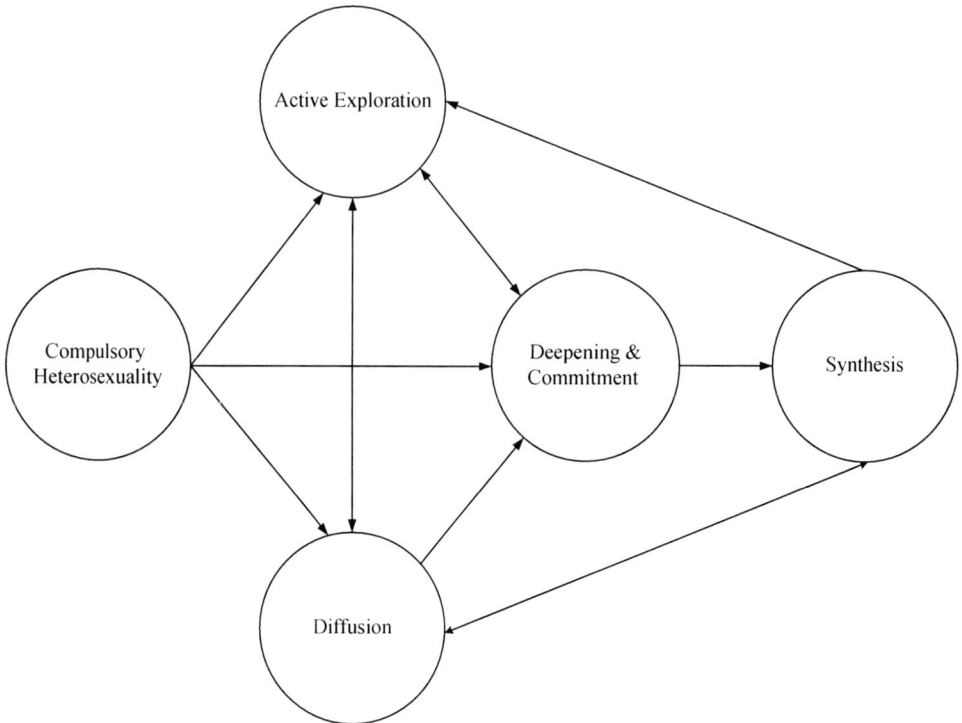

Fig. 27.2 Processes of sexual identity development

posited to occur within five discernible sexual identity development statuses—described in the next section of the chapter (see Fig. 27.2): (a) compulsory heterosexuality [a term first proposed by Rich (1980) and more recently adopted by Mohr (2002)], (b) active exploration, (c) diffusion, (d) deepening and commitment, and (e) synthesis. Although the unifying model represents an attempt to describe developmental phenomena, we emphasize that there are opportunities for circularity and revisiting of statuses throughout the lifespan for a given individual. Thus, points in the model should be thought of as nonlinear, flexible, and fluid descriptions of statuses through which people may pass as they develop their sexual identity over the lifespan. As can be seen in Fig. 27.2, which illustrates the hypothesized processes underlying sexual identity development, there are many different trajectories and outcomes of sexual identity development.

As described earlier in the chapter, individual sexual identity includes, but is not limited to, sexual orientation identity. As in the heterosexual identity model, sexual identity in the universal model is understood as a multi-dimensional construct that includes sexual orientation identity and numerous other domains of human sexuality (e.g., sexual needs, sexual values, preferred sexual activities, preferred characteristics of sexual partners, preferred modes of sexual expression) (see Fig. 27.1). The social identity process involves group membership identity, or the recognition of oneself as a member of a group of individuals with similar sexual identities, and attitudes toward other sexual identity groups (see Ashmore, Deaux, & McLaughlin-Volpe, 2004, for more on group membership identity theory). It is important to note that the recognition of oneself as a member of a group of persons with similar *sexual identities* differs from the recognition of one's *sexual orientation identity*. The former is a broader group membership identification which includes both sexual orientation identity and other salient aspects of human sexuality. For instance, a person could identify as heterosexual (a sexual orientation identity), while also considering oneself as a member of other sexuality-related social groups [e.g., celibates (Abbott, 1999), swingers (de Visser & McDonald, 2007), nudists (Story, 1987), voyeurs (Rye & Meaney, 2007), exhibitionists (Långström & Seto, 2006), practitioners of sadomasochism (Moser & Klienplatz, 2006)]. We expect that dimensions of the larger construct of individual sexual identity evolve and interact with the processes of group membership identity and attitudes toward sexual identity groups (See Fig. 27.1). For example, an individual who has (a) negative attitudes toward sexual minority individuals and (b) a group membership identity grounded in societal heterosexism may not want to engage in sexual activities that involve homoerotic taboos.

Regardless of whether a person is sexually active or celibate, sexual identity development may occur on both conscious and unconscious levels throughout all stages of the model. For instance, exploration can involve cognitive or behavioral activities (or both) and is not limited to behavioral experimentation. Furthermore, as suggested by identity status literature (e.g., Pastorino, Dunham, Kidwell, Bacho, & Lamborn, 1997), we expect that persons experience different sexual identity statuses (and related dimensions) at different times due to individual differences in developmental context. Thus, the model allows for many different individual trajectories and outcomes of identity development.

Statuses of Sexual Identity Development in the Unified Model

Compulsory heterosexuality. The title of this status is based on the term coined by Rich (1980) and applied by Mohr (2002) to describe the presumption across societal systems that (a) heterosexuality is normal and universal and (b) women and men are innately attracted to each other emotionally and sexually. Compulsory heterosexuality refers to individuals of any sexual

orientation who accept and adopt the compulsory heterosexuality as a sexual orientation identity that is institutionalized and required by socialization in many cultures. Compulsory heterosexuality also reflects microsocial (e.g., familial) and macrosocial (e.g., societal) mandates for "appropriate" gender roles and sexual behavior and/or avoidance of sexual self-exploration, which may preempt sexual exploration. Because of societal assumptions about normative development, most people are likely to experience very little conscious thought about their adoption of compulsory heterosexuality. People exhibiting the compulsory heterosexuality identity status can be of any age. For example, prepubescent boys and girls may not have had much opportunity to consider their sexuality at a conscious level. Similarly, many adults may never have considered any alternatives to heterosexuality.

Because heterosexuality is so strongly circumscribed in most cultures, compulsory heterosexuality is likely to be the starting point for most individuals, regardless of whether they later self-identify as heterosexual or as a sexual minority. As a result, this status represents an externally imposed identity rather than a self-ascribed identity, even when an individual identifies outwardly as heterosexual. This status closely resembles the foreclosed identity status in Marcia's model of identity development (see Kroger & Marcia, Chapter 2, this volume). Movement out of compulsory heterosexuality is likely to be permanent because entry into one of the other statuses ultimately precludes the type of naive commitment to sexual identity characteristic of this status (see the *Deepening and commitment* status sub-section of the chapter for our descriptions of two related sub-statuses of *Deepening and commitment—committed heterosexuality* and *committed compulsory heterosexuality*).

In terms of group membership identity, individuals of any sexual orientation in compulsory heterosexuality tend to operate within culturally prescribed norms for heterosexist assumptions about normative behavior on the part of others. Concrete, all-or-nothing thinking tends to characterize conceptions of different sexual identity groups. For instance, attitudes toward heterosexuals are "group appreciating" (cf. Atkinson, Morten, & Sue, 1995). The presumption that heterosexuality is normal and good is accepted without question. Awareness that heterosexuals are a privileged, dominant majority group is either denied or repressed from awareness or accepted without question as normal, understandable, and justifiable. Attitudes toward sexual minority individuals are "group depreciating" among individuals in the compulsory heterosexuality status (cf. Atkinson et al., 1995). People in this status are likely to assume that everyone in their microsocial contexts (e.g., familial, work, and other immediate social circles) is heterosexual. As such, sexual minority individuals are understood only in abstract, stereotypic terms. For individuals who have same-sex or other-sex sexual orientations, the nature of this status suggests that attitudes toward sexual minority individuals are likely to be at the condemnation end of Herek's (1984) *condemnation—tolerance* continuum, reflecting prejudice toward same-sex sexual orientation and sexual minority individuals (Herek, Gillis, & Cogan, 2009).

Active exploration. Purposeful exploration, evaluation, or experimentation of one's sexual needs, values, orientation and/or preferences for activities, partner characteristics, or modes of sexual expression are typical of the active exploration status. Active exploration of individual sexual identity is distinguished from naive behavioral experimentation in three important ways that have implications for other statuses in the model. First, exploration can be cognitive or behavioral. Although there may be a bias toward behavioral sexual exploration in modern society, cognitive forms of exploration (e.g., fantasy) are possible as well and may be the preferred form of exploration among individuals; particularly those who engage in abstinence-oriented lifestyles. Second, active exploration is purposeful and usually tends to be goal directed, such as purposefully experimenting (in thought or action) with different modes of sexual expression, different characteristics of sexual partners, and/or sexual acts. Third, the socially mandated aspects of heterosexuality—those that

characterize compulsory heterosexuality—are thought to be questioned or abandoned by individuals of any sexual orientation when active exploration occurs. However, contextual influences can constrain or promote sexual identity exploration within socially acceptable boundaries. For example, this occurs when a person is raised in a family, culture, or religion that instructs that acceptable sexual partners are only persons of the same race, different gender, similar age, same socioeconomic status, and same religion. Although these constraints vary from person to person depending on a number of dimensions of social context (e.g., gender, culture, age, religious orientation), active exploration occurs when the individual engages in cognitive or behavioral exploration of individual sexual identities beyond that which is socially mandated within one's social context. For instance, even if one is raised in the above-described context, active exploration regarding preferred characteristics of a sexual partner for some might entail the development of sexual or romantic relationships with people having different types of physical, social, economic, or spiritual characteristics. For others, active exploration might entail such things as experimenting with different types of sexual activities, transcending gender roles through adoption of gender atypical modes of sexual expression, engaging in sex with more than one partner (e.g., group sex), reading books about sex, and so on. As a result, active exploration could be characterized very differently depending on contextual factors. Furthermore, there is a wide range of levels of exploration (e.g., type, depth, and duration of exploration). Thus, our notion of active exploration is inclusive and flexible enough to account for between and within-group differences exhibited by same-sex- and other-sex-oriented individuals, as suggested by Savin-Williams' (Chapter 28, this volume) differential developmental trajectories perspective on sexual identity development.

Active exploration will most typically coincide with biological maturation (e.g., physical capacity), but could occur at nearly any point during the course of the lifespan. This status closely resembles Marcia's (Kroger & Marcia,

Chapter 2, this volume) moratorium status, which is characterized by a suspension of commitment in favor of active exploration. Due to the powerful impact of systemic homonegativity and sexual prejudice, many heterosexually identified individuals who enter this status are likely to primarily explore needs, values, and preferences for activities, partner characteristics (with the exception of gender), and modes of sexual expression—but they will likely not explore sexual orientation identity alternatives.

Sexual minority individuals are more likely to explore options in all areas of their sexual identities. Entry into the active exploration status for sexual minority individuals may be prompted by awareness of homoerotic feelings, behaviors, and exploration (Fassinger & Miller, 1996). These experiences may lead to re-labeling of sexual orientation identity (e.g., from heterosexual to lesbian, gay, or bisexual) during active exploration. Although some heterosexuals in this status may also consciously experiment with symbolic (fantasy) or real sexual activities with same-sex partners, most are expected to identify as "straight" to preserve the privileged status associated with it. Others may reflect on the possibility that their compulsory heterosexual orientation identity does not fit them and may consider or adopt another sexual orientation identity (e.g., gay, lesbian, bisexual, queer). We conceptualized only two pathways out of active commitment: (a) into deepening and commitment following active exploration or (b) into diffusion. This process is described in subsequent sections of the chapter.

The group membership identity process is hypothesized to be more salient for individuals in the active exploration status in comparison to the compulsory heterosexuality status. Recognition of same-sex attractions might result in (a) questioning the privileged status of heterosexuality in society, (b) maintaining negative attitudes toward oneself and toward sexual minority individuals (Szymanski, Kashubeck-West, & Meyer, 2008), or (c) exploring one's own attitudes toward sexual minorities as a group, as well as the possibility of membership in that group (Fassinger & Miller, 1996). When a person recognizes her or his membership in a dominant heterosexual group, such recognition might result in (a) questioning the justice of the privileged heterosexual majority position or (b) further asserting the privileges of the heterosexual majority. In active exploration, the interaction of individual and social processes of identity development is thought to become considerably intertwined. For example, a willingness to violate cultural sanctions against sexual self-exploration may result in recognition and understanding of ordinate–subordinate group dynamics and majority group privilege by individuals of any sexual orientation identity. As such, individuals of any sexual orientation identity may be aware of and associate with persons from different sexual minority groups more often than persons in the compulsory heterosexuality status.

Identifying as heterosexual (a privileged group membership status) in active exploration can sometimes be reserved as a visible orientation (i.e., passing as straight) by individuals of any sexual orientation. Homoerotic thoughts, feelings, and behaviors can be dismissed as transient, concealed, and denigrated; or may be accepted as congruent with one's of sexual, romantic, and affectional arousal and desire. Many individuals in active exploration can overtly or secretly experiment with behaviors that involve more than one partner and/or one or more same-sex partners without ever identifying with a sexual orientation identity minority group (Diamond, 2008; McConaghy et al., 1994; Worthington & Reynolds, 2009). Thus, sexual behaviors and sexual orientation identity can be conveniently separated by some. For instance, this discrepancy could occur when persons identify as heterosexual to serve an "ego preservation" function, protecting individuals with heterosexist and self-stigmatizing beliefs from threatening thoughts and feelings (Moradi, van den Berg, & Epting, 2006). Earlier related research (Herek, 1984) also suggests that expressing negative attitudes toward lesbian and gay individuals may serve as an expression of positive self-concept for the individual (e.g., negative attitudes that are part of one's religious identity; Mohr, 2002). Not surprisingly, separation of gayness from one's

self-concept has been identified as a component of internalized homophobia as reported by
self-identified lesbian and gay adults (Moradi,
van den Berg, & Epting, 2009). Alternatively, as
noted above, some individuals in active exploration may more openly associate with (and come
to identify with) LGB individuals and groups
through friendship patterns, sexual exploration,
and other types of affiliation. This process is
thought to be more likely for persons who either
(a) are less restricted by heterosexist contextual
influences (e.g., growing up in an environment
in which sexual diversity is normative, acceptable, and even desirable; Savin-Williams, 2005,
this volume), or (b) who demonstrate resilience
against such constraints (Sanders & Kroll, 2000).

Attitudes toward other sexual orientation identity groups are likely to vary considerably both
within and between individuals in the active
exploration status. However, we posit that an orientation toward active self-exploration is likely to
correspond with more positive attitudes toward
sexual minority individuals and with less self-
stigma compared to compulsory heterosexuality.
This hypothesis is partially supported by our earlier work, which found that exploration was positively associated with LGB-affirmative attitudes
and negatively related to homonegativity among
one sample of heterosexual adults (Worthington
et al., 2005) and another sample of individuals
from heterosexual, gay, lesbian, and bisexual sexual orientation identity groups (Worthington &
Reynolds, 2009). In another study, we found that
exploration was related to psychotherapists' self-
efficacy to affirmatively work with sexual minor
ity clients (Dillon, Worthington, Soth-McNett, &
Schwartz, 2008).

Diffusion. Diffusion has been defined as the
absence of commitment and of systematic exploration (Marcia, 1987). It is one of the more complex identity statuses. Identity literature describes
two types of diffusion—*diffused diffusion* and
carefree diffusion (Luyckx, Goossens, Soenens,
Beyers, & Vansteenkiste, 2005; Luyckx et al.,
2008; Marcia, 1976, 1989). The carefree diffusion status reflects someone who is unconcerned
and content with not having strong commitments
or having actively explored. In fact, carefree

diffusion does not always include the maladjustment commonly thought to accompany it
(Luyckx et al., 2005, 2008). Thus, in terms of sexual identity development, people exhibiting carefree diffusion are similarly expected to indicate
low levels of commitment or exploration, and
apathy regarding commitment and exploration
(e.g., "I don't care"). Any sexual identity-related
exploration by carefree diffusers is expected to
appear to be a random willingness to try or be
almost anything related to sexual identity without
distress. The diffused diffusion status has been
suggested to reflect an underlying uncertainty or
insecurity and is more likely to be distressed by
lack of commitments (Archer & Waterman, 1990;
Luyckx et al., 2005, 2008).

Whether due to insecure apathy or a carefree lack of commitment, individuals in diffusion may be more likely to ignore or reject
social and cultural prescriptions for sexual values, behavior, and identity. In some cases, diffusion may be difficult to distinguish from active
exploration, because the infrequent and random
experimentation (in thought or action) characteristic of this status might resemble active
exploration. However, diffusion typically lacks
goal-directed intentionality—one of the criteria necessary for active exploration to occur
(Soenens & Vansteenkiste, Chapter 17, this
volume). Although carefree diffusion may be
characterized by a lack of distress, it is important to note that diffusion typically coincides
with a number of forms of psychological distress (Schwartz, Zamboanga, Weisskirch, &
Rodriguez, 2009). Thus, wc posit that people
experiencing diffusion are likely to have identity confusion in other aspects of their lives.
They may also express a lack of self-awareness
about their underlying motives or intentions
that might characterize people in other statuses
(see Soenens & Vansteenkiste, Chapter 17, this
volume, Luyckx, Schwartz, Goossens, Beyers, &
Missotten, Chapter 4, this volume).

Because emerging research suggests that individuals in diffusion can transition into either foreclosure or moratorium (Meeus, van de Schoot,
Keijsers, Schwartz, & Branje, 2010), pathways
out of diffusion could include returning to

compulsory heterosexuality or progressing into active exploration, which in some cases may be facilitated through professional psychological services or other interventions to address potential psychological distress (Schwartz et al., 2009). We expect that individuals are vulnerable to enter this status from any of the other identity statuses—but most likely compulsory heterosexuality or active exploration— while experiencing high levels of distress (e.g., distress resulting from stigma and/or harassment associated with sexual exploration or taboo behaviors). Research is needed to examine this assumption and to identify types of distress that could potentially influence entry into diffusion. Furthermore, given that individuals in more integrated levels of identity are less likely to regress into diffusion (Meeus et al., 2010), we assume a similar dynamic in sexual identity.

Deepening and commitment. Individuals of any sexual orientation identity in the deepening and commitment status exhibit a movement toward greater commitment to their identified sexual needs, values, sexual orientation and/or preferences for activities, partner characteristics, and modes of sexual expression. This status most closely resembles Marcia's achieved identity status (Marcia, 1987; see Kroger & Marcia, Chapter 2, this volume).

A critical distinction between deepening and commitment and Marcia's achieved identity status is that deepening and commitment in our model is hypothesized to be possible (or even likely) without the individual's engaging in active exploration. We posit that moving to deepening/commitment of lesbian, gay, bisexual persons almost always involve active exploration, whereas movement to deepening/commitment of heterosexual identity may or may not involve active exploration. Some individuals may move directly from compulsory heterosexuality into deepening and commitment as a function of maturational changes in life experiences, cognitions, and behaviors that do not meet the criteria for active exploration. For instance, heterosexual individuals entering deepening and commitment may be more likely to transition into

this status from compulsory heterosexuality than from active exploration. For such individuals, the deepening and commitment that occurs during this status is contained within their compulsory heterosexuality. As such, their compulsory heterosexuality becomes a *committed compulsory heterosexuality* that is characterized by a more profound commitment to compulsory heterosexuality.

It is also possible that heterosexuals could move from compulsory heterosexuality to deepening and commitment via active exploration. We expect such individuals to differ from individuals in committed compulsory heterosexuality in several ways. Individuals moving into this status from active exploration may be more likely to question the presumption that heterosexuality is the only normal and appropriate sexual orientation identity, and to question the need for the institutionalization of heterosexuality as the only sexual orientation identity through, for example, legislation banning same-sex marriages. In terms of group membership identity, individuals in deepening and commitment who commit to a heterosexual identity orientation after active exploration are expected to question heterosexist assumptions about normative behavior on the part of others. Heterosexist assumptions and attitudes (e.g., heterosexuality is normal and universal; women and men should only be attracted to each other emotionally and sexually) are expected to be maintained or strengthened among heterosexuals entering deepening and commitment from compulsory heterosexuality without active exploration (i.e., committed compulsory heterosexuality).

Deepening and commitment following active exploration is thought to be the most common identity development process for LGB individuals. The active inquiry into different sexual needs, values, orientation, and partner characteristics in active exploration is thought to yield a great amount of self-understanding and knowledge (McCarn & Fassinger, 1996; Riggle, Whitman, Olson, Rostosky, & Strong, 2008). This heightened sense of self-understanding is hypothesized to lead to greater levels of clarity and choices about one's sexuality. This process is also thought to be linked to a greater level of acceptance than earlier described statuses, and more willingness to further examine one's overall sexual identity.

Attitudes toward heterosexuals may still be "group appreciating" (cf. Atkinson et al., 1995) on the part of individuals of any sexual orientation identity. Persons who have entered the deepening and commitment status are thought to deny that heterosexuals are a privileged, dominant majority group if they have engaged in active exploration. This is because the socially mandated aspects of heterosexuality—those that characterize compulsory heterosexuality—are thought to be questioned or abandoned by individuals when active exploration occurs. Both LGB persons in deepening and commitment and heterosexuals in deepening and commitment following active exploration are hypothesized to express less "group depreciating" attitudes toward sexual minority individuals compared to heterosexuals characterized by committed compulsory heterosexuality.

For sexual minority individuals and committed heterosexuals in this status, group membership identity processes and attitudes toward sexual orientation identity groups also begin to deepen and crystallize into conscious, coherent perspectives on dominant/non-dominant group relations, privilege or loss of privilege, and oppression or marginalization. This process of crystallization may take virtually any form along the continuum of attitudes toward sexual minority individuals as well as toward heterosexuals (the dominant group), from condemnation to tolerance to affirmation (Herek, 1984; Worthington et al., 2005). Based on general identity literature, we expect that individuals may move out of deepening and commitment via three pathways: (a) into synthesis (described below), (b) into active exploration, or (c) into diffusion (Stephen, Fraser, & Marcia, 1992; Meeus et al., 2010).

Synthesis. Potentially the most mature and adaptive status of sexual identity is characterized by a state of congruence between the individual and social identity processes of sexual identity development that were described earlier in the chapter (see also Fassinger & Miller, 1996). In the synthesis status, people come to an understanding of sexual identity that fulfills their self-definitions

and carries over to their attitudes and behaviors toward both LGB-identified and heterosexually identified individuals. Individual sexual identity, group membership identity, and attitudes toward dominant and marginalized sexual orientation identity groups merge into an overall sexual self-concept, which is conscious, congruent, and volitional (see Soenens & Vansteenkiste, Chapter 17, this volume). Other aspects of identity are likely to blend into the synthesis status—in the sense that intersecting identities (e.g., along lines of gender, race/ethnicity, religious orientation) will have a high degree of coherence and consistency in relation to sexual identity. Thus, we expect that a coherent sexual identity will correlate with coherence and consolidation within other types of identity.

We posit only one pathway into synthesis, through deepening and commitment. However, we hypothesize that synthesis may also require active exploration. Individuals who experience deepening and commitment directly from compulsory heterosexuality are not likely to demonstrate all of the qualities of synthesis. For instance, we hypothesize that more active exploration is associated with more affirmative and flexible thinking with respect to sexual diversity for sexual minority and heterosexual individuals (Worthington & Reynolds, 2009; Worthington et al., 2005). Thus, individuals in synthesis are likely to experience little or no self-stigma or internalized heterosexism/homophobia, to understand human sexuality as a continuous and nuanced—rather than all-or-nothing—phenomenon, and to be more affirmative toward LGB individuals. However, the difficulty of transitioning into synthesis does not preclude an individual from moving out of synthesis for one reason or another, which we hypothesize to occur via either active exploration or diffusion.

Preliminary Research Supporting a Unifying Model of Sexual Identity Development

Several empirical studies have informed the development of the unifying model. One study involved the development of a measure that quantitatively assesses the statuses associated with sexual identity development (Worthington et al., 2008). The measure, called the *measure of sexual identity exploration and commitment* (MoSIEC), was designed to assess sexual identity statuses among individuals, regardless of sexual orientation or identity. Initial psychometric investigations yielded promising evidence of reliability and validity in national adult samples (Worthington & Reynolds, 2009; Worthington et al., 2008).

Similar to other literature that supports the measurement of identity status (Luyckx et al., 2005, 2008; Meeus et al., 2010), the MoSIEC yields four empirically derived dimensions: (a) *commitment*, (b) *exploration*, (c) *sexual orientation identity uncertainty*, and (d) *synthesis/integration*. The MoSIEC factor structure reflects constructs from Marcia's theory that describe two dimensions of exploration (i.e., exploration factor and sexual orientation identity uncertainty factor) and two commitment-related dimensions (i.e., commitment factor and synthesis/integration factor). The four factors also represent constructs from the unifying sexual identity development model: (a) active exploration indicated by the exploration factor, (b) compulsory heterosexuality and deepening and commitment represented by the commitment factor, and (c) synthesis characterized by the synthesis/integration factor.

The sexual orientation identity uncertainty factor reflects what Marcia referred to as *moratorium* (delay of commitment during exploration) or what recently has been termed *reconsideration of commitment* (the comparison of present commitments with possible alternatives because the current commitments are no longer satisfactory; Crocetti, Rubini, Luyckx, & Meeus, 2008). Construct validity for this factor has been demonstrated through its positive correlation with exploration and its negative correlations with commitment and synthesis. An analysis of patterns of between-groups differences on sexual orientation identity uncertainty indicated that participants who were bisexual, lesbian, or gay tended to endorse these items more strongly compared to those individuals who identified as

heterosexual (Worthington & Reynolds, 2009; Worthington et al., 2008).

Recent studies employing the MoSIEC have also supported the unified model. For instance, significant between-group differences in sexual identity development statuses have been found among self-identified sexual minority individuals (e.g., Worthington & Reynolds, 2009). For instance, "mostly straight" women differed from "exclusively straight" women, showing higher levels of identity exploration and uncertainty (and marginally lower levels of synthesis) than their exclusively straight counterparts. In addition, in support of the unified model, differences in sexual behaviors among participants in Thompson and Morgan (2008) did not necessarily constitute differences in sexual identity development status (mostly straight women shared similar levels of exploration, uncertainty, and synthesis with both bisexual and lesbian women although they reported different sexual behaviors). This finding specifically supports the notion advanced by the universal model that sexual behavior is only part of sexual identity.

As previously mentioned, the unifying model of sexual identity development hypothesizes that individuals who have engaged in active exploration are more likely to hold positive attitudes toward LGB individuals and less internalized heterosexism or self-stigma. As noted earlier, this hypothesis was partially supported by prior research using an earlier version of the MoSIEC (Worthington & Reynolds, 2009; Worthington et al., 2005). More specifically, these authors found that exploration and sexual orientation identity uncertainty were positively associated with LGB-affirmative attitudes (i.e., LGB civil rights, knowledge, and internalized affirmativeness) and that exploration was negatively related to homonegativity (i.e., religious conflict and hate) among self-identified heterosexuals. Future research is needed to explore whether (and how) internalized heterosexism and self-stigma (Herek et al., 2009; Moradi, van den Berg, et al., 2009; Szymanski et al., 2008) differ across self-identified lesbian, gay, and bisexual persons who range in endorsement of commitment, exploration, sexual orientation identity uncertainty, and synthesis/integration dimensions. Worthington and Reynolds (2009) recently began this line of research in a study indicating within-group differences among bisexual men and women, gay men, and heterosexual women in terms of sexual identity development dimensions and LGB-related knowledge and attitudes.

The MoSIEC studies also report links of sexual identity dimensions with age, religiosity, sexual conservatism, and multiple aspects of sexual self-awareness (Worthington & Reynolds, 2009; Worthington et al., 2008). Age was positively linked with commitment and synthesis/integration. Individuals who were lower on religiosity and less sexually conservative appeared more likely to engage in exploration and exhibit uncertainty, whereas sexual assertiveness and sexual self-consciousness were associated with commitment, exploration, and synthesis/integration.

Future Research

The unifying sexual identity development model and the MoSIEC can be applied to a host of additional research questions and social issues. The various dimensions of sexual identity development are theorized to relate to a range of sexual behaviors and outcomes, including unintended pregnancy, sexually transmitted diseases, safer sex practices, sexual agency, and sexual risk behaviors. Research is needed to examine these hypothesized links with the goal of understanding and impacting these behaviors. Furthermore, the unifying model and measure could be useful in examining the relations between sexual identity statuses and sexual health awareness and help seeking. Future research might also investigate whether educational and psychological interventions targeting various social issues (e.g., risky sexual practices, antigay attitudes and behavior, and heterosexism and homonegativity) can be tailored according to aspects of sexual identity present in the target groups to increase the effectiveness of these strategies. An integrated sexual identity model can also facilitate research

integrating sexual identity with other types of identity, including racial/ethnic, gender, and religious/spiritual (among others). Ultimately, this model can be a starting point from which an extensive program of research on sexual identities can be produced.

Conclusion

The proposed unifying model of sexual identity development incorporates what has been learned from years of theory and research concerning sexuality, LGB and heterosexual identity development, attitudes toward sexual minority individuals, and the meaning of ordinate and subordinate group membership. We have attempted to describe the intersection of various contextual factors that influence the individual and social processes underlying sexual identity development. The unifying model is innovative in its applicability across sexual orientation identities, as well as its inclusion of a wide range of dimensions of sexual identity and possible developmental trajectories. We hope this innovation allows researchers, educators, and practitioners to develop interventions and conduct investigations on broader questions about human sexuality without being constrained to gay–straight dichotomies of sexual orientation and the related methodological limitations that have characterized sexual identity theory and research in the past.

References

Abbott, E. (1999). *A history of celibacy*. Cambridge, MA: Da Capo Press.

American Psychological Association. (2003). *Lawrence vs. Texas: Brief for amicus curiae, Supreme Court of the United States*. Washington, DC. Retrieved February 25, 2008, from http://www.apa.org/about/offices/ogc/amicus/lawrence.pdf

American Psychological Association Task Force on Appropriate Therapeutic Responses to Sexual Orientation (2009). *Report of the task force on appropriate therapeutic responses to sexual orientation*. Washington, DC: American Psychological Association.

Archer, S. L., & Waterman, A. S. (1990). Varieties of identity diffusions and foreclosures: An exploration of subcategories of the identity statuses. *Journal of Adolescent Research, 5,* 96–111.

Ashmore, R. D., Deaux, K., & McLaughlin-Volpe, T. (2004). An organizing framework for collective identity: Articulation and significance of multidimensionality. *Psychological Bulletin, 130,* 80–114.

Atkinson, D. R., G. Morten, & D. W. Sue (Eds.). (1995). *Counseling American minorities: A cross cultural perspective* (5th ed.). Dubuque, IA: William C. Brown.

Bell, A. P., Weinberg, M. S., & Hammersmith, S. K. (1981). *Sexual preference: Its development in men and women.* Bloomington, IN: Indiana University Press.

Bieschke, K. (2002). Charting the waters. *The Counseling Psychologist, 30,* 575–581.

Bronfenbrenner, U. (1977). Toward an experimental ecology of human development. *American Psychologist, 32,* 513–531.

Buhrke, R. A., Ben-Ezra, L. A., Hurley, M. E., & Ruprecht, L. J. (1992). Content analysis and methodological critique of articles concerning lesbian and gay male issues in counseling journals. *Journal of Counseling Psychology, 39,* 91–99.

Cass, V. C. (1979). Homosexual identity formation: A theoretical model. *Journal of Homosexuality, 4,* 219–235.

Chung, Y. B., & Katayama, M. (1996). Assessment of sexual orientation in lesbian/gay/bisexual studies. *Journal of Homosexuality, 30,* 49–62.

Clark, W. M., & Serovich, J. M. (1997). Twenty years and still in the dark? Content analysis of articles pertaining to gay, lesbian, and bisexual issues in marriage and family therapy journals. *Journal of Marital and Family Therapy, 23,* 239–253.

Crocetti, E., Rubini, M., Luyckx, K., & Meeus, W. (2008). Identity formation in early and middle adolescents from various ethnic groups: From three dimensions to five statuses. *Journal of Youth and Adolescence, 37,* 983–996.

Davidson, J. K., Darling, C. A., & Norton, L. (1995). Religiosity and the sexuality of women: Sexual behavior and sexual satisfaction revisited. *Journal of Sex Research, 32,* 235–243.

de Visser, R., & McDonald, D. (2007). Swings and roundabouts: Management of jealousy in heterosexual 'swinging' couples. *British Journal of Social Psychology, 46,* 459–476.

Diamond, L. M. (2000). Sexual identity, attractions, and behavior among young sexual-minority women over a two-year period. *Developmental Psychology, 36,* 241–250.

Diamond, L. M. (2003a). Was it a phase? Young women's relinquishment of lesbian/bisexual identities over a 5-year period. *Journal of Personality and Social Psychology, 84,* 352–364.

Diamond, L. M. (2003b). What does sexual orientation orient? A biobehavioral model distinguishing romantic love and sexual desire. *Psychological Review, 110,* 173–192.

Diamond, L. M. (2008). Female bisexuality from adolescence to adulthood: Results from a 10-year longitudinal study. *Developmental Psychology, 44,* 5–14.

Diamond, L. M., & Savin-Williams, R. C. (2000). Explaining diversity in the development of same-sex sexuality among young women. *Journal of Social Issues, 56,* 297–313.

Dillon, F. R., Worthington, R. L., Soth-McNett, A. M., & Schwartz, S. J. (2008). Gender and sexual identity based predictors of lesbian, gay, and bisexual affirmative counseling self-efficacy. *Professional Psychology: Research and Practice, 39,* 353–360.

Drescher, J. (1998a). Contemporary psychoanalytic psychotherapy with gay men: With a commentary on reparative therapy of homosexuality. *Journal of Gay and Lesbian Psychotherapy, 2,* 51–74.

Drescher, J. (1998b). I'm your handyman: A history of reparative therapies. *Journal of Homosexuality, 36,* 19–42.

Drescher, J., Stein, T. S., & Byne, W. (2005). Homosexuality, gay and lesbian identities, and homosexual behavior. In B. J. Sadock & V. A. Sadock (Eds.), *Kaplan and Sadock's comprehensive textbook of psychiatry* (8th ed.). Baltimore: Lippincott Williams & Wilkins.

Eliason, M. J. (1995). Accounts of sexual identity formation in heterosexual students. *Sex Roles, 32,* 821–834.

Ellis, A. L., & Mitchell, R. W. (2000). Sexual orientation. In L. T. Szuchman & F. Muscarella (Eds.), *Psychological perspectives on human sexuality* (pp. 196–231). New York: John Wiley.

Ellis, L., & Ames, M. A. (1987). Neurohormonal functioning and sexual orientation: A theory of homosexuality-heterosexuality. *Psychological Bulletin, 101,* 233–258.

Erikson, E. H. (1950). *Childhood and society.* New York: Norton.

Fassinger, R. E. (1997). *Gay identity questionnaire.* Unpublished instrument, University of Maryland.

Fassinger, R. E., & McCarn, S. (1997). *Lesbian identity questionnaire.* Unpublished instrument, University of Maryland.

Fassinger, R. E., & Miller, B. A. (1996). Validation of an inclusive model of sexual minority identity formation on a sample of gay men. *Journal of Homosexuality, 32,* 53–78.

Gilbert, L. A., & Scher, M. (1999). *Gender and sex in counseling and psychotherapy.* Boston: Allyn & Bacon.

Goodman, M. B., & Moradi, B. (2008). Attitudes and behaviors toward lesbian and gay persons: Critical correlates and mediated relations. *Journal of Counseling Psychology, 55,* 371–384.

Haldeman, D. C. (1991). Sexual conversion therapy for gay men and lesbians: A scientific examination. In J. C. Gonsiorek & J. D. Weinrich (Eds.), *Homosexuality: Research implications for public policy* (pp. 149–160). Newbury Park, CA: Sage.

Haldeman, D. C. (1994). The practice and ethics of sexual orientation conversion therapy. *Journal of Consulting and Clinical Psychology, 62,* 221–227.

Hardiman, R., & Jackson, B. W. (1992). Racial identity development: Understanding racial dynamics in college classrooms and on campus. *New Directions for Teaching and Learning, 53,* 21–37.

Herek, G. M. (1984). Attitudes toward lesbians and gay men: A factor-analytic study. *Journal of Homosexuality, 10,* 39–51.

Herek, G. M., & Capitanio, J. (1996). "Some of my best friends": Intergroup contact, concealable stigma, and heterosexuals' attitudes toward gay men and lesbians. *Personality and Social Psychology Bulletin, 22,* 412–424.

Herek, G. M., Gillis, J. R., & Cogan, J. C. (2009). Internalized stigma among sexual minority adults: Insights from a social psychological perspective. *Journal of Counseling Psychology, 56,* 32–43.

Horowitz, J. L., & Newcomb, M. D. (2001). A multidimensional approach to homosexual identity. *Journal of Homosexuality, 42,* 1–19.

Huang, Y. P., Brewster, M., Moradi, B., Goodman, M., Wiseman, M., & Martin, A. (2009). Content analysis of literature about LGB people of color. *The Counseling Psychologist,* Advance online publication. doi:10.1177/0011000009335255.

Johnson, M. E., Brems, C., & Alford-Keating, P. (1997). Personality correlates of homophobia. *Journal of Homosexuality, 34,* 57–69.

Kinnish, K. K., Strassberg, D. S., & Turner, C. W. (2005). Sex differences in the flexibility of sexual orientation: A multidimensional retrospective assessment. *Archives of Sexual Behavior, 34,* 173–183.

Kinsey, A. C., Pomeroy, W. B., & Martin, C. E. (1948). *Sexual behavior in the human male.* Philadelphia: W. B. Saunders.

Kinsey, A. C., Pomeroy, W. B., Martin, C. E., & Gebhard, P. (1953). *Sexual behavior in the human female.* Philadelphia: W. B. Saunders.

Klein, F. (1993). *The bisexual option* (2nd ed.). New York: Haworth Press.

Klein, F., Sepekoff, B., & Wolf, T. J. (1985). Sexual orientation: A multi-variable dynamic process. *Journal of Homosexuality, 11,* 35–49.

Långström, N., & Seto, M. C. (2006). Exhibitionistic and voyeuristic behavior in a Swedish national population survey. *Archives of Sexual Behavior, 35,* 427–435.

Levitt, H. M., Ovrebo, E., Anderson-Cleveland, M. B., Leone, C., Jae, Y. J., Arm, J. R., et al. (2009). Balancing dangers: GLBT experience in a time of anti-GLBT legislation. *Journal of Counseling Psychology, 56,* 67–81.

Luyckx, K., Goossens, L., Soenens, B., Beyers, W., & Vansteenkiste, M. (2005). Identity statuses based on 4 rather than 2 identity dimensions: Extending and refining Marcia's paradigm. *Journal of Youth and Adolescence, 34,* 605–618.

Luyckx, K., Schwartz, S. J., Berzonsky, M. D., Soenens, B., Vansteenkiste, M., Smits, I., et al. (2008). Capturing ruminative exploration: Extending the four-dimensional model of identity formation in late adolescence. *Journal of Research in Personality, 42,* 58–82.

Mahalik, J. R., Locke, B. D., Ludlow, L. H., Diemer, M. A., Scott, R. P., Gottfried, M., et al. (2003). Development of the conformity to masculine norms inventory. *Psychology of Men and Masculinity, 4,* 3–25.

Mahalik, J. R., Morray, E. B., Coonerty-Femiano, A., Ludlow, L. H., Slatterly, S. M., & Smiler, A. (2005). Development of the conformity to feminine norms inventory. *Sex Roles, 52,* 417–434.

Marcia, J. E. (1976). Identity six years after: A follow-up study. *Journal of Youth and Adolescence, 5,* 145–160.

Marcia, J. E. (1987). Identity in adolescence. In J. Adelson (Ed.), *Handbook of adolescent psychology.* New York: Wiley.

Marcia, J. E. (1989). Identity diffusion differentiated. In M. A. Luszcz & T. Nettelbeck (Eds.), *Psychological development: Perspectives across the life-span* (pp. 123–137). Dordrecht: Elsevier.

Masters, W. H., & Johnson, V. E. (1979). *Homosexuality in perspective.* New York: Bantam Books.

McCarn, S. R., & Fassinger, R. E. (1996). Revisioning sexual minority identity formation: A new model of lesbian identity and its implications for counseling and research. *The Counseling Psychologist, 24,* 508–534.

McConaghy, N., Buhrich, N., & Silove, D. (1994). Opposite sex- linked behaviors and homosexual feelings in the predominantly heterosexual male majority. *Archives of Sexual Behavior, 23,* 565–577.

Meeus, W., van de Schoot, R., Keijsers, L., Schwartz, S. J., & Branje, S. (2010). On the progression and stability of adolescent identity formation: A five-wave longitudinal study in early-to-middle and middle-to-late adolescence. *Child Development, 81,* 1565–1581.

Meyer, I. H., & Wilson, P. A. (2009). Sampling lesbian, gay, and bisexual populations. *Journal of Counseling Psychology, 56,* 23–31.

Mohr, J. J. (2002). Heterosexual identity and the heterosexual therapist: An identity perspective on sexual orientation dynamics in psychotherapy. *The Counseling Psychologist, 30,* 532–566.

Money, J. (1987). Sin, sickness, or status? Homosexual gender identity and psychoneuroendocrinology. *American Psychologist, 43,* 384–399.

Moradi, B., Mohr, J. J., Worthington, R. L., & Fassinger, R. E. (2009). Counseling psychology Research on sexual (orientation) minority issues: Conceptual and methodological challenges and opportunities. *Journal of Counseling Psychology, 56,* 5–22.

Moradi, B., van den Berg, J., & Epting, F. (2009). Internalized lesbian and gay threat and guilt: Links with intrapersonal and interpersonal identity stressors. *Journal of Counseling Psychology, 56,* 119–131.

Moradi, B., van den Berg, J., & Epting, F. R. (2006). Intrapersonal and interpersonal manifestations of anti lesbian/gay prejudice: An application of personal construct theory. *Journal of Counseling Psychology, 53*, 57–66.

Moser, C., & Kleinplatz, P. J. (2006). Introduction: The state of our knowledge on SM. *Journal of Homosexuality, 50*, 1–15.

Parent, M., & Moradi, B. (2009). Confirmatory factor analysis of the *conformity to masculine norms inventory* and development of the CMNI-46. *Psychology of Men and Masculinity, 10*, 175–189.

Parent, M., & Moradi, B. (2010). Confirmatory factor analysis of the conformity to feminine norms inventory and development of the CFNI-45. *Psychology of Women Quarterly, 34*, 97–109.

Pastorino, E., Dunham, R. M., Kidwell, J., Bacho, R., & Lamborn, S. D. (1997). Domain-specific gender comparisons in identity development among college youth: Ideology and relationships. *Adolescence, 32*, 559–577.

Phillips, J. C., Ingram, K. M., Smith, N. G., & Mindes, E. J. (2003). Methodological and content review of lesbian-, gay-, and bisexual-related articles in counseling journals: 1990–1999. *The Counseling Psychologist, 31*, 25–62.

Reynolds, A. L., & Hanjorgiris, W. F. (2000). Coming out: Lesbian, gay, and bisexual identity development. In R. M. Perez, K. A. DeBord, & K. Bieschke (Eds.), *Handbook of counseling and psychotherapy with lesbian, gay, and bisexual clients* (pp. 35–55). Washington, DC: American Psychological Association.

Rich, A. (1980). Compulsory heterosexuality and lesbian existence. *Signs: Journal of Women in Culture and Society, 5*, 631–660.

Riggle, E. D. B., Whitman, J. S., Olson, A., Rostosky, S. S., & Strong, S. (2008). The positive aspects of being a lesbian or gay man. *Professional Psychology: Research and Practice, 39*, 210–217.

Robinson, W. L., & Calhoun, K. S. (1982). Sexual fantasies, attitudes and behavior as a function of race, gender and religiosity. *Imagination, Cognition and Personality, 2*, 281–290.

Rosario, M., Schrimshaw, E. W., Hunter, J., & Braun, L. (2006). Sexual identity development among lesbian, gay, and bisexual youths: Consistency and change over time. *Journal of Sex Research, 43*, 46–58.

Rostosky, S. S., Riggle, E. D. B., Horne, S. G., & Miller, A. D. (2009). Marriage amendments and psychological distress in lesbian, gay, and bisexual (LGB) adults. *Journal of Counseling Psychology, 56*, 56–66.

Rust, P. (2003). Reparative science and social responsibility: The concept of a malleable core as theoretical challenge and psychological comfort. *Archives of Sexual Behavior, 32*, 449–451.

Rye, B. J., & Meaney, G. J. (2007). Voyeurism: It is good as long as we do not get caught. *International Journal of Sexual Health, 19*, 47–56.

Sanders, G. L., & Kroll, I. T. (2000). Generating stories of resilience: Helping gay and lesbian youth and their families. *Journal of Marital and Family Therapy, 26*, 433–442.

Savin-Williams, R. C. (2005). *The new gay teenager.* Cambridge, MA: Harvard University Press.

Savin-Williams, R. C., & Diamond, L. M. (2000). Sexual identity trajectories among sexual-minority youths: Gender comparisons. *Archives of Sexual Behavior, 29*, 419–440.

Schwartz, S. J., Zamboanga, B. L., Weisskirch, R. S., & Rodriguez, L. (2009). The relationships of personal and ethnic identity exploration to indices of adaptive and maladaptive psychosocial functioning. *International Journal of Behavioral Development, 33*, 131–144.

Sell, R. L., Wells, J. A., & Wypij, D. (1995). The prevalence of homosexual behavior and attraction in the United States, the United Kingdom and France: Results of national population-based samples. *Archives of Sexual Behavior, 24*, 235–248.

Shively, M. G., & DeCecco, J. P. (1977). Components of sexual identity. *Journal of Homosexuality, 3*, 41–48.

Stein, E. (1999). *The mismeasure of desire: The science, theory, and ethics of sexual orientation.* New York: Oxford University Press.

Stephen, J., Fraser, E., & Marcia, J. E. (1992). Moratorium-achievement (Mama) cycles in lifespan identity development: Value orientations and reasoning system correlates. *Journal of Adolescence, 15*, 283–300.

Storms, M. D. (1980). Theories of sexual orientation. *Journal of Personality and Social Psychology, 38*, 783–792.

Story, M. D. (1987). A comparison of social nudists and non-nudists on experience with various sexual outlets. *Journal of Sex Research, 23*, 197–211.

Sullivan, P. (1998). Sexual identity development: The importance of target or dominant group membership. In R. L. Sanlo (Ed.), *Working with lesbian, gay, bisexual, and transgender college students: A handbook for faculty and administrators* (pp. 3–12). Westport, CT: Greenwood.

Szymanski, D. M., Kashubeck-West, S., & Meyer, J. (2008). Internalized heterosexism: A historical and theoretical overview. *The Counseling Psychologist, 36*, 525–574.

Thompson, E. M., & Morgan, E. M. (2008). Mostly straight young women: Variations in sexual behavior and identity development. *Developmental Psychology, 44*, 15–21.

Tolman, D. L., & Diamond, L. M. (2001). Desegregating sexuality research: Cultural and biological perspectives on gender and desire. *Annual Review of Sex Research, 12*, 33–74.

Tozer, E. E., & Hayes, J. A. (2004). Why do individuals seek conversion therapy: The role of religiosity, internalized homonegativity, and identity development. *The Counseling Psychologist, 32*, 716–740.

Troiden, R. R. (1988). Homosexual identity development. *Journal of Adolescent Health Care, 9*, 105–113.

Troiden, R. R. (1993). The formation of homosexual identities. In L. Garnets & D. Kimmel (Eds.), *Psychological perspectives on lesbian and gay male experiences* (pp. 191–217). New York: Columbia University Press.

Weinberg, M. S., Williams, C. J., & Pryor, D. W. (1994). *Dual attraction: Understanding bisexuality.* New York: Oxford University Press.

Weinrich, J. D., & Klein, F. (2003). Bi-gay, bi-straight, and bi-bi: Three bisexual subgroups identified using cluster analysis of the Klein sexual orientation grid. *Journal of Bisexuality, 2,* 111–139.

West, C., & Zimmerman, D. H. (1987). Doing gender. *Gender and Society, 1,* 125–151.

Worthington, R. L., Dillon, F. R., & Becker-Schutte, A. M. (2005). Development, reliability, and validity of the LGB knowledge and attitudes scale for heterosexuals (LGB-KASH). *Journal of Counseling Psychology, 52,* 104–118.

Worthington, R. L., Navarro, R. L., Savoy, H. B., & Hampton, D. (2008). Development, reliability, and validity of the measure of sexual identity exploration and commitment. *Developmental Psychology, 44,* 22–33.

Worthington, R. L., & Reynolds, A. L. (2009). Within-group differences in sexual orientation and identity. *Journal of Counseling Psychology, 56,* 44–55.

Worthington, R. L., Savoy, H., Dillon, F. R., & Vernaglia, E. R. (2002). Heterosexual identity development: A multidimensional model of individual and group identity. *The Counseling Psychologist, 30,* 496–531.

Yang, A. (2000). *From wrong to rights: Public opinions on gay and lesbian Americans' move toward equality.* Washington, DC: National Gay and Lesbian Task Force Institute.

Zucker, K. J., & Bradley, S. J. (1995). *Gender identity disorder and psychosexual problems in children and adolescents.* New York: Guilford.

Identity Development Among Sexual-Minority Youth

Ritch C. Savin-Williams

Abstract

Sexual identity is the name and meaning individuals assign to themselves based on the most salient sexual aspects of their life – such as sexual attractions, fantasies, desires, and behaviors. Sexual identities usually fall within existing social categories, such as straight, bisexual, or lesbian/gay, and are historically and culturally specific. Youth in today's cohort have expanded the list of sexual identities, moving beyond traditional notions of a gay, bisexual, or heterosexual orientation to include gender identity and partner characteristics. Social scientists from a variety of disciplines have proposed models of sexual identity. In this chapter, the most frequently cited and tested sexual identity model, Cass's homosexual identity formation model, is evaluated. An alternative perspective, differential developmental trajectories, has recently been proposed that focuses on developmental milestones that contribute to a sexual identity. Besides recognizing the inherent uniqueness of every life, this perspective proposes that in many developmental processes, sexual-minority youth are similar to all other adolescents of their sex, ethnicity, class, and cohort. Also discussed are the possibility of a "straight sexual identity" and two major problems with sexual identity models – the instability of sexual identity over time and its occasional inconsistency with sexual behavior and attraction. The distinctive aspects of growing up lesbian or gay have greatly diminished as the current cohort of youth has increasingly accepted sexual diversity as normative, acceptable, and even desirable. Thus, the demise of sexual identity is forecast as youth of all sexualities are refusing and resisting sexual identity labels.

Sexual Identity, Sexual Orientation Label, Sexual Orientation

Sexual identity is the term an individual assigns to himself or herself based on the most salient sexual aspects of his or her life – such as sexual attractions, fantasies, desires, behaviors, and relationships. It gives meaning and significance

R.C. Savin-Williams (✉)
Department of Human Development, Cornell University, Ithaca, NY, USA
e-mail: rsw36@cornell.edu

This chapter is an update of my previous writings, particularly Savin-Williams, 2005, 2009, portions of which have been modified for the current chapter.

S.J. Schwartz et al. (eds.), *Handbook of Identity Theory and Research*,
DOI 10.1007/978-1-4419-7988-9_28, © Springer Science+Business Media, LLC 2011

to the configuration of feelings, perceptions, and cognitions that an individual has about the various domains of sexuality in her or his life. When based on one's sexual orientation (see below), these sexual identities usually fall within existing social categories such as straight, bisexual, or lesbian/gay. The self-ascribed term may accurately reflect the totality of the individual's sexuality. Alternatively, it may give priority to some domains over others (e.g., sexual attractions over sexual behavior), or may consciously (or unconsciously) attempt to deceive the self or others about the nature of the individual's sexuality.

Furthermore, sexual identity is historically and culturally specific and can be altered over one's life course – or even from day to day. Many youth in today's cohort have expanded the list of sexual identities, often moving beyond traditional notions of sexual orientation. These may include elements of gender identity (transqueer dyke), politics (pomosexual – post-modern sexuality), partner characteristics (pansexual – not the genitalia of the person but her/his personality, for example), or idiosyncrasies (squiggly). Increasingly there is recognition that variations in sexual behavior may also become a sexual identity – slut, swinger, polyamorist, BDSM (i.e., bondage, discipline, dominance, submission, sadism, and masochism) practitioner, serial monogamist.

Sexual identity is frequently mistaken for or equated with *sexual orientation label – sometimes* referred to as sexual orientation identity. I use sexual orientation label rather than sexual orientation identity for two reasons. First, the term "label" reduces confusion with the more general concept of sexual identity. Second, I refrain from using the term "identity" with reference to sexual orientation because it seems too presumptuous to assume that individuals are doing anything other than labeling their sexual orientation when we ask them to describe, label, or identify their sexual orientation. Label is a more descriptive term; identity carries too much weight. Currently, most researchers use five sexual orientation labels: heterosexual, mostly heterosexual, bisexual, mostly homosexual, and homosexual.

For clarity, *sexual orientation* is a deeply rooted predisposition toward erotic or sexual fantasies, thoughts, affiliations, affection, or bonding with members of one's sex, the other sex, both sexes, or, perhaps, neither sex (asexuality). Sexual orientation label is thus the term applied to that predisposition. Although sexual identity and sexual orientation label are alterable, it is generally understood that sexual orientation is not because of its genetic and/or prenatal environmental genesis. Few individuals state they chose their sexual orientation; most recognize they can easily choose and un-choose a sexual identity. One's awareness of her or his sexual orientation may, however, be fluctuating and subject to greater information and familiarity with the various domains of sexuality – this may be particularly noteworthy during adolescence when sexuality is increasingly expressed through sexual behavior.

The distinctions among sexual identity, sexual orientation label, and sexual orientation are often conflated and are sources of considerable misunderstandings and debate. For example, a young woman could be sexually attracted primarily to other females, engage in sex with both sexes, and romantically fall in love with males. She might label her sexual orientation as mostly heterosexual and sexually identify as straight. A young man could be attracted to both sexes, engage in no sexual activity, and romantically fall in love with females. He might label his sexual orientation as bisexual and identify his sexuality as gay.

My focus in this chapter is on sexual identity, with multiple references to sexual orientation label, sexual orientation, and various aspects of sexuality. To make sense of sexual identity, social scientists from a variety of disciplines have proposed models of sexual identity and coming out (i.e., disclosure to others) development. In nearly all cases, however, sexual identity models have been devoted to sexual minorities and not to heterosexuals (one exception is Dillon, Worthington, & Moradi, Chapter 27, this volume). In this chapter, I briefly review the most frequently cited and tested sexual identity model, Cass's (1979) homosexual identity formation (HIF) model, and evaluate the empirical support it has garnered. A number of scholars have critiqued sexual identity models in general, and Cass's model in particular, and I add my own perspective on the value of these critiques. An alternative perspective, a differential developmental trajectory framework, is proposed which argues that, in their sexual development, sexual-minority youth are similar to all other adolescents. Thus, I briefly discuss the possibilities of a "straight sexual identity" and two major problems with sexual-minority sexual identity models – the instability of sexual identity over time and its inconsistency with two domains of sexual orientation – sexual behavior and attractions. Because the distinctive aspects of growing up as lesbian or gay have greatly diminished as the current cohort of youth has increasingly accepted sexual diversity as normative, acceptable, and even desirable, I forecast the demise of sexual identity because youth of all sexualities are refusing and resisting sexual identity labels. Evidence for this qualitative change in attitudes toward sexual minorities, and the consequences of this change, are summarized, resulting in the possible disappearance of the "gay teenager."

Sexual Identity Models

Naming one's sexuality as a means to achieve a personal and positive understanding to a life narrative is a relatively recent development. From the beginning of this endeavor, attempts to understand this process were enhanced by the construction of sexual identity models, but only for non-heterosexual (i.e., sexual-minority) youth. Heterosexual youth were not viewed as having a sexual identity. These theoretical proposals were initially and variously referred to as "coming out" or "sexual identity" (the terms were used interchangeably) models. These constructions charted the process by which a young adult moved from knowing that she/he was not heterosexual to identifying to her/himself and eventually (perhaps) to others as lesbian or gay, but rarely as bisexual (Savin-Williams, 2005). Attention to the identity aspect of human sexuality emanated not from early sexologists such as Kinsey (Kinsey,

Pomeroy, & Martin, 1948), who rather saw heterosexuality, bisexuality, and homosexuality as sexual behaviors/feelings rather than as an inherent characteristic of an individual, but from the theoretical and clinical writings of the 1960s and 1970s (Dank, 1971; Gagnon & Simon, 1973; Hooker, 1965; Warren, 1974; Weinberg, 1970). Identifying or coming out as homosexual implied the creation of a new cognitive category for individuals who came to recognize that they were not heterosexual and of a new social category for individuals who, by virtue of their public declarations, became an "outsider" (Dank, 1971). Thus, from the "invention of homosexuality" during the modern era, idealized sexual identity models of how one "becomes gay/lesbian" soon evolved. Neglected by nearly all of these writers were comparable concerns about how those who were not lesbian or gay became something else (e.g., heterosexual, unlabeled). For example, Malcolm (2008) argued that Cass's model does not address the experiences of individuals who engage in same-sex behavior but who are not proceeding toward a gay/lesbian identity.

Although elaborations on this identity process were based on various theoretical perspectives, most sexual identity models were derived from Erikson (1968). Commensurate with the prevailing view of his time, Erikson assumed a link between positive identity and heterosexuality: heterosexuality was an inevitable part of *healthy* identity development in adolescence and early adulthood – a stance for which he has received some criticism (Eliason, 1995; Gilligan, 1982; Moore & Rosenthal, 1993). According to Erikson, heterosexuality is merely a "natural" aspect of one's personal identity. Given this postulate, a *positive* personal identity coalescing around a perceived deviant sexual status was not initially seen as possible, certainly not by Erikson, who believed that a homosexual identity was a rebellion against parental values and an acceptance of "all those identifications and roles which, at critical stages of development, had been presented to them as most undesirable or dangerous and yet also as most real" (Erikson, 1968, p. 174). Homosexuality was a negative, desperate attempt to regain mastery and equilibrium when routes toward positive identity were unachievable.

Sexual identity models were first proposed in the 1970s and have continued over time (Horowitz & Newcomb, 2001; Morris, 1997). The authors of these identity models have come from various professions, usually psychiatry, psychology, sociology, or social work, and have proposed theoretical perspectives (Cass, 1979; Coleman, 1982; Malyon, 1981; Troiden, 1979; Weinberg, 1978). Sometimes relying on qualitative data, but rarely on quantitative data, these scholars offered theoretical interpretations of the coming-out process, most of which evolved into developmental stage models. Adolescence and young adulthood were presumed to represent critical developmental times for tracing the transition from the feeling during late childhood that "something isn't quite right" to the early adolescent recognition that "something" was same-sex desire, to middle adolescent sexual exploration, to late adolescent (however reluctantly) acceptance of a lesbian/gay identity, and to young adult commitment to, integration of, and pride with this identity. These theoretical notions are strongly reflected in research from an identity status perspective, with its focus on identity exploration and commitment (Kroger & Marcia, Chapter 2, this volume).

Cass's Homosexual Identity Formation Model

Although more than two dozen experts have created what they assert to be *unique* models of sexual identity development, the six-stage model proposed by Cass (1979, 1984, 1990, 1996) has become, by near unanimous acclaim, the standard bearer of sexual identity models. Unlike the other models, Cass's model has been continually refined and expanded since Cass first proposed it during her pre-doctoral days in the late 1970s. Indeed, it is the only one, to my knowledge, that has been subjected to empirical verification – including generating its own assessment tool, the Gay Identity Questionnaire (Brady & Busse,

1994), to test its hypothetical sequence of identity progression.

Despite claims by nearly all sexual identity models that they offer something unique and are not intended to apply to all individuals, most model constructions (including Cass) reify "master" narratives to explain how individuals shift from *thinking* gay, to *doing* gay, to *being* gay in such a way that "stages" are presented as occurring in a uniform, though not inevitable, fashion. To Cass, what young people are to avoid as developmentally detrimental is becoming diffused or foreclosed about one's identity; testing one's identity and advancing toward identity synthesis is to be encouraged as developmentally beneficial (McConnell, 1994). Briefly, the six stages are as follows:

1. *Identity confusion.* Individuals recognize that their sexual feelings, actions, or thoughts could be homosexual but they are not yet prepared to accept this possibility. Emotional tension, bewilderment, and anxiety are common at this point (cf. Luyckx et al., 2008).

2. *Identity comparison.* Individuals compare their sexual feelings with those of others and may tentatively accept that they might be gay/lesbian. They evaluate this possibility as desirable (true self), as too costly (alienation from family and friends), or as a temporary aberration (bisexual, a special case).

3. *Identity tolerance.* Individuals begin with the tentative belief that they are likely gay/lesbian and end this stage with near certainty but not full acceptance that they are lesbian/gay. They explore how this identity might affect other domains of the self, initial contacts with similar others are made, and trusted (safe) others are informed.

4. *Identity acceptance.* With acceptance individuals gain a clearer and more positive image of themselves as lesbian/gay. Greater comfort leads to selective disclosures, although "passing as straight" might occur in special circumstances (e.g., grandparents, sports teams).

5. *Identity pride.* Incongruity between the homosexual and heterosexual worlds dichotomizes the universe into in-group versus out-group dynamics (Spears, Chapter 9, this volume):

gay/lesbian (pride) versus not-gay/lesbian (anger with heterosexism). The inevitable confrontations inspire a preference for associations with like-minded people and help to engender a sense of pride in one's sexual identity.

6. *Identity synthesis.* Individuals integrate their sense of self as a sexual minority with other aspects of the self. Being lesbian or gay is an important but not exclusive aspect of the self. They are at peace, feel self-actualized, and not defensive, and have positive interactions with heterosexuals.

Corresponding to the number of sexual identity models are questions about whether they match people's real lives. These criticisms have been broad and penetrating (Diamond, 2008; Savin-Williams, 2001a, 2005). The most common criticism of these models has been that they present sexual identity from an essentialist perspective, as if it were a series of discrete, universalized stages without regard to contextual influences. Within sexual lives, well-defined and universal starting and ending points in the search for a sexual identity seldom exist. Stage boundaries inherently place brackets around something that is difficult to bracket. Sexual identity development is also socially constructed and, hence, variable. That is, individuals may or may not feel or recognize that they are different from their peers and that this difference is because of their sexuality. If they are aware, they may or may not give this "different sexuality" a name or tell others about their secretive discovery. Uncertain as well is the extent to which they will integrate their same-sex sexuality with their sense of self; these steps may occur in no particular order or developmental timeline. As will be clear in the next section, there is no empirical evidence to suggest that sexual identity development occurs in stages.

One analysis determined that the majority of sexual identity models can be reduced to four common themes: self-awareness, self-acceptance, disclosure to others, and integration into personal identity (Horowitz & Newcomb, 2001). A more parsimonious interpretation of the empirical evidence reviewed below suggests

that the process can be more accurately reduced to the relatively simplistic three stages of pre-awareness, awareness, and post-awareness (disclosure to others). The first process is rarely represented in research because of the difficulty in recruiting individuals in the midst of a process of which they are not yet aware; our knowledge of pre-awareness is frequently retrospective, with whatever accompanying distortions and biases that might exist. Those who progress in their sexual identity development may remember or report their initial stages as more traumatic than they actually were, as a way to execute a cultural script that expects such ordeals, to gain sympathy, or to garner praise for their current recovery or psychic strength. Perhaps awareness and post-awareness are not stages of development per se but rather simply reflect different types of individuals who choose, for various justifiable or non-justifiable reasons, whether others are to know that they are lesbian/gay. Thus, awareness individuals know that they are not heterosexual but essentially decide to tell few others that they are lesbian/gay, whereas post-awareness individuals want everyone who knows them to know about their sexuality.

Empirically Testing Sexual Identity Models

My focus here is to assess whether there is empirical support for these models, especially Cass's homosexual identity formation model (see Dillon, Worthington, & Moradi, Chapter 27, this volume, for a broader discussion). That is, if sexual identity stage models describe an unfolding of sexual-minority development, then they should be observable and verifiable across time and space in the lives of at least a substantial number (if not most) of same-sex-attracted individuals.

The empirical base for these models is, however, scant so much that Eliason (1996, p. 53) noted that people appear to be wedged or "forced into stages, rather than stages made to fit people's situations." Weinberg (1984, p. 78) wondered whether sexual identity models were being portrayed as "frameworks superimposed on phenomena by researchers and [that] may be real only for their inventors." The first to supply empirical data was Cass (1984) herself, to test her six-stage model. Unfortunately, 70% of her subjects were in stage 4 (acceptance) or 6 (synthesis), and she was consequently unable to assess the identity development of those in the first three stages. She conceded that this finding "in no way provides evidence for the concept of progress" (Cass, 1984, p. 162). In addition, she granted that her six stages could be reduced to four, largely because of the difficulty of recruiting individuals in the first three stages. By definition, such individuals were highly improbable to participate in research on an identity they were unable or unwilling to acknowledge or accept.

A decade later, despite Cass's own conclusions on the lack of empirical verifiable evidence that sexual identity progresses, Brady and Busse (1994) developed "The Gay Identity Questionnaire" (GIQ) to assess the progressive nature of Cass's six-stage model. Similar to Cass (1984), few of the individuals recruited were classified in the first three stages (8%) or in stage 5 (pride, 9%), leaving nearly everyone either in stage 4 (acceptance) or in stage 6 (synthesis). As a result, Brady and Busse could not provide evidence that individuals transitioned through early stages or that individuals who accepted their sexuality would eventually evolve to identity pride or identity synthesis. Indeed, they reduced Cass's repositioned four stages to "a two-stage process" (Brady & Busse, 1994, p. 13).

Another decade later, perhaps unaware of previous findings regarding the failure of the GIQ as an acceptable measure of identity progress, Halpin and Allen (2004) and Halpin (2008) used the GIQ and rediscovered that nearly all subjects were in stage 4 or 6. They concluded, however, that their results supported Cass's "progressive stage nature" of homosexual sexual identity. Given the lack of longitudinal evidence, a more parsimonious explanation is that individuals in acceptance and synthesis stages represented two statuses, with the latter exhibiting, by definition, greater happiness, life satisfaction, and self-esteem. With an adult sample, Johns and

Probst (2004) also concluded that Cass's stages could be reduced to two – individuals who have an unintegrated or fully integrated sense of their sexual identity.

Sexual Identity Models Reconsidered

Historically, sexual identity models helped to establish "gay/lesbian adolescence" as a field for developmental scholarship and clinical concern. However, they also simplified a complex, evolving process and did so with little empirical support. Though initially promising, these models have failed to broadly represent the life experiences of many individuals with same-sex sexuality and, consequently, they do not adequately characterize the dynamic lives of contemporary adolescents and young adults. Unless a sexual identity model explicitly incorporates social, cultural, and historical contextual relativity, it fails to capture what is most critical in the young lives of those with same-sex attractions and desires. The erroneous assumption that one model covers all, without regard to discrepant sex, socioeconomic, cohort, and ethnic backgrounds, is inherently limiting. Sexual identity development is not dictated by an essentialist program – a predetermined unfolding of collective proportions. Indeed, this calls for a more contextual approach in which sexual lives are configured, including sexual identity development has a rich history (Hammack, 2005; Hammack & Cohler, 2009; McAdams, 2005; Savin-Williams, 2005) but has failed to garner much research attention (Diamond, 2005).

What should replace these models? Alternatives to stage models that reflect the diverse, unpredictable, and ever-changing lives of contemporary teens are few (for examples of such life stories, see Hammack & Cohler, 2009). Thus, several social constructionist scholars have proposed alternative, "multidimensional" models of sexual identity (Glover, Galliher, & Lamere, 2009; Horowitz & Newcomb, 2001; Kinnish, Strassberg, & Turner, 2005). These "holistic" proposals emphasize that the various domains of sexual identity, such as sexual desire, behavior, attraction, and orientation, are not combined in a unitary construct but are fluid and complex with meaningful differences among individuals (Glover et al., 2009).

This option, to tweak existing sexual identity models until they better reflect the real lives of sexual-minority youth, is unwise from my vantage point. I believe that, fundamentally, the notion of psychological or social stages/phases of sexual identity development from either an essentialist or a social constructionist perspective is a flawed and fairly limited concept – for all the reasons noted above. There must be other alternatives.

Differential Developmental Trajectories

Given the definition of sexual identity that opened this chapter – an organized and inclusive configuration of cognitions, perceptions, and feelings that individuals have about the meaning and significance of their sexual attractions, desires, behaviors, and relationships – I believe there have been many misunderstandings in regard to its character and hence its characteristics. One alternative that I suggested a decade ago was a *differential developmental trajectory* framework (Savin-Williams, 1998, 2001b). *Differential* refers to the variability inherent within and across sexual domains and individuals, *developmental* signifies the sexual milestones and processes that occur throughout the life course, and *trajectories* indicate individual pathways in their sexual development that occur across time. Neither an essentialist nor a social constructionist position is necessary or adequate because the different developmental trajectory framework assumes an interactive approach to development. The four basic tenets are as follows:

1. Same-sex-oriented youth are similar to all other adolescents in their developmental trajectories. They are subject to the same biological, psychological, and social influences that affect other youth, regardless of sexuality. To exclusively focus on the consequences of homoeroticism runs the danger of misattributing normal adolescent experiences to a sexual orientation.

2. Same-sex-oriented youth are dissimilar from other-sex-oriented adolescents in their developmental trajectories. Perhaps due to a unique biologically mediated constitution (e.g., a brain that is organized in a sex-atypical manner that causes, for example, boys, similar to girls, to be attracted to boys) and cultural heterocentrism and sexual prejudice, especially manifested in negative social treatment for displaying gender-atypical behavior, temperament, and interests, same-sex-oriented teens negotiate their psychological development in a manner at variance from other-sex-oriented youth.

3. Same-sex-oriented youth vary among themselves in their developmental trajectories, often congruent with the ways in which other-sex-oriented teens vary among themselves. The influences of gender, ethnicity, geography, socioeconomic status, and cohort, among many other variables, result in distinctive trajectories among teens. It is imprudent to characterize same-sex desire as a monolith – a single entity with similar developmental trajectories and outcomes.

4. Same-sex-oriented youth follow their own unique developmental trajectories, dissimilar to any other person who has ever lived. Given the profound diversity inherent in individual lives, general descriptions of group mean differences and similarities may be irrelevant when applied to a specific individual.

Over the past 25 years, my empirical work has highlighted tenet #1 by demonstrating the "no sexual orientation difference" in a number of developmental and mental health domains, including pubertal onset (Savin-Williams, 1995; Savin-Williams & Ream, 2006), self-esteem (Savin-Williams, 1990, 1995), aspects of ethnicity (Dubé & Savin-Williams, 1999), gender socialization (Diamond & Savin-Williams, 2000; Savin-Williams & Diamond, 2000), and suicide attempts (Savin-Williams, 2001c; Savin-Williams & Ream, 2003). What I have not done, however, is to apply the different developmental trajectory perspectives to help us understand how sexual-minority sexual identity development is similar or different from sexual identity development among heterosexuals.

To do this, the first task is to understand the development of sexual identity for individuals of all sexualities, a task complicated by the reality that sexual identity is usually a topic reserved for investigations of same-sex- or, more rarely, both-sex-oriented individuals. The logical follow-up question is this: Do heterosexual individuals have a straight sexual identity?

Straight Sexual Identity

The sexual privilege conferred on heterosexual individuals as possessing the normative or desirable sexuality usually prevents thoughtful or empirical consideration of whether youth do or can have a "straight" sexual identity.[1] Because, in mainstream North America, heterosexuality has often been hyper-normalized, with historically minimal attention given to same-sex attractions, desires, or behaviors (Bolton & MacEachron, 1988; Gagnon & Simon, 1973; Marsiglio, 1988). Frankel (2003, p. 83) concluded that young male heterosexuals may be aware of themselves as sexual beings but that there is little evidence that they have a sexual identity: "This is the paradox of heterosexuality: It is ubiquitous as an orientation yet invisible as a sexual identity." Establishing a straight sexual identity requires conscious thought and action about one's heterosexual orientation and its everyday meaning. To "have" a straight sexual identity implies being aware of possessing a heterosexuality that has meaning and significance for who one is as a person. It also involves a process by which other-sex-oriented individuals integrate their sexual orientation into a personal and social life such that their heterosexuality affects their self-concept and alters their personal history and relationships with others and with society. We know that heterosexuals have a sexual orientation; that they sexually fantasize, become sexually aroused, engage in sexual behavior, and develop sexual and romantic relationships with (usually) similarly other-sex-oriented individuals; and

that they can label their sexual orientation as "heterosexual" or "mostly heterosexual." The critical question is whether heterosexually oriented individuals understand their sexual orientation as evidence for a sexual identity.

The usual empirical procedure to investigate this issue, unfortunately, assesses not sexual identity but sexual orientation label, even though the resulting categorization is (mis)labeled "sexual identity." For example, Konik and Stewart (2004) asked nearly 400 undergraduates, "How would you identify your sexual orientation?" with response options considered to be indicators of sexual identity (including heterosexual). Indeed, a fair number of these "heterosexually identified" youth had bisexual attractions, fantasies, and behaviors (Hoburg, Konik, Williams, & Crawford, 2004) – but it is not clear whether these inconsistencies affected their sexual identity. In another study, a heterosexual sexual identity was defined as "someone who is interested in members of the other sex" (Boratav, 2006, p. 218), and then youth were asked about the origins, consistency, and effect of this identity. Although it is doubtful that this question assessed anything other than sexual orientation, the author suggested that most participants were foreclosed in their *identity* development. Certainly, the Turkish college students in that study experienced their sexual identity, feelings, and behaviors as "always having been the same" (p. 219). Finally, in another study of "heterosexual-identified" youth, sexual identity was asked, "When you think about your sexual orientation, what term do you *most* identify with?" (Morgan, Steiner, & Thompson, 2010, p. 5). Given the questions asked, I believe that all three studies assessed not sexual identity but sexual orientation label.

Exceptions to this tendency to equate heterosexual orientation with identity include the small-scale study by Eliason (1995) and the dissertation study by Frankel (2003, 2004). In her qualitative interviews with 26 well-educated, other-sex-oriented college students about their sexual identity, Eliason (1995, p. 826) reported that the most common themes were "outside forces [e.g., gender socialization] made me heterosexual" and "never thought about it." It was not so much that their heterosexuality was inborn or fixed, a common perspective among sexual-minority young people, but that "the question of how my sexual identity formed really left me stumped" (Eliason, 1995, p. 826). Frankel (2003, 2004) asked 154 young men to complete a "Who Am I?" exercise and discovered that less than 10% spontaneously mentioned their sexual identity (or even their sexual orientation) among their top 15 characteristics. Those who did were not more likely than other young men to have questioned their sexuality or to be attracted to other males.

In their research with heterosexually oriented college men, Morgan and associates (2010) reported that over half had questioned their heterosexuality. What differentiated them were not masculine ideology, beliefs about civil rights for sexual minorities, or sexual identity exploration but rather higher affiliations with sexual-minority individuals and openness to being a sexual minority (likely due to a greater sexual identity uncertainty and lower levels of sexual identity commitment, integration, and synthesis).

In general, research participants' reports have been consistent with Marcia's (1966, 1980; Kroger & Marcia, Chapter 2, this volume) identity-diffused status (no active sense of identity with neither exploration nor commitment to an identity) and identity foreclosure (accepting an identity imposed by others or by societal expectations without critique or exploration). Straight young people generally have not been known to "come out" to themselves or others as straight-identified. It is my impression that they seldom say after their first sex with a girl/boy, "Wow! I'm a heterosexual!" Rarely do they wake up one morning and divulge to their mother or best friend, "Hey, I have something to tell you. I think I'm straight." In a far larger and more contemporary study, Thompson and Morgan (2008), using the Worthington sexual identity measure (Worthington, Navarro, Savoy, & Hampton, 2008), reported that compared with lesbian, bisexual, and mostly straight college women, exclusively straight women were significantly lower in sexual identity exploration (open to or actively experimenting with the same

sex in the past, currently, or in the future) and identity uncertainty (uncertain or unclear about one's sexual needs or desires).

If other-sex-oriented young people are to become aware of the developmental processes that create their sexual identity, they must adjust their deep-seated cognitive, affective, and behavioral understanding of themselves in such a manner as to include sexual domains. Similar to the findings of Thompson and Morgan (2008), Diamond (2008, p. 58) argued that relatively few heterosexual women think about their sexual identity because the presumption of mandated heterosexuality is unquestioned. It is when a woman violates the heterosexual norm that she begins to contemplate her sexual identity. If other-sex-oriented individuals are unaware of how their sexuality has any impact on their sense of self – which appears to be the current norm – the question remains, Do they have a sexual identity? Because the overwhelming answer to this question reported by heterosexual youth is "no," this supports the *unmarked* nature of heterosexuality. That is, other-sex-oriented individuals assume that they have a "normal" sexuality not that they have a straight identity. It is precisely this naturalness of heterosexuality that has dictated the virtual absence of research or theories about straight identity development. The notable exception is a primarily theoretical model of heterosexual identity development proposed by Worthington et al. (2008; Dillon et al., Chapter 27, this volume).

Given the above speculations, sexual-minority youth would be considered unique (tenet #2) in their development of a sexual identity, not because of a biologically mediated factor but because of social constructions of sexual identity. A counter-argument would be that other-sex-oriented individuals have a sexual identity but simply have not been asked about it by researchers because straightness is not considered a worthy topic to investigate. Although heterosexually oriented individuals, especially women (Diamond, 2008), are certainly capable of moving from a weak or nonexistent straight identity to an identity based on a growing realization of being attracted to same-sex others, a recent review of the empirical literature on adolescent sexuality included only sexual minorities when discussing sexual identity, largely because of the paucity of data about heterosexuals' sexual identity (Diamond & Savin-Williams, 2009).

Stability and Consistency of a Sexual-Minority Sexual Identity

Stability

Tenet #3 of the differential developmental trajectory framework proposes that same-sex-oriented youth vary among themselves in their sexual identity progression.[2] This divergence in pathways was noted in several early research studies (Herdt & Boxer, 1993; Savin-Williams, 1990; Sears, 1991). Somewhat later, Schneider (2001) proposed that sexual-minority women manifested one of four trajectories:

1. Consistent women had an early awareness of same-sex attractions and knew their sexual-minority status during adolescence.
2. Adult onset women were convinced that they were heterosexual during adolescence and became lesbian/bisexual in mid-life, usually after falling in love with a woman.
3. Vacillating women experienced confusion during adolescence because of their sexual attractions, with the possibility that they would accept a bisexual label.
4. Uncertain women felt they did not fit in, sexually floated through adolescence, and deferred sexuality or were not very interested in sex with anyone.

Although little is known about this diversity in sexual identity trajectories, the presence of sexual identity instability among sexual-minority youth, especially among young women (Diamond, 2008), over time has recently been investigated. Youth maintain that their sexual identity (straight yesterday, bisexual today, gay/lesbian tomorrow) is, by its very nature, subject to change, especially during adolescence and young adulthood (Friedman et al., 2004). Several retrospective studies provide support for an instability conclusion among sexual-minority populations. Among community and college youth, nearly two-thirds of gay/lesbian and bisexual individuals thought at one time during their development that they were bisexual or gay/lesbian, respectively (Rosario et al., 1996). In another study, participants aged 36–60 years and of various sexualities rated themselves on components of sexuality, including sexual identity, for repeated 5-year periods beginning with ages 16–20 years and ending with their current age (Kinnish et al., 2005). Even though each identity category represented a significant alteration in self-representation, over time many sexual minorities, but few heterosexuals, changed their identity label (Table 28.1). Women were more likely than men to change, and bisexuals were more so than gays/lesbians or heterosexuals. For example, whereas most gay men had always been identified as gay, only about one-third of lesbians had always been identified as lesbian – over half of current bisexuals at one time identified as heterosexual.

Diamond (2008) discovered that she could not predict from her longitudinal study which young

Table 28.1 Stability among identity groups over time: current identification of individuals (*x*-axis) who had once identified under another category (*y*-axis)

Identity	Heterosexual only (%)	Gay only (%)	Lesbian only (%)	Bisexual only (%)	Multiple identities (%)
Heterosexual	97	0	0	3	1
Gay	11	61	–	19	9
Lesbian	39	–	35	10	16
Bisexual male	50	12	–	34	4
Bisexual female	63	–	6	23	8

women would be stable or would relinquish their sexual identity over a 10-year period. Nearly two-thirds changed their identity label at least once, often because the identity categories did not adequately capture the diversity of their sexual and romantic feelings for female and male partners. Over time, lesbian and bisexual identities lost the most adherents, and heterosexual and unlabeled identities gained the most. What remained relatively unchanged were reports of sexual and romantic attractions. That is, young women might change their sexual identity from bisexual to heterosexual to unlabeled without undergoing a comparable change in their sexual orientation.

Consistency

Given this instability in sexual identity over time, investigators have attempted to predict consistency of sexual identity with components of sexual orientation within a time period or across time periods. Results have not been encouraging. Only about 20% of US adults who were same-sex oriented on one component (identity, attraction, or behavior) reported being same-sex oriented on the other two (Laumann, Gagnon, Michael, & Michaels, 1994). Among Dutch men who reported having had sex with another male, one-third said they were not attracted to males and just half of these same-sex behaving men identified as gay/bisexual or had ever been in love with a male (Sandfort, 1997). The most telling youth data come from an anonymous questionnaire study conducted with a representative sample of Minnesota junior and senior high school students. Youth who reported same-sex fantasies, attractions, or behaviors seldom reported being same-sex oriented in the other domains or reported having a gay, lesbian, or bisexual identity (Remafedi, Resnick, Blum, & Harris, 1992).

A substantial body of literature supports the finding that the vast majority of those who *identify* as a sexual minority also engage in same-sex *behavior* – *even* though gay virgins do exist. Less empirically convincing, however, is the transposition: although a higher proportion

of sexual-minority than straight-identified youth engage in same-sex behavior, the sexual partners of sexual-minority youth usually identify as heterosexual. Indeed, in terms of pure numbers, similar to adult men (Pathela et al., 2006), most adolescents with a same-sex experience identify as straight – three-quarters in one study (Remafedi et al., 1992). The reverse is also true: a heterosexual encounter is as likely or more likely to be reported by a sexual-minority as by a straight-identified youth (DuRant, Krowchuk, & Sinal, 1998; Garofalo, Wolf, Kessel, Palfrey, & DuRant, 1998). This seeming contradiction, that a majority of gay- and lesbian-identified youth report other-sex behavior, is reflected in the finding that exclusive same-sex behavior in populations of adolescents and young adults is relatively rare, usually less than 1% (D'Augelli & Hershberger, 1993; Garofalo, Wolf, Wissow, Woods, & Goodman, 1999; Remafedi et al., 1992; Savin-Williams, 1998). These findings are supported by cross-cultural data in Switzerland, where over 80% of adolescents reporting same-sex activity identified as heterosexual (Narring, Stronski Huwiler, & Michaud, 2003; see also van Griensven et al., 2004 in Thailand; and Eskin, Kaynak-Demir, & Demir, 2005 in Turkey).

The consistency between sexual *attraction* and *identity* is also weak, at best. Minnesota public school students were four times more likely to report same-sex attractions than a same-sex identity, especially for girls, and only 5% of those with same-sex attractions identified as a sexual minority (Remafedi et al., 1992). Among Swiss adolescent girls, 73% of those with same-sex attraction (83% of those with same-sex fantasies) identified not as lesbian or bisexual but as heterosexual; for Swiss boys, the proportions were lower but in the same direction (Narring et al., 2003). These findings were replicated among Turkish college students but not among Thai adolescents (Eskin et al., 2005; van Griensven et al., 2004).

The generally weak relationships among sexual components are also present in the National Longitudinal Study of Adolescent Health dataset, a national study of US youth (Savin-Williams & Ream, 2007). During Wave 3, less than 2% of the young women who reported having exclusively same-sex romantic attraction or same-sex behavior identified as exclusively or mostly lesbian; among young men, 13 and 3%, respectively, identified as gay. Of those who had *both* exclusive same-sex attraction and behavior, 41% of young women and 82% of young men identified as mostly or exclusively lesbian or gay. Thus, same-sex attraction plus same-sex behavior were better than either alone in predicting young adult sexual identity. Further illustrating the inconsistency among sexual components, of adolescents who engaged in same-sex behavior at Wave 1, fewer than one in twenty-five males and one in five females identified as a sexual minority at Wave 3. A worthy research pursuit would be to test whether different sexual components, such as sexual behavior or romantic feelings, have different meanings or salience for sexual identity at various ages and across sexes.

Stability and Consistency

Based on the available data, a sexual-minority identity (but not, as far as we know, straight identity) tends toward instability over time and toward inconsistency with other components of sexuality. Changes can be multidirectional and seemingly unpredictable. Individuals leave and enter a sexual identity stage or status, perhaps once or several times, at different rates and for different reasons. Although nearly all individuals who identify as a sexual minority also report same-sex attraction, arousal, and behavior, a relatively small minority of those with same-sex attraction, arousal, or behavior identify as gay, lesbian, or bisexual – they might, however, and are increasingly identified as "mostly heterosexual" (Vrangalova & Savin-Williams, 2010). Adolescents are far more likely to report same-sex attraction, fantasy, or desire than to identify as something other than heterosexual. The possibility that this identity instability and inconsistency uniquely reflect adolescent developmental phenomena is doubtful because similar findings have emerged in adult populations (Dunne, Bailey, Kirk, & Martin, 2000; Laumann et al., 1994;

Pathela et al., 2006; Savin-Williams & Ream, 2006, 2007; Smith, Rissel, Richters, Grulich, & de Visser, 2003).

These findings suggest a greater sexual orientation/identity alignment among heterosexuals than sexual minorities and among young men than young women. This is the conventional wisdom – but I remain unconvinced until more comprehensive data are produced. Although these inconsistencies have been interpreted as manifestations of "sexual fluidity" (Diamond, 2003, 2008) or "erotic plasticity" (Baumeister, 2000) among sexual-minority young women, I question whether erotic plasticity is solely the province of young women. In recent investigations across several countries, more young women *and* men reported that they are "mostly straight" in their sexual orientation identity or attractions/fantasies than say they are gay or bisexual (Busseri, Willoughby, Chalmers, & Bogaert, 2008; Dickson, Paul, & Herbison, 2003; Ellis, Robb, & Burke, 2005; Thompson & Morgan, 2008; Wichstrøm & Hegna, 2003).

How or why individuals transform their sexuality or their understanding of their sexuality, or remain stable and consistent, is unknown. Nevertheless, in their lives, these discrepancies exist. A young woman may be romantically attracted to women, but she does not thus necessarily give up her desire to identify as straight. Or she identifies as lesbian as a means to bond with a community of women, as heterosexual to please her parents, or as unlabeled because she does not want to be pigeon-holed into one identity category. A young man has consistent and persistent longings for sex with males, falls deeply in love with a woman, has sexual experiences with both sexes, and identifies as heterosexual as a means to secure his chosen career. Developmental movement across the life course from assumed heterosexuality to non-heterosexuality and back to heterosexuality is characteristic among youth who have a singular idealized, hero-worship infatuation with a coach or a teacher that is interpreted as a romantic crush; engage in a curiosity-driven sexual experience that may be sporadic or continuous; or say gay or bisexual to be "in" or to fit the image of the rebellious teen. Youth want to be accepted, and the moving target of popularity may motivate various sexual identifications. Of course, passages among various sexual identities may also be understood as "finally" recognizing one's authentic self (cf. Soenens & Vansteenkiste, Chapter 17, this volume; Waterman, Chapter 16, this volume), even if that acknowledgement is merely temporary.

Alternatively: No Sexual Identity

Given the findings summarized in this chapter – the low incidence of sexual identity among heterosexually oriented individuals, the instability of sexual identity among sexual minorities, and the lack of consistency between sexual identity and other aspects of sexuality – an alternative perspective would be a reasonable undertaking. My starting point is tenet #1 of a differential developmental trajectory framework: irrespective of sexual orientation, same-sex-oriented adolescents are, first and foremost, adolescents. As such, I propose that current cohorts of youth with some degree of same-sex sexuality are similar to their other-sex-oriented peers, rather than replicating previous generations of sexual-minority youth, in two regards. First, they often prefer not to reference their sexuality with a sexual identity label. During a 2009 workshop I conducted, one 16-year-old male wrote when asked to describe his sexual identity, "I don't desire to identify my sexuality. I just am me. Get over it." An 18-year-old young woman wrote, "I like what I like regardless of what's down their pants. If someone's attractive, they're attractive. The end." Second, when asked, many in today's cohort of youth prefer to describe their sexuality in complex and often non-traditional terms that frequently combine notions of gender with sexuality. In the workshop, an 18-year-old young woman wrote, "Pansexual. I like gender blenders, the mixtures, the people that look like both boys and girls. Then it's a 'special surprise inside' when you discover them in a sexual situation." A 17-year-old young man wrote, "I guess I'm straight but curious because maybe I haven't met the right guy yet. Right now, straight, but open to possibilities."

It is not that today's youth cannot name their sexual orientation, attractions, or desires. They can certainly say or describe their sexual orientation as heterosexual, mostly heterosexual, bisexual, mostly gay, or gay. What I believe is happening in the lives of modern-day youth, regardless of their sexuality, is that they are eliminating the need to label their sexual identity, either altogether or in traditional terms. These developments are radical solutions to the sexual identity conundrum, the categorical boxes that adults have asked youth to own up to. It is not that youth deny or reject their sexuality or its role in their lives; rather, many believe that sexual identity labels, especially the traditional ones, limit them and their sexuality. They are inadequate, confusing, and misplaced. The mere creation of sexual categories reifies the labels across time and place and exaggerates false differences among sexualities (Muehlenhard, 2000) and between them and their friends.

Yet we know little about sexual-minority youth who prefer not to identify their sexuality as gay, lesbian, or bisexual. How do they differ from sexual-minority youth who continue to use the traditional labels? We cannot answer this question in part because the non-identifying youth tend to opt out of research, educational programs, and support groups targeted for "lesbian/gay/bisexual youth." I suspect that they likely reject a sexual identity for various reasons. Some may experience their sexuality as more fluid than most sexual labels tolerate, and others may object for philosophical reasons. They protest against attempts to place their sexuality into "identity boxes." As such, they view sexual identity in general as artificial, as a balkanization of sexuality into inflexible, distinct boundaries, and personally as failing to capture the full extent of their complex sexuality. Or they may raise objections to the sexual and political connotations of a particular identity label. Lesbian sounds too clinical; bisexual emphasizes the sexual; and gay signifies gay politics, rights, and queer lifestyles. They may wish to separate their sexual desire from the friction of politics. To them, sexuality cannot be compartmentalized; it is not about politics but rather about pleasure and happiness (D'Erasmo, 2001).

These trends have been reported for a number of years – but primarily only among young women who were more likely than men to allow, and be okay with, inconsistencies in their romantic/sexual fantasies, behavior, and identity. As a result, they often made sense of their erotic desires and behaviors with reference to *new notions* of sexuality (Diamond, 2008; Pattatucci & Hamer, 1995; Rothblum, 2000; Rust, 2000, 2002). Even when asked to label their sexuality, adolescent girls often preferred to create their own identity label rather than to choose one offered by researchers (Hillier et al., 1998). This is the result, according to Rust (2000), of gender socialization that encourages women to seek their identity through relationships, to have sex within that context, and to change their identity in response to this variability.

Others, however, have noted these trends among young men as well. Green (1998) observed that adolescents of both sexes often refused to become embroiled in sexual identity politics, which they perceived as important issues for older generations. They simply wanted to love and have sex with the person(s) they desired, regardless of the individual's biological sex. Green speculated that, although these youth threaten both the gay/lesbian and the straight establishments, they might well be the future in a post-sexual identity society. Similarly, Dixit (2001) reported in *Rolling Stone* that same-sex-attracted college men no longer felt that identifying as gay was a primary aspect of their personal identity. One student suggested, "There's a prevailing attitude of, because I'm gay, it doesn't mean that's my life. I'm not a 'gay person,' I'm a person who happens to be gay." These young adult men knew their same-sex attractions and desires but they chose not to have their same-sex sexuality define them or to be the major decider in their personal identity. Rather than obsessing over their sexuality, these young adult men were occupied with typical college pursuits, including sports, fraternities, and careers. Few asserted either a gay identity or a gayness that

defined them relative to their straight peers. "No one really cares or objects to you if you're gay. In fact, making a big deal about being gay is seen as distasteful."

What has led to this development is a matter of considerable speculation, but two possibilities are noteworthy (Savin-Williams, 2005). First, as same-sex sexuality has become more visible and prevalent among today's cohort of youth, youth may feel that a distinctive sexual identity as an aspect of their personal identity adds little of significance. In this, they are becoming more similar to their other-sex-oriented peers (tenet #1). Young people with same-sex desires look and act like other youth, value marriage and family life, have the same career aspirations, and hold the same diverse range of attitudes toward mainstream values. Real changes in North American politics, laws, and consciousness toward sexual minorities have raised the possibility that sexual orientation may feel to teens to be irrelevant to their personal identity. Whether similar processes are taking shape in other less-Westernized societies is unknown but worthy of documentation in the coming decade.

One indication of this widespread change in the US cultural landscape is national poll data which indicate that attitudes toward sexual minorities have become strikingly more positive over the past two decades (Campo-Flores, 2008). For example, a December 2008 *Newsweek* poll indicated that a majority of Americans believe that gays/lesbians should serve openly in the military; that same-sex unions or partnerships should be legally sanctioned; that gays and lesbians should be able to legally adopt children; and that sexual minorities should have inheritance rights, Social Security benefits, hospital visitation rights, and equal job and housing opportunities. The latter grouping is endorsed by more than two-thirds of all Americans, and these proportions have increased since the questions were asked in the early 1990s, in large part because attitudes have become considerably more progressive among younger cohorts (Campo-Flores, 2008). For example, 58% of those 18–34-year-olds support same-sex marriage; this drops to 42% among 35–64-year-olds and 24% among those 65 years and older (Steinhauser, 2009). This secular trend might partially be the result of an increase in those who know a sexual-minority individual. In the *Newsweek* poll, one-third of Americans have a sexual-minority family member, two-thirds have a sexual-minority friend, and three-quarters know someone who is gay or lesbian. Those who befriend gay people tend to have more positive attitudes toward them (Morrison & Bearden, 2007), though cause and effect are difficult to determine. That is, perhaps those with positive attitudes toward sexual diversity are more likely to befriend a gay individual.

Among adolescents and young adults, these attitudes toward gay people are especially positive (Campo-Flores, 2008; Savin-Williams, 2005). For example, whereas 39% of Americans over the age of 18 support legally sanctioned same-sex marriage (Campo-Flores, 2008), among high school seniors and college freshmen, same-sex marriage endorsement exceeds 60% (Broverman, 2006; Hamilton College, 2001; Vara-Orta, 2007). The percentage of 18–29-year-olds who find homosexuality "acceptable" is 62; among their parents' generation, 46 (Evans & Salazar, 2007). In addition to knowing someone who is gay, the increased visibility of sexual diversity in youth culture may also be causal in this shift toward progressive attitudes among contemporary cohorts. This shift might be attributable to several factors. One is the proliferation of gay/straight alliances, of which there are now over 4,000 in US secondary schools (glsen.org, 2009). These are student-run, school-sanctioned clubs that work to improve the social and interpersonal climate for all students, regardless of sexual orientation or gender identity/expression. A second is the frequent portrayal of same-sex desire in the youth-oriented online and offline worlds (see Savin-Williams, 2005, for example). As Doig (2007, p. 49) noted, "During the course of the 1990s, homosexuality went from being largely invisible to shockingly visible to fairly pedestrian." The culture of contemporary teenagers easily incorporates its homoerotic members. It is more than being gay friendly; it is being gay blind.

A second possible liberalizing factor is the public's belief that individuals do not choose their sexual orientation. Whereas 30 years ago only, 1 in 10 US citizens believed that an individual is born gay, today more than 4 in 10 agree that homosexuality is something a person is born with rather than a result of upbringing or the environment (Saad, 2007). Consequently, the majority of the US public accepts that sexual orientation cannot be changed (Gandossy, 2007). This belief matters because those who express strong antigay attitudes tend to view homosexuality as "temporary" and not biologically based (Haslam & Levy, 2006).

A counter argument to the secular trend hypothesis is that scholars previously overestimated the prevalence and importance of a sexual identity among sexual-minority youth because they included in their research only youth who had a strong sense of their sexual identity. Sexual-minority youth were defined as those who had a gay, a lesbian, or a bisexual *sexual identity*; excluded were those who had no such identification or for whom their sexuality was a minor aspect of their personal identity. Evidence for this is apparent in a state-wide survey of Massachusetts high school students which revealed that just over 2% identified themselves as gay, lesbian, or bisexual (Garofalo et al., 1998). Yet, in a national representative study of the same age group conducted a few years later, over three times that many reported that they had same-sex romantic attractions (identity was not assessed) (Russell & Joyner, 2001). Were the 2% in 1998 representative of the 6% in 2001? One indication that they might not be is that suicide attempt rates dramatically differed: 35% for the self-identified sexual minorities and 13% for the same-sex-attracted youth. In another study of Massachusetts youth, fewer than 3% identified as gay, lesbian, or bisexual, even though over 11% ascribed to themselves same-sex attractions, fantasies, or behavior (Orenstein, 2001). Again, were the 3% representative of the 11%? Thus, it matters for research findings whether the population sampled is based on sexual identity or some other aspect of sexual orientation.

Conclusion

The notion that the development of a sexual identity involves a predetermined trajectory as predicted by sexual identity or coming-out models is belied by recent scholarship. Sexuality is but one facet of an interactive system that comprises a youth's personal identity, and this is true regardless of sexual orientation. Whether contemporary cohorts of same-sex-oriented youth are mirroring other-sex-oriented youth in their sexual identity development is difficult to assess at this point because of the dearth of comparable research on straight identity and the limitations of research on sexual minorities. However, any presumption that teens have more in common with others of their sexual orientation than with their peers in general simply because of that orientation is questionable and perhaps implausible. The most accurate conclusion is that sexual orientation dictates some (but not all) of the essence of a personal identity and that this contribution varies across individuals and across developmental time. Thus, to understand the development of sexual identity among same-sex-oriented teenagers, scientists must first understand the development of personal identity in general. A critical aspect of this understanding is the recognition that sexual diversity is becoming normalized among current cohorts of youth.

Same-sex-oriented adolescents have the same developmental concerns, assets, and liabilities as do other-sex-oriented adolescents. Contemporary same-sex-attracted teenagers want to pursue diverse personal goals, one of which is choosing unconventional sexual identities or forgoing a sexual identity altogether. How prevalent is this "trend?" It is difficult to assess given the scholarship available. What is clear is that for many adolescents, the old sexual identity categories do not fit so well anymore.

Notes

1. This section is based in part on a dissertation by Frankel (2003).

2. This section is based in large part on my earlier writing (Savin-Williams, 2009).

References

Baumeister, R. F. (2000). Gender differences in erotic plasticity: The female sex drive as socially flexible and responsive. *Psychological Bulletin, 126,* 247–374.

Bolton, F. G., & MacEachron, A. E. (1988). Adolescent male sexuality: A developmental perspective. *Journal of Adolescent Research, 3,* 259–273.

Boratav, H. B. (2006). Making sense of heterosexuality: An exploratory study of young heterosexual identities in Turkey. *Sex Roles, 54,* 213–225.

Brady, S., & Busse, W. J. (1994). The Gay Identity Questionnaire: A brief measure of homosexual identity formation. *Journal of Homosexuality, 26,* 1–22.

Broverman, N. (2006, February, 14). By the numbers: Gay rights. *Advocate,* 36.

Busseri, M. A., Willoughby, T., Chalmers, H., & Bogaert, A. R. (2008). On the association between sexual attraction and adolescent risk behavior involvement: Examining mediation and moderation. *Developmental Psychology, 44,* 69–80.

Campo-Flores, A. (2008). A gay marriage surge: Public support grows, according to the new Newsweek Poll. Retrieved December 5, 2008, from www.newsweek.com/id/172399.

Cass, V. C. (1979). Homosexual identity formation: A theoretical model. *Journal of Homosexuality, 4,* 219–235.

Cass, V. C. (1984). Homosexual identity: A concept in need of a definition. *Journal of Homosexuality, 9,* 105–126.

Cass, V. C. (1990). The implications of homosexual identity formation for the Kinsey model and scale of sexual preference. In D. P. McWhirter, S. A. Sanders, & J. M. Reinisch (Eds.), *Homosexuality/heterosexuality: Concepts of sexual orientation* (pp. 239–266). New York: Oxford University Press.

Cass, V. C. (1996). Sexual orientation identity formation: A Western phenomenon. In R. P. Cabaj & T. S. Stein (Eds.), *Textbook of homosexuality and mental health* (pp. 227–251). Washington, DC: American Psychiatric Press.

Coleman, E. (1982). Developmental stages of the coming out process. *Journal of Homosexuality, 7,* 31–43.

Dank, B. M. (1971). Coming out in the gay world. *Psychiatry, 34,* 180–197.

D'Augelli, A. R., & Hershberger, S. L. (1993). Lesbian, gay, and bisexual youth in community settings: Personal challenges and mental health problems. *American Journal of Community Psychology, 21,* 421–448.

D'Erasmo, S. (2001, October, 14). Polymorphous normal: Has sexual identity – gay, straight or bi – outlived its usefulness? *New York Times Magazine,* 104–107.

Diamond, L. M. (2003). Was it a phase? Young women's relinquishment of lesbian/bisexual identities over a

5-year period. *Journal of Personality and Social Psychology, 84*, 352–364.

Diamond, L. M. (2005). Toward greater specificity in modeling the ecological context of desire. *Human Development, 48*, 291–297.

Diamond, L. M. (2008). *Sexual fluidity: Understanding women's love and desire.* Cambridge, MA: Harvard University Press.

Diamond, L. M., & Savin-Williams, R. C. (2000). Explaining diversity in the development of same-sex sexuality among young women. *Journal of Social Issues, 56*, 297–313.

Diamond, L. M., & Savin-Williams, R. C. (2009). Adolescent sexuality. In R. M. Lerner & L. Steinberg (Eds.), *Handbook of adolescent psychology* (3rd ed., pp. 479–523). New York: Wiley.

Dickson, N., Paul, C., & Herbison, P. (2003). Same-sex attraction in a birth cohort: Prevalence and persistence in early adulthood. *Social Science & Medicine, 56*, 1607–1615.

Dixit, J. (2001, October 11). To be gay at Yale. Rolling Stone, Issue 879, Available at http://jaydixit.com/writing/gayatyale.htm

Doig, W. (2007, July, 17). America's *real* first family. *The Advocate*, 46–50.

Dubé, E. M., & Savin-Williams, R. C. (1999). Sexual identity development among ethnic sexual-minority male youths. *Developmental Psychology, 35*, 1389–1399.

Dunne, M. P., Bailey, J. M., Kirk, K. M., & Martin, N. G. (2000). The subtlety of sex-atypicality. *Archives of Sexual Behavior, 29*, 549–565.

DuRant, R. H., Krowchuk, D. P., & Sinal, S. H. (1998). Victimization, use of violence, and drug use at school among male adolescents who engage in same-sex sexual behavior. *Journal of Pediatrics, 132*, 113–118.

Eliason, M. J. (1995). Accounts of sexual identity formation in heterosexual students. *Sex Roles, 32*, 821–834.

Eliason, M. J. (1996). Identity formation for lesbian, bisexual and gay persons: Beyond a "minoritizing" view. *Journal of Homosexuality, 30*, 31–58.

Ellis, L., Robb, B., & Burke, D. (2005). Sexual orientation in United States and Canadian college students. *Archives of Sexual Behavior, 34*, 569–581.

Erikson, E. H. (1968). *Identity: Youth and crisis.* New York: Norton.

Eskin, M., Kaynak-Demir, H., & Demir, S. (2005). Same-sex sexual orientation, childhood sexual abuse, and suicidal behavior in university students in Turkey. *Archives of Sexual Behavior, 34*, 185–195.

Evans, D., & Salazar, V. (2007). *USA Today* Retrieved February 8, 2007, from www.usatoday.com/news/graphics/hs_acceptance

Frankel, L. B. W. (2003). *Do heterosexual men have a sexual identity? An exploratory study.* Unpublished doctoral dissertation, Cornell University, Ithaca, NY.

Frankel, L. B. (2004). An appeal for additional research about the development of heterosexual male sexual

identity. *Journal of Psychology & Human Sexuality, 16*, 1–16.

Friedman, M. S., Silvestre, A. J., Gold, M. A., Markovic, N., Savin-Williams, R. C., Huggins, J., et al. (2004). Adolescents define sexual orientation and suggest ways to measure it. *Journal of Adolescence, 27*, 303–317.

Gagnon, J. H., & Simon, W. (1973). *Sexual conduct: The social sources of human sexuality.* Chicago: Aldine.

Gandossy, T. (2007). Poll majority: Gays' orientation can't change. Retrieved July 7, 2007, from www.cnn.com/2007/LIVING/personal.

Garofalo, R., Wolf, R. C., Kessel, S., Palfrey, J., & DuRant, R. H. (1998). The association between health risk behaviors and sexual orientation among a school-based sample of adolescents. *Pediatrics, 101*, 895–902.

Garofalo, R., Wolf, R. C., Wissow, L. S., Woods, E. R., & Goodman, E. (1999). Sexual orientation and risk of suicide attempts among a representative sample of youth. *Archives of Pediatric Adolescent Medicine, 153*, 487–493.

Gilligan, C. (1982). *In a different voice: Psychological theory and women's development.* Cambridge, MA: Harvard University Press.

Glover, J. A., Galliher, R. V., & Lamere, T. G. (2009). Identity development and exploration among sexual minority adolescents: Examination of a multidimensional model. *Journal of Homosexuality, 56*, 77–101.

glsen.org (2009). Retrieved June 28, 2009, from www.glsen.org

Green, B. C. (1998). Thinking about students who do not identify as gay, lesbian, or bisexual, but. . . . *Journal of American College Health, 47*, 89–91.

Halpin, S. A. (2008). *Psychosocial well-being and gay identity development.* Unpublished doctoral dissertation, University of Newcastle, Callaghan, Australia.

Halpin, S. A., & Allen, M. W. (2004). Changes in psychosocial well-being during stages of gay identity development. *Journal of Homosexuality, 47*, 109–126.

Hamilton College (with Zogby International) (2001, August, 28). High school seniors liberal on gay issues. *USA Today*, 8D.

Hammack, P. L. (2005). The life course development of human sexual orientation: An integrative paradigm. *Human Development, 48*, 267–290.

Hammack, P. L., & Cohler, B. J. (Eds.) (2009). *The story of sexual identity: Narrative perspectives on the gay and lesbian life course.* New York: Oxford University Press.

Haslam, N., & Levy, S. R. (2006). Essentialist beliefs about homosexuality: Structure and implications for prejudice. *Personality and Social Psychology Bulletin, 32*, 471–485.

Herdt, G., & Boxer, A. M. (1993). *Children of Horizons: How gay and lesbian teens are leading a new way out of the closet.* Boston: Beacon Press.

Hillier, L., Dempsey, D., Harrison, L., Beale, L., Matthews, L., & Rosenthal, D. (1998). *Writing themselves in: A national report on the sexuality,* health and well-being of same-sex attracted young people (Australian Research Centre in Sex, Health and Society, National Centre in HIV Social Research, La Trobe University) Carlton, Australia.

Hoburg, R., Konik, J., Williams, M., & Crawford, M. (2004). Bisexuality among self-identified heterosexual college students. *Journal of Bisexuality, 4*(1/2), 25–36.

Hooker, E. (1965). Male homosexuals and their worlds. In J. Marmor (Ed.), *Sexual inversion* (pp. 83–107). New York: Basic Books.

Horowitz, J. L., & Newcomb, M. D. (2001). A multidimensional approach to homosexual identity. *Journal of Homosexuality, 42*, 1–19.

Johns, D. J., & Probst, T. M. (2004). Sexual minority identity formation in an adult population. *Journal of Homosexuality, 47*, 81–90.

Kinnish, K. K., Strassberg, D. S., & Turner, C. W. (2005). Sex differences in the flexibility of sexual orientation: A multidimensional retrospective assessment. *Archives of Sexual Behavior, 34*, 173–183.

Kinsey, A. C., Pomeroy, W. B., & Martin, C. E. (1948). *Sexual behavior in the human male*. Philadelphia: W. B. Saunders.

Konik, J., & Stewart, A. (2004). Sexual identity development in the context of compulsory heterosexuality. *Journal of Personality, 72*, 815–844.

Laumann, E. O., Gagnon, J., Michael, R. T., & Michaels, S. (1994). *The social organization of sexuality: Sexual practices in the United States*. Chicago: University of Chicago Press.

Luyckx, K., Schwartz, S. J., Berzonsky, M. D., Soenens, B., Vansteenkiste, M., Smits, I., et al. (2008). Capturing ruminative exploration: Extending the four-dimensional model of identity formation in late adolescence. *Journal of Research in Personality, 42*, 58–82.

Malcolm, J. P. (2008). Heterosexually married men who have sex with men: Marital separation and psychological adjustment. *Journal of Sex Research, 45*, 350–357.

Malyon, A. K. (1981). The homosexual adolescent: Developmental issues and social bias. *Child Welfare, 60*, 321–330.

Marcia, J. E. (1966). Development and validation of ego identity status. *Journal of Personality and Social Psychology, 3*, 551–558.

Marcia, J. E. (1980). Identity in adolescence. In J. Adelson (Ed.), *Handbook of adolescent psychology* (pp. 159–172). New York: Wiley.

Marsiglio, W. (1988). Adolescent male sexuality and heterosexual masculinity: A conceptual model and review. *Journal of Adolescent Research, 3*, 285–303.

McAdams, D. P. (2005). Sexual lives: The development of traits, adaptations, and stories. *Human Development, 48*, 298–302.

McConnell, J. H. (1994). Lesbian and gay male identities as paradigms. In S. L. Archer (Ed.), *Interventions for adolescent identity development* (pp. 103–118). Thousand Oaks, CA: Sage.

Moore, S., & Rosenthal, D. (1993). *Sexuality in adolescence*. New York: Routledge.

Morgan, E. M., Steiner, M. G., & Thompson, E. M. (2010). Processes of sexual orientation questioning among heterosexual men. *Men and Masculinities, 12*, 425–443.

Morris, J. F. (1997). Lesbian coming out as a multidimensional process. *Journal of Homosexuality, 33*, 1–22.

Morrison, T. G., & Bearden, A. G. (2007). The construction and validation of the homopositivity scale: An instrument measuring endorsement of positive stereotypes about gay men. *Journal of Homosexuality, 52*, 63–89.

Muehlenhard, C. L. (2000). Categories and sexuality. *Journal of Sex Research, 37*, 101–107.

Narring, F., Stronski Huwiler, S. M., & Michaud, P. (2003). Prevalence and dimensions of sexual orientation in Swiss adolescents: A cross-sectional survey of 16 to 20-year-old students. *Acta Paediatric, 92*, 233–239.

Orenstein, A. (2001). Substance use among gay and lesbian adolescents. *Journal of Homosexuality, 41*, 1–15.

Pathela, P., Hajat, A., Schillinger, J., Blank, S., Sell, R., & Mostashari, F. (2006). Discordance between sexual behavior and self-reported sexual identity: A population-based survey of New York City men. *Annals of Internal Medicine, 145*, 416–425.

Pattatucci, A. M. L., & Hamer, D. H. (1995). Development and familiality of sexual orientation in females. *Behavior Genetics, 25*, 407–420.

Remafedi, G., Resnick, M., Blum, R., & Harris, L. (1992). Demography of sexual orientation in adolescents. *Pediatrics, 89*, 714–721.

Rosario, M., Meyer-Bahlburg, H. F. L., Hunter, J., Exner, T. M., Gwadz, M., & Keller, A. M. (1996). The psychosexual development of urban lesbian, gay, and bisexual youths. *Journal of Sex Research, 33*, 113–126.

Rothblum, E. D. (2000). Sexual orientation and sex in women's lives: Conceptual and methodological issues. *Journal of Social Issues, 56*, 193–204.

Russell, S. T., & Joyner, K. (2001). Adolescent sexual orientation and suicide risk: Evidence from a national study. *American Journal of Public Health, 91*, 1276–1281.

Rust, P. C. (2000). Bisexuality:A contemporary paradox for women. *Journal of Social Issues, 56*, 205–221.

Rust, P. C. (2002). Bisexuality: The state of the union. *Annual Review of Sex Research, 13*, 180–240.

Saad, L. (2007, May 29). Tolerance for gay rights at high-water mark. Retrieved May 29, 2007, from www.poll.gallup.com

Sandfort, T. G. M. (1997). Sampling male homosexuality. In J. Bancroft (Ed.), *Researching sexual behavior: Methodological issues* (pp. 261–275). Bloomington, IN: Indiana University Press.

Savin-Williams, R. C. (1990). *Gay and lesbian youth: Expressions of identity*. Washington, DC: Hemisphere.

Savin-Williams, R. C. (1995). An exploratory study of pubertal maturation timing and self-esteem among gay and bisexual male youths. *Developmental Psychology, 31*, 56–64.

Savin-Williams, R. C. (1998). *". . . and then I became gay." Young men's stories*. New York: Routledge.

Savin-Williams, R. C. (2001a). A critique of research on sexual-minority youth. *Journal of Adolescence, 24*, 15–23.

Savin-Williams, R. C. (2001b). *Mom, Dad. I'm gay. How families negotiate coming out*. Washington, DC: American Psychological Association.

Savin-Williams, R. C. (2001c). Suicide attempts among sexual-minority youth: Population and measurement issues. *Journal of Consulting and Clinical Psychology, 69*, 983–991.

Savin-Williams, R. C. (2005). *The new gay teenager*. Cambridge, MA: Harvard University Press.

Savin-Williams, R. C. (2009). Who's gay? It depends on how you measure it. In D. A. Hope (Ed.), *Nebraska symposium on motivation: Contemporary perspectives on lesbian, gay, and bisexual identities*. Lincoln, NE: University of Nebraska Press.

Savin-Williams, R. C., & Diamond, L. M. (2000). Sexual identity trajectories among sexual-minority youth: Gender comparisons. *Archives of Sexual Behavior, 29*, 419–440.

Savin-Williams, R. C., & Ream, G. L. (2003). Suicide attempts among sexual-minority male youth. *Journal of Clinical Child and Adolescent Psychology, 32*, 509–522.

Savin-Williams, R. C., & Ream, G. L. (2006). Pubertal onset and sexual orientation in an adolescent national probability sample. *Archives of Sexual Behavior, 35*, 279–286.

Savin-Williams, R. C., & Ream, G. L. (2007). Prevalence and stability of sexual orientation components during adolescence and young adulthood. *Archives of Sexual Behavior, 36*, 385–394.

Schneider, M. S. (2001). Toward a reconceptualization of the coming-out process for adolescent females. In A. R. D'Augelli & C. J. Patterson (Eds.), *Lesbian, gay, and bisexual identities and youth: Psychological perspectives* (pp. 71–96). New York: Oxford University Press.

Sears, J. T. (1991). *Growing up gay in the South: Race, gender, and journeys of the spirit*. New York: Harrington Park Press.

Smith, A. M. A., Rissel, C. E., Richters, J., Grulich, A. E., & de Visser, R. O. (2003). Sexual identity, sexual attraction and sexual experience among a representative sample of adults. *Australian and New Zealand Journal of Public Health, 27*, 138–145.

Steinhauser, P. (2009). CNN poll: Generations disagree on same-sex marriage. Retrieved May 4, 2009, from www.cnn.com/2009;US/05/04/samesex.marriage.poll/index

Thompson, E., & Morgan, E. M. (2008). "Mostly straight" young women: Variations in sexual behavior and identity development. *Developmental Psychology, 44*, 15–21.

Troiden, R. R. (1979). Becoming homosexual: A model of gay identity acquisition. *Psychiatry, 42*, 362–373.

van Griensven, F., Kilmarx, P. H., Jeeyapant, S., Manopaiboon, C., Korattana, S., Jenkins, R. A., et al. (2004). The prevalence of bisexual and homosexual orientation and related health risks among adolescents in Northern Thailand. *Archives of Sexual Behavior, 33*, 137–147.

Vara-Orta, F. (2007, January, 19). Majority of freshmen view gay marriage as OK. *Los Angeles Times*, 1 (Living section).

Vrangalova, Z., & Savin-Williams, R. C. (2010). Correlates of same-sex sexuality in heterosexually-identified young adults. *Journal of Sex Research, 47*, 92–102.

Warren, C. A. B. (1974). *Identity and community in the gay world*. New York: Wiley.

Weinberg, M. S. (1970). Homosexual samples: Differences and similarities. *Journal of Sex Research, 6*, 312–325.

Weinberg, T. S. (1978). On "doing" and "being" gay: Sexual behavior and homosexual male self-identity. *Journal of Homosexuality, 4*, 143–156.

Weinberg, T. S. (1984). Biology, ideology, and the reification of developmental stages in the study of homosexual identities. *Journal of Homosexuality, 10*, 77–84.

Wichstrøm, L., & Hegna, K. (2003). Sexual orientation and suicide attempt: A longitudinal study of the general Norwegian adolescent population. *Journal of Abnormal Psychology, 112*, 144–151.

Worthington, R. L., Navarro, R. L., Savoy, H. B., & Hampton, D. (2008). Development, reliability, and validity of the measure of sexual identity exploration and commitment (MoSIEC). *Developmental Psychology, 44*, 22–33.

Part VI
Economic and Civic Participation

Occupational Identity

Vladimir B. Skorikov and Fred W. Vondracek

Abstract

Occupational identity refers to the conscious awareness of oneself as a worker. The process of occupational identity formation in modern societies can be difficult and stressful. However, establishing a strong, self-chosen, positive, and flexible occupational identity appears to be an important contributor to occupational success, social adaptation, and psychological well-being. Whereas previous research has demonstrated that the strength and clarity of occupational identity are major determinants of career decision-making and psychosocial adjustment, more attention needs to be paid to its structure and contents. We describe the structure of occupational identity using an extended identity status model, which includes the traditional constructs of moratorium and foreclosure, but also differentiates between identity diffusion and identity confusion as well as between static and dynamic identity achievement. Dynamic identity achievement appears to be the most adaptive occupational identity status, whereas confusion may be particularly problematic. We represent the contents of occupational identity via a theoretical taxonomy of general orientations toward work (Job, Social Ladder, Calling, and Career) determined by the prevailing work motivation (extrinsic vs. intrinsic) and preferred career dynamics (stability vs. growth). There is evidence that perception of work as a calling is associated with positive mental health, whereas perception of work as a career can be highly beneficial in terms of occupational success and satisfaction. We conclude that further research is needed on the structure and contents of occupational identity and we note that there is also an urgent need to address the issues of cross-cultural differences and intervention that have not received sufficient attention in previous research.

Occupational identity, also alluded to as vocational, work, professional, or career identity, refers to the conscious awareness of oneself as a worker. On the one hand, occupational identity represents one's perception of occupational

V.B. Skorikov (✉)
Department of Psychology, University of Hawaii, Hilo, HI, USA
e-mail: skorikov@hawaii.edu

interests, abilities, goals, and values (Kielhofner, 2007). On the other hand, occupational identity represents a complex structure of meanings in which the individual links his or her motivation and competencies with acceptable career roles (Meijers, 1998). Occupational identity has frequently been conceptualized as a major component of one's overall sense of identity (Kroger, 2007; Skorikov & Vondracek, 2007). From this perspective, it represents a core, integrative element of identity, serving not only as a determinant of occupational choice and attainment, but also as a major factor in the emergence of meaning and structure in individuals' lives (Erikson, 1968). Although there is no universal agreement regarding the domains of identity that are most relevant, the domain of occupation appears to be a central element of identity (Schwartz, 2001). Over the past 50 years, research on the structure, functions, and development of occupational identity has been conducted by scholars from a variety of disciplines, with the majority of the studies conducted within the field of vocational psychology.

Vocational and developmental psychologists view forming an occupational identity as a critical developmental task of adolescence, and vocational identity formation is taken to represent an overall index of progress in career development (Kroger, 2007; Savickas, 1985; Vondracek, 1995; Zimmer-Gembeck & Mortimer, 2006). Thus, it is not surprising that the concept of occupational identity has been incorporated in almost every major theory of career development (e.g., Bordin, 1984; Holland, 1985; Peatling & Tiedeman, 1977; Super, Savickas, & Super, 1996; Tiedeman & O'Hara, 1963). Nevertheless, only two of these theoretical perspectives on occupational identity continue to be widely utilized. One is a personality-theory-based approach established by Holland (1985), and the other stems from a psychosocial approach based on Erikson's (1963, 1968) theory of identity.

John Holland, the author of a popular theory about the relationships between personality types and work environments, known as the Person-Environment Fit Theory (1985), added the construct of identity to his theory in the 1970s. Holland's objective was to use both personality types and subjective awareness of one's occupational preferences to predict occupational choice and occupational success. He defined occupational identity (vocational identity in his terminology) as a clear, stable, and coherent picture of one's career goals, interests, and abilities (Holland, 1985; Holland, Daiger, & Power, 1980; Holland, Gottfredson, & Power, 1980). Holland's definition of occupational identity has been subsequently integrated into another major career theory, Super's Life-span, Life-space Theory (Super et al., 1996) and stimulated considerable research over the past 30 years.

Although Holland (1985) noted that vocational identity develops during childhood and adolescence through increasing differentiation among preferred activities, interests, competencies, and values, his approach focused on the strength of identity while largely ignoring its structure and the complexity of developmental processes involved in its formation. Holland's rather simplistic perspective on identity has been criticized by developmentally minded vocational psychologists, particularly because of its inability to differentiate among identity achievement and foreclosure (Brisbin & Savickas, 1994; see also Kroger & Marcia, Chapter 2, this volume) and to capture the differentiation, coherence, and stability (as well as clarity) of occupational self-concept (Vondracek, 1992). Since the 1970s, an alternative approach to the construct of occupational identity, based on Erikson's ego identity theory (Erikson, 1963, 1968; see Kroger & Marcia, Chapter 2, this volume), has become widely accepted (Blustein & Noumair, 1996; Munley, 1977; Savickas, 1985; Vondracek, 1992). Given that Erikson considered occupational choice and commitment to be the core elements of identity and noted that the inability to settle on an occupation is especially disturbing during the transition to adulthood (Erikson, 1968), his approach has been readily embraced by vocational psychologists.

Erikson described identity as the experience of "wholeness" characterized by a sense of individuality, continuity, and integration of personal goals and values, potentially achieved through the psychosocial crisis of adolescence (Erikson, 1968). According to Erikson, failure to establish a sense of personal identity during adolescence leads to confusion with regard to future adult roles and can be associated with an array of adjustment problems. The dynamic nature and complexity of adult roles in modern societies make the process of identity formation difficult and stressful. Although some individuals can adopt a foreclosed identity based on premature early identification with parents, peers, and other role models, establishing a true sense of identity involves a relatively long period of psychosocial moratorium, characterized by active role experimentation and postponing making adult role commitments. In contrast to Holland's model, the Eriksonian perspective suggests considerable differences in the consequences of identity commitments characterized by foreclosure versus those characterized by achievement and assumes that the state and strength of occupational identity should be interpreted from the perspective of developmental stages. Thus, during the period of identity moratorium, adolescents may appear to be vocationally maladjusted as they experience an identity crisis, but this period of internal instability is an important developmental precursor for further occupational and psychosocial adaptation (Erikson, 1963, 1968).

The operationalization of occupational identity within the Eriksonian approach has most frequently been guided by Marcia's (1966) identity status construct (see Kroger & Marcia, Chapter 2, this volume). Identity status refers to a characteristic way of dealing with the salient identity issues characterized by exploration and decision-making crisis on the one hand, and by personal investment and commitment on the other (Marcia, 1966, 1993). Following Marcia, many vocational researchers (e.g., Dellas & Jernigan, 1981; Melgosa, 1987; Munson & Widmer, 1997) have described occupational identity *Achievement* as a strong commitment to self-chosen occupational goals and values acquired through occupational exploration. In contrast, occupational identity *Foreclosure* is characterized by occupational commitments made without much occupational- and self-exploration.

Occupational identity *Moratorium* represents an active process of exploration and crisis and temporary inability to make a lasting career commitment. Occupational identity *Diffusion* is characterized by lack of effective exploration and inability to make commitments, regardless of whether one has already experienced a period of crisis.

Marcia's identity status categories have been effectively used in research on occupational identity directly or with minor modifications (e.g., Goossens, 2001; Meeus, Dekovic, & Iedema, 1997; Skorikov & Vondracek, 1998). There have also been attempts to refine and extend the identity status paradigm (Luyckx, Goossens, Soenens, Beyers, & Vansteenkiste, 2005; Skorikov & Vondracek, 2007). Revisions to the original identity status paradigm were suggested, in part, by Marcia's recognition that some individuals appear to be characterized by fluctuations between moratorium and achievement, which he called the *MAMA cycles* (Stephen, Fraser, & Marcia, 1992). Individuals in MAMA cycles have made identity commitments, but did not disengage from the process of exploration, which assumes a state of identity characterized by continuously updated, dynamic, and flexible choices rather than a static commitment. Recognition of the importance of differentiating between lack of interest and involvement in exploring identity issues (identity diffusion) and failure to secure a sense of identity despite having completed the process of exploration (identity confusion), described by Erikson as a potentially dangerous role confusion (Erikson, 1963), provided further impetus to expand the identity status paradigm. The resulting expanded model of occupational identity status proposed by Skorikov and Vondracek (2007) is shown in Table 29.1.

Although this expansion of the identity status paradigm is a step in the right direction, it still does not fully capture occupational identity as the complex, evolving structure of meanings in which the individual links his or her motivation and competencies with acceptable career roles (Meijers, 1998; Savickas, 1985; Vondracek, 1992). Accordingly, a recent volume dedicated to

Table 29.1 Occupational identity status classification

Occupational commitment	Occupational self-exploration		
	Limited	Active	Completed
Not made	Occupational identity diffusion	Occupational identity moratorium	Occupational identity confusion
Made	Occupational identity foreclosure	Dynamic occupational identity achievement	Static occupational identity achievement

occupational identity research in Europe (Brown, Kirpal, & Rauner, 2007) outlined a few important observations about the nature of modern occupational identities:

– Occupational identity is characterized by both continuity and change
– Occupational identity is shaped by the changing system of interpersonal relationships around which it is constructed
– Individuals make a significant contribution to the construction of their occupational identity
– Individual occupational identities are constrained by social-economic structures and processes (also see Oyserman & James, Chapter 6, this volume)
– There is considerable variation in the salience of occupational identity within the person's overall sense of identity

These generalizations are consistent with a recent analysis of occupational identity (Skorikov & Vondracek, 2007), which utilized the developmental contextual perspective on career development (Vondracek, Lerner, & Schulenberg, 1986). Skorikov and Vondracek described occupational identity as a dynamic organization of occupational self-perception, shaped by "qualitative and quantitative changes in the structure and form of identification with the role of a worker that occurs as a result of the interaction between the epigenetic unfolding of the person's capabilities and learning through self-chosen and socially assigned vocational, educational, and leisure activities" (p. 146). Additionally, the process of constructing one's occupational identity is influenced by relevant significant relationships and broader social factors, such as societal norms and expectations and economic and technological change.

Whereas the structural aspects of occupational identity have been extensively studied at least since the 1980s, its content has received considerably less attention in the literature. The importance of significant differences in occupational identities, and the ways in which these differences are associated with the underlying assumptions about the meaning of work, have been largely ignored in theory and research on careers and on identity (Blustein, 2006). Developing an understanding of occupational identity as a system of meanings associated with the worker role requires attending to its contents as well as its structure. Thus, a distinction between work as a job versus as a career has been re-emphasized in recent European studies, as the "job" perspective appears to be characterized by lack of a long-term perspective and of a sense of uniqueness, along with passive adoption of an ascribed identity. The "career" perspective, on the other hand, is marked by an active construction of occupational identity and focus on long-term career prospects and occupational success from a highly individualized perspective (FAME Consortium, 2007). Other authors have drawn upon a more traditional triad of the meanings of work as a job, as a career, or as a calling (Walsh & Gordon, 2008; Wrzesniewski, McCauley, Rozin, & Schwartz, 1997). However, the rationale for these traditionally utilized groupings has not been clearly articulated. Thus, in an attempt to develop a logically consistent taxonomy of general orientations toward work, Skorikov (2008) suggested a two-dimensional approach. First, an individual's meaning of work can be described in terms of the relative importance of extrinsic and intrinsic work motivation (see Soenens & Vansteenkiste, Chapter 17, this volume; Waterman, Chapter 16,

Table 29.2 Taxonomy of work orientations

	Preferred career dynamics	
Prevailing work motivation	Stability	Growth
Extrinsic	Work as a job	Work as a social ladder
Intrinsic	Work as a calling	Work as a career

this volume). Whereas most workers value occupational rewards and conditions as well as the work that they actually do, one is typically more important than the other within the individual's system of work preferences. Second, from the perspective of career dynamics, the meaning of work may be characterized by orientation toward professional growth versus stability. The corresponding theoretical model is presented in Table 29.2.

An empirical assessment of this logical taxonomy of general orientations toward work indicated that the four categories indeed represent empirically independent types of subjective meanings assigned to work in accord with one's sense of identity (McKeague, Skorikov, & Serikawa, 2002). Of course, many additional aspects of the contents of identity should be considered to provide a comprehensive description of the range of individual perceptions of work and of one's role as a worker. Among those, one's commitment to a particular occupational field as well as work role salience and its relative subjective importance among other life roles are also critical (Brown et al., 2007; Super et al., 1996). We address these issues in the sections that follow.

Occupational Identity and the Overall Identity Structure

As noted above, in accord with Erikson's theoretical propositions, occupational identity can be considered as a core element of identity (Skorikov & Vondracek, 1998). In the modern world, occupation is often viewed not only as the major source of income, but also as the main mechanism of social integration and the means of developing and expressing one's identity (Christiansen, 1999). Empirical studies

confirm that engaging in occupational exploration and making occupational commitments leads not only to establishing a sense of occupational identity, but also to constructing one's identity in general from childhood through adulthood (Flum & Blustein, 2006; Kroger, 2007; Skorikov, 2007; Vondracek, Silbereisen, Reitzle, & Wiesner, 1999).

Numerous cross-sectional studies have found positive associations between occupational identity and more general conceptions of identity in adolescence and young adulthood (Blustein, Devenis, & Kidney, 1989; Nauta & Kahn, 2007; Savickas, 1985; Skorikov & Vondracek, 1998). Whereas identity development is often marked by asynchrony and relatively low congruence across different domains (Goossens, 2001; Meeus, Iedema, Helsen, & Vollebergh, 1999; Solomontos-Kountouri & Hurry, 2008), adolescents are more likely to be characterized by identity achievement in the occupational domain than in any other domain (Grotevant & Thorbecke, 1982; Skorikov & Vondracek, 1998). Skorikov and Vondracek (1998) found that identity development in the domains of lifestyle, ideology, religion, and politics was correlated with, but lagged behind, occupational identity development, and these authors concluded that occupational identity plays the leading role in the process of adolescent identity formation.

The effects of occupational identity on identity in general are likely to be particularly strong during the transition from school to work (Danielsen, Lorem, & Kroger, 2000). During that period, successful employment strengthens the sense of occupational identity and its salience within the overall identity structure, whereas failure to find adequate employment increases the subjective importance of relational identity, which may then replace occupational identity as a main source of meaning and psychological well-being (Meeus et al., 1997; Skorikov & Vondracek, 2007). Interestingly, in a Norwegian study of recent high-school graduates, work was found to be the primary influence on overall identity regardless of whether the participants were attending college, working, or unemployed (Danielsen et al., 2000). In young and middle adulthood, the relationships between occupational identity and other identity domains become progressively reciprocal as individuals recognize the need to balance their work, family, religious, and other commitments (Dorn, 1992; Friend, 1973; Kroger, 2007). However, there is also evidence that identity development in the occupational domain consistently outpaces development in other domains in adulthood and is most congruent with identity development at the overall level (Fadjukoff, Pulkkinen, & Kokko, 2005).

Functions of Occupational Identity

The formation of an occupational identity is an important career and developmental task of adolescence (Erikson, 1968; Flum & Blustein, 2006; Lapan, 2004; Vondracek et al., 1986). From a career development perspective, occupational identity represents the central mechanism of agentic control over one's career development (Meijers, 1998; Vondracek & Skorikov, 1997), because it serves as a principal cognitive structure that controls the assimilation and integration of self- and occupational knowledge and allows for making logical and systematic career decisions even when facing a serious career problem. Without a clear and strong occupational identity, individuals would be unable to make self-endorsed career choices, resulting in feelings of distress. This could further impede the capacity for adaptive information processing and decision making (Saunders, Peterson, Sampson, & Reardon, 2000). Indeed, the strength of occupational identity is closely associated with various indices of overall career development progress, such as career maturity (Holland, Johnston, & Asama, 1993; Leong & Morris, 1989; Savickas, 1985; Turner et al., 2006).

Theoretically, possessing an established occupational identity allows for making relatively easy, rational, and mature career decisions in the face of occupational ambiguities (Holland, 1985; Raskin, 1985; Saunders et al., 2000). This proposition has been supported in numerous studies of adolescents and young adults where positive associations have been reported between occupational identity and career decision-making skills, career search and decision-making self-efficacy, career choice readiness, and career decidedness (Gushue, Scanlan, Pantzer, & Clarke, 2006; Hirschi & Läge, 2007; Holland et al., 1993; Solberg, 1998). In contrast, career indecision is correlated with a less established sense of occupational identity (Conneran & Hartman, 1993; Holland & Holland, 1977). Longitudinal studies of occupational identity in adults provide further evidence of its functional importance. For example, occupational identity achievement was found to be a significant predictor of both occupational attainment and re-establishing the worker's role in the process of occupational rehabilitation (Braveman, Kielhofner, Albrecht, & Helfrich, 2006; Schiller, 1998).

Another important function of occupational identity is to provide the person with a sense of direction and meaning and to establish a framework for occupational goal setting and self-assessment (Christiansen, 1999; Meijers, 1998; Raskin, 1985; Solberg, Close, & Metz, 2002). Experimental research has demonstrated that vocational identity is a strong predictor of the quality of reasoning about future career challenges and opportunities (Klaczynski & Lavallee, 2005). Additionally, naturalistic studies suggest that one's sense of vocational direction is an important predictor of success during the transition from school to work (Lapan, 2004; Mortimer, Zimmer-Gembeck, Holmes, & Shanahan, 2002), particularly for disadvantaged adolescents (Diemer & Blustein, 2006; Ladany, Melincoff, Constantine, & Love, 1997).

Adult occupational identity incorporates both (a) an understanding of who one has been and (b) a sense of desired and possible directions for one's future, and it serves as a means of self-definition and a blueprint for future action (Kielhofner, 2007). The organizing role of occupational identity has been consistently supported in research on workers in a variety of occupations. For example, studies have shown that occupational identity is an important predictor of continuity in one's work role, occupational and organizational commitment, and work performance (Baruch & Cohen, 2007; Kidd & Frances, 2006; Suutari & Makela, 2007). Research also suggests that occupational identity serves as a control mechanism that regulates adult career stability and the range of acceptable career options (King, Burke, & Pemberton, 2005).

Finally, many theorists have argued that possessing a strong occupational identity contributes to psychosocial adjustment, well-being, and life satisfaction (Christiansen, 1999; Kroger, 2007; Raskin, 1985; Vondracek, 1995). Indeed, empirical studies have provided strong and consistent evidence for positive relationships between occupational identity and psychosocial functioning. During the transition from high school to work, occupational identity achievement appears to be predictive of mental health (De Goede, Spruijt, Iedema, & Meeus, 1999; Meeus et al., 1997) and may help to protect against drug use in men (Frank, Jacobson, & Tuer, 1990). In college students, strength of occupational identity was positively associated with life satisfaction and adjustment, and was negatively associated with distress (Leong & Morris, 1989; Lopez, 1989; Strauser, Lustig, Cogdal, & Uruk, 2006). In working adults, the strength of occupational identity was found to be a strong predictor of affective health, manifested in lower levels of depression and anxiety, and life satisfaction even when controlling for the effects of occupational status, income, education, and self-esteem (McKeague et al., 2002; Schiller, 1998; Skorikov, 2008). A number of cross-sectional studies provide converging evidence that perceiving work as a calling can be highly beneficial in terms of adult workers' psychological health and well-being (Kidder, 2006; Skorikov, 2008; Vaughan & Roberts, 2007; Wrzesniewski et al., 1997). Longitudinal research is needed, however, to clarify the nature of these associations and to test causal hypotheses about the role of occupational identity in human lives.

Occupational Identity Development

From a developmental point of view, occupational identity formation represents a lifelong process of constructing, shaping, and reshaping the self as a worker (FAME Consortium, 2007). At any given point in time, occupational identity reflects accumulated life experiences organized into an understanding of who one is and wishes to become (Kielhofner, 2007). Adolescence is often considered the stage of development during which the process of identity formation begins, as the limitations of children's cognition and activity may not permit establishing complex, integrated, and stable self-representations (Kroger, 2007). However, childhood experiences very likely provide a foundation for one's occupational identity formation (Skorikov & Vondracek, 2007).

Although children's perceptions of work do not seem to be incorporated into an identity-like cognitive structure (Barak, Feldman, & Noy, 1991; Cook & Simbayi, 1998; Sellers, Satcher, & Comas, 1999), early vocational experiences and preferences may have lasting effects on the process of occupational identity construction. For example, informal observations of family members' work behavior and attitudes, societal expectations and cultural stereotypes, and mass media gradually shape the individual meaning of work (Danto, 2003), and by middle childhood a relatively stable system of vocational preferences can be established. Under favorable conditions, these preferences can facilitate future occupational identity formation (Vondracek et al., 1999). However, they can also exert negative effects. For instance, early experience of restrictive gender-role stereotypes and confined social class roles can limit the range of exploration and perceived career opportunities in adolescence (Gottfredson, 2005).

It is not uncommon for a child to adopt an occupational identity at a young age as a result of identifying with an adult or accepting an occupational identity assigned by others (Kalil, Levine, & Ziol-Guest, 2005). In that case, the child's identity would be almost inevitably ascribed and characterized as foreclosed rather than self-chosen and characterized as achieved (Brisbin & Savickas, 1994; Erikson, 1963; Vondracek et al., 1986). Furthermore, early occupational commitments are often based on an unrealistic self-assessment and change quickly during the transition from school to work (Vondracek & Skorikov, 1997). For example, there is evidence that athletic occupational identity formed at a relatively young age can be remarkably stable throughout childhood and adolescence, but is frequently associated with failure to explore alternative occupations, poor career decision-making skills, and low career maturity (Brown, Glastetter-Fender, & Shelton, 2000; Murphy, Petitpas, & Brewer, 1996). Most importantly, such foreclosed identities rarely allow for implementing one's vocational plans in the world of adult work (Brown et al., 2000). Thus, many identity researchers argue that an early occupational or major educational choice does not provide an optimal context for psychosocial identity development and future adjustment (e.g., Danielsen et al., 2000). Some children, however, may be much more capable of forming realistic ideas about their future work roles than traditionally assumed, and in those cases there may be positive effects of establishing early vocational preferences (that are, however, open to revision) on subsequent identity development (Vondracek et al., 1999).

Occupational identity development during adolescence may be quite variable, with some adolescents remaining identity diffused in the absence of clear expectations in regard to work preparation and positive role models, while others, when pressured to make decisions about their occupational future, quickly accept a foreclosed occupational identity, especially if they strongly identify with their parents (Vondracek et al., 1986). During the high-school years, however, many adolescents begin questioning and reconsidering the work and career attitudes, beliefs, and values held by adult family members (Stead, 1996), a process referred to by Erikson (1968) as an identity crisis. This process typically leads to occupational identity moratorium, characterized by engagement in exploratory behavior that lays the groundwork for making important career decisions, but that is also usually accompanied by a lengthy delay in making occupational commitments (Erikson, 1968). Inability to make progress toward achieving an occupational identity can lead to vocational role confusion

and career stagnation, whereas the emergence of self-understanding and acceptance during the period of moratorium facilitates subsequent occupational identity achievement and helps to promote occupational adjustment (Salomone & Mangicaro, 1991).

Empirical studies have demonstrated that developmental changes in occupational identity cannot be detected over short periods of time and that there is no predictable pattern of change in any given individual's occupational identity status (Dellas & Jernigan, 1987; Meeus & Dekovic, 1995; Meeus et al., 1999; Van Hoof, 1999). Nevertheless, over longer periods of time, there is a clear developmental progression in occupational identity toward identity achievement and a decline in occupational identity diffusion during adolescence and adulthood (Fadjukoff et al., 2005; Pulkkinen & Kokko, 2000; Skorikov & Vondracek, 1998). A possible exception to this pattern is represented by occupationally foreclosed adolescents, who are most likely to retain their status, frequently well into adulthood (Dellas & Jernigan, 1987; Fadjukoff et al., 2005).

The period of occupational identity moratorium can be a long and difficult part of late adolescence and young adulthood, especially because many adolescents do not exhibit much progress in career development during high school (Vondracek & Skorikov, 1997). Research on career and identity development during the transition to adulthood consistently suggests that today's adolescents and young adults around the world have considerable, long-lasting difficulties with formulating career goals and making occupational commitments (Bloor & Brook, 1993; Fadjukoff et al., 2005; Mortimer et al., 2002; Skorikov, 2007). Identity development in the occupational domain is expected to be particularly difficult and stressful (Erikson, 1968). The extent to which young adults benefit from extending the period of occupational moratorium into their late 20s and early 30s may depend on how they approach the processes of individualization and identity formation. Recent research has suggested that young adults who approach these processes proactively and with a strong sense of agency (i.e., they accept responsibility for the course of their life; they own their decisions and accept the consequences; they are confident that they can overcome barriers and obstacles) are more likely to engage in exploration and make flexible commitments and less likely to be conforming and avoiding (Schwartz, Côté, & Arnett, 2005).

Some longitudinal data suggest that postponing a transition to the adult work roles can facilitate further occupational identity development toward identity achievement (Fadjukoff, Kokko, & Pulkkinen, 2007). These findings dovetail with theorizing about the developmental relevance of a long period of occupational identity moratorium, which allows for exploring oneself and one's career options without making definitive decisions about one's occupational future (Ladany et al., 1997). However, many young people seem to postpone making occupational commitments without engaging in active and systematic career exploration (Côté, 2000; Salomone & Mangicaro, 1991). Their pattern of occupational behavior, described as floundering (Super, 1957), is marked by an apparently meaningless succession of random jobs and lack of progress in their occupational identity (Mortimer et al., 2002). Floundering is likely to be caused by a diffused identity, which prevents adolescents from making meaningful occupational decisions and from learning from their experiences (Salomone & Mangicaro, 1991). Thus, developing at least a general sense of direction and a tentative occupational identity by the beginning of the transition from school to work is an important conclusion to the process of occupational identity formation throughout childhood and adolescence.

There has been very little research on the developmental trends in occupational identity in adulthood. What is known, however, is that from young to middle adulthood there is a strong trend toward making occupational commitments, but the end result can be identity foreclosure as well as achievement (Fadjukoff et al., 2005; Pulkkinen & Kokko, 2000). This finding is consistent with the results of cross-sectional research, which shows that in working adults the strength of occupational identity is positively correlated with age (Skorikov, 2008). Interestingly, the growth of an occupational commitment also increases the salience of the work role within the person's overall identity structure (Pulkkinen & Kokko, 2000). Unfortunately, little is known about the role of adult work experience in the construction and reconstruction of occupational identities (Brown et al., 2007). Although positive work experience promotes occupational identity development through strengthening of occupational commitments (e.g., Fagerberg & Kihlgren, 2002), adults must constantly renegotiate the balance between their occupational and life dreams and aspirations and the realities of the job market (Lips-Wiersma & McMorland, 2006). Inability to successfully implement one's occupational identity due to the limitations imposed by personal and contextual factors can lead to regressive shifts in occupational identity and even to identity loss (Brown et al., 2007; Fadjukoff et al., 2005; Vrkljan & Polgar, 2007). Moreover, in the process of work transitions, employment experience and occupational identity are likely to exert strong, reciprocal effects, but the exact nature of their influences on each other in adulthood has not been systematically studied.

Influences on Occupational Identity Formation

Theoretically, occupational identity development is shaped by the person's activities and experiences and a variety of individual (e.g., personality and gender) and contextual (e.g., family, peer group, social and economic conditions) factors, as well as their interaction (Skorikov & Vondracek, 2007). Contextual factors can have direct effects on identity via social stereotypes, modeling, perceived opportunity structure, and environmental constraints (see Oyserman & James, Chapter 6, this volume). At the same time, contextual variables can exert indirect effects on identity formation by regulating the direction and repertoire of individual actions.

Individual Activities and Experiences

Vondracek et al. (1986) argued that both vocational and avocational activities can serve as the means of self- and occupational exploration throughout the lifespan and thus can contribute to the process of occupational identity development. Indeed, Vondracek and Skorikov (1997) found that middle- and high-school students derive ideas about their occupational interests, aspirations, and abilities from a variety of work, school, and leisure activities and do not seem to differentiate among those as sources of their preferences and self-assessment. Participation in various organized youth activities, particularly service, faith-based, community, and vocational activities, has also been found to be a positive factor in shaping adolescent identity (Hansen, Larson, & Dworkin, 2003; Vondracek, 1994).

The role of early work experience in the process of occupational identity development has received increasing attention (e.g., Bynner, 1998; Mortimer, 2003; Mortimer & Zimmer-Gembeck, 2007; Skorikov & Vondracek, 1997). However, the actual work activities of children and even adolescents may have limited implications for developing ideas about one's occupational future and testing one's capacity to perform adult work roles. First, many cultures discourage formal employment until the completion of mandatory schooling (Ferreira, Santos, Fonseca, & Haase, 2007). Second, even in countries where many adolescents work while attending school, such as the United States, their jobs are typically located within unskilled manual labor and service occupations. These jobs are not perceived by young workers as relevant to their career plans as adults and do not provide significant opportunities for occupational exploration (Arnett, 2000; Skorikov & Vondracek, 1997). Nevertheless, adolescent work experience was found to be positively related to occupational goal setting (Zimmer-Gembeck & Mortimer, 2006) and development of the work value system (Porfeli, 2007; Skorikov & Vondracek, 1997). Early work experience can also have an indirect, delayed effect on occupational identity during the transition from school to work by increasing youths' employability

and potential for securing higher quality jobs (Mortimer et al., 2002). In contrast, youth unemployment and poor quality of the work environment during the transition to adulthood can inhibit the development of occupational identity (Danielsen et al., 2000; De Goede et al., 1999; Peregoy & Schliebner, 1990).

Children and adolescents in most parts of the world spend much of their waking time participating in educational activities. Schooling is a significant determinant of occupational identity formation, because it facilitates the acquisition of work skills, contributes to the development of occupational interests, and provides direct and indirect career guidance (Bynner, 1998; Dellas & Gaier, 1975; Vondracek & Skorikov, 1997). However, little research has been conducted on the specific effects of schools and academic activities on occupational identity, and the results of the few available studies have been inconsistent. For example, Meeus (1993) and Vondracek (1994) found that academic achievement facilitates occupational identity development in adolescence, but other studies did not find significant associations between academic achievement and occupational identity (Penick & Jepsen, 1992; Turner et al., 2006). Considerable variation among school systems makes it difficult to generalize any conclusions about the effects of educational contexts and activities on student occupational identity. There is converging, international evidence, however, that incorporating an occupational perspective in the academic curriculum (via magnet schools with special curricula that attract students from beyond the usual boundaries of school districts, similar to "special schools" in Great Britain, apprenticeships, internships, job shadowing for high-school students that involves following a member of an occupation for a day or longer to observe their activities, etc.,) promotes occupational identity development (Flaxman, Guerrero, & Gretchen, 1999; Heinz, Kelle, Witzel, & Zinn, 1998; Remer, O'Neill, & Gohs, 1984; Zimmer-Gembeck & Mortimer, 2006). In contrast, purely academic school systems may delay the process of occupational identity formation by depriving students of opportunities to engage in occupationally relevant exploratory activities (Vondracek & Skorikov, 1997). Apprenticeships seem to be particularly beneficial in terms of promoting occupational identity development (Hamilton, 1990; Zimmer-Gembeck & Mortimer, 2006). However, their success depends on the student's ability to integrate complementary as well as contradictory learning experiences (Harris, Simons, Willis, & Carden, 2003). Thus, adolescents who have already formed at least some sense of identity are likely to benefit most from apprenticeships (Skorikov & Vondracek, 2007).

Extracurricular and leisure activities can have numerous and varied effects on identity development as well (Hansen et al., 2003). High-school students who were more advanced in their occupational identity development were also more likely to be involved in extracurricular activities and sports (Vondracek, 1994). Similar findings were obtained in studies of college students (Munson & Savickas, 1999; Munson & Widmer, 1997). However, existing correlational studies do not preclude the possibility of the reverse effect: engaging in specific types of extracurricular and leisure activities can be an outcome of occupational identity development rather than its cause. For example, volunteerism and sports participation are frequently used by career-concerned high-school students to increase their chances of admission to elite colleges.

Personality

Erikson's (1963) theory suggests that successful identity formation during adolescence depends on stable, trait-like, adaptive ego qualities, such as optimism, autonomy, and sense of agency and industry, acquired in the process of accomplishing the developmental tasks of childhood. These ego qualities can be seen as personality traits evolving through life experiences on the basis of innate, temperamental characteristics. Thus, as a major component of overall identity, occupational identity formation is expected to be affected by personality. Indeed, studies on middle school, high school, and college students have consistently found positive associations between occupational identity development and adaptive personality characteristics (e.g., openness to new experiences, flexibility, curiosity) and negative associations between occupational identity and self-defeating traits (e.g., narcissism, rigidity, defensiveness). In adolescence and young adulthood, occupational identity strength and occupational identity achievement are positively correlated with self-esteem (Munson, 1992; Santos, 2003), proactivity and goal directedness (Santos, 2003; Turner et al., 2006), self-regulation, internal locus of control and orientation toward personal growth (Robitschek & Cook, 1999), and rational decision making (Saunders et al., 2000). In contrast, occupational identity is negatively correlated with general indecisiveness (Lucas & Epperson, 1990; Santos, 2001), goal instability (Santos, 2003), and trait anxiety and depression (Lopez, 1989; Saunders et al., 2000). Unfortunately, there have been no longitudinal studies on the relationships between personality traits and occupational identity, and the hypothesized direction of effects has not been tested.

Gender

Historically, sex-related differences have frequently been theorized to be a major influence on identity in general and on occupational identity in particular (Erikson, 1968; Josselson, 1987). However, numerous empirical studies conducted on early, middle, and late adolescent samples in different countries over the past 20 years have found few or no gender differences in the process of occupational identity formation and its outcomes (Archer, 1989; Diemer & Blustein, 2006; Munson, 1992; Skorikov & Vondracek, 1998). Some studies indicate that girls can be somewhat more advanced than boys in their occupational exploration and commitment during middle and late adolescence (Meeus & Dekovic, 1995; Skorikov & Vondracek, 1998), which may be partially explained by the developmental lag in pubertal and maturational processes during adolescence in boys compared with girls (Skorikov & Vondracek, 2007).

In an early study by Grotevant and Thorbecke (1982), occupational identity was positively related to masculinity in both male and female high-school students. Studies on young adults suggest, however, that gender-related differences in societal demands and expectations may actually promote occupational identity formation in women. For example, Savickas (1985) found that, among medical school students, young adult women were more committed to their career goals, more likely to explore their career options, and had better-defined occupational identities compared to their male counterparts. Savickas explained his findings in terms of the women's need to possess a more stable occupational identity in order to choose and enter a male-dominated occupation. This explanation was supported in a study of Belgian college students majoring in engineering and psychology, in which women were much more likely than men to be assigned to the occupational identity achievement status (Goossens, 2001).

For modern women, the need to progress toward occupational identity achievement can represent a general, rather than occupation-specific, demand. As adolescent girls move into adulthood, contemporary societal expectations promote multiple role conflicts within the female identity (Barnett & Hyde, 2001), but studies of adult women suggest that employment is now the most important role in the hierarchy of role identities for the majority of women (Graham, Sorell, & Montgomery, 2004). To cope with various role conflicts, a working woman needs to possess a clear picture of herself as a worker – and this portrayal must be well integrated into her overall identity. In light of the above, it may not be surprising that, in a long-term study of identity development in Finland (Fadjukoff et al., 2005), women were found to clearly outpace men in terms of progress toward occupational identity achievement from young through middle adulthood. By the age of 42, almost 70% of women in the Finnish sample were identity achieved in the occupational domain, compared to just over 50% of men. In contrast, men were twice as likely to experience regressive changes (transitions in the direction opposite to the hypothesized

progressive sequence, which moves from identity diffusion to foreclosure to moratorium to achievement) in their occupational identity compared to women – 37% versus 19%. Whereas both men and women showed a strong tendency to make occupational commitments, as they grew older, men were more likely than women to adopt a foreclosed identity.

Despite similarities in the level of occupational identity development in adolescence, there are considerable gender differences in the relationships of occupational identity with other domains of identity (Goossens, 2001). Adolescent girls may be more advanced than boys in the family role domain of their identities (Archer, 1989) and may consider their relational identity more important than their occupational identity (Meeus & Dekovic, 1995). The occupational identity of high-school boys appears to be separated from the issues of gender and family, whereas in female high-school students, gender identity begins playing a central role in perceived occupational interests and abilities (Hollinger, 1988). In the process of negotiating their identities, girls begin balancing the occupational and other domains of identity earlier than boys and become progressively sensitive to the issues of family and relationships when making educational and occupational choices in late adolescence (Vondracek et al., 1986). By the end of adolescence, career commitment appears to be negatively related to intimacy (Seginer & Noyman, 2005), and some young women may change their previous occupational plans in favor of their family plans, whereas many professional women decide not to have children in order to pursue their careers. However, the distinction between the occupational and family domains of identity in women has been contested in the literature. Thus, Merrick (1995) argued that adolescent childbearing in some instances can be regarded as a career choice through which young women implement their sense of identity and which represents their adult occupation. Indeed, in some studies of occupational identity, motherhood and child rearing were considered an occupational choice for women (e.g., Frank et al., 1990).

Gender differences and similarities observed in research on occupational identity certainly depend on the historic trends in the interpretation of gender roles and cultural norms given that social context is a strong determinant of occupational identity salience, as well as of the relative importance of different identity domains (Shorter-Gooden & Washington, 1996; Solomontos-Kountouri & Hurry, 2008; Stead, 1996). To date, most research on gender issues in occupational identity has been conducted in Europe and North America, and findings cannot be generalized to other social and historical contexts. In fact, even among post-industrial societies, there is considerable variation in the relationships among various domains of identity (Solomontos-Kountouri & Hurry, 2008). A South African study of the perceived relevance of identity domains in adolescence (Alberts, Mbalo, & Ackermann, 2003) provides an interesting example of such cultural differences. In that study, adolescent girls were more likely than boys to see their future career as very important, whereas relationships with the opposite sex were surprisingly more important for boys than girls.

Family and Peers

The influence of significant others has always been considered a major factor in the process of identity development in general (Danielsen et al., 2000) and occupational identity in particular (Vondracek et al., 1986). Research on children and adolescents suggests that significant figures in their lives, such as parents, friends, and teachers, exert a major impact on their occupational identity (Mortimer et al., 2002). However, these effects are complex and depend on the nature of the underlying interpersonal relationships (Li & Kerpelman, 2007) and the entire pattern of social interactions (Flaxman et al., 1999). For example, the density of the social network that provides mentoring is – surprisingly – negatively related to the clarity of occupational identity during the transition from college to work (Dobrow & Higgins, 2005). A possible explanation is that increasing the breadth, rather than depth,

of exploration does not immediately promote career planning and decision making, but rather intensifies the experience of an occupational identity moratorium (Porfeli & Skorikov, 2010; Schwartz, Zamboanga, Weisskirch, & Rodriguez, 2009).

Family of origin is considered a key factor in child and adolescent career development in general (e.g., Bryant, Zvonkovic, & Reynolds, 2006; Hartung, Porfeli, & Vondracek, 2005; Vondracek et al., 1986). However, empirical research on the effects of family on occupational identity formation has been largely inconclusive. For example, Lopez (1989) reported that the overall strength of occupational identity was correlated with family dynamics (i.e., how family members relate to one another), whereas others (e.g., Hartung, Lewis, May, & Niles, 2002) have not found a significant association. Moreover, when the associations among family variables are statistically controlled, very few characteristics of the family exert independent effects on occupational identity (Hargrove, Creagh, & Burgess, 2002; Johnson, Buboltz, & Nichols, 1999). Hargrove, Inman, and Crane (2005) found no association between strength of high-school students' occupational identity and any of the family environment characteristics studied, including quality of family relationships, family goal orientations, and degree of organization and control within the family system. In a study of 11th graders, Penick and Jepsen (1992) found that the strength of occupational identity was also independent of the family's socioeconomic status, and that there was no consistent pattern of associations with family characteristics reported by students, mothers, and fathers. Similarly, a large-scale study conducted on 12–24-year-old Dutch adolescents found that the effects of family on occupational identity status were small, and that the process of occupational identity formation appeared to be influenced more strongly by peers than parents (Meeus & Dekovic, 1995). Similar findings were reported in a study of commitment to career choice among American college students (Feldsman & Blustein, 1999). In contrast, Berríos-Allison (2005) reported more consistent associations between occupational identity status and family differentiation, connectedness, and separateness.

The influence of peers on occupational identity may be particularly strong in middle adolescence, when membership in adolescent crowds is predictive of occupational interests and preferences in early adulthood (Johnson, 1987). Meeus (1993) found that support provided by high-school friends facilitated progress toward occupational identity achievement, and that the effects of peers remained consistently important in educational and work settings after high school graduation (see also Meeus & Dekovic, 1995). The influence of peers on adolescent occupational identity has been interpreted in terms of mutual reinforcement within the peer group, which is typically characterized by similar occupational interests and career goals (Flaxman et al., 1999).

Nevertheless, family should not automatically be considered less important than peers in terms of effects on occupational identity development (Skorikov & Vondracek, 2007). First, the formation of a peer group and peer interactions are undoubtedly influenced by upbringing in the family (e.g., Granic, Dishion, & Hollenstein, 2003). Second, the effects of family can be lagged and indirect, and there is evidence that families that promote exploration, independence, and achievement facilitate long-term progress in the process of occupational identity formation, whereas growing up in a dysfunctional family can jeopardize forming an adaptive occupational identity. In contrast, the immediate effects of family can be limited to only some of the occupational identity prerequisites, such as occupational exploration (Flum & Blustein, 2006). Clearly, the effects of family on vocational development are complex and determined by multivariate relationships rather than by simple associations.

Modern Social and Economic Conditions

Occupational identity, as well as identity in general, can be viewed as a form of adaptation to the social context (Baumeister & Muraven, 1996; Kielhofner, 2007), which is effective only

in relation to the changing social, economic, and cultural contexts of human lives (Blustein & Noumair, 1996; Law, Meijers, & Wijers, 2002). In the past, many traditional societies assigned an occupational identity to the child based on the basis of cultural norms and traditions, and some cultures may still promote early acceptance of a foreclosed, ascribed identity (Waterman, 1999). However, assigning an occupational identity may not be possible – or at least effective – in modern, post-industrial societies, which encourage active identity exploration and facilitate construction of a highly individualized sense of identity (Kroger, 2007). The growing trend toward individualization of the life course and increased variability in the nature and timing of developmental transitions leaves young people with few normative resources with which to develop a clear occupational identity (Côté, 2000; Mortimer et al., 2002).

Ongoing changes in the world of work have important implications for understanding the current context for occupational identity formation and implementation. Those changes include globalization, rapid shifts in occupational structures and the labor market, continuous technological innovation and lifelong learning, a growing demand for flexibility and mobility at work, a dramatic decrease in loyalty within employee-employer relationships, coupled with a decrease in the availability of normative, predictable, long-term career paths, as well as growing diversity in the workplace (Blustein, 2006; Hall, 2002; Kirpal, 2004; Patton & McMahon, 2006; also see Haslam & Ellemers, Chapter 30, this volume). In Europe, Australia, and North America, these changes have already resulted in the recognition of the growing importance of self-centered, flexible, and proactive careers (Briscoe & Hall, 2006; Brown et al., 2007; Kirpal, 2004; Patton & McMahon, 2006). Accordingly, adjustment to the nature of careers in modern economies progressively depends on establishing and maintaining a strong sense of proactive, dynamic, and highly individualized occupational identity (Skorikov & Vondracek, 2007). For workers with a traditional, rigid occupational identity, characterized by a high level of identification with a narrowly defined occupation and expectations of loyalty and stability in employer-employee relationships, changes at work present a great challenge (Kirpal, 2004).

Forming an adaptive occupational identity is both important and challenging during the transition to adulthood. Traditionally, following in parents' footsteps has been the common path toward forming an occupational identity and a major mechanism of the intergenerational transmission of occupational status as well as career advancement (Kalil et al., 2005). However, due to vast and rapid changes in social and economic conditions, educational requirements, and career patterns over the past three decades, children can no longer rely on their parents as adequate career role models. Their career success and satisfaction depend on developing a highly individualized occupational identity characterized by dynamic achievement, but they are offered few opportunities to engage in adequate career exploration and preparation. Furthermore, as adults, they are progressively challenged by massive layoffs, organizational restructuring, and dramatic shifts in the nature of jobs in many occupations in response to technological innovations. Often, individuals are forced to change careers in their 40s or 50s as a result of outsourcing, downsizing, and other corporate decisions. Recent publications make a strong case in favor of the critical role played by the worker's occupational identity in these career transitions (Fouad & Bynner, 2008). Whereas possessing a strong yet flexible occupational identity has been shown to be particularly important in high-status occupations (Kidd & Frances, 2006; Suutari & Makela, 2007), future research needs to investigate the forms of occupational identity and their implications among lower-status workers, particularly those in non-professional, blue-collar occupations. Some studies suggest that occupational identity could be one of the major factors promoting employability following a job loss among members of those occupations (McArdle, Waters, Briscoe, & Hall, 2007).

Another important line of future research involves a detailed examination of cultural differences and similarities in occupational identity (Blustein & Noumair, 1996; Flum & Blustein,

2006; Toporek & Pope-Davis, 2001). Modern societies are becoming progressively multiethnic and multicultural (see Jensen, Arnett, & McKenzie, Chapter 13, this volume; Huynh, Nguyen, & Benet-Martínez, Chapter 35, this volume), and greater attention should be paid to the cultural and socioeconomic aspects of the meaning of work and of occupational identity construction in ethnic and cultural minority groups. However, only a few empirical studies have addressed the issues of ethnic differences and minority status in occupational identity (e.g., Diemer & Blustein, 2006; Gushue et al., 2006; Leong, 1991; Turner et al., 2006). Although there has been a promising increase in the number of such publications in the past few years, the overall scope of this line of research has been limited. Nevertheless, recent findings clearly demonstrate that developing a strong, positive, and flexible occupational identity is very important for economically disadvantaged and minority youth, who face significant career barriers associated with their status within the society (Diemer & Blustein, 2006, 2007; also see Oyserman & James, Chapter 6, this volume).

In addition, little is known about the functions of occupational identity and its relationships with other domains of identity in non-Western cultural contexts (Fouad & Bynner, 2008). However, the few available studies suggest that the process of vocational identity development in less individualistic, less industrialized, and more religiously based cultures may differ from that observed in the North American and Western European samples that comprise most of the literature (e.g., Solomontos-Kountouri & Hurry, 2008). Further research on international labor force migration, which is frequently associated with renegotiating an occupational identity in the process of occupational and social adaptation (Cooke, 2007), is also urgently needed.

Occupational Identity Interventions

There has been little research on targeted interventions in the process of occupational identity development and their effects on career and life trajectories. Both identity and career theorists have frequently noted the importance of vocational guidance (e.g., Erikson, 1968; Raskin, 1989; Vondracek, 1993) but the evidence suggests that few adolescents obtain any professional help with finding appealing career paths or developing their occupational identities (Mortimer et al., 2002). To successfully promote the process of occupational identity development, interventions should take into account developmental differences in occupational identity formation and status (Raskin, 1994). Such interventions might begin in childhood by helping children to acquire a sense of industry (Vondracek, 1993) and exposing them to positive occupational role models. In adolescence, occupational identity interventions are particularly appropriate, as there is evidence that they may significantly enhance career exploration opportunities and facilitate active and systematic exploration guided by a tentative career choice (Raskin, 1989; Salomone & Mangicaro, 1991). The impact of such interventions can be particularly positive if they include active involvement and support of the family (Berríos-Allison, 2005).

During middle and late adolescence, occupational identity formation can be significantly enhanced by providing career mentors and establishing apprenticeships (Hamilton, 1990; Long, Sowa, & Niles, 1995). In late adolescence, with the emergence of serious concerns about one's career prospects, even simple, short-term interventions, such as career development courses, have been found to be valuable in terms of motivating adolescents to explore identity issues and clarify their sense of occupational identity (Anderson, 1995; Barnes & Herr, 1998; Scott & Ciani, 2008). Modern interventions with adolescents should also incorporate the use of the Internet, which has already become a powerful tool in the process of occupational identity construction, and should facilitate establishing a relatively flexible occupational identity, necessary for adjustment and success in the labor market (Terêncio & Soares, 2003).

During the transition to adulthood, an important task is assisting youth with the process of integrating the occupational domain with other domains of identity, particularly the family

domain (Dorn, 1992; Graham et al., 2004; Skorikov & Vondracek, 2007). Yet the most critical task is assisting youth with a successful transition from occupational identity exploration to occupational identity implementation. This transition can be challenging – research suggests that many adolescents do not possess a realistic picture of their occupational opportunities and prospects (Mortimer et al., 2002), and they are further handicapped by insufficient skills and environmental constraints during the transition to the role of an adult worker (FAME Consortium, 2007). As career paths become more changeable and work transitions become more common, there is a growing need to address the corresponding changes and adjustments in occupational identity during middle adulthood (Fouad & Bynner, 2008). One of the key issues for appropriate occupational identity interventions is facilitating adaptability and flexibility. Numerous studies indicate that a narrow and rigid occupational identity is often a major obstacle for occupational success and satisfaction in the modern economy (Brown et al., 2007).

Successful future interventions require a much deeper understanding of occupational identity than has been achieved so far. Clearly, further longitudinal studies are needed to identify the mechanisms underlying occupational identity formation and its outcomes, particularly during the transition to adulthood. Previous research, for the most part, has been conducted on college students and has utilized cross-sectional designs. Findings from such studies provide little information about the nature of the relationships of occupational identity to other aspects of career development and to other identity domains, or about the developmental processes underlying the formation of occupational identity. A systematic investigation of the roles played by schools and family in constructing occupational identities is a critical direction for future research. In this regard, intervention studies could also provide a valuable tool in developing a better understanding of the development and implementation of occupational identity. A careful assessment of intervention outcomes can shed light on the mechanisms of promoting an adaptive identity, as well as on those factors that can jeopardize the progression toward successful identity achievement and implementation. A serious commitment on the part of intervention professionals to understand and deal with the full complexity of individuals trying to develop a firm occupational identity in challenging contexts would benefit not only these individuals but also their families and communities.

References

Alberts, C., Mbalo, N. F., & Ackermann, C. J. (2003). Adolescents' perceptions of the relevance of domains of identity formation: A South African cross-cultural study. *Journal of Youth and Adolescence, 32,* 169–184.

Anderson, K. J. (1995). The use of a structured career development group to increase career identity: An exploratory study. *Journal of Career Development, 21,* 279–291.

Archer, S. L. (1989). Gender differences in identity development: Issues of process, domain and timing. *Journal of Adolescence, 12,* 117–138.

Arnett, J. J. (2000). Emerging adulthood: A theory of development from the late teens through the twenties. *American Psychologist, 55,* 469–480.

Barak, A., Feldman, S., & Noy, A. (1991). Traditionality of children's interests as related to their parents' gender stereotypes and traditionality of occupations. *Sex Roles, 24,* 511–524.

Barnes, J. A., & Herr, E. L. (1998). The effects of interventions on career progress. *Journal of Career Development, 24,* 179–193.

Barnett, R. C., & Hyde, J. S. (2001). Women, men, work and family. *American Psychologist, 56,* 781–796.

Baruch, Y., & Cohen, A. (2007). The dynamics between organizational commitment and professional identity formation at work. In A. Brown, S. Kirpal, & F. Rauner (Eds.), *Identities at work* (pp. 241–260). Dordrecht: Springer.

Baumeister, R. F., & Muraven, M. (1996). Identity as adaptation to social cultural and historical context. *Journal of Adolescence, 19,* 405–416.

Berríos-Allison, A. C. (2005). Family influences on college students' occupational identity. *Journal of Career Assessment, 13,* 233–247.

Bloor, D., & Brook, J. (1993). Career development of students pursuing higher education. *New Zealand Journal of Educational Studies, 28,* 57–68.

Blustein, D. L. (2006). *The psychology of working.* Mahwah, NJ: Erlbaum.

Blustein, D. L., Devenis, L. E., & Kidney, B. A. (1989). Relationship between the identity formation process and career development. *Journal of Counseling Psychology, 36,* 196–202.

Blustein, D. L., & Noumair, D. A. (1996). Self and identity in career development: Implications for theory and practice. *Journal of Counseling & Development, 74,* 433–441.

Bordin, E. S. (1984). Psychodynamic model of career choice and satisfaction. In D. Brown & L. Brooks (Eds.), *Career choice and development* (pp. 94–136). San Francisco: Jossey-Bass.

Braveman, B., Kielhofner, G., Albrecht, G., & Helfrich, C. (2006). Occupational identity, occupational competence and occupational settings (environment): Influences on return to work in men living with HIV/AIDS. *Work: Journal of Prevention, Assessment & Rehabilitation, 27,* 267–276.

Brisbin, L. A., & Savickas, M. L. (1994). Career indecision scales do not measure foreclosure. *Journal of Career Assessment, 2,* 352–363.

Briscoe, J. P., & Hall, D. T. (2006). The interplay of boundaryless and protean careers: Combinations and implications. *Journal of Vocational Behavior, 69,* 4–18.

Brown, C., Glastetter-Fender, C., & Shelton, M. (2000). Psychosocial identity and career control in college student-athletes. *Journal of Vocational Behavior, 56,* 53–62.

Brown, A., Kirpal, S., & Rauner, F. (Eds.) (2007). *Identities at work.* Dordrecht: Springer.

Bryant, B. K., Zvonkovic, A. M., & Reynolds, P. (2006). Parenting in relation to child and adolescent vocational development. *Journal of Vocational Behavior, 69,* 149–175.

Bynner, J. (1998). Education and family components of identity in the transition from school to work. *International Journal of Behavioral Development, 22,* 29–53.

Christiansen, C. H. (1999). Defining lives: Occupation as identity: An essay on competence, coherence, and the creation of meaning. *American Journal of Occupational Therapy, 53,* 547–558.

Conneran, J. M., & Hartman, B. W. (1993). The concurrent validity of the self directed search in identifying chronic career indecision among vocational education students. *Journal of Career Development, 19,* 197–208.

Cook, J., & Simbayi, L. C. (1998). The effects of gender and sex role identity on occupational sex role stereotypes held by white South African high school pupils. *Journal of Vocational Behavior, 53,* 274–280.

Cooke, F. E. (2007). 'Husband's career first': Renegotiating career and family commitment among migrant Chinese academic couples in Britain. *Work, Employment and Society., 21,* 47–65.

Côté, J. E. (2000). *Arrested adulthood: The changing nature of maturity and identity.* New York: New York University Press.

Danielsen, L. M., Lorem, A. E., & Kroger, J. (2000). The impact of social context on the identity-formation process of Norwegian late adolescents. *Youth & Society, 31,* 332–362.

Danto, E. (2003). Americans at work: A developmental approach. In D. P. Moxley & J. R. Finch (Eds.), *Sourcebook of rehabilitation and mental health practice* (pp. 11–26). New York: Kluwer.

De Goede, M., Spruijt, E., Iedema, J., & Meeus, W. (1999). How do vocational and relationship stressors and identity formation affect adolescent mental health? *Journal of Adolescent Health, 25*, 14–20.

Dellas, M., & Gaier, E. L. (1975). The self and adolescent identity in women: Options and implications. *Adolescence, 10*, 399–407.

Dellas, M., & Jernigan, L. P. (1981). Development of an objective instrument to measure identity status in terms of occupation crisis and commitment. *Educational and Psychological Measurement, 41*, 1039–1050.

Dellas, M., & Jernigan, L. P. (1987). Occupational identity status development, gender comparisons, and internal-external control in first-year air force cadets. *Journal of Youth and Adolescence, 16*, 587–600.

Diemer, M. A., & Blustein, D. L. (2006). Critical consciousness and career development among urban youth. *Journal of Vocational Behavior, 68*, 220–232.

Diemer, M. A., & Blustein, D. L. (2007). Vocational hope and vocational identity: Urban adolescents career development. *Journal of Career Assessment, 15*, 98–118.

Dobrow, S. R., & Higgins, M. C. (2005). Developmental networks and professional identity: A longitudinal study. *Career Development International, 10*, 567–583.

Dorn, F. J. (1992). Occupational wellness: The integration of career identity and personal identity. *Journal of Counseling & Development, 71*, 176–178.

Erikson, E. H. (1963). *Childhood and society* (2nd ed.). New York: Norton.

Erikson, E. H. (1968). *Identity: Youth and crisis.* New York: Norton.

Fadjukoff, P., Kokko, K., & Pulkkinen, L. (2007). Implications of timing of entering adulthood for identity achievement. *Journal of Adolescent Research, 22*, 504–530.

Fadjukoff, P., Pulkkinen, L., & Kokko, K. (2005). Identity processes in adulthood: Diverging domains. *Identity, 5*, 1–20.

Fagerberg, I., & Kihlgren, M. (2002). Experiencing a nurse identity: The meaning of identity to Swedish registered nurses 2 years after graduation. *Journal of Advanced Nursing, 34*, 137–145.

FAME Consortium. (2007). Vocational identity in theory and empirical research: Decomposing and recomposing occupational identities – a survey of theoretical concepts. In A. Brown, S. Kirpal, & F. Rauner (Eds.), *Identities at work* (pp. 13–44). Dordrecht: Springer.

Feldsman, D. E., & Blustein, D. L. (1999). The role of peer relatedness in late adolescent career development. *Journal of Vocational Behavior, 54*, 279–295.

Ferreira, J. A., Santos, E. J. R., Fonseca, A. C., & Haase, R. F. (2007). Early predictors of career development: A 10-year follow-up study. *Journal of Vocational Behavior, 70*, 61–77.

Flaxman, E., Guerrero, A., & Gretchen, D. (1999). *Career development effects of career magnets versus comprehensive schools.* Berkeley, CA: National Center for Research in Vocational Education.

Flum, H., & Blustein, D. L. (2006). Reinvigorating the study of vocational exploration: A framework for research. *Journal of Vocational Behavior, 56*, 380–404.

Fouad, N. A., & Bynner, J. (2008). Work transitions. *American Psychologist, 63*, 241–251.

Frank, S. J., Jacobson, S., & Tuer, M. (1990). Psychological predictors of young adults' drinking behaviors. *Journal of Personality and Social Psychology, 59*, 770–780.

Friend, J. G. (1973). *Personal and vocational interplay in identity building: A longitudinal study.* Oxford, UK: Branden.

Goossens, L. (2001). Global versus domain-specific statuses in identity research: A comparison of two self-report measures. *Journal of Adolescence, 24*, 681–699.

Gottfredson, L. S. (2005). Applying Gottfredson's theory of circumscription and compromise in career guidance and counseling. In S. D. Brown & R. W. Lent (Eds.), *Career development and counseling: Putting theory and research to work* (pp. 71–100). New York: Wiley.

Graham, C. W., Sorell, G. T., & Montgomery, M. J. (2004). Role-related identity structure in adult women. *Identity, 4*, 251–254.

Granic, I., Dishion, T. J., & Hollenstein, T. (2003). The family ecology of adolescence: A dynamic systems perspective on normative development. In G. R. Adams & M. D. Berzonsky (Eds.), *Blackwell handbook of adolescence* (pp. 60–91). Oxford, UK: Blackwell.

Grotevant, H. D., & Thorbecke, W. L. (1982). Sex differences in styles of occupational identity formation in late adolescence. *Developmental Psychology, 18*, 396–405.

Gushue, G. V., Scanlan, K. R. L., Pantzer, K. M., & Clarke, C. P. (2006). The relationship of career decision-making self-efficacy, vocational identity, and career exploration behavior in African American high school students. *Journal of Career Development, 33*, 19–28.

Hall, D. T. (2002). *Careers in and out of organizations.* Thousand Oaks, CA: Sage Publications.

Hamilton, S. F. (1990). *Apprenticeship for adulthood: Preparing youth for the future.* New York: Free Press.

Hansen, D. M., Larson, R. W., & Dworkin, J. B. (2003). What adolescents learn in organized youth activities: A survey of self-reported developmental experiences. *Journal of Research on Adolescence, 13*, 25–55.

Hargrove, B. K., Creagh, M. G., & Burgess, B. L. (2002). Family interaction patterns as predictors of vocational identity and career decision-making self-efficacy. *Journal of Vocational Behavior, 61*, 185–201.

Hargrove, B. K., Inman, A. G., & Crane, R. L. (2005). Family interaction patterns, career planning attitudes, and vocational identity of high school adolescents. *Journal of Career Development, 31*, 263–278.

Harris, R., Simons, M., Willis, P., & Carden, P. (2003). Exploring complementarity in on- and off-job training for apprenticeships. *International Journal of Training and Development, 7,* 82–92.

Hartung, P. J., Lewis, D. M., May, K., & Niles, S. G. (2002). Family interaction patterns and college student career development. *Journal of Career Assessment, 10,* 78–90.

Hartung, P. J., Porfeli, E. J., & Vondracek, F. W. (2005). Child vocational development: A review and reconsideration. *Journal of Vocational Behavior, 66,* 385–419.

Heinz, W. R., Kelle, U., Witzel, A., & Zinn, J. (1998). Vocational training and career development in Germany: Results from a longitudinal study. *International Journal of Behavioral Development, 22,* 77–101.

Hirschi, A., & Läge, D. (2007). Holland's secondary constructs of vocational interests and career choice readiness of secondary students. *Journal of Individual Differences, 28,* 205–218.

Holland, J. L. (1985). *Making vocational choices: A theory of vocational personalities and work environments* (2nd ed.). Englewood Cliffs, NJ: Prentice Hall.

Holland, J. L., Daiger, D. C., & Power, P. G. (1980). *My vocational situation: Manual.* Palo Alto, CA: Consulting Psychologists Press.

Holland, J. L., Gottfredson, D. C., & Power, P. G. (1980). Some diagnostic scales for research in decision making and personality: Identity, information, and barriers. *Journal of Personality and Social Psychology, 39,* 1191–1200.

Holland, J. L., & Holland, J. E. (1977). Vocational indecision: More evidence and speculation. *Journal of Counseling Psychology, 24,* 404–414.

Holland, J. L., Johnston, J. A., & Asama, N. F. (1993). The vocational identity scale: A diagnostic and treatment tool. *Journal of Career Assessment, 1,* 1–12.

Hollinger, C. L. (1988). Toward an understanding of career development among G/T female adolescents. *Journal for the Education of the Gifted, 12,* 62–79.

Johnson, J. A. (1987). Influence of adolescent social crowds on the development of vocational identity. *Journal of Vocational Behavior, 31,* 182–199.

Johnson, P., Buboltz, W. C., & Nichols, C. N. (1999). Parental divorce, family functioning, and vocational identity of college students. *Journal of Career Development, 26,* 137–146.

Josselson, R. (1987). *Finding herself: Pathways to identity development in women.* San Francisco: Jossey-Bass.

Kalil, A., Levine, J. A., & Ziol-Guest, K. M. (2005). Following in their parents' footsteps: How characteristics of parental work predict adolescents' interest in parents' jobs. In B. Schneider & L. J. Waite (Eds.), *Being together, working apart: Dual-career families and the work-life balance* (pp. 422–442). New York, NY: Cambridge University Press.

Kidd, J. M., & Frances, G. (2006). The careers of research scientists: Predictors of three dimensions of career commitment and intention to leave science. *Personnel Review, 35,* 229–251.

Kidder, J. (2006). "It's the job that I love": Bike messengers and edgework. *Sociological Forum, 21,* 31–54.

Kielhofner, G. (2007). *Model of human occupation: Theory and application* (4th ed.). Baltimore: Lippincott Williams & Wilkins.

King, Z., Burke, S., & Pemberton, J. (2005). The 'bounded' career: An empirical study of human capital, career mobility and employment outcomes in a mediated labour market. *Human Relations, 58,* 981–1007.

Kirpal, S. (2004). Researching work identities in a European context. *Career Development International, 9,* 199–221.

Klaczynski, P. A., & Lavallee, K. L. (2005). Domain-specific identity, epistemic regulation, and intellectual ability as predictors of belief-biased reasoning: A dual-process perspective. *Journal of Experimental Child Psychology, 92,* 1–24.

Kroger, J. (2007). *Identity development: Adolescence through adulthood* (2nd ed.). Thousand Oaks, CA: Sage.

Ladany, N., Melincoff, D. S., Constantine, M. G., & Love, R. (1997). At-risk urban high school students' commitment to career choices. *Journal of Counseling & Development, 76,* 45–52.

Lapan, R. T. (2004). *Career development across the K-16 years: Bridging the present to satisfying and successful futures.* Alexandria, VA: American Counseling Association.

Law, B., Meijers, F., & Wijers, G. (2002). New perspectives on career and identity in the contemporary world. *British Journal of Guidance & Counselling, 30,* 431–449.

Leong, F. T. (1991). Career development attributes and occupational values of Asian American and white American college students. *Career Development Quarterly, 39,* 221–230.

Leong, F. T., & Morris, J. (1989). Assessing the construct validity of Holland, Daiger, and Power's measure of vocational identity. *Measurement & Evaluation in Counseling & Development, 22,* 117–125.

Li, C., & Kerpelman, J. (2007). Parental influences on young women's certainty about their career aspirations. *Sex Roles, 56,* 105–115.

Lips-Wiersma, M., & McMorland, J. (2006). Finding meaning and purpose in boundaryless careers: A framework for study and practice. *Journal of Humanistic Psychology, 46,* 147–167.

Long, B. E., Sowa, C. J., & Niles, S. G. (1995). Differences in student development reflected by the career decisions of college seniors. *Journal of College Student Development, 36,* 47–52.

Lopez, F. G. (1989). Current family dynamics, trait anxiety, and academic adjustment: Test of a family-based model of vocational identity. *Journal of Vocational Behavior, 35,* 76–87.

Lucas, M. S., & Epperson, D. L. (1990). Types of vocational undecidedness: A replication and refinement. *Journal of Counseling Psychology, 37,* 382–388.

Luyckx, K., Goossens, L., Soenens, B., Beyers, W., & Vansteenkiste, M. (2005). Identity statuses based upon four rather than two identity dimensions: Extending and refining Marcia's paradigm. *Journal of Youth and Adolescence, 34*, 605–618.

Marcia, J. E. (1966). Development and validation of ego identity status. *Journal of Personality and Social Psychology, 3*, 551–558.

Marcia, J. E. (1993). The status of the statuses: Research review. In J. E. Marcia, A. S. Waterman, D. R. Matteson, S. L. Archer & J. Orlofsky (Eds.), *Ego identity: A handbook for psychosocial research* (pp. 22–41). New York: Springer.

McArdle, S., Waters, L., Briscoe, J. P., & Hall, D. T. (2007). Employability during unemployment: Adaptability, career identity and human and social capital. *Journal of Vocational Behavior, 71*, 247–264.

McKeague, T., Skorikov, V., & Serikawa, T. (2002). Occupational identity and workers' mental health. In C. Weikert, E. Torkelson, & J. Pryce (Eds.), *Occupational health psychology: Empowerment, participation, and health at work* (pp. 113–117). Nottingham, UK: I-WHO Publications.

Meeus, W. (1993). Occupational identity development, school performance, and social support in adolescence: Findings of a Dutch study. *Adolescence, 28*, 809–818.

Meeus, W., & Dekovic, M. (1995). Identity development, parental and peer support in adolescence: Results of a national Dutch survey. *Adolescence, 30*, 931–944.

Meeus, W., Dekovic, M., & Iedema, J. (1997). Unemployment and identity in adolescence: A social comparison perspective. *Career Development Quarterly, 45*, 369–380.

Meeus, W., Iedema, J., Helsen, M., & Vollebergh, W. (1999). Patterns of adolescent identity development: Review of literature and longitudinal analysis. *Developmental Review, 19*, 419–461.

Meijers, F. (1998). The development of a career identity. *International Journal for the Advancement of Counselling, 20*, 191–207.

Melgosa, J. (1987). Development and validation of the occupational identity scale. *Journal of Adolescence, 10*, 385–397.

Merrick, E. N. (1995). Adolescent childbearing as career "choice": Perspective from an ecological context. *Journal of Counseling & Development, 73*, 288–295.

Mortimer, J. T. (2003). *Working and growing up in America*. Cambridge, MA: Harvard University Press.

Mortimer, J. T., & Zimmer-Gembeck, M. J. (2007). Adolescent paid work and career development. In V. Skorikov & W. Patton (Eds.), *Career development in childhood and adolescence* (pp. 255–276). Rotterdam, The Netherlands: Sense Publishers.

Mortimer, J. T., Zimmer-Gembeck, M. J., Holmes, M., & Shanahan, M. J. (2002). The process of occupational decision making: Patterns during the transition to adulthood. *Journal of Vocational Behavior, 61*, 439–465.

Munley, P. H. (1977). Erikson's theory of psychosocial development and career development. *Journal of Vocational Behavior, 10*, 261–269.

Munson, W. W. (1992). Self-esteem, vocational identity, and career salience in high school students. *Career Development Quarterly, 40*, 361–368.

Munson, W. W., & Savickas, M. L. (1999). Relation between leisure and career development of college students. *Journal of Vocational Behavior, 53*, 243–253.

Munson, W. W., & Widmer, M. A. (1997). Leisure behavior and occupational identity in university students. *Career Development Quarterly, 46*, 190–198.

Murphy, G. M., Petitpas, A. J., & Brewer, B. W. (1996). Identity foreclosure, athletic identity, and career maturity in intercollegiate athletes. *Sport Psychologist, 10*, 239–246.

Nauta, M. M., & Kahn, J. H. (2007). Identity status, consistency and differentiation of interests, and career decision self-efficacy. *Journal of Career Assessment, 15*, 55–65.

Patton, W., & McMahon, M. (2006). *Career development and systems theory: Connecting theory and practice*. Rotterdam: Sense Publishers.

Peatling, J. H., & Tiedeman, D. V. (1977). *Career development: Designing self*. Muncie, IN: Accelerated Development.

Penick, N. I., & Jepsen, D. A. (1992). Family functioning and adolescent career development. *Career Development Quarterly, 40*, 208–222.

Peregoy, J. J., & Schliebner, C. T. (1990). Long-term unemployment: Effects and counseling interventions. *International Journal for the Advancement of Counseling, 13*, 193–204.

Porfeli, E. J. (2007). Work values system development during adolescence. *Journal of Vocational Behavior, 70*, 42–60.

Porfeli, E. J., & Skorikov, V. B. (2010). Specific and diversive career exploration during late adolescence. *The Journal of Career Assessment, 18*, 46–58.

Pulkkinen, L., & Kokko, K. (2000). Identity development in adulthood: A longitudinal study. *Journal of Research in Personality, 34*, 445–470.

Raskin, P. M. (1985). Identity and vocational development. *New Directions for Child Development, 30*, 25–42.

Raskin, P. M. (1989). Identity status research: Implications for career counseling. *Journal of Adolescence, 12*, 375–388.

Raskin, P. M. (1994). Identity and the career counseling of adolescents: The development of vocational identity. In S. L. Archer (Ed.), *Interventions for adolescent identity development* (pp. 155–173). Thousand Oaks, CA: Sage.

Remer, P., O'Neill, C. D., & Gohs, D. E. (1984). Multiple outcome evaluation of a life-career development course. *Journal of Counseling Psychology, 31*, 532–540.

Robitschek, C., & Cook, S. W. (1999). The influence of personal growth initiative and coping styles on career exploration and vocational identity. *Journal of Vocational Behavior, 54*, 127–141.

Salomone, P. R., & Mangicaro, L. L. (1991). Difficult cases in career counseling: IV – floundering and occupational moratorium. *Career Development Quarterly, 39*, 325–337.

Santos, P. J. (2001). Predictors of generalized indecision among Portuguese secondary school students. *Journal of Career Assessment, 9*, 381–396.

Santos, P. J. (2003). Goal instability, self-esteem, and vocational identity of high school Portuguese students. *Análise Psicológica, 21*, 229–238.

Saunders, D. E., Peterson, G. W., Sampson, J. P. J., & Reardon, R. C. (2000). Relation of depression and dysfunctional career thinking to career indecision. *Journal of Vocational Behavior, 56*, 288–298.

Savickas, M. L. (1985). Identity in vocational development. *Journal of Vocational Behavior, 27*, 329–337.

Schiller, R. A. (1998). The relationship of developmental tasks to life satisfaction, moral reasoning, and occupational attainment at age 28. *Journal of Adult Development, 5*, 239–254.

Schwartz, S. J. (2001). The evolution of Eriksonian and Neo-Eriksonian identity theory and research: A review and integration. *Identity, 1*, 7–58.

Schwartz, S. J., Côté, J. E., & Arnett, J. J. (2005). Identity and agency in emerging adulthood: Two developmental routes in the individualization process. *Youth and Society, 37*, 201–229.

Schwartz, S. J., Zamboanga, B. L., Weisskirch, R. S., & Rodriguez, L. (2009). The relationships of personal and ethnic identity exploration to indices of adaptive and maladaptive psychosocial functioning. *International Journal of Behavioral Development, 33*, 131–144.

Scott, A. B., & Ciani, K. D. (2008). Effects of an undergraduate career class on men's and women's career decision-making self-efficacy and vocational identity. *Journal of Career Development, 34*, 263–285.

Seginer, R., & Noyman, M. S. (2005). Future orientation, identity and intimacy: Their relations in emerging adulthood. *European Journal of Developmental Psychology, 2*, 17–37.

Sellers, N., Satcher, J., & Comas, R. (1999). Children's occupational aspirations: Comparisons by gender, gender role identity, and socioeconomic status. *Professional School Counseling, 2*, 314–317.

Shorter-Gooden, K., & Washington, N. C. (1996). Young, black, and female: The challenge of weaving an identity. *Journal of Adolescence, 19*, 465–475.

Skorikov, V. B. (2007). Continuity in adolescent career preparation and its effects on adjustment. *Journal of Vocational Behavior, 70*, 8–24.

Skorikov, V. B. (2008). Occupational identity and human lives in the 21st century. In E. Avram (Ed.), *Psychology in modern organizations* (pp. 25–38). Bucharest: University Press.

Skorikov, V. B., & Vondracek, F. W. (1997). Longitudinal relationships between part-time work and career

development in adolescents. *The Career Development Quarterly, 45*, 221–235.

Skorikov, V., & Vondracek, F. W. (1998). Vocational identity development: Its relationship to other identity domains and to overall identity development. *Journal of Career Assessment, 6*, 13–35.

Skorikov, V. B., & Vondracek, F. W. (2007). Vocational identity. In V. B. Skorikov & W. Patton (Eds.), *Career development in childhood and adolescence* (pp. 143–168). Rotterdam: Sense Publishers.

Solberg, V. S. (1998). Assessing career search self-efficacy: Construct evidence and developmental antecedents. *Journal of Career Assessment, 6*, 181–193.

Solberg, V. S., Close, W., & Metz, A. J. (2002). Promoting success pathways for middle and high school students: Introducing the adaptive success identity plan for school counselors. In C. L. Juntunen & D. R. Atkinson (Eds.), *Counseling across the lifespan: Prevention and treatment* (pp. 135–157). Thousand Oaks, CA: Sage.

Solomontos-Kountouri, O., & Hurry, J. (2008). Political, religious and occupational identities in context: Placing identity status paradigm in context. *Journal of Adolescence, 3*, 241–258.

Stead, G. B. (1996). Career development of black South African adolescents: A developmental-contextual perspective. *Journal of Counseling & Development, 74*, 270–275.

Stephen, J., Fraser, E., & Marcia, J. E. (1992). Moratorium-achievement (Mama) cycles in lifespan identity development: Value orientations and reasoning system correlates. *Journal of Adolescence, 15*, 283–300.

Strauser, D. R., Lustig, D. C., Cogdal, P. A., & Uruk, A. C. (2006). Trauma symptoms: Relationship with career thoughts, vocational identity, and developmental work personality. *The Career Development Quarterly, 54*, 346–360.

Super, D. E. (1957). *The psychology of careers*. New York: Harper & Row.

Super, D. E., Savickas, M. L., & Super, C. M. (1996). The life-span, life-space approach to career development. In D. Brown, L. Brooks, & Associates (Eds.), *Career choice and development* (3rd ed., pp. 121–178). San Francisco: Jossey-Bass.

Suutari, V., & Makela, K. (2007). The career capital of managers with global careers. *Journal of Managerial Psychology, 22*, 628–648.

Terêncio, M. G., & Soares, D. H. P. (2003). Internet as a tool for professional identity development. *Psicologia em Estudo, 8*, 139–145.

Tiedeman, D. V., & O'Hara, R. P. (1963). *Career development: Choice and adjustment*. New York: College Entrance Examination Board.

Toporek, R. L., & Pope-Davis, D. B. (2001). Comparison of vocational identity factor structures among African American and white American college students. *Journal of Career Assessment, 9*, 135–151.

Turner, S. L., Trotter, M. J., Lapan, R. T., Czajka, K. A., Yang, P., & Brissett, A. E. A. (2006). Vocational skills and outcomes among Native American adolescents: A test of the integrative contextual model of career development. *Career Development Quarterly, 54*, 216–226.

Van Hoof, A. (1999). The identity status field re-reviewed: An update of unresolved and neglected issues with a view on some alternative approaches. *Developmental Review, 19*, 497–556.

Vaughan, K., & Roberts, J. (2007). Developing a 'productive' account of young people's transition perspectives. *Journal of Education and Work, 20*, 91–105.

Vondracek, F. W. (1992). The construct of identity and its use in career theory and research. *Career Development Quarterly, 41*, 130–144.

Vondracek, F. W. (1993). Promoting vocational development in early adolescence. In R. M. Lerner (Ed.), *Early adolescence: Perspectives on research, policy, and intervention* (pp. 277–292). Hillsdale, NJ: Erlbaum.

Vondracek, F. W. (1994). Vocational identity development in adolescence. In R. K. Silbereisen & E. Todt (Eds.), *Adolescence in context: The interplay of family, school, peers, and work in adjustment* (pp. 284–303). New York: Springer.

Vondracek, F. W. (1995). Vocational identity across the life-span: A developmental-contextual perspective on achieving self-realization through vocational careers. *Man and Work, 6*, 85–93.

Vondracek, F. W., Lerner, R. M., & Schulenberg, J. E. (1986). *Career development: A life-span developmental approach*. Hillsdale, NJ: Erlbaum.

Vondracek, F. W., Silbereisen, R. K., Reitzle, M., & Wiesner, M. (1999). Vocational preferences of early adolescents: Their development in social context. *Journal of Adolescent Research, 14*, 267–288.

Vondracek, F. W., & Skorikov, V. B. (1997). Leisure, school, and work activity preferences and their role in vocational identity development. *Career Development Quarterly, 45*, 322–340.

Vrkljan, B. H., & Polgar, J. M. (2007). Linking occupational participation and occupational identity: An exploratory study of the transition from driving to driving cessation in older adulthood. *Journal of Occupational Science, 14*, 30–39.

Walsh, K., & Gordon, J. R. (2008). Creating an individual work identity. *Human Resource Management Review, 18*, 46–61.

Waterman, A. S. (1999). Identity, the identity statuses, and identity status development: A contemporary statement. *Developmental Review, 19*, 591–621.

Wrzesniewski, A., McCauley, C. R., Rozin, P., & Schwartz, B. (1997). Jobs, careers, and callings: People's relations to their work. *Journal of Research in Personality, 31*, 21–33.

Zimmer-Gembeck, M. J., & Mortimer, J. T. (2006). Adolescent work, vocational development, and education. *Review of Educational Research, 76*, 537–566.

S. Alexander Haslam and Naomi Ellemers

Abstract

In recent years, theory and research on issues of identity have addressed a range of topics relevant to organizations, such as leadership, motivation, communication, decision-making, negotiation, productivity, stress and well-being. Identities in organizations can be defined at different levels, including the *individual* (people's personal identity within the organization), *group* (teams within an organization), *organizational* (the organization as a whole) and *cultural* (commonalities in identity within a society as a whole). Moreover, identity processes can manifest themselves as context-determined consequences of organizational life, as strategic responses to organizational conditions, as motivators of organizational goals and behaviour, as determinants of normative and organizational influence, and as organizational and political projects in their own right. Organizations make us who we are, and who we are determines the type of organizations that we make. A key goal of this chapter is to place this very diverse body of work within the broader canvas of organizational and social psychological research. We consider theoretical and practical contributions to our understanding of both organizations and the nature of identity, by first outlining key identity processes specified with social identity theory (SIT) and self-categorization theory (SCT) and then demonstrating how these provide the basis for an integrated analysis of three central organizational topics: leadership, motivation and stress. A fundamental point that emerges from this review is that processes pertaining to organizational identity are central to the meaning, form and dynamics of organizational life — as well as to the fact that organizational life is possible at all.

Over the past 20 years, industrial and organizational psychologists' interest in identity and related concepts has increased at a phenomenal rate. An early catalyst for this work was the publication in 1989 of a landmark article by Blake Ashforth and Fred Mael in the *Academy of Management Review*. In this, they applied the insights of Henri Tajfel and John Turner's *social*

S.A. Haslam (✉)
School of Psychology, University of Exeter, Exeter, UK
e-mail: a.haslam@exeter.ac.ak

identity theory to issues in management and organizational science. This paper has now been cited over 2,000 times, and at least 15 other publications on identity and organizations have been cited more than 300 times. These are listed in Table 30.1, and it is worth noting that more than 30 other publications in this area have been cited over 100 times, with the 40 most highly cited papers together having been cited over 15,000 times.

From these crude statistics it can clearly be seen that, far from being a peripheral concern, issues of identity have become a major interest within the organizational field. From the range of outlets in which this work is published and the dramatic increase in interest that has been witnessed in recent years (for details, see Haslam, 2004, p. xxv; Haslam, Postmes, & Ellemers, 2003), it is also apparent that this research is having an increasingly broad and deep impact on our understanding of organizational dynamics.

The goal of this chapter is to chart and explain the contribution made by research into identity processes in organizations – first by clarifying the importance of (social) identity processes to organizational life, and then demonstrating how an integrated understanding of these processes can be used to develop accounts of key organizational phenomena that are both novel and powerful.

In line with these objectives, the first part of this chapter provides an overview of some of the key identity processes that have been of interest to organizational researchers. Following Ashforth and Mael, this discussion is heavily informed by work in the social identity tradition (specifically, social identity theory, *SIT*; Tajfel & Turner, 1979, 1986; and self-categorization theory, *SCT*; Turner, Hogg, Oakes, Reicher, & Wetherell, 1987; Turner, Oakes, Haslam, & McGarty, 1994; see also Spears, Chapter 9, this volume).

Following on from this, the second part looks at the ways in which appreciation of these various processes can be used to provide an integrated understanding of specific organizational topics. Because a detailed review would fill several books (e.g., see Bartel, Blader, & Wrzesniewski,

2006; Haslam, 2001; Haslam, van Knippenberg, Platow, & Ellemers, 2003), the treatment here is necessarily selective. Accordingly, we focus our analysis on just three core topics: leadership, motivation and stress. Although necessarily selective, these are topics that have proved to be of particular interest to organizational theorists and practitioners. Accordingly, our focus on these topics is a useful way of showcasing what the study of identity can bring to organizational science.

The chapter ends with a reflection on the way in which identity serves as an integrative theme for organizational science. A key conclusion here is that, although many issues remain to be resolved, an appreciation of identity processes in organizations has become, and will remain, central to the study of organizational behaviour. This is because it is our collective sense of who we are – and what we might be – that provides the psychological foundation for the structures and achievements of the organizational world. Indeed, identity lies not only at the centre of organizational psychology, but at the heart of the organization itself.

Part 1: Identity Processes and Their Relevance to Organizational Life

The Definition and Structure of Organizational Identity

Within social psychology, the concept of *social identity* grew from an awareness of the psychological reality and importance of the social group and of its distinctive contribution to cognition and behaviour. As defined by Tajfel (1972), social identity is an "individual's knowledge that he [or she] belongs to certain social groups together with some emotional and value significance to him [or her] of this group membership" (p. 31). A core idea here is that groups are not only external features of the world, but can also be *internalized* and thereby contribute to a person's *sense of self*. In this way, group memberships make a fundamental contribution to a person's sense of 'who they are' (Turner, 1975).

Table 30.1 Publications on 'identity' and 'organization' that have been cited more than 300 times[a]

Authors	Year	Title	Outlet	Citations	Citations per year
Ashforth & Mael	1989	Social identity theory and the organization	*Academy of Management Review*	2,061	98.1
Kogut & Zander	1996	What firms do? Coordination, identity, and learning	*Organization Science*	1,280	91.4
Dutton, Dukerich, & Harquail	1994	Organizational images and member identification	*Administrative Science Quarterly*	1,236	77.3
Albert & Whetten	1985	Organizational identity	*Research in Organizational Behavior*	1,183	47.3
Dutton & Dukerich	1991	Keeping an eye on the mirror: image and identity in organizational adaptation	*Academy of Management Journal*	1,092	57.5
Czarniawska-Joerges & Czarniawska	1997	*Narrating the organization: dramas of institutional identity*	Book	1,064	81.8
Hogg & Terry	2000	Social identity and self-categorization processes in organizational contexts	*Academy of Management Review*	897	89.7
Mael & Ashforth	1992	Alumni and their alma mater: a partial test of the reformulated model of organizational identification	*Journal of Organizational Behavior*	739	41.0
Haslam	2001	*Psychology in organizations: the social identity approach*	Book (2 editions)	725	81.0
Ashforth & Humphrey	1993	Emotional labour in service roles: The influence of identity	*Academy of Management Review*	717	42.2
Gioia, Schultz, & Corley	2000	Organizational identity, image and adaptive instability	*Academy of Management Review*	549	54.9
Akerlof & Kranton	2005	Identity and the economics of organizations	*Journal of Economic Perspectives*	439	87.8
Alvesson & Willmott	2002	Identity regulation as organizational control: producing the appropriate individual	*Journal of Management Studies*	435	54.4
Scott & Lane	2000	A stakeholder approach to organizational identity	*Academy of Management Review*	391	39.1

Table 30.1 (continued)

Authors	Year	Title	Outlet	Citations	Citations per year
Hatch & Schultz	1997	Relations between organizational culture, identity and image	*European Journal of Marketing*	334	25.7
Parker	2000	*Organizational culture and identity: unity and division at work*	Book	307	30.7

Note: [a]Data abstracted from Google Scholar, April 6, 2010.

In organizational contexts, this means that the organizations to which we belong (and the units within those organizations; e.g., teams, sections and departments) can also provide us with a sense of social identity – an *organizational social identity* (or *organizational identity* for short). Reflecting this, when we engage with these organizations or organizational units, we commonly refer to their members as '*we*' and '*us*' not just 'them' (Fiol, 2002; Gioia, Schultz, & Corley, 2000). Importantly, this is not simply a metaphorical allusion. Instead, it speaks to aspects of those organizations that we perceive to be real and important, and which (as we will see) are likely to impact upon our thoughts and actions in significant ways. For this reason, the capacity for organizations to furnish their members with a sense of social identity (and for them to project this identity to the world at large) is commonly considered to be one of their defining features (e.g., Statt, 1994).

Elaborating further on the nature and structure of social identity, Turner (1982) subsequently argued that this and other cognitive representations of the self take the form of *self-categorizations*. Within SCT, the self is seen as a member of a particular class or category of stimuli, and as such is perceived to be (a) more or less equivalent to other stimuli in that category, and (b) more or less distinct from stimuli in other categories. For example, if a female dentist categorizes herself as a dentist, she acknowledges her similarity to other dentists and her difference from, say, patients or doctors. Following Rosch (1978), SCT argues that these identity-defining categories exist at different levels of abstraction with higher-level identities

(e.g., health professional) being more inclusive than those defined at lower levels (e.g., doctor, dentist).

In the organizational domain, this means that identities can be realized at many different levels, each of which provides a different framework for both organizational behaviour and its interpretation (Cornellissen, Haslam, & Balmer, 2007; Schultz, Hatch, & Larsen, 2000). In this vein, A.D. Brown (2001) identifies four relevant levels of analysis: *individual* (relating to people's *personal identity* as unique individuals within the organization; Turner, 1982), *group* (relating to the shared identity of organizational teams and sections), *organizational* (relating to the identity of the organization as a whole) and *cultural* (relating to commonalities in identity across organizations and within a particular culture or society). Importantly, from the perspective of SCT, identities at all these levels of abstraction are equally 'real' and just as much a reflection of a person's 'true' self (Oakes, Haslam, & Turner, 1994). This means that no single level of self-categorization is inherently more appropriate or useful than another, and hence that none is in any sense more fundamental to who or what the person is. It is worth noting as well that this proposition goes against a general tendency for industrial and organizational psychologists (after Münsterberg, 1913; in keeping with many other theorists; e.g., see Skorikov & Vondracek, Chapter 29, this volume; Soenens & Vansteenkiste, Chapter 17, this volume; Waterman, Chapter 16, this volume) to accord privileged status to personal identity – as if a person's 'true' self is always defined by their individuality (see Asch, 1952; Oakes, 1996).

The Motivation for Positive, Distinct and Enduring Organizational Identity

As noted elsewhere in this Handbook (e.g., Spears, Chapter 9, this volume), a specific empirical catalyst for early social identity work was the series *of minimal group studies* conducted by Tajfel and his colleagues in the early 1970s (Tajfel, 1970; Tajfel, Flament, Billig, & Bundy, 1971). These studies sought to identify the minimal conditions that would lead members of one group to discriminate in favour of the *ingroup* to which they belonged and against another *outgroup* to which they did not belong. The robust finding that emerged from these studies was that even the most stripped-down conditions – in which groups had no pre-existing meaning and no obvious self-relevance – were sufficient to encourage ingroup-favouring responses. This suggested that the mere act of individuals *categorizing themselves* as group members was sufficient to lead them to display ingroup favouritism (Turner, 1975). Moreover, self-categorization of this form can be seen to provide the psychological underpinnings of group behaviour in general. In other words, it is a sense of shared social identity that makes group behaviour possible (Turner, 1982), just as it is a shared sense of organizational identity that makes organizational behaviour possible (Haslam, Postmes, & Ellemers, 2003).

Organizational research has shown that the basic patterns revealed in minimal group settings are reproduced in a range of work contexts. For example, in an early study of wage negotiations, R. J. Brown (1978) found that different professional groups were motivated not simply to earn as much as possible, but to preserve wage *differentials* which ensured that their own group earned more than others. Indeed, as was found in the minimal group studies, this motivation meant that group members would sacrifice absolute gain in order to preserve their ingroup's relative advantage.

In this regard, one of the key points that the minimal group studies brought home to Tajfel (1972) was that, when people categorize themselves as members of a social group, they are motivated to establish a social identity that is *positive* and *distinct*. That is, when their sense of self is defined in terms of group membership, people want to feel that this group is 'special'. They are motivated to behave in ways which establish the superiority of the ingroup relative to comparison outgroups and aim to preserve that state of affairs over time, by protecting their identity against circumstances that may challenge their group's superiority or undermine its distinctiveness.

Consistent with these motivations, Albert and Whetten (1985) argued that organizational identities tend to be defined by anchors that provide some continuity in capturing an organization's central and distinctive features (e.g., mission statements and other organizational pronouncements that define 'us' as different from, and better than, 'them'; Dutton, Dukerich, & Harquail, 1994; Haslam & Ellemers, 2005). Moreover, in line with this insight, the significance of people's desire for organizational identities that are positive, distinct and enduring is revealed in multiple strands of organizational research. In particular, these motivations become apparent in the context of organizational *change* – for example, when firms are undergoing merger, acquisition or restructuring. Here, a large body of research attests to the fact that employees whose sense of identity is bound up with their membership of a particular organizational unit typically find change to that unit intensely threatening, and hence are likely to resist it (e.g., Ellemers, 2003; Jetten, O'Brien, & Trindall, 2002; Terry, 2003; van Leeuwen & van Knippenberg, 2003). This is especially true when change is driven by agencies external to the group itself. For related reasons, loss or devaluation of organizational identity (e.g., resulting from the fact that after organizational change, a self-defining organizational group no longer exists in its original form) is also found to be a source of profound organizational stress (Haslam & Reicher, 2006a; see below).

The Contribution of Perceived Social Structure to Strategies of Identity Enhancement

In the minimal group studies, participants achieved positive distinctiveness through a strategy of *social competition* that led them to favour their ingroup over an outgroup. However, within SIT, social competition is conceptualized as only one of three strategies that individuals can pursue in order to achieve a sense of positive social identity. Two other strategies that can achieve this objective are *individual mobility* and *social creativity*. Which of these three strategies a person resorts to is seen to depend on three structural elements: the perceived *permeability* of group boundaries, and the perceived *stability* and *legitimacy* of an ingroup's position relative to other groups (Tajfel & Turner, 1979; see also Ellemers, 1993; Spears, Chapter 9, this volume).

Without going into too much detail, if members of low-status groups believe that group boundaries are permeable, then in order to deal with the negative identity that is associated with their group's low status, they should tend to favour a strategy of individual mobility that leads them to act individually and seek out a new positive group identity. For example, if a woman finds that her gender identity is a bar to preferment and promotion in her place of work, she may seek to disavow this identity and act like 'one of the boys' in order to get ahead (Ellemers, Van den Heuvel, De Gilder, Maass, & Bonvini, 2007; Schmitt, Ellemers, & Branscombe, 2003).

On the other hand, if individuals perceive group boundaries to be impermeable (so that group membership is fixed and one's low status is inescapable) individual mobility is not an option. Here, if social relations are *secure* (i.e., seen as both stable and legitimate), members of low-status groups are predicted to engage in social creativity – striving to accentuate their positivity in alternative ways that are irrelevant to the status-defining dimension. They might do this by endorsing beliefs of the form 'We may not be as wealthy/intelligent/qualified as them, but we're more down-to-earth/friendly/kind' (Terry, Carey, & Callan, 2001). As an example of this,

Terry and Callan (1998) examined the reactions of employees in two hospitals (one high-status, one low-status) that were going through the process of a merger. Here, those who had been in the low-status hospital acknowledged the inferiority of their ingroup on the status-relevant dimensions of clinical excellence, but compensated for this by accentuating their superiority on status-irrelevant dimensions such as friendliness and sociability. Likewise, Ashforth and Kreiner (1999) examined the ways in which people who do 'dirty work' (i.e., who have low-status jobs) respond to the challenge that their low-status profession poses for their sense of work-based identity (see also Lupton, 2000). The researchers observed that these workers deal with the potentially negative implications of their occupation for the self by defining it in creative ways that focus on positives rather than negatives. For example, garbage collectors draw attention to the fact that their job involves working outdoors, dog catchers focus on their flexible hours, and exotic dancers highlight the fact that they have plenty of opportunities to meet new people.

Yet if relations are impermeable and *insecure* (i.e., seen to be unstable and/or illegitimate), then members of low-status groups generally prove less willing to accept their low status and to try to 'work around' it. It is here that they are more likely to define themselves in terms of their group membership and strive to engage in social competition with a view to achieving some form of *social change*. As in the minimal group studies, this may involve challenging the outgroup, and its status, head on. Consistent with this analysis, experimental research by Wright and his colleagues has shown that, if members of low-status groups are vying to gain entrance to an organizational élite, they are far more likely to pursue a strategy of collective conflict when access to the high-status group is impossible and the behaviour of that group appears illegitimate. Under other conditions – especially when the high-status group promotes some 'token' low-status group members to cultivate the appearance of boundary permeability – members of the low-status group are much less likely to challenge the status quo

(Wright, 2000; see also Reicher & Haslam, 2006; Reynolds, Turner, & Haslam, 2000; Taylor et al., 1987).

The Salience of Organizational Identities and Variation in Individuals' Ability to Embody Them

We can see from the previous section that SIT is focused largely on the psychological and behavioural implications of individuals coming (or not coming) to define themselves in terms of social identity. However, the theory does not deal in any great detail with the question of how particular social identities become salient in the first place. In contrast, these questions are of primary importance within SCT.

A key process here is that of *self-stereotyping*. This allows the self to be perceived as categorically interchangeable with other ingroup members – a process Turner (1982) termed *depersonalization*. Most theory and research in psychology defines the individual, 'who one is' (and therefore what one *does* and *seeks* to do) almost exclusively in terms of idiosyncratic personal attributes (i.e., personal identity). Complementing this view, SCT posits that when people self-stereotype as group members (i.e., when social identity is salient), the self (and the actions and aspirations dictated by this self) is defined in terms of stereotypical attributes (e.g., values and goals) that are shared with others who are perceived to be representative of the same social category. Building upon this point, SCT goes on to provide an analysis of *social identity salience* (Oakes, 1987; Turner, 1985). Here, SCT specifies the processes that dictate *whether* people define themselves in terms of personal or social identity and, when social identity is salient, *which* particular group membership serves to guide behaviour. In any given organization, when will employees see themselves and others as members of the department or team to which they belong, or as members of the organization as a whole, rather than acting as individuals? Answering such questions is important, because, as we intimated above, the *particular* level at which organizational members define themselves has distinctive implications both for their own behaviour and for the functioning (and analysis) of the organization as a whole (Ellemers, de Gilder, & van den Heuvel, 1998; van Dick, 2004; van Dick, Wagner, Stellmacher, & Christ, 2004).

Evidence garnered by self-categorization theorists suggests that social identity salience is the product of an interaction between two processes: *perceiver readiness* (or *accessibility*) and *fit* (Oakes, 1987; Oakes, Turner, & Haslam, 1991; after Bruner, 1957). This means that people are more likely to define themselves in terms of a particular social identity if this identity has prior meaning for them and if it allows them to make sense of the particular reality with which they are confronted in any given setting. We are more likely to define ourselves as psychologists if we have been working as psychologists for a long time, and if it makes sense to do so in the context that we find ourselves –for example, if we are at a psychology conference rather than a football match.

The process of perceiver readiness ensures that categorization always depends, at least in part, on the expectations, goals and theories which the perceiver brings into any situation – many of which derive from their group memberships and the socialization experiences associated with them. People thus organize and construe the world in ways that reflect the groups to which they already belong and in this way their social histories lend stability, predictability and continuity to ongoing experience (Fiol, 2001; Oakes et al., 1994; Peteraf & Shanley, 1997; Reicher, 1996; Rousseau, 1998; Turner & Giles, 1981). Along these lines, it is apparent that particular social group memberships are more likely to be used as a basis for self-definition if they are valued and self-involving, and contribute to an enduring sense of identity. For this reason, *identification* with a given social category (e.g., a work team, a department, an organization) is one particularly important factor that affects a person's readiness to use that category in order to define themselves across situations (e.g., Ellemers, Spears, & Doosje, 2002; Turner, 1999). When a person identifies strongly with a given organization, for example, they will be more prepared to interpret the world, and their own place within it, in a manner consistent with that organization's values, ideology and culture (Kramer, Brewer, & Hanna, 1996; Mael & Ashforth, 1992; Rousseau, 1998).

Yet, as well as being determined by prior experience, social categorization is also determined by features of the immediate context with which the perceiver is confronted. The principle of *comparative fit* explains how people adapt their self-definitions to different comparative contexts, depending on the salience of specific dimensions of judgement and relevant others in that context. Specifically, the likelihood that people define themselves in terms of a particular social category increases to the extent that the differences among members *within* that category are perceived to be smaller than the differences *between* members of different categories (Turner, 1985). One broad implication of this principle is that employees will be more likely to categorize themselves as members of a particular organizational group in intergroup rather than intragroup contexts (Haslam, Oakes, Turner, & McGarty, 1995). For example, teachers in different schools should be more likely to define themselves as teachers rather than as employees of a particular school in situations where they are in competition with other professions (rather than with each others' schools; Van Dick & Wagner, 2002). This same principle is also illustrated in research on the formation of *faultlines* and the emergence of intergroup conflict as a result of employee diversity in organizations. This work has argued and shown that employees in organizations are more likely to form different subgroups when they can be distinguished from each other on multiple dimensions of comparison – for instance, when young female employees with a university degree work together with older male employees with professional training (Lau & Murningham, 1998; Thatcher, Jehn, & Zanutto, 2003). This can be explained as a consequence of the fact that the convergence of multiple characteristics which differentiate between groups of individual workers increases the comparative fit of these subgroups.

In addition to comparative fit, the likelihood that people will invoke a particular categorization to make sense of the world also depends on the *normative fit* of that category to a specific context. Whereas comparative fit speaks to the distinctive salience of category characteristics, the principle of normative fit relates to the meaningfulness of category *content* as a basis for distinguishing between individuals. This principle also helps perceivers to understand and predict how individuals will respond or behave in a particular situation. For instance, the distinction between managers versus workers is more likely to predict employees' respective positions in discussions about working unpaid overtime, than in a discussion about the selection of snacks in the canteen. In other words, people are more likely to see themselves and others as members of distinct categories when the *nature* of the differences between them is consistent with category-related expectations (Oakes et al., 1991). If these content-related expectations are not met (e.g., when different attitudes about overtime work cut across the distinction between managers and workers), the social categorization will not be invoked to make sense of events or to define the perceiver's own action.

The way in which prior experience and current context interact to determine the salience of organizational identities is summarized schematically in Fig. 30.1. The key point to note here is that organizational identity salience and organizational identification are dynamically interrelated. That is, whether an organizational identity becomes salient at a given point in time is interactively determined by the accessibility of organizational self-categories and current organizational conditions. However, once people develop a strong organizational identity in this way, this in turn helps to foster an ongoing sense of organizational identification that will enhance the salience of organizational identities in the future.

Importantly, principles of fit do not just play a role in determining social identity salience. They also help determine *which aspects* of any given organizational identity will be seen to define that

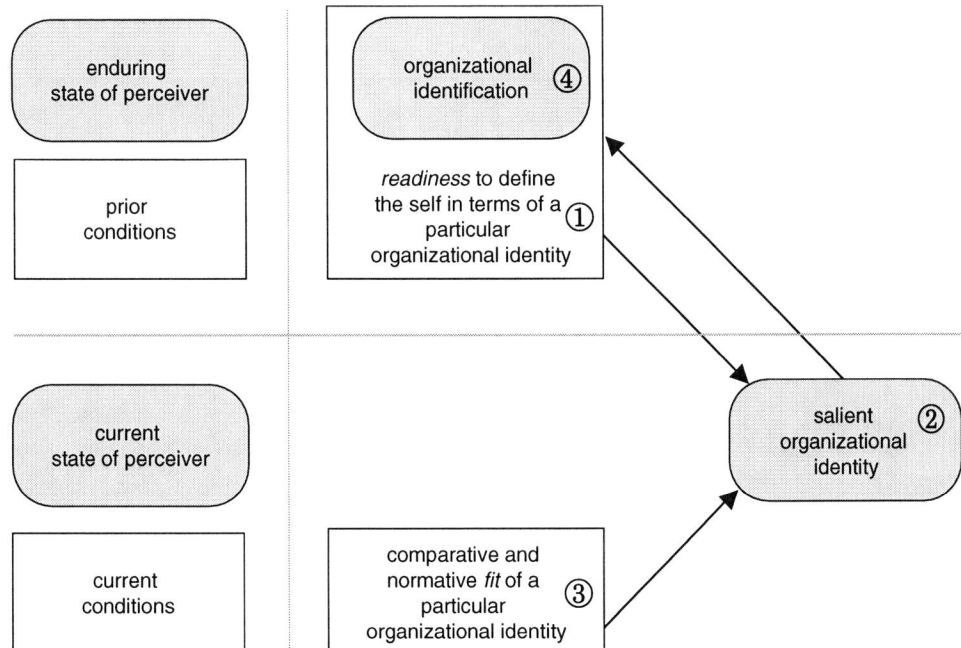

Fig. 30.1 The inter-relationship between organizational identification and organizational identity salience (adapted from Haslam, Postmes, & Ellemers, 2003) *Note:* Organizational identification reflects a person's relatively enduring identification with an organization or organizational unit (i.e., their pre-existing *readiness* ① to use an organizational category to define their sense of self (what Rousseau, 1998, refers to as *deep-structure identification*). Organizational identity salience ② (what Rousseau, 1998, calls *situated identification*) reflects the impact of organizational identification in interaction with perceptions of the specific set of contextual conditions that impact on the perceiver in the current context ③ (i.e., perceiver readiness in interaction with the *fit* of a particular self-categorization; Oakes, 1987). In this way, current and prior conditions contribute to the current state of the perceiver which in turn contributes to his or her long-term state ④ (Fiol, 2002; Haslam, Postmes & Ellemers, 2003; Rousseau, 1998). This long-term state then becomes one of the prior conditions that contributes to the perceiver's current state at some time in the future

identity best in any given context. In particular, just as comparative fit is a partial determinant of *which* social categories perceivers use to define themselves and others, so too it is a partial determinant of the *internal structure* of those categories. This idea follows from the theorizing of cognitive psychologists (e.g., Barsalou, 1987; Rosch, 1978), which suggests that categories have an internally *graded structure* so that, for any individual category, some features (e.g., particular behaviours, attributes or individuals) will define it better than others. This means that, although all category members are seen as to some extent representative (or *prototypical*) of the category, they also differ in the extent to which they are perceived to be representative or prototypical of it. All academics may be seen as

intelligent, but some are perceived to be more intelligent than others.

It also follows from this idea that whether any particular group member is seen as prototypical of the group's identity will depend on which other groups are salient in a given context, and on how these groups are being compared (i.e., on what dimensions; Turner, 1987). In particular, a given individual will appear to be more prototypical of a group to the extent that he or she is both similar to other ingroup members *and* different from relevant outgroup members. In a comparison with cleaners, a relatively intellectual administrator may be quite prototypical of the category 'administrator' because she partly embodies the stereotypical *difference* between administrators and cleaners with administrators being relatively more intellectual as a group. But in comparison with academics that same person's prototypicality for the category of administrators will tend to decrease. In this comparative context, an administrator who is more practical and 'hands on' would seem more prototypical for the category, as this latter dimension embodies the stereotypical difference between administrators and academics (Haslam, Oakes, McGarty, Turner, & Onorato, 1995; Hogg, Turner, & David, 1990; McGarty, Turner, Hogg, David, & Wetherell, 1992).

The Ability of Shared Organizational Identity to Generate Influence and Power

Critically, once a particular organizational identity has become salient for a particular group of people, and once particular facets of the organization (e.g., norms, values and individuals) have come to define it, this should have an impact on the psychology of individuals but it should also help translate that psychology into *collective* products – plans and visions, goods and services, organizations and institutions. In particular, this is because, as a form of social identity, shared organizational identity is a basis not only for people to perceive and interpret their world in similar ways, but also for processes of *mutual social influence* which allow them to coordinate (and *expect* to coordinate) their behaviour in ways that lead to concerted social action and collective products (Haslam, 2001; Turner, 1987, 1991). To the extent that someone embodies a salient shared organizational identity (i.e., to the extent that this person is seen to represent the meaning of 'us'), others will perceive him/her as carrying features of social and organizational reality that bear upon that identity. Indeed, this is one reason why people tend to look towards particular individuals to provide guidance concerning the appropriate shape and direction for their activities within the organization (Ellemers, De Gilder, & Haslam, 2004; Haslam & Platow, 2001a; Turner & Haslam, 2001).

Moreover, as Mayo (1949) first acknowledged, it is precisely through individuals'

conformity to norms that are perceived to be shared with others in a particular context that their potentially idiosyncratic views become socially organized and consensual. Through this process, individual views are coordinated and transformed into *shared* values, beliefs and behaviours. These values and beliefs have particular force because they are no longer experienced as subjective but instead articulate a common, as-if-objective, view (Haslam, Turner, Oakes, McGarty et al., 1998; Moscovici, 1984). In this way *personal opinion* can become *social fact*. '*I think* it is important to work overtime' can become '*It is* important to work overtime'; '*I think* we are the best' can become '*We are* the best'. Indeed, at the most general level, it is apparent that identity-based processes of social influence are central to the transformation of low-level individual inputs (e.g., opinions, attitudes) into higher-order organizational products (e.g., norms, values, culture).

Organizational evidence attesting to the utility of these ideas has been provided by multiple strands of research. For example, studies of communication and group productivity show that factors that serve to increase a sense of social identity (e.g., as a member of a team or organization) make people (a) more willing to communicate with each other, (b) more open to other's communications and (c) more likely to interpret communicative acts in similar ways and in the spirit in which they are intended (e.g., Lea, Spears, & Rogers, 2003; Moreland, Argote, & Krishnan, 1996; Postmes, Spears, & Lea, 1998). At the same time, such processes also increase the likelihood that individual group members will develop shared understandings (e.g., transactive memory systems and shared mental models) that allow them to produce collaborative products that exceed what would be expected on the basis of group members' potentialities as individuals (Haslam, 2001; Postmes, 2003). In short, shared organizational identity (or the lack of it) is responsible for the oft-noted difference between a team of champions and a champion team.

In exactly this way, shared organizational identity can be seen to be the basis for forms of 'collective mind' akin to those observed in research by Weick and Roberts (1993) into the inter-related activities of flight deck crews on aircraft carriers. Here, it was the fact that the crews had a shared identity-based understanding of their roles, relationships and responsibilities that allowed them to *trust* each other and work together at the high intensity that their work demanded and without needing to refer to written rules or constantly checking what others were doing (see also Platow, Haslam, Foddy, & Grace, 2003).

Ultimately then, the particular significance of organizational identity as an analytic construct derives from the fact that it is an embodiment of the dialectic relationship between, on the one hand, individual psychology and, on the other, collective organizational products (Haslam, Postmes, & Ellemers, 2003). Recognition of the fact that individual psychology is socially structured means that the psychological analysis of organizational life is not necessarily reductionist in the way that some critics have suggested (e.g., MacKenzie, 1978). At the same time, the fact that collective products are always underpinned and made possible by individual psychology means that organizational analysis does not have to skirt around issues of psychology in order to capture and account for high-level organizational realities.

Part II: Integrated Analyses of Identity Processes in Organizations

The first part of this chapter provided some insight into a range of identity processes that shape and structure the dynamics of organizational life. From this treatment, though, it may be difficult to get a sense of the way in which these various processes interact and combine, and hence how they allow for an integrated appreciation of particular facets of organizational activity – especially as these are conventionally examined by organizational theorists and practitioners. Accordingly, with this goal in mind, the second part of the chapter is devoted to a more detailed exploration of three key topics in the organizational field. Although this review is

necessarily selective, the aim here is to provide a window onto the ways in which these topics in fact centre on issues of identity – even though this is not how they are routinely understood.

Leadership

Leadership is the process of influencing other people so that they are motivated to contribute to the achievement of group goals. Leadership allowed the Romans to build their empire, it enabled astronauts to land on the moon, it took Exeter City to promotion through two divisions of the English football league in successive seasons from 2007 to 2009, and it led to the extermination of six million Jews in the Holocaust. To any such list one can always add more – some widely recognized, some widely ignored; some widely celebrated, some widely condemned. Accordingly, leadership is probably the most widely studied topic in the organizational field, and it is one into which most people have some insight on the basis of their own experience.

However, a common theme in most theoretical treatments is that, almost without exception, they embrace *individualistic* models that see leadership as a process that is fundamentally grounded in a leader's individuality. In this way, leadership is seen to arise from a distinctive psychology that sets the minds and lives of great leaders apart from those of others – as superior, special, different. The most obvious examples are provided by personality theories that suggest that it is the possession of a unique constellation of traits and abilities that distinguishes great (or merely good) leaders from the rank and file.

There are many problems with individualistic accounts of this form (for a recent review, see Haslam, Reicher, & Platow, 2011). Probably the most serious of these is that empirical support for their various premises is typically very weak. In particular, following extensive reviews by Stogdill (1948) and Mann (1959), researchers have generally failed to identify any particular personality profile that has the ability to identify leaders predictively. Moreover, this fact does not change markedly when such profiles are incorporated into contingency models (e.g., Fiedler, 1978) that see leadership as the mechanical product of an interaction between fixed personality characteristics and specified situational variables.

In contrast to such accounts, analysis informed by social identity and self-categorization principles sees leadership not as a process that revolves around individuals acting and thinking in isolation, but as a *group process* in which leaders and followers are joined together – *and perceive themselves to be joined together* – in a collaborative endeavour (e.g., see Ellemers et al., 2004; Haslam et al., 2011; Hogg & van Knippenberg, 2004; Turner & Haslam, 2001). Critically, then, this process centres on a sense of *shared identity* that defines both leaders and followers as 'us'. In these terms, individuals are able to lead (i.e., to exert influence over other group members) not as a result of their 'I-ness', but by virtue of their capacity both to represent what it is that 'we' means in any given context and to promote interests associated with that collective self-definition.

In this way, a social identity approach encourages us to see leadership not as a process that is concerned with leaders alone, but as one that, by necessity, also involves the followers with whom those leaders forge a psychological connection and whose effort is required to do the work that drives the group forward (Hollander, 1985). Two processes that we focused on in the first part of this chapter are critical here: *social categorization* and *social influence*. Social categorization is important because it determines whether, and to what degree, leaders and followers see themselves as members of the same psychological group. Social influence is important because this is the process through which leaders and followers coordinate their activities. It is also this that ultimately determines – and defines – the success of leadership.

Leaders as ingroup prototypes. In this regard, one important way in which SCT conceptualizes a leader is as someone who is *prototypical* of a given ingroup (Turner, 1987). Indeed, it follows from the arguments outlined above that, the more

prototypical a person is of a group, the more they will represent what that group stands for, and, on this basis, the more influence they will exert over other members of the group (von Cranach, 1986). Importantly, though, as we noted above, a person's prototypicality with regard to a given social category is not fixed and so is not a stable property that they 'possess'. Instead, it varies predictably as a function of social context (Turner, 1987).

Consistent with this view, programmatic research by Platow and colleagues (e.g., Haslam & Platow, 2001a; Platow et al., 1997, 1998; Platow & van Knippenberg, 2001; see also Hogg, Hains, & Mason, 1998) has shown that group members' willingness to support and be influenced by a leader varies as a function of changes to the comparative context within which the group is defined. In particular, in intragroup contexts (i.e., contexts in which only the ingroup is salient) group members are observed to favour leaders who treat ingroup members fairly and equally, but in intergroup contexts (where one or more outgroups is also salient) they favour leaders who allocate more rewards to ingroup members than to outgroup members (i.e., treating people *un*fairly and *un*equally) – as this helps to differentiate the ingroup positively from the comparison outgroup. Such findings support predictions derived from both SIT and SCT in demonstrating that leadership – and the value of particular leader characteristics (e.g., fairness) – is contingent both on leaders' capacity to contribute to the positive distinctiveness of a social identity that they share with followers and on their context-determined prototypicality with respect to that identity.

As with contingency theories (e.g., Fiedler, 1978), this analysis can be seen to provide a partial explanation for the fact that different leaders (or different leadership styles) are considered appropriate and prove effective in different situations. Nevertheless, unlike most other accounts, from a social identity perspective the properties of the individual associated with these variations are seen to derive not from qualities inherent in the person *as an individual* (e.g., their personality or personal style) but from features of the individual *as a representative of a contextually defined social category*. It is not always easy to distinguish the two, if only because many groups like to think of themselves in terms of positive characteristics such as initiative or competence, or because a range of situations may give rise to similar behavioural norms (e.g., associated with fairness or cooperation), resulting in converging leadership preferences. However, it is important to keep in mind that these preferences stem from contextually defined social identities, not from individual leadership qualities *per* se. As an extreme example of what this implies, in an experiment on leadership selection it was demonstrated that the majority of participants who thought that the outgroup had an extremely intelligent leader voted for an ingroup leader who was considerate and dedicated, but *un*intelligent (Haslam, 2001; Turner & Haslam, 2000). Thus, while standard leadership accounts emphasize personal leadership qualities as aspects of an individual-level analysis, our approach in terms of self-categorization and social identity processes helps understand why leaders with all the 'right' qualities are not always successful, and predicts when groups are likely to express unconventional leadership preferences.

Leaders as entrepreneurs of identity. Although leadership flows from a person's ability to represent a given social identity in context, it is not the case that this process is entirely passive. Leaders are not puppets of prototypicality but rather play an active role in its definition. More specifically, in the terminology of Reicher and Hopkins (1996; see also Haslam et al., 2011; Reicher, Haslam, & Hopkins, 2005), leaders can be seen as '*entrepreneurs of identity*'. So, for example, where would-be leaders espouse views that are not representative of their group, they may seek to restructure the social context, as a means of increasing their own ingroup prototypicality. They might do this by arguing for the appropriateness of particular social categorizations – especially those that distinguish between 'us' and 'them' in a manner that enables both the leader and the ingroup to be seen as positive and distinct. Reicher and Hopkins (1996) provide a number of case studies of these processes in action – for example, through an examination of the contributions of political leaders to debate about the 1984–1985 British miners' strike. Here, the leaders of the two main political parties, Margaret Thatcher and Neil Kinnock, attempted to construe events surrounding the strike in such a way that (a) their party could be seen as representative of a positively defined ingroup which (unlike the negatively defined outgroup) encompassed almost the entire population and (b) the policies that their leadership advocated were consonant with the definition of that ingroup identity. For example, the conservative Thatcher defined her government as representative of "a moderate and responsible majority … fighting for great and good causes" that was opposed to an "organized revolutionary minority" of "thugs and bullies" and which, for this reason, was committed to a policy of political and industrial conflict (Reicher & Hopkins, 1996, pp. 360–361). Along similar lines, longitudinal research by Fiol (2001) shows how industry leaders who are seeking to promote organizational change use rhetorical tools (e.g., defining new identities positively and old identities negatively) to redefine organizational identities and thereby transform a workforce.

As an extension of this point, the position of a leader in power can be strengthened by backing up the rhetoric of 'us versus them' with actual hostility towards an outgroup. Experimental support for this idea also comes from research by Rabbie and Bekkers (1978) which found that leaders whose positions within their group were unstable were more likely to choose to engage in intergroup conflict than leaders whose positions were secure (see also Platow & van Knippenberg, 2001). Clearly too, this strategy is one to which political leaders who face dissent from their constituents routinely resort and one which has played a role in the escalation of a great number of conflicts (R.J. Brown, 1988). Most recently, this has been witnessed in the actions of leaders in Iran, Iraq, Israel, Venezuela, the United Kingdom and the United States.

Leader charisma as a product of identity advancement. In researchers' attempts to identify the source of the 'special something' that surrounds great leaders and our relationship with them, one attribute that they have often focused on is that of *charisma*. This attribute was first explored in depth by Weber (1921/1946) and although the term has multiple meanings (including the power to perform miracles, and the ability to make prophecies; Marturano & Arsenault, 2008) it is generally taken to refer to the idea of a 'special gift' that allows leaders to motivate, enthuse and influence others. Weber himself argued that this gift was partly bestowed by others, but in line with the individualistic leanings of the leadership literature, contemporary analyses tend to regard it as characteristic of the person (Platow, van Knippenberg, Haslam, van Knippenberg, & Spears, 2006). That is, leaders are seen as effective because they *have* the charisma (or the charismatic personality) that allows them to articulate a vision for a given group of followers and to generate enthusiasm for that vision.

In contrast to this view, and in keeping with the conception of successful leaders as entrepreneurs of identity described above, a social identity approach suggests that charisma results from individuals' ability to define (or, more typically, *re*define) a group's identity and objectives in a way that enhances both the shared self-concept of its members and therefore the leader's own relative influence (House & Shamir, 1993). In other words, charisma can be seen as an *emergent product* of self-categorization processes that serve to define a positive (i.e., self-enhancing) identity-based relationship between leaders and followers, as well as between their group and others (Haslam, Platow et al., 2001). Charisma is thus *conferred* by followers and is an *expression* of the leader–group dynamic as perceived by those followers in a specific social context. This is not to deny that there may be individual difference variables (such as adaptability to changing circumstances, sensitivity to the expectations of others) that can make it easier to successfully achieve such a relationship with one's followers. However, in contrast to standard approaches that focus on charisma as an inherent personal characteristic or personality trait,

the social identity approach we propose emphasizes the group dynamic processes involved in the emergence and maintenance of leadership that is experienced as charismatic.

Support for these ideas has emerged from a number of recent studies (for a review, see Haslam et al., 2011). For example, experiments by Platow et al. (2006) showed that students' perceptions of a (male) leader's charisma flowed from his being defined (by the experimenters) as prototypical of their own student group. Moreover, this prototypicality-based charisma also determined the leader's perceived persuasiveness. In short, the leader had to be defined as 'one of us' in order to be seen as charismatic, and, when he was, it was this identity-based charisma that made him persuasive. Along related lines, earlier studies by Haslam and colleagues (Haslam, Platow et al., 2001) also showed that perceptions of charisma were enhanced when a leader was associated with a dramatic upturn in an organization's fortunes (e.g., an increase in profits; replicating Pillai & Meindl, 1991), but that this was also contingent upon the leader having previously acted in ways that promoted a valued group identity (e.g., by displaying ingroup favouritism). These results are at odds with the suggestion that followers confer charisma *wherever* they find organizational success. Instead, they support the view that such perceptions depend upon the implications of a leader's behaviour for the social identity that he or she is expected to represent. Followers thus appear to entertain few romantic illusions about a leader who is clearly not 'doing it for us' (Haslam & Platow, 2001b; see also Kulich, Ryan, & Haslam, 2007).

Extending this point, this same research also provided evidence that attributions of charisma are a reflection of the *intellectual work* that followers sometimes need to do in order to explain (both to themselves and others) why they are influenced and inspired by a person who is not a straightforward embodiment of salient ingroup norms and why, indeed, that person has encouraged them to redefine the meaning of 'weness'. In much the same way, we can see that when people acknowledge the charisma of people like Nelson Mandela, Martin Luther King Jr. or Barack Obama, there is a sense in which they acknowledge that this person has played a role in redefining and restructuring their identity. Such experiences can also be seen as genuinely *transformational* (in the sense implied by Burns, 1978) not only because the leader has forged a new path, but also because his or her behaviour motivates followers to contribute *creatively* both to a collective redefinition of self and to profoundly new forms of social and organizational behaviour (see also Adarves-Yorno, Postmes, & Haslam, 2007).

Motivation

The theories of motivation that are typically advanced in the organizational literature tend to focus on individual workers and on the way in which their needs, goals and rewards affect their work behaviour (cf. Soenens & Vansteenkiste, Chapter 17, this volume). In particular, such theories aim to understand (a) the conditions that encourage people to invest energy in their work (*energize*), (b) the activities that they focus their efforts on (*direct*) and (c) what makes them sustain these efforts over time (*persist*). For instance, various models point to ways in which workers can be energized by appealing to the particular needs that they seek to satisfy (these being specified within particular needs *hierarchies*; e.g., Alderfer, 1972; Herzberg, 1966; after Maslow, 1943). Other models provide insight into the direction that workers' efforts are likely to take by examining the behavioural choices they make (e.g., Mowday, 1979; Vroom, 1964). Finally, theories derived from principles of psychological learning seek to understand why certain organizational behaviours are more likely to be sustained than others (e.g., Komaki, Coombs, & Schepman, 1996; for reviews, see Ellemers et al., 2004; Ellemers, De Gilder, & Haslam, 2008).

Although these various approaches all have some merit, as with dominant approaches to leadership, one of their common features is that they construe motivation primarily as an issue that

relates to the behaviour of people *as separate agents*. However, in most contemporary organizational settings, it is apparent that individuals typically have to work *together* with others in teams and collaborative work groups. For this reason, motivation in the contemporary world of work is at least as much about 'we' as it is about 'I'. Accordingly, there is a demand for theoretical approaches that account for motivation at *both* individual and collective (team or organizational) levels. In this regard, a key attraction of the social identity approach is that it provides a framework that allows us to explain the capacity for people to conceive of themselves, and act, either as separate individuals or as part of a collective (Ellemers, Spears, & Doosje, 2002; Turner, 1985).

Motivation as a product of variable self-categorization. As with issues of leadership, questions of identity provide an important starting point for thinking about questions of motivation. More specifically, to understand a person's motivations, it can be useful to reflect on their likely response to the question 'Who do you think you are?' (for related arguments, see Handy, 1976; Oyserman & Packer, 1996; Shamir, 1991). As we noted in the first part of this chapter, SCT suggests that a question of this form can be answered at varying levels of abstraction (Turner, 1985). These range from conceptions of the self in terms of one's personal identity as a unique individual, through group-based self-definitions in terms of a salient social identity, to more abstract representations of self as a human being, or at an even higher level as an animal (i.e., sharing identity with other living creatures).

Importantly too, each of these different levels of self-definition is likely to be associated with a distinct set of needs. In particular, when people categorize themselves at a personal level, they should be motivated to do those things that promote their personal identity as individuals; but when they categorize themselves at a social level, they should be motivated to do those things that promote their social identity as group members. In this way, needs associated with a salient personal identity should be more specialized and idiosyncratic than those associated with a social identity, which in turn should be more specialized

Table 30.2. The relationship between level of self-categorization and hierarchies of need identified by major theorists (Maslow, Aldferer and Herzberg) (adapted from Haslam, 2001; Haslam, Powell, & Turner, 2000)

Level of self-categorization	Content	Associated needs as identified by the hierarchies proposed by key motivational theorists		
		Maslow	Alderfer	Herzberg
Personal	Self as individual (in contrast to ingroup members)	Self-actualization	Growth	Motivators
Social	Self as group member (in contrast to outgroup members)	Esteem	Relatedness	
		Love		Hygienes
Human	Self as human (in contrast to other animals)	Safety	Existence	
Animal	Self as animal (in contrast to non-animals)	Physiological		

and idiosyncratic than those associated with a human or animal identity (Haslam, Powell, & Turner, 2000).

As Table 30.2 indicates, the actual content of the needs associated with each of these different levels of self-definition can be seen to correspond closely with the different categories of needs that are identified within the hierarchies of need identified by researchers such as Maslow, Alderfer and Herzberg. So, when personal identity is salient, this should be associated with needs to self-actualize and to enhance personal interests through personal advancement and growth (Ouwerkerk et al., 1999). On the other hand, when social identity is salient, this should be associated with the need to enhance social self-esteem through a sense of relatedness, respect, peer recognition and the achievement of group goals (Bagozzi, 2000; Hogg & Abrams, 1990, 1993). And when human or animal identities are salient, needs should be more existence-, security- and safety-related.

As we have seen in the first part of this chapter, SCT presents a framework for understanding when and why particular levels of self-categorization become salient. This suggests that *identity salience* is the key process that determines which particular category of needs guides a person's behaviour. Thus, although we are generally motivated to live up to norms and to achieve

goals that are relevant to our self-definition, the definition of self varies with context. Moreover, given the argument that no level of self-definition is any more real or essential than any other, it follows from this perspective that there is no sense in which 'higher-level' needs are inherently more important, superior, valuable or valid than 'lower-level' needs. Nevertheless, this same theoretical framework also explains why there is such a strong resemblance between various needs hierarchies and why these hierarchies have the structure they do. We argue that this is the case because they all map onto an underlying hierarchy of self, in which personal, social and human identities are organized in a hierarchical system of nested categorizations (Ellemers & Rink, 2005).

Contrary to the assertions of many needs theorists (e.g., Maslow, 1943), there is therefore nothing special about personal self-actualization that makes it an inherently better motivator than the need to stand well with one's peers or to achieve collective goals (Leavitt, 1995). Consistent with this analysis, a large number of studies have shown that people can quite easily change the focus of their needs and trade one type of motivator for another, depending on the conditions in which they find themselves and the opportunities these offer. For instance, when group boundaries are perceived to be permeable (e.g., when it is seen to be possible to be promoted from a low-status group to a high-status one), members of low-status groups tend to define themselves in terms of personal identity and so are motivated to work hard as individuals in order to advance their personal career within an organization. However, once boundaries are impermeable, individuals are more likely to define themselves in terms of social identity and so become more attuned to the needs and advancement of the group as a whole (e.g., Ellemers, 1993; Reicher & Haslam, 2006; Taylor, Moghaddam, Gamble, & Zellerer, 1987).

Organizational identification as a multi-level determinant of motivation. When Ashforth and Mael (1989) first outlined the potential applications of SIT to organizational settings, much of their discussion focused on the importance of organizational identification (i.e., the extent to which an individual identifies with a given organization or organizational unit; Cornelissen et al., 2007), as they proposed that this might be a very good predictor of a range of significant organizational behaviours, including turnover, adherence to organizational values and willingness to perform extra-role duties. Indeed, these researchers argued that identification may be a particularly useful construct in this regard because it relies upon *internalization* of the organization's goals, whereas other rival theoretical constructs (e.g., those relating to incentive) may only reflect attraction to the resources that the organization offers, as an external or extrinsic source of motivation (O'Reilly & Chatman, 1986). Consistent with these claims, a number of studies have shown that organizational identification is a powerful predictor of a range of important organizational behaviours. For example, an early study by Mael and Ashforth (1992) found that organizational identification (in this case former students' identification with the college of which they were alumni) was associated with alumni being more willing to contribute funds to their college, to send their children there, and to attend college functions.

As a variant on this position, van Knippenberg and van Schie (2000) note that, in many organizational contexts, employees' primary identification will not be with the organization as a whole but rather with their specific workgroup or team (see also Barker & Tomkins, 1994; Brewer, 1995; Kramer, 1993; Van Dick, Wagner, Stellmacher, & Christ, 2005). Indeed, this prediction follows from principles of positive distinctiveness and comparative fit that we discussed in the first part of this chapter (Deschamps & Brown, 1983; Tajfel & Turner, 1979; Turner, 1985). These principles suggest that, in many organizational contexts, identities are likely to become salient at a level below that of the organizational category as a whole (e.g., at a departmental, divisional or work-team level) because in an intra-organizational context (a) sub-organizational identities allow employees to feel that their ingroup is in some way 'special' and distinct from others and (b) people should be more likely to make comparisons between different work groups than between different organizations.

Supporting these assertions, van Knippenberg and van Schie (2000) found that, in several different organizational samples, individuals' identification with their immediate workgroup was higher than their identification with the organization as a whole. Moreover, identification with this lower-level (i.e., less inclusive) self-category was a much better predictor of a range of key work-related variables (including job satisfaction, job involvement and intention to continue working for the organization) than was identification with the organization as a whole. Similar patterns have also been observed by other researchers who note that workers often identify more with particular organizational constituencies than with an organization as a whole (Becker & Billings, 1993; Hunt & Morgan, 1994; Reichers, 1986; see Ouwerkerk et al., 1999).

Along related lines, Ouwerkerk et al. (1999) argue that individuals' identification with their workgroup can also be differentiated from their commitment to *personal* organizational goals (which they refer to as *career commitment*; see Skorikov & Vondracek, Chapter 29, this volume).

This claim was supported in studies conducted by Ellemers, De Gilder and van den Heuvel (1998), in which workgroup identification emerged as a far better predictor of employees' willingness to engage in extra-role helping behaviour and other acts of organizational citizenship. In line with arguments presented in the previous section, it thus appears that, when work behaviour is determined by a salient personal identity, people are likely to engage in activities that advance their personal status (e.g., by obtaining additional qualifications). On the other hand, when employees act in terms of a salient social identity, they are likely to work hard to promote the interests of the group with which that identity is associated (e.g., by doing unpaid overtime and performing other 'thankless' tasks). To the extent that organizational researchers are interested in predicting and encouraging collective forms of behaviour (as they often are), they may therefore need to focus less on motivation associated with personal identity and more on motivation rooted in social identification.

Motivation as a product of identity fit. As well as specifying that motivation is determined by the level at which identity is defined, SCT principles also lead us to expect that motivation should vary as a function of people's perceptions of the degree to which they are representative of a given organizational group. In particular, those who are on the periphery of an organization (or organizational unit) and who find it hard to move towards the centre should display lower levels of organizational identification (Jetten, Branscombe, Spears, & McKimmie, 2003; Jetten, Spears, & Manstead, 1997) and, as a result, display lower levels of motivation.

Amongst other things, this analysis helps us understand why women's motivation levels are found to drop relative to men's if the organization of which they are part has a masculine or male-dominated culture. Evidence of this process emerges from research with female surgeons and police officers conducted by Peters, Ryan, Haslam, and Hersby (2009; see also van Vianen & Fischer, 2002). In these studies, women who perceived their own approach to work as differing from that of people who were in leadership positions in the organization were found to have lower levels of ambition and a greater desire to exit their profession – a relationship that was fully mediated by the perceived lack of fit between their own identity and that of the organization. Similar results also emerged from studies in which fit was experimentally manipulated (Peters et al., 2009). Here, to the extent that women police officers were led to believe that their own characteristics matched those of prototypical group members, they displayed greater desire to stay, and to get ahead, in the police service.

On the basis of such findings, these researchers concluded that the atrophy of ambition among women once they reach managerial positions (sometimes referred to as the 'opt out revolution'; e.g., Belkin, 2003; Wallis, 2004; see also Lyness & Judiesch, 2001) does not arise because they are inherently less motivated than men to scale organizational heights (e.g., as a result of their biological drive to go off and have children). Rather, their disengagement is better understood as an adaptive response to the particular social and organizational realities they encounter (Ryan, Haslam, Hersby, Kulich, & Atkins, 2007; Ryan, Haslam, Hersby, Kulich, & Wilson-Kovacs, 2008; Schmitt, Branscombe, & Postmes, 2003). Accordingly, if one is trying to encourage members of minority groups to advance in organizations, this should be construed not as a battle against biology but as an issue of identity.

Stress

Despite the fact that the value of leadership and motivation is always dependent on the content of the identities with which they are associated (so that these things can be used in the service of evil as well as good; e.g., Haslam & Reicher, 2007), organizations typically seek to encourage and promote both of these processes. Stress, on the other hand, is something that organizations are typically very keen to reduce – not least because it can be very costly. Indeed, estimates suggest that stress-related costs arising from absenteeism, inefficiency and demands on health care may account for anything up to 1% of national gross domestic product and 10% of company profit (Martin, 1997). Furthermore, stress can be seen to reflect the potential for 'positive' organizational processes like leadership and motivation to have a 'down side' that impacts negatively on employees' well-being (Cooper, Dewe, & O'Driscoll, 2001). For example, leaders who work hard to champion change may place a heavy psychological burden both on themselves and on those they lead (Quick, Cooper, Gavin, & Quick, 2002; Terry et al., 2001). Likewise, motivational and productivity demands may put staff under extreme pressure (Bourassa & Ashforth, 1998; Parker, 1993).

As a result, researchers and practitioners are routinely charged with trying both to understand the nature and basis of stress in the workplace and with trying to do something to reduce it. Their strategies in this respect take a number of forms, including stress counselling, cognitive behaviour therapy and the delivery of other forms of personal advice and guidance. Despite their variety, a common feature of these approaches is that they tend to regard stress as a phenomenon grounded in the psychology of the individual *as an individual* (Folkman & Moskowitz, 2004). Typically, then, because stress is seen as a problem of (and for) the individual, remedial interventions are targeted at workers in isolation, rather than their condition being seen as something that is grounded in their experience with respect to social and organizational groups.

In contrast, a social identity approach suggests that group memberships are central to people's experiences of, and reactions to, social and environmental stressors (Branscombe, Schmitt, & Harvey, 1999; Haslam, 2004; Ryan et al., 2008; Van Dick & Wagner, 2001). Not least, this is because individuals' experience of stress in the workplace is often interwoven with the existence of groups and with individuals' membership in these groups. It is clear, for example, that stress can arise from the activities that particular occupational groups have to perform (e.g., caring for others), from the way in which groups are treated by others (e.g., being abused by customers), from a person's relationship to a group (e.g., as a newcomer) and from norms that develop within a group (e.g., to treat people disrespectfully; Haslam, 2004).

Reflecting the dynamics that surround these facets of organizational experience, the social identity approach argues that group life plays a key role in shaping the psychology of stress through its capacity to inform and structure our sense of self — and the sense of belonging, worth, purpose and potential that goes with it (Haslam, Jetten, Postmes, & Haslam, 2009). Most particularly, the sense of social identity that underpins group membership plays a key role in determining whether stressful conditions change us for the worse or whether we combine with others to change them for the better (Haslam & Reicher, 2006a).

Social identity as a basis for primary stress appraisal. One of the most basic predictions that flows from principles articulated within the social identity approach is that if a person's social identity is salient, then his or her *appraisal* of social stressors will be influenced by the perspective and condition of his or her ingroup. In line with this suggestion, a body of research has confirmed that social identity salience is an important determinant of *primary appraisal* – that is, the assessment of a given stressor as threatening to self (Lazarus & Folkman, 1984). This is for the simple reason that such appraisal is necessarily dependent on how the self is defined.

These ideas were initially supported in experimental research by Levine and Reicher (1996). These researchers found that female sportswomen found the threat of a knee injury more stressful than the threat of a facial scar when their identity as sportspeople was made salient; however, the opposite pattern emerged when their gender identity was salient (see also St. Claire, Clift, & Dumbelton, 2008). In a subsequent study, Levine (1999) also showed that secretaries' responses to stressors that were relevant to their professional identity (e.g., restricted manual dexterity, back pain) were perceived to be more stressful when their professional identity had first been made salient.

A related prediction is that employees' responses to organizational stressors should also be structured by their level of identification with the organizational unit that is the source of those stressors. Amongst other things, this is because stressors that emanate from a source with which one identifies (e.g., requests from teammates to work unpaid overtime) are more likely to be seen as self-generated and under one's control than those which emanate from a source with which one does not identify (e.g., the same requests from senior managers). The resulting hypothesis is that employees will respond more positively to organizational stressors to the extent that they have high levels of organizational identification. This prediction has been supported by large-scale studies of call-centre workers (Wegge, van Dick, Fisher, Wecking, & Moltzen, 2006), schoolteachers (van Dick & Wagner, 2002) airline pilots (Peters, Tevichapong, Haslam, & Postmes, 2010) and office workers (Knight & Haslam, 2010a, 2010b).

One interesting feature of a number of organizational stressors is that responses to them are often *shared* among members of a particular work community. This is true, for example, of complaints such as Sick Building Syndrome (SBS) and Repetitive Strain Injury (RSI), which are typically found to be concentrated among employees in a particular organizational culture at a particular point in time (Bartholomew & Wessely, 2002). In line with principles articulated within SCT, this can be seen to reflect the fact that members of particular organizational communities perceive themselves to share social identity and, on this basis, group members play a key role in shaping each others' appraisal of their work environment. This is a point that van Steenbergen, Ellemers, Haslam and Urlings (2008) discuss in relation to the potential stress that attempting to maintain work–life balance poses for working women – showing that whether women respond positively or negatively to this challenge depends very much on how others around them respond.

In contrast to the picture that might emerge from alternative approaches, it is typically not the case, then, that individuals appraise particular stressors from a position of isolation and then decide matter-of-factly whether or not a particular stimulus is threatening. Instead, they talk to their peers and come to shared understandings about the meaning and significance of their experiences. And it is partly on this basis that they come to see the air as stale or fresh, the work demands as unreasonable or reasonable, and their manager as a help or a hindrance (Mayo, 1949).

Indicative evidence of the role that social identity can play in such appraisals emerges from an experimental study in which students were presented with a message about the stressfulness of a series of arithmetic tasks from someone described as an ingroup member (a fellow student) or an outgroup member (a stress sufferer; Haslam, Jetten, O'Brien, & Jacobs, 2004). When they performed the task themselves, students' stress was reduced only when the message encouraged them to perceive the task as an enjoyable challenge and it was provided by a fellow ingroup member. As suggested by SCT (Turner, 1991), this can be seen to reflect the fact that only a person with the same identity-based perspective as the perceivers was qualified to inform them about the meaning of the social reality they confronted.

Social identity as a basis for secondary stress appraisal. As well as affecting primary appraisal, social identity salience also serves as a basis for *secondary appraisal* – that is, the assessment of one's capacity to cope with a particular stressor (Lazarus & Folkman, 1984). In particular, this is because a person's sense of shared group membership is central to the dynamics of *social support* (i.e., whether they give and receive assistance from others, and how they respond to it; Cohen & Wills, 1985; Underwood, 2000). SCT principles predict that, to the extent that a person defines themselves in terms of a social identity that they share with another person, they should be more willing to help that person out and provide them with various forms of support – instrumental, emotional, companionship and informational.

This idea was supported in research by Levine, Prosser, Evans and Reicher (2005), who showed that a person's willingness to help a stranger in distress (the phenomenon of 'bystander intervention'; Darley & Latané, 1968) is enhanced when the stranger in question is perceived to share social identity with the prospective helper (see also Levine, Cassidy, Brazier, & Reicher, 2002). As a corollary, it should also be the case that the likelihood of a person *receiving* support from others depends on whether or not he or she is perceived by the support provider to be an ingroup member. The same process should also determine whether any particular act of support is interpreted in the spirit in which it was intended. This is important because, as work by Nadler (e.g., Nadler, Fisher, & Streufert, 1974) suggests, there is considerable opportunity for *mis*interpretation of social support where the salient identities of provider and recipient are not matched. Indeed, this may help to explain why, in many organizational contexts, social support is found to have mixed benefits and can actually prove counterproductive (Dunkel-Schetter, Blasband, Feinstein, & Herbert, 1992; Terry, Callan, & Sartori, 1996; Underwood, 2000). Nevertheless, where the providers and recipients of social support do share the same social identity, there is plenty of evidence that this can play a key role in buffering groups – especially those with low status – from adverse environmental threats. In particular, this has been found in studies of the work-related stress experienced by ethnic minority groups (James, 1997) and in studies of Black Americans' responses to discrimination and prejudice (Branscombe et al., 1999; Postmes & Branscombe, 2002).

Research with bomb disposal experts and bar staff also supports suggestions that shared social identity can offset the effects of stress because it serves as a basis for the receipt of effective support from ingroup members (Haslam, O'Brien, et al., 2005). In this study, employees' identification with their colleagues was found to be significantly correlated with job satisfaction, and this relationship was mediated by the perception that those colleagues were an important source of material, emotional and intellectual support.

Interestingly, this same research also indicated that employees' assessment of their capacity to cope with particular stressors was moderated by their membership of specific occupational groups. Thus, although bar staff reported that handling bombs would be much more problematic than doing bar work, bomb disposal experts reported the very opposite pattern. Bar staff were thus relatively unfazed by the stresses of bar work, and bomb handlers by the stresses of handling bombs. This pattern of findings suggests that groups' collective experiences (e.g., during training and in the course of actually doing their job) allow them to *normalize* aspects of work that might otherwise be quite abnormal and threatening (Ashforth, 2001). More generally, these research findings suggest that (a) the nature and strength of a person's workgroup identity, and (b) the meaning of a specific stressor in relation to that identity, are both very important determinants of any given stressor's impact.

Lack of social identity as a basis for burnout. The research discussed in the previous two sections was generally conducted with opportunity samples of 'normal' workers and hence only provides insight into stress of a relatively unexceptional nature. A key question is thus whether the analysis we have outlined is relevant to work environments where stressors are much more toxic. In particular, can the social identity approach help us to understand the dynamics of *burnout* — that is, chronic stress associated with exhaustion, a profound sense of lack of accomplishment, and callousness (a lack of concern for others' welfare; Maslach & Leiter, 1996)?

Some evidence that it might comes from a study by O'Brien and Haslam (2003) of an organization that had been issued with the first Stress Improvement Notice by the UK Health and Safety Executive. In this study, low levels of social identification (at both team and organizational levels) were found to be significant predictors of employees' burnout levels (which were extremely high in some workgroups). Moreover, as in Haslam et al.'s (2005) study, this relationship between low identification and burnout was mediated by a lack of social support. In other words, in this organization, one reason why many workers experienced high levels of burnout was that their psychological connection to the organization was weak and, as a result, they found themselves both isolated and unsupported (see also Haslam, Jetten, & Waghorn, 2009).

Yet, like many other studies of stress (and other organizational processes), the above study employed only correlational methods and was reliant on employees' self-reports of their psychological states. A study with the unique capacity to overcome these weaknesses and to provide a much closer inspection of these processes at work (as well as allowing for a more general analysis of the contribution of social identity to group and organizational functioning) was the BBC Prison Study (Haslam & Reicher, 2006a, 2006b; Reicher & Haslam, 2006). In this study, participants were randomly assigned to groups of Prisoners and Guards, and their behaviour within a simulated prison environment was studied closely over a period of 8 days. The goal of the research was to manipulate factors that would impact upon the Prisoners' degree of social identification and to examine the impact of this on group functioning (see Reicher & Haslam, 2006, for more detail).

In line with the arguments outlined in previous sections, it was clear from psychological, physiological and observational data that higher levels of social identification were generally associated with more positive stress-related outcomes (i.e., *eu*stress – the opposite of distress; Suedfeld, 1997). As events unfolded, the Prisoners' increasing identification with their group led them to become increasingly resistant to the strains of their predicament (e.g., physical confinement, poor diet, lack of privileges) and increasingly willing to impose strain on the Guards (e.g., by challenging their position, by subjecting them to humiliation and bullying). At the same time, as the Guards' sense of shared identity declined, they became increasingly distressed. Not least, this was because they became increasingly isolated and failed to provide each other with the support necessary to maintain their authority and resist the various challenges posed by the Prisoners. Ultimately, the Guards'

failure to run the prison effectively led to them experiencing high levels of burnout.

In its entirety, this study thus allowed for an integrated examination of the complex roles that social identification and emergent intra- and intergroup dynamics play in the stress process, and in organizational dynamics more generally (e.g., clarifying the role that social identity plays in leadership and motivation, as argued in preceding sections; see Haslam & Reicher, 2008; Reicher et al., 2006). On the one hand, then, the experiences of the Prisoners illustrate how an emergent sense of shared social identity allows individuals to resist strain and turn adversity into advantage. On the other hand, the experiences of the Guards demonstrate how the erosion of social identity exposes individuals to stress and how, if it contributes to collective failure, it can ultimately pave the way to burnout. In this way, the study confirms the point that stress is not simply a problem of individual biology, physiology or personality. It is also (and perhaps primarily) a problem of group life. And yet, at the same time, group life is also the key to its amelioration.

Conclusion: Identity as an Integrative Principle for Organizational Science

Our goal in this chapter has been to identify some of the main identity processes that operate in organizational contexts, and then to demonstrate how an appreciation of these processes allows for an integrated understanding of key organizational topics. Our analysis has drawn heavily on principles originally specified within SIT and SCT, but it has also shown how these theories can be extended through their application to the organizational domain. We have also attempted to show that this exercise provides powerful new insights into traditional topics and challenges a number of deeply held assumptions along the way. In doing so, the approach allows us to tackle some of the core problems of traditional organizational psychology – in particular, its piecemeal empiricism, its individualism, its obsession with taxonomy, and its restricted conceptions of the self (see Haslam & Ellemers, 2005; Pfeffer, 1997).

In this and other work, a key contribution of the social identity approach has been to question static approaches that view measurement and classification of particular organizational features as the primary path to theoretical and practical understanding. Above all, the approach reveals the capacity for contextual factors to redefine the nature and meaning of both (a) particular organizational properties and structures, and (b) the sense of self that underpins individuals' psychological orientations towards them. Furthermore, this redefinition has *qualitative*, not just quantitative, implications. This is because social identities are emergent higher-order products that are *transformed* by context, rather than merely aggregated from it (Turner & Oakes, 1986). This means that relevant psychological states and processes (e.g., leadership, culture, gender) cannot be discovered within the dissembled parts of wholes in the manner that classical organizational approaches suggest. Rather, these identity-based processes need to be understood, and studied, as irreducibly socio-contextual. Organizational contexts do not merely provide milieus within which identity operates – they also contribute to the creation of *new* identities, just as those identities themselves motivate the creation of new organizational contexts (Gioia et al., 2000). The organizational world shapes who we are, but who we are (and want to be) also shapes the organizational world. This dynamic is central to organizational psychology and, moreover, is a basic source of organizational vitality and adaptiveness.

In conclusion, it is worth noting that the ideas and research we have focused on in this chapter have not paid much heed to questions of how social identity can be used and managed in organizations. For organizational psychologists in particular, this has been a significant issue and one that has underscored debate surrounding issues of negotiation, diversity and change (e.g., see Jackson, 1992; Reynolds, Turner, & Haslam, 2003; van Knippenberg & Haslam, 2003). In all of these areas, core questions centre on the way in which (perceptions of) group and individual differences can be managed in order to promote harmonious group relations and to achieve positive organizational outcomes (e.g., employee satisfaction, enhanced productivity).

This is not the place to discuss the range of options that researchers have outlined and to weigh their relative strengths and weaknesses (see Haslam & Ellemers, 2005, for a discussion). Nevertheless, an important point that emerges from the body of work that has been conducted in this area is that relevant organizational goals are far more likely to be reached when organizational agents (e.g., managers, leaders, policy-makers) take steps to discover, develop and *work with* relevant identities rather than ignore or work against them (e.g., see Haslam, Eggins, & Reynolds, 2003). Moreover, by attempting to come to terms with the political as well as the psychological dimensions of identity, such activities allow for a more fruitful dialogue between the various parties whose interests converge around this fundamental topic.

This dialogue is both intellectually rewarding and of supreme practical importance for the shape, structure and sustainability of organizational life. For it is only through an awareness of our shared organizational identity that we are able to organize ourselves, and it is only through the content of that identity that we know what form our organization needs to take. Identity, then, determines not only the work we do in the world, but also the world in which we do the work.

Acknowledgments Work on this chapter was supported by a grant from the Economic and Social Research Council (RES-062-23-0135).

References

Adarves-Yorno, I., Postmes, T., & Haslam, S. A. (2007). Creative innovation or crazy irrelevance? The contribution of group norms and social identity to creative behaviour. *Journal of Experimental Social Psychology, 43*, 410–416.

Akerlof, G. A., & Kranton, R. E. (2000). Economics and identity. *Quarterly Journal of Economics, 3*, 715–753.

Albert, S., Ashforth, B. E., & Dutton, J. E. (2000). Organizational identity and identification. *Academy of Management Review, 25*, 13–17.

Albert, S. & Whetten, D. A. (1985). Organizational identity. In L. L. Cummings & B. M. Staw (Eds.), *Research in organizational behavior* (Vol. 8, pp. 263–295). Greenwich, CT: JAI Press.

Alderfer, C. P. (1972). *Existence, relatedness and growth: Human needs in organizational settings.* New York: Free Press.

Asch, S. E. (1952). *Social psychology.* Englewood Cliffs, NJ: Prentice Hall.

Ashforth, B. E. (2001). Which hat to wear? The relative salience of multiple identities in organizational contexts. In M. A. Hogg & D. J. Terry (Eds.), *Social identity processes in organizational contexts* (pp. 31–48). Philadelphia: Psychology Press.

Ashforth, B. E. (2001). *Role transitions in organizational life: An identity-based perspective.* Mahwah, NJ: Erlbaum.

Ashforth, B. E., Harrison, S. H., & Corley, K. G. (2008). Identification in organizations: An examination of four fundamental questions. *Journal of Management, 34*, 325–374.

Ashforth, B.E., & Kreiner, G. E. (1999). "How can you do it?": Dirty work and the challenge of constructing a positive identity. *Academic of Management Review, 24*, 413–434.

Ashforth, B. E., & Mael, F. (1989). Social identity theory and the organization. *Academy of Management Review, 14*, 20–39.

Bagozzi, R. P. (2000). On the concept of intentional social action in consumer behavior. *Journal of Consumer Research, 27*, 388–396.

Barker, J., & Tomkins, P. (1994). Identification in the self-managing organization. *Human Communication Research, 21*, 223–240.

Barsalou, L. W. (1987). The instability of graded structure: Implications for the nature of concepts. In U. Neisser (Ed.), *Concepts and conceptual development: Ecological and intellectual factors in categorization.* Cambridge: Cambridge University Press.

Bartel, C., Blader, S., & Wrzesniewski, A. (Eds.) (2006). *Identity and the modern organization.* New York: Erlbaum.

Bartholomew R. E., & Wessely, S. (2002). Protean nature of mass sociogenic illness: From possessed nuns to chemical and biological terrorism fears. *British Journal of Psychiatry, 180*, 300–306.

Becker, T. E., & Billings, R. S. (1993). Profiles of commitment: An empirical test. *Journal of Organizational Behavior, 14*, 177–190.

Belkin, L. (2003). Q: Why don't more women choose to get to the top? A: They choose not to. *New York Times Magazine, 58*, 42–47.

Bourassa, L., & Ashforth, B. E. (1998). You are about to party *Defiant* style: Socialization and identity onboard an Alaskan fishing boat. *Journal of Contemporary Ethnography, 27*, 171–196.

Branscombe, N. R., Schmitt M. T., & Harvey, R. D. (1999). Perceiving pervasive discrimination among African Americans: Implications for group identification and well-being. *Journal of Personality and Social Psychology, 77*, 135–149.

Brewer, M. B. (1995). Managing diversity: The role of social identities. In S. E. Jackson & M. N. Ruderman (Eds.), *Diversity in work teams: Research paradigms for a changing workplace* (pp. 47–68). Washington, DC: American Psychological Association.

Brown, A.D. (2001). Organization studies and identity: Towards a research agenda. *Human Relations, 54*, 113–121.

Brown, R. J. (1978). Divided we fall: Analysis of relations between different sections of a factory workforce. In H. Tajfel (Ed.), *Differentiation between social groups: Studies in the social psychology of intergroup relations* (pp. 395–429). London: Academic Press.

Brown, R. J. (1988). *Group processes: Dynamics within and between groups.* Oxford: Blackwell.

Bruner, J. S. (1957). On perceptual readiness. *Psychological Review, 64*, 123–152.

Burns, J. M. (1978). *Leadership.* New York: Harper & Row.

Cohen, S., & Wills, T. A. (1985). Stress, social support and the buffering hypothesis. *Psychological Bulletin, 98*, 310–357.

Cooper, C. L., Dewe, P. J., & O'Driscoll, M. P. (2001). *Organizational stress: A review and critique of theory, research and applications.* London: Sage.

Cornelissen, J. P., Haslam, S. A., & Balmer, J. M. T. (2007). Social identity, organizational identity and corporate identity: Towards an integrated understanding of processes, patternings and products. *British Journal of Management, 18*, 1–16.

Dunkel-Schetter, C., Blasband, D. E., Feinstein, L. G., & Herbert, T. B. (1992). Elements of supportive interaction: When are attempts to help effective? In S. Spacapan & S. Oskamp (Eds.), *Helping and being helped in the real world.* Newbury Park, CA: Sage.

Dutton, J. E., Dukerich, J. M., & Harquail, C. V. (1994). Organizational images and member identification. *Administrative Science Quarterly, 39*, 239–263.

Ellemers, N. (1993). The influence of socio-structural variables on identity enhancement strategies. *European Review of Social Psychology, 4*, 27–57.

Ellemers, N. (2003). Identity, culture, and change in organizations: A social identity analysis and three illustrative cases. In Haslam, A., Van Knippenberg, D., Platow, M., & Ellemers, N. (Eds.), *Social identity at work: Developing theory for organizational practice* (pp. 191–204). New York, Hove: Psychology Press.

Ellemers, N., De Gilder, D., & Haslam, S. A. (2004). Motivating individuals and groups at work: A social identity perspective on leadership and group performance. *Academy of Management Review, 29*, 459–478.

Ellemers, N., De Gilder, D., & Haslam, S. A. (2008).
Motivating individuals and groups at work in the
21st Century. In C. Wankel (Ed.), *Handbook of 21st
Century Management*. (Vol. 2, pp.182–192). Thousand
Oaks, CA: Sage.

Ellemers, N., De Gilder, D., & Van den Heuvel, H. (1998).
Career-oriented versus team-oriented commitment and
behavior at work. *Journal of Applied Psychology, 83*,
717–730.

Ellemers, N., Haslam, S.A., Platow, M., & van
Knippenberg, D. (2003). Social identity at work:
Developments, debates, directions. In: S. A. Haslam,
D. van Knippenberg, M. J. Platow, & N. Ellemers
(Eds.), *Social identity at work: Developing theory
for organizational practice* (pp. 3–28). New York:
Psychology Press.

Ellemers, N., & Rink, F. (2005). Identity in work
groups: The beneficial and detrimental consequences
of multiple identities and group norms for collaboration and group performance. *Advances in Group
Processes, 22*, 1–41.

Ellemers, N., Spears, R., & Doosje, B. (2002). Self and
social identity. *Annual Review of Psychology, 53*, 161–
186.

Ellemers, N., Van den Heuvel, H., De Gilder, D., Maass,
A., & Bonvini, A. (2007). The underrepresentation
of women in science: Differential commitment or
the Queen-bee syndrome? *British Journal of Social
Psychology, 43*, 1–24.

Elsbach, K. D., & Kramer, R. D. (1996). Members'
responses to organizational identity threats:
Encountering and countering the Business Week
rankings. *Administrative Science Quarterly, 41*,
442–476.

Fiedler, F. E. (1978). The contingency model and the
dynamics of the leadership process. In L. Berkowitz
(Ed.), *Advances in Experimental Social Psychology*
(Vol. 11), New York: Academic Press.

Fiol, C. M. (2001). Revisiting an identity-based view
of sustainable competitive advantage. *Journal of
Management, 27*, 691–699.

Fiol, C. M. (2002). Capitalizing on paradox: The role
of language in transforming organizational identities.
Organizational Science, 13, 653–666.

Folkman, S., & Moskowitz, J. T. (2004). Coping: Pitfalls
and promise. *Annual Review of Psychology, 55*,
745–774.

Gioia, D.A., Schultz, M., & Corley, K. G. (2000).
Organizational identity, image and adaptive instability.
Academy of Management Review, 25, 63–81.

Handy, C. B. (1976). *Understanding organizations*.
Harmondsworth: Penguin.

Haslam, S. A. (2001). *Psychology in organizations: The
social identity approach* (1st ed.). London: Sage.

Haslam, S. A. (2004). *Psychology in organizations: The
social identity approach* (2nd ed.). London: Sage.

Haslam, S. A., Eggins, R. A., & Reynolds, K. J. (2003).
The ASPIRe model: Actualizing social and personal
identity resources to enhance organizational outcomes.
*Journal of Occupational and Organizational
Psychology, 76*, 83–113.

Haslam, S. A., & Ellemers, N. (2005). Social identity in industrial and organizational psychology:
Concepts, controversies and contributions. In G. P.
Hodgkinson & J. K. Ford (Eds.), *International review
of industrial and organizational psychology* (Vol. 20,
pp. 39–118). Chichester: Wiley.

Haslam, S. A., Jetten, J., O'Brien, A., & Jacobs, E.
(2004). Social identity, social influence, and reactions
to potentially stressful tasks: Support for the self-
categorization model of stress. *Stress and Health, 20*,
3–9.

Haslam, S. A., Jetten, J., Postmes, T., & Haslam, C. (Eds.)
(2009). Social identity, health and well-being. Special
Issue of *Applied Psychology: An International Review,
58*, 1–192.

Haslam, S. A., Jetten, J., & Waghorn, C. (2009).
Social identification, stress, and citizenship in teams:
A five-phase longitudinal study. *Stress and Health, 25*,
21–30.

Haslam, S. A., Oakes, P. J., McGarty, C., Turner, J. C., &
Onorato, R. (1995). Contextual shifts in the prototypicality of extreme and moderate outgroup members. *European Journal of Social Psychology, 25*,
509–530.

Haslam, S. A., O'Brien, A., Jetten, J., Vormedal, K., &
Penna, S. (2005). Taking the strain: Social identity,
social support and the experience of stress. *British
Journal of Social Psychology, 44*, 355–370.

Haslam, S. A., & Platow, M. J. (2001a). The link between
leadership and followership: How affirming a social
identity translates vision into action. *Personality and
Social Psychology Bulletin, 27*, 1469–1479.

Haslam, S. A., & Platow, M. J. (2001b). Your wish is
my command: How a leader's vision becomes a fol-
lower's task. In M. A. Hogg & D. J. Terry (Eds.),
Social identity processes in organizational contexts
(pp. 213–228). Philadelphia: Psychology Press.

Haslam, S. A., Platow, M. J., Turner, J. C., Reynolds, K. J.,
McGarty, C., Oakes, P. J., Johnson, S., Ryan, M. K., &
Veenstra, K. (2001). Social identity and the romance of
leadership: The importance of being seen to be 'doing
it for us'. *Group Processes and Intergroup Relations,
4*, 191–205.

Haslam, S. A., Postmes, T., & Ellemers, N. (2003).
More than a metaphor: Organizational identity
makes organizational life possible. *British Journal of
Management, 14*, 357–369.

Haslam, S. A., Powell, C., & Turner, J. C. (2000).
Social identity, self-categorization and work motivation: Rethinking the contribution of the group
to positive and sustainable organizational outcomes.
Applied Psychology: An International Review, 49,
319–339.

Haslam, S. A., & Reicher, S. D. (2006a). Stressing the
group: Social identity and the unfolding dynamics of
responses to stress. *Journal of Applied Psychology, 91*,
1037–1052.

Haslam, S. A., & Reicher, S. D. (2006b). Social identity and the dynamics of organizational life: Insights from the BBC Prison Study. In C. Bartel, S. Blader, & A. Wrzesniewski (Eds.), *Identity and the modern organization* (pp. 135–166). New York: Erlbaum.

Haslam, S. A., & Reicher, S. D. (2007). Beyond the banality of evil: Three dynamics of an interactionist social psychology of tyranny. *Personality and Social Psychology Bulletin, 33*, 615–622.

Haslam, S. A., Reicher, S. D., & Platow, M. J. (2011). *The new psychology of leadership: Identity, influence and power.* London: Psychology Press.

Haslam, S. A., Turner, J. C., Oakes, P. J., McGarty, C., & Reynolds, K. J. (1998). The group as a basis for emergent stereotype consensus. *European Review of Social Psychology, 9*, 203–239.

Haslam, S. A., & Van Dick, R. (2010). A social identity approach to workplace stress. In K. Murnighan, D. De Cremer, & R. van Dick (Eds.), *Social Psychology in Organizations* (pp. 325–352). New York: Taylor & Francis.

Haslam, S. A., van Knippenberg, D., Platow, M., & Ellemers, N. (Eds.) (2003). *Social identity at work: Developing theory for organizational practice.* Philadelphia: Psychology Press.

Herzberg, F. (1966). *Work and the nature of man.* Cleveland, OH: World Publishing Co.

Hogg, M. A., & Abrams, D. (1990). Social motivation, self-esteem and social identity. In D. Abrams & M. A. Hogg (Eds.), *Social identity theory: Constructive and critical advances* (pp. 28–47). London: Harvester Wheatsheaf.

Hogg, M. A., & Abrams, D. (1993). Towards a single-process uncertainty-reduction model of social motivation in groups. In M. A. Hogg & D. Abrams (Eds.), *Group motivation: Social psychological perspectives* (pp. 173–90). London: Harvester Wheatsheaf.

Hogg, M. A., Hains, S. C., & Mason, I. (1998). Identification and leadership in small groups: Salience, frame of reference, and leader stereotypicality effects on leader evaluations. *Journal of Personality and Social Psychology, 75*, 1248–1263.

Hogg M. A., & Terry, D. J. (2000). Social identity and self-categorization processes in organizational contexts. *Academy of Management Review, 25*, 121–140.

Hogg, M. A., Turner, J. C., & David, B. (1990). Polarized norms and social frames of reference: A test of the self-categorization theory of group polarization. *Basic and Applied Social Psychology, 11*, 77–100.

Hogg, M. A., & van Knippenberg, D. (2004). Social identity and leadership processes in groups. *Advances in Experimental Social Psychology, 35*, 1–52.

Hollander, E. P. (1985). Leadership and power. In G. Lindzey & E. Aronson (Eds.), *The handbook of social psychology* (3rd ed., pp. 485–537). New York: Random House.

House, R. J., & Shamir, B. (1993). Toward the integration of transformational, charismatic, and visionary theories. In M. M. Chemers & R. Ayman (Eds.), *Leadership theory and research: Perspectives and directions* (pp. 81–107). Orlando, FL: Academic Press.

Hunt, S. D., & Morgan, R. M. (1994). Organizational commitment: One of many commitments or key mediating construct? *Academy of Management Journal, 37*, 1568–1587.

Jackson, S. E. (1992). Team composition in organizational settings: Issues in managing an increasingly diverse workforce. In S. Worchel, W. Wood &, J. A. Simpson (Eds.), *Group processes and productivity* (pp. 136-180). Newbury Park, CA: Sage.

James, K. (1997). Worker social identity and health-related costs for organizations: A comparative study between ethnic groups. *Journal of Occupational Health Psychology, 2*, 108–117.

Jetten, J., Branscombe, N. R., Spears, R., & McKimmie, B. M. (2003). Predicting the paths of peripherals: The interaction of identification and future possibilities. *Personality and Social Psychology Bulletin, 29*, 130–140

Jetten, J., O'Brien, A., & Trindall, N. (2002). Changing identity: Predicting adjustment to organizational restructure as a function of subgroup and superordinate identification. *British Journal of Social Psychology, 41*, 281–297.

Jetten J., Spears R., & Manstead, A. S. R. (1997). Distinctiveness threat and prototypicality: Combined effects on intergroup discrimination and collective self-esteem. *European Journal of Social Psychology, 27*, 635–657.

Knight, C., & Haslam, S. A. (2010a). Your place or mine? Organizational identification and comfort as mediators of relationships between the managerial control of workspace and employees' satisfaction and well-being. *British Journal of Management, 21*, 717–735.

Knight, C., & Haslam, S. A. (2010b). The relative merits of lean, enriched, and empowered offices: An experimental examination of the impact of workspace management strategies on well-being and productivity. *Journal of Experimental Psychology: Applied, 16*, 158–172.

Komaki, J., Coombs, T., & Schepman, S. (1996). Motivational implications of reinforcement theory. In R. M. Steers, L. W. Porter, & G. A. Bigley (Eds.), *Motivation and leadership at work* (6th ed., pp. 34–52). New York: McGraw-Hill.

Kramer, R. M. (1993). Cooperation and organizational identification. In J. K. Murnigham (Ed.), *Social psychology in organizations: Advances in theory and research* (pp. 244–268). Englewood Cliffs, NJ: Prentice Hall.

Kramer, R. M, Brewer, M. B., & Hanna, B. A. (1996). Collective trust and collective action: The decision to trust as a social decision. In R. M. Kramer & T. R. Tyler (Eds.), *Trust in organizations: Frontiers of theory and research* (pp. 357–389). Thousand Oaks, CA: Sage.

Kulich, C., Ryan, M. K., & Haslam, S. A. (2007). Where is the romance for women leaders? The effects of gender on leadership attributions and performance-based pay. *Applied Psychology: An International Review*, *56*, 582–601.

Lau, D. C., & Murnighan, J. K. (1998). Demographic diversity and faultlines: The compositional dynamics of organizational groups. *Academy of Management Review*, *23*, 325–340.

Lazarus, R. S., & Folkman, S. (1984). *Stress, appraisal and coping*. New York: Springer Publishing Company.

Lea, M., & Spears, R., & Rogers, P. (2003). Social processes in electronic team work: The central issue of identity. In S. A. Haslam, D. van Knippenberg, M. J. Platow, & N. Ellemers (Eds.), *Social identity at work: Developing theory for organizational practice* (pp. 99–115). Philadelphia: Psychology Press.

Leavitt, H. J. (1995). 'Suppose we took groups seriously . . .' In B. M. Staw (Ed.), *Psychological dimensions of organizational behavior* (2nd ed.). Englewood Cliffs, NJ: Prentice Hall.

Levine, R. M. (1999). Identity and illness: The effects of identity salience and frame of reference on evaluation of illness and injury. *British Journal of Health Psychology*, *4*, 63–80.

Levine R. M., Cassidy, C., Brazier, G., & Reicher S. D. (2002). Self-categorization and bystander non-intervention: Two experimental studies. *Journal of Applied Social Psychology*, *32*, 1452–1463.

Levine, R. M., Prosser, A., Evans, D., & Reicher, S.D. (2005). Identity and emergency intervention: How social group membership and inclusiveness of group boundaries shapes helping behavior. *Personality and Social Psychology Bulletin*, *31*, 443–453.

Levine, R. M., & Reicher, S. D., (1996). Making sense of symptoms: Self-categorization and the meaning of illness and injury. *British Journal of Social Psychology*, *35*, 245–256.

Lupton, B. (2000). Maintaining masculinity: Men who do "women's work". *British Journal of Management, 11*, 33–48.

Lyness, K. S., & Judiesch, M. K. (2001). Are female managers quitters? The relationship of gender, promotions, and family leaves of absence to voluntary exit. *Journal of Applied Psychology, 86*, 1167–1178.

Mackie, D. M., & Cooper, J. (1984). Attitude polarization: The effects of group membership. *Journal of Personality and Social Psychology*, *46*, 575–585.

Mael, F. A., & Ashforth, B. E. (1992). Alumni and their alma mater: A partial test of the reformulated model of organizational identification. *Journal of Organizational Behavior*, *13*, 103–123.

Mann, R. D. (1959). A review of the relationship between personality and performance in small groups. *Psychological Bulletin*, *56*, 241–270.

Martin, P. (1997). *The sickening mind: Brain, behaviour, immunity and disease*. London: Flamingo.

Marturano, A., & Arsenault, P. (2008). Charisma. In A. Marturano & J. Gosling (Eds.) *Leadership: The key concepts* (pp. 18–22). New York: Routledge.

Maslach, C., & Leiter, M. P. (1996). *The truth about burnout: How organizations cause personal stress and what to do about it*. San Francisco: Jossey Bass.

Maslow, A. H. (1943). A theory of motivation. *Psychological Review*, *50*, 370–396.

Mayo, E. (1949). *The social problems of an industrial civilization*. London: Routledge and Kegan Paul.

McGarty, C., Turner, J. C., Hogg, M. A., David, B., & Wetherell, M. S. (1992). Group polarization as conformity to the prototypical group member. *British Journal of Social Psychology*, *31*, 1–20.

McGarty, C., Turner, J. C., Oakes, P. J., & Haslam, S. A. (1993). The creation of uncertainty in the influence process: The roles of stimulus information and disagreement with similar others. *European Journal of Social Psychology*, *23*, 17–38.

Moreland, R. L., Argote, L., & Krishnan, R. (1996). Socially shared cognition at work: Transactive memory and group performance. In J. Nye & A. Brower (Eds.), *What's social about social cognition? Research on socially shared cognition in small groups* (pp. 57–84). Newbury Park, CA: Sage.

Moscovici, S. (1984). The phenomenon of social representations. In R. M. Farr & S. Moscovici (Eds.), *Social Representations*. Cambridge: Cambridge University Press.

Mowday, R. T. (1979). Equity theory predictions of behavior in organizations. In R. M. Steers & L. W. Porter (Eds.), *Motivation and work behavior* (pp. 124–146). New York: McGraw Hill.

Münsterberg, H. (1913). *Psychology and industrial efficiency*. Boston: Houghton Mifflin.

Nadler, A., Fisher, J.D., & Streufert, S. (1974). Donors' dilemma: Recipients' reactions to aid from friend or foe. *Journal of Applied Social Psychology*, *4*, 275–285.

Oakes, P. J. (1987). The salience of social categories. In J. C. Turner, M. A. Hogg, P. J. Oakes, S. D. Reicher, & M. S. Wetherell (Eds.), *Rediscovering the social group: A self-categorization theory* (pp. 117–141). Oxford: Blackwell.

Oakes, P. J. (1996). The categorization process. Cognition and the group in the social psychology of stereotyping. In W. P. Robinson (Ed.), *Social groups and identities: Developing the legacy of Henri Tajfel*. Oxford: Butterworth–Heinemann.

Oakes, P. J., Haslam, S. A., & Turner, J. C. (1994). *Stereotyping and social reality*. Oxford: Blackwell.

Oakes, P. J., Turner, J. C., & Haslam, S. A. (1991). Perceiving people as group members: The role of fit in the salience of social categorizations. *British Journal of Social Psychology*, *30*, 125–144.

O'Brien, A.T., & Haslam S. A. (2003). *Shaping the future — Measuring and managing stress among hospital employees: A report responding to the first Health and Safety Executive improvement notice*. School of Psychology: University of Exeter.

O'Reilly, C.A., Chatman, J., & Caldwell, D.F. (1991). People and organizational culture: A profile-comparison approach to assessing person-organization fit. *Academy of Management Journal, 34*, 487–516.

Organ, D. W. (1988). *Organizational citizenship behavior: The good soldier syndrome.* Lexington, MA: Lexington.

Ouwerkerk, J. W., Ellemers, N., & De Gilder, D. (1999). Group commitment and individual effort in experimental and organizational contexts. In N. Ellemers, R. Spears, & B. J. Doosje (Eds.), *Social identity: Context, commitment, content* (pp. 184–204). Oxford: Blackwell.

Oyserman, D., & Packer, M. J. (1996). Social cognition and self concept: A socially contextualized model of identity. In J. Nye & A. Brower (Eds.), *What's social about social cognition? Research on socially shared cognition in small groups* (pp. 174–201). Newbury Park, CA: Sage.

Parker, M. (1993). Industrial relations myth and shop floor reality: The team concept in the auto industry. In N. Lichtenstein & J. H. Howell (Eds.), *Industrial democracy in America* (pp. 249–274). Cambridge: Cambridge University Press.

Peteraf, M., & Shanley, M. (1997). Getting to know you: A theory of strategic group identity. *Strategic Management Journal, 18*, 165–186.

Peters, K. O., Ryan, M. K., Haslam, S. A., & Hersby, M. (2009). *How fit fuels ambition: The contribution of perceived self–leader congruence to women's career aspirations.* Unpublished manuscript: University of Exeter.

Peters, K., Tevichapong, P., Haslam, S. A., & Postmes, T. (2010). Making the organizational fly: Organizational identification and citizenship in full-service and low-cost airlines. *Journal of Personnel Psychology, 9*, 145–148.

Pfeffer, J. (1997). *New directions for organization theory: Problems and prospects.* New York: Oxford University Press.

Pillai, R., & Meindl, J. R. (1991). The impact of a performance crisis on attributions of charismatic leadership: A preliminary study. *Best paper proceedings of the 1991 Eastern Academy of Management Meetings.* Hartford, CT.

Platow, M. J., Haslam, S. A., Foddy, M., & Grace, D. M. (2003). Leadership as the outcome of self-categorization processes. In D. van Knippenberg & M. A. Hogg (Eds.), *Leadership and power: Identity processes in groups and organizations* (pp. 34–47). London: Sage.

Platow, M. J., Hoar, S., Reid, S., Harley, K., & Morrison, D. (1997). Endorsement of distributively fair or unfair leaders in interpersonal and intergroup situations. *European Journal of Social Psychology, 27*, 465–494.

Platow, M. J., Reid, S. A., & Andrew, S. (1998). Leadership endorsement: The role of distributive and procedural behavior in interpersonal and intergroup contexts. *Group Processes and Intergroup Relations, 1*, 35–47.

Platow, M. J., & van Knippenberg, D. (2001). A social identity analysis of leadership endorsement: The effects of leader ingroup prototypicality and distributive intergroup fairness. *Personality and Social Psychology Bulletin, 27*, 1508–1519.

Platow, M. J., van Knippenberg, D., Haslam, S. A., van Knippenberg, B., & Spears, R. (2006). A special gift we bestow on you for being representative of us: Considering leadership from a self-categorization perspective. *British Journal of Social Psychology, 45*, 303–320.

Postmes, T. (2003). A social identity approach to communication in organizations. In S. A. Haslam, D. van Knippenberg, M. J. Platow, & N. Ellemers (Eds.), *Social identity at work: Developing theory for organizational practice* (pp. 81–97). Philadelphia: Psychology Press.

Postmes, T., & Branscombe, N. (2002). Influence of long-term racial environmental composition on subjective-well-being in African Americans. *Journal of Personality and Social Psychology, 83*, 735–751.

Quick, J. D., Cooper, C. L., Gavin, J. H., & Quick, J. C. (2002). Executive health-building: Self-reliance for challenging times. *International Review of Industrial and Organizational Psychology, 17*, 187–216.

Rabbie, J. M., & Bekkers, F. (1978). Threatened leadership and intergroup competition. *European Journal of Social Psychology, 8*, 9–20.

Reicher, S. D. (1996). Social identity and social change: Rethinking the context of social psychology. In P. Robinson (Ed.), *Social groups and identities: Developing the legacy of Henri Tajfel.* Oxford: Butterworth–Heinemann.

Reicher, S. D., & Haslam, S. A. (2006). Rethinking the psychology of tyranny: The BBC Prison experiment. *British Journal of Social Psychology, 45*, 1–40.

Reicher, S. D., Haslam, S. A., & Hopkins, N. (2005). Social identity and the dynamics of leadership: Leaders and followers as collaborative agents in the transformation of social reality. *Leadership Quarterly, 16*, 547–568.

Reicher, S. D., & Hopkins, N. (1996). Seeking influence through characterising self-categories: An analysis of anti-abortionist rhetoric. *British Journal of Social Psychology, 35*, 297–311.

Reichers, A. E. (1986). Conflict and organizational commitments. *Journal of Applied Psychology, 71*, 508–514.

Reynolds, K. J., Turner, J. C., & Haslam, S. A. (2000). When are we better than them and they worse than us? A closer look at social discrimination in positive and negative domains. *Journal of Personality and Social Psychology, 78*, 64–80.

Reynolds, K. J., Turner, J. C., & Haslam, S. A. (2003). Social identity and self-categorization theories' contribution to understanding identification, salience and diversity in teams and organizations. In M.A. Neale

& Mannix, E. (Series Eds.) & J. Polzer (Vol. Ed.), *Research on managing groups and teams: Identity issues in groups* (Vol. 5, pp. 279–304). Oxford: Elsevier Science.

Rosch, E. (1978). Principles of categorization. In E. Rosch & B. B. Lloyd (Eds.), *Cognition and categorization* (pp. 27–48). Hillsdale, NJ: Erlbaum.

Rousseau, D. M. (1998). Why workers still identify with organizations. *Journal of Organizational Behavior, 19,* 217–233.

Ryan, M. K., Haslam, S. A., Hersby, M. D., Kulich, C., & Atkins, C. (2007). Opting out or pushed off the edge? The glass cliff and the precariousness of women's leadership positions. *Social and Personality Psychology Compass, 1,* 266–279.

Ryan, M. K., Haslam, S. A., Hersby, M. D., Kulich, C., & Wilson-Kovacs, M. D. (2008). The stress of working on the edge: Examining the implications of glass cliffs for both women and organizations. In M. Barreto, M. K. Ryan, & M. Schmitt (Eds.), *The glass ceiling in the 21st Century: Understanding barriers to gender equality* (pp. 153–169). New York: American Psychological Association.

Schmitt, M. T., Branscombe, N. R., & Postmes, T. (2003). Women's emotional responses to the perception of pervasive gender discrimination. *European Journal of Social Psychology, 33,* 297–312.

Schmitt, M. T., Ellemers, N., & Branscombe, N. R. (2003). Perceiving and responding to gender discrimination in organizations. In S. A. Haslam, D. van Knippenberg, M. J. Platow, & N. Ellemers (Eds.), *Social identity at work: Developing theory for organizational practice* (pp. 277–292). Philadelphia: Psychology Press.

Schultz, M., Hatch, M. J., & Larsen, M. H. (Eds.) (2000). *The expressive organization: Identity, reputation and corporate branding.* Oxford: Oxford University Press.

Shamir, B. (1991). Meaning, self and motivation in organizations. *Organizational Studies, 12,* 405–24.

Spears, R., Doosje, B., & Ellemers, N. (1997). Self-stereotyping in the face of threats to group status and distinctiveness: The role of group identification. *Personality and Social Psychology Bulletin, 23,* 538–553.

Statt, D. A. (1994). *Psychology and the world of work.* Basingstoke: Macmillan.

St. Claire, L., Clift, A., & Dumbelton, L. (2008). How do I know what I feel? Evidence for the role of self-categorisation in symptom perceptions. *European Journal of Social Psychology, 38,* 173–186.

Stogdill, R. M. (1948). Personality factors associated with leadership: A survey of the literature. *Journal of Psychology, 25,* 35–71.

Suedfeld, P. (1997). The social psychology of 'Invictus': Conceptual and methodological approaches to indomitability. In C. McGarty & S. A. Haslam (Eds.), *The message of social psychology: Perspectives on mind in society* (pp. 328–341). Oxford: Blackwell.

Tajfel, H. (1970). Experiments in intergroup discrimination. *Scientific American, 223,* 96–102.

Tajfel, H. (1972). La catégorisation sociale (English transl.). In S. Moscovici (Ed.), *Introduction à la psychologie sociale.* Paris: Larousse.

Tajfel, H., Flament, C., Billig, M. G., & Bundy, R. F. (1971). Social categorization and intergroup behaviour. *European Journal of Social Psychology, 1,* 149–177.

Tajfel, H., & Turner, J. C. (1979). An integrative theory of intergroup conflict. In W. G. Austin & S. Worchel (Eds.), *The social psychology of intergroup relations* (pp. 33–47). Monterey, CA: Brooks/Cole.

Tajfel, H., & Turner, J. C. (1986). The social identity theory of intergroup behavior. In: S. Worchel & W.G. Austin (Eds.). *Psychology of intergroup relations.* Monterey, CA: Brooks/Cole.

Taylor, D. M., Moghaddam, F., Gamble, I. Z., & Zellerer, E. (1987). Disadvantaged group responses to perceived inequality: From passive acceptance to collective action. *Journal of Social Psychology, 127,* 259–272.

Terry, D. J. (2003). A social identity perspective on organizational mergers: The role of group status, permeability, and similarity. In S. A. Haslam, D. van Knippenberg, M. J. Platow, & N. Ellemers (Eds.), *Social identity at work: Developing theory for organizational practice* (pp. 223–240). Philadelphia: Psychology Press.

Terry, D. J., & Callan, V. J. (1998). Ingroup bias in response to an organizational merger. *Group Dynamics: Theory, Research and Practice, 2,* 67–81.

Terry, D. J., Callan, V. J., & Sartori, G. (1996). Employee adjustment to an organizational merger: Stress, coping and intergroup differences. *Stress Medicine, 12,* 105–122.

Thatcher, S. M. B., Jehn, K. A., & Zanutto, E. (2003). Cracks in diversity research: The effects of diversity faultlines on conflict and performance. *Group Decision and Negotiation, 12,* 217–241.

Turner, J. C. (1975). Social comparison and social identity: Some prospects for intergroup behaviour. *European Journal of Social Psychology, 5,* 5–34.

Turner, J. C. (1982). Towards a cognitive redefinition of the social group. In H. Tajfel (Ed.), *Social identity and intergroup relations* (pp. 15–40). Cambridge: Cambridge University Press.

Turner, J. C. (1985). Social categorization and the self-concept: A social cognitive theory of group behaviour. In E. J. Lawler (Ed.), *Advances in group processes* (Vol. 2, pp. 77–122) Greenwich, CT: JAI Press.

Turner, J. C. (1987). The analysis of social influence. In J. C. Turner, M. A. Hogg, P. J. Oakes, S. D. Reicher, & M. S. Wetherell (Eds.), *Rediscovering the social group: A self-categorization theory* (pp. 68–88). Oxford: Blackwell.

Turner, J. C. (1991). *Social influence.* Milton Keynes: Open University Press.

Turner, J. C. (1999). Some current issues in research on social identity and self-categorization theories. In N. Ellemers, R. Spears, & B. Doosje (Eds.), *Social identity: Context, commitment, content* (pp. 6–34). Oxford: Blackwell.

Turner, J. C., & Giles, H. (Eds.) (1981). *Intergroup behaviour*. Oxford: Blackwell.

Turner, J. C., & Haslam, S. A. (2001). Social identity, organizations and leadership. In M. E. Turner (Ed.), *Groups at work: Advances in theory and research* (pp. 25–65). Hillsdale, NJ: Erlbaum.

Turner, J. C., Hogg, M. A., Oakes, P. J., Reicher, S. D., & Wetherell, M. S. (1987). *Rediscovering the social group: A self-categorization theory*. Oxford: Blackwell.

Turner, J. C., & Oakes, P. J. (1986). The significance of the social identity concept for social psychology with reference to individualism, interactionism, and social influence. *British Journal of Social Psychology, 25*, 237–252.

Turner, J. C., Oakes, P. J., Haslam, S. A., & McGarty, C. A. (1994). Self and collective: Cognition and social context. *Personality and Social Psychology Bulletin, 20*, 454–463.

Tyler, T. R., & Blader, S. (2000). *Co-operation in groups: Procedural justice, social identity and behavioral engagement*. Philadelphia: Psychology Press.

Underwood, P. W. (2000). Social support: The promise and reality. In B. H. Rice (Ed.) *Handbook of stress, coping and health* (pp. 367–391). Newbury Park, CA: Sage.

Van Dick, R. (2004). My job is my castle: Identification in organizational contexts. In C. L. Cooper & I. T. Robertson (Eds.), *International Review of Industrial and Organizational Psychology* (Vol. 19, pp. 171–204). Chichester: Wiley.

Van Dick, R., & Wagner, U. (2001). Stress and strain in teaching: A structural equation approach. *British Journal of Educational Psychology, 71*, 243–259.

Van Dick, R., & Wagner, U. (2002). Social identification among school teachers: Dimensions, foci, and correlates. *European Journal of Work and Organizational Psychology, 11*, 129–149.

Van Dick, R., Wagner, U., Stellmacher, J., & Christ, O. (2004). The utility of a broader conceptualization of organizational identification: Which aspects really matter? *Journal of Occupational and Organizational Psychology, 77*, 171–191.

Van Dick, R., Wagner, U., Stellmacher, J., & Christ, O. (2005). Category salience and organizational identification. *Journal of Occupational and Organizational Psychology, 78*, 273–285.

van Knippenberg, D., & Haslam, S. A. (2003). Harnessing the diversity dividend: Exploring the subtle inter-play between identity, ideology and reality. In S. A. Haslam, D. van Knippenberg, M. J. Platow, & N. Ellemers (Eds.), *Social identity at work: Developing theory for organizational practice* (pp. 61–77). Philadelphia: Psychology Press.

van Knippenberg, D., & Hogg, M. A. (Eds.) (2003). *Leadership and power: Identity processes in groups and organizations*. London: Sage.

van Knippenberg, D., & van Schie, E. C. M. (2000). Foci and correlates of organizational identification. *Journal of Occupational and Organizational Psychology, 73*, 137–147.

van Leeuwen, E., & van Knippenberg, D. (2003). Organizational identification following a merger: The importance of agreeing to differ. In S. A. Haslam, D. van Knippenberg, M. J. Platow, & N. Ellemers (Eds.), *Social identity at work: Developing theory for organizational practice* (pp. 205–221). Philadelphia: Psychology Press.

van Steenbergen, E. F., Ellemers, N., Haslam, S. A., & Urlings, F. (2008). There is nothing either good or bad but thinking makes it so: Informational support and cognitive appraisal of the work–family interface. *Journal of Occupational and Organizational Psychology, 81*, 349–367.

van Vianen A. E. M., & Fischer A. H. (2002). Illuminating the glass ceiling: The role of organizational culture preferences. *Journal of Occupational and Organizational Psychology, 75*, 315–337.

von Cranach, M. (1986). Leadership as a function of group action. In C. F. Graumann & S. Moscovici (Eds.), *Changing conceptions of leadership* (pp. 115–134). New York: Springer Verlag.

Vroom, V. H. (1964). *Work and motivation*. New York: Wiley.

Wallis, C. (2004). The case for staying home: Why more young moms are opting out of the rat race. *Time, 22*, 52–58.

Weber, M. (1921/1946). The sociology of charismatic authority. In H. H. Gerth & C. W. Milles (Eds. & Trans.), *Max Weber: Essays in sociology* (pp. 245–252). New York: Oxford University Press.

Wegge, J., Van Dick, R., Fisher, G.K., Wecking, C., & Moltzen, K. (2006). Work motivation, organizational identification, and well-being in call centre work. *Work and Stress, 20*, 60–83.

Weick, K. E., & Roberts, K. H. (1993). Collective mind in organizations: Heedful interrelating on flight decks. *Administrative Science Quarterly, 38*, 357–381.

Wright, S.C. (2000). Strategic collective action: Social psychology and social change. In: R. Brown & S. Gaertner (Eds.). *Blackwell handbook of social psychology: Intergroup processes* (pp. 409–430). Oxford: Blackwell.

Material and Consumer Identities

Helga Dittmar

Abstract

One increasingly powerful context in which individuals construct and express their identities is the material and consumer culture we live in. Having the 'right' material goods has become vital to many, not so much because of these goods themselves, but because of hoped-for psychological benefits, such as moving closer to an ideal identity, creating a desired social image, and achieving positive emotional states. Having, buying, and desiring material goods has a profound impact on individuals' identities and their well-being (Dittmar, 2008). This chapter starts with a sketch of contemporary material and consumer culture as a significant context for identity processes, and develops a theoretical framework for understanding how material goods become incorporated into identity. Second, it outlines an integrative model of identity-related functions of material goods, and reviews pertinent research with respect to each function, in relation to both favourite personal possessions and acquiring new consumer goods. Third, although material goods can, and do, have positive functions for individuals' identity, a strong emphasis on having and buying goods in order to make ourselves feel better and move closer to an ideal identity can have negative consequences for well-being. This is illustrated in a selective review of research on the link between materialistic values and well-being, as well as on the search for a better self in compulsive buying, a dysfunctional consumer behaviour, in both conventional and online buying environments. Thus, interventions are needed to protect vulnerable individuals from a maladaptive pursuit of material and consumer identities.

As this book attests, identity is multi-faceted and complex, with diverse self-representations in different identity domains. One increasingly powerful context in which individuals construct and express their identities is the material and consumer culture we live in. Having the 'right' material goods has become vital to many, not

H. Dittmar (✉)
School of Psychology, University of Sussex, Falmer, Brighton, UK
e-mail: h.e.dittmar@sussex.ac.uk

S.J. Schwartz et al. (eds.), *Handbook of Identity Theory and Research*,
DOI 10.1007/978-1-4419-7988-9_31, © Springer Science+Business Media, LLC 2011

so much because of these goods themselves, but because of hoped-for psychological benefits, such as moving closer to an ideal identity, creating a desired social image, and achieving positive emotional states. Celebrities, fashion models, media stars, even computer game heroes or toys, influence who children and adolescents aspire to be and what they want to look like. Having, buying, and desiring material goods has a profound impact on individuals' identities and well-being (Dittmar, 2008). Material and consumer identities are still relatively novel topics in mainstream psychology, whereas substantial literatures exist in consumer, marketing, and advertising research, as well as social sciences such as sociology (e.g. Sassatelli, 2007; Slater, 1997) and anthropology (e.g. Douglas & Isherwood, 1979).

This chapter cannot possibly give an exhaustive account of the many ways in which material goods are linked to individuals' identity and well-being, but it offers three things. First, it sketches contemporary material and consumer culture as a significant context for identity processes, and develops a theoretical framework for understanding how material goods become incorporated into identity. Second, it outlines an integrative model of identity-related functions of material goods, and reviews pertinent research with respect to each function, in relation to both favourite personal possessions and acquiring new consumer goods. Third, although material goods can, and do, have positive functions for individuals' identity, a strong emphasis on having and buying goods in order to make ourselves feel better and move closer to an ideal identity can have negative consequences for well-being. This is shown in research on the link between a materialistic value orientation and lower well-being, as well as dysfunctional consumer behaviour. Thus, interventions are needed to protect vulnerable individuals from a maladaptive pursuit of material and consumer identities.

Living in a 'Material World': Context, Identity, and Identity Processes

It is hard to overestimate the significance of material and consumer culture. The mass media

generally, and advertising specifically, are full of idealised images of desirable material goods, perfect appearance, and affluent lifestyles, reflecting a core cultural ideal: the 'material good life' (Dittmar, 2008). They contain 'lifestyle and identity instructions' of how to look, how to act, and what goods to aspire to (Arnould & Thompson, 2005). In these images, the pursuit of material goods and achievement of affluence is associated not only with success, control, and autonomy, but also with a positive identity, satisfying personal life, happiness, and rewarding intimate relationships. The link between material goods on the one hand and identity and well-being on the other is heavily emphasised. Goods are marketed and presented as symbolic bridges towards an 'ideal self', with the message that buyers consume not only the actual goods advertised, but also their symbolic meanings (successful, happy, glamorous), thus moving closer to the ideal identity portrayed by media models. Of course, nobody takes these messages at face value, but it is very hard – if not impossible – to remain unaffected by the continuous exposure to the 'material good life' ideal. Current estimates are that individuals in developed consumer societies see as many as 3,000 ads a day (Kalkbrenner, 2004). Even if they do not process them in an aware and explicit manner, repeated media exposure shifts perceptions of social reality, because we come to see socio-cultural ideals as increasingly normative, desirable, and expected (Gerbner, Gross, Morgan, & Signorelli, 2002; Shrum, 2002).

Mass Consumer Society and Identity

Although material culture has played an important role for individuals and society for a long time, linked economic-structural, socio-cultural, and psychological transformations in the last three or four decades have created particularly dramatic changes in the thoughts, feelings, and behaviours of consumers. The existence of continuing, or even growing, inequalities in wealth means that some individuals live in poverty in developed mass consumer societies, but – overall – the rise of disposable incomes has given people increasingly greater spending power. Complementing greater disposable incomes are mushrooming credit facilities: it is now easier than ever to spend money that one does not, in fact, have (at least before the 'credit crunch', i.e. the lowering of credit limits, raising of interest rates, and increased lender scrutiny since 2008). Between 1970 and 1990, the number of credit cards in the United Kingdom multiplied more than fourfold (Rowlingson & Kempson, 1994) and the average number of credit cards per US household in 2005 was given as 12.75 (Harper's Index, 2005). Alongside growing opportunities for credit that outstrip individuals' ability to repay, consumption has come to play a central socio-cultural role, with overwhelming consumer choice, and leisure activities that increasingly involve having and buying material goods. There is growing concern about the consequences for children of growing up in a consumer culture that is all-pervading (Schor, 2004).

Parallel with these economic and socio-cultural transformations is a stronger psychological role of consumer culture and material goods in people's lives. One reason for this greater psychological significance is that traditional, stable means of identity construction – such as community, class, religion, family, or nationality – have become eroded to some extent, particularly in urban environments, leading to an 'empty self' (Cushman, 1990). Instead of being *ascribed*, identity is increasingly *achieved* by the individual herself or himself (Côté & Levine, 2002; Kroger & Marcia, Chapter 2, this volume). A highly significant element of such achieved identity is the acquisition, ownership, and consumption of material goods. They have become contemporary means of acquiring, expressing, and attempting to enhance identity: they signify social status, express unique aspects of the person, and symbolise hoped-for, better, more ideal identities (Benson, 2000; Dittmar, 2004a, 2004b, 2008; see also Oyserman & James, Chapter 6, this volume).

Material Goods as Identity Extensions

The terms 'self', 'self-concept', and 'self-identity' are all related to identity, but have been given complex and sometimes inconsistent definitions in psychology. In the present chapter, identity is defined as the subjective concept (or representation) that a person holds of herself or himself, in agreement with authors such as Vignoles (Chapter 18, this volume) and Gregg, Sedikides, and Gebauer (Chapter 14, this volume). What is important about this definition is that identity focuses on subjective psychological experience, and that it is inclusive, involving individual, relational, and group levels of self-representation.

The fact that material goods are extensions of our identity has long been recognised, as in this famous and oft-quoted passage of William James's *Principles of Psychology*: '… it is clear that between what a man calls *me* and what he simply calls *mine* the line is difficult to draw… *a man's self is the sum total of what he CAN call his'* (1981/1890, pp. 279–80, emphases in original). Supporting evidence comes from studies that demonstrate directly that material goods are perceived by people as a part of an extended sense of self, such as 'my house' or 'my car' (Belk, 1988; Prelinger, 1959), and are named spontaneously as elements of the self by children, adolescents, and adults (Dixon & Street, 1975; Gordon, 1968). The link between identity and possessions is also strong when measured implicitly, that is, when people are not conscious of what is being measured (Oyamot, 2004). Possessions become 'me' the more people are attached to them, the more they symbolise close interpersonal relationships or autonomous identity and the stronger their role for individuals' past, present, or future selves (Schultz-Kleine, Kleine, & Allen, 1995).

If we use material goods for defining an extended identity, it follows that their unintended loss should be experienced as a lessening of self. Indeed, burglary victims experience rather more psychological trauma than is often credited to the loss of 'mere things', due to perceptions of violation and shrinkage of self (Van den Bogaard & Wiegman, 1991). Similar reactions occur when personal possessions are lost in natural disasters, where the loss of treasured objects is linked systematically to identity (Ikeuchi, Fujihara, &

Dohi, 2000). Experimental studies confirm that threats to spatial-symbolic extensions of the self are experienced as identity threats (Burris & Rempel, 2004). Thus, individuals perceive and experience material goods as integral parts of their extended identity: identity has boundaries that extend beyond the physical body (Dittmar, 1992a, 2008).

A Meadian Approach to Material Identity Development

My account of how the symbolic meanings of material goods become incorporated to form part of individuals' identity is informed by, but also goes beyond, Meadian symbolic interactionist principles. The present analysis is broad, and better understood as a 'meta-theory', but it nevertheless shares several components of the structural symbolic interactionist extension reflected in identity theory, discussed by Serpe and Stryker (Chapter 10, this volume), particularly a multi-faceted view of identity and the concept of identity salience.

The body of thought outlined by Mead (e.g. 1913, 1934), commonly referred to as *symbolic interactionism*, has as its core the notion that developing a sense of identity stems from the human ability for self-reflexivity, or viewing oneself from the *perspective of the other*. Imagining how we appear from the standpoint of others is bound up with socially shared systems of meaning, and a Meadian perspective therefore has unique potential for mapping the symbolic significance of material goods for identity development (Dittmar, 1992a, 2008). Material objects, or rather the symbolic meanings associated with them, can also serve as imaginary points of view from which to see the self. Within consumer culture, a Rolex watch is seen as a symbol of wealth and success, and by looking at myself on the basis of these symbolic meanings, I can view myself as a person who is wealthy and successful. Children's early interactions with material objects, such as toys or dolls, are intimately bound up with social interactions in which the symbolic meanings of these material objects are

established and internalised. So, symbolic communication about material goods is involved in how children become aware of themselves, and develop and maintain an identity, particularly in the context of contemporary consumer culture's emphasis on the material 'good life' ideal.

The process of children developing an identity is a gradual one, progressing in stages. With respect to taking the perspective of another person, a child at first can only adopt the perspective of a specific person with whom she/he interacts directly, and thus internalises the attitudes of that individual towards him or her as part of their self-concept. Subsequently, the child is able to adopt the perspective of several specific others simultaneously and thus comes to see herself or himself from the viewpoints of, for instance, her or his whole family or group of playmates all at once. Consequently, self-attitudes become more complex and integrated. But Mead speaks of a fully developed identity only when particular attitudes of specific others towards the individual are integrated and generalised, so that they become an internalised *set* of representations, which reflect the attitudes of larger social units, and even society as a whole. This process can also be applied to the link between material symbols and identity. Gradually, young children learn the symbolic meanings of material goods through observing and imaginatively taking part in others' interactions with objects, be it directly or on the mass media. For example, a mother might comment during a children's TV programme that the person who owns this beautiful, large house is very clever and successful. In this way, children are introduced to the idea that material objects provide symbolic information about the characteristics of the owner.

To give an empirical example, we can consider how dolls influence young girls' identity and body image (Dittmar, Halliwell, & Ive, 2006). Dolls like Barbie can serve as an imaginary point of reference for social comparisons, from which young girls can see their own bodily self, where they come to understand the meaning of beauty and perfection through pretending to be their dolls. If dolls signify a socio-cultural ideal of the female body that equates beauty with thinness, such as Barbie, then the thin beauty ideal is gradually internalised through fantasy and play. Thus, the primary meaning of the term 'role model' for Mead is a cultural representation that becomes internalised to form part of the child's emerging identity. This process involves different phases of play, where young children initially imitate, and identify with, 'beautiful' Barbie in a direct, non-reflexive manner, but then – gradually – come to internalise thinness as a salient feature of what it means to be beautiful. Eventually, the internalised thin appearance ideal can become a significant element of their ideal, if not easily actual, identity, and thus a guiding principle for their thoughts, emotions, and behaviours.

This conceptualisation of identity as a social product, accomplished through symbolic communication, is a meta-theoretical framework of identity development. It forms a backdrop throughout this chapter. However, in subsequent sections, specific social psychological models and theories are adapted and integrated in order to understand the social psychological processes which link material goods and individuals' identity, as well as vulnerability factors for negative well-being resulting from the pursuit of particular material and consumer identities.

Identity-Related Functions of Material Goods

When people own material possessions, this can serve various identity functions, such as expressing or enhancing their identity, as well as symbolising relatedness with others. Such identity functions also play a role in motivating people to buy new consumer goods, even though the act of 'buying' is separate from attachments to specific possessions. This review of different identity-related functions of material goods is concerned with motivated identity, as discussed by Gregg et al. (Chapter 14, this volume) and Oyserman and James (Chapter 6, this volume), and presents a framework that has important links

with some core identity motives (reviewed by Vignoles, Chapter 18, this volume).

Model of Identity-Related Functions of Material Goods

Based on extensive research in which diverse respondents provided open-ended accounts of the reasons why their favourite material possessions were important to them (Dittmar, 1992a, 2008), a model of seven main categories emerges, as shown in the left column of Table 31.1. These bottom-up identity functions in the context of material goods show strong connections with most of the identity motives identified by Vignoles (Chapter 18, this volume), shown in the right column of Table 31.1. In recent work, these identity motives have been found to be related to individuals' identification with brands (Kreuzbauer, Vignoles, & Chiu, 2009), as well as to material possessions (Vignoles et al., 2011).

Identity functions have been examined in qualitative research that uses the 'favourite possessions paradigm', where respondents explain in their own words why treasured objects are important to them. Buying motives for new consumer goods have been researched with a number of methodologies, including shopping diaries, interviews, and questionnaires, both in social psychology (Dittmar, 2008) and in consumer research (Banwari, 2006).

Instruments of control and mastery. Individuals give accounts of how their material possessions enable them to do specific activities and enhance their independence, freedom, and autonomy, for instance referring to their laptop computer. This effectiveness function closely resembles the self-efficacy identity motive, where individuals strive to feel competent and capable of influencing their environment. Based on an extensive cross-cultural and developmental interview study with children, adolescents, and adults from America, Israeli kibbutzim, and Israeli cities, Furby (1978) argues that effectance motivation, or the need for mastery, is the main defining characteristic of why possessions are psychologically important. Given that the

Table 31.1 Identity-related functions of material goods and identity motives

Dittmar's identity-related functions	Vignoles' identity motives
Effectiveness Control, independence, autonomy	*Self-efficacy* Feel competent and capable of influencing environment
Emotional regulation Regulate/enhance mood, comfort, security	
Actual identity Individuality/differentiation, symbol of personal qualities, values, goals	*Distinctiveness* Distinguish self from other people *Continuity* Perceive identity as continuous over time
Ideal identity[a] Identity repair, moving closer to ideal self, fantasy self	*Self-esteem* See self in positive light
Personal history Link to past/childhood, symbol of self-continuity	*Continuity* Perceive identity as continuous over time
Symbolic interrelatedness Relationships with specific others, symbolic company *Social identity* Social category, group membership, sub-culture, status	*Belongingness* Be included and accepted within social circles Also esteem, and distinctiveness for social identity
	Meaning Perceive life as ultimately meaningful

[a]This category was added after the 1992 book.

three cultures studied differ on individualism–collectivism (Smith, Chapter 11, this volume) and have different values with respect to possessions, with kibbutzim highly collectivist and non-materialistic in contrast to the individualist culture in US and Israeli cities, Furby interprets her findings as support for a universal effectance motivation, which is reflected in a strong link between individuals' sense of self and their material possessions, regardless of developmental stage or cultural context. The psychological significance of possessions is seen as residing mainly in the control they afford their owner over the physical and social environment, and they are closely linked to identity for precisely that reason. The magnitude of control an individual has over their possessions is of the same order as the control they exert over their body, and it is this powerful control, which leads to possessions becoming a part of people's sense of self. The proposal that material possessions are linked to individuals' identity because they help them exercise control and experience a sense of mastery echoes the effectiveness identity function

and self-efficacy identity motive described in Table 31.1.

Although the implication that the psychological significance of possessions resides primarily in fulfilling control and mastery motives may hold for young children, others functions are likely to become equally, or even more, important for adolescents and adults. The effectiveness, control, or self-efficacy motive is well supported in all of the research using open-ended accounts, not only by Furby and myself, but also by US studies with different age groups (Csikszentmihalyi & Rochberg-Halton, 1981; Kamptner, 1991). In addition, there is experimental evidence for this. A study on self-completion, a process of compensating for aspects of self perceived as inadequate, examined the link between possessions and control motivation through manipulating people's sense of personal control and then collecting their judgements of the extent to which their possessions give them control and mastery (Beggan, 1991). The findings confirmed that those who suffer control deprivation (being told that they had failed on an experimental task) overemphasise the control their possessions give them, compared to those who experience control gain, but this result emerged only for those respondents who believed in general that they have control over their life (internal locus of control).

Thus, material goods clearly play an important role for identity through fulfilling needs for effectiveness, mastery, and self-efficacy (see also literature review by Pierce, Kostova, & Dirks, 2003). Self-determination theory (Ryan & Deci, 2000; Soenens & Vansteenkiste, Chapter 17, this volume) identifies competence and autonomy as intrinsic psychological needs that require fulfilment for people's well-being. It therefore makes sense that material goods can have a beneficial effect for people if they contribute towards a sense of effective identity.

Emotional expression and regulation. Emotion 'work' emerged strongly in both qualitative and quantitative work on identity functions, where individuals use material goods to express, regulate or enhance their mood, find emotional comfort, derive a sense of emotional security, vent their frustration, or escape from unwanted emotional states. This facet of material identity is not reflected in Vignoles' review of identity motives. Although emotional expression or regulation is not necessarily linked to identity, it may have some connection to various of his identity motives: to self-esteem (people strive to feel better about themselves); to belongingness (having a nice car can help to 'fit in' in a wealthy social group), or continuity (people who live in the same house for years may be better adjusted than those who move around a lot). The mood people are in is reflected in their subjective evaluation of consumer goods they own or desire to own, such that they evaluate goods more positively when in a positive rather than negative mood, although this mood-congruent pattern is moderated by personality differences (Ciarrochi & Forgas, 2000).

Significantly, emotional functions of material goods emerge as highly prominent concerns when people buy new consumer goods, both in typologies of buyers (Stone, 1954) and surveys of buying motives. Emotional functions appear as hedonic, compared to utilitarian, benefits from shopping in consumer research (Babin, Darden, & Griffin, 1994), but we found that emotional buying motives form a coherent, internally consistent dimension separate from other types of buying motives, reflecting concerns such as 'I get a real buzz from buying things' or 'I often buy things because it puts me in a better mood' (Dittmar, 2008).

Although emotional regulation is likely to fulfil beneficial functions for identity, particularly the emotional comfort and security provided by treasured personal possessions that symbolise personal history and interrelatedness with others, there are also indications that mood regulation in the context of buying new consumer goods – 'retail therapy' – may have negative consequences. In one study, we asked respondents about potential difficulties with uncontrolled spending, such as finding it easy to spend money without realising, and found that emotional motives were a significant predictor of perceived ease of spending in shops and stores (Dittmar, 2008). This suggests that emotional involvement in buying goods can facilitate overspending. Indeed, as we will see in a later section, escape from negative mood states, such as anxiety or depression, are prominent features of dysfunctional consumer behaviour.

Expressing actual identity. Material goods can symbolise, both to self and others, an individual's unique qualities, values, and personal goals, expressing their personal identity and their differentiation from others. The desire to be differentiated from others, to stand out from the crowd, and to be unique may be particularly strong in Western, individualist cultures, but has been identified as an important general identity motive (Vignoles, Regalia, Manzi, Golledge, & Scabini, 2006). Scabini and Manzi (Chapter 23, this volume) discuss the differentiation motive in the context of identity and family processes. The motive to be distinct from others also finds expression when people buy new consumer goods. We collected open-ended accounts of buying motives in women's shopping diaries. These diaries showed that concerns with expressing identity, such as 'something that fits "me"' or 'just how I want to look', were reported as frequently as non-identity concerns with whether goods are useful or good value for money, and more frequently than mood change (Dittmar, 2001, 2005a). We also demonstrated that the motive to buy 'because it expresses what is unique about me' is commonly endorsed (overall ratings fell above the scale midpoint; Dittmar, 2008). However, this motive differs by type of consumer good, such that mean ratings are significantly higher for clothes, which are high in identity-symbolising potential, than for basic body care items such as shampoo (Dittmar & Bond, 2010).

The close link between material goods and actual identity is also highlighted in a literature review (Pierce et al., 2003), which identifies self-identity as one of three main functions of possessions. Moreover, it appears that material possessions are viewed as a particularly useful source of information about others' identity, and that identity inferences show a degree of accuracy. A US study showed that 84% of observers preferred possessions over other sources of information, and that those who made identity inferences on the basis of possessions were more accurate (in the sense that they agreed more strongly with owners' self-ratings) than observers who had chosen information about behaviours or activities (Burroughs, Drews, & Hallman, 1991). This suggests that the function of material goods to express actual identity is not only strong, but can be successful. However, the relationship between owners' personal qualities and observers' inferences becomes more complex once it is taken into account that there are differences between what individuals want to express through their favourite material goods, and what they think other people will infer about them on the basis of photographs of those goods (Anderson, 2007).

In the consumer and academic marketing research literatures, there is a substantial body of work on self-congruity, which focuses on the match between attributes of consumers and the same attributes applied to products or brands. The closeness of the self-product match is then used as a predictor of different facets of consumer attitudes and behaviours, such as perceived advertising effectiveness (Sirgy, 1982).

The self-congruity effect is explained through a self-consistency motive, according to which individuals are motivated to behave in ways consistent with how they see themselves, their actual identity, which may also be linked to Vignoles' self-continuity motive. Lack of consistency in a person's self-concept is linked to the subjective experience of emotional distress (Gramzow, Sedikides, Panter, & Insko, 2000).

Taken together, this evidence suggests that material goods – both already owned and considered for purchase – serve an important function through helping individuals to express their actual identity. Identity symbolism has a communicative role, in the sense that material goods can be used by people to make inferences about owners, which can be reasonably accurate. Identity expression is linked to the need to maintain self-consistency, and possibly self-continuity, which are beneficial for psychological well-being.

Striving for an ideal identity. Self-congruity research has also studied the fit between ideal identity and product image, again finding that a greater fit (modestly) predicts stronger liking for goods or brands, and stronger purchase motivations, with some indication that effects are stronger for ideal compared to actual identity (Sirgy, 1985). This effect is explained by self-esteem and self-enhancement motives, whereby ideal self-product congruity can help people to reduce discrepancies between their actual and ideal self.

Qualitative research confirms that people use material symbols to bolster or enhance aspects of their identity and, in our survey research on buying motives, ideal identity motives emerged as a coherent, internally consistent, and conceptually distinct set of buying motives, with 'makes me feel more like the person I want to be' as an example item (Dittmar, 2008). A perspective that is conceptually rich and has proved fruitful for my own research is symbolic self-completion theory, which proposes that people make use of material possessions, among other strategies, to compensate for perceived inadequacies in their self-concept (Wicklund & Gollwitzer, 1982). Because of their communicative power, material symbols have identity-creating and identity-enhancing features. Within limits (of gender, age, or social role), people attempt to move closer to their ideal identity by engaging in symbolic self-completion. For instance, business students who had a weak symbolic basis for a business career, in the sense that their qualifications were less good, displayed more relevant material symbols, such as an expensive watch, briefcase, or business suit, compared to students with better career prospects (Braun & Wicklund, 1989). The subjective importance people attach to an identity – its salience – is important, however, because the compensatory relationships between a weak identity and increased use of relevant material symbols holds only for those people who were committed to that particular identity. This implies that people pursue material symbols in order to reduce discrepancies between their actual and ideal self, which raises the question of whether material goods are a beneficial strategy for dealing with identity deficits. This interesting issue is discussed later, in the sections on materialism and dysfunctional consumer behaviour.

In summary, the pursuit of an ideal identity seems a particularly powerful function of material goods, linked to various identity motives. Ideal identity is linked to self-esteem, in the sense that people are motivated to improve their self-image and see themselves in a positive light, similar to the self-enhancement motive highlighted by Gregg et al. (Chapter 14, this volume). Yet, at the same time, ideal identity is also concerned with identity repair, since the motive to move closer to an ideal self implies that aspects of the actual self are perceived as lacking, incomplete, or undesirable.

Personal history, identity maintenance, and self-continuity. Early evidence that possessions help people to maintain a general sense of identity and integrity can be found in Goffman's (1961, 1968) classic analyses of 'self mortification' in prisons and mental hospitals. He offers a vivid account of the identity-maintaining features of personal possessions by outlining how admission procedures where 'inmates' are stripped of all personal belongings take away most of the previous basis of self-identification. Goffman (1968) argues that these procedures not only are

humiliating, but also deprive inmates of their 'identity-kit', which includes clothing, make-up, and other personal possessions, which function as 'embodiments of self'. Investigations concerned with relocations and major life transitions demonstrate that people adjust better if they can take their treasured possessions with them, because they symbolise a person's life experiences, and thus the historical continuity of self. Elderly people coped much better with the trauma of moving into a nursing home (Wapner, Demick, & Redondo, 1990), and emigration to a different country is also easier (Mehta & Belk, 1991).

This research highlights that symbolic aspects of possessions help people to maintain a general sense of identity, integrity, and self-continuity, providing a symbolic record of their personal history. This identity function of possessions is very closely related to the self-continuity motive reviewed by Vignoles (Chapter 18, this volume). Life-span investigations of personal possessions and identity (Csikszentmihalyi & Rochberg-Halton, 1981; Kamptner, 1991) characterise late adulthood as a life stage where this identity function becomes particularly prominent because people are engaged with a retrospective life review process, where reminders of the past and relationships aid in the maintenance and assessment of their lifelong sense of self.

Symbolic interrelatedness. The desire for interpersonal attachments has been described as a fundamental human motivation (Baumeister & Leary, 1995), and the need for interrelatedness with others is identified as an intrinsic motive that has to be fulfilled to achieve well-being (Ryan & Deci, 2000). Material goods emerge as important symbols of personal relationships with others in the 'favourite possessions paradigm' studies, where photos, heirlooms, and gifts are prominent examples of symbolic interrelatedness, symbolising close relationships with friends and family (Dittmar, 1992a).

Material goods can also be used to communicate and negotiate identities within relationships. For instance, giving gifts often involves more than constituting a token of love: it can be likened to the imposition of an identity, in the sense that it is one of the ways in which we announce and transmit the image we have of somebody, and the receiver's acceptance of the gift entails an acceptance of the giver's ideas about her or his identity. Imagine the difference between giving a woman a black, tailored cocktail dress versus a flowery, cotton dress with puffed sleeves.

Clearly, material goods can play an important beneficial role in symbolising and strengthening close personal relationships, a function that is closely related to Vignoles' belonging motive. When material possessions provide a psychological sense of actual interrelatedness, then this is likely to be beneficial for well-being. However, people sometimes pursue material goods in order to compensate for unsatisfactory, damaged relationships, which can be detrimental for their well-being.

Symbols of status, wealth, and group membership. Moving on to material goods as categorical symbols and as signs of social identities, clothes are perhaps the most obvious example of our possessions through which we can signify group affiliations and social standing, including sex-role identification, political orientation, or socio-economic status (Solomon, 1985). Material goods can also serve to signify membership in smaller sub-cultures, such as punks (Hebdige, 1979).

Inspired by Veblen's (1899) seminal essay on wasteful conspicuous consumption, more systematically researched material expressions of a person's standing are status symbols, investigated mainly by sociologists (Goffman, 1951). Status symbols change over time. Objects cease to serve as status symbols once they become shared too widely to denote exclusiveness. There are both 'trickle-down' and 'trickle-up' effects, where aspiring low status groups imitate and adopt the status symbols of those groups slightly more affluent than they are, until higher status groups discard these markers and, in turn, adopt new ones to differentiate themselves. Yet, it is important to recognise the power of an advertising-driven mass fashion which simultaneously informs, influences, and is adopted by social groups at many levels of the social–material hierarchy (Sproles, 1985).

Work on brand loyalty emphasises the significance of social brand community, that is, an actual group where members have contact with each other, as well as psychological brand community, which suggests a sense of identification with an anonymous collection of individuals because they share the same brand preference (Carlson, Suter, & Brown, 2008). In other words, people can identify with other brand admirers as a virtual group in the absence of any social interaction: 'I'm an Armani man, myself.' However, people also actively choose goods in order to be different from members of other social groups, selecting cultural tastes including material possessions, which distinguish them from other groups and abandoning tastes when other social groups adopt them, in order both to communicate identity and to avoid others making undesired identity inferences (Berger & Heath, 2007).

Stereotypes of different social groups are typically examined through personal qualities ascribed to in-group and out-group members, but stereotypes of different groups exist also in terms of material possession profiles. I (Dittmar, 1994) asked respondents from three different socio-economic groups – business employees, students, and unemployed – to list objects they thought of as favourite possessions, both for themselves and for members of the other two groups. Two findings emerged that are typical features of stereotyping: out-group homogeneity and between-group differentiation. Members of other groups are perceived as being more similar to each other than they really are, in that possessions listed for other groups were less diverse than those for one's own group. Differences between groups are perceived as greater than they actually are, given that goods related to the socio-economic differences between groups in terms of (relative) wealth and status were overemphasised.

If people use material possession profiles to locate individuals in socio-economic terms and if they hold stereotypes associated with those profiles, it follows that first impressions of the very same person should differ, depending on whether that person is surrounded with material objects that denote a relatively higher, compared to lower, level of wealth. This was examined in an experimental study (Dittmar, 1992b), where respondents from middle-class or working-class backgrounds watched a short video that depicted a young person, whose profile of material possessions denoted either relative affluence (e.g. an expensive designer pine kitchen, state-of-the-art music equipment, high status car) or a lack of affluence (e.g. basic kitchen and hi-fi equipment, small car). As expected, the middle-class respondents described the affluent video as more similar to their family background, whereas the working-class respondents saw the less affluent video as more similar. This material similarity between video character and observer is important, because social identity theory (Brown & Hewstone, 2005; Spears, Chapter 9, this volume) proposes that people should form more positive impressions of in-group members, in this case the video character with a similar material background. In contrast, wealth stereotypes profiled in consumer culture may be so pervasive that they are shared across different SES groups, so that impressions would differ only on the basis of the video character's material possessions profile. The findings supported the second hypothesis. The same person, when portrayed with affluent material goods rather than inexpensive possessions, was perceived by both groups as significantly more intelligent, more assertive, and more in control – all of which are highly valued culturally in Western societies. Yet, she/he was also seen as less warm and expressive. Thus, the wealth stereotype combines less interpersonal warmth with a set of attributes that are overwhelmingly positive and important for success. These findings have been replicated since (Christopher & Schlenker, 2000; Dittmar & Pepper, 1994).

Thus, material goods symbolise membership of, or sense of belonging to, diverse social groups, such as social categories, smaller groups, and even virtual groups whose members do not interact directly. They also signify social status and wealth, with associated beliefs about owners' personal qualities. This identity function resonates with several of the identity motives reviewed by Vignoles (Chapter 18, this volume): belongingness, distinctiveness, and esteem.

Identity Variations: Life-span, Culture, Socio-economic Status, and Gender

The evidence to support the existence and importance of the seven identity functions of material goods outlined in Table 31.1 is strong, drawn from my own research as well as from different literatures in psychology, sociology, consumer, marketing, and advertising research. Their relative importance to a person is influenced by a number of factors, such as stage in the life-span, culture, socio-economic status, and gender.

Life-span. Changes from infancy to old age have been documented consistently, where concerns with control, mastery, and independence are gradually overtaken by a focus on the symbolic functions of goods, first with respect to one's own identity, and then increasingly with respect to close personal relationships with others, such as friends and family. This trajectory of change has been interpreted as reflecting different life stages, or tasks, of identity development, that are thought to apply universally. However, the relevant evidence was collected typically in individualist, Western cultures, and thus it may not reflect universal stages. Indeed, recent findings provide support for the symbolic interactionist framework adopted in this chapter, which suggests that different orientations towards material goods can occur at every stage of identity development, depending on social context.

Infants often establish a special relationship with just one or two material possessions, usually a 'cuddly' toy or 'transitional' object (Winnicott, 1953), which has been argued to play a significant role in the child's development from total dependency towards autonomy by giving emotional comfort and – as the first 'not me' possession – helping the child to draw a boundary between self and the external world. Yet, cross-cultural research shows socialisation influences rather than cuddlies constituting a necessary, and therefore universal, step in infants' successful individuation and construction of identity. Whereas most children in developed Western countries have a cuddly, children in developing countries typically have almost continuous body contact with their nurturer, but no cuddly (Gulerce, 1991).

Studies of different age groups and generations (Csikszentmihalyi & Rochberg-Halton, 1981; Kamptner, 1991) found that children treasured possessions predominantly in terms of the active functions they fulfil for them in establishing independence and autonomy, whereas the oldest generation was concerned with the symbolic record that photographs and memorabilia provided of their lives and relationships with their loved ones. In between, adolescents were concerned with peer-group ties associated with their favourite objects and the aspects of identity they expressed. Young adults also talked about the interpersonal ties their cars, jewellery, photographs, and general memorabilia symbolised. In middle adulthood, photographs and jewellery take increasingly prominent places as favoured objects, with a growing emphasis on the social and family networks they signify, and the emotions and memories associated with them. To explain these changes, Kamptner (1991) draws on Erikson's (1980) model of identity development, according to which the central identity tasks at different life stages are as follows: build a sense of competence, mastery, and independence in childhood; develop an autonomous identity in adolescence; find intimate relationships in young adulthood; establish social links with different generations in middle adulthood; and engage in a retrospective life review process in late adulthood.

Thus, life-span changes are reflected in a gradual shift of emphasis, initially from effectiveness to self-expressive and then, finally, to the social-symbolic functions of material goods, depending on the main identity tasks people are engaged in. However, this life-span approach should not be taken to imply that there is a universal pattern for the links between identity and material possessions. As with the meanings of cuddlies in early childhood, there is evidence that culture influences these links.

Culture. As discussed by Smith (Chapter 11, this volume), a growing literature in social psychology documents that identity construction differs across cultures. Individualist cultures, such as the United States or the United Kingdom, tend to privilege an independent form of self-construal, such that identity is separate from others and defined by personal goals, whereas collectivist cultures emphasise interdependent self-construal, such that identity is defined through connectedness with others and the importance of group goals (Markus & Kitayama, 1991). A study comparing favourite possessions and their meaning among US residents with those in a traditional, tribal community in Niger (Wallendorf & Arnould, 1988) found not only that the objects named were radically different, but also that the reasons why they were treasured focused predominantly on symbolising personal history in the United States, in contrast to symbolising status within the community and commitment to shared values in Niger. Although this study was not designed to assess identity construction directly, its findings are consistent with the proposal that material possessions are likely to symbolise personal identity in an individualist culture, and social identity in a collectivist society.

We (Bond, Dittmar, Singelis, Papadopoulou, & Chiu, 2002) examined the hypothesis that identity functions of material possessions would reflect culturally prevalent modes of identity construction in a cross-cultural comparison of respondents from the United States, the United Kingdom, and Hong Kong. The findings support the hypothesis that there is some match between cultural-level individualism (higher in the United States and the United Kingdom than in Hong Kong) and the identity functions of emotional regulation and actual (unique) identity expression: emotional regulation was rated as more important in the United States and the United Kingdom than in Hong Kong, and possessions were valued as symbols of a unique identity most strongly in the United States, followed by the United Kingdom, and least strongly in Hong Kong. Thus, there are systematic differences between cultures so that identity functions that reflect culturally privileged forms of self-construal are perceived as more important. Yet, self-construal differences exist not only between, but also within, cultures.

Socio-economic status. Socio-economic status (SES) is a further influence on the relative emphasis that individuals place on different identity functions of their material goods. High SES, middle-class business managers are more concerned with their utility, leisure, and sentimental possessions as unique symbols of their personal history and development, whereas low SES, working-class unemployed individuals focus more on the functional, active, and emotional uses of their leisure and utility objects, such as 'switching off' or 'escaping' (Dittmar, 1991). This reflects a highly individualised, long-term perspective on self-development in those of a high social–material position, in contrast to a short-term, functional perspective more likely to be adopted by individuals from a low social–material position, arising at least in part from a constantly enforced concern with economic and emotional security. A US study also showed that high and low SES individuals engage differently with symbolic and material culture, reflecting different notions of identity (Snibbe & Markus, 2005). High SES participants and their preferred cultural products (such as music CDs) emphasise the expression of uniqueness, control, and power, whereas less educated, low SES respondents and their preferred products emphasise maintaining integrity and adjusting selves.

Gender. The 'favourite possessions' studies reviewed earlier, as well as my own research (Dittmar, 1989), confirm that women and men tend to differ in the importance they attach to different identity functions. Compared to women, men refer more strongly to control and effectiveness functions, whereas women concentrate more on the role of goods as symbols of interpersonal relationships and their emotional significance. These gender differences can be understood as reflecting the ways in which women and men typically construct their identity. Men tend towards a more *in*dependent form of identity construction (separateness from others, being able to do things) in contrast to women's more *inter*dependent identity (embeddedness in close personal relationships). Of course, women and men can, and do, use both independent and interdependent forms of identity construction, but gender differences have been demonstrated consistently in their typical preferences (Cross & Madson, 1997). These are reflected in the identity-related functions that women and men value most in the material possessions they already own, but also in buying motives for new consumer goods. In particular, gender differences emerge with respect to emotional regulation, where the importance of buying goods in order to cheer oneself up and feel happier is significantly greater for women than for men (Dittmar, 2008).

This section has documented the diverse identity functions that material goods fulfil for individuals. These functions can change throughout the life course, but rather than reflecting universally applicable stages of individual development, variations occur and can be analysed as reflections of privileged modes of identity construction in the social context, as suggested by a Meadian perspective, whether this be culture, SES, or gender. It also suggested that material goods, particularly treasured possessions, often play a positive role for individuals, thus contributing to their well-being because they can help fulfil identity needs seen as intrinsic from the self-determination perspective, discussed by Soenens and Vansteenkiste (Chapter 17, this volume). Material goods can increase individuals' effectiveness and autonomy, aid identity expression, maintenance and continuity, or, as symbolic markers of interrelatedness, increase their sense of affiliation and connectedness with others. However, there is a dark side to the close link between material goods and identity.

Maladaptive Pursuits of Material and Consumer Identities

The pursuit of materialistic values – money, fame, material goods – is highly profiled in consumer culture as a pathway to a happy, satisfied life and has been seen as central to the success of modern economies. Yet, there is growing concern and evidence that an orientation to the *material good life* undermines psychological well-being. Drawing on several influential social psychological theories, I have developed a model that aims to identify who is most vulnerable to negative effects from pursuing material goods, wealth, and the *material good life* ideal, and to outline the identity processes through which these pursuits come to impact individuals' well-being (Dittmar, 2008). A brief summary is given below in four points.

First, comparisons with images prevalent in the media and consumer culture can make people feel bad about themselves. The core of Social Comparison Theory is that people have a need to evaluate themselves through comparing themselves to others (Festinger, 1954), and consumers are affected because they cannot help but compare themselves with idealised media images, implicitly and explicitly (Richins, 1991). Given that the great majority of individuals fall far short of the *material good life* typically portrayed, social comparisons with media models lead many people to negative self-evaluation and discontent. However, in order for this negative effect to occur, individuals need to attach psychological importance to the central qualities of these media images, such as an affluent lifestyle and expensive goods.

Second, this psychological importance depends on individuals' underlying value system. From a self-determination perspective, an orientation that emphasises money, material goods, fame, and image is based on extrinsic life goals, guided by external influences, such as approval by others, rewards, or coercion, as opposed to intrinsic goals, such as relationships, community involvement, or self-development (Soenens & Vansteenkiste, Chapter 17, this volume). The *material good life* ideal can be internalised by individuals, so that it forms a personal system of values or goals, which guides how individuals construe themselves, the ideals they pursue, and the motivations that drive their behaviour. Depending on the extent to which they internalise a materialistic value orientation, some individuals, or groups of people, are more

vulnerable to detrimental consumer culture effects than others.

Third, and most central, are psychological processes related to identity. Self-Discrepancy Theory (Higgins, 1987) postulates negative psychological consequences when individuals experience discrepancies, or gaps, between how they see themselves (actual identity) and how they would ideally like to be (ideal identity). Thus, comparisons with idealised models can lead to salient actual-ideal identity deficits, particularly when individuals already endorse material ideals as a personal goal. In this way, consumer culture highlights identity deficits, and can also contribute to their development in the first place. Yet, it also offers a supposed remedy: consumers need only buy the promoted products to get closer to their ideal identity, and experience more positive emotions. Whether they are aware of it or not, people engage in identity and mood repair through consumption by acquiring relevant material symbols, as suggested by Symbolic Self-Completion Theory (Wicklund & Gollwitzer, 1982). For instance, people might buy a 'glamorous' outfit in order to feel more glamorous and self-confident. Although this may work for some people, at least in the short term, it is unlikely to provide a long-term solution for those who have chronic identity deficits.

Fourth, putting the previous three points together, the central thesis of the model emerges. Material culture encourages value internalisation and construction of a negative identity in vulnerable people, so that they feel far away from their ideal, and bad about this gap. At the same time, it offers supposed, but illusory, solutions for managing and repairing identity deficits and negative emotions through consumption. The particular motivations for buying material goods emphasised by the *material good life* ideal focus on identity repair and mood management, captured in the material culture slogans of 'retail therapy' and 'I shop, therefore I am' (Dittmar, 2008). And identity repair and mood management are precisely the identity functions that are detrimental to well-being.

The Pursuit of the 'Material Good Life' and Subjective Well-being

There is a substantial body of research that examines links between a materialistic value orientation and individuals' well-being (for reviews, see Dittmar, 2008; Kasser & Kanner, 2004). The review provided here is selective, focusing on the role of identity processes in the materialism–well-being link. Materialism is concerned with people's *desire* for material goods and wealth, not with people's actual wealth. It can be defined as the importance that people ascribe to the ownership and acquisition of material goods in achieving their life goals, and associated beliefs about the identity-related benefits that material goods will bring, such as status, positive identity, or happiness (Dittmar, 2008; Kasser & Kanner, 2004; Richins, 2004). The most prominent explanation for why materialism may be linked to lower well-being comes from the self-determination perspective (Kasser & Ryan, 1996; Soenens & Vansteenkiste, Chapter 17, this volume), proposing that such an extrinsic goal orientation is unlikely to lead to, or may even undermine, the fulfilment of essential psychological needs for relationships, autonomy, and competence. In short, the pursuit of material goods and wealth takes time and energy away from intrinsic goals, and therefore leads to lower well-being.

Contrary to the pervasive belief that more money and material goods will improve our lives considerably, profiled so strongly in the media and consumer culture, the evidence demonstrates that those with a strong materialistic value orientation have lower life satisfaction, are less happy, suffer from more psychological and physical problems, and experience lower subjective well-being. Subjective well-being includes long-term satisfaction with one's life as a cognitive component, and the presence of positive emotions combined with an absence of negative emotions as an affective component. Correlational studies consistently report a negative association between a materialistic value orientation and well-being, not only in the United States where the majority of research has been conducted (e.g. Kasser & Ryan, 1993, 1996; Richins & Dawson, 1992; Sirgy, 1998), but also in other countries, including Europe, the Far East, the former Soviet bloc, and – recently – developing countries (Dittmar & Kapur, in press; Garðarsdóttir, Dittmar, & Aspinall, 2009; Jankovic & Dittmar, 2006; Kasser & Ahuvia, 2002; Ryan et al., 1999). Perhaps the most persuasive piece of evidence linking materialism to lower well-being is a cross-temporal meta-analysis of psychopathology among young Americans from 1938 to 2007, showing that there are strong generational increases in psychopathology and that this increase fits best with a cultural shift model towards increasing extrinsic goals (Twenge et al., 2010).

Notwithstanding the consistency of a negative link between materialism and well-being, the strength of association is typically small, or moderate at best. An explanation can be found in the recent goals–motives debate, suggesting that this negative link may only hold with respect to particular motives for wanting money and possessions (Garðarsdóttir et al., 2009; Srivastava, Locke, & Bartol, 2001). People may pursue affluence and material goods for many diverse reasons, and the motive to secure a pleasant home environment for one's family may well have a different link to well-being, compared to the motive to feel superior to the neighbours by displaying higher status goods.

Srivastava et al. (2001) examined 10 different motives for holding materialistic values classified into three types. *Freedom of action* motives, such as spending time and resources pursuing leisure activities, had no effect on subjective well-being, and *positive* motives were labelled as such because they showed a (mild) positive relationship with SWB, including supporting a family, feeling proud of oneself, and getting just compensation for one's efforts. *Negative* motives were found to be linked to lower well-being, with the central motives focused on overcoming self-doubt and status seeking, such as proving that one is not a failure or dumb, and having a house and cars that are better than those of the neighbours. Consistent with previous research, Srivastava et al. (2001) reported a significant negative link between materialism and SWB, but found that this link was reduced to non-significance once underlying motives were taken into account. However, from a self-determination perspective, research challenges this conclusion by demonstrating that it is both the money (goal content) and the motives behind the goals that affect subjective well-being independently (Sheldon, Ryan, Deci, & Kasser, 2004). These authors argue that negative motives (operationalised as externally controlled rather than autonomously motivated) and extrinsic goal content, such as the pursuit of money, share significant features and are therefore both important when it comes to predicting SWB, so that the link with SWB is not reducible to one or the other predictor.

We conducted a follow-up study with students and employees in the public and private sector (Garðarsdóttir et al., 2009). The two motives that are of central interest for this chapter are the motive for a happier self, where people want affluence in order to improve positive emotions and lead a happier life, and the motive for a better identity, where people want money to deal with identity deficits and seek better status. As expected, we found small, but significant negative associations between materialism and SWB. When we took motives into account, both the motives for a happier self and a better identity were significant, and stronger, negative predictors of SWB. At the same time, the previously significant association between materialism and SWB disappeared. Thus, our conclusion concurs with Srivastava et al. (2001): The pursuit of money and expensive goods is not necessarily linked to lower well-being. Instead, specific identity motives which influence such a pursuit for money and goods seem toxic: the motive for greater happiness and the motive for a more ideal identity.

The 'Bricks' and 'Clicks' of Dysfunctional Consumer Behaviour

Compulsive buying, often called shopping addiction in the media, is a dysfunctional consumer behaviour that has serious negative consequences

for individuals: debt, distress, and impairment. This dysfunctional behaviour can come to dominate individuals' lives to such an extent that it has to be considered a clinical disorder, listed in the DSM-TR-IV (American Psychiatric Association, 2000). Although there is no agreed upon specific definition, broad consensus exists on three core features: the urge to buy is experienced as irresistible, individuals lose control over their buying behaviour, and they continue with excessive buying despite adverse consequences in their personal, social, or occupational lives, as well as financial debt (Dittmar, 2004b; Faber & O'Guinn, 2008).

Moreover, the problem is growing (Neuner, Raab, & Reisch, 2005). As many as half a million people in the United Kingdom, one million in Germany, and 15 million in the United States may be affected by compulsive buying (Dittmar, 2004b; Koran, Faber, Boujaoude, Large, & Serpe, 2006), and many more are likely to suffer from sub-clinical dysfunctional consumer behaviour: a tendency towards compulsive buying, which can be measured with clinically validated screener questionnaires. Several comprehensive overviews of the compulsive buying literature are available (Benson, 2000; Benson, Dittmar, & Wolfsohn, 2010; Dittmar, 2004b; Faber & O'Guinn, 2008). Compulsive buying is multi-determined, and the aim here is to provide a selective review with respect to identity functions and motives linked to material goods. This summary from an interview with a recovering compulsive shopper illustrates not only the agreed on core characteristics (printed in italics), but also the two identity motives of central interest: emotional regulation and striving for an ideal identity (printed in bold):

For Nancy, 35 years old, there is only impulse buying. If she sees something in a shop she likes, she *must have it*. She *can't stop* herself. It is always clothes and jewellery, smart clothes mainly, **a size 12 which she desires to be**... It does **lift her up** for a few hours... It is *all her fault*, she thinks. She *feels guilty*. She has ridden the family into *debt*. She says that she *cannot tell her husband*, because he would walk out on her.... her repayments will add up to about £15,000 ($22,500). (Dittmar, 2004b, p. 412 emphases added)

Nancy refers to emotional regulation ('lifts her up'), which is also prominently discussed in the clinical literature, where compulsive buying has been described as relieving anxiety and 'self-medication' for depression (Black, 2006; Lejoyeux, Adés, Tassian, & Solomon, 1996). She also illustrates that compulsive buyers typically seek to move closer to their ideal identity through buying identity-relevant consumer goods, in her case an attractive, slim body ideal through size 12 clothes. This is consistent with clinical reports that compulsive buyers are highly selective in their purchases – for women it is usually clothes, appearance-related goods, and accessories (Dittmar, 2004b, 2008).

We have carried out diary, interview, survey, and experimental studies with UK respondents in which we assessed compulsive buying tendencies (Dittmar, 2001, 2005a, 2005b, 2008; Dittmar & Bond, 2010). The scale employed (d'Astous, Maltais, & Roberge, 1990) cannot be used for clinical diagnosis, but it does have a cut-off point, which identifies individuals whose score indicates dysfunctional buying attitudes and behaviours, even though these may be subclinical. Our figures from several UK surveys are therefore higher than clinical prevalence estimates of around 5% (Koran et al., 2006), but we are concerned with identifying the prevalence of consumer behaviour that implies a degree of negative well-being that is sufficient to give cause for concern and indicates a need for intervention. Among an adult sample that excluded respondents who either had been in contact with a self-help organisation or responded to appeals concerning shopping problems, 13% scored above the cut-off point. For students, it was 20%, rising to 28% among consumer research panellists for a multinational corporation, who are likely to be particularly strongly involved with consumer culture. Among 16–18-year-old adolescents, 44% scored beyond the dysfunctional cut-off point. Although this should be interpreted with caution, given that adolescence is a developmental stage marked by extreme behaviours in various consumption domains (e.g. drinking alcohol), it does indicate that potentially problematic shopping and spending habits are widespread among adolescents.

Given our proposal that identity-related functions of material goods are important predictors of dysfunctional consumer behaviour, we examined the role played by endorsement of a materialistic value orientation. Research on over 200,000 US students suggests that today's young adults are more materialistic in orientation than ever: the proportion who report that it is *very important or essential* that they become *very well off financially* increased dramatically between the 1970s and the present from about a third to over three quarters of respondents (Pryor, Hurtado, Saenz, Santos, & Korn, 2007). Thus, age needs to be examined as well as materialism, given that compulsive buying tendencies are negatively correlated with age. They may also be stronger in women. Therefore, I examined age, gender, and materialistic value orientation as predictors of compulsive buying tendency (Dittmar, 2005b), controlling for income and education. In a hierarchical multiple regression, gender and age were examined first, showing mildly greater dysfunctional buying for women, and for younger respondents. Yet, when added as a predictor, materialistic values not only proved a powerful predictor of increasingly stronger compulsive buying tendencies, but it also reduced age differences. Indeed, younger people held significantly stronger materialistic values, which are associated with stronger dysfunctional buying behaviour. These findings are important because they demonstrate that younger people's stronger compulsive buying tendencies are due, at least in part, to their greater endorsement of materialistic values.

The importance of demonstrating that materialistic values are a powerful risk factor for dysfunctional consumer behaviour lies in the proposal that identity-related processes are likely to take maladaptive forms when they are associated with materialism. Similar to Symbolic Self-Completion Theory (Wicklund & Gollwitzer, 1982), I propose that gaps or discrepancies in a person's self-concept produce a motivation to self-complete through reducing gaps and discrepancies. Given that a materialistic value orientation entails the belief that material goods are an ideal route to achieve a more ideal identity, we propose that the psychological salience of a person's identity deficits should predict their compulsive buying tendency if they also endorse a materialistic value orientation. We developed our own measure of identity deficits, which draws on Self-Discrepancy Theory (Higgins, 1987), but is different from Higgins' Selves Questionnaire. Rather than asking respondents separately about their actual and ideal self, we developed the Self-Discrepancy Index (SDI), in which respondents are asked directly about their identity deficits, and the psychological salience of these deficits. In the first, qualitative, part, respondents complete a number of sentences, usually five, of the format 'I. . ., but I would like. . .', and then, in the second, quantitative part, they rate each self-discrepancy they generate in terms of its magnitude (size of discrepancy) and psychological importance (concern or worry about the discrepancy). The SDI can be used as a global measure (calculated by summing the products of the magnitude and importance ratings of each self-discrepancy and then dividing by the number of statements, following Dittmar, Beattie, & Friese, 1996), or as a measure of self-discrepancies in a specific identity domain (calculated by summing the products of the magnitude and importance ratings of each relevant self-discrepancy), such as appearance (Dittmar, Halliwell, & Stirling, 2009; Halliwell & Dittmar, 2006).

We have good evidence that materialistic values lead to dysfunctional buying behaviour when they are accompanied by identity deficits (Dittmar, 2001, 2004a, 2005a). For the purpose of illustration, I selected 40 women from one sample of almost 300 (Dittmar, 2004b), in order to create four groups of ten women each, with two groups non-materialistic and the other two with a strong materialistic value orientation. Within the non-materialistic and materialistic women, half were selected because they feel quite close to how they would like to be (low SDI), and the other half because they were highest in identity deficits (high SDI). Our two-factor model predicts that only women who are *both* materialistic *and* high in identity deficits should have strong

compulsive buying tendencies, while the other three groups should not. This is, indeed, the case. Compared to the mean score of these three groups of women (17.6, 25.6, and 30.9), the ten women in this quadrant had a mean score (56.5) that falls beyond the scale's cut-off point for dysfunctional buying (43). In fact, every single one of these ten women scored higher than the cut-off point. In contrast, for men, we found that materialistic value orientation was a strong predictor of compulsive buying tendency, but not of identity deficits (Dittmar, 2005a). This may be due to women's identities still being more closely bound up with shopping than men's, or to the fact that the scale used to measure dysfunctional buying focuses predominantly on high street shopping. Our two-factor model may be supported if we examine dysfunctional consumer behaviour that is more prevalent among men, such as pathological collecting of expensive goods, or addiction to bidding in auctions.

Finally, let us consider a direct examination of emotional regulation and ideal identity seeking as buying motives, which we propose as intervening processes in the association between materialism and compulsive buying tendency. Compulsive buying does not only take place in the 'bricks' of conventional shops and stores, but also in the 'clicks' of online buying: the Internet is fast becoming a serious alternative to conventional buying (Dittmar, 2008), and the Internet may even be more conducive to excessive buying, because 'clicking' does not feel like spending 'real' money (Dittmar, Long, & Meek, 2004), with limitless access 24 hours a day. In a survey of young online buyers (Dittmar, Long, & Bond, 2007), we hypothesised that a materialistic value orientation should manifest itself in emotional and ideal identity buying motives. The more individuals believe that the acquisition of material goods will bring them happiness – improved emotions and mood – the more they should be motivated to buy goods in order to obtain these emotional benefits. The same should hold for beliefs that material goods bring them social status and a more ideal identity: the more individuals endorse such materialistic beliefs, the more they should seek social and personal identity gains when they buy goods. The proposed model thus conceptualises internalisation of materialistic values as a more distal, or general, predictor of compulsive buying tendency, exerting its impact through the more proximal, or direct, predictors of emotional and ideal identity buying motives. Controlling for general Internet use, we found, as expected, that materialistic value orientation positively and strongly predicts compulsive buying tendency online, thus replicating our findings for conventional buying. Yet, when emotional and ideal identity buying motives are added as mediators, the direct link between materialism and compulsive buying tendency online drops to near zero. Given that individuals' internalisation of materialistic values strongly predicts both the emotion-regulation motive and the identity gain motive, and that these two motives, in turn, significantly predict compulsive buying tendency online, we can see that the link of materialism to compulsive buying is fully accounted for by these buying motives. Moreover, the explanatory power of the model is substantially increased through the inclusion of these two identity motives from 29 to 56% of the variance in compulsive online buying tendencies.

When considering these findings, one should bear in mind that compulsive buying is multi-determined. However, we can nevertheless conclude that the same two identity motives identified as leading to lower subjective well-being when pursuing the *material good life* also play a significant role in predicting dysfunctional buying. These findings are consistent with the proposal that these identity motives are unrealistic when they are pursued through material goods. A judgement that some motives are more unrealistic than others is not an easy one to make, and the view presented here should be understood mainly as an aid in interpreting the effects of the motives. These motives have negative associations with well-being, because it seems unlikely that people can find fulfilment through obtaining wealth or material goods. Research shows that greater actual wealth has surprisingly little impact on individuals' happiness and well-being

beyond the fulfilment of such basic needs as adequate nutrition and reasonable housing (Diener & Biswas-Diener, 2002), and that it may even be detrimental (Eaton & Eswaran, 2009). It is also unlikely that material goods would solve underlying self-doubts and identity deficits. Positive emotions, happiness, and a positive identity are more likely to be achieved by pursuing goals other than financial success, and engaging in activities other than buying consumer goods. Supportive interpersonal relationships and a meaningful life (e.g. job satisfaction, spirituality, community involvement) are particularly strong predictors of well-being (Diener & Seligman, 2005).

Conclusions and Implications for Intervention

The evidence is persuasive that material goods are perceived as parts of the extended self, so that there is not an absolute dividing line between an extended identity and a core identity; rather material goods emerge as constituent parts of a person's identity. Material goods, both treasured possessions already owned and new consumer goods, fulfil diverse identity functions for individuals, whose relative importance reflects privileged modes of identity construction in the social context a person finds themselves in. This pattern of findings supports the Meadian framework on how material goods are incorporated into identity outlined near the start of this chapter. The analysis of identity functions demonstrated that material goods can have positive effects for people's identity and well-being, particularly in aiding effectiveness, control and autonomy, maintenance and continuity of identity over time, and providing a sense of interrelatedness with others. These are related to the three intrinsic needs identified by Self-Determination Theory: competence, autonomy, and relatedness. This has implications for practitioners helping people to maintain and stabilise their identity during periods of change and crisis, such as immigration to a new country, moving into an institution (e.g. nursing home, hospital), or the challenging transition from adolescence to adulthood.

However, in the analysis of identity functions and buying motives, there were already indications of a possible 'dark side' of certain identity motives, namely, emotional regulation and identity repair to move closer to one's ideal. These motives are interrelated: individuals do not only want to feel better, they also want to feel better about themselves. However, material goods are unlikely to deliver these hoped-for benefits when people seek long-term solutions to identity deficits, insecurity, and unhappiness. Often, goods provide nothing more than a momentary high, where people fantasise about who they would like to be, and where browsing through goods and purchasing seems to offer an avenue for moving closer to that ideal person, which then quickly turns into a dead end. These maladaptive pursuits of material and consumer identities have to be taken very seriously, given the wide and increasing spread of a materialistic value orientation and sub-clinical levels of dysfunctional buying behaviour.

The pursuit of wealth and material goods is not necessarily damaging to individuals' well-being. Rather it is a more specific type of materialistic value orientation that is problematic, namely, the emotional regulation and ideal identity motives for desiring affluence and goods which are linked to lower subjective well-being. These kinds of motives may already play a role in children's internalisation of materialistic values: we (Banerjee & Dittmar, 2008) found that 8–11-year olds endorse materialistic values because they believe that, in order to be 'cool' and popular among their peers, they have to have the right material goods. We are currently extending this work to examine links with children's well-being (Dittmar & Banerjee, 2011).

Compulsive buying is clearly a detrimental consumer behaviour, psychologically and financially, which appears to be on the increase, at least as far as sub-clinical dysfunctional buying is concerned. It is more prominent in younger people, and adolescents may be at particular risk of engaging in uncontrolled buying and spending. The central risk factors identified across a series of studies are individuals' materialistic value orientation, as well as identity deficits, and buying motives that focus on seeking identity and enhancing mood. Given the exponential growth of online buying, and the increasing sophistication of retail sites in mimicking visual and experiential aspects of conventional shopping, virtual compulsive buying could represent a future trend that increasingly affects young consumers.

The research presented in this chapter provides convergent evidence that pursuing material goods in order to fulfil emotion regulation and ideal identity motives is detrimental to the well-being of adults, adolescents, and most likely children, too, suggesting the need for intervention. Given that these motives are likely to be promoted and reinforced by media and advertising messages that stress the 'material good life' as a road to ideal identity and happiness, one possibility could be to change advertising policies (see, for example, the anti-consumerist Canadian magazine *Adbusters* at www.adbusters.org), although this seems unlikely to be instituted any time soon. With respect to compulsive buying tendencies, curbing credit opportunities that are likely to over-indebt consumers could be beneficial, and changes to lender practices are under discussion in the United Kingdom (Elliott, 2005).

At the level of the individual, information and advice could help people to develop a more critical stance towards the unrealistic nature of the materialistic ideal, which proclaims that consumer goods offer viable means of solving emotional and identity-related problems. Clinical, consumer advice, and educational practitioners may wish to guide individuals towards critical reflection on materialistic values, both in terms of their personal value system and media literacy aimed at critical reflection on advertising messages that emphasise unrealistic psychological benefits from buying new consumer goods. It should be acknowledged, however, that attempts to curb a materialistic value orientation are probably a difficult route, because they run counter to the prevailing economic and consumer climate geared towards increasing consumption. For this reason, critical reflection on a materialistic value orientation may stand the best chance of providing a basis for prevention and consumer education when it is encouraged early, such as pre-adolescents being advised in their school curricula about unrealistic expectations of material goods, and about why and how to avoid uncontrolled spending and buying. Given that children as young as 8 years old already believe that having 'cool things' will help them get accepted by their peers, it would seem important to target individuals as young as possible, preferably in both school and home environments.

Thus, in conclusion, this chapter highlights that identity functions and identity processes hold the key to understanding important consumer phenomena, which increasingly dominate our everyday lives. One the one hand, material goods can, and do, play a powerful positive role in identity development, maintenance, and transition through fulfilling diverse identity functions conducive to psychological need fulfilment. On the other hand, two particular motives for desiring money and expensive possessions – emotion regulation and identity repair – are toxic for well-being, jeopardising personal well-being and facilitating overspending and overshopping. Indeed, in order to understand the impact of consumer culture on children's, adolescents', and adults' identities and well-being, we need to understand the role of identity-related processes centred on mood and identity repair.

References

American Psychiatric Association. (2000). *Diagnostic and statistical manual for mental disorders, 4th ed., Text Revision (DSM-IV-TR)*. Washington, DC: Author.

Anderson, N. (2007). *Shopping for identity: The symbolic role of consumer goods in fulfilling individuals' identity needs*. D.Phil thesis, University of Sussex.

Arnould, E. J., & Thompson, C. J. (2005). Consumer culture theory (CCT): Twenty years of research. *Journal of Consumer Research, 31*, 868–882.

Babin, B. J., Darden, W. R., & Griffin, M. (1994). Work and/or fun: Measuring hedonic and utilitarian shopping value. *Journal of Consumer Research, 20*, 644–656.

Banerjee, R., & Dittmar, H. (2008). Individual differences in children's materialism: The role of peer relations. *Personality and Social Psychology Bulletin, 34*, 17–31.

Banwari, M. (2006). I, me, and mine – how products become consumers' extended selves. *Journal of Consumer Behaviour, 5*, 550–562.

Baumeister, R. F., & Leary, M. R. (1995). The need to belong: Desire for interpersonal attachment as a fundamental human motivation. *Psychological Bulletin, 117*, 497–529.

Beggan, J. K. (1991). Using what you own to get what you need: The role of possessions in satisfying control motivation. In F. W. Rudmin (Ed.), *To have possessions: A handbook on ownership and property*. Special issue of the *Journal of Social Behavior and Personality, 6*, 129–146.

Belk, R. W. (1988). Possessions and the extended self. *Journal of Consumer Research, 15*, 139–168.

Benson, A. (Ed.). (2000). *I shop therefore I am: Compulsive buying and the search for self*. New York: Aronson.

Benson, A., Dittmar, H., & Wolfsohn, R. (2010). Compulsive buying: Cultural contributors and consequences. In E. Aboujaoude & L. M. Koran (Eds.), *Impulse control disorders* (pp. 23–33). New York: Cambridge University Press.

Berger, J., & Heath, C. (2007). Where consumers diverge from others: Identity signalling and product domains. *Journal of Consumer Research, 34*, 121–124.

Black, D. W. (2006). Compulsive shopping. In E. Hollander & D. J. Stein (Eds.), *Clinical manual of impulse-control disorders* (pp. 203–228). Arlington, VA: American Psychiatric Publishing.

Bond, R., Dittmar, H., Singelis, T., Papadopoulou, K., & Chiu, M. (2002). Identity-related functions of material possessions in individualist and collectivist cultures. BPS Social Section Annual Conference, September, Huddersfield, England. Part of symposium organized by Dittmar, H. (2002). To have is to be: The social psychology of material goods and identity.

Braun, O. L., & Wicklund, R. A. (1989). Psychological antecedents of conspicuous consumption. *Journal of Economic Psychology, 10*, 161–187.

Brown, R., & Hewstone, M. (2005). An integrative theory of intergroup contact. In M. P. Zanna (Ed.), *Advances in experimental social psychology* (Vol. 37, pp. 255–343). San Diego, CA: Elsevier-Academic Press.

Burris, B. T., & Rempel, J. K. (2004). 'It's the end of the world as we know it': Threat and the spatial-symbolic self. *Journal of Personality and Social Psychology, 86*, 19–42.

Burroughs, W. J., Drews, D. R., & Hallman, W. K. (1991). Predicting personality from personal possessions: A self-presentational analysis. In F. W. Rudmin (Ed.), *To have possessions: A handbook on ownership and property*. Special issue of *Journal of Social Behavior and Personality, 6*, 147–164.

Carlson, B. D., Suter, T. A., & Brown, T. J. (2008). Social versus psychological brand community: The role of psychological sense of brand community. *Journal of Business Research, 61*, 284–291.

Christopher, A. N., & Schlenker, B. (2000). The impact of perceived material wealth and perceiver personality on first impressions. *Journal of Economic Psychology, 21*, 1–19.

Ciarrochi, J., & Forgas, J. (2000). The pleasure of possessions: Affective influences and personality in the evaluation of consumer items. *European Journal of Social Psychology, 30*, 637–649.

Côté, J. E., & Levine, C. G. (2002). *Identity formation, agency, and culture*. Mahwah, NJ: Erlbaum.

Cross, S. E., & Madson, L. (1997). Models of the self: Self-construals and gender. *Psychological Bulletin, 122*, 3–37.

Csikszentmihalyi, M., & Rochberg-Halton, E. (1981). *The meaning of things: Domestic symbols and the self*. Cambridge: Cambridge University Press.

Cushman, P. (1990). Why the self is empty: Toward a historically situated psychology. *American Psychologist, 45*, 599–611.

D'Astous, A., Maltais, J., & Roberge, C. (1990). Compulsive buying tendencies of adolescent consumers. *Advances in Consumer Research, 17*, 306–313.

Diener, E., & Biswas-Diener, R. (2002). Will money increase subjective well-being? A literature review and guide to needed research. *Social Indicators Research, 57*, 119–169.

Diener, E., & Seligman, M. E. P. (2005). Beyond money: Toward an economy of well-being. *Psychological Science in the Public Interest, 5*, 1–31.

Dittmar, H. (1989). Gender identity-related meanings of personal possessions. *British Journal of Social Psychology, 28*, 159–171.

Dittmar, H. (1991). Meanings of material possessions as reflections of identity: Gender and social-material position in society. In F. W. Rudmin (Ed.), *To have possessions: A handbook on ownership and property*. Special issue of *Journal of Social Behavior and Personality, 6*, 165–186.

Dittmar, H. (1992a). *The social psychology of material possessions: To have is to be*. Hemel Hempstead: Harvester Wheatsheaf & New York: St. Martin's Press.

Dittmar, H. (1992b). Perceived material wealth and first impressions. *British Journal of Social Psychology, 31*, 379–392.

Dittmar, H. (1994). Material possessions as stereotypes: Material images of different socio-economic groups. *Journal of Economic Psychology, 15*, 561–585.

Dittmar, H. (2001). Impulse buying in ordinary and 'compulsive' consumers. In E. Weber, J. Baron, & G. Loomes (Eds.), *Conflicts and tradeoffs in decision making* (pp. 110–135). Cambridge Series on Judgment and Decision Making. New York: Cambridge University Press.

Dittmar, H. (2004a). Understanding and diagnosing compulsive buying. In R. Coombs (Ed.), *Handbook of addictive disorders: A practical guide to diagnosis and treatment* (pp. 411–450). New York: Wiley.

Dittmar, H. (2004b). Are you what you have? Consumer society and our sense of identity. *Psychologist, 17*, 206–210.

Dittmar, H. (2005a). A new look at 'compulsive buying': Self-discrepancies and materialistic values as predictors of compulsive buying tendency. *Journal of Social and Clinical Psychology, 24*, 806–833.

Dittmar, H. (2005b). Compulsive buying behavior – a growing concern? An empirical exploration of the role of gender, age, and materialism. *British Journal of Psychology, 96*, 467–491.

Dittmar, H. (2008). *Consumer culture, identity, and well-being*. European Monographs in Social Psychology. London and New York: Psychology Press.

Dittmar, H., & Banerjee, R. (2011). Children's internalisation of consumer culture ideals and well-being. Manuscript in preparation.

Dittmar, H., Beattie, J., & Friese, S. (1996). Objects, decision considerations and self-image in men's and women's impulse purchases. *Acta Psychologica* (special issue on Decision-making and Emotions), *93*, 187–206 (Also available at: http://www.ukc.ac.uk/ESRC).

Dittmar, H., & Bond, R. (2010). I want it and I want it now: Self-discrepancies and materialistic values as predictors of ordinary and compulsive buyers' temporal discounting of different consumer goods. *British Journal of Psychology, 101*, 751–776.

Dittmar, H., Halliwell, E., & Ive, S. (2006). Does Barbie make girls want to be thin? The effect of experimental exposure to images of dolls on the body image of 5–8-year-old girls. *Developmental Psychology, 42*, 283–292.

Dittmar, H., Halliwell, E., & Stirling, E. (2009). Understanding the impact of thin media models on women's body-focused affect: The roles of thin-ideal internalization and weight-related self-discrepancy activation in experimental exposure effects (Part of special issue on Mass media, body image and eating behaviours). *Journal of Social and Clinical Psychology, 28*, 43–72.

Dittmar, H., & Kapur, P. (in press). Consumerism and well-being in India and the UK: identity projection and emotion regulation as underlying psychological processes. *Psychological Studies*, special issue on Self and Identity.

Dittmar, H., Long, K., & Bond, R. (2007). When a better self is only a button click away: Associations between materialistic values, emotional and identity-related buying motives, and compulsive buying tendency online. *Journal of Social and Clinical Psychology, 26*, 334–361.

Dittmar, H., Long, K., & Meek, R. (2004). Buying on the internet: Gender differences in online and conventional buying motivations. *Sex Roles, 50*(5/6), 423–444.

Dittmar, H., & Pepper, L. (1994). To have is to be: Materialism and person perception in working-class and middle-class British adolescents. *Journal of Economic Psychology, 15*, 233–251.

Dixon, J. C., & Street, J. W. (1975). The distinction between self and not-self in children and adolescents. *Journal of Genetic Psychology, 127*, 157–162.

Douglas, M., & Isherwood, B. (1979). *The world of goods: Towards an anthropology of consumption.* London: Allen Lane.

Eaton, B. C., & Eswaran., M. (2009). Well-being and affluence in the presence of a Veblen good. *Economic Journal, 119*, 1088–1104.

Elliott, A. (2005). *Not waving but drowning: Over-indebtedness by misjudgement.* London & New York: Centre for the Study of Financial Innovation (CSFI).

Erikson, E. (1980). *Identity and the life-cycle: A re-issue.* New York: Norton.

Faber, R. J., & O'Guinn, T. C. (2008). Compulsive buying: Review and reflection. In C. P. Haugtvedt, P. M. Herr, & F. R. Frank (Eds.), *Handbook of consumer psychology, marketing and consumer psychology series* (pp. 1039–1056). New York: Taylor & Francis/Lawrence Erlbaum.

Festinger, L. (1954). A theory of social comparison processes. *Human Relations, 7*, 117–140.

Furby, L. (1978). Possessions: Toward a theory of their meaning and function throughout the life cycle. In P. B. Baltes (Ed.), *Life span development and behavior* (Vol. 1, pp. 297–336). New York: Academic Press.

Garðarsdóttir, R., Dittmar, H., & Aspinall, C. (2009). It's not the money, it's the quest for a happier self: Money motives impact the link between materialism and subjective well-being. *Journal of Social and Clinical Psychology, 28*, 1100–1127.

Gerbner, G., Gross, L., Morgan, M., & Signorelli, N. (2002). Growing up with television: The cultivation perspective. In J. Bryant & D. Zillmann (Eds.), *Media effects: Advances in theory and research* (2nd ed., pp. 43–67). Mahwah, NJ: Lawrence Erlbaum Associates.

Goffman, E. (1951). Symbols of class status. *British Journal of Sociology, 2*, 294–304.

Goffman, E. (1961). *Asylums.* New York: Anchor.

Goffman, E. (1968). The inmate world. In C. Gordon & K. J. Gergen (Eds.), *The self in social interaction, Vol. 1: Classic and contemporary perspectives* (pp. 267–274). New York: Wiley.

Gordon, C. (1968). Self conceptions: Configurations and contents. In C. Gordon & K. J. Gergen (Eds.), *The self in social interaction, Vol. 1: Classic and contemporary perspectives* (pp. 115–136). New York: Wiley.

Gramzow, R. H., Sedikides, C., Panter, A. T., & Insko, C. A. (2000). Aspects of self-regulation and self-structure as predictors of perceived emotional distress. *Personality and Social Psychology Bulletin, 26*, 188–205.

Gulerce, A. (1991). Transitional objects: A reconsideration of the phenomenon. In F. W. Rudmin (Ed.), *To have possessions: A handbook on ownership and property.* Special issue of the *Journal of Social Behavior and Personality, 6*, 187–208.

Halliwell, E., & Dittmar, H. (2006). The role of appearance-related self-discrepancies for young adults' affect, body image, and emotional eating: A comparison of fixed-item and respondent-generated self-discrepancy measures. *Personality and Social Psychology Bulletin, 32*, 447–458.

Harper's Index (2005). Online issue of Harper's Magazine, December, last accessed June 6, 2009 at http://www.harpers.org/archive/2005/12/0080830.

Hebdige, D. (1979). *Subculture: The meaning of style.* London: Routledge.

Higgins, E. T. (1987). Self-discrepancy: A theory relating self to affect. *Psychological Review, 94*, 319–340.

Ikeuchi, H., Fujihara, T., & Dohi, I. (2000). Involuntary loss of the extended self: Survey results on the loss of important possessions by a great earthquake. *Japanese Journal of Social Psychology, 16*, 27–38.

James, W. (1981/1890). The consciousness of self. In *Principles of psychology* (Vol. 1, pp. 279–379). Cambridge, MA: Harvard University Press.

Janković, J., & Dittmar, H. (2006). The componential nature of materialistic values and subjective well-being: A comparison of students in Croatia, Germany and the UK. In A. Delle Fave (Ed.), *Dimensions of well-being: Research and intervention* (pp. 34–52). Milano: Franco Angeli.

Kalkbrenner, P. (2004). Advertising damages mental health. Portland Independent Media Centre. Last accessed July 4, 2006 at http://portland.indymedia.org/en/2004/06/290078.shtml.

Kamptner, N. (1991). Personal possessions and their meanings: A life-span perspective. In F. W. Rudmin (Ed.), *To have possessions: A handbook on ownership and property.* Special issue of the *Journal of Social Behavior and Personality, 6*, 209–228.

Kasser, T., & Ahuvia, A. (2002). Materialistic values and well-being in business students. *European Journal of Social Psychology, 32*, 137–146.

Kasser, T., & A. D. Kanner (Eds.). (2004). *Psychology and consumer culture: The struggle for a good life in a materialistic world.* Washington, DC: APA.

Kasser, T., & Ryan, R. M. (1993). A dark side of the American dream: Correlates of financial success as a central life aspiration. *Journal of Personality and Social Psychology, 65*, 410–422.

Kasser, T., & Ryan, R. M. (1996). Further examining the American dream: Differential correlates of intrinsic and extrinsic goals. *Personality and Social Psychology Bulletin, 22*, 280–287.

Koran, L. M., Faber, R. J., Boujaoude, M. A., Large, M. D., & Serpe, R. T. (2006). Estimated prevalence of compulsive buying behavior in the United States. *American Journal of Psychiatry, 163*, 1806–1812.

Kreuzbauer, R., Vignoles, V. L., & Chiu, C. -Y. (2009). Motivational foundations of brand identification.

Unpublished manuscript, University of Illinois at Urbana Champaign.

Lejoyeux, M., Adés, J., Tassian, V., & Solomon, J. (1996). Phenomenology and psychopathology of uncontrolled buying. *American Journal of Psychiatry, 153,* 1524–1529.

Markus, H., & Kitayama, S. (1991). Culture and the self: Implications for cognition, emotion, and motivation. *Psychological Review, 98,* 224–253.

Mead, G. H. (1913). The social self. *Journal of Philosophy,* 374–380.

Mead, G. H. (1934). *Mind, self, and society.* Chicago: University of Chicago Press.

Mehta, R., & Belk, R. W. (1991). Artifacts, identity, and transition: Favorite possessions of Indians and Indian immigrants to the United States. *Journal of Consumer Research, 17,* 398–411.

Neuner, M., Raab, R., & Reisch, L. A. (2005). Compulsive buying in maturing consumer societies: An empirical re-inquiry. *Journal of Economic Psychology, 26,* 509–522.

Oyamot, C. M. (2004). Me, myself, and mine: The incorporation of possessions into the self. *Dissertation Abstracts International (Section-B), 65,* 2149.

Pierce, J. L., Kostova, T., & Dirks, K. T. (2003). The state of psychological ownership: Integrating and extending a century of research. *Review of General Psychology, 7,* 84–107.

Prelinger, E. (1959). Extension and structure of the self. *Journal of Psychology, 47,* 13–23.

Pryor, J. H., Hurtado, B., Saenz, V. B., Santos, J. L., & Korn, W. S. (2007). *The American freshman: Forty-year trends, 1966–2006.* Los Angeles: Higher Education Research Institute.

Richins, M. (2004). The material values scale: Measurement properties and development of a short form. *Journal of Consumer Research, 31,* 209–219.

Richins, M., & Dawson, S. (1992). Materialism as a consumer value: Measure development and validation. *Journal of Consumer Research, 19,* 303–316.

Richins, M. L. (1991). Social comparison and the idealized images of advertising. *Journal of Consumer Research, 18,* 71–83.

Rowlingson, K., & Kempson, E. (1994). *Paying with plastic: A study of credit card debt.* London: Policy Studies Institute.

Ryan, R. M., Chirkov, V. I., Little, T. D., Sheldon, K. M., Timoshina, E., & Deci, E. L. (1999). The American dream in Russia: Extrinsic aspirations and well-being in two cultures. *Personality and Social Psychology Bulletin, 25,* 1509–1524.

Ryan, R. M., & Deci, E. L. (2000). Self-determination theory and the facilitation of intrinsic motivation, social development, and well-being. *American Psychologist, 55,* 68–78.

Sassatelli, R. (2007). *Consumer culture: History, theory, and politics.* London: Sage.

Schor, J. B. (2004). *Born to buy: The commercialized child and the new consumer culture.* New York: Scribner.

Schultz-Kleine, S. S., Kleine, R. E., & Allen, C. T. (1995). How is a possession 'me' or 'not me'? Characterizing types and an antecedent of material possession attachment. *Journal of Consumer Research, 22,* 327–343.

Sheldon, K. M., Ryan, R. M., Deci, E. L., & Kasser, T. (2004). The independent effects of goal contents and motives on well-being: It's both what you pursue and why you pursue it. *Personality and Social Psychology Bulletin, 30,* 475–486.

Shrum, L. J. (2002). Media consumption and perceptions of social reality: Effects and underlying processes. In J. Bryant & D. Zillmann (Eds.), *Media effects: Advances in theory and research* (2nd ed., pp. 69–95). Mahwah, NJ: Lawrence Erlbaum Associates.

Sirgy, M. J. (1982). Self-concept in consumer behavior: A critical review. *Journal of Consumer Research, 9*(3), 287–300.

Sirgy, M. J. (1985). Using Self-Congruity and Ideal Congruity to Predict Purchase Motivation. *Journal of Business Research, 13,* 195–206.

Sirgy, M. J. (1998). Materialism and quality of life. *Social Indicators Research, 43,* 227–260.

Slater, D. (1997). *Consumer culture and modernity.* Cambridge: Polity Press.

Snibbe, A. C., & Markus, H. R. (2005). You can't always get what you want: Educational attainment, agency, and choice. *Journal of Personality and Social Psychology, 68,* 703–720.

Solomon, M. R. (1985). *The psychology of fashion.* Lexington, MA: Lexington Books.

Sproles, G. B. (1985). Behavioral science theories of fashion. In M. R. Solomon (Ed.), *The psychology of fashion* (pp. 55–70). Lexington: D. C. Heath/Lexington Books.

Srivastava, A., Locke, E. A., & Bartol, K. M. (2001). Money and subjective well-being: It's not the money, it's the motives. *Journal of Personality and Social Psychology, 80,* 959–971.

Stone, G. P. (1954). City shoppers and urban identification: Observations of the social psychology of city life. *American Journal of Sociology, 60,* 36–45.

Twenge, J. M., Gentile, B., DeWall, C. M., Ma, D., Lacefield, K., & Schurtz, D. R. (2010). Birth cohort increases in psychopathology among young Americans, 1038–2007: A cross-temporal meta-analysis of the MMPI. *Clinical Psychology Review, 30,* 145–154.

Van den Bogaard, J., & Wiegman, O. (1991). Property crime victimization: The effectiveness of police services for victims of residential burglary. In F. W. Rudmin (Ed.), *To have possessions: A handbook on ownership and property.* Special issue of the *Journal of Social Behavior and Personality. 6,* 329–362.

Veblen, T. (1899). *The theory of the leisure class.* New York: McMillan.

Vignoles, V. L., Dittmar, H., Spencer, L. G. F., Langton, T. A. D., Wright, A. E., & Anderson, N. (2011). The material self: Identity motives and the symbolic value of material possessions. Manuscript in preparation, University of Sussex, UK.

Vignoles, V. L., Regalia, C., Manzi, C., Golledge, J., & Scabini, E. (2006). Beyond self-esteem: The influence of multiple motives on identity construction. *Journal of Personality and Social Psychology, 90*, 308–333.

Wallendorf, M., & Arnould, E. J. (1988). My favourite things: A cross-cultural inquiry into object attachment, possessiveness and social linkage. *Journal of Consumer Research, 14*, 531–547.

Wapner, S., Demick, J., & Redondo, J. P. (1990). Cherished possessions and adaptation of older people to nursing homes. *International Journal of Aging and Human Development, 31*, 219–235.

Wicklund, R. A., & Gollwitzer, P. M. (1982). *Symbolic self-completion*. Hillsdale, NJ: Erlbaum.

Winnicott, D. W. (1953). Transitional objects and transitional phenomena: A study of the first not-me possession. *International Journal of Psycho-Analysis, 24*, 89–97.

Civic Identity

32

Daniel Hart, Cameron Richardson, and Britt
Wilkenfeld

Notions of citizenship and civic identity are central to political theory and
political psychology. We explore the various meanings of civic identity, and
suggest that the concept is best understood as having subjective, ethical, and
political facets. The prominence of civic identity in constructions of citizenship is then considered. We use civic identity embedded in the context
of citizenship to refract contemporary debates concerning globalization and
immigration. Our review suggests that civic identity figures prominently in
each debate, with proponents of different perspectives in these debates varying in their views about the kinds of civic identities morally desirable and
politically necessary. In the final section, data from a large international survey of adolescents are used to explore the relations of different facets of civic
identity and citizenship. We conclude with suggestions for future research
and conceptual exploration.

Civic identity lies at the heart of common notions of citizenship and civic participation. A sense of civic identity leads people to volunteer to help their neighbors and their neighbors' children, vote in local and national elections, join the military and risk their lives to protect national interests, and pay taxes to provide for fellow citizens who are unable to earn enough to pay for housing, food, and medical care. The sense of oneself as a civic actor empowers political discussion, protest of governmental policies judged unfair or illegal, and participation in many facets of political life. Civic identity infuses meaning in, and provides the motivation for civic behavior. As Leydet (2006) points out, "A strong civic identity can itself motivate citizens to participate actively in their society's political life." To give one empirical example, American adults surveyed in the General Social Survey were asked how much pride, on a 5-point scale, they had in being American and whether they had voted in the 1992 election. Seventy-five percent of those who claimed to be "extremely proud" of being American reported having voted, a substantially higher percentage compared to the 64% voting rate among those who reported only being "somewhat proud" of being American.[1]

D. Hart (✉)
Center for Children and Childhood Studies, Rutgers
University, Camden, NJ, USA
e-mail: daniel.hart@rutgers.edu

S.J. Schwartz et al. (eds.), *Handbook of Identity Theory and Research*,
DOI 10.1007/978-1-4419-7988-9_32, © Springer Science+Business Media, LLC 2011

The absence of a sense of oneself as a member of a community, to which one is emotionally attached and for which one feels responsible, reframes civic behavior within judgments of utility; the personal benefits derived from civic behavior are so few—utility is so low—that voting, volunteering, jury duty, and so on become nearly irrational and consequently are to be avoided. It is because civic identity is considered so central to motivating civic life that societies develop elaborate practices—civics and national history classes, for example—to inculcate their young into the synthesis of emotions, beliefs, and obligations constituting civic identity.

Our goals in this chapter are to explore the nature of civic identity, contemporary debates about civic identity, and the connections of civic identity and citizenship to context. To anticipate one theme that appears throughout the chapter, civic identity, citizenship, and context have become ubiquitous notions in contemporary political science and social policy, largely because of the consequences—real and imagined—of globalization.

The Nature of Civic Identity

Connotations of Identity

Identity has become a frequently used term in social discourse (as demonstrated within this volume). One consequence of its ubiquity has been a wide—and diffuse—range of meanings. As Brubaker and Cooper (2000) point out, identity has been used in political discussions to refer to (a) a subset of interests that are particular rather than general (e.g., "I am a train hobbyist"), (b) group memberships (e.g., gender and race "identities"), (c) a social role that is formed in social or political movements, and (d) a specific aspect of self that shifts according to social or temporal circumstances. Brubaker and Cooper note that these various uses of the term identity are not necessarily compatible with each other. This is because so many different fields have used "identity" to mean different things—hence the confusion (see Schwartz, Vignoles, & Luyckx, Chapter 1, this

volume). For example, identity in the philosophical literature often refers to the persistence of objects and persons over time (Nozick, 1981). A person has an "identity" in the sense that the individual can make judgments about the future based upon his or her views concerning which qualities of self will persist over time. Gender, race, and other enduring qualities of self (meaning (b) of identity) can be viewed to constitute an identity in this sense. This notion of identity can be inconsistent with notions of identity which emphasize transient, context-specific patterns of behavior (meaning (d)) often described in social psychology.

A second inconsistency among connotations concerns the authority of the individual in determining identity. Some scholars use "identity" in ways that indicate that an individual's view concerning himself or herself is largely irrelevant in assigning an identity to that person for analytical purposes. That is, an individual might be labeled as having a particular identity based on physical features, occupation, group or tribal membership, and so on, independent of whether the individual perceives any of these characteristics as part of the self. For example, an individual might be of Asian heritage, and viewed as an "Asian" by some; yet the same individual might not identify closely with any Asian country or culture (see Umaña-Taylor, Chapter 33, this volume). The theorist or analyst assigning the identity simply infers that a characteristic is sufficiently important in social interaction that important facets of a person's life can be better understood by reference to this characteristic: if a person looks to be of Asian heritage, then that fact—or assigned identity—likely captures some facets of that person's life and experience.

Other philosophers and psychologists view identity as essentially subjective and, consequently, necessarily dependent upon the individual's own view of self and of the self's qualities (see for example Cameron, 2004). William James, for example, discerned identity in the continuity of consciousness over time, a phenomenon that is necessarily subjective. This view opens up the possibility that a characteristic of an individual salient to others—gender or race, for example—might be viewed by the individual as peripheral to his or her sense of identity. We adopt this perspective in this chapter.

Identity and Civic Life

Centrality of civic life to the sense of self. In our view, civic identity is best understood as a set of beliefs and emotions about oneself as a participant in civic life. Forms of participation overlap with the actions characteristic of citizenship, and consequently may include voting, holding or running for political office, jury duty, and so on. These forms of participation can be associated with strongly held views of the self. For example, a South African voter, recalling the history of Apartheid policy and his own memories of police abuse in childhood, writes that "to stand in a long line of black and white people waiting patiently together to vote remains an emotional experience for most of us" (Wende, 2009). The American revolutionary war hero Nathan Hale felt so deeply for his nascent country that he is reported to have said just prior to being hanged as a spy by the British that "I regret that I have but one life to give for my country." Shadid (2005) quotes an Iraqi citizen discussing the risks and benefits of voting in his country's first democratic election in 50 years "Whatever they [terrorists] would do, I would still vote. . . Even if I was dead, I would still participate. The vote comes from the bottom of my heart." All of these quotes illustrate how central civic participation can become to civic identity and to one's sense of identity in general.

The salience of civic identifications within the sense of self varies from person to person, among historical eras, and across countries. Polls suggest, for example, that pride in one's country, a component of civic identity as we discuss in a later section, varies across Europe with only 23% of Germans, but 57% of Spaniards, reporting being "very proud" of their countries (Harris Poll, 2004). Not everyone eligible to vote feels as deeply about the importance of voting as does the Iraqi cited above; indeed, a concern of many political scientists and policy-makers is that the

centrality of civic obligations to the sense of self is declining in many societies throughout the world with worrisome implications for civic participation (Rahn, 2008), a topic to which we return in a later section of the chapter.

Similarities of civic identity to moral and national identities. Civic identity is usually linked to communities and societies, each of which is attached to a specific geographical location. An individual might think of herself as concerned about her neighborhood, as an active citizen of her town, or a proud, contributing member of her country.

An important question taken up by philosophers is whether civic identity *must* or *ought* to be linked to geography. For example, "citizen of the world" is a term often used to characterize individuals who seek to contribute to the welfare of others in communities other than their own. Leydet (2006) provides a particularly thorough exposition of the philosophical debate on the issues related to civic identity, citizenship, and links to specific communities. Those who favor a locale-based notion for civic identity and citizenship argue that a connection to a specific place and culture is necessary for civic action to be motivated and to be effective. In a world in which people move freely from location to location, without constructing local bonds with others, there are no political units capable of effective self-governance, there are only "casual aggregates" (Walzer, 1983), that is, groups of individuals moving independently of each other. On the other hand, some theorists argue that a sense of civic identity and citizenship may be constructed independently of attachment to particular locations and social groups. The argument made by Kymlicka (2001), for example, is that the demands of justice supersede boundaries of political groups and their associated territories. A world citizen, then, may be an individual who seeks the widest possible spheres for justice.

The balance between the larger concern with justice and a more local civic identity may be what Nelson Mandela (1999) was describing when he saw his future, following his departure from the presidency of South Africa, "as part of an international community of men and women who have chosen the world as the theatre of their operations in pursuit of justice; and as an ordinary citizen of a nation that has won the world's admiration not by prowess in war but by the dedication of its people of every background to celebrate their humanity." In our view, as the notion of civic identity is unlinked from specific communities and societies, it begins to become indistinguishable from a broad moral orientation or moral identity concerned with universal moral concerns (cf. Hardy & Carlo, Chapter 19, this volume). Mandela's goal to join others in the "pursuit of justice" seems a straightforward moral goal rather than one that is best described as an aim or reflection of civic activity. There may be no explanatory benefit to a notion like civic identity if it is identical with concepts like moral identity.

In our view, the notion of civic identity is most useful when it is linked to particular social groups located in specific geographical areas—and in such ways, can be distinguished from moral identities. However, civic identity should also be distinguished from simple identifications with these social groups. For example, one's civic identity is at least potentially distinct from one's national identity; one might view oneself as fully German, or Mexican, or Norwegian, participating in the cultures of the countries, without viewing oneself as a participant in the group's civic affairs. Civic identity, in the connotation advanced here, necessarily implies participation in the civic life of the community. In contrast to the universalistic moral aspirations of a "world citizen" moral identity, civic identity is bound to particular social groups; in contrast to national identities, civic identity implies action in a public arena governed by a concern with rights and responsibilities for all.

Citizenship and Civic Identity

The meaning of civic identity is best understood in relation to traditional notions of citizenship. By citizenship, we refer, as is common, to three qualities: *membership*, *rights*, and *participation* (Bellamy, 2008). Membership refers to the sense of belonging to the nation and communities of

which one is a citizen. Citizens are entitled to rights by virtue of membership, and as citizens, they participate in shaping these rights. Full citizenship requires participation in the life of society.

Citizenship demands some degree of subjective identification with other citizens. Participation in democratic government often presumes that those who vote and those who govern identify, to some degree, with the people and institutions constituting the state. Indeed, democracy is thought to function best when those individuals holding elected positions are concerned for the well-being of their constituents and for the state itself. Although it is usually understood that politicians have their own interests that they hope to fulfill while holding public office—whether these be psychological or material in nature—the public ordinarily expects these interests to be subjugated to the public good. The United States and many other countries have laws and regulations intended to diminish government officials' inclinations to pursue private goals at the expense of the public good.

Similarly, some sense of identification with the state is often seen as a prerequisite for citizenship. To the extent that voters and representatives act out of self-interest and, relatedly, an interest in the prosperity of one's community, citizenship guarantees a certain protection for the state—in the form of citizens' investment in their communities and nations. For example, it would seem unwise to allow citizens and residents of Australia to vote or run for office in local elections within the United States. Australian residents presumably have no interests in the governance of, for instance, Cheyenne, Wyoming, and, consequently, are likely to make ill-informed and poorly considered decisions. One might imagine a resident of Australia running for office in America in order to benefit Australians (e.g., restrict trade between the United States and all other countries except Australia). In contrast, citizens of Cheyenne are motivated by their own collective interests (e.g., I want my home prices to remain high, so I will vote for a candidate who restricts highway development near residential neighborhoods) and a concern for their fellow residents and local institutions to make careful choices for electoral office.

As noted previously, functioning democracy requires that citizens feel that their lives are joined in important ways with their fellows. The absence of such a sentiment reduces civic life to the point where it is expressed as instrumental action intended to fulfill purely selfish interests—and such a scenario is incompatible with healthy democracy. Although it is possible to assign the identity of "citizen" to an individual who feels no identification with fellow citizens—indeed, every democratic society has citizens for whom this is true—this is not the kind of civic identity that can serve as the goal toward which analysis and practice ought to build.

To summarize, a full civic identity contains elements of the three constituents of identity: membership, participation, and a concern for rights. Like a national identity (e.g., "I'm a Canadian"), it includes a sense of membership; like a moral identity (e.g., "I'm a citizen of the world") it includes, but is not limited to, concerns for rights. And, finally, a civic identity motivates, is maintained, and is structured by participation in civic life.

Developmental Emergence of Civic Identity and Citizenship

Civic identity includes experiences, beliefs, and emotions concerning membership, rights, and participation (Bellamy, 2008). Although, as noted previously, these three qualities are conceptually related, psychologically they are likely to be partially independent. It is conceptually possible, for example, for one to identify with one's fellow citizens, and yet be little involved in civic life; similarly, an individual might be concerned about the rights of citizens without identifying with others in the community and absent political participation. Although these different facets of civic identity do cohere—as we demonstrate in a later section—one's view of oneself in civic life is open to psychological, social, and political influences that make civic identity more fluid than other more stable identities (e.g., sexual identity).

For example, the 2008 presidential election in the United States, featuring the charismatic Barack Obama as a candidate, was thought to enlarge and energize the civic identities of many voters who had previously been disconnected from civic and political concerns.

Because of the openness of civic identity to a variety of influences, different facets of civic identity are likely to follow partially independent developmental trajectories. Moreover, the salience, elaboration, and content of each quality are likely to reflect slightly different influences.

The developmental trajectories of the sense of membership and of rights are quite surprising in that both seem to emerge at very young ages. For example, Barrett, Wilson, and Lyons (2003) demonstrated that English schoolchildren as young as 5 years of age were able to distinguish between British citizens and those from America and Germany. Moreover, even young children preferred citizens of their own nations to those of others (for further evidence of in-group preference, see Abrams, Rutland, & Cameron, 2003; Brewer, 1999; also see Spears, Chapter 9, this volume). Barrett et al. (2003) found that the importance of national identity increased over the course of childhood, with older children judging nationality to be more important to them than gender and age-based identities. In comparing their results to those of other researchers, Barrett et al. conclude that there is considerable variation in findings across countries and that developmental trajectories are yet to be fully identified. However, variations in methods that have been used in different studies in different countries make conclusive comparisons about cross-national differences and developmental trajectories impossible.

Young children are also able to infer that citizens have rights. In a series of studies, Helwig and colleagues (Helwig, 1998; Helwig, Arnold, Tan, & Boyd, 2003; Helwig, Arnold, Tan, & Boyd, 2007; Neff & Helwig, 2002) have shown that children and adolescents believe that citizens have rights that should not be violated through governmental actions. In Canada, the United States, and China, 6-year-old children have been shown to judge, based on the principle of fairness, that citizens should not be prevented by legislation or authority from criticizing the government (Helwig, 1998). Although older children's judgments on the principle of fairness are more differentiated and more pragmatic about the consequences of such actions (e.g., it might be dangerous to voice opposition to government policies if the country officially opposes free speech) compared to those of 6-year-olds, it appears that a fundamental sensitivity to citizens' rights emerges early in life. Moreover, sensitivity to rights appears even in countries that are traditionally viewed as less rights-oriented than Western democracies, such as China (Helwig et al., 2003).

Less is known about children's sense of themselves as civic actors. However, children do volunteer, a precursor to adult forms of civic participation (Hart, Donnelly, Youniss, & Atkins, 2007), and by adolescence, volunteering is viewed by some adolescents as integral to their senses of self (Hart & Yates, 1997).

Contemporary Debates Concerning Civic Identity

Civic identity and citizenship have become central topics in the controversies arising from the recent transformations in social, economic, and political life collectively referred to as *globalization*. A computer search of works published in 1990 suggests that of the approximately 4,500 articles with the keyword "citizenship" in the bibliographic record, only 187, or 4%, also contained the keyword "globalization." In contrast, of the 29,300 bibliographic records for works published in 2008 with the keyword "citizenship," 45% also contained the keyword "globalization." It is unknown whether the increase from 4,500 to 29,000 published works with the keyword "citizenship" reflects greater interest in citizenship, bibliographic records with more information, or more publications. However, what is clear is that contemporary discussions of citizenship are intertwined with the various threads of globalization to a degree that makes it impossible to discuss one without consideration of the other. In contrast,

it appears that the vast majority of discussions of citizenship just 20 years ago did not feature considerations of globalization (see Jensen et al., Chapter 13, this volume, for a discussion of globalization and identity).

One reason for this interest is immigration. Many countries have had protracted debates about extensions of citizenship to residents who are currently accorded neither the full rights nor the responsibilities of citizens (see Schildkraut, Chapter 36, this volume; Licata, Sanchez-Mazas, & Green, Chapter 38, this volume; Stepick, Dutton Stepick, & Vanderkooy, Chapter 37, this volume, for additional discussions). In the United States, for example, there are both (a) groups seeking to provide paths to citizenship to the millions of illegal immigrants within the borders and (b) groups advocating for the immediate return of illegal immigrants to their countries of origin (Lowenstein, 2006). Germany, too, has had an enduring debate concerning the rights of immigrants, with this discussion focusing particularly on first- and second-generation Turks. Versions of the arguments heard in the United States and Germany can be found throughout Europe, Africa, and North America, as citizens of countries on each of these continents examine their responsibilities to new residents and reflect upon their willingness to grant these new residents the rights and responsibilities of citizenship (see Koopmans, Statham, Giugni, & Passy, 2005, for an example of this discourse).

Immigration raises not only questions concerning the rights and responsibilities of immigrants, but about *identities* as well. An important issue is whether immigrants see themselves as citizens of the countries in which they reside. Merely living in a country is not sufficient to ensure identification with it (Zhou, Morris, & Benet-Martínez, 2008). Immigrants to Sweden, for example, may be willing to accept the social welfare benefits of residence in Sweden, but fail to perceive themselves to be Swedish or Swedish-like. This lack of identification might be reflected in an unwillingness to acquire the language, habits, and practices common in Sweden (Caldwell, 2006; see also chapters in this volume by Jensen et al., Chapter 13, Licata et al., Chapter 38, Vanderkooy et al., Chapter 37, Huynh et al., Chapter 35, Umaña-Taylor, Chapter 33, and Schildkraut, Chapter 36).

Huntington (2004) has suggested that recent immigrants to the United States might not incorporate key elements of the national identity into their own belief systems, and, consequently, might not view themselves to be Americans—at least when it comes to "American" values (but see Schildkraut, Chapter 36, this volume). Specifically, Huntington argued that Mexican immigrants might be particularly likely not to identify with core American values, and that this lack of identification occurs for a number of reasons. First, Mexico is contiguous with the United States, meaning that immigrants who live near the border can maintain their social and institutional affiliations in Mexico. The maintenance of a connection to Mexico reduces the likelihood of parallel and new affiliations developing in the United States. Second, Huntington suggests that the size of the Mexican immigrant community in the United States allows immigrants to bond with each other rather than create relationships with other Americans with whom traditional American values and norms can be modeled.

Huntington (2004, pp. 44–45) foresees "dangerous" consequences for the United States resulting from this lack of identification: "Continuation of this large immigration (without improved assimilation) could divide the United States into a country of two languages and two cultures...[resulting in] the end of the America we have known for more than three centuries." The same concern has been raised by commentators in other Western democracies experiencing large influxes of immigrants.

Ethnic and racial diversity among *citizens* poses some of the same challenges as those arising from immigration. Putnam (2007) has reported that increasing racial and ethnic diversity—both forms increasing in many Western democracies—is often accompanied by decreases in social capital. Social capital, according to Putnam, is constituted of social networks characterized by reciprocity and trustworthiness.

Those who have access to more social capital tend to be healthier, wealthier, and happier (Kawachi, Kennedy, Lochner, & Prothrow-Stith, 1997). Most importantly for our purposes in this chapter, social capital is positively associated with civic participation, such as volunteering, voting, protesting, and military service (Kahne & Sporte, 2008).

Ethnic and racial diversity may undermine social capital because citizens of different races and ethnicities can view themselves in competition with each other for limited resources (Perlmutter, 2002), the consequences of which can be increased bias favoring those who share the same racial and ethnic identities and derogation of those who do not (see Spears, Chapter 9, this volume). There is evidence that this occurs even in countries that are known for their tolerance of others, such as the Nordic nations (Pred, 2000).

Collier (2009) suggests that many of the problems in governance that characterize the world's poorest nations result from diversity. For example, Collier attributes the corruption and inequitable distribution of national resources characteristic of poorly functioning African states in part to ethnic diversity:

> Although the instant states that came into being with the dissolution of the colonial empires were ancient societies with a multiplicity of strong ethnic loyalties, usually they lacked national loyalty: people's primary allegiance was to their ethnic group. As I have argued, this severely impeded the provision of public goods. Anything public was simply up for grabs: a common pool resource, the control of which depended upon winning the political struggle between the various ethnic groups. Much of the surest way of overcoming this problem would be to follow the earlier model of nation building: gradually erode ethnic identities and replace them with a national identity (Collier, 2009, p. 178).

Moreover, Collier reports that ethnic identification is *positively* related to educational attainment and political mobilization in nine African countries. The implication is that high levels of ethnic identification—and low levels of national identification—are unlikely to disappear as a result of modernization.

Finally, Collier (2009) describes several lines of research suggesting that the sense of citizenship may be particularly submerged in countries that are characterized by *both* high levels of poverty and diversity. That is, there is an *interaction* between diversity and poverty that exacerbate the effects of each on civic identity. High levels of diversity and high levels of poverty are common in many African countries, and it is for this reason that many of these countries have difficulty in creating functional democracies. In these countries, there is no shared collective identity to moderate conflicts posed by the shortage of resources. To the extent that globalization alleviates poverty, it can contribute to the decline of such conflicts; but for the reasons noted earlier, the processes related to globalization may not lead to more inclusive civic identities.

To summarize, globalization has led to increases in immigration and diversity, each of which has the potential to pose problems for the development of citizenship and civic identity. Political scientists have been particularly focused on the potential for immigration and diversity to suppress the sense of identification with fellow residents and citizens, which theorists since Aristotle have seen as central for democracy. At the same time, results from studies in intergroup relations within the field of psychology (e.g., Halevy, Bornstein, & Sagiv, 2008) suggest that the implications of diversity and immigration are complex and can be beneficial in certain contexts.

Psychological, Political, and Demographic Contexts of Civic Identity

The overview of contemporary discussions suggests that civic identity is embedded within the social and political contexts in which the individual functions. In this section, we identify the connections of civic identity to psychological, political, and demographic contexts.

Psychological Influences on Civic Identity

Trust. Trust—the expectation that others are fair, trustworthy, and will reciprocate—is the cornerstone of the psychological foundation of citizenship (Flanagan, 2003). Adults high in trust participate in civic life to a much greater degree than do those who lack trust (Putnam, 2000). Similarly, adolescents who are high in trust report more conventional civic engagement, and more intended civic engagement in adulthood, compared to adolescents who lack trust in political institutions (Hart & Gullan, 2010). Consequently, research suggests that trust facilitates civic participation, a central component of civic identity; it also seems likely, although research evidence is lacking, that trust will increase the propensity for identification with others and an interest in rights.

Civic knowledge. Civic knowledge, or knowledge of democratic principles (Torney-Purta, 2002) and of domestic and international history and government (Rubin, 2007), is important as well. Civic knowledge is associated with political participation and respect for rights (Galston, 2001). Indeed, the association of civic knowledge with citizenship is foundational for most civics curricula, based on the assumption that those who know will translate that knowledge into action, although this assumption is not as well-substantiated as many proponents of civics education imagine (Hart et al., 2007; Youniss & Hart, 2005).

Belonging. From a peer relations perspective, the need to belong seems to be a primary motivator for many people, leading even to greater acceptance of negative behavior when it is a norm in the group in which membership is desired (Duffy & Nesdale, 2009). It is likely that individuals also feel a need to belong to a nation, even in childhood (Barrett, 2007). It is unclear the extent to which a need to belong to a nation will affect one's civic identity, though a sense of belonging is certainly related to the formation of a national versus ethnic identity (Berry, Phinney, Sam, & Vedder, 2006)

Political Influences on Civic Identity

Civic identity is also likely to be the product of political climate. Civic identity is likely to be expressed differently in societies characterized by repression of dissenting views than it is in societies open to a variety of competing perspectives. For example, Hart and Gullan (2010) have suggested that the emergence of political activism is influenced by the openness of a society to political protest. Relatedly, the absence of explicit political activism does not imply satisfaction or complicity in the state of affairs of a nation, but may simply reflect the acknowledgment of the danger of activism in a society closed to opposition (Turiel, 2003; Turiel & Perkins, 2004). Torney-Purta, Wilkenfeld, and Barber (2008) found that *political efficacy*, the sense that one is an effective actor in the political sphere, which may influence civic identity, was actually lower in countries in which more political rights and civil liberties are accorded to citizens.

Demographic Influences on Civic Identity

Economic conditions. The functioning of the national economy is one frequently examined influence on how individuals view themselves civically. Generally, it is assumed that desperate economic times make civic identity and citizenship difficult. Poor economic conditions may adversely affect civic identity in multiple ways.

Ethnic heterogeneity. As noted earlier, ethnic heterogeneity has often been assumed to interfere with individuals' sense of citizenship. Putnam (2000) and Huntington (1996) have both suggested that countries that are ethnically diverse might have difficulty creating social capital (Putnam, 2000) and promoting national identification (Huntington, 1996).

Child saturation. One demographic quality of populations that may be associated with civic identity is the percentage of the population that is composed of children (Hart, Atkins, Markey, & Youniss, 2004)—child saturation. The idea that child saturation is an important index for understanding civic life has received some credence from work by political scientists. For example, Moller (1968) has linked youth bulges, corresponding to high levels of child saturation, to the Protestant Reformation, and to revolutions in eighteenth-century France and twentieth-century Indonesia, and Huntington (1996) has suggested that youth are generally more attracted to such movements than are adults. Goldstone (1999) pointed out that youth may be less invested in the existing social and religious structures—they are less likely than adults to be married, have children, occupy prestigious positions in their communities and churches, and so on—and that as a consequence, youth may be more open to movements that seek to overthrow or revise existing orthodoxies. Although there is a great deal of fascinating writing on the relation of child saturation to the emergence of powerful social and religious movements (e.g., Moller, 1968), there is as yet a dearth of systematic research.

Hart et al. (2004) suggest that those who grow up in communities and societies with large cohorts of children (child-saturated contexts) are less influenced by adults, compared to children who grow up in communities and societies where adults constitute large majorities of the population (adult-saturated contexts). Hart et al. hypothesized that growing up in adult-saturated contexts results in a more thorough transmission of knowledge of, and respect for, the culture and society. This transmission is possible because, in adult-saturated contexts, a large percentage of a child's interactions will naturally involve adults, who typically possess knowledge about society and culture. In contrast, in child-saturated contexts, children interact frequently with other children, and less transmission of cultural information can take place because there are fewer adults available to transmit information about their societies. Indeed, Hart et al. (2004) demonstrated empirically that children living in child-saturated communities in the United States have less civic knowledge compared to children living in adult-saturated communities, and showed as well that children in child-saturated countries possess less civic knowledge compared to children in adult-saturated countries. Hart et al. suggested, but have not empirically demonstrated, that youth who possess little civic knowledge are more likely to become involved in radical political and social activism compared to those who possess more civic knowledge. In summary, Hart et al. argue that members of youth bulges have less civic knowledge compared to youth of the same age who were not socialized in large cohorts of children, and that a deficit in civic knowledge can lead to participation in extremist political activities. An interesting question is whether civic identities are involved in terrorist activities. Clearly, at least some terrorists view themselves in terms of collective identifications (Post, Sprinzak, & Denny, 2003). One line for future research might be to contrast civic identities, traditionally construed in terms of the framework provided by explorations of citizenship, with the identities motivating terrorism.

An International Examination

Perhaps because civic identity has only recently become prominent in political science discourse, there is little research on the relations of facets of civic identity to the psychological, political, and demographic influences outlined in the previous section. In this section, we aim to contribute some knowledge on these issues by reporting new analyses from the International Association for the Evaluation of Educational Achievement (IEA) Civic Education Study (Torney-Purta, Lehmann, Oswald, & Schulz, 2001).

The IEA Civic Education Study (CIVED) was a rigorous international study of adolescents' civic knowledge, attitudes, and behavior in 28 countries (representing countries in Eastern and Western Europe, Asia, and Latin America, as well as the United States and Australia). Adolescents (age 14) completed surveys of civic attitudes and anticipated civic participation, as well as a 38-item assessment of civic knowledge. The sample across all countries totals nearly 90,000 adolescents.

Because the CIVED is international, it permits an examination of the associations of demographic and political characteristics of countries to facets of civic identities. Moreover, because the Civic Education Study assessed knowledge and trust in adolescents, it is also possible to estimate the association of these psychological qualities to civic identity.

Indicators of Citizenship and Civic Identity

The CIVED includes indicators of the three qualities of citizenship and civic identity discussed in previous sections: *membership*, *participation*, and *rights*. Membership was assessed by asking for a judgment of agreement with three statements such as "this country [the country in which the adolescent was resident] should be proud of what it has achieved." Scores on these three items were combined to form a scale that we consider to assess *nationalism* and a sense of membership (details about this scale, and the others in the CIVED data, are found in Lehman & Torney-Purta, n.d.). Presumably adolescents who agree with such statements feel that they belong to the countries of which they are proud. The questionnaire also assessed adolescents' views about conventional participation, with adolescents judging the importance of participation in ways such as "voting in every election." Ratings on six such items were combined to form a scale of *conventional participation*. Finally, support for rights is indicated by adolescents' judgments concerning the rights and opportunities for women. Adolescents reported the extent of their agreement with five statements such as "women should have the same rights as men in every way." Scores for the five statements were combined to form an index of support for *women's rights*.

In addition to the measures conceptually related to civic identity and citizenship, CIVED also contained an 8-item attitudinal measure concerning immigration (sample item "Immigrants should have all the same rights that everyone else in a country has"). High scores indicate a favorable attitude toward immigrants.

Predictors of Citizenship and Civic Identity

Knowledge and trust. The survey included sets of multiple choice questions tapping civic knowledge (e.g., "In a democratic system, which of the following ought to govern the country?") and political trust (e.g., "how much of the time can you trust each of the following institutions... the courts"). Scales measuring each were formed by combining relevant items.

Political and demographic influences. Kaufmann, Kraay, and Mastruzzi (2008) have combined hundreds of survey scale items (none from the CIVED study), ratings from non-governmental organizations, and other forms of data to create a measure of a country's *voice and accountability*, which we use in these analyses to index tolerance for political dissent. *Voice and accountability* refers to "the extent to which a country's citizens are able to participate in selecting their government, as well as freedom of expression, freedom of association, and a free media" (Kaufmann et al., 2008, p. 7). Our prediction is that adolescents are more likely to perceive themselves to be citizens in countries tolerant of political dissent (high in *voice and accountability*).

The World Bank Development Indicator data set was the source for *child saturation* (the percentage of children under the age of 15) for each of the 28 countries in the IEA study. Country-level economic vitality was indexed by using a country's per capita *gross domestic product (GDP)*, also drawn from the World Bank Indicator data set.

Finally, estimates of ethnic diversity within countries are drawn from Alesina, Devleeschauwer, Easterly, Kurlat, and Wacziarg (2003). These authors used a variety of data sources to estimate ethnic diversity within nations.

Analyses

Correlations among the various indicators of civic identity and hypothesized predictors are presented in Table 32.1 (a correlation matrix was computed separately for each country; to aggregate the matrices, we used the r-to-z transformation, averaged the 28 matrices, and then transformed the z scores back). Two general observations are important. The first is that correlations among the indicators of civic identity are small in magnitude: nationalism, conventional participation, and support for women's rights are only weakly related to each other. The second observation is that the hypothesized predictors are all generally related to one or more of the indicators for civic identity.

Nationalism, reflected partly by self-reported pride in one's membership in a country, is positively correlated with *conventional participation* and support for *women's rights*. Those who identified strongly with their countries were more likely than those with weak attachments to the nation to support the importance of jury duty, voting, and the rights of women to participate fully in society. Nationalism was also positively related to trust. Adolescents who reported high levels of trust in the political institutions in their country were more patriotic than adolescents distrustful of their national bureaucracies. Interestingly, nationalism was essentially unrelated to civic knowledge; apparently even those with very little understanding of how democratic governments work can identify with their countries just as strongly as can those with sophisticated understandings of political functioning.

Table 32.1 Average within-nation correlations among indicators of civic identity and psychological factors[a]

Variable	Nationalism	Conventional participation	Women's rights	Trust
Conventional participation	0.18			
Women's rights	0.12	0.04		
Trust	0.22	0.25	0.07	
Civic knowledge	0.01	–0.01	0.29	0.04

[a]$N > 91,000$.

Table 32.2 Correlations of aggregated indicators of civic identity with demographic and political predictors[a]

Variable	Nationalism	Conventional participation	Women's rights	Trust	Civic knowledge	Voice	Saturation	Per capita GDP
Conventional participation	0.65							
Women's rights	−0.01	−0.33						
Trust	0.04	−0.03	0.66					
Civic knowledge	0.28	0.01	0.12	0.21				
Voice	−0.16	−0.41	0.73	0.43	0.14			
Child saturation	0.44	0.39	0.14	0.12	−0.41	−0.30		
Ethnic diversity	−0.31	0.03	−0.44	−0.36	−0.34	−0.46	0.15	
Per capita GDP	−0.42	−0.46	0.77	0.60	0.16	0.67	−0.23	−0.20

[a] $N > 91,000$.

Table 32.2 presents the correlations of the national average scores for the markers of civic identity with national level demographic and political variables (it should be noted that these correlations reflect differences between nations in mean levels of civic identity, and thus they cannot tell us anything about the differences between the individuals within those nations [see Trzesniewski, Donnellan, & Robins, 2008 for a good explanation of these kinds of correlations]). At the level of demographics, nationalism was positively associated with child saturation (the percentage of the population under the age of 15); it appears that countries with young populations inspired more identification and patriotism than countries with older populations. Predictably, given the literature reviewed in an earlier section, ethnic diversity was inversely correlated with nationalism. Surprisingly, however, so too was per capita gross domestic product (GDP); adolescents residing in affluent countries were less likely to report high levels of nationalism than were adolescents living in poor countries.

Adolescents' judgments about the importance of civic participation showed a pattern of associations similar to that observed with nationalism. Adolescents were more likely to judge different forms of civic participation to be important if they were high in trust and lived in countries high in child saturation. Somewhat surprisingly, adolescents were less likely to endorse conventional participation in countries with high per capita GDPs and in which political dissent was common (voice). Finally, support for the rights of women was highest among adolescents who trusted the political institutions in their countries, were knowledgeable about civic functioning, and who lived in countries that were supportive of political dissent, relatively affluent, and ethnically homogeneous.

Although the indicators used in these analyses of civic identity—nationalism, endorsement of conventional participation, and support for women's rights—are all very limited and indirect reflections of membership, participation, and rights, the pattern of correlations suggest that civic identity rests upon trust in political institutions to a much greater degree than it does upon

civic knowledge. Many societies seek to inculcate civic spirit primarily through civics instruction; the findings presented here suggest that social context and attitudes may be more important for educators interested in influencing civic spirit. It is possible that effective preparation of future citizens ought to be concerned with providing adolescents with experiences in which they can observe and participate in effective, fair functioning of political processes, with the hope that these experiences result in heightened trust in political institutions. Too little is known about the effectiveness of intentional interventions to spur increased trust to suggest that trust-building ought to be the aim of civic education. On the other hand, the findings in Table 32.1 suggest that civic knowledge is largely independent of civic identity.

Although trust is related similarly with each of the indicators of civic identity, this pattern is something of an anomaly—none of the other indicators showed such a consistent pattern. For example, political voice is negatively associated with nationalism, but positively associated with support for women's rights; per capita GDP is positively correlated with support for women's rights, but negatively associated with endorsement of conventional participation; and so on. This suggests (though better data such as data resulting from longitudinal studies and from natural experiments are needed to make stronger claims) that the factors that make salient some elements of civic identity may at the same time depress other elements. Elements of civic identity may be in dynamic tension with each other. Future research should examine this possibility.

We discussed earlier that the increased interest in civic identity witnessed over the past two decades is in part a consequence of concerns resulting from globalization and immigration. It is interesting, therefore, to examine the relation of the indicators of civic identity to attitudes toward immigration. It is noteworthy that all three indicators of civic identity are positively associated with favorable attitudes about immigrants. Figure 32.1 depicts the association of nationalism and positive attitudes toward

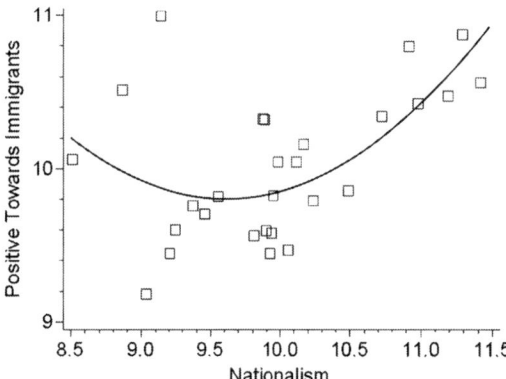

Fig. 32.1 Relation of positive attitudes toward immigrants with nationalism. Each point in the graph corresponds to the average for a country. A quadratic regression *line* is fitted to the plot. That the quadratic trend depicted here for data aggregated at the level of country also characterizes the relation of positive attitudes toward immigrants with nationalism at the level of the individual was confirmed using multi-level modeling, with participants at level 1 and countries at level 2 (details of this analysis are available upon request from the authors)

immigration. Each data point corresponds to a country and reflects the average for nationalism and positive attitudes toward immigrants living in that country. Superimposed on the graph is a quadratic trend, indicating that very little difference, and perhaps change in a negative direction, in positive attitudes toward immigrants is observed as countries change from low- to average levels of nationalism; however, attitudes toward immigrants become sharply more positive as countries change from about average in nationalism to high in nationalism. One possible interpretation of the trend is that in countries characterized by low levels of identification (low nationalism), positive attitudes toward immigrants are possible because adolescents seem little concerned about protecting the country from the possible threat posed by non-citizens. As identification increases, concerns about threats to the integrity of the society increase, and immigration is seen as a threat. At high levels of identification and pride in the country, however, adolescents apparently are confident that their countries are able to assimilate immigrants and accommodate to cultural traditions immigrants bring with them.

The strands of civic identity traced throughout this review—membership, participation, and rights—are related to each other and to psychological, political, and demographic influences. The strands are only loosely wound, and each is pulled and stretched by its own combination of influences. The consequence is that civic identity can assume very different profiles in comparisons between individuals (one person might be high in the sense of membership, whereas another might be focused on participation) or within individuals considered over time (high in the sense of oneself as a participant in early adulthood, more focused on membership in later adulthood). These findings suggest that understanding civic identity requires a consideration of its contexts.

Conclusion

Our goals in this chapter were to explore the nature of civic identity, consider contemporary debates about civic identity, and assess connections of civic identity and citizenship to context. We have suggested that civic identity is subjective and is best captured in relation to the qualities of citizenship. This means that civic identity refers to the individual's sense of self as a member of a community or society, as an actor contributing to the management and welfare of that group, and as a participant in that society bearing rights and responsibilities. Civic identity from this perspective excludes some connotations of identity (the notion advocated here rests on the subject's view of the self, and does not extend to attributing civic identities to individuals simply because they live in social groups), as well as distinguishes civic identity from other forms of identity that may be similar (national identities, moral identities).

Contemporary fascination with civic identity has arisen in large measure in reaction to, and concern with, the effects of diversity resulting from globalization and immigration. Our review touched upon claims that rapidly increasing cultural and racial diversities are problematic for the sense of membership and identification with the community that are central to civic identity and citizenship. Philosophers and social scientists are exploring the intersections of diversity, identity, and citizenship, and consequently much interesting scholarship has emerged with much more work on the near horizon.

Finally, our analyses of the CIVED data set were used to illustrate the intertwining of civic identity with psychological, political, and demographic contexts. The elaboration of civic identity and its psychological salience depend substantially on social, demographic, and political contexts. Perhaps more so than other identities, civic identity—the individual's sense of membership, participation, civic rights, and responsibilities—reflects one's psychological and social environments. We showed, for example, that nationalism, which reflects civic identity to some degree, varies according to the youthfulness of a country's population.

Our review of the research also identified gaps in our knowledge. For example, a great deal needs to be learned about civic identity before its explanatory power can be accurately assessed. As we noted, contemporary discussions are very much concerned with the consequences of globalization for civic identity and citizenship. Yet we know very little about the importance of civic identity, and the relative salience of different aspects of civic identity, for successful functioning of communities and societies. Our intuitions lead us to assume the importance of these identities, and there are certainly many facts consistent with this inference; but in fact, there is a dearth of careful empirical work disentangling civic identity from moral obligations, political considerations, and so on. Moreover, it is unclear whether it is even accurate to characterize an individual as having a single civic identity—perhaps multiple civic identities would be more accurate. The latter might be particularly true for immigrants, for example. If indeed multiple civic identities might exist in the same individual, the question then arises as to how these identities relate to each other and the conditions under which one identity assumes regulatory dominance over others in civic and political life (see Schildkraut, Chapter 36, this volume; and Stepick et al., Chapter 37, this volume, for more on this).

Secondly, although there are many views about how civic identity is best inculcated in children and adolescents (see Youniss & Hart, 2005, 2006 for several examples), we know very little about how civic identity can be intentionally and successfully fostered. Our analyses presented in this chapter suggest that teaching adolescents the facts and principles of civic life is not sufficient, as civic knowledge was not tightly connected to civic identity. Moreover, the successful transmission of civic knowledge is itself a complicated process that is not fully understood (see Hart et al., 2007, for one discussion of the limitations of civic knowledge for understanding civic life). It seems likely that the openness of civic identity to a variety of influences means that a range of interventions can be effective. Perhaps, at the time the second edition of this handbook is prepared, there will be sufficient knowledge to make recommendations to those concerned with social policy on this issue.

Despite the need for more careful theoretical and empirical work on civic identity, we believe it to be a construct whose time has arrived. The very real issues arising from immigration and globalization highlight the possibilities for exploration of political and civic life through the lens of civic identity.

Note

1. Details of this analysis are available upon request.

References

Abrams, D., Rutland, A., & Cameron, L. (2003). The development of subjective group dynamics: Children's judgments of normative and deviant in-group and out-group individuals. *Child Development, 74,* 1840–1856.

Alesina, A., Devleeschauwer, A., Easterly, W., Kurlat, S., & Wacziarg, R. (2003). Fractionalization. *Journal of Economic Growth, 8*(2), 155–194.

Barrett, M. (2007). *Children's knowledge, beliefs, and feelings about nations and national groups.* Hove, UK: Psychology Press.

Barrett, M., Wilson, H., & Lyons, E. (2003). The development of national ingroup bias: English children's attributions of characteristics to English, American, and German people. *British Journal of Developmental Psychology, 21,* 193–220.

Bellamy, R. (2008). *Citizenship: A very short introduction.* Oxford, UK: Oxford University Press.

Berry, J. W., Phinney, J. S., Sam, D. L., & Vedder, P. (2006). *Immigrant youth in cultural transition: Acculturation, identity, and adaptation across national contexts.* Mahwah, NJ: Lawrence Erlbaum Associates.

Brewer, M. B. (1999). The psychology of prejudice: Ingroup love or outgroup hate? *Journal of Social Issues, 55,* 429–444.

Brubaker, R., & Cooper, F. (2000). Beyond "identity". *Theory and Society, 29,* 1–47.

Caldwell, C. (2006, February, 5). Islam on the outskirts of the welfare state. *The New York Times*

Cameron, J. E. (2004). A three-factor model of social identity. *Self and Identity, 3,* 239–262.

Collier, P. (2009). *Wars, guns, and votes: Democracy in dangerous places.* New York: HarperCollins.

Duffy, A. L., & Nesdale, D. (2009). Peer groups, social identity, and children's bullying behavior. *Social Development, 18,* 121–139.

Flanagan, C. A. (2003). Trust, identity, and civic hope. *Applied Developmental Science, 7*(3), 165–171.

Galston, W. A. (2001). Political knowledge, political engagement, and civic education. *Annual Review of Political Science, 4,* 217–234.

Goldstone, J. A. (1999). Population and pivotal states. In R. Chase, E. Hill, & P. Kennedy (Eds.), *US strategy and pivotal states* (pp. 247–269). New York: W.W. Norton.

Halevy, N., Bornstein, G., & Sagiv, L. (2008). "In-group love" and "out-group hate" as motives for individual participation in intergroup conflict. *Psychological Science, 19,* 405–411.

Harris Interactive | News Room – National Pride Varies Greatly Across Europe. (2004). Retrieved January 22, 2010, from http://www.harrisinteractive.com/news/all newsbydate.asp?NewsID=815

Hart, D., Atkins, R., Markey, P., & Youniss, J. (2004). Youth bulges in communities: The effects of age structure on adolescent civic knowledge and civic participation. *Psychological Science, 15,* 591–597.

Hart, D., Donnelly, T. M., Youniss, J., & Atkins, R. (2007). High school community service as a predictor of adult voting and volunteering. *American Educational Research Journal, 44,* 197–219.

Hart, D., & Gullan, R. (2010). The sources of adolescent activism: Historical and contemporary findings.

In L. Sherrod, J. Torney-Purta, & C. Flanagan (Eds.), *Handbook of research on civic engagement in youth.*

Hart, D., & Yates, M. (1997). Identity and self in adolescence. In R. Vasta (Ed.), *Annals of Child Development, 1996* (pp. 207–242). London: Jessica Kingsley.

Helwig, C. C. (1998). Children's conceptions of fair government and freedom of speech. *Child Development, 69,* 518–531.

Helwig, C. C., Arnold, M. L., Tan, D., & Boyd, D. (2003). Chinese adolescents' reasoning about democratic and authority-based decision making in peer, family, and school contexts. *Child Development, 74,* 783–800.

Helwig, C. C., Arnold, M. L., Tan, D., & Boyd, D. (2007). Mainland Chinese and Canadian adolescents' judgments and reasoning about the fairness of democratic and other forms of government. *Cognitive Development, 22,* 96–109.

Huntington, S. P. (1996). *The clash of civilizations and the remaking of world order.* New York: Simon & Schuster.

Huntington, S. P. (2004). *Who are we? The challenges to America's national identity.* New York: Simon & Schuster.

Kahne, J. E., & Sporte, S. E. (2008). Developing citizens: The impact of civic learning opportunities on students' commitment to civic participation. *American Educational Research Journal, 45,* 738–766.

Kaufmann, D., Kraay, A., & Mastruzzi, M. (2008). *Governance matters VII: Aggregate and individual governance indicators, 1996–2007* (World Bank Policy Research Working Paper No. 4654). Washington, DC: World Bank.

Kawachi, I., Kennedy, B. P., Lochner, K., & Prothrow-Stith, D. (1997). Social capital, income inequality, and mortality. *American Journal of Public Health, 87,* 1491–1498.

Koopmans, R., Statham, R., Giugni, M., & Passy, F. (2005). *Contested citizenship immigration and cultural diversity in Europe.* Minneapolis, MN: University of Minnesota Press.

Kymlicka, W. (2001). *Politics in the vernacular: Nationalism, multiculturalism, and citizenship.* New York: Oxford University Press.

Lehman, R., & Torney-Purta, J. (n.d.). IEA Civic Education Study, 1999: Civic Knowledge and Engagement Among 14-Year-Olds in 23 European Countries, 2 Latin American Countries, Hong Kong, Australia, and the United States. Retrieved January 27, 2010, from http://dx.doi.org/10.3886/ICPSR21661

Leydet, D. (2006). Citizenship. *Stanford Encyclopedia of Philosophy.* Retrieved January 11, 2010, from http://plato.stanford.edu/entries/citizenship/

Lowenstein, R. (2006). The immigration equation. *New York Times*

Mandela, N. (1999). Nelson Mandela Foundation. Retrieved January 19, 2010, from http://www.foundationweb.co.za/website/speeches/pub_view.asp?pg=item&ItemID=NMS084&txtstr=youth%20day

Moller, H. (1968). Youth as a force in the modern world. *Comparative Studies in Sociology and History*, *10*, 238–260.

Neff, K. D., & Helwig, C. C. (2002). A constructivist approach to understanding the development of reasoning about rights and authority within cultural contexts. *Cognitive Development*, *17*, 1429–1450.

Nozick, R. (1981). *Philosophical explanations*. Cambridge, MA: Belknap Press.

Perlmutter, P. (2002). Minority group prejudice. *Society*, *39*(3), 59–65.

Post, J. M., Sprinzak, E., & Denny, L. M. (2003). The terrorists in their own words: Interviews with 35 incarcerated Middle Eastern terrorists. *Terrorism and Political Violence*, *15*(1), 171–184.

Pred, A. R. (2000). *Even in Sweden:* Racisms, racialized spaces, and the popular geographical imagination. Berkeley, CA: University of California Press.

Putnam, R. D. (2000). *Bowling alone: The collapse and revival of American community*. New York: Simon & Schuster.

Putnam, R. D. (2007). E pluribus unum: Diversity and community in the twenty-first century. *Scandinavian Political Studies*, *30*(2), 137–174.

Rahn, W. M. (2008). Globalization, the decline of civic commitments, and the future of democracy. In P. F. Nardulli (Ed.), *International perspectives on contemporary democracy* (pp. 134–157). Champaign, IL: University of Illinois Press.

Rubin, B. C. (2007). "There's still not justice": Youth civic identity development amid distinct school and community contexts. *Teachers College Record*, *109*, 449–481.

Shadid, A. (2005, January, 31). Iraqis Defy Threats as Millions Vote (washingtonpost.com). Retrieved January 18, 2010, from http://www.washingtonpost.com/wp-dyn/articles/A48454-2005Jan30.html

Torney-Purta, J. (2002). The school's role in developing civic engagement: A study of adolescents in twenty-eight countries. *Applied Developmental Science*, *6*(4), 203–212.

Torney-Purta, J., Lehmann, R., Oswald, H., & Schulz, W. (2001). *Citizenship and education in twenty-eight countries*. Amsterdam: International Association for the Evaluation of Educational Achievement.

Torney-Purta, J., Wilkenfeld, B., & Barber, C. (2008). How adolescents in twenty-seven countries understand, support, and practice human rights. *Journal of Social Issues*, *64*(4), 857–880.

Trzesniewski, K. H., Donnellan, M. B., & Robins, R. W. (2008). Is" Generation Me" really more narcissistic than previous generations? *Journal of Personality*, *76*, 903–918.

Turiel, E. (2003). Resistance and subversion in everyday life. *Journal of Moral Education*, *32*(2), 115–130.

Turiel, E., & Perkins, S. A. (2004). Flexibilities of mind: Conflict and culture. *Human Development*, *47*, 158–178.

Walzer, M. (1983). *Spheres of justice: A defense of pluralism and equality*. New York: Basic Books.

Wende, H. (2009). In the Field: Hear from CNN reporters across the globe Blog Archive – Voting in South Africa an emotional experience « – Blogs from CNN.com. Retrieved January 15, 2010, from http://inthefield.blogs.cnn.com/2009/04/22/voting-in-south-africa-an-emotional-experience/

Youniss, J., & Hart, D. (2005). The intersection of social institutions with civic development. In L. A. Jensen & R. W. Larson (Eds.), *New directions in child development: New horizons in developmental theory and research* (Vol. 109, pp. 73–81). San Francisco: Jossey-Bass.

Youniss, J., & Hart, D. (2006). The virtue in youth civic participation. *Diskurs Kindhiets- und Jugenforschung*, *2*, 229–243.

Zhou, X., Morris, M. W., & Benet-Martínez, V. (2008). Identity motives and cultural priming: Cultural (dis)identification in assimilative and contrastive responses. *Journal of Experimental Social Psychology*, *44*, 1151–1159.

Part VII
Ethnic and Cultural Identities

Adriana J. Umaña-Taylor

Abstract

The current chapter reviews existing empirical work on ethnic identity and its relation to psychosocial functioning among ethnic minorities in the United States. A working definition of the construct of ethnic identity is presented, followed by an overview of the theoretical frameworks that have informed the literature on ethnic identity. Existing work with Latino, Black, Asian, and American Indian samples is then reviewed and the strengths and limitations of this work are presented. Although there is much heterogeneity in ethnic identity experiences within and among ethnic minority groups in the United States, the current review of the existing research suggests that, among all groups, ethnic identity appears to serve a promotive and/or protective function for individuals' psychosocial functioning. Despite this potential commonality, it is recommended that researchers not assume homogeneity in ethnic identity experiences and outcomes within or among ethnic minority groups. Suggestions for future research are presented and focus largely on conducting longitudinal work that captures multiple developmental periods and that considers (a) within group diversity, (b) the influence of community ethnic concentration, and (c) the interaction of ethnic identity and other salient social identities in informing individuals' psychosocial functioning and development.

Identity formation is a critical developmental task throughout the lifespan (Erikson, 1968). As outlined within several chapters in this volume (e.g., Haslam & Ellemers, Chapter 30; Savin-Williams, Chapter 28; Spears, Chapter 9), individuals are defined by multiple social identities. One such social identity is informed by an individual's ethnicity, which is defined by one's culture of origin and is often associated with specific cultural values, attitudes, and behaviors (Phinney, 1996). The United States has a long history of placing a strong societal emphasis on ethnicity, such that the country is frequently described as a land of immigrants who came from diverse places across

A.J. Umaña-Taylor (✉)
School of Social and Family Dynamics, Program
in Family and Human Development, Arizona State
University, Tempe, AZ, USA
e-mail: adriana.umana-taylor@asu.edu

S.J. Schwartz et al. (eds.), *Handbook of Identity Theory and Research*,
DOI 10.1007/978-1-4419-7988-9_33, © Springer Science+Business Media, LLC 2011

the world, and equality among ethnic groups is often emphasized as a core value of the country (Devos & Banaji, 2005; Schildkraut, Chapter 36, this volume). Unfortunately, ethnicity also is particularly salient in the United States because significant disparities exist in access to power and resources based on ethnic group membership, with ethnic minority group members experiencing significant discrimination and marginalization (Devos & Banaji, 2005). Because of this sociohistorical context, ethnic group membership can be especially salient for the identities of ethnic minority individuals in the United States, particularly compared to their European American ethnic majority counterparts (Tsai, Morensen, Wong, & Hess, 2002).

The identity that develops as a function of one's ethnic group membership can be generally referred to as one's ethnic identity. Ethnic identity is conceptualized as a component of one's overall identity, and will vary in its salience across individuals, as introduced above. Given the diversity in disciplinary backgrounds among researchers who have studied ethnic identity, a wide range of definitions and conceptualizations of ethnic identity exists. Such conceptualizations have ranged from simple self-identification labels (e.g., Chinese American) to complex and multifaceted typologies informed by one's orientation and attachment toward one's ethnic heritage. For the most part, scholars have moved toward these more complex conceptualizations in recent work, given increased recognition that ethnic identity is a multifaceted and complex construct that cannot be reduced to a self-identification label (Phinney, 1996; Umaña-Taylor, Diversi, & Fine, 2002). Reducing ethnic identity to a self-identification label overlooks important variability that exists within groups, such as individuals' attachment or sense of commitment to their ethnic group, and the degree to which individuals have explored their ethnic group membership. Different people within the same ethnic group may have dramatically different degrees of ethnic identity. Importantly, this variability is often associated with individuals' psychosocial adjustment, given that the connection one feels to the group can determine whether or not membership in that group will have an impact on one's sense of self (Phinney, 1989; Spears, Chapter 9, this volume).

Researchers studying ethnic minority group members living in the United States have examined ethnic identity as a multifaceted construct that is comprised of various components such as exploration, resolution, and affirmation of ethnicity. Such research has identified significant associations between ethnic identity and various indices of psychosocial functioning. Members of ethnic minority groups in the United States are disproportionately likely to face negative experiences associated with their ethnic background, such as ethnic discrimination (e.g., Fisher, Wallace, & Fenton, 2000), that are, in turn, associated with negative psychosocial outcomes such as anxiety and depression (e.g., Romero, Carvajal, Valle, & Orduña, 2007). As a result, research designed to identify factors that can protect against these negative experiences and/or that predict positive psychosocial functioning among ethnic minority group members is particularly important. Specifically, basic research that focuses on promotive or protective factors among ethnic minority group members, such as ethnic identity, is critically necessary for developing effective preventive intervention programs designed to minimize negative outcomes among ethnic minority group members. In fact, several scholars (e.g., Case & Robinson, 2003; Hollon et al., 2002; Prado et al., 2006), as well as the US surgeon general (Thompson, 2001), have called for an increased focus on prevention research with members of ethnic minority groups in the United States, particularly because of the increased risk that members of ethnic minority groups face with respect to indices of maladjustment such as delinquency, school failure or dropout, physical health problems, and mental health problems. As such, the current chapter provides an overview of existing work in which the construct of ethnic identity has been examined in relation to psychosocial functioning (i.e., general psychosocial adjustment such as self-esteem; internalizing behaviors such as depressive symptoms; externalizing behaviors such as drug or alcohol use) among ethnic minorities in the United States. Strengths and limitations of existing work are reviewed, and suggestions for future theoretical and empirical advances are presented. Throughout the remainder of this chapter, terms such as Asian, Black, and Latino are used to refer to individuals who live in the United States and have ethnic origins in these groups. The term "American" is not added to these descriptors (e.g., Asian American) unless this is the terminology used in the original published work that is being discussed. Although all research reviewed pertains to studies conducted on ethnic minority groups in the United States, adding the qualifier "American" would be inaccurate for some group members who, despite residing in the United States, do not identify with the label "American."

Theoretical Background

Although existing conceptualizations of ethnic identity have been guided by numerous theoretical frameworks, among the most prevalent theoretical perspectives upon which scholars have drawn when studying ethnic identity are Erikson's (1968) theory of identity development (see Kroger & Marcia, Chapter 2, this volume) and social identity theory (Tajfel, 1981; Tajfel & Turner, 1986; see Spears, Chapter 9, this volume). Specifically, Phinney (1989, 1993) applied these theoretical frameworks, along with Marcia's (1980, 1994) operationalization of Erikson's theory, to derive a new conceptualization of ethnic identity development. Based on Marcia's operationalization of Erikson's theory, which outlined four possible identity statuses (i.e., diffuse, foreclosed, moratorium, achieved; see Kroger & Marcia, Chapter 2, this volume, for a review) in which individuals could be classified based on their degree of exploration of identity issues and commitment to a personal identity, Phinney (1993) proposed a three-stage model of ethnic identity. Phinney's work, which focused largely on adolescence, emphasized the need to acknowledge and understand the psychosocial meaning that individuals developed with respect to their ethnic group membership. That is, what does a person's ethnicity mean to her or him? How

central is it to her or his sense of self? Does the person regard her or his ethnicity positively or negatively, and to what extent?

From a developmental perspective, similar to identity status (see Kroger & Marcia, Chapter 2, this volume), ethnic identity formation includes processes of exploration and commitment/resolution (Phinney, 1993; Umaña-Taylor, Yazedjian, & Bámaca-Gómez, 2004). *Exploration* involves increasing one's understanding and exposure to one's group by doing things such as reading about one's ethnic background, talking to others about one's ethnic group, or searching the Internet for information about one's ethnic group (Umaña-Taylor et al., 2004). Making a commitment toward one's ethnic identity pertains to individuals' sense of *resolution* regarding their ethnic group membership; in particular, *resolution* of ethnic identity involves a sense of understanding regarding what an individual's ethnic group membership means to her or him and the extent to which it plays an important role in her or his life. The concepts of *exploration* and *resolution* are drawn largely from Erikson's (1968) and Marcia's (1980) work on identity formation and provide a useful framework for understanding how the psychological meaning of ethnicity develops and eventually may contribute to the individual's general sense of self.

Social identity theory has provided a sociological and social-psychological approach toward understanding ethnic identity, with a specific emphasis on the affect that individuals develop toward their ethnic group. The construct of ethnic identity *affirmation* has emerged largely from social identity theory (Spears, Chapter 9, this volume; Tajfel, 1981; Tajfel & Turner, 1986) and is based on the notion that, in an effort to maintain a positive self-concept, individuals strive to achieve a positive social identity. One way in which such a positive social identity can be developed is by adopting a positive outlook toward the social groups to which one belongs. Thus, ethnic identity *affirmation* pertains generally to whether individuals feel positively or negatively about their ethnic group membership (Umaña-Taylor et al., 2004). This dimension is sometimes also referred to as private regard (Fuligni, Witkow, & Garcia, 2005; Rivas-Drake, Hughes, & Way, 2009).

Viewed as a social-developmental process, ethnic identity has been theorized to become increasingly important during adolescence (Phinney, 1993), but it is also considered a salient process that can occur throughout the lifespan (Phinney, 1996; Syed, Azmitia, & Phinney, 2007). Furthermore, ethnic identity serves as an important predictor of individuals' psychosocial functioning and development. Conceptually, a secure sense of ethnic identity contributes significantly to positive psychosocial functioning among ethnic minority group members (Phinney & Kohatsu, 1997). Existing research, conducted primarily with adolescent populations, has generally supported the notion that ethnic identity may promote positive adjustment, although findings vary somewhat according to the specific ethnic minority group studied. In the sections that follow, I review research that has examined ethnic identity in relation to indices of psychosocial functioning, with an emphasis on understanding whether findings are consistent across ethnic groups and across developmental periods. I identify general patterns and make recommendations regarding directions for future work in this area.

Overview of Empirical Findings

The past decade has seen a significant increase in the number of studies published focused on ethnic identity among members of four pan-ethnic minority groups in the United States (i.e., Latino, Black, Asian, and American Indian) and potential links between ethnic identity and psychosocial functioning among these populations. Much of this work has been driven by an interest in identifying the degree to which ethnic identity can serve a protective function for ethnic minority group members, who have been identified in previous research as being at increased risk for negative psychosocial adjustment (e.g., Lee, 2003; Mossakowski, 2003; Romero & Roberts, 2003; Walker, Wingate, Obasi, & Joiner, 2008).

Within this body of work, some studies have examined ethnic identity among samples that collapse across multiple ethnic minority groups (i.e., the sample includes Blacks, Latinos, and Asians; and analyses are conducted across ethnic groups). When studies have analyzed data based on individual ethnic groups, however, findings are somewhat different than when pooled ethnic samples are examined. A review of this work, as well as a discussion of this discrepancy, follows.

Pooled ethnic samples. When samples are examined collapsing across ethnic groups, ethnic identity appears to be significantly associated with favorable psychosocial outcomes. For example, researchers have found that higher levels of ethnic identity affirmation are associated with lower levels of drug use among ethnic-minority early adolescents (Marsiglia, Kulis, & Hecht, 2001; Marsiglia, Kulis, Hecht, & Sills, 2004), and that exploration and resolution are each positively associated with self-esteem among ethnic-minority high school and college students (Umaña-Taylor et al., 2004). In addition, in studies in which a composite ethnic identity score was examined (i.e., scores are summed across exploration, resolution, and affirmation), higher levels of ethnic identity were associated with higher self-esteem among ethnic-minority high school students (Bracey, Bámaca-Gomez, & Umaña-Taylor, 2004), higher overall quality of life among ethnic-minority adults (Utsey, Chae, Brown, & Kelly, 2002), and lower levels of personality characteristics commonly linked to drug use, such as rebelliousness and impulsivity, among ethnic-minority young adults (Brook, Duan, Brook, & Ning, 2007).

Latino samples. In contrast, findings from studies that examined ethnic identity among ethnically homogenous samples (or studies that included multiple ethnic groups in their sample but where analyses were carried out separately for specific ethnic groups) have been more mixed. Research with Latinos is a good example of this, in that some findings suggest that higher ethnic identity is associated with more positive adjustment, others suggest that ethnic identity is positively associated with *mal*adjustment, and yet others fail to find an association between Latinos' ethnic identity and individuals' psychosocial functioning. For instance, studies have found composite ethnic identity scores to be positively associated with self-esteem among both early adolescents (Schwartz, Zamboanga, & Jarvis, 2007) and older adolescents (Bracey, Bámaca-Gómez, & Umaña-Taylor, 2004; Umaña-Taylor, 2004), and positively associated with coping, mastery, and optimism among early adolescents (Roberts et al., 1999). In addition, exploration and resolution were each uniquely and positively associated with self-esteem among Latino high school (Umaña-Taylor & Updegraff, 2007; Umaña-Taylor, Vargas-Chanes, Garcia, & Gonzales-Backen, 2008) and college (Umaña-Taylor & Shin, 2007) students. Group esteem, which appears analogous to ethnic identity affirmation, has been found to be negatively associated with delinquency in late adolescents (French, Kim, & Pillado, 2006). Furthermore, ethnic identity affirmation has also emerged as a protective factor by minimizing (a) the negative association between discrimination and self-esteem among Mexican-origin adolescents (Romero & Roberts, 2003) and (b) the positive association between salient risk factors (e.g., peer drug use) and drug use among Puerto Rican adolescents (Brook, Whiteman, Balka, Win, & Gursen, 1998). Thus, many studies suggest a positive link with adjustment, or, put differently, a negative link with maladjustment.

A few studies with Latinos, however, have found ethnic identity to be associated with increased maladjustment. For instance, using composite ethnic identity scores, researchers have found ethnic identity to be positively associated with alcohol use in Mexican American college students (Zamboanga, Raffaelli, & Horton, 2006), and positively associated with alcohol and marijuana use in early adolescents (Zamboanga, Schwartz, Jarvis, & Van Tyne, 2009). In addition, researchers studying Latino early adolescents have found ethnic identity exploration to be associated with increased delinquency (French, Seidman, Allen, & Aber, 2006), and ethnic identity affirmation to be associated with an increased alcohol use (Marsiglia et al., 2004). Finally, McCoy and Major (2003) found that prejudice was more strongly and positively associated with depressive symptoms among college students who were highly ethnically identified, suggesting that ethnic identity may serve as a risk enhancer in this context.

Finally, in other studies, researchers failed to find a significant association between ethnic identity and depressive symptoms among Latino early adolescents (Roberts et al., 1999) and found that ethnic identity affirmation was not associated with self-esteem among older adolescents and college students (Umaña-Taylor & Shin, 2007; Umaña-Taylor et al., 2004). More longitudinal work is needed with samples that capture *multiple* developmental periods, such as early adolescence through adulthood, to gain a clearer understanding of the potential links of ethnic identity to psychosocial functioning throughout the lifespan and, further, to better understand which, if any, of the ethnic identity components are linked to these outcomes. There is some empirical support for the notion that ethnic identity affirmation is a protective factor that can reduce or buffer the negative effects of risk on Latino adolescents' psychosocial functioning. Furthermore, it appears that the most consistent finding with Latinos across developmental periods is that both ethnic identity exploration and resolution are positively associated with indices of adaptive psychosocial adjustment (e.g., self-esteem, coping, optimism, lower delinquency), although there was one study that found a link between ethnic identity exploration and delinquency during early adolescence (i.e., French et al., 2006). Interestingly, only one study, using a sample of early adolescents, examined depressive symptoms as an outcome of interest with Latinos, and that study found no association between a composite ethnic identity score and depressive symptoms (Roberts et al., 1999). Given Latinos' increased risk for mental health disorders such as depression (Roberts, Roberts, & Chen, 1997; Siegel, Yancey, Aneshensel, & Schuler, 1999), it is important to examine this association among other samples of Latinos, including high school and college students, as well as adults, to determine whether the findings regarding ethnic identity and depressive symptoms are generalizable across age groups. Findings from this work will have important implications for preventive intervention work with Latinos.

Black samples. Research examining the associations between ethnic identity and psychosocial functioning, internalizing, and externalizing behaviors among Black samples has more consistently yielded promotive effects. In fact, of the studies identified in the current review, only one was found in which ethnic identity affirmation (labeled "group esteem") was associated with increased delinquency among African American early and middle adolescents (French et al., 2006). Overall, findings from studies of Black early adolescents have indicated that composite ethnic identity scores were associated with fewer externalizing behaviors (Arbona, Jackson, McCoy, & Blakely, 1999), lower risky sexual attitudes (Belgrave, Van Oss Marin, & Chambers, 2000), and lower levels of aggressive behaviors and beliefs (McMahon & Watts, 2002). Similarly, composite ethnic identity scores have been inversely linked with depressive symptoms among early and middle adolescents (e.g., McHale, Whiteman, Kim, & Crouter, 2007; McMahon & Watts, 2002; Wong, Eccles, & Sameroff, 2003; Yasui, Dorham, & Dishion, 2004), lower levels of loneliness among early adolescents (Roberts et al., 1999), and higher self-esteem among high school students (Bracey et al., 2004; Roberts et al., 1999).

When individual ethnic identity components were examined, similar findings emerged. With respect to Black adolescents' externalizing behaviors, ethnic identity exploration was associated with lower levels of delinquency among early and middle adolescents (French et al., 2006); and ethnic identity affirmation was associated with fewer sexual behaviors among early adolescents (Wills et al., 2007) and more positive school attitudes and fewer problem behaviors among early and middle adolescents (Resnicow, Soler, Braithwaite, Selassie, & Smith, 1999). In terms of psychosocial functioning and internalizing behaviors, ethnic identity affirmation was positively associated with self-esteem among early, middle, and late adolescents (Resnicow et al., 1999; Umaña-Taylor & Shin,

2007), and negatively associated with depressive symptoms (Gaylord-Harden, Ragsdale, Mandara, Richards, & Petersen, 2007) among early adolescents. In addition, ethnic identity exploration and resolution were each positively associated with self-esteem among African American college students (Umaña-Taylor & Shin, 2007).

Furthermore, consistent with findings from studies that examined Latinos, among Black youth, ethnic identity affirmation has emerged as a significant protective factor against drug use (Brook & Pahl, 2005) and alcohol consumption (Nasim, Belgrave, Jagers, Wilson, & Owens, 2007). Moreover, when measured as a composite variable, ethnic identity appeared to reduce the positive association between depressive symptoms and suicidal ideation among Black college students (Walker et al., 2008). In addition, early adolescents' connection to their ethnic group attenuated the negative effects of discrimination on adolescents' academic achievement, self-competency, and problem behaviors (Wong et al., 2003). In sum, the association between ethnic identity and positive psychosocial functioning and adjustment appears to be clear among Black samples. Ethnic identity is not only clearly linked to positive outcomes among Black youth, but ethnic identity affirmation, in particular, may play a significant protective function in the face of negative external influences. As with research on Latinos, there is limited research on developmental periods beyond late adolescence and, thus, it is unclear whether ethnic identity functions in a similar manner among Black adults. This is an area ripe for future research, particularly because the findings have significant implications for preventive intervention work in light of the potentially protective nature of ethnic identity.

Asian samples. Research conducted with Asian samples is most distinguishable from research with Latino samples in that many studies have focused on specific national origin groups (e.g., Filipinos, Koreans) rather than on pan-ethnic populations (e.g., Asian, Latino). In addition, unlike Blacks and Latinos, several studies have examined adult Asian samples. Findings for Asians appear to be more mixed compared to those with Latino or Black samples. For instance, ethnic identity tended to be linked with greater maladjustment for Cambodian and Hawaiian adolescents, such that higher composite ethnic identity scores were associated with more delinquency among Cambodian adolescents (Go & Le, 2005) and more misconduct (Hishinuma et al., 2005) and suicide attempts (Yuen, Nahulu, Hishinuma, & Miyamoto, 2000) among Native Hawaiian adolescents living in Hawaii. On the contrary, in another study, ethnic identity affirmation was associated with lower levels of violence among Hawaiian adolescents and adults (Austin, 2004). Furthermore, when studying pan-ethnic Asian samples, composite ethnic identity scores have been associated with higher self-esteem among high school students (Bracey et al., 2004) and lower depressive symptoms among college students (Juang, Nguyen, & Lin, 2006). In addition, among college students, ethnic identity affirmation was found to be positively associated with self-esteem (Umaña-Taylor & Shin, 2007) and negatively associated with depressive symptoms (Mahalingam, Balan, & Haritatos, 2008). Higher composite ethnic identity scores were also linked with fewer depressive symptoms among Filipino adults (Mossakowski, 2003). Interestingly, among a sample of Korean college students, there was no significant association between composite ethnic identity and either self-esteem or depressive symptoms (Hovey, Kim, & Seligman, 2006). Given the limited research on specific Asian ethnic groups, it is not clear whether these pan-ethnic findings are a function of the mixture of national origins in these samples or of some other participant characteristics. What these findings highlight, however, is the importance of examining specific Asian ethnic groups, as findings with pan-ethnic samples may not necessarily be generalizable to all specific ethnic groups within the pan-ethnic group. Findings obtained using a sample that is largely Chinese, for example, may obscure important findings for Vietnamese, Korean, Asian Indian, Hmong, and other Asian groups that may be less well represented in the sample. Unlike Latinos, Asian groups do not share a common language and, furthermore, several Asian groups (e.g., Sri Lankans, Vietnamese, and Chinese) differ considerably from one another with respect to conditions of immigration to the United States, context of reception, and religion, for example. It is likely that the differences across Asian cultures – particularly the lack of a common language, which is believed to be an important ethnic marker (Alba, 1990; Padilla, 1999; Sridhar, 1988) – may partially explain the discrepant findings across Asian groups.

With respect to the potential protective nature of ethnic identity, findings from two studies of Filipino adults, each utilizing a composite ethnic identity score, indicated that ethnic identity attenuated the negative effects of discrimination on depressive symptoms (Mossakowski, 2003) and on total prescription drug use (i.e., use and misuse; Gee, Delva, & Takeuchi, 2007). In another study, which included a pan-ethnic Asian American sample of college students, Lee (2003) also examined the potential moderating role of ethnic identity in the association between discrimination and both self-esteem and depressive symptoms, but found no evidence of moderation. All three studies used a composite score of ethnic identity and, in fact, used the same measure. The main difference, however, was that Lee's study utilized a pan-ethnic Asian American college student sample and an Asian Indian college student sample, whereas Mossakowski and Gee et al., each studied Filipino adult samples. Given the differences in the samples, it is unclear whether the protective nature of ethnic identity may be specific to the national origin group under study or to the developmental period (i.e., college students versus adults).

Another significant moderator that has emerged in existing work with Asian samples involved the Asian ethnic concentration within individuals' schools or communities. Juang et al. (2006) found a significant association between ethnic identity and depressive symptoms when Asian American college students were in an ethnically concentrated context (i.e., at the community level, Asians comprised 31% of the total population); however, this relation did not emerge as significant for Asian American college students in a primarily White American context (i.e., at the community level, Asians comprised only 8% of the total population and Whites comprised 81%). Somewhat contrary to Juang's findings, but consistent with the notion that ethnic concentration of context is a variable worthy of study, Umaña-Taylor and Shin (2007) found that ethnic identity exploration, resolution, and affirmation were unrelated to self-esteem among Asian American college students in California, whereas resolution and affirmation were both positively associated with self-esteem among Asian American college students in the Midwest. The two studies differed significantly in the outcome variable of interest (i.e., depressive symptoms versus self-esteem) and the nature of the context (e.g., the California sample for Umaña-Taylor and Shin's study was not a particularly Asian-concentrated context, but it was more ethnically diverse than the Midwest sample). Thus, it is inaccurate to present these findings as completely contradictory; however, they are being presented to illustrate that within both of these studies, community ethnic concentration played a significant moderating role and should be considered in future research.

In sum, research findings from studies with Asian American samples are more mixed, and it is not clear whether ethnic identity generally plays a promotive role vis-à-vis psychosocial functioning and adjustment for Asian Americans in general, or whether findings must be qualified for specific Asian groups. Furthermore, the specific role that community ethnic concentration plays is unclear, but it appears to be an influential variable. Studies examining ethnic identity must pay special attention to the characteristics of the communities in which individuals' lives are embedded, particularly with respect to ethnic composition. As explained by Juang et al. (2006), it is possible that Asians living in an ethnic-concentrated context and who identify strongly with their ethnicity may experience a better fit with the norms and values of the context, and this may lead to greater well-being. These ideas are consistent with notions from a goodness-of-fit framework (Lerner & Lerner, 1983; Thomas & Chess, 1977) and suggest that individuals' adjustment may depend on the degree to which their

ethnic identity is consistent with the demands and resources of their community (Juang et al., 2006).

American Indian samples. Although researchers have examined ethnic identity among American Indian populations, this pan-ethnic group has been the least represented in the existing work on ethnic identity. One study found that ethnic identity affirmation was negatively associated with drug use (Kulis, Napoli, & Marsiglia, 2002). A second study (Newman, Sontag, & Salvato, 2006) found that a composite ethnic identity score was positively associated with self-esteem and negatively associated with social problems, but there was no significant association between ethnic identity and depressive symptoms. Finally, Marsiglia et al. (2004) found that ethnic identity affirmation was positively associated with drug use among American Indian early adolescents. Given the few studies in which ethnic identity has been examined among American Indian populations, it is difficult to speculate about the value of ethnic identity for this pan-ethnic population. Furthermore, given the diversity that exists within the American Indian population (e.g., numerous tribes, languages, and traditions), it may be difficult to draw generalizations from existing work in which the focus has been a pan-ethnic population (e.g., including multiple tribal affiliations).

Summary. Together, findings suggest that the construct of ethnic identity appears to serve a promotive function, particularly among adolescent and college student populations. This seems to be most consistent for Blacks in the United States, and least consistent for Asians in the United States. Although the findings from research with American Indian samples suggest that ethnic identity is associated with positive adjustment, the limited number of studies and the vast diversity that exists among this pan-ethnic population limits the ability to draw generalizable conclusions from existing findings. Importantly, the findings reviewed above demonstrate the need to acknowledge the diversity that exists both among and within ethnic minority groups. Studies that reported findings based on pooled ethnic samples revealed only promotive associations between ethnic identity and outcome variables. However, studies focusing on specific ethnic minority groups, as described above, yielded discrepant findings. The limitations of this work and ideas for advancing this literature are reviewed below.

Empirical and Conceptual Limitations and Directions for Future Research

Within-Group Diversity. Although findings from existing studies provide a starting point from which to understand the relevance of ethnic identity for various ethnic minority group members in the United States, they also underscore the need to account for the tremendous heterogeneity that exists among and within ethnic minority populations in the United States, and could possibly apply to dynamics for certain populations in other countries (e.g., South Asians in England, North Africans in France). First, the divergent findings for pooled samples and ethnic homogenous samples demonstrate the need to conduct analyses for specific ethnic groups. Further, the inconsistent findings within ethnic minority groups (e.g., Asians) suggest that perhaps analyses should be conducted by specific national origin groups, rather than an assumed homogenous pan-ethnic population; for instance, separate analyses would be conducted for Chinese, Vietnamese, and Cambodian Americans, rather than combining all groups and analyzing data for an assumed homogenous "Asian" group. In fact, one characteristic that distinguished research on Asians (in which findings were most mixed) from research on Latinos, Blacks, and American Indians was that, in most studies on Asians, analyses were conducted by specific national-origin groups, whereas analyses were largely conducted on pan-ethnic populations for the other three groups. This may help to explain why findings appear to be more consistent across Blacks than across Latinos. Among samples of Blacks, it is possible that few Black immigrants are represented in the samples and, rather, the findings are being driven by African American participants who share a long group

history in the United States. Among Latinos, however, findings may be driven by one group when conducted in a certain region of the United States (e.g., Cubans in Florida; Mexicans in California; Puerto Ricans and Dominicans in the Northeast) and, thus, the most dominant national-origin group in each sample may be driving the findings in each study – perhaps accounting for the inconsistent findings across studies.

Developmental Period Studied. Another notable limitation of the existing work is the lack of focus on adult populations. Although it is understandable that a vast majority of research on ethnic identity would focus on adolescents and emerging adults, given the central focus on identity formation during this developmental period (Arnett, 2000; Erikson, 1968), ethnic identity is a process that is expected to be revisited throughout the lifespan (Phinney, 1996; Syed et al., 2007) and, thus, there is a need to understand this process beyond adolescence. Further, studies that have examined adult populations suggest that ethnic identity may serve a protective function by offsetting the negative effects of discrimination on depressive symptoms (cf. Mossakowski, 2003) and prescription drug use and misuse (Gee et al., 2007). Moreover, using a sample of ethnic minority adults (pooled across ethnic groups), Utsey et al. (2002) found that a stronger sense of ethnic identity was associated with higher quality of life. Thus, it will be important for future research to determine whether ethnic identity functions in a similar promotive manner among adults from other ethnic minority backgrounds. There is some work (i.e., Snyder, Cleveland, & Thornton, 2006) to suggest that ethnic identity may moderate the association between demographic variables and attitudes toward affirmative action among Asian, Black, and Latino adults; thus, future work should consider ethnic identity as a potential moderator of the relations between stressful experiences and adult adjustment.

Longitudinal Studies. Another important research gap involves the need for more longitudinal work that follows the progression of ethnic identity across multiple developmental periods. Given the costly and labor-intensive nature of longitudinal studies, coupled with the relatively recent advancement of ethnic identity as a construct worthy of study, it is not surprising that few longitudinal studies focused on ethnic identity have been published. The few longitudinal studies that have been conducted to date have focused on early to middle adolescence (French et al., 2006) and middle to late adolescence (Pahl & Way, 2006; Umaña-Taylor, Gonzales-Backen, & Guimond, 2009). These studies have focused on African Americans and Latinos, and did not include Asian Americans or American Indians, and developmental periods beyond adolescence have not been examined. Nevertheless, findings suggest significant growth in ethnic identity affirmation and exploration during middle adolescence for Black and Latino youth (French et al., 2006) as well as significant growth in ethnic identity exploration and resolution from middle to late adolescence for Latino girls and growth in ethnic identity affirmation during this same time period for both Latino boys and girls (Umaña-Taylor et al., 2009). In a third study, Pahl and Way (2006) found no change in ethnic identity affirmation, and a decrease in ethnic identity exploration, between middle and late adolescence in a sample of Black and Latino adolescents. Again, however, community ethnic concentration may play a role in these inconsistent results across studies: Pahl and Way studied an urban sample of Black and Latino youth in New York City, whereas Umaña-Taylor et al.,'s sample consisted of Latino youth attending Midwestern schools that were predominately European American. It is possible that differences in the salience of ethnicity across the two samples could be contributing to the different trajectories observed. The inconsistent findings, at the very least, underscore the importance of considering the potential influence of community ethnic concentration on ethnic identity formation.

Finally, Syed et al. (2007) examined changes in ethnic identity in a short-term longitudinal study (i.e., examining change in college students' ethnic identity between Fall and Spring quarters within a single academic year) utilizing a typology approach based on Phinney's (1993) theoretical work on ethnic identity (described above). In their study, they examined whether individuals' ethnic identity status classification (i.e., unexamined, moratorium, achieved) changed over time. Individuals who reported low levels of exploration and resolution were classified as unexamined, those with high levels of exploration but low levels of resolution were classified as being in moratorium, and those suggesting high levels of both exploration and resolution were classified as achieved. Syed et al.'s (2007) findings supported existing theory in that the emerging adults in their sample were generally moving toward, rather than away from, the achieved status. Furthermore, these findings are consistent with existing theory and empirical work on developmental patterns of change in identity statuses (for a review, see Kroger & Marcia, Chapter 2, this volume). Their approach, focusing on shifts in ethnic identity status membership over time, is consistent with existing ethnic identity theory (i.e., Phinney, 1993), which is built on the notion of identity status typologies and classifications (Marcia, 1980). Although it is analytically challenging to examine change in ethnic identity using typology classifications, particularly with longer term longitudinal studies in which the possible trajectories are numerous, it is an important methodological step that would significantly advance the field's understanding of how ethnic identity formation unfolds. Syed and colleagues' study was limited to college students and spanned only one semester; it would be worthwhile to replicate this work following early adolescents through emerging adulthood. Given the centrality of the developmental task of identity formation during adolescence (Erikson, 1968), coupled with the increased social and cognitive maturity that accompanies this developmental period (Elliott & Feldman, 1990; Keating, 1990) and makes the abstract construct of ethnicity increasingly salient to youth, it is likely that much change in ethnic identity formation takes place during the period from early adolescence through emerging adulthood. Furthermore, following individuals for a longer period of time will allow for a clearer understanding of possible trajectories and their potential links to outcomes. Meeus, van de Schoot, Keijsers, Schwartz, and

Branje (2010) provide an example of an analytic approach that may be useful to apply to ethnic identity research. Meeus and colleagues longitudinally examined identity status transitions (i.e., their focus was on personal identity - assessing interpersonal and ideological domains) using a combination of latent class analysis and latent transition analysis. With this dual-method strategy, they were able to identify the prevalence of specific identity statuses at distinct developmental periods and, importantly, to track patterns of identity transitions over time. It will be useful to apply such an approach to analyze longitudinal data on ethnic identity.

Composite Ethnic Identity Scores versus Examination of Individual Components

Generally, scholars have moved toward an examination of individual ethnic identity components (e.g., affirmation, exploration), rather than an examination of a composite ethnic identity score that encompasses multiple ethnic identity components (e.g., via the use of a sum score or a mean across multiple subscales). In early work on ethnic identity, the Multigroup Ethnic Identity Measure (MEIM; Phinney, 1992) was one of, if not *the*, most widely used measures to assess ethnic identity (Helms, 2007). However, psychometric analyses of the MEIM by multiple research teams (e.g., Pegg & Plybon, 2005; Ponterotto, Gretchen, Utsey, Stracuzzi, & Saya, 2003; Worrell, 2000) including Phinney herself (see Phinney & Ong, 2007) have repeatedly suggested that this measure is characterized by a single factor, rather than the original three-factor model that guided the development of the scale. This has led much of the work on ethnic identity to be based on an examination of a composite ethnic identity score, which combined individuals' scores on multiple ethnic identity components such as exploration, resolution, and affirmation. Umaña-Taylor et al. (2004) argued that a new measure, in which one could uniquely examine the multiple components of ethnic identity, was necessary to be more consistent with existing theory (for a detailed account of this argument, see Umaña-Taylor & Alfaro, 2006; Umaña-Taylor, 2005). Thus, the Ethnic Identity Scale (EIS; Umaña-Taylor et al., 2004), which allowed for the unique assessment of three components of ethnic identity (i.e., exploration, resolution, and affirmation), was developed. Also recognizing the need to independently assess the components of ethnic identity, Phinney and Ong (2007) published a revised version of the MEIM (i.e., MEIM-R), which consists of two distinct subscales (i.e., exploration and commitment). The EIS and MEIM-R both allow for examination of individual components of ethnic identity.

The examination of individual components of ethnic identity has proven worthwhile, given that the components have been differentially linked to predictors and outcomes. For instance, Umaña-Taylor et al. (2004) found that familial ethnic socialization significantly predicted ethnic identity exploration and resolution, but not ethnic identity affirmation, among both university and high school students from various ethnic groups. Supple, Ghazarian, Frabutt, Plunkett, and Sands (2006) replicated this finding with a sample of Latino youth. Furthermore, Supple and colleagues found that ethnic identity affirmation, but not exploration or resolution, significantly predicted teacher-reported school performance. Finally, in a longitudinal study of Latino youth (Umaña-Taylor et al., 2009), growth in ethnic identity exploration, but not affirmation or resolution, significantly predicted growth in self-esteem from middle to late adolescence. Together, these findings suggest that utilizing a composite ethnic identity score may be less informative, given that the specific associations for certain ethnic identity components may be masked. Furthermore, measurement of individual components and examination of typology classifications using various combinations of levels of different ethnic identity components (as described above in Syed et al., 2007, work) are most consistent with the theoretical frameworks guiding existing work on ethnic identity and, thus, make the measurement of individual ethnic identity components most compelling.

The Role of Community Ethnic Concentration. Existing research also is limited in its understanding of the role that social context plays in individuals' ethnic identity formation and, in turn, its association with various predictors and outcomes. Although a few studies have examined ethnic identity in distinct contexts based on the ethnic composition of adolescents' schools (e.g., Juang et al., 2006; Umaña-Taylor, 2004; Umaña-Taylor & Shin, 2007), there is a need for a more systematic examination of this aspect of the social context. In particular, it will be important for future research to consider not only the proximal social context (e.g., school ethnic composition), but also the more distal community ethnic concentration, such as the geographical region in which individuals' lives are embedded. For example, ethnic identity may be protective against drug and alcohol use in highly Hispanic areas in the Southwestern United States (Marsiglia et al., 2001, 2004), but it may represent a risk for drug and alcohol use in parts of the American Midwest, where White Americans comprise an overwhelming majority of the local population (Zamboanga et al., 2009).

Findings from existing studies on the effects of community ethnic concentration on ethnic identity have been somewhat mixed, but it is difficult to compare across studies because they have examined different populations (e.g., Asian American adolescents versus Latino adolescents). Furthermore, existing studies have assessed the proximal community ethnic concentration by measuring the ethnic density of adolescents' schools or universities, but the geographical region in which adolescents were raised has not been tested as a contributing variable in existing studies. Representation of some ethnic groups is much greater in certain regions of the United States than others. For instance, the Latino population is more heavily concentrated in the Southwest than in the Northwest. As a more specific example, if one were to focus on specific national-origin groups, it would be important to recognize that, within the state of California, the experiences related to ethnic identity would likely be significantly different for Mexican-origin Latinos, who make up a majority

of the Latino population in California, and Puerto Rican Latinos, who are a double-minority in California because they are a numerical minority within the Latino population (which in turn is a minority within the United States as a whole). However, if the same study were conducted in New York, Puerto Ricans would be the majority Latino group, and Mexican-origin Latinos would be a double-minority.

It is a complex endeavor to account for the distinct social contexts in which individuals' lives are embedded (Bronfenbrenner, 1989), and even more challenging to identify which ecological variables should be examined as significant contributors or moderators in studies of ethnic identity. However, it will be critical for research to move in this direction, particularly because of existing work that has demonstrated that ethnic group density and history in a particular geographic context can have a significant impact on ethnic identity development via the resources available for ethnic socialization and the potential barriers that result from lack of representation of one's group (Schwartz et al., 2007; Umaña-Taylor & Bámaca, 2004). Thus, there is a need for future studies on ethnic identity to focus on specific national-origin groups and obtain their samples from at least two distinct geographical regions, in which a key distinguishing factor is the ethnic representation and history of the group of interest. Ideally, researchers would study two groups within the same pan-ethnic group (e.g., Chinese and Vietnamese; Mexican and Puerto Rican) who had opposite histories and representation in the geographical regions where the data were being gathered, such as Cubans and Mexicans in Florida and California.

Examining the potential influence of community ethnic concentration in studies of ethnic identity is not only important for understanding how ethnic identity develops, but also for understanding the functions of ethnic identity in individuals' lives. Based on social identity theory (Tajfel, 1981; Tajfel & Turner, 1986), individuals' self-concepts are informed, in part, by their membership in social groups and their perceptions of others' evaluations of their group. In particular, individuals seek to maintain a positive sense of self via positively evaluating their group. When one's group is viewed negatively, individuals may engage in identity protection strategies (see Spears, Chapter 9, this volume) that enable them to reconcile negative views of their group and, thus, to not be negatively impacted by disparaging views of their group (Roberts, Settles, & Jellison, 2008). Furthermore, social identity theory suggests that antagonistic intergroup relations (e.g., experiences with discrimination) can heighten identification with and positive attachment to one's group (Tajfel & Turner, 1986). Thus, the history of an individual's ethnic group in a particular area, and the resulting context of reception that the individual's group experiences (Portes & Rumbaut, 2006), is likely to impact one's self-concept and, specific to ethnic identity, the degree to which one's ethnic identity is linked to perceptions of the self. As described above, it is possible that individuals who identify strongly with their ethnic group, but whose group is devalued and/or lacks representation in their respective communities may, in turn, have poorer adjustment due to a poor fit between their identity and their environment.

Multiple Social Identities. A final limitation within the literature is the limited understanding of the interface of ethnic identity and other social identities. Individuals' identities are made up of multiple social identities, such as ethnic identity, gender identity, sexual identity, and racial identity, to name a few (e.g., Bussey, Chapter 25, this volume; Savin-Williams, Chapter 28, this volume). All of these social identities contribute to the individual's global sense of self. Few studies have examined how multiple social identities intersect and the degree to which they develop in a uniform or distinct manner. Most of the studies that have examined the intersection of ethnic identity with other social identities have focused on ethnic identity and gender identity, and there are a few that have examined ethnic identity in relation to other identities such as American identity (i.e., Kiang, Yip, & Fuligni, 2008), but these studies are limited in number and, thus, it is difficult to draw general conclusions regarding the intersection of these identities. A majority of the work on the intersection of ethnic and

gender identity has been conducted by the same research team (i.e., Pittinsky, Shih, & Ambady, 1999; Shih, Pittinsky, & Ambady, 1999; Shih, Pittinsky, & Trahan, 2006), although others also have contributed to this area (Abu-Ali, 1999; Hoffman, 2006; Sinclair, Hardin, & Lowery, 2006). Findings suggest that gender identity development and ethnic identity development may follow similar trajectories, such that women from an ethnically diverse sample who had an achieved gender identity also tended to have an achieved ethnic identity and vice versa (Hoffman, 2006). Interestingly, in a study of Muslim adolescent girls living in the United States, Abu-Ali (1999) found that higher levels of ethnic identity affirmation were associated with higher scores on femininity; however, there was no significant association between ethnic identity achievement and femininity.

With a more experimental design, Shih et al. (2006) found that Asian American college females performed better on verbal tests when their gender identity was made salient than when their ethnic identity was made salient. Conversely, a previous study by the same research group found that Asian American women assigned to an experimental group scored higher than those assigned to a control group on a math test when their Asian American identity was made salient and worse than the control group when their gender identity was made salient. The control group consisted of Asian American women for whom neither identity was made salient (Shih et al., 1999). In both studies, researchers suggested that it was not the particular identity that influenced individuals' performance on math or verbal tests, but rather the stereotype associated with the identity that was made salient. This explanation is somewhat consistent with the concept of stereotype threat, which suggests that when a stereotype of a group to which one belongs is made salient, it can affect one's behavior in a manner that confirms the stereotype (Steele, 1997). Interestingly, the concept of stereotype threat has been generally discussed with respect to negative stereotypes about one's group; in the case of Shih and colleagues' work, it seems that both negative and positive stereotypes may actually affect behavior in a manner that is consistent with the stereotype that exists about the group.

In another study that examined ethnic and gender identities, Pittinsky et al. (1999) examined Asian women's affect toward their social identities in three separate conditions: a context in which Asian ethnic identity was adaptive (i.e., a math test), a context in which female gender identity was adaptive (a verbal test), and a context in which neither identity was relevant (control). Findings indicated that participants generated more positive memories related to their gender than their ethnicity in the verbal test condition, whereas they generated more positive memories related to their ethnicity than their gender in the math test condition. In the control situation, there were no significant differences in the positive or negative memories participants generated regarding their gender or ethnic identities. These findings suggest that individuals may activate different social identities in different contexts and that the characteristics of a particular context may prime a certain type of affect (i.e., positive or negative) toward a specific social identity. Though informative, these studies do not speak directly to the intersectionality of gender and ethnic identity. It would be interesting, for example, to examine whether gender identity would be strongest for those with high levels of ethnic identity in cultures that follow more rigid gender socialization patterns. For instance, in cultures that adhere to more rigid distinctions between males and females, would those who are most strongly ethnically identified also tend to demonstrate the strongest gender identities? And, in turn, would this strengthen the association between the particular identity and psychosocial, externalizing, or internalizing outcomes?

Interestingly, researchers generally have not examined the intersection of ethnic identity and racial identity (for an exception see Worrell & Gardner-Kitt, 2006). Although sometimes used synonymously, the terms race and ethnicity refer to considerably different constructs. A person's race is based on external physical characteristics, such as skin color (Phinney, 1996). Ethnicity, on the other hand, is based on cultural traditions

and values that are transmitted over generations (Spencer & Markstrom-Adams, 1990) and tends to be more subjective than race, which is more heavily grounded in the sociohistorical and cultural milieu of a particular country or region. There can be multiple races found within any ethnic group. For example, some Cuban Americans are racially White and others are racially Black. Whereas ethnic identity is based on identification with an ethnic group, racial identity pertains to individuals' identification with their racial group, including a shared history as a result of being a member of a particular race (Helms, 1990). For example, for Black individuals, racial identity would involve overcoming oppression and related struggles that result from historical oppression and racism that have existed throughout US history. Scholars suggest that the construct of race is not particularly meaningful for Latinos, as evidenced by the large proportion of the Latino population in the United States that does not answer the race question or refuses to identify with a single standard race in the US Census (Hirschman, 2004; Perez & Hirschman, 2009). Thus, it is possible that the construct of race is most salient for Blacks and least salient for Latinos, and that the construct of ethnicity is particularly salient for Latinos and perhaps less salient for Blacks.

Although it is not often discussed in the literature, it is possible for individuals to have both a racial identity and an ethnic identity, with racial identity being based on individuals' experiences with and understanding of the societal factors that affect their racial group, and ethnic identity being based on cultural characteristics that are transmitted from one generation to the next (Umaña-Taylor, 2003). For example, while Black Haitian Americans and Black African Americans would both have racial identities associated with being Black in the United States, Haitian Americans' ethnic identity would be based on their Haitian heritage, and African Americans' ethnic identity may be based on their African tribal heritage. The lack of understanding regarding how individuals' ethnic and racial identities intersect is among the largest limitations of the existing work on ethnic and racial identity.

This is an area in need of future research, particularly for Latinos who are tremendously racially diverse, with many having African roots, others having indigenous roots, and others having European roots. In fact, scholars question the arbitrary distinction between current conceptualizations of race and ethnicity, particularly because they do not adequately reflect the experiences of Latinos in the United States (see Hitlin, Brown, & Elder, 2007). Thus, it will be important for future research to understand the contexts within which racial versus ethnic identity is more salient to individuals (similar to research described above for gender and ethnic identity). Are there contexts in which individuals draw on both racial and ethnic identities for protection? For example, when faced with discrimination, are individuals more likely to rely on both their racial and ethnic identity to find ways to cope with the discriminatory behavior, rather than just one or the other? Does it depend on the type of discrimination that one is experiencing? It also is important to acknowledge (and to understand more fully) the notion that, for some groups and individuals, racial identity may be more salient, whereas for others, ethnic identity may be more salient.

Conclusion

In closing, existing work on ethnic identity among ethnic minority group members in the United States has advanced tremendously in the past several decades. The current review of existing empirical studies on the associations among ethnic identity and various indices of psychosocial functioning indicates that it is important to consider specific ethnic groups and, particularly, not to assume homogeneity in ethnic identity experiences and outcomes within or among ethnic minority groups. Furthermore, despite the heterogeneity within ethnic minority groups, ethnic identity appears to serve a promotive and/or protective function for individuals' psychosocial functioning. What will be important to understand more clearly, however, is the specific function that ethnic identity serves for each specific ethnic minority group. As previously discussed, the various ethnic groups that comprise the population of the United States are diverse with respect to, for example, their immigration history (e.g., some groups are predominately voluntary immigrants while others are involuntary immigrants), the context of reception that their group has experienced in the United States, and the structure of economic opportunities that sometimes differ by group because of different labor needs in specific geographic areas where certain ethnic groups tend to disproportionately settle (Baca Zinn & Wells, 2000). Since this diversity may account for some of the differences observed across groups with respect to the importance placed on and the protective nature of ethnic identity, future research should systematically study the potential impact of factors such as immigration history and context of reception in the United States.

In addition, although existing work has advanced the field's understanding with respect to ethnic identity among adolescents and emerging adults, there is a significant gap in the literature regarding ethnic identity beyond late adolescence and emerging adulthood. This may be due, in part, to a majority of this work being guided by Erikson's (1968) theory of identity formation, which emphasized adolescence as a central developmental period for identity formation. Nevertheless, scholars agree that identity is a process that is revisited throughout the lifespan (Kroger & Marcia, Chapter 2, this volume; Luyckx, Schwartz, Goossens, Beyers, & Missotten, Chapter 4, this volume). As a result, there is a need for more attention to ethnic identity during adulthood. In sum, given the limitations and directions for future research discussed above, the path to a more complete understanding of the process of ethnic identity development and its association with psychosocial outcomes will require more longitudinal work that captures multiple developmental periods and considers within group diversity, the influence of community ethnic concentration, and the interaction of ethnic identity and other salient social identities in informing individuals' psychosocial functioning and development.

Acknowledgment A special thanks to Aaron Foley for his assistance with a search of the literature on ethnic identity and externalizing behaviors.

References

Abu-Ali, A. (1999). Gender role identity among adolescent Muslim girls living in the US. *Current Psychology, 18*, 185–192.

Alba, R. D. (1990). *Ethnic identity: The transformation of white America*. New Haven, CT: Yale University Press.

Arbona, C., Jackson, R. H., McCoy, A., & Blakely, C. (1999). Ethnic identity as a predictor of attitudes of adolescents toward fighting. *Journal of Early Adolescence, 19*, 323–340.

Arnett, J. J. (2000). Emerging adulthood: A theory of development from the late teens through the twenties. *American Psychologist, 55*, 469–480.

Austin, A. A. (2004). Alcohol, tobacco, other drug use, and violent behavior among native Hawaiians: Ethnic pride and resilience. *Substance Use and Misuse, 39*, 721–746.

Baca Zinn, M., & Wells, B. (2000). Diversity within Latino families: New lessons for family social science. In D. Demo, K. Allen, & M. A. Fine (Eds.), *Handbook of family diversity* (pp. 252–273). Oxford, UK: Oxford University Press.

Belgrave, F. Z., Van Oss Marin, B., & Chambers, D. B. (2000). Cultural, contextual, and intrapersonal predictors of risky sexual attitudes among urban African American girls in early adolescence. *Cultural Diversity and Ethnic Minority Psychology, 6*, 309–322.

Bracey, J. R., Bámaca-Gómez, M. Y., & Umaña-Taylor, A. J. (2004). Examining ethnic identity and self-esteem among biracial and monoracial adolescents. *Journal of Youth and Adolescence, 33*, 123–132.

Bronfenbrenner, U. (1989). Ecological systems theory. *Annals of Child Development, 6*, 187–249.

Brook, J. S., Duan, T., Brook, D. W., & Ning, Y. (2007). Pathways to nicotine dependence in African American and Puerto Rican young adults. *American Journal on Addictions, 16*, 450–456.

Brook, J. S., & Pahl, K. (2005). The protective role of ethnic and racial identity and aspects of an Afrocentric orientation against drug use among African American young adults. *Journal of Genetic Psychology, 166*, 329–345.

Brook, J. S., Whiteman, M., Balka, E. B., Win, P. T., & Gursen, M. D. (1998). Drug use among Puerto Ricans: Ethnic identity as a protective factor. *Hispanic Journal of Behavioral Sciences, 20*, 241–254.

Case, M. H., & Robinson, W. L. (2003). Interventions with ethnic minority populations: The legacy and promise of community psychology. In G. Bernal, J. E. Trimble, A. K. Burlew, & F. T. L. Leong (Eds.), *Handbook of racial and ethnic minority psychology* (pp. 573–590). Thousand Oaks, CA: Sage.

Devos, T., & Banaji, M. R. (2005). American = White? *Journal of Personality and Social Psychology, 88*, 447–466.

Elliott, G., & Feldman, S. (1990). *At the threshold: The developing adolescent*. Cambridge, MA: Harvard University Press.

Erikson, E. H. (1968). *Identity: Youth and crisis*. New York: Norton.

Fisher, C. B., Wallace, S. A., & Fenton, R. E. (2000). Discrimination distress during adolescence. *Journal of Youth and Adolescence, 29*, 679–695.

French, S. E., Kim, T. E., & Pillado, O. (2006). Ethnic identity, social group membership, and youth violence. In N. G. Guerra & E. P. Smith (Eds.), *Preventing youth violence in a multicultural society* (pp. 47–73). Washington, DC: American Psychological Association.

French, S. E., Seidman, E., Allen, L., & Aber, J. L. (2006). The development of ethnic identity during adolescence. *Developmental Psychology, 42*, 1–10.

Fuligni, A. J., Witkow, M., & Garcia, C. (2005). Ethnic identity and the academic adjustment of adolescents from Mexican, Chinese, and European backgrounds. *Developmental Psychology, 41*, 799–811.

Gaylord-Harden, N. K., Ragsdale, B. L., Mandara, J., Richards, M. H., & Petersen, A. C. (2007). Perceived support and internalizing symptoms in African American adolescents: Self-esteem and ethnic identity as mediators. *Journal of Youth and Adolescence, 36*, 77–88.

Gee, G. C., Delva, J., & Takeuchi, D. T. (2007). Relationships between self-reported unfair treatment and prescription medication use, illicit drug use, and alcohol dependence among Filipino Americans. *American Journal of Public Health, 97*(5), 933–940.

Go, C. G., & Le, T. N. (2005). Gender differences in Cambodian delinquency: The role of ethnic identity, parental discipline, and peer delinquency. *Crime & Delinquency, 51*(2), 220–237.

Helms, J. E. (1990). *Black and White racial identity: Theory, research, and practice*. New York: Greenwood.

Helms, J. E. (2007). Some better practices for measuring racial and ethnic identity. *Journal of Counseling Psychology, 54*, 235–246.

Hirschman, C. (2004). The origins and demise of the concept of race. *Population and Development Review, 30*, 385–415.

Hishinuma, E. S., Johnson, R. C., Kim, S. P., Nishimura, S. T., Makini, G. K., Jr., Andrade, N. N., et al. (2005). Prevalence and correlates of misconduct among ethnically diverse adolescents of native Hawaiian/Part-Hawaiian and non-Hawaiian ancestry. *International Journal of Social Psychiatry, 51*(3), 242–258.

Hitlin, S., Brown, J. S., & Elder, G. H. (2007). Measuring Latinos: Racial versus ethnic classification and self-understandings. *Social Forces, 86*, 587–611.

Hoffman, R. M. (2006). Gender self-definition and gender self-acceptance in women: Intersections with feminist, womanist, and ethnic identities. *Journal of Counseling and Development, 84*, 358–372.

Hollon, S. D., Muñoz, R. F., Barlow, D. H., Beardslee, W. R., Bell, C. C., Bernal, G., et al. (2002). Psychosocial intervention development for the prevention and treatment of depression: Promoting innovation and increasing access. *Biological Psychiatry, 52*, 610–630.

Hovey, J. D., Kim, S. E., & Seligman, L. D. (2006). The influences of cultural values, ethnic identity, and language use on the mental health of Korean American college students. *Journal of Psychology, 140*, 499–511.

Juang, L. P., Nguyen, H. H., & Lin, Y. (2006). The ethnic identity, other-group attitudes, and psychosocial functioning of Asian American emerging adults from two contexts. *Journal of Adolescent Research, 21*, 542–568.

Keating, D. P. (1990). Adolescent thinking. In S. S. Feldman & G. R. Elliott (Eds.), *At the threshold: The developing adolescent* (pp. 54–89). Cambridge, MA: Harvard University Press.

Kiang, L., Yip, T., & Fuligni, A. J. (2008). Multiple social identities and adjustment in young adults from ethnically diverse backgrounds. *Journal of Research on Adolescence, 18*, 643–670.

Kulis, S., Napoli, M., & Marsiglia, F. F. (2002). Ethnic pride, biculturalism, and drug use norms of urban American Indian adolescents. *Social Work Research, 26*(2), 101–112.

Lee, R. M. (2003). Do ethnic identity and other-group orientation protect against discrimination for Asian Americans? *Journal of Counseling Psychology, 50*, 133–141.

Lerner, R. M., & Lerner, J. V. (1983). Temperament and adaptation across life: Theoretical and empirical issues. In P. B. Baltes & O. G. Brim, Jr. (Eds.), *Life-span development and behaviors* (Vol. 5, pp. 197–231). New York: Academic Press.

Mahalingam, R., Balan, S., & Haritatos, J. (2008). Engendering immigrant psychology: An intersectionality perspective. *Sex Roles, 59*, 326–336.

Marcia, J. E. (1980). Identity in adolescence. In J. Adelson (Ed.), *Handbook of adolescent psychology* (pp. 159–187). New York: Wiley.

Marcia, J. E. (1994). The empirical study of ego identity. In H. A. Bosma, T. G. Graafsma, H. D. Grotevant, & D. J. de Levita (Eds.), *Identity and development: An interdisciplinary approach* (4th ed., pp. 281–321). Belmont, CA: Wadsworth.

Marsiglia, F. F., Kulis, S., & Hecht, M. L. (2001). Ethnic labels and ethnic identity as predictors of drug use among middle school students in the southwest. *Journal of Research on Adolescence, 11*, 21–48.

Marsiglia, F. F., Kulis, S., Hecht, M. L., & Sills, S. (2004). Ethnicity and ethnic identity as predictors of drug norms and drug use among preadolescents in the US southwest. *Substance Use and Misuse, 39*, 1061–1094.

McCoy, S. K., & Major, B. (2003). Group identification moderates emotional responses to perceived prejudice. *Personality and Social Psychology Bulletin, 29*, 1005–1017.

McHale, S. M., Whiteman, S. D., Kim, J., & Crouter, A. C. (2007). Characteristics and correlates of sibling relationships in two-parent African American families. *Journal of Family Psychology, 21*, 227–235.

McMahon, S. D., & Watts, R. J. (2002). Ethnic identity in urban African American youth: Exploring links with self-worth, aggression, and other psychosocial variables. *Journal of Community Psychology, 30*, 411–431.

Meeus, W., van de Schoot, R., Keijsers, L., Schwartz, S. J., & Branje, S. (2010). On the progression and stability of adolescent identity formation: A five-wave longitudinal study in early-to-middle-to-late adolescence. *Child Development, 81*, 1565–1581.

Mossakowski, K. N. (2003). Coping with perceived discrimination: Does ethnic identity protect mental health? *Journal of Health and Social Behavior, 44*, 318–331.

Nasim, A., Belgrave, F. Z., Jagers, R. J., Wilson, K. D., & Owens, K. (2007). The moderating effects of culture on peer deviance and alcohol use among high-risk African-American adolescents. *Journal of Drug Education, 37*, 335–363.

Newman, D. L., Sontag, L. M., & Salvato, R. (2006). Psychosocial aspects of body mass and body image among rural American Indian adolescents. *Journal of Youth and Adolescence, 35*, 281–291.

Padilla, A. (1999). Psychology. In J. A. Fishman (Ed.), *Handbook of language and ethnic identity* (pp. 109–121). New York: Oxford University Press.

Pahl, K., & Way, N. (2006). Longitudinal trajectories of ethnic identity among urban Black and Latino adolescents. *Child Development, 77*, 1403–1415.

Pegg, P. O., & Plybon, L. E. (2005). Toward the theoretical measurement of ethnic identity. *Journal of Early Adolescence, 25*, 250–264.

Perez, A. D., & Hirschman, C. (2009). The changing racial and ethnic composition of the US population: Emerging American identities. *Population and Development Review, 35*, 1–51.

Phinney, J. S. (1989). Stages of ethnic identity development in minority group adolescents. *Journal of Early Adolescence, 9*, 34–49.

Phinney, J. S. (1992). The multigroup ethnic identity measure: A new scale for use with diverse groups. *Journal of Adolescent Research, 7*, 156–176.

Phinney, J. S. (1993). A three-stage model of ethnic identity development. In G. P. Knight & M. E. Bernal (Eds.), *Ethnic identity: Formation and transmission among Hispanics and other minorities* (pp. 61–79). Albany, NY: State University of New York Press.

Phinney, J. S. (1996). When we talk about American ethnic groups, what do we mean? *American Psychologist, 51*, 918–927.

Phinney, J. S., & Kohatsu, E. L. (1997). Ethnic and racial identity development and mental health. In J. Schulenberg, J. L. Maggs, & K. Hurrelmann (Eds.), *Health risks and developmental transitions during adolescence* (pp. 420–443). New York: Cambridge University Press.

Phinney, J. S., & Ong, A. D. (2007). Conceptualization and measurement of ethnic identity: Current status and future directions. *Journal of Counseling Psychology, 54*, 271–281.

Pittinsky, T. L., Shih, M., & Ambady, N. (1999). Identity adaptiveness: Affect across multiple identities. *Journal of Social Issues, 55*, 503–518.

Ponterotto, J. G., Gretchen, D., Utsey, S. O., Stracuzzi, T., & Saya, R. (2003). The multigroup ethnic identity measure (MEIM): Psychometric review and further validity testing. *Educational and Psychological Measurement, 63*, 502–515.

Portes, A., & Rumbaut, R. G. (2006). *Immigrant America: A portrait* (3rd ed.). Berkeley, CA: University of California Press.

Prado, G., Schwartz, S. J., Pattatucci-Aragón, A., Clatts, M., Pantin, H., Fernández, M. I., et al. (2006). The prevention of HIV transmission in Hispanic adolescents. *Drug and Alcohol Dependence, 84S*, S43–S53.

Resnicow, K., Soler, R. E., Braithwaite, R. L., Selassie, M. B., & Smith, M. (1999). Development of a racial and ethnic identity scale for African American adolescents: The survey of black life. *Journal of Black Psychology, 25*, 171–188.

Rivas-Drake, D., Hughes, D., & Way, N. (2009). A preliminary analysis of associations among ethnic-racial socialization, ethnic discrimination, and ethnic identity among urban sixth graders. *Journal of Research on Adolescence, 19*, 558–584.

Roberts, L. M., Settles, I. H., & Jellison, W. A. (2008). Predicting strategic identity management of gender and race. *Identity: An International Journal of Theory and Research, 8*, 269–306.

Roberts, R. E., Phinney, J. S., Masse, L. C., Chen, Y. R., Roberts, C. R., & Romero, A. (1999). The structure of ethnic identity of young adolescents from diverse ethnocultural groups. *Journal of Early Adolescence, 19*, 301–322.

Roberts, R. E., Roberts, C. R., & Chen, Y. R. (1997). Ethnocultural differences in prevalence of adolescent depression. *American Journal of Community Psychology, 25*, 95–110.

Romero, A. J., Carvajal, S. C., Valle, F., & Orduña, M. (2007). Adolescent bicultural stress and its impact on mental well-being among Latinos, Asian Americans, and European Americans. *Journal of Community Psychology, 35*, 519–534.

Romero, A. J., & Roberts, R. E. (2003). The impact of multiple dimensions of ethnic identity on discrimination and adolescents' self-esteem. *Journal of Applied Social Psychology, 33*, 2288–2305.

Schwartz, S. J., Zamboanga, B. L., & Jarvis, L. H. (2007). Ethnic identity and acculturation in Hispanic early adolescents: Mediated relationships to academic grades, prosocial behaviors, and externalizing symptoms. *Cultural Diversity and Ethnic Minority Psychology, 13*, 364–373.

Shih, M., Pittinsky, T. L., & Ambady, N. (1999). Stereotype susceptibility: Identity salience and shifts in quantitative performance. *Psychological Science, 10*, 80–83.

Shih, M., Pittinsky, T. L., & Trahan, A. (2006). Domain-specific effects of stereotypes on performance. *Self and Identity, 5*, 1–14.

Siegel, J. M., Yancey, A. K., Aneshensel, C. S., & Schuler, R. (1999). Body image, perceived pubertal timing, and adolescent mental health. *Journal of Adolescent Health, 25*, 155–165.

Sinclair, S., Hardin, C. D., & Lowery, B. S. (2006). Self-stereotyping in the context of multiple identities. *Journal of Personality and Social Psychology, 90*, 529–542.

Snyder, L. A., Cleveland, J. N., & Thornton, G. C. (2006). Support for affirmative action initiatives among diverse groups: The role of ethnic identity. *Journal of Applied Social Psychology, 36*, 527–551.

Spencer, M. B., & Markstrom-Adams, C. (1990). Identity Processes among racial and ethnic minority children in America. *Child Development, 61*, 290–310.

Sridhar, K. K. (1988). Language maintenance and language shift among Asian-Indians: Kannadigas in the New York area. *International Journal of Sociology of Language, 69*, 73–87.

Steele, C. M. (1997). A threat in the air: How stereotypes shape intellectual identity and performance. *American Psychologist, 52*, 613–629.

Supple, A. J., Ghazarian, S. R., Frabutt, J. M., Plunkett, S. W., & Sands, T. (2006). Contextual influences on Latino adolescent ethnic identity and academic outcomes. *Child Development, 77*, 1427–1433.

Syed, M., Azmitia, M., & Phinney, J. S. (2007). Stability and change in ethnic identity among Latino emerging adults in two contexts. *Identity: An International Journal of Theory and Research, 7*, 155–178.

Tajfel, H. (1981). *Human group and social categories.* Cambridge: Cambridge University Press.

Tajfel, H., & Turner, J. C. (1986). The social identity theory of intergroup behavior. In S. Worschel & W. Austin (Eds.), *Psychology of intergroup relations*. Chicago: Nelson Hall.

Thomas, A., & Chess, S. (1977). *Temperament and development.* New York: Brunner/Mazel.

Thompson, T. G. (2001). *Culture, race, and ethnicity: A supplement to mental health: A report of the Surgeon General.* Washington, DC: Department of Health and Human Services.

Tsai, J. L., Morensen, H., Wong, Y., & Hess, D. (2002). What does "being American" mean? A comparison of Asian American and European American young adults. *Cultural Diversity and Ethnic Minority Psychology, 8*, 257–273.

Umaña-Taylor, A. J. (2003). Ethnic and racial identities. In J. R. Miller, R. M. Lerner, L. B. Schiamberg, & P. M. Anderson (Eds.), *Human ecology: An encyclopedia of children, families, communities, and environments* (pp. 245–247). Santa Barbara, CA: ABC-Clio.

Umaña-Taylor, A. J. (2004). Ethnic identity and self-esteem: Examining the role of social context. *Journal of Adolescence, 27*, 139–146.

Umaña-Taylor, A. J. (2005). The Ethnic Identity Scale. In K. A. Moore & L. H. Lippman (Eds.), *What do children need to flourish? Conceptualizing and measuring indicators of positive development* (pp. 75–91). New York: Springer.

Umaña-Taylor, A. J., & Alfaro, E. C. (2006). Ethnic identity among US Latino adolescents: Theory, measurement, and implications for well being. In F. A. Villaruel & T. Luster (Eds.), *The crisis in youth mental health: Disorders in adolescence* (pp. 195–211). Westport, CT: Greenwood Publishing.

Umaña-Taylor, A. J., & Bámaca, M. Y. (2004). Immigrant mothers' experiences with ethnic socialization of adolescents growing up in the US: An examination of Colombian, Guatemalan, Mexican, and Puerto Rican mothers. *Sociological Focus, 37*, 329–348.

Umaña-Taylor, A. J., Diversi, M., & Fine, M. A. (2002). Ethnic identity and self-esteem among Latino adolescents: Making distinctions among the Latino populations. *Journal of Adolescent Research, 17*, 303–327.

Umaña-Taylor, A. J., Gonzales-Backen, M. A., & Guimond, A. (2009). Latino adolescents' ethnic identity: Is there a developmental progression and does growth in ethnic identity predict growth in self-esteem? *Child Development*

Umaña-Taylor, A. J., & Shin, N. (2007). An examination of the ethnic identity scale with diverse populations: Exploring variation by ethnicity and geography. *Cultural Diversity and Ethnic Minority Psychology, 13*, 178–186.

Umaña-Taylor, A. J., & Updegraff, K. (2007). Latino adolescents' mental health: Exploring the role of discrimination, ethnic identity, acculturation, and self-esteem. *Journal of Adolescence, 30*, 549–567.

Umaña-Taylor, A. J., Vargas-Chanes, D., Garcia, C. D., & Gonzales-Backen, M. (2008). A longitudinal examination of Latino adolescents' ethnic identity, coping with discrimination, and self-esteem. *Journal of Early Adolescence, 28*, 16–50.

Umaña-Taylor, A. J., Yazedjian, A., & Bámaca-Gómez, M. Y. (2004). Developing the ethnic identity scale using Eriksonian and social identity perspectives. *Identity: An International Journal of Theory and Research, 4*, 9–38.

Utsey, S. O., Chae, M. H., Brown, C. F., & Kelly, D. (2002). Effect of ethnic group membership on ethnic identity, race-related stress, and quality of life. *Cultural Diversity and Ethnic Minority Psychology, 8*, 366–377.

Walker, R. L., Wingate, L. R., Obasi, E. M., & Joiner, T. E. (2008). An empirical investigation of acculturative stress and ethnic identity as moderators for depression and suicidal ideation in college students. *Cultural Diversity and Ethnic Minority Psychology, 14*, 75–82.

Wills, T. A., Murry, V. M., Brody, G. H., Gibbons, F. X., Gerrard, M., Walker, C., et al. (2007). Ethnic pride and self-control related to protective and risk factors: Test of the theoretical model for the strong African American families program. *Health Psychology, 26*, 50–59.

Wong, C. A., Eccles, J. S., & Sameroff, A. (2003). The influence of ethnic discrimination and ethnic identification on African American adolescents' school and socioemotional adjustment. *Journal of Personality, 71*, 1197–1232.

Worrell, F. C. (2000). A validity study of scores on the multigroup ethnic identity measure based on a sample of academically talented adolescents. *Educational and Psychological Measurement, 60*, 439–447.

Worrell, F. C., & Gardner-Kitt, D. L. (2006). The relationship between racial and ethnic identity in Black adolescents: The cross racial identity scale (CRIS) and the multigroup ethnic identity measure (MEIM). *Identity: An International Journal of Theory and Research, 6*, 293–315.

Yasui, M., Dorham, C. L., & Dishion, T. J. (2004). Ethnic identity and psychological adjustment: A validity analysis for European American and African American adolescents. *Journal of Adolescent Research, 19*, 807–825.

Yuen, N. Y. C., Nahulu, L. B., Hishinuma, E. S., & Miyamoto, R. H. (2000). Cultural identification and attempted suicide in native Hawaiian adolescents. *Journal of the American Academy of Child and Adolescent Psychiatry, 39*, 360–367.

Zamboanga, B. L., Raffaelli, M., & Horton, N. J. (2006). Acculturation status and heavy alcohol use among Mexican American college students: Investigating the moderating role of gender. *Addictive Behaviors, 31*, 2188–2198.

Zamboanga, B. L., Schwartz, S. J., Jarvis, L. H., & Van Tyne, K. (2009). Acculturation and substance use among Hispanic early adolescents: Investigating the mediating roles of acculturative stress and self-esteem. *Journal of Primary Prevention, 30*, 315–333.

Jennifer B. Unger

Abstract

Cultural identity represents an individual's identity as a member of a group with shared characteristics, which often (but not always) include racial, ethnic, or geographical origins. Cultural identity influences multiple life domains, including the ways in which people make decisions about performing behaviors that ultimately influence their health. This chapter reviews the role of cultural identity in public health. I present a theoretical model in which the effects of cultural identity on health-related behaviors are mediated by perceptions of risk of disease, perceptions of cultural norms, desire to self-present as a member of a cultural group, functional meanings of behaviors, and cultural values. Through these mediated pathways, cultural identity can influence the likelihood that individuals will engage in health-protective behaviors, seek early detection of illness, and obtain treatment for existing illness. These pathways also can be moderated by enabling factors such as access to care, information, and resources. These mediating and moderating mechanisms are then illustrated with examples from multiple domains of public health research such as genetic testing, smoking, healthcare decision-making, and adolescent drug use. Further research is needed to develop improved measures of cultural identity, understand the effects of changes in cultural identity on health-related behaviors, understand the interactions between the individual's cultural identity and the larger cultural context, and develop health education interventions that are compatible with patients' cultural identities. The theoretical model presented in this chapter could be a useful starting point for researchers, interventionists, and evaluators to include cultural identity in public health efforts.

Cultural identity pervades all aspects of life, including interpretations of situations and events, patterns of interpersonal communication, values and priorities, and day-to-day behaviors. Therefore, it is not surprising that cultural identity affects health and illness as well. Cultural identity has been associated with various aspects

J.B. Unger (✉)
Institute for Health Promotion and Disease Prevention Research, University of Southern California Keck School of Medicine, Alhambra, CA, USA
e-mail: unger@usc.edu

S.J. Schwartz et al. (eds.), *Handbook of Identity Theory and Research*,
DOI 10.1007/978-1-4419-7988-9_34, © Springer Science+Business Media, LLC 2011

of health, including people's understanding of their vulnerability to various illnesses and their likelihood of performing health-risk and health-protective behaviors, obtaining medical screenings for disease, and seeking treatment. This chapter reviews the role of cultural identity in public health. I propose a new theoretical model of potential mediators and moderators of the associations between cultural identity and health behaviors, and I provide examples of these processes from previous research on health-related behaviors such as genetic testing, smoking, healthcare decision-making, and adolescent drug use.

A Working Definition of Cultural Identity

Before examining the role of cultural identity in public health, it is necessary to clarify our definition of cultural identity. For the purposes of this chapter, I use the term "cultural identity" rather than "ethnic identity" because these terms differ in breadth. The main difference is that ethnicity usually refers to a person's ancestral geographic origin, whereas cultures are groups of people who share knowledge, beliefs, norms, and behaviors (Geertz, 1973). Cultures can include ethnic groups as well as other groups of people whose membership is based not on geography but on other shared traits, interests, knowledge, or behaviors (e.g., gay culture, deaf culture, hip-hop culture). The term "cultural identity" implies that an individual has a number of different possible identities at different levels, because each individual belongs to numerous overlapping and non-overlapping cultural and subcultural groups (Raman, 2006; Spears, Chapter 9, this volume). In this chapter, I use the term "cultural identity" to describe a person's identity as a member of a cultural group, which often (but not always) consists of people of similar ethnic, racial, and/or national origins. Therefore, cultural identity usually includes ethnic identity, but it also can be broader than ethnic identity.

Cultural identity, like culture itself, is a complex and abstract phenomenon that is difficult to

define and measure (Matsumoto, 2003). Trimble (2000) describes cultural identity as an "affiliative construct"; individuals view themselves and others as belonging to a particular group with shared characteristics (Spears, Chapter 9, this volume). People's judgments about whether they or others belong to a cultural group can be influenced by the person's physical appearance (e.g., the person's physical similarity to others in the group), the person's ancestral origin, or the person's behaviors (e.g., celebration of holidays, choice of clothing, manner of speech, etc.,) (Cheung, 1993).

According to Phinney, 1990, 2000, 2003), a person claims an identity within the context of a group that has a common ancestry and shares a similar culture, race, religion, language, kinship, or place of origin. This identity includes self-identification, sense of belonging to a cultural group, attitudes toward the cultural group, social participation, and cultural practices. Referring to people who immigrate to a new culture or belong to a cultural minority group, cultural identity also includes people's subjective orientation (a) toward their families' culture(s) of origin (b) toward one or more "dominant" cultures, or (c) toward a combination of these cultures. Cultural identity also refers to the degree to which one has explored and committed to a sense of who one is in a cultural sense (see Umaña-Taylor, Chapter 33, this volume). In the case of immigrants, because there are usually differences between the sending and receiving cultures, and because there may be heterogeneity within each of these cultures, people can develop cultural identities that are a blend of multiple cultures (Howard, 2000). For example, Fig. 34.1 depicts the self-reported cultural identities of 1,963 Hispanic/Latino high school students in Southern California in 2005 (Unger et al., unpublished manuscript). The students were asked, "Do you live by or follow the – way of life?" (Oetting & Beauvais, 1990). These students might be expected to have cultural identities comprised of elements of their Hispanic cultures of origin, the US culture where they live, or a combination of the two. Although most students identified primarily with aspects of the Hispanic/Latino (92%) and

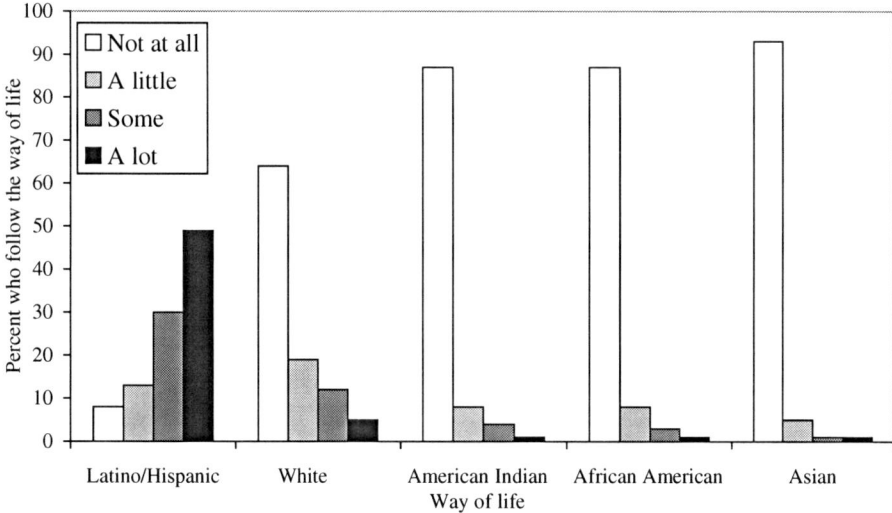

Fig. 34.1 Cultural/ethnic identity among Hispanic/Latino high school students in Southern California

White (36%) cultures, some students also identified with aspects of African American (13%), American Indian (13%), and Asian American (7%) cultures. These adolescents' multicultural identities are not surprising, given that they are living in a culturally diverse urban context where they are exposed to a wide variety of cultural norms, values, and behavioral expressions. Even members of "dominant" or majority cultures can adopt cultural identities that include elements of minority cultures, as evidenced by non-African-American adolescents in the United States adopting elements of African-American cultural identity such as music and clothing styles.

Cultural identity formation has been described recently as a continuous and dynamic process that evolves over the entire life course and also shifts from moment to moment, depending on the social context (Weinreich, 2009). Although Phinney (2003) describes cultural identity formation as a developmental process in adolescence and young adulthood rather than a lifelong process, she also acknowledges that it can continue to change over the life course and across situational contexts. Cultural identity is not a final decision, but a constantly shifting understanding of one's identity in relation to others. Recent writings on cultural identity formation (Weinreich, 2009) have emphasized the active role of the

agentic individual in building a cultural identity by selecting individual features of multiple cultures to incorporate into the self-identity, rather than a passive individual being changed by a dominant culture (see Huynh, Nguyen, & Benet-Martínez, Chapter 35, this volume). In other words, individuals repeatedly explore the meaning of various cultural identities, including those of their ancestors and those of the people in their current social networks. They can choose elements of these identities to incorporate into their own self-identities. The salience of any particular aspect of the cultural identity varies according to the situational context.

How Does Cultural Identity Influence Health?

Cultural identity does not necessarily determine people's health status directly, but it can influence their decisions about engaging in behaviors that affect their health status. Because cultural identity shapes people's understanding of the physical and social world and their role in it, cultural identity also shapes people's beliefs about health and disease, including criteria for labeling oneself as healthy or sick, actions taken to avoid disease, decisions about seeking early detection of disease, and decisions about whether, when, and how to treat disease (Mechanic, 1986). In the public health field, health-related behaviors can be classified as primary prevention (preventing disease from occurring), secondary prevention (detecting disease in its early stages), and tertiary prevention (treating existing disease). These classes of behaviors are described in detail below.

Primary prevention. Primary prevention includes behaviors undertaken to maintain health or prevent disease from occurring (Friis & Sellers, 2009). These include health-enhancing behaviors such as physical activity and appropriate dietary choices, behaviors to protect against disease and injury such as hand-washing and wearing seatbelts, and avoidance of behaviors that threaten health such as smoking or unsafe sex. Cultural identity may influence primary prevention behaviors by influencing people's perceptions of which behaviors are related to health and disease (e.g., is diabetes caused by diet or by experiencing strong emotions? [Hatcher & Whittemore, 2007]); which behaviors are normative and accepted among members of their cultural group (e.g., is it acceptable for women to smoke? [Unger et al., 2003]); and the cultural assets and resources upon which the person can draw to make decisions about engaging in risky and protective behaviors (e.g., do extended family members or religious leaders influence these decisions? [Turner, 2000]).

Secondary prevention. The goal of secondary prevention is to identify and detect disease in its earliest stages, before symptoms develop, when it is most likely to be treated successfully (Friis & Sellers, 2009). Early detection and diagnosis can make it possible to cure a disease, slow its progression, prevent or minimize complications, and limit disability. Cultural identity could influence secondary prevention behaviors by influencing people's perceptions of themselves as members of high-risk groups (e.g., whether they are aware of their ethnic, racial, and national origins and the specific diseases that are prevalent among those groups) and their desire to become aware of their disease risk (e.g., do people want to know about a cancer diagnosis, or would they rather not know and remain optimistic? [Powe & Finnie, 2003]).

Tertiary prevention. Tertiary prevention involves treating disease after it has occurred (Friis & Sellers, 2009). For diseases that cannot be cured, this includes improving the patient's quality of life by managing symptoms and pain, limiting complications and disabilities, reducing the severity and progression of disease, and providing rehabilitation. Cultural identity could influence tertiary prevention behaviors by influencing people's preferences about how medical treatment decisions should be made (e.g., should the patient make treatment decisions autonomously, or should family members relieve the patient of the burden of decision-making? [Kagawa-Singer & Blackhall, 2001]) and the extent of medical intervention that they are willing to receive to prolong their lives (Kagawa-Singer & Blackhall, 2001).

Theoretical Model

In this chapter, I propose a theoretical model of the role of cultural identity in people's decisions about engaging in specific health behaviors. I posit that cultural identity influences these decisions, and that there are mediators and moderators of these effects. The theoretical model is diagrammed in Fig. 34.2, and the paths in the model are described in detail below.

Mediating Factors in the Association between Cultural Identity and Health-Related Behaviors. Paths (1) and (2) in the model show a causal chain leading from cultural identity to the mediating factors to health-related behavior. Mediators are steps within a causal pathway (Baron & Kenny, 1986). They represent the mechanism by which one phenomenon (e.g., cultural identity) influences another phenomenon (e.g., health-related behavior). In this model, I posit that the causal pathway from cultural identity to health-related behaviors is mediated by cognitions such as the following:

- *Perception of risk of disease among the cultural group* (i.e., does this cultural group have a relatively high prevalence of a particular

Fig. 34.2 Theoretical model

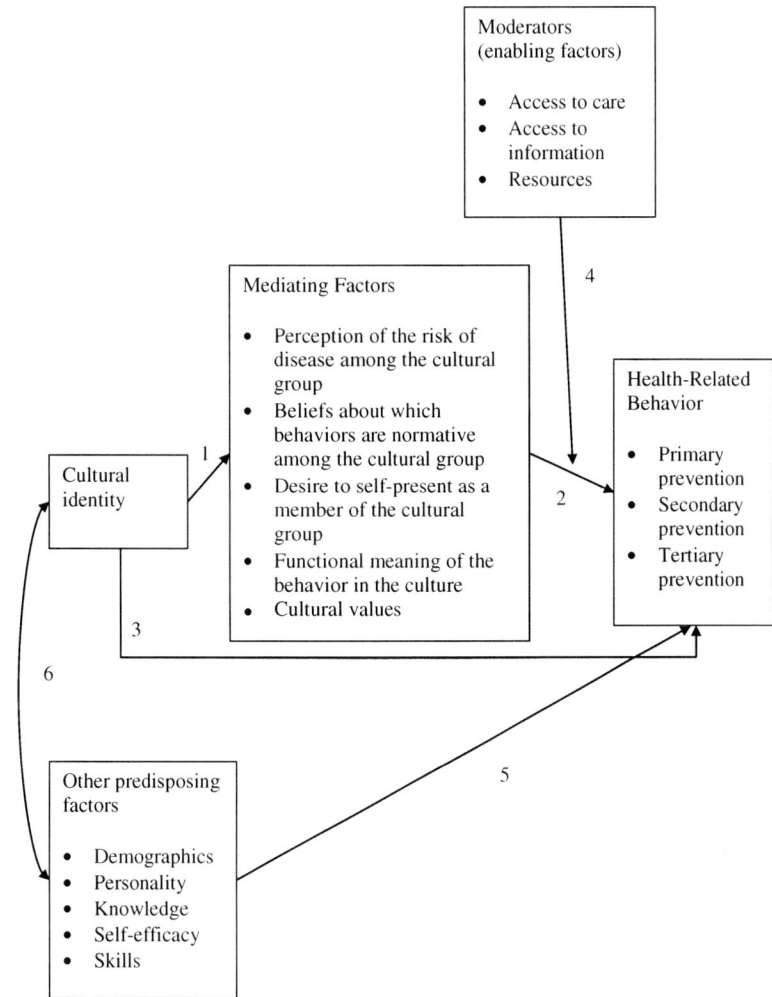

disease, relative to other groups?) [Janz & Becker, 1984]

- *Perception of normative behaviors among the cultural group* (i.e., is this behavior common among this cultural group? Is this behavior viewed as acceptable and desirable among this cultural group?) [Fishbein & Ajzen, 1975]
- *Desire to self-present as a member of the cultural group* (i.e., do I want people to view me as a member of this cultural group? Will this behavior contribute to my image as a member of this cultural group?) [Baumeister, 1982]
- *Functional meaning of the behavior among the cultural group* (i.e., In this cultural group, what do people believe are the positive

and negative consequences of this behavior?) [Spruijt-Metz, 1995]

- *Cultural values* (e.g., individualism vs. collectivism, as well as group-specific cultural values such as familism, filial piety, "respeto," "simpatia," and saving face) [McElroy & Jezewski, 2000]

Unmediated Effect of Cultural Identity on Health-Related Behavior. Path (3) in the model leads directly from cultural identity to health-related behavior. This path indicates a directional and causal association between cultural identity and health-related behavior that is not mediated by the hypothesized mediating factors. This path leaves open the possibility that other undiscovered mediators may exist.

Moderators of the Path from Cultural Identity to Health-Related Behavior. Path (4) in the model indicates that other factors (sometimes referred to as "enabling factors" in other theories [Green & Kreuter, 1999]) can facilitate or block the path from cultural identity to health-related behavior. Moderators are variables that influence the strength of the association between a predictor and an outcome (Baron & Kenny, 1986). For example, women whose cultural beliefs are consistent with early detection of breast cancer may be more likely to obtain mammograms, but only *if* mammograms are conveniently available and affordable. Women who lack access to mammography will be unlikely to obtain mammograms, regardless of their cultural identities. Enabling factors such as access to care, access to information, and resources are shown in the box at the top of Fig. 34.2. The arrow pointing down from these enabling factors indicates that they moderate the association between the mediating factors and behavior.

Other Predisposing Factors. Of course, cultural identity is not the only factor that influences health-related behaviors. Path (5) in the model shows the effects of other variables such as demographic characteristics (e.g., age, gender, socioeconomic status), personality (e.g., general tendency to take risks [Llewellyn, 2008]), knowledge (e.g., knowledge of the risks and benefits of various behaviors), self-efficacy (i.e., confidence in one's ability to perform a health-protective behavior [Bandura, 1986]), and skills (i.e., one's actual ability to perform the behavior correctly). Path (6) in the model indicates that some of these other predisposing factors also may be correlated with cultural identity.

A key assumption of this model is that people are motivated to maintain consistency between their self-image and their behaviors (see Oyserman & James, Chapter 6, this volume). This notion has been expressed in several psychological theories such as cognitive dissonance (Festinger, 1957), self-consistency (Aronson, 1968; 1999), and self-affirmation theories (Steele, 1988). These theories assert that people develop conceptualizations of themselves as individuals, with specific preferences, personal and moral values, skills, and priorities. People are most comfortable when they act in ways that affirm their self-images. When people act in ways that are inconsistent with the self-image (for example, if a person with an "honest" self-image tells a lie), they feel discomfort and take action to resolve the discrepancy, either by revising the self-image or by finding a way to rationalize the aberrant behavior.

I posit that, whenever possible, people will engage in health-related behaviors that are consistent with their chosen cultural identities, that is, behaviors that are salient among the cultural group with which they identify, behaviors that are normative and valued by that cultural group, behaviors that strengthen their identity as members of the cultural group, behaviors that serve a valued function among members of the cultural group, and behaviors that are consistent with the core values of the cultural group.

Of course, all human behavior occurs within a sociocultural context (Bronfenbrenner, 1979). Systems outside the individual, including family, social network, social institutions (schools, workplaces, churches), community, and the sociopolitical context also exert influences on health-related behaviors. Although these ecological influences are not the focus of this chapter, it is important for the reader to keep in mind that the larger social and cultural context likely influences individual-level associations between cultural identity and health behaviors.

Examples of the Role of Cultural Identity in Health-Related Behaviors

Cultural identity can influence primary, secondary, and tertiary preventive health behaviors through the pathways depicted in Fig. 34.2. The remainder of this chapter describes some examples of how cultural identity can influence health decision making through the mediating mechanisms described above. I describe a different behavioral health issue for each mediating mechanism to illustrate the variety of health behaviors that are influenced by cultural identity. These examples illustrating possible mediating mechanisms are by no means exhaustive; they are just illustrations of associations between cultural identity and health behaviors.

Perceptions about Risk of Disease in the Cultural Group

Genetic Screening among Ashkenazi Jews. Cultural identity can influence people's decisions about whether to be screened for disease by influencing their perceptions of whether they are at risk for a particular disease. Individuals might be more likely to seek screening tests if they identify with a cultural group that is viewed as having a high risk for a given disease. Research has identified two genes, BRCA1 and BRCA2, which are strongly linked to hereditary breast and ovarian cancers (King, Marks, & Mandell, 2003). People with a mutation in one of these genes have a lifetime risk of breast cancer as high as 82%. These genetic mutations are especially common among people of central and eastern European (Ashkenazi) Jewish descent. Therefore, it is typically recommended that Ashkenazi Jewish women, especially those with a family history of breast cancer, should consider being tested for the specific BRCA mutations that are common in this population. Women who test positive for BRCA mutations may elect to have prophylactic surgery such as mastectomy or oophorectomy (removal of the ovaries), or they may elect to receive frequent mammograms to detect breast cancer in its early stages.

Theories of health behavior (e.g., Janz & Becker, 1984) posit that people will be more likely to seek screening if they believe that they are personally susceptible to the disease. Perceptions of susceptibility can be influenced by a number of factors, including people's beliefs about the quality of their health in general, their beliefs about whether they tend to be more or less lucky than others (Weinstein, 1980), and their subjective perceptions about whether they fit the profile of the typical person who is likely to get the disease. Women may be more likely to seek breast cancer screening if they believe they fit the profile of the "typical" woman who is at risk for

breast cancer, and this belief may be influenced by their cultural identities, as described below.

In recent years, the media have publicized the high prevalence of breast cancer genes among Ashkenazi Jews, highlighting this group as a high-risk group for breast cancer (Hoffman-Goetz, Clarke, & Donelle, 2005). Self-identification as an Ashkenazi Jew may increase a woman's subjective perception of her breast cancer risk, which may make her more interested in being tested for BRCA mutations. However, many factors may influence women's cultural identification with the Ashkenazi Jewish population. Jewish identity is a complex construct that includes aspects of heritage, religious beliefs, and cultural belongingness. Many people have a Jewish biological lineage but do not participate in the Jewish community. Others consider themselves members of the Jewish culture but not religiously observant. In addition, because of the history of migration of the Jewish diaspora, many people of Jewish descent cannot trace their families back to specific countries, and there are likely many people with Jewish ancestors who are not aware of this ancestry. For example, one of the BRCA1 mutations was found among six non-Jewish Americans of Spanish ancestry living in Colorado (Mullineaux et al., 2003). Although none of them knew of a Jewish ancestor, one researcher hypothesized that they were descendants of Marranos, Spanish Jews who pretended to convert to Christianity in the fourteenth and fifteenth centuries to avoid persecution (Long, 2004). In most of the original studies of BRCA1/2 mutations, there were no consistent criteria for identifying Ashkenazi Jews; families were identified based on their self-reports, or even their physicians' assumptions, that they were Ashkenazi Jews (Brandt-Rauf, Raveis, Drummond, Conte, & Rothman, 2006). Therefore, the cultural identities that people choose, and the cultural identities that they present to their physicians, could influence the types of screening that they seek out or are offered.

Jewish cultural identity illustrates how cultural identity can influence people's perceptions of disease risk, which in turn can influence their screening behaviors and potentially prevent cancer mortality. Messages about the high prevalence of breast cancer susceptibility genes among Ashkenazi Jews may resonate more with people who have a strong Jewish identity. Jews who are more immersed in the Jewish community may have more opportunities to learn about their risk for breast cancer and may be more likely to find this risk personally relevant.

Perception of Normative Behaviors among the Cultural Group

Smoking among Women. Cultural identity can influence perceived social norms about the appropriateness or desirability of health-risk and health-protective behaviors. Cultural norms dictate which behaviors are appropriate for which segments of the population. Therefore, cultural identity may influence people's decisions about which behaviors would be appropriate for them personally. Tobacco smoking is a health-risk behavior that is associated with over 443,000 premature deaths in the United States each year (Adhikari, Kahende, Malarcher, Pechacek, & Tong, 2008). The demographic patterns of smoking differ across cultural contexts. For example, within White American culture and in many European cultures, the prevalence of cigarette smoking is similar among men and women (Hammond, 2009). These cultures lack strong social norms about whether smoking is more appropriate among one gender than among the other. However, in some Asian cultures, smoking is considered appropriate among men but undesirable among women (Hsia & Spruijt-Metz, 2008; Tsai, Tsai, Yang, & Kuo, 2008). Since the cultural meaning of women's smoking varies across cultural contexts, individual women's cultural identities will influence their decisions about smoking.

Cultural influences on smoking might not be so obvious among Asian women who are living in Asian cultural contexts, because they share an Asian cultural identity and share the norm that smoking is not acceptable among women. However, when Asian women move to the United

States or Europe (or when daughters of Asian immigrants grow up in the United States or Europe), the influence of cultural identity on smoking may become especially salient. Among those with Asian cultural identities, smoking will still likely be viewed as unacceptable for women. Among those Asian women who have adopted more Westernized cultural identities, smoking may be less taboo. In fact, women may actually use smoking as a way to demonstrate to their peers that they have adopted a more Westernized identity. Consequently, acculturation to American culture is associated with an increased risk of smoking among Asian women and girls, but not among Asian men and boys (Chae, Gavin, & Takeuchi, 2006; Hofstetter et al., 2004; Kim, Ziedonis, & Chen, 2007). For example, in studies of Chinese, Filipino, South Asian, Japanese, Korean, and Vietnamese American adults in California (An, Cochran, Mays, & McCarthy, 2008) and of Chinese, Korean, Vietnamese, and Cambodian women in Pennsylvania and New Jersey (Ma et al., 2004), endorsement of an American cultural identity was associated with an increased prevalence of smoking among women but not among men. Similar patterns have been found among Asian-American adolescents, with higher levels of US cultural identity being associated with a higher prevalence of smoking and stronger social norms about the acceptability of smoking among girls but not among boys (Weiss & Garbanati, 2006). The patterns of smoking among Asian women illustrate one way in which cultural identity can affect health-risk behaviors: because of cross-cultural differences in social norms and the social acceptability of smoking among women, an Asian cultural identity may be protective against smoking among Asian-heritage women, whereas a Westernized cultural identity may be a risk factor for smoking.

Desire to Self-present as a Member of the Cultural Group

Menthol smoking among African Americans. People may choose to adopt certain health-related behaviors as a way of demonstrating their cultural identity to others. If a behavior is viewed as typical among a certain cultural group, people can use that behavior as a way of demonstrating that they belong to that group. One example of this is menthol cigarette smoking among African Americans. Menthol cigarettes have become associated with an African American cultural identity, so people may smoke menthols as a way of demonstrating that they identify with African American culture. Over 70% of African American smokers, compared with 30% of White smokers, prefer menthol cigarettes (Gardiner, 2004). Multiple factors have interacted over the past century to create an association between African American identity and menthol smoking. It is likely that the association between African American cultural identity and menthol smoking has its roots in traditional Deep South African American culture, in which mentholated products were frequently used as folk medicine cures for numerous ailments (Castro, 2004). The tobacco industry capitalized on this association between menthol and medicinal benefits to market mentholated cigarettes to the African American community as a healthier alternative to regular cigarettes. Tobacco companies later began to use culturally tailored images and messages to "African Americanize" menthol cigarettes (Gardiner, 2004). Mentholated tobacco products, such as Kool cigarettes, were promoted as young, hip, new, and healthy. More recently, tobacco companies have selectively marketed menthol cigarettes in African American neighborhoods (Yerger, Przewoznik, & Malone, 2007) and in African American magazines (Landrine et al., 2005). They have also associated menthol smoking with genres of music that have been popular with African Americans, such as jazz and hip-hop (Gardiner, 2004). The result of this marketing is the creation of a strong cultural norm that African Americans smoke menthols, whereas White Americans do not.

Now that this norm has been established, it may influence people's decisions about smoking menthols. For example, many African Americans may try menthol cigarettes first because their parents or other relatives smoke menthol brands. Depending on the extent of their identification with the African American community and its media-generated image, they may decide to continue smoking menthols (and thus reinforce their African American identity) or switch to a non-mentholated brand (and thus turn away from the norm in the African American community) (Allen & Unger, 2007). The decision to smoke menthols, in turn, may affect their risk for tobacco-related diseases because menthol smokers tend to inhale more deeply and therefore expose themselves to more nicotine and other harmful chemicals per cigarette compared to non-menthol smokers (Ahijevych & Garrett, 2004).

Figure 34.3 compares African American smokers who smoke menthols exclusively, those who smoke non-menthols exclusively, and those who smoke both types of cigarettes. In this study

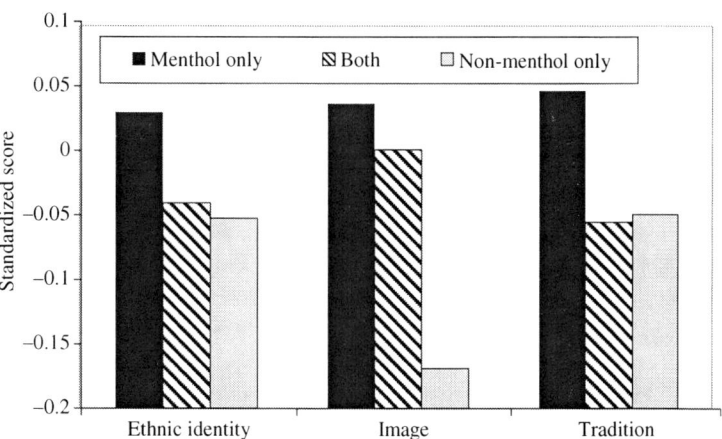

Fig. 34.3 Identity-related measures among African American smokers in Southern California

(described by Unger, Allen, Leonard, Wenten, & Cruz, in press), a representative sample of 720 African American smokers in Southern California, recruited through a quota sampling approach at retail locations in census tracts with large proportions of African Americans, completed a survey about their smoking behavior and associated attitudes and beliefs. Among the respondents, 57% smoked menthols only, 15% smoked non-menthols only, and 28% smoked both. The respondents answered questions about their African American cultural identity (Phinney, 1992), beliefs that menthol smoking is consistent with the African American cultural image, and beliefs that menthol smoking is consistent with African American traditions. The "image" measure was the mean of six items, e.g., "Smoking menthols shows that African Americans identify more with their culture" (Cronbach's alpha=0.75). The "tradition" measure was the mean of five items, e.g., "African Americans have chewed mint and used mint tea since the time of slavery," (Cronbach's alpha=0.77). As shown in Fig. 34.3, menthol smokers have stronger ethnic self-identification, stronger beliefs that menthol smoking is consistent with the African American image, and stronger beliefs that menthol is an African American tradition, as compared with non-menthol smokers or respondents who smoke both types of cigarettes.

Ironically, the association between African American cultural identity and menthol smoking may be changing, as Whites who wish to emulate the African American culture have also been reported to smoke menthol cigarettes (Richter, Beistle, Pederson, & O'Hegarty, 2008). This illustrates that people can adopt cultural identities that differ from their own cultural backgrounds, and these adopted cultural identities can also influence their health behaviors. This example illustrates how industry marketing can create an association between a specific cultural identity and a health-risk behavior, and how that newly created norm can then influence people's behavior according to their personal cultural identities.

Functional Meaning of the Behavior among the Cultural Group

Individual- versus Family-based Medical Decision Making across Cultural Groups. Health-related behaviors have different meanings across cultures. Therefore, people's cultural identities may influence the extent to which they ascribe certain meanings to behaviors, which in turn will influence the extent to which they practice the behaviors in question. This is evident in the ways in which healthcare decisions are made – do patients choose treatment options independently, as a way of maintaining their autonomy and control, or do family members participate in the decision-making or even assume full responsibility for decision-making? In the United States and most Western cultures, personal autonomy in healthcare decision-making is viewed as a basic right (Bowman & Hui, 2000). Whenever possible, patients are given all available information about their condition and the treatment options, and the patient makes the final decision about which treatment to pursue. Medical systems in most Western cultures operate under the assumption that making one's own decisions is a way for the patient to maintain control, dignity, autonomy, and privacy. Typically the doctor first informs the patient about the diagnosis and prognosis, leaving it to the discretion of the patient whether or not to inform family members.

However, in more collectivist cultures including many cultures in Asia (Bowman & Hui, 2000) and Latin America (Galanti, 2003), medical decision-making is viewed as a family activity and an opportunity for family members to help the patient by relieving him/her of the burden of making difficult choices alone. Collectivist cultures view the person as a "relational self" – a self for whom social relationships, rather than rationality and individualism, provide the basis for decision-making (see Chen et al., Chapter 7, this volume). Therefore, the entire family is involved in decisions about medical procedures. The family may designate one member – often someone other than the patient – to receive medical information from the physician, confer with the family, and communicate the family's decision back to the physician. Often the patient is not told the details of her/his prognosis, because bad news might cause excessive worry that could impede recovery. Personal autonomy in healthcare decision-making is viewed not as a human right but as a burden and a stressor; family members are obligated to protect the patient from upsetting information and excessive stress by making decisions on the patient's behalf (Blackhall, Murphy, Frank, Michel, & Azen, 1995). In a study of adults in the United States (Blackhall et al., 1995), individuals of Korean and Mexican descent were more likely to hold a family-centered model of medical decision-making, whereas European American and African American respondents preferred patient-centered decision-making.

The distinction between individual decision-making and family decision-making illustrates a major source of variation in cultural identities across cultural groups. According to Markus and Kitayama (1991, 1995) and Smith, (Chapter 11, this volume), there are two types of self-construal: independent and interdependent. The independent self-construal, which is emphasized in Western cultures, views the self as a self-contained set of internal attributes (preferences, traits, abilities, motives, values, and rights). In this view, each person's set of internal attributes is separate and unique. The individual constructs her/his own identity and makes her/his own autonomous decisions. This can still include consideration of the consequences to other people, but the self is seen as a distinct entity with inherent boundaries and rights.

The interdependent self-construal, which is emphasized in non-Western cultures, views the self not as a separate entity but instead as fundamentally interdependent with the family, social group, and community. This does not imply that the person with an interdependent view of the self has no conception of a unique self, but rather that the self is viewed in the context of its relationships with others (cf. Chen et al., Chapter 7, this volume). Thus, a person's priorities include occupying one's proper place in the group, engaging in collectively appropriate actions, and promoting

the goals of the group. Independent and interdependent self-construals are present to some extent in every culture, but cultures vary in ways in which these orientations are weighted in social life and manifest in behavior, including medical decision-making. One study (Kim, Smith, & Gu, 1999) found that people with high levels of interdependent self-construal were more likely to prefer healthcare decisions made by the physician or the family, whereas people with high levels of independent self-construal were more likely to prefer patient decision-making. This is an example of how one's cultural identity can shape perceptions about the functional meaning of behaviors such as healthcare decision-making.

Cultural Values

Cultural Values and Health-Risk Behaviors among Adolescents. Cultural values refer to attitudes, beliefs, priorities, and behaviors that are emphasized, encouraged, and viewed as desirable by members of a particular social group at a specific time (McElroy & Jezewski, 2000). Cultural values shape people's attitudes toward performing various behaviors, including those related to health. Examining the values of multiple cultures, one can easily observe parallels. Many cultures have values that emphasize the importance of harmonious social relationships, including agreeableness, politeness, and avoidance of blatant disagreement, including the traditionally Hispanic value of simpatía and the traditionally Asian value of saving face (Griffith, Joe, Chatham, & Simpson, 1998; Triandis, 1984). Some cultures endorse collectivist values that emphasize the well-being of the group (family, community, etc.,) over the well-being of the individual (Triandis, 1995). Some collectivist values, such as the traditionally Hispanic value of familism, emphasize a sense of obligation to, and connectedness with, immediate and extended family, as well as fictive kin (e.g., close family friends; "adopted" aunts, uncles, and cousins who are not biological relatives) (Cuellar, Arnold, & Gonzalez, 1995). Other values imply a more vertical, hierarchical power structure, emphasizing that lower-status people such as children should obey and respect higher-status people such as family and community elders, for the good of the larger group (Triandis, 1995). For example, the traditionally Hispanic value of Respeto and the traditionally Asian value of filial piety emphasize a child's duty to show respect for, take care of, and obey the advice of parents and other authority figures such as doctors, teachers, and community elders (Garcia, 1996; Ho, 1994). Internalization of certain cultural values could influence people's decisions about health-related behaviors. For example, a study of students in a culturally diverse high school (Unger et al., 2002) found that filial piety was associated with a lower risk for substance use, presumably because students who internalized the value of filial piety were more likely to obey their parents' rules about substance use. Another study of Asian American and Hispanic middle school students (Unger et al., 2006) found that the values of respect for adults (a combination of filial piety and respeto) and politeness (importance of smooth, harmonious interpersonal interactions, saving face) were inversely associated with tobacco use. This example illustrates that cultural identity can shape cultural values, which in turn can affect people's decisions about engaging in health-related behaviors.

Conclusions

This chapter has proposed a new theoretical model of the mechanisms by which cultural identity might influence health-related behaviors, including primary preventive behaviors (preventing disease before it occurs), secondary preventive behaviors (detecting disease early), and tertiary preventive behaviors (treating existing disease). The effects of cultural identity on health-related behaviors are likely mediated by cognitive and affective factors such as perceptions of the risk of disease in a particular cultural group, perceptions of the normative behaviors of the cultural group, desire to self-present as a member of the cultural group, and internalization of the values of the cultural group. In addition, it is likely that these effects can be facilitated or hindered by enabling factors such as access to care and knowledge. Although this hypothesized model provides a framework with which to organize and understand the role of cultural identity in health, future research will be necessary to garner support for the pathways proposed in the model.

Recommendations for Future Research and Practice

The theoretical model and the examples discussed in this chapter suggest several gaps in the research and recommendations for service providers who work with diverse populations:

Develop Improved Measures of Cultural Identity. Many psychometric instruments exist to assess various constructs related to cultural identity, including acculturation, ethnic identity formation, and cultural values. These constructs overlap to some extent, and there has been great variation across studies in the definition of cultural identity and the measures used, making it difficult to compare results across studies. Brief, valid survey measures are needed to assess cultural identity in ways that are not too cumbersome for inclusion in large-scale studies (see Umaña-Taylor, Chapter 33, this volume).

Conduct Research to Understand the Effects of Changes in Cultural Identity on Health-Related Behaviors. As described above, cultural identity is not static; it changes throughout the life course and across situations, and it also changes as a result of acculturation. Research is needed to understand how long-term and short-term changes in cultural identity affect people's decisions about health-related behaviors. For example, do processes of cultural identity exploration or changes in cultural identity lead to changes in health behaviors? Does the salience of a person's cultural identity in a given situation influence the person's immediate decisions about performing health behaviors that are consistent or inconsistent with that cultural identity?

Conduct Research on the Interactions between an Individual's Cultural Identity and the Larger Cultural Context. Although all human behavior occurs within a cultural context, most studies of cultural identity merely examine individual-level associations between cultural identity and behavior. Research is needed to determine whether matches or mismatches between an individual's cultural identity and the larger cultural context also influence behavior (Schwartz, Unger, Zamboanga, & Szapocznik, 2010). For example, does cultural identity influence behavior more when the individual is in a cultural minority because the individual's cultural identity is more salient? Or does cultural identity influence behavior more when the individual is in the cultural majority because the prevailing social norms support that behavior?

Practitioners Should Understand Patients' Cultural Identities and Present Medical Advice in Ways that Are Compatible with Patients' Cultural Identities. A common complaint among practitioners is that patients do not comply with medical recommendations (Winnick, Lucas, Hartman, & Toll, 2005). It may be possible to increase compliance by taking the time to learn about patients' cultural identities and make recommendations that are consistent with these identities. In many cases, it may be sufficient merely to mention a health-related behavior and ask the patient whether this behavior is acceptable in her/his cultural group. For example, Bowman and Hui (2000) describe a case of a Chinese man with a medical condition. The physician simply asked the man whether he was more comfortable making medical decisions himself or whether he preferred another family member to receive his medical information and convey the family's decision. The man designated his son as the family spokesperson – a solution that was acceptable to everyone. Because cultural identity is such a pervasive determinant of human behavior, and health is such a central quality of the human experience, it is crucial to continue to gain more information about the complex associations between cultural identity and health. Such information will likely help respect the cultural values of individuals and their families, as well as to improve the health of the public.

References

Adhikari, B., Kahende, J., Malarcher, A., Pechacek, T., & Tong, V. (2008). Smoking-attributable mortality, years of potential life lost, and productivity losses – United States, 2000–2004. *Morbidity & Mortality Weekly Reports*, 57, 1226–1228.

Ahijevych, K., & Garrett, B. E. (2004). Menthol pharmacology and its potential impact on cigarette smoking behavior. *Nicotine and Tobacco Research*, 6, S17–S28.

Allen, B., & Unger, J. B. (2007). Sociocultural correlates of menthol cigarette smoking among adult African Americans in Los Angeles. *Nicotine and Tobacco Research*, 9, 447–451.

An, N., Cochran, S. D., Mays, V. M., & McCarthy, W. J. (2008). Influence of American acculturation on cigarette smoking behaviors among Asian American subpopulations in California. *Nicotine and Tobacco Research*, 10, 579–587.

Aronson, E. (1968). Dissonance theory: Progress and problems. In R. P. Abelson, E. Aronson, W. J. McGuire, T. M. Newcomb, M. J. Rosenberg, & P. H. Tannenbaum (Eds.), *Theories of cognitive consistency: A sourcebook* (pp. 5–27). Chicago: Rand McNally.

Aronson, E. (1999). Dissonance, hypocrisy, and the self-concept. In E. Harmon-Jones & J. Mills (Eds.), *Cognitive dissonance: Progress on a pivotal theory in social psychology* (pp. 103–126). Washington, DC: American Psychological Association.

Bandura, A. (1986). *Social foundations of thought and action: A social cognitive theory*. Englewood Cliffs, NJ: Prentice-Hall.

Baron, R. M., & Kenny, D. A. (1986). The moderator-mediator variable distinction in social psychological research: Conceptual, strategic, and statistical considerations. *Journal of Personality and Social Psychology*, 51, 1173–1182.

Baumeister, R. F. (1982). A self-presentational view of social phenomena. *Psychological Bulletin*, 91, 3–26.

Blackhall, L. J., Murphy, S. T., Frank, G., Michel, V., & Azen, S. (1995). Ethnicity and attitudes toward patient autonomy. *Journal of the American Medical Association*, 274, 820–825.

Bowman, K. W., & Hui, E. C. (2000). Bioethics for clinicians: 20. Chinese bioethics. *Canadian Medical Association Journal*, 163, 1481–1485.

Brandt-Rauf, S. I., Raveis, V. H., Drummond, N. F., Conte, J. A., & Rothman, S. M. (2006). Ashkenazi Jews and breast cancer: The consequences of linking ethnic identity to genetic disease. *American Journal of Public Health*, 96, 1979–1988.

Bronfenbrenner, U. (1979). *The ecology of human development: Experiments by nature and design*. Boston: Harvard University Press.

Castro, F. G. (2004). Physiological, psychological, social, and cultural influences on the use of menthol cigarettes among Blacks and Hispanics. *Nicotine and Tobacco Research*, 6, S29–S41.

Chae, D. H., Gavin, A. R., & Takeuchi, D. T. (2006). Smoking prevalence among Asian Americans: Findings from the National Latino and Asian American Study (NLAAS). *Public Health Reports, 121*, 755–763.

Cheung, Y. W. (1993). Approaches to ethnicity: Clearing roadblocks in the study of ethnicity and substance abuse. *International Journal of Addictions, 28,* 1209–1226.

Cuellar, I., Arnold, B., & Gonzalez, G. (1995). Cognitive referents of acculturation: Assessment of cultural constructs in Mexican Americans. *Journal of Community Psychology, 23*, 339–356.

Festinger, L. (1957). *A theory of cognitive dissonance.* Stanford, CA: Stanford University Press.

Fishbein, M., & Ajzen, I. (1975). *Belief, attitude, intention, and behavior.* Reading, MA: Addison-Wesley.

Friis, R. H., & Sellers, T. A. (2009). *Epidemiology for public health practice.* Boston: Jones & Bartlett.

Galanti, G. A. (2003). The Hispanic family and male-female relationships: An overview. *Journal of Transcultural Nursing, 14*, 180–185.

Garcia, W. (1996). Respeto: A Mexican base for interpersonal relationships. In S. Ting-Toomey & W. B. Gudykunst (Eds.), *Communication in personal relationships across cultures* (pp. 137–155). Thousand Oaks, CA: Sage Publications.

Gardiner, P. S. (2004). The African Americanization of menthol cigarette use in the United States. *Nicotine and Tobacco Research, 6*, S55–S65.

Geertz, C. (1973). *The interpretation of cultures.* New York: Basic Books.

Green, L. W., & Kreuter, M. W. (1999). *Health promotion planning: An educational and ecological approach* (3rd ed.). Mountain View, CA: Mayfield.

Griffith, J. D., Joe, G. W., Chatham, L. R., & Simpson, D. D. (1998). The development and validation of a simpatia scale for Hispanics entering drug treatment. *Hispanic Journal of Behavioral Sciences, 20*, 468–482.

Hammond, S. K. (2009). Global patterns of nicotine and tobacco consumption. In J. E. Henningfield, E. D. London, & S. Pogun (Eds.), *Nicotine psychopharmacology* (pp. 3–28). Berlin: Springer.

Hatcher, E. & Whittemore, R. (2007). Hispanic adults' beliefs about type 2 diabetes: Clinical implications. *Journal of the American Academy of Nurse Practitioners, 19*, 536–545.

Ho, D. (1994). Filial piety, authoritarian moralism, and cognitive conservatism in Chinese societies. *Genetic, Social, and General Psychology Monographs, 120,* 349–365.

Hoffman-Goetz, L., Clarke, J. N., & Donelle, L. (2005). Ethnicity, genetics, and breast cancer: Media portrayal of disease identities. *Ethnicity and Health, 10,* 185–197.

Hofstetter, C. R., Hovell, M. F., Lee, J., Zakarian, J., Park, H., & Paik, H. Y., et al. (2004). Tobacco use and acculturation among Californians of Korean descent:

A behavioral epidemiological analysis. *Nicotine and Tobacco Research, 6*, 481–489.

Howard, J. A. (2000). Social psychology of identities. *Annual Review of Sociology, 26*, 367–393.

Hsia, F. N., & Spruijt-Metz, D. (2008). Gender differences in smoking and meanings of smoking in Asian-American college students. *Journal of Health Psychology, 13*, 459–463.

Janz, N. K., & Becker, M. H. (1984). The health belief model: A decade later. *Health Education and Behavior, 11*, 1–47.

Kagawa-Singer, M., & Blackhall, L. J. (2001). Negotiating cross-cultural issues at the end of life: "You got to go where he lives". *Journal of the American Medical Association, 286*, 2993–3001.

Kim, M. S., Smith, D. H., & Gu, Y. (1999). Medical decision making and Chinese patients' self-construals. *Health Communication, 11*, 249–260.

Kim, S. S., Ziedonis, D., & Chen, K. W. (2007). Tobacco use and dependence in Asian Americans: A review of the literature. *Nicotine and Tobacco Research, 9*, 169–184.

King, M., Marks, J. H., & Mandell, J. B. (2003). Breast and ovarian cancer risks due to inherited mutations in BRCA1 and BRCA2. *Science, 302*, 643–646.

Landrine, H., Klonoff, E. A., Fernandez, S., Hickman, N., Kashima, K., & Parekh, B., et al. (2005). Cigarette advertising in Black, Latino, and White magazines, 1998–2002: An exploratory investigation. *Ethnicity and Disease, 15*, 63–67.

Llewellyn, D. J. (2008). The psychology of risk taking: Toward the integration of psychometric and neuropsychological paradigms. *American Journal of Psychology, 121*, 363–376.

Long, H. J. (2004). Identification of germline 185delAG BRCA1 mutations in non-Jewish Americans of Spanish ancestry from the San Luis Valley, Colorado. *Cancer, 100*, 434–435.

Ma, G. X., Tan, Y., Toubbeh, J. I., Su, X., Shive, S. E., & Lan, Y. (2004). Acculturation and smoking behavior in Asian-American populations. *Health Education Research, 19*, 615–625.

Markus, H. R., & Kitayama, S. (1991). Culture and the self: Implications for cognition, emotion, and motivation. *Psychological Review, 98*, 224–253.

Markus, H. R., & Kitayama, S. (1995). A collective fear of the collective: Implications for selves and theories of selves. *Personality and Social Psychology, 20*, 568–579.

Matsumoto, D. (2003). The discrepancy between consensual-level culture and individual-level culture. *Culture and Psychology, 9*, 89–95.

McElroy, A., & Jezewski, M. A. (2000). Cultural variation in the experience of health and Illness. In G. Albrecht, R. Fitzpatrick, & S. Scrimshaw (Eds.), *Social studies in health and medicine* (pp. 191–209). Thousand Oaks, CA: Sage.

Mechanic, D. (1986). The concept of illness behavior: Culture, situation and personal predisposition. *Psychological Medicine, 16*, 1–7.

Mullineaux, L. G., Castellano, T. M., Shaw, J., Axell, L., Wood, M. E., & Diab, S., et al. (2003). Identification of germline 185delAG BRCA1 mutations in non-Jewish Americans of Spanish ancestry from the San Luis Valley, Colorado. *Cancer, 98*, 597–602.

Oetting, E. R., & Beauvais, F. (1990). Orthogonal cultural identification theory: The cultural identification of minority adolescents. *International Journal of the Addictions, 25*, 655–685.

Phinney, J. (1992). The Multi-group Ethnic Identity Measure: A new scale for use with adolescents and you adults from diverse groups. *Journal of Adolescent Research, 7*, 156–176.

Phinney, J. (2000). Ethnic identity. In A. E. Kazdin (Ed.), *Encyclopedia of psychology* (Vol. 3, pp. 254–259). New York: Oxford University Press.

Phinney, J. (2003). Ethnic identity and acculturation. In K. Chun, P. B. Organista, & G. Marin (Eds.), *Acculturation: Advances in theory, measurement, and applied research* (pp. 63–81). Washington, DC: American Psychological Association.

Phinney, J. S. (1990). Ethnic identity in adolescents and adults: Review of research. *Psychological Bulletin, 108*, 499–514.

Powe, B. D., & Finnie, R. (2003). Cancer fatalism: The state of the science. *Cancer Nursing, 26*, 454–465.

Raman, S. (2006). Cultural identity and child health. *Journal of Tropical Pediatrics, 52*, 231–234.

Richter, P., Beistle, D., Pederson, L., & O'Hegarty, M. (2008). Small-group discussions on menthol cigarettes: Listening to adult African American smokers in Atlanta, Georgia. *Ethnicity and Health, 13*, 171–182.

Schwartz, S. J., Unger, J. B., Zamboanga, B. L., & Szapocznik, J. (2010). Rethinking the concept of acculturation: Implications for theory and research. *American Psychologist, 65*, 237–251.

Spruijt-Metz, D. (1995). Personal incentives as determinants of adolescent health behavior: The meaning of behavior. *Health Education Research, 10*, 355–364.

Steele, C. M. (1988). The psychology of self-affirmation: Sustaining the integrity of the self. In L. Berkowitz (Ed.), *Advances in experimental social psychology* (Vol. 21, pp. 261–302). San Diego, CA: Academic Press.

Triandis, H. C. (1984). A theoretical framework for the more efficient construction of cultural assimilators. *International Journal of Intercultural Relations, 8*, 301–330.

Triandis, H. C. (1995). *Individualism and collectivism*. Boulder, CO: Westview Press.

Trimble, J. E. (2000). Social psychological perspectives on changing self-identification among American Indians and Alaska Natives. In R. H. Dana (Ed.), *Handbook of cross-cultural and multicultural personality assessment* (pp. 197–222). Mahwah, NJ: Lawrence Erlbaum Associates.

Tsai, Y. W., Tsai, T. I., Yang, C. L., & Kuo, K. N. (2008). Gender differences in smoking behaviors in an Asian population. *Journal of Women's Health, 17*, 971–978.

Turner, W. L. (2000). Cultural considerations in family-based primary prevention programs in drug abuse. *Journal of Primary Prevention, 21*, 285–303.

Unger, J. B., Allen, B., Leonard, E., Wenten, M., & Cruz, T. B. (2010). Menthol and non-menthol cigarette use among Black smokers in Southern California. *Nicotine and Tobacco Research, 12*, 398–407.

Unger, J. B., Cruz, T., Shakib, S., Mock, J., Shields, A., & Baezconde-Garbanati, L., et al. (2003). Exploring the cultural context of tobacco use: A transdisciplinary framework. *Nicotine and Tobacco Research, 5*, S101–S117.

Unger, J. B., Ritt-Olson, A., Teran, L., Huang, T., Hoffman, B. R., & Palmer, P. (2002). Cultural values and substance use in a multiethnic sample of adolescents. *Addiction Research and Theory, 10*, 257–279.

Unger, J. B., Shakib, S., Gallaher, P., Ritt-Olson, A., Mouttapa, M., & Palmer, P. H., et al. (2006). Cultural/interpersonal values and smoking in an ethnically diverse sample of Southern California adolescents. *Journal of Cultural Diversity, 13*, 55–63.

Weinreich, P. (2009). 'Enculturation', not 'acculturation': Conceptualising and assessing identity processes in migrant communities. *International Journal of Intercultural Relations, 33*, 124–139.

Weinstein, N. D. (1980). Unrealistic optimism about future life events. *Journal of Personality and Social Psychology, 39*, 806–820.

Weiss, J. W., & Garbanati, J. A. (2006). Effects of acculturation and social norms on adolescent smoking among Asian-American subgroups. *Journal of Ethnicity in Substance Abuse, 5*, 75–90.

Winnick, S., Lucas, D. O., Hartman, A. L., & Toll, D. (2005). How do you improve compliance? *Pediatrics, 115*, 718–724.

Yerger, V. B., Przewoznik, J., & Malone, R. E. (2007). Racialized geography, corporate activity, and health disparities: Tobacco industry targeting of inner cities. *Journal of Health Care for the Poor and Underserved, 18*(4 Suppl), 10–38.

Que-Lam Huynh, Angela-MinhTu D. Nguyen, and Verónica Benet-Martínez

Abstract

Given the growing numbers of bicultural individuals in the United States and around the world, bicultural identity integration (BII) is an important construct that helps researchers to better capture the diversity within this group. In this chapter, we organize and summarize the limited literature on individual differences in bicultural identity, with a special focus on BII. First, we discuss and define biculturalism and cultural identity in general. Second, we introduce individual differences in bicultural identity and the ways in which these differences have been studied. Third, we define BII, summarize research on this construct, and introduce the latest applications of BII theory to other areas of identity research. In unpacking the construct of BII, we first define it along with its components (harmony and blendedness) and nomological network. We also discuss what we believe to be the process involved in integrating one's dual cultural identities. We then present correlates of BII, including self-group personality perceptions, culturally related behaviors and values, and sociocultural and psychological adjustment. Finally, we discuss how BII relates to other important social-cognitive constructs, such as cultural frame switching or code switching. We end with a brief overview of the latest applications of BII theory (e.g., to gay identity) and suggestions for future research on bicultural identity. In summary, our goal for this chapter is to introduce BII and to help readers understand the importance of culture in identity.

Since 1970, international migration has doubled worldwide. According to a recent report by the United Nations, about 175 million people are living in a country other than where they were born, and about 1 in 10 persons in "more developed" regions is an international migrant (United Nations Department of Economic and Social Affairs, 2002). In addition to these changes in international migration, advances in technology have drastically increased cross-cultural contact and cultural diversity across the globe (Arnett, 2002), and changes in attitudes and laws about

Q.-L. Huynh (✉)
Department of Psychology, San Diego State University,
San Diego, CA, USA
e-mail: huynh.quelam@gmail.com

S.J. Schwartz et al. (eds.), *Handbook of Identity Theory and Research*,
DOI 10.1007/978-1-4419-7988-9_35, © Springer Science+Business Media, LLC 2011

inter-ethnic marriage in some parts of the world have led to more inter-ethnic families whose children have mixed cultural backgrounds. Overall, people have more opportunities now than ever before to interact with those who are culturally different from them due to international migration, globalization, travel, and the Internet (cf. Arnett Jensen et al., Chapter 13, this volume). As a result of this cross-cultural exposure, there has been a large increase in the number of bicultural individuals – people who have internalized at least two cultures. It is essential for those interested in issues of identity to understand how dual-cultural identities operate within bicultural persons.

Broadly speaking, bicultural individuals may be immigrants, refugees, sojourners, indigenous people, ethnic minorities, or mixed-ethnic individuals (Berry, 2003; Padilla, 2006). However, bicultural individuals are not necessarily cultural minorities or those in non-dominant ethnocultural groups. For example, individuals from the dominant group (e.g., non-Hispanic White Americans) who have lived abroad or in ethnic enclaves, and those in inter-ethnic relationships, may also be bicultural. More strictly defined, bicultural individuals are those who have been exposed to and have internalized two cultures (Benet-Martínez, in press; Benet-Martínez & Haritatos, 2005; Nguyen & Benet-Martínez, 2007, 2010), so the cultural domain of identity is especially important for them. The focus of this chapter is on bicultural identity, specifically bicultural identity integration (BII; Benet-Martínez & Haritatos, 2005), as outlined below. We explore the diversity of the bicultural experience, present BII as a way to understand individual differences in biculturalism, and discuss the implications of and suggest future directions for BII.

Types of Biculturals

From the acculturation literature, biculturalism is conceived as one of four possible acculturation strategies: (a) the integration strategy (i.e., biculturalism) refers to involvement in both dominant and ethnic cultures, (b) the assimilation strategy is involvement in the dominant culture only, (c) the separation strategy is involvement in the ethnic culture only, and (d) marginalization is involvement in neither culture (Berry, 2003). Traditionally, cultural psychologists have focused on differences *between* bicultural individuals (those using the integration acculturation strategy) and other acculturating groups (those using the assimilation, separation, or marginalization acculturation strategies). However, empirical research, mostly conducted on young adults and adolescents, has shown that the majority of acculturating individuals are bicultural (Berry, 2003; Van Oudenhoven, Ward, & Masgoret, 2006). Therefore, it may be more fruitful to focus on differences *among* bicultural individuals, rather between bicultural individuals and other acculturating individuals. For example, do all bicultural individuals integrate their two cultures in the same way, in the same contexts, and for the same reasons? Until recently, there has been little research exploring differences within this large group that uses the integration strategy and whether these differences are meaningful. New research, however, suggests that bicultural or integrated individuals do not comprise a homogeneous group and that there are clearly variations among them (Schwartz & Zamboanga, 2008).

One of the earliest typologies of bicultural individuals, obtained with a sample of Latinos in the United States, included (a) the synthesized multicultural individual, (b) the functional multicultural individual with a mainstream cultural orientation, and (c) the functional multicultural individual with a Latino cultural orientation (Ramirez, 1984). The synthesized multicultural individual represents the "true" bicultural individual who is competent in and committed to both cultures. The functional multicultural individual is competent in both cultures but is committed to or identified with only one culture – either the mainstream or Latino (or other ethnic) culture. Although this typology was developed for Latinos, it may apply more broadly to other bicultural individuals. See Table 35.1 for a summary and comparison of typologies of bicultural individuals.

Table 35.1 Types of Biculturals Identified in Previous Research

Description	Theorists					
	Ramirez (1984)	LaFromboise et al. (1993)	Birman (1994)	Phinney and Devich-Navarro (1997)	Benet-Martínez et al. (2002)	Benet-Martínez and Haritatos (2005)
Competent in and identified with both dominant and ethnic cultures		Fused	Blended	Blended	High BII	High blendedness and/or high harmony
	Synthesized	Alternating		Alternating	Low BII	Low blendedness and/or low harmony
Competent in both cultures, identified with dominant culture only	Functional/ mainstream		Integrated			
Competent in both cultures, identified with ethnic culture only	Functional/ ethnic					
Competent in both cultures, identified with neither dominant nor ethnic culture			Instrumental			

Subsequently, LaFromboise, Coleman, and Gerton (1993) proposed two bicultural modes: alternation and fusion. Alternating bicultural individuals "alternate" or shift between their two cultures in accordance with the situation, whereas fused bicultural individuals subscribe to a "fused" or emergent third culture created by mixing and recombining their two cultures. Building on the above conceptualizations, Birman (1994) described three types of bicultural individuals: (a) blended, which is similar to LaFromboise et al.,'s (1993) fused category, (b) instrumental, which includes individuals competent in both cultures but identified with neither, and (c) integrated, which is similar to Ramirez's (1984) functional multicultural individual with a Latino cultural orientation. To empirically test these theoretical propositions regarding types of bicultural individuals, Phinney and Devich-Navarro (1997) conducted a study with Mexican American and

African American adolescents using both quantitative and qualitative methods. They found support for two types of bicultural individuals: blended and alternating. Although both types feel positively about their two cultures, alternating bicultural individuals appear to feel conflicted about having two cultures, whereas blended bicultural individuals do not.

The above researchers are credited with calling attention to bicultural individuals and for advancing this area of research. However, a conceptual limitation of these typologies is their confounding of identity and behavioral markers. Specifically, whereas the labels "blended" and "fused" refer to identity-related aspects of the bicultural experience (e.g., seeing oneself as Asian American or Chicano), the label "alternating" refers to the behavioral domain, that is, the ability to engage in cultural frame switching (Hong, Morris, Chiu, & Benet-Martínez, 2000).

Naturally, individuals' subjective experience of their identity and their behavior/competencies may not necessarily map onto each other (Roccas & Brewer, 2002). For instance, a bicultural individual may have a blended or fused identity (e.g., someone who sees himself/herself as a product of both Jewish and American cultures and accordingly identifies as Jewish American) *and* also alternates between speaking mainstream English and Yiddish depending on the context. Thus, researchers should be aware that labels such as "blended" and "alternating" do not tap different types of bicultural individuals but rather different components of the bicultural experience (i.e., identity vs. behaviors, respectively). In other words, blending one's two cultural identities is not incompatible with alternating between different cultural behavioral repertoires. Given this, the validity of the above "blended" versus "alternating" groupings (e.g., Phinney & Devich-Navarro, 1997) as separate types of biculturals is unclear.

To address the above shortcomings of the biculturalism literature, Benet-Martínez, Leu, Lee, and Morris (2002) introduced the construct of BII, an individual difference variable which captures the phenomenology of managing one's dual cultural identities. More recently, Benet-Martínez and Haritatos (2005) demonstrated that BII is not a unitary construct, but instead that it encompasses two different and psychometrically independent components (Benet-Martínez & Haritatos, 2005): (a) cultural *blendedness* versus compartmentalization – the degree of dissociation versus overlap perceived between the two cultural orientations (e.g., "I see myself as a Chinese in the United States" vs. "I am a Chinese-American"); and (2) cultural *harmony* versus conflict – the degree of tension or clash versus compatibility perceived between the two cultures (e.g., "I feel trapped between the two cultures" vs. "I do not see conflict between the Chinese and American ways of doing things").[1] In other words, for bicultural individuals, cultural blendedness is subjective distance, which varies among people and is more relevant and meaningful than the objective distance between two cultures (Rudmin, 2003). Cultural blendedness and cultural harmony are psychometrically

independent components and are differentially related to important contextual and personality variables. Specifically, lower blendedness is linked to personality and performance-related challenges (e.g., lower openness to new experiences, greater language barriers, and living in more culturally isolated surroundings), whereas lower harmony stems from other personality traits and strains that are largely interpersonal in nature (e.g., higher neuroticism, greater perceived discrimination, more strained intercultural relations, and greater language barriers – see Benet-Martínez, in press; Benet-Martínez & Haritatos, 2005, for a full discussion and graphing of these results). Bicultural individuals can have any combination of high or low blendedness and high or low harmony.

The BII framework emphasizes the subjective (i.e., perceptual) elements of perceived blendedness and harmony between the two cultures. This emphasis is a strength of the theory, as a study of over 7,000 first- or second-generation immigrant adolescents in 13 countries found that objective cultural differences do not relate to adjustment (Berry, Phinney, Sam, & Vedder, 2006). Objective cultural difference was operationalized as the difference in countries' scores determined by Hofstede (1983) on his dimensions of individualism-collectivism, power distance, masculinity-femininity, uncertainty avoidance, and long- versus short-term orientation.

Measurement of BII

Early versions of the Bicultural Identity Integration Scale. The Bicultural Identity Integration Scale – Pilot version (BIIS-P) is comprised of a short descriptive vignette that bicultural individuals rate on an 8-point Likert-type scale (1 = definitely not true, 8 = definitely true) with regard to how much it reflects their bicultural identity experiences. This measure was used in the first study of BII (Benet-Martínez et al., 2002) to assess the perceived compartmentalization (lack of blending) and conflict (lack of harmony) between two cultures in a multi-statement paragraph. Although this measure has high face validity with respondents, it confounds the two components of BII, cultural blendedness and harmony, by requiring participants to rate a statement that contains both of these elements. The Bicultural Identity Integration Scale – Version 1 (BIIS-1) is an eight-item measure of BII blendedness (4 items) and harmony (4 items; Benet-Martínez & Haritatos, 2005). These items are rated on a 5-point Likert-type scale (1 = strongly disagree, 5 = strongly agree). Although the BIIS-1 is adequately internally consistent ($\alpha_{blendedness}$ =0.69, $\alpha_{harmony}$ =0.74; Benet-Martínez & Haritatos, 2005), the reliability of scores yielded by this instrument is not ideal. In addition, the few items assessing each component of BII do not adequately cover all relevant content domains of BII. Therefore, in a series of development and validation studies, Huynh (2009) improved the measurement of BII with the Bicultural Identity Integration Scale – Version 2 (BIIS-2).

After generating items using qualitative data (open-ended essays written by self-identified bicultural college students) and item evaluation by subject-matter experts and pilot testers, Huynh (2009) administered 45 new items of the BIIS-2 to an ethnically diverse group of more than 1,000 self-identified bicultural college students. Approximately half of the participants (55.5%) were women, and the mean age of the sample was 19.3 years. The majority of participants were either Latinos/as (32.1%) or Asian Americans (48.6%), and most participants were either first- (34.6%, mean years in the United States = 10.6 years) or second- (55.9%) generation Americans. The final BIIS-2 consists of 19 items rated on a 5-point Likert-type scale (1 = strongly disagree, 5 = strongly agree; see Appendix A for sample items). These items yield reliable (blendedness vs. compartmentalization α = .86 for 9 items; harmony vs. conflict α = .81 for 10 items) and stable (n = 240; M = 6.93 days, SD = 0.90 days; Time 1 and Time 2 correlations: $0.74 < r < .78$) scores across ethnic groups. In addition, results from both exploratory and confirmatory factor analyses suggest that the BIIS-2 is comprised of separate blendedness and

harmony components. Finally, the BIIS-2 showed measurement invariance (i.e., that the structure of the BIIS-2 is similar across groups) for two ethnic groups (Asian American and Latino) and two generational groups (first and second generation). Across groups, the blendedness and harmony components were moderately correlated (r = .36), but they were distinguishable in the exploratory and confirmatory factor analyses described above.

Previous Findings on BII

Previous literature suggests that BII has important implications for bicultural individuals' adjustment, cognition, and behaviors. We first review earlier literature on BII when it was still considered a unitary construct, and then we review more recent literature on the blendedness and harmony components of BII. Regarding adjustment, researchers have found that BII was associated with greater adjustment (i.e., higher self-esteem, greater life satisfaction, greater subjective happiness, lower depression, lower anxiety, and less loneliness) for Mainland Chinese adult immigrants in Hong Kong, native-born college students in Hong Kong, and native-born college students in Mainland China (Chen, Benet-Martínez, & Bond, 2008). Further support for the relation between BII and adjustment comes from research on multicultural identity integration (MII, an extension of BII from two to three cultures: e.g., ethnic culture, English Canadian culture, French Canadian culture) in Quebec. Researchers also found a link between MII and greater psychological well-being (i.e., self-acceptance, positive relations with others, autonomy, environmental mastery, purpose in life, and personal growth) in young adults from diverse backgrounds in Quebec (Downie, Koestner, ElGeledi, & Cree, 2004; Downie, Mageau, Koestner, & Liodden, 2006). In summary, individuals higher on BII tend to be better adjusted.

To understand the cognitive correlates of global BII (i.e., BII as measured by the BIIS-P), Benet-Martínez, Lee, and Leu (2006) compared the cognitive complexity of Chinese American undergraduate students high versus low on BII. They found that individuals low on BII had more cognitively complex representations of culture because they provided more abstract and dense descriptions of their cultures than did those high on BII. In other words, individuals low on BII described culture using multiple perspectives, compared and contrasted those different perspectives, included more ideas and words in their descriptions, and made evaluative judgments of each culture. Benet-Martínez and colleagues reasoned that the more systematic and careful processing of cues that underlies the monitoring of conflictual information (Botvinick, Braver, Barch, Carer, & Cohen, 2001) would lead low BIIs to develop cultural representations that are more complex (e.g., richer in content, more differentiated and integrated) than high BIIs. This finding is in agreement with the work of Suedfeld and colleagues (Suedfeld, Bluck, Loewen, & Elkins, 1994; Suedfeld & Wallbaum, 1992), which showed that conflict between desired but contradictory values (e.g., individual freedom and social equality) leads to more complex descriptions of each value.

Differences between individuals high versus low on BII also extend into social networks (Mok, Morris, Benet-Martínez, & Karakitapoglu-Aygun, 2007). In a sample of Chinese American undergraduate students, graduate students, visiting scholars, and their spouses, the social network of individuals high on BII included more dominant-culture friends, and their dominant-culture and ethnic-culture friends were more interconnected. In summary, variations in BII levels are associated with variations in cognitive complexity and social behavior.

In terms of the two components of BII, recent studies have helped to delineate the unique links between these components and adjustment, sociocognitive variables, and behavioral variables. Across multiple studies with bicultural individuals from several different ethnic groups in university and community settings, BII harmony (but not BII blendedness) was related to lower rates of depression and/or anxiety symptoms (Benet-Martínez, Haritatos, & Santana,

2010). However, regarding social perceptions such as self- and group-stereotypes, BII blendedness (but not BII harmony) was consistently related to higher overlap among personality ratings that Latino college students and Cuban American adults ascribed to the self, a typical Latino, and a typical American (Miramontez, Benet-Martínez, & Nguyen, 2008). This suggests that, as theorized, BII blendedness captures the organization and structure of one's two cultural orientations, whereas BII harmony indexes the feelings and attitudes toward those cultures. Finally, it appears that BII blendedness and BII harmony are associated with different aspects of the acculturation process (Nguyen, Huynh, & Benet-Martínez, 2010). In a sample of Vietnamese American bicultural individuals, BII harmony was related to acculturation in terms of values, such that individuals who only endorsed one set of cultural values (e.g., only American values) perceived more harmony between their cultures than those who endorsed both sets of cultural values. Furthermore, BII blendedness was related to behavioral acculturation, such that individuals who engaged in behaviors associated with both cultures had blended rather than compartmentalized identities.

Building on the Nomological Network for BII

Using the BIIS-2, Huynh (2009) found further support for the notion that blendedness represents the behavioral or performance-related component, whereas harmony represents the affective component of BII. Meaningful relations have been found between these BII dimensions and acculturation, identity, personality traits, and psychological adjustment. BII blendedness was correlated with orientation to American culture (e.g., years in the United States, English language proficiency and use, and US cultural identification). This suggests that exposure to American culture is related to perceiving one's heritage and receiving cultures as more similar, and that this exposure is important in forming a combined identity. Furthermore, supporting previous research on the relationship between BII blendedness and acculturation strategies (Benet-Martínez & Haritatos, 2005), there were small to moderate correlations between BII blendedness and stronger integration attitudes and weaker separation attitudes. This suggests that bicultural individuals who wish to integrate their two cultures and do not endorse separation from the mainstream culture are more likely to find it easy to combine their two cultural identities. In addition, BII blendedness was only weakly related to acculturation stressors (e.g., perceived discrimination, problematic intercultural relations, work challenges), well-being, anxiety, depression, and hostility, further supporting the claim that blendedness is the less affect-laden component of BII. These findings also suggest that the perception of compartmentalization between two cultures is not likely linked to either contextual pressures or to psychological adjustment.

Regarding findings for BII harmony, there were small to moderate positive correlations between this BII component and ethnic identity affirmation, a dimension of ethnic identity that emphasizes positive attitudes toward one's ethnic group. In addition, BII harmony generally was moderately and negatively correlated with contextual acculturation stressors and neuroticism. This supports the claim that BII harmony involves affective elements of bicultural identity and is driven more strongly by contextual pressures compared to BII blendedness (Benet-Martínez & Haritatos, 2005). In addition, BII harmony had small to moderate positive correlations with measures of mental health (higher general well-being and lack of depressive symptoms). This suggests that there are links between the perception of conflict between a person's two cultures and lower psychological well-being and higher psychological distress (Chen et al., 2008). In general, BII harmony evidenced weak relationships with traditional acculturation variables (e.g., years in the United States, language proficiency, cultural identification, bicultural competence, cultural orientation, acculturation attitudes; Benet-Martínez & Haritatos, 2005) – providing further evidence that the two BII dimensions are largely separate.

Huynh (2009) also examined the antecedents and consequences of BII via path analyses and found that personality and acculturation variables influence individuals' perceptions about their dual identities (BII), which in turn influences adjustment [tests of model fit: $\chi^2(34) = 220.86$, $p < 0.0001$, CFI $= 0.93$; RMSEA $= 0.07$ (90% CI $= 0.06$–0.08); SRMR $= 0.05$]. Specifically, these analyses indicate that individuals who perceive the greatest harmony between their cultures are those who are more emotionally stable (or less neurotic); those who have harmonious intercultural relations, few culture-related work challenges, and few linguistic problems in English; and those who live in culturally diverse areas (i.e., personality and acculturation variables predict BII harmony). Consequently, individuals who perceive harmony between their cultures, as well as those who are emotionally stable, suffer the least from depressive symptoms (i.e., personality and BII harmony both predict psychological adjustment). Furthermore, individuals who blend their cultures most are those with few linguistic problems in English, those strongly identified with their ethnic culture, those highly oriented to American culture, and those preferring the integration strategy. In other words, acculturation variables predict BII blendedness, which in turn is *not* predictive of adjustment.

Development of an Integrated Bicultural Identity

BII may be determined by a variety of factors, ranging from personality to the immediate social environment to the larger historical, political, and economic context of one's cultural group. Although research on BII has been limited to correlational data, which does not allow for causal inferences, we can advance some theoretical propositions regarding the developmental process of BII. First, the history and current status of one's cultural group within the dominant culture may determine the range of one's BII level. For example, Phinney and Devich-Navarro (1997) found that the majority of African American adolescents were blended biculturals (e.g., high BII), whereas the majority of Mexican American adolescents were alternating biculturals (e.g., low BII). It is possible that African Americans' long and stable history in the United States, allowing for the development of a widespread African American culture, facilitates their cultural blendedness. Conversely, despite their long history in the United States, Mexican Americans are at the center of often controversial immigration debates, which impose on them an ever-present immigrant status even for those who are not immigrants. These tensions may predispose them to being alternating biculturals. Although BII has been found to be valid across highly diverse cultural and ethnic groups (Huynh, 2009), these groups may differ in the relative level of BII blendedness or harmony experienced.

In addition to larger contextual factors, variations in BII might be further influenced by dispositional factors, such as one's personality. For example, more neurotic or less emotionally stable individuals tend to perceive lower harmony between their cultures. Moreover, those who are more open to new experiences tend to perceive greater blendedness between their cultures (Benet-Martínez & Haritatos, 2005).

Finally, the actual degree of BII reported by a given person also may be determined by his/her immediate social environment and experiences. For example, previous research on large, diverse samples of bicultural individuals (Benet-Martínez & Haritatos, 2005; Huynh, 2009) showed that experiences with discrimination, interpersonal problems with culturally different others, and linguistic barriers were associated with bicultural individuals' perception of lower harmony between their two cultures. Furthermore, path analyses in those studies indicated that linguistic barriers and culturally isolated environments were associated with bicultural individuals' perception of lower blendedness between their two cultures.

In addition to these antecedents of BII, we believe that, although blendedness and harmony are theoretically independent and only weakly correlated, BII blendedness may precede BII harmony (see Fig. 35.1 for a pictorial depiction of the proposed developmental process of BII). Researchers have proposed that bicultural individuals with two cultures that are considerably different experience lower identity integration and greater identity conflict than those with two cultures that are more similar to one another

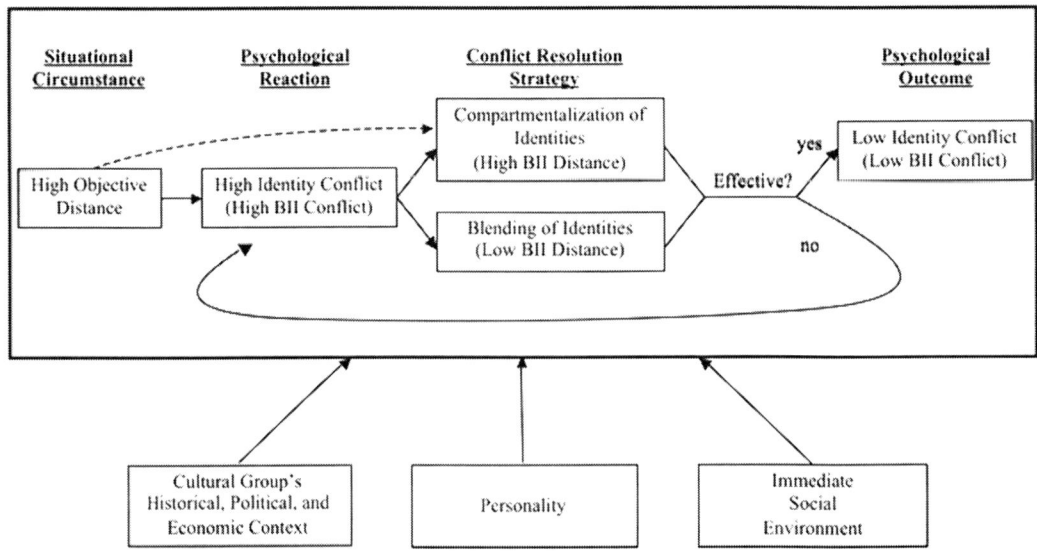

Fig. 35.1 Development of an integrated bicultural identity

(Amiot, de la Sablonnière, Terry, & Smith, 2007; Ward, 2008). In other words, high objective cultural distance [e.g., difference in countries' scores on Hofstede's (1983) dimensions] may lead to high BII conflict (low harmony). However, if the two cultures are kept separate, bicultural individuals may not recognize or perceive conflict at all (Amiot et al., 2007). As an attempt to resolve identity conflict, individuals may choose to blend or integrate different aspects of one's two identities into a new, merged identity in order to reconcile conflict, or they may choose to compartmentalize or separate their identities in order to avoid conflict (Amiot et al., 2007; Ashforth, Kreiner, & Fugate, 2000; Baumeister, Shapiro, & Tice, 1985). In other words, subjective cultural distance (low blendedness or high compartmentalization) may be a response to high BII conflict (low harmony). Alternatively, *objective* cultural distance also may have a direct influence on *subjective* cultural distance, such that bicultural individuals may be forced to keep their cultures compartmentalized if the two cultural identities represent truly different ways of being (e.g., marriage for love vs. arranged marriage).

Note that blending versus compartmentalizing one's identities is only an attempt, and thus may not be successful, at resolving conflict. For example, the blending of some norms from two cultural systems (e.g., dating and marital preferences) may not be possible and cannot be used to resolve cultural conflicts. Therefore, whereas some individuals with either blended or compartmentalized identities may not perceive any conflict between their two cultures, other individuals with either blended or compartmentalized identities may still perceive conflict. In other words, whether identity conflict is decreased or remains high may depend on the effectiveness of blending or compartmentalizing identities, which is not always possible given cultural and situational constraints. This would lend further support to the theoretical and empirical independence of BII blendedness and harmony. In summary, we believe that the degree to which one's two cultures are objectively different (high objective cultural distance) would influence one's perception of conflict between the two cultures (low BII harmony), which in turn might influence the degree to which one either blends or compartmentalizes the two cultures (BII blendedness or subjective cultural distance). These theoretical propositions await empirical examination, and findings from such studies would further our understanding of the development of BII and biculturalism.

BII and Cultural Frame Switching

Biculturalism includes the adoption of two sets of behavioral repertoires (Rotheram-Borus, 1993) as well as the ability to switch between two sets of cultural schemas and norms (Hong et al., 2000). This shifting of cultural thoughts and behaviors in response to cultural cues or primes is referred to as cultural frame switching (Hong et al., 2000). Cultural frame switching has been shown to occur for cognitive styles (Hong et al., 2000), personality (Ramirez-Esparza, Gosling, Benet-Martínez, Potter, & Pennebaker, 2006), self-identification and cultural values (Verkuyten & Pouliasi, 2002), self-construal (See Smith, Chapter 11, this volume), affect (Perunovic, Heller, & Rafaeli, 2007), and decision making (Briley, Morris, & Simonson, 2005), among others. Although cultural frame switching is characteristic of bicultural individuals, individuals high versus low on BII frame-switch in different ways (Benet-Martínez et al., 2002; Cheng, Lee, & Benet-Martínez, 2006; Zou, Morris, & Benet-Martínez, 2008). More specifically, individuals high on BII respond to cultural cues by performing prime-consistent behaviors (e.g., behaving in Chinese ways after being primed with Chinese culture), whereas individuals low on BII respond to cultural cues by displaying prime-resistant behaviors (e.g., behaving in American ways after being primed with Chinese culture). Because individuals high in BII perceive their cultures as non-oppositional, it may be easier for them to switch between cultural frames in a fluid manner, by responding to cultural cues in culturally consistent ways. On the other hand, individuals low in BII perceive their cultures as oppositional and may chronically polarize their two cultures, which in turn may lead to cognitive linking of the cultures as a single dichotomy (i.e., viewing the two cultures as evaluative/conceptual opposites). Thus, priming one culture (e.g., Chinese) would lead to the activation of the other culture (e.g., American; Hong et al., 2000), perhaps through a process of comparison and contrast (see Benet-Martinez, in press; for a more detailed account of this phenomenon). This suggests that BII may be associated with cultural comfort and expertise, where individuals high in BII are able to respond appropriately to cultural primes from each of their respective cultural backgrounds.

Constructs Related to BII

Given the paucity of research on biculturalism and BII, we discuss suggestions for future research. Theoretically, there are several constructs, both within and outside the cultural area, that may relate to BII; however, empirical data are needed to determine whether these constructs are distinct. Baumeister et al.,'s (1985) identity compartmentalization, which refers to the separation of identities into different domains or situations, may relate to low BII blendedness, and their construct of identity conflict, which refers to the perception of incompatibility between two identities, may relate to low BII harmony. Moreover, Ward's (2008) ethnocultural identity conflict, which refers to the perception of conflict between one's ethnic and dominant cultures, may relate to low BII harmony. In addition, Ogbu's (1993) oppositional identity (vs. non-oppositional identity), which refers to an identity that involves two groups that are in conflict with one another, may relate to low BII harmony. Finally, identity synthesis (vs. confusion; Schwartz, 2006), which refers to a coherent and consolidated identity, may relate to both components of BII. All of these associations are in need of empirical investigation.

Another construct relevant to BII is social identity complexity, which may provide further insight into individual differences in biculturalism. Roccas and Brewer (2002) proposed four types of social identity representations based on the structure of individuals' two social identities and how those identities create a perceived in-group. First, individuals in the intersection mode only perceive those sharing both their identities as the in-group (e.g., Mexican Americans). Second, individuals in the dominance mode view those sharing their more dominant identity (e.g., either Mexican or American) as in-group members. Third, individuals in the compartmentalization mode define their in-group members depending on the situation (e.g., Americans in American settings, Mexicans in Mexican settings). Finally, those in the merger mode view their in-group members as those who share at least one of their identities (e.g., Mexican Americans, Mexicans, and Americans). Further research is needed to understand how these social identity representations map onto cultural identities and BII. For example, it is likely that individuals low on blendedness may be in the compartmentalization mode. However, it is uncertain whether individuals high on blendedness would be in the intersection or merger mode. Future research may help to determine whether individuals high on blendedness comprise a heterogeneous group and whether further delineation of this BII component is needed.

Beyond Cultural Applications of BII

Applications of BII theory. The principles of BII are not necessarily restricted to ethnocultural identities. They may apply to any other type of dual identities, such as sexual, religious, or professional identities. For example, Fingerhut, Peplau, and Ghavami (2005) examined lesbian women's identification with lesbian culture and their identification with the mainstream heterosexual culture. Ideas from the BII literature could be incorporated into a study such as this by asking participants whether they perceive conflict between lesbian and heterosexual cultures and whether they compartmentalize their affiliations with these two cultures. Furthermore, in addition to extending to identities other than ethnocultural identities (e.g., racial identities),

BII theory can also extend to multiple (more than two) identities, as in the case of multiracial identity integration (Cheng & Lee, 2009) or multicultural identity integration for tricultural individuals such as Chinese Canadians in English-French Quebec (Downie et al., 2004). Overall, the processes associated with BII are likely to generalize to other identities, such as career identity (see Skorikov & Vondracek, Chapter 29, this volume), religious/spiritual identity (see MacDonald, Chapter 21, this volume; Roehlkepartain, Benson, & Scales, Chapter 22, this volume), and sexual identity (see Dillon et al., Chapter 27, this volume; Savin-Williams, Chapter 28, this volume). For example, BII theory may apply to the integration of one's Buddhist identity with the dominant culture's Christian identity. These identities may also be described as conflictual or compartmentalized; however, further research is needed to determine whether the integration of other types of identities follows the same principles as the integration of cultural identities.

Not only can BII be applied to dual identities within a single category (e.g., Buddhist and Christian religious identities), but it can also be applied to dual identities from two different categories (e.g., cultural identity and religious identity). For example, Verkuyten and Yildiz (2007) examined Turkish-Dutch Muslims' identification with their ethnic (Turkish) culture, their dominant (Dutch) culture, and their religious (Muslim) culture. BII could have contributed to this study by capturing the degree of perceived blendedness and harmony among Turkish, Dutch, and Muslim cultures, and the Muslim culture may be contrasted with the secular Dutch culture – given that most Dutch people do not endorse organized religion. BII could also be used to examine the degree of harmony versus conflict perceived between the sexual identity and religious identity of Muslim gay men (of Pakistani descent in the United Kingdom; Jaspal & Cinnirella, 2010) and Jewish gay men (in the United Kingdom; Coyle & Rafalin, 2000). In a study of female engineers, BII was applied to examine the degree of compartmentalization between participants'

identities as women (i.e., gender identity) and as engineers (e.g., professional identity; Cheng, Sanchez-Burks, & Lee, 2008). They found that female engineers with more integrated identities designed more creative products than those who perceived lower blendedness between their gender and professional identities. Other research within the work domain, such as that on women who are both African Americans and professionals (Bell, 1990) and men who are both fathers and managers (DeLong & DeLong, 1992), may also benefit from the introduction of BII into their research paradigm.

Suggestions for future research. Concepts from sociology, anthropology, ethnic studies, and education that have the potential for further elucidating the construct of BII include biculturation, hybridity, pan-ethnicity, segmented assimilation, and intersectionality. [See also Jensen, Arnett, and McKenzie's (Chapter 13, this volume) chapter on globalization and hybridity.] First, biculturation refers to the process of adapting to two cultures (Polgar, 1960; Sadao, 2003; Valentine, 1971). Biculturation differs from acculturation, which presupposes that one (ethnic) culture is learned first, followed by the second (dominant) culture (Berry, 2003); biculturation allows for the possibility of individuals learning their two cultures simultaneously (Birman, 1994; Padilla, 2006; Szapocznik, Kurtines, & Fernandez, 1980). Biculturation is more appropriate for and more inclusive to the experiences of bicultural individuals, such as mixed-ethnic individuals and second-generation children of immigrants or refugees. Analogous to the comparison of acculturation versus biculturation is the comparison of coordinate bilingualism versus compound bilingualism within the area of psycholinguistics (Ervin & Osgood, 1954). Coordinate bilinguals learn one language before the other, learn their two languages in different contexts, and organize their two language systems separately, whereas compound bilinguals learn their two languages at the same time and in the same context, and the organization of their two language systems tend to overlap. It thus follows that bicultural individuals who learn their two cultures simultaneously should be more likely to have overlapping identities (high blend-edness) than those who learn one culture before the other; however, further research is needed to test this hypothesis.

Second, hybridity, or an emergent third cul-ture, is a concept that has received increasing attention (Hermans & Kempen, 1998; Hutnyk, 2005; Lowe, 1996; Oyserman, Sakamoto, & Lauffer, 1998). Hybridity refers to a new culture that emerges from a dynamic interaction, rather than merely a summation, of existing cultures. It is also known as ethnogenesis (Flannery, Reise, & Yu, 2001) or transculturation (Comas-Diaz, 1987). A well-known example of hybridity is Chicano culture, which is comprised of Mexican culture, US American culture, as well as Mexican American culture and other cultures (Garza & Lipton, 1982). Another example is British Indian culture (including the recently invented chicken tikka masala dish) which stems from but is dis-tinctly different from both mainstream British culture and Indian culture as found on the Indian subcontinent (Cook, 2001). There seem to be many parallels between hybridity and blended-ness, and it is therefore important for future research to identify the distinctions and overlap between these two constructs.

Third, pan-ethnicity refers to the identification with a racial or pan-ethnic group (e.g., Asian, Latino) rather than with their specific ethnic group (e.g., Chinese, Mexican; Rumbaut, 1994). It is also known as panethnogenesis, or the cre-ation of a culture based on ethnicity. A pan-ethnic culture might consists of values and behaviors common among hyphenated ethnic cultures of that pan-ethnicity (e.g., all Asian Americans) but not found in the cultures of origin (e.g., cultures in Asia) – for example, identification as "AZN" (shortened form of "Asian"), driving a modified ("tricked-out") imported vehicle, and drinking boba (a drink with tapioca pearls). Pan-ethnically identified individuals tend to belong to later generations, to have experienced discrimina-tion, and to have higher socioeconomic status (Masuoka, 2006; Rumbaut, 2005). It is possible that blendedness for these individuals involves the merging of multiple hyphenated ethnic cultures of that pan-ethnicity along with the

dominant culture, rather than merely the merging of their ethnic culture with the dominant culture. Moreover, because pan-ethnic labels were created by US institutions to classify groups of individ-uals (Espiritu, 1996; Lopez & Espiritu, 1990), a pan-ethnic culture may also include the blending of the dominant group's perceptions of the pan-ethnic group with actual characteristics of the pan-ethnic group (e.g., the term "Hispanic" is a US-American grouping of 21 Latin American groups). Future research is needed to under-stand the conceptualization of blendedness among pan-ethnically identified bicultural individuals.

Fourth, segmented assimilation refers to an orientation to neither the dominant culture nor the ethnic culture, but rather an orientation to the culture of an impoverished, under-privileged, lower-class, inner-city, and reactive racial-minority segment of dominant society (Portes & Zhou, 1993). For example, some low-income Vietnamese Americans in New Orleans identify with and are friends with the tradi-tionally low-income, marginalized group in that city: African Americans (Bankston & Zhou, 1997). As with pan-ethnicity, individuals partic-ipating in segmented assimilation tend to belong to later generations and to have experienced discrimination. However, unlike pan-ethnically identified individuals, those participating in seg-mented assimilation tend to have lower socioeco-nomic status and to experience greater economic and class inequality (Portes, Fernandez-Kelly, & Haller, 2005; Portes & Zhou, 1993). Baumeister et al. (1985) proposed that individuals resolve identity conflict by either blending or compart-mentalizing their identities. Segmented assimila-tion may be a third possible response to identity conflict. As a way of resolving conflicts between their two cultures, individuals may choose to or be forced to withdraw from both cultures and seek refuge in another culture, a culture for those who face racial and economic conflicts and hardships. Future research is needed to deter-mine whether segmented assimilation is related to low BII harmony, or possibly to the marginal-ization acculturation strategy (Nguyen, Huynh, & Benet-Martínez, 2009).

Finally, the dual identities from different categories alluded to earlier (e.g., cultural and religious identities, gender and professional identities) are often referred to as intersectionality. Intersectionality is defined as the unique experience associated with having multiple identities and multiple types of oppression (e.g., gender, race, sexual orientation, religion, class, ability; Cole, 2009; Collins, 1998; Stirratt, Meyer, Ouellette, & Gara, 2008; Warner, 2008). Individuals with multiple subordinate identities (e.g., African American lesbian women) face unique obstacles, such as intersectional invisibility (Purdie-Vaughns & Eibach, 2008), whereby they are not recognized as traditional members of any of their groups. Thus, BII, especially the harmony component, is relevant to and can inform the study of intersectionality and the interaction of multiple identities. Research on BII and intersectionality can both be advanced by the study of these constructs in conjunction with each other.

Concluding Remarks

In this chapter, we have reviewed the importance of biculturalism and of variations among bicultural individuals within the larger framework of studying identity. We believe that bicultural individuals are the key to uncovering the dynamics of culture and identity, and the field of biculturalism offers many new and exciting opportunities for future inquiries. Attention to variations in bicultural identity (e.g., LaFromboise et al., 1993; Phinney & Devich-Navarro, 1997) has propelled the field forward, and BII is a part of this exciting new movement (Benet-Martínez, in press; Benet-Martínez & Haritatos, 2005; Benet-Martínez et al., 2002; Huynh, 2009; Nguyen & Benet-Martínez, 2007).

Thus far, across different ethnic groups and geographic locations, researchers have found that BII consists of two components: blendedness and harmony. These components are distinct, and they are related to different personality and situational variables. In addition, they are differentially related to emotional stability and adjustment, supporting previous

theoretical propositions that blendedness is the more organizational, behavioral, and performance-related component of BII, whereas harmony is the more affective, psychological component of BII. There is an increasing body of empirical research on BII and its nomological network or set of correlates (e.g., Benet-Martínez & Haritatos, 2005; Benet-Martínez et al., 2006; Huynh, 2009; Miramontez et al., 2008; Nguyen et al., 2010), but much still remains to be discovered about dual identity integration.

Although topics from across the social sciences such as biculturation, emergent third culture and hybridity, pan-ethnicity, segmented assimilation, and intersectionality offer promising new directions to the field of biculturalism, they have been relatively unexplored within psychology. To further move the field forward, it is essential to gather empirical evidence to examine the commonalities and differences between these constructs and psychological constructs such as BII. Moreover, with increasing diversity, other dual identities and the intersection of multiple identities require more research. The BII framework can be used within these areas of research to elucidate how people affectively and cognitively manage their various, and sometimes potentially incompatible, identities.

Given the important changes in international migration and increasing cultural exposure around the world within the past few decades, empirical work on biculturalism from an individual differences perspective is a surprisingly new and under-researched area of inquiry in psychology. Much more research is needed to understand how increasing cultural diversity and global interconnectedness affect people's identities, which has important implications for individuals as well as for societies.

Note

1. Note that Benet-Martínez and Haritatos (2005) initially named the two components of BII distance versus blendedness and conflict

versus harmony. However, recently, we have renamed the dimensions blendedness versus compartmentalization (not distance, to better capture the dissociation, rather than objective distance, between the cultures) and harmony versus conflict (to take focus away from the negative pole of the dimensions). For ease of reading, we will refer to the blendedness versus compartmentalization component as "blendedness" and the harmony versus conflict component as "harmony" from now on.

Appendix

Examples of the Bicultural Identity Integration Scale–Version 2

Items are rated on a 1 (strongly disagree) to 5 (strongly agree) scale; an asterisk indicates a reverse-scored item to measure the positive pole of the BII component.

Blendedness versus compartmentalization:

I feel _____ and American at the same time.

I do not blend my _____ and American cultures.*

Harmony versus conflict:

I find it easy to harmonize _____ and American cultures.

I feel that my _____ and American cultures are incompatible.*

For the full BIIS-2 scale, please see Huynh (2009), or contact Que-Lam Huynh at qhuynh@projects.sdsu.edu.

References

Amiot, C. E., de la Sablonnière, R., Terry, D. J., & Smith, J. R. (2007). Integration of social identities in the self: Toward a cognitive-developmental model. *Personality and Social Psychology Review, 11*, 364–388.

Arnett, J. J. (2002). The psychology of globalization. *American Psychologist, 57*, 774–783.

Ashforth, B. E., Kreiner, G. E., & Fugate, M. (2000). All in a day's work: Boundaries and micro role transitions. *Academy of Management Review, 25*, 472–491.

Bankston, C. L., & Zhou, M. (1997). The social adjustment of Vietnamese American adolescents: Evidence for a segmented-assimilation approach. *Social Science Quarterly, 78*, 508–523.

Baumeister, R. F., Shapiro, J. P., & Tice, D. M. (1985). Two kinds of identity crisis. *Journal of Personality, 53*, 407–424.

Bell, E. L. (1990). The bicultural life experience of career-oriented black women. *Journal of Organizational Behavior, 11*, 459–477.

Benet-Martínez, V. (in press). Multiculturalism: Cultural, personality, and social processes. In K. Deaux & M. Snyder (Eds.), *Handbook of personality and social psychology*. Oxford, UK: Oxford University Press.

Benet-Martínez, V., & Haritatos, J. (2005). Bicultural identity integration (BII): Components and psychosocial antecedents. *Journal of Personality, 73*, 1015–1050.

Benet-Martínez, V., Haritatos, J., & Santana, L. (2010). *Bicultural Identity Integration (BII) and well-being*. Unpublished manuscript. Riverside: University of California.

Benet-Martínez, V., Lee, F., & Leu, J. (2006). Biculturalism and cognitive complexity: Expertise in cultural representations. *Journal of Cross-Cultural Psychology, 37*, 386–407.

Benet-Martínez, V., Leu, J., Lee, F., & Morris, M. (2002). Negotiating biculturalism: Cultural frame switching in biculturals with oppositional versus compatible cultural identities. *Journal of Cross-Cultural Psychology, 33*, 492–516.

Berry, J. W. (2003). Conceptual approaches to acculturation. In K. M. Chun, P. B. Organista, G. Marín (Eds.), *Acculturation: Advances in theory, measurement, and applied research* (pp. 17–37). Washington, DC: American Psychological Association.

Berry, J. W., Phinney, J. S., Sam, D. L., & Vedder, P. (2006). *Immigration youth in cultural transition: Acculturation, identity, and adaptation across national contexts*. Mahwah, NJ: Lawrence Erlbaum.

Birman, D. (1994). Acculturation and human diversity in a multicultural society. In E. J. Trickett, R. J. Watts, D. Birman (Eds.), *Human diversity: Perspective on people in context* (pp. 261–284). San Francisco: Jossey-Bass.

Botvinick, M., Braver, T., Barch, D., Carer, C., & Cohen, J. (2001). Conflict monitoring and cognitive control. *Psychological Review, 108*, 624–652.

Briley, D. A., Morris, M. W., & Simonson, I. (2005). Cultural chameleons: Biculturals, conformity motives, and decision making. *Journal of Consumer Psychology, 15*, 351–362.

Chen, S. X., Benet-Martínez, V., & Bond, M. H. (2008). Bicultural identity, bilingualism, and psychological adjustment in multicultural societies: Immigration-based and globalization-based acculturation. *Journal of Personality, 76*, 803–838.

Cheng, C., Lee, F., & Benet-Martínez, V. (2006). Assimilation and contrast effects in cultural frame-switching: Bicultural Identity Integration (BII) and valence of cultural cues. *Journal of Cross-Cultural Psychology*, *37*, 742–760.

Cheng, C. -Y., & Lee, F. (2009). Multiracial identity integration: Perceptions of conflict and distance among multiracial individuals. *Journal of Social Issues*, *65*, 51–68.

Cheng, C. -Y., Sanchez-Burks, J., & Lee, F. (2008). Connecting the dots within: Creative performance and identity integration. *Psychological Science*, *19*, 1178–1184.

Cole, E. (2009). Intersectionality and research in psychology. *American Psychologist*, *64*, 170–180.

Collins, P. H. (1998). It's all in the family: Intersections of gender, race, and nation. *Hypatia*, *13*(3), 62–82.

Comas-Diaz, L. (1987). Feminist therapy with mainland Puerto Rican women. *Psychology of Women Quarterly*, *11*, 461–474.

Cook, R. (2001, April 19). Robin Cook's chicken tikka masala speech: Extracts from a speech by the foreign secretary to the Social Market Foundation in London. Retrieved November 22, 2009, from http://www.guardian.co.uk/world/2001/apr/19/race. britishidentity

Coyle, A., & Rafalin, D. (2000). Jewish gay men's accounts of negotiating cultural, religious and sexual identity: A qualitative study. *Journal of Psychology and Human Sexuality*, *12*, 21–48.

DeLong, T. J., & DeLong, C. C. (1992). Managers as fathers: Hope on the homefront. *Human Resource Management*, *31*, 171–181.

Downie, M., Koestner, R., ElGeledi, S., & Cree, K. (2004). The impact of cultural internalization and integration on well-being among tricultural individuals. *Personality and Social Psychology Bulletin*, *30*, 305–314.

Downie, M., Mageau, G. A., Koestner, R., & Liodden, T. (2006). On the risk of being a cultural chameleon: Variations in collective self-esteem across social interactions. *Cultural Diversity and Ethnic Minority Psychology*, *12*, 527–540.

Ervin, S. M., & Osgood, C. E. (1954). Second language learning and bilingualism. *Journal of Abnormal and Social Psychology*, *49*, 139–146.

Espiritu, Y. L. (1996). Crossroads and possibilities: Asian Americans on the eve of the twenty-first century. *Amerasia Journal*, *22*(2), vii–xii.

Fingerhut, A. W., Peplau, L. A., & Ghavami, N. (2005). A dual-identity framework for understanding lesbian experience. *Psychology of Women Quarterly*, *29*, 129–139.

Flannery, W. P., Reise, S. P., & Yu, J. (2001). An empirical comparison of acculturation models. *Personality and Social Psychology Bulletin*, *27*, 1035–1045.

Garza, R. T., & Lipton, J. P. (1982). Theoretical perspectives on Chicano personality development. *Hispanic Journal of Behavioral Sciences*, *4*, 407–432.

Hermans, H. J. M., & Kempen, H. J. G. (1998). Moving cultures: The perilous problem of cultural dichotomies

in a globalizing society. *American Psychologist*, *53*, 1111–1120.

Hofstede, G. (1983). Dimensions of national cultures in fifty countries and three regions. In J. B. Deregowski, S. Dziurawiec, R. C. Annis (Eds.), *Expiscations in cross-cultural psychology* Swets and Zeitlinger: Lisse.

Hong, Y. Y., Morris, M. W., Chiu, C. Y., & Benet-Martínez, V. (2000). Multicultural minds: A dynamic constructivist approach to culture and cognition. *American Psychologist*, *55*, 709–720.

Hutnyk, J. (2005). Hybridity. *Ethnic and Racial Studies*, *28*, 79–102.

Huynh, Q. -L. (2009). *Variations in biculturalism: Measurement, validity, mental and physical health/psycho-social correlates, and group differences of identity integration*. Unpublished doctoral dissertation. Riverside: University of California.

Jaspal, R., & Cinnirella, M. (2010). Coping with potentially incompatible identities: Accounts of religious, ethnic and sexual identities from British Pakistani men who identify as Muslim and Gay. *British Journal of Social Psychology*, *49*, 849–870.

LaFromboise, T., Coleman, H. L., & Gerton, J. (1993). Psychological impact of biculturalism: Evidence and theory. *Psychological Bulletin*, *114*, 395–412.

Lopez, D., & Espiritu, Y. L. (1990). Panethnicity in the United States: A theoretical framework. *Ethnic and Racial Studies*, *13*, 198–224.

Lowe, L. (1996). *Immigrant acts: On Asian American cultural politics*. Durham, NC: Duke University.

Masuoka, N. (2006). Together they become one: Examining the predictors of panethnic group consciousness among Asian Americans and Latinos. *Social Science Quarterly*, *87*, 993–1011.

Miramontez, D. R., Benet-Martínez, V., & Nguyen, A. -M. D. (2008). Bicultural identity and self/group personality perceptions. *Self and Identity*, *7*, 430–445.

Mok, A., Morris, M., Benet-Martínez, V., & Karakitapoglu-Aygun, Z. (2007). Embracing American culture: Structures of social identity and social networks among first-generation biculturals. *Journal of Cross-Cultural Psychology*, *38*, 629–635.

Nguyen, A. -M. D., & Benet-Martínez, V. (2007). Biculturalism unpacked: Components, individual differences, measurement, and outcomes. *Social and Personality Psychology Compass*, *1*, 101–114.

Nguyen, A. -M. D., & Benet-Martínez, V. (2010). Multicultural identity: What it is and why it matters. In R. Crisp (Ed.), *The psychology of social and cultural diversity* (pp. 87–114). Oxford, UK: Wiley-Blackwell.

Nguyen, A. -M. D., Huynh, Q. -L., & Benet-Martínez, V. (2009). Bicultural identities in a diverse world. In J. L. Chin, (Ed.), *Diversity in mind and in action* (Vol. 1., pp. 17–31). Westport, CT: Praeger.

Nguyen, A. -M. D., Huynh, Q. -L., & Benet-Martínez, V. (2010). The interaction of values and perceived cultural harmony in bicultural individuals. Manuscript under review.

Ogbu, J. U. (1993). Differences in cultural frame of reference. *International Journal of Behavioral Development*, *16*, 483–506.

Oyserman, D., Sakamoto, I., & Lauffer, A. (1998). Cultural accommodation: Hybridity and the framing of social obligation. *Journal of Personality and Social Psychology*, *74*, 1606–1618.

Padilla, A. M. (2006). Bicultural social development. *Hispanic Journal of Behavioral Sciences*, *28*, 467–497.

Perunovic, W. Q. E., Heller, D., & Rafaeli, E. (2007). Within-person changes in the structure of emotion: The role of cultural identification and language. *Psychological Science*, *18*, 607–613.

Phinney, J. S., & Devich-Navarro, M. (1997). Variations in bicultural identification among African American and Mexican American adolescents. *Journal of Research on Adolescence*, *7*, 3–32.

Polgar, S. (1960). Biculturation of Mesquakie teenage boys. *American Anthropologist*, *62*, 217–235.

Portes, A., Fernandez-Kelly, P., & Haller, W. (2005). Segmented assimilation on the ground: The new second generation in early adulthood. *Ethnic and Racial Studies*, *28*, 1000–1040.

Portes, A., & Zhou, M. (1993). The new second generation: Segmented assimilation and its variants. *Annals of the American Academy of Political and Social Science*, *530*, 74–96.

Purdie-Vaughns, V., & Eibach, R. P. (2008). Intersectional invisibility: The distinctive advantages and disadvantages of multiple subordinate-group identities. *Sex Roles*, *59*, 377–391.

Ramirez-Esparza, N., Gosling, S., Benet-Martínez, V., Potter, J., & Pennebaker, J. (2006). Do bilinguals have two personalities? A special case of cultural frame-switching. *Journal of Research in Personality*, *40*, 99–120.

Ramirez, M. (1984). Assessing and understanding biculturalism-multiculturalism in Mexican-American adults. In J. Martinez, R. Mendoza (Eds.), *Chicano psychology* (pp. 77–94). Orlando, FL: Academic.

Roccas, S., & Brewer, M. B. (2002). Social identity complexity. *Personality and Social Psychology Review*, *6*, 88–107.

Rudmin, F. W. (2003). Critical history of the acculturation psychology of assimilation, separation, integration, and marginalization. *Review of General Psychology*, *7*, 3–37.

Rumbaut, R. G. (1994). The crucible within: Ethnic identity, self-esteem, and segmented assimilation among children of immigrants. *International Migration Review*, *28*, 748–794.

Rumbaut, R. G. (2005). Assimilation, dissimilation, and ethnic identities: The experience of children of immigrants in the United States. In M. Rutter, M. Tienda (Eds.), *Ethnicity and causal mechanisms* (pp. 301–334). Cambridge, UK: Cambridge University.

Sadao, K. C. (2003). Living in two worlds: Success and the bicultural faculty of color. Review of Higher Education. *Journal of the Association for the Study of Higher Education*, *26*, 397–418.

Schwartz, S. J. (2006). Predicting identity consolidation from self-construction, eudaimonistic self-discovery, and agentic personality. *Journal of Adolescence*, *29*, 777–793.

Schwartz, S. J., & Zamboanga, B. L. (2008). Testing Berry's model of acculturation: A confirmatory latent class approach. *Cultural Diversity and Ethnic Minority Psychology*, *14*, 275–285.

Stirratt, M. J., Meyer, I. H., Ouellette, S. C., & Gara, M. A. (2008). Measuring identity multiplicity and intersectionality: Hierarchical classes analysis (HICLAS) of sexual, racial, and gender identities. *Self and Identity*, *7*, 89–111.

Suedfeld, P., Bluck, S., Loewen, L., & Elkins, D. (1994). Sociopolitical values and integrative complexity of members of student political groups. *Canadian Journal of Behavioral Science*, *26*, 121–141.

Suedfeld, P., & Wallbaum, A. B. (1992). Modifying integrative complexity in political thought: Value conflict and audience disagreement. *International Journal of Psychology*, *26*, 19–36.

Szapocznik, J., Kurtines, W., & Fernandez, T. (1980). Bicultural involvement and adjustment in Hispanic American youths. *International Journal of Intercultural Relations*, *3*, 15–47.

United Nations Department of Economic and Social Affairs (2002). International migration report 2002. Retrieved April 22, 2009 from http://www.un.org/esa/population/publications/ittmig 2002/2002ITTMIGTEXT22-11.pdf.

Valentine, C. A. (1971). Deficit, difference, and bicultural models of Afro-American behavior. *Harvard Educational Review*, *2*, 137–157.

Van Oudenhoven, J. P., Ward, C., & Masgoret, A. -M. (2006). Patterns of relations between immigrants and host societies. *International Journal of Intercultural Relations*, *30*, 637–651.

Verkuyten, M., & Pouliasi, K. (2002). Biculturalism among older children: Cultural frame switching, attributions, self-identification, and attitudes. *Journal of Cross-Cultural Psychology*, *33*, 596–609.

Verkuyten, M., & Yildiz, A. A. (2007). National (dis)identification and ethnic and religious identity: A study among Turkish-Dutch Muslims. *Personality and Social Psychology Bulletin*, *33*, 1448–1462.

Ward, C. (2008). Thinking outside the Berry boxes: New perspectives on identity, acculturation and intercultural relations. *International Journal of Intercultural Relations*, *32*, 105–114.

Warner, L. R. (2008). A best practices guide to intersectional approaches in psychological research. *Sex Roles*, *59*, 454–463.

Zou, X., Morris, M. W., & Benet-Martínez, V. (2008). Identity motives and cultural priming: Cultural (dis)identification in assimilative and contrastive responses. *Journal of Experimental Social Psychology*, *44*, 1151–1159.

Part VIII

National Identity, Cohesion, and Conflict

National Identity in the United States

36

Deborah J. Schildkraut

Abstract

This chapter explores many facets of the question "What does it mean to be American?" The topic of American national identity is explored from the perspective of political science, while drawing on history, political philosophy, and psychology. The chapter begins with an exploration of the concepts of nationalism and patriotism, and discusses how they play a role in American public opinion. Next it examines the notion of identity attachment, which refers to the extent to which people think of themselves first and foremost as American. The question of identity attachment is often salient when societies have high levels of immigration, as the United States has had over the past several decades. As such, this section pays particular attention to the study of ethnic and racial differences in identity attachment. The factors that influence such attachment are discussed, as are the consequences of such attachment – or lack thereof – on political outcomes, such as trust in political institutions and political behavior. The final section of the chapter investigates the content of American identity, which involves the set of norms that people think constitutes American identity, such as the norms of free speech, active citizenship, and Protestantism. It looks at what these norms are, how they have evolved over time, the extent to which they are adopted by various segments of the American population. As with the section on identity attachment, this final section specifically addresses ethnic and racial differences in how people define what it means to be American.

This chapter explores many facets of the age-old question: "What does it mean to be American?" The topic of American national identity is explored from the perspective of political science, while also drawing on history, philosophy, and psychology. The chapter begins with a discussion of the concepts of nationalism and patriotism, and discusses their role in American public opinion. Next, it examines the notion of identity attachment, which refers to the extent to which people think of themselves first and foremost as Americans instead of as members of

D.J. Schildkraut (✉)
Department of Political Science, Packard Hall, Tufts University, Medford, MA, USA
e-mail: deborah.schildkraut@tufts.edu

particular ethnic or national origin groups (for more on these types of identity attachments, see Umaña-Taylor, Chapter 33, this volume). Identity attachment is often salient when societies have high levels of immigration, as the United States has had over the past several decades. National origin quotas in place for the first part of the twentieth century kept immigration levels low, but reforms in 1965 and again in 1986 ushered in a new era of immigration. As a consequence, the percentage of foreign-born residents in the country has been rising steadily, from a low of roughly 4% in 1970 to approximately 13% today. And although in the past American immigration politics primarily concerned immigrants from various European and Asian countries, today the focus is largely on immigrants from Latin America, and especially from Mexico, in addition to Asia.[1] As such, this section of the chapter attends closely to the study of ethnic and racial differences in identity attachment. The factors that influence such attachment are discussed, as are the consequences of such attachment – or lack thereof – on political outcomes, such as political behavior and trust in political institutions. The final section of the chapter deals with the content of American identity, which involves the set of norms that people regard as constituting American identity, such as the norms of free speech, active citizenship, and Protestantism. I examine what these norms are, how they have evolved over time, and the extent to which they are adopted by various segments of the American population.

Americans have been concerned with American national identity since the country's founding. This preoccupation with what it means to be American exists because the nation has typically been characterized as being founded on ideas, not culture or ethnicity (Hackney, 1997; Hartz, 1955). Ancestry was pushed aside, and the notion that a common set of principles constituted the essential meaning of American identity took center stage. Gunnar Myrdal (1944) wrote in the 1940s that American identity is based on a collection of ideals that he termed the American Creed. These ideals include individualism, the notion and promise of hard work, a belief in the rule of law, freedom, and equality.

Whether these liberal principles have, in practice, encompassed the full range of ideas constituting American identity has been a matter of debate (Banning, 1986; Mills, 1997; Schildkraut, 2005a; Smith, 1993, 1997). Yet the conventional wisdom remains that the Creed is a central component of what it means to be American and that America is unique among nations in being defined by the Creed instead of by culture or ancestry. Though other nations of immigrants, such as Canada or Australia, may be able to make similar claims that ancestry and national identity are separate, popular culture in the United States maintains that the United States is "exceptional" in this regard.

Even among people who believe in the Creed's centrality to the notion of American identity, some wonder whether ideas are enough to hold such a diverse country together (Hackney, 1997; Huntington, 2004; Schlesinger, 1998). Samuel Huntington, for instance, points to former communist countries as examples of places that were unable to sustain unity over time when the sole basis for that unity was a set of political ideas. Upon the demise of their communist regimes, he notes, many of these countries became embroiled in conflicts over culture and ethnicity as new elites sought to redefine their national identities in ethnic terms (Huntington, 2004).[2] One can also see this tendency emerge when dictatorships topple, as in the recent case of Iraq. This type of concern has received renewed attention lately in the United States as immigration politics have returned to the foreground of the political landscape. In particular, the fear is that the latest wave of immigrants are too culturally distinct from the American mainstream such that the stability of the nation is threatened even if immigrants claim to support political ideals such as individualism and equality.

In this regard, it is important to note that another reason Americans have been preoccupied with the question of what it means to be American is because the American population consists in large part of voluntary immigrants or the descendants of voluntary immigrants. Since 1990, close to (or more than) one million legal immigrants have been admitted to the United States each year (Department of Homeland Security, 2008). It is estimated that roughly another 500,000 enter illegally per year (Passel, 2006). As noted earlier, the foreign born currently comprise about 13% of the population in the United States, and in eight states (California, New York, New Jersey, Nevada, Florida, Hawaii, Texas, and Arizona), they represent over 15% of population.[3] In the 2006 General Social Survey (GSS), 43.1% of respondents said that at least one of their grandparents was born outside of the United States, and 22.6% said that at least one of their parents was born outside of the United States.[4] Thus, the immigration experience is a very real component of the day-to-day lives and memories of many Americans. This high level of immigration has resulted in a country that is quite ethnically diverse. The Census Bureau recently estimated that the population of the United States is 12.8% Black, 14.8% Latino, and 4.4% Asian, and six states (Arizona, California, Florida, New Mexico, Nevada, and Texas) are over 20% Latino (U.S. Census Bureau, 2008). Though American identity is popularly conceived of as unique due to such diversity, it is important to note that there is no reason to think that any process discussed in this chapter is in fact unique to the United States. Any diverse democracy will need to consider the issues under investigation here, and existing research on immigration and identity suggests that attitudes develop similarly across countries (Citrin & Sides, 2008; de Figueiredo & Elkins, 2003; Fetzer, 2000; also see Licata, Sanches-Mazas, & Green, Chapter 38, this volume).

Patriotism and Nationalism

Despite concerns over whether a set of ideals is enough to unify and sustain a nation, Americans are a highly patriotic group of people, and a key source of that patriotism – or love of country – are those ideals, embodied in the country's political system: freedom, individualism, and egalitarianism. Americans consistently report that they are very or extremely proud of their country and its achievements. In 1996, the GSS asked respondents how important being American is to them on a scale from 0 to 10 where 10 indicated that being American is the most important thing in the person's life (Davis & Smith, 1996). Fully 45% of the respondents said being American is the most important thing in their lives. Another 25% rated being American as an 8 or 9. In that same survey, over 80% said they were very or somewhat proud of the way American democracy works and of America's history. In the 2004 National Election Study (NES), 80% of respondents said they feel extremely or very good when they see the American flag flying (The National Election Studies, 2004). As illustrated in Fig. 36.1, survey data between 1983 and 2006 consistently show over half of the population as "very patriotic," with at least another 20% as "somewhat patriotic." Over the entire 23-year period, at least 90% of the population deemed itself either "very" or "somewhat" patriotic. The group claiming to be "not very" patriotic did not exceed 7%.

Even with these consistently high numbers, patterns of change can still be detected. For instance, American patriotism peaked during the Gulf War in 1991 and immediately after the September 11, 2001 terrorist attacks. The other high point in "very patriotic" sentiment followed highly publicized US military attacks on targets in Libya in 1986, which also coincided with centennial celebrations of the Statue of Liberty. Its lowest levels were in the summer of 1989, before the fall of the Berlin Wall, and in the summer of 2006, just before a tumultuous Congressional election and when the war in Iraq was unpopular.[5]

It should be noted that Americans are not necessarily unique in their high levels of patriotism. Of 70 countries surveyed in the 1999–2004 wave of the World Values Survey, only 23 had fewer than 80% of the population claiming to be very or quite proud to be a citizen of their country, and only 7, such as Japan and Lithuania, had fewer than 60% (World Values Survey, 2004). The United States had more than 90%, which puts it in the company of 28 other countries including Canada, Iceland, Indonesia, Nigeria, Peru, Poland, Portugal, Iran, Jordan, and Singapore.

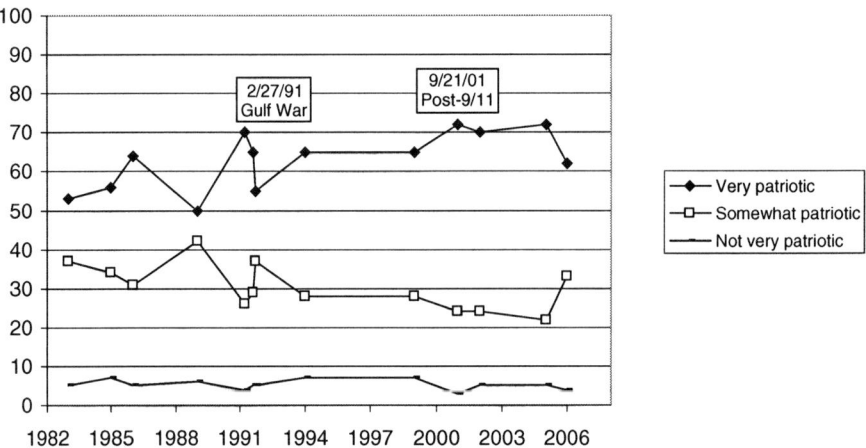

Fig. 36.1 Patriotic sentiment in the US, 1983–2006 (Source: The Roper Center for Public Opinion Research, iPoll Databank. Surveys from CBS News, *The New York* *Times*, Gallup, *The Washington Post*, The Kaiser Family Foundation, and ABC News)

There have been vigorous debates in the literature regarding the different manifestations of patriotism, how to measure its variations, and whether certain types – such as "blind" patriotism – are more worrisome than others – such as "constructive" patriotism (Schatz, Staub, & Lavine, 1999). "Blind" patriotism does not allow room for criticism and is characterized by an unquestioning loyalty to the nation. When someone tells a critic to "love it or leave it," he or she is exhibiting this kind of patriotism. "Constructive" patriotism, on the other hand, is motivated by a desire to improve the nation, and therefore permits criticism (Schatz et al., 1999). Protestors of domestic and/or foreign policy who see their actions as trying to help the country live up to its ideals embody this type of patriotism. Survey research indicates that many Americans are sympathetic to the constructive variant of patriotism. In June 2008, Gallup asked Americans how patriotic it is to protest American policies that they oppose; 38% of respondents said that doing so displays a great amount of patriotism, and another 28% said that it displays a moderate amount (poll data in this paragraph obtained from the Roper Center for Public Opinion Research). A 2006 poll by CBS News found that 83% of Americans said that one could be patriotic and still oppose the Iraq war. In September 2002, before the war began, 67% of respondents in a

Newsweek poll said that it is patriotic to raise questions about a possible war with Iraq. A similar question was asked by the *Los Angeles Times* during the first Gulf War in 1991, and 70% of respondents said it was possible to protest the war and still be patriotic.

Whether high levels of patriotism are "good" or "bad" is a question that is perennially debated. Cultivating patriotism has long been advocated as a means of encouraging individual citizens to overcome selfish impulses and contribute to the public good. As Elizabeth Theiss-Morse (2006, p. 6) noted, "one of the best predictors of helping behavior is shared group membership". Additionally, Theiss-Morse (2006, p. 24) found that, "whether people give to charity, volunteer in their community, help in a crisis, or support increased government spending on education is significantly affected by whether they feel deeply attached to and embedded in their national community." She concludes that having a strong national identity can therefore be quite good for the country (for more on the positive aspects of group attachments, see Spears, Chapter 9, this volume).

Moreover, it is argued that love of country promotes civic and political engagement. Huddy and Khatib (2007) found that people who said being American is important to them were more likely than others to pay attention to politics and to vote. They posited that this relationship stems from the fact that identifying oneself with the national group leads to a greater likelihood of adhering to group norms, and these scholars rightly note that political participation is an important American norm, one that is admittedly more widely endorsed in principle than in practice (Schildkraut, 2005b, 2007). And as noted earlier, constructive patriotism can motivate people to support and promote efforts to improve the country.

Alexis de Tocqueville (1835/1990, p. 243) observed strong patriotic feelings among the many people he encountered during his travels in the United States in the 1830s, and he wondered how Americans could have developed so strong a love of country in such a short period of time. The reason, he concluded, was because "everyone, in his sphere, takes an active part in the government of society." In other words, participating in public life makes one proud of the community, and that pride, in turn, encourages further action directed toward the public good.

The scholarly consensus is thus that patriotism itself is generally unproblematic, but that it is *nationalism* that presents a cause for concern. Nationalism is commonly understood to mean a belief in the superiority and dominance of one's own country relative to other countries (de Figueiredo & Elkins, 2003, p. 175). It is typically measured by asking people whether they agree that their country is a better country than most others and that the world would be a better place if more countries were like their own. Nationalism and patriotism are correlated, but factor analyses have suggested that they are distinct concepts (Citrin, Wong, & Duff, 2001; de Figueiredo & Elkins, 2003; Kosterman & Feshbach, 1989; McDaniel & Nooruddin, 2008).[6] In their study of patriotism and nationalism using the 1996 GSS, Citrin and colleagues found that the mean score on a patriotism scale (ranging from 0 to 1) was 0.80, whereas the mean score on a nationalism scale was 0.59 (Citrin et al., 2001). Although levels of nationalism are generally not as high as levels of patriotism, data from the GSS indicate that levels of nationalism in the United States rose between 1996 and 2004, most likely in response to terrorist attacks in 2001 and the war in Iraq (McDaniel & Nooruddin, 2008).

A potential reason why nationalism is considered to be more problematic than patriotism is that, whereas patriotism promotes civic engagement, nationalism has been shown to promote xenophobia, anti-immigrant attitudes, a greater willingness to define American identity in ascriptive terms (e.g., saying that true Americans are Christian), and a greater support for nuclear armament (Citrin et al., 2001; de Figueiredo & Elkins, 2003; Kosterman & Feshbach, 1989; McDaniel & Nooruddin, 2008; and Licata, Sanchez-Mazas, & Green, Chapter 38, this volume). Recent research, however, has called into question whether patriotism continues to be benign. Analyses by McDaniel and Nooruddin (2008) suggest that although nationalists held more nativist ideas about the meaning of American identity than patriots in 1996, this difference was greatly diminished by 2004. They argue that 9/11 and the wars in Iraq and Afghanistan have "blurred" the line between nationalism and patriotism. Their research powerfully suggests that the external political context is an important consideration when assessing the implications of a highly patriotic population.

National Attachment and Self-Identification

Recently, the issue of patriotism has been a concern in the United States, not only because of the country's "War on Terror" but also because of the demographic changes it has been experiencing. As the American population has become more diverse over the past several decades, some have begun to wonder whether immigrants and their descendants truly "become American." As Patrick Buchanan, a conservative media commentator and former presidential candidate, charges, "millions [of immigrants] bring no allegiance to America and remain loyal to the lands of their birth. And though they occupy more and more rooms in our home, they are not part of our family. Nor do they wish to be" (Buchanan, 2006, p. 13). Many Americans likewise compare today's "bad" immigrants to yesterday's "good" immigrants when talking about immigration (Schildkraut, 2005a). Indeed, because many Americans today are immigrants or children of immigrants of varying ethnicities, it is important to consider whether there are racial and ethnic differences in the extent to which people feel patriotic and consider being American to be an important part of their identity. If differences exist, we need to consider the implications (also see Hart, Richardson, & Wilkenfeld, Chapter 32, this volume; see Huynh, Nguyen, & Benet-Martínez; and Umaña-Taylor, Chapter 35, this volume).

American Identity, Ethnic Identity, and National Origin Identity

One method of gauging attachment to being American has been to ask people whether they think of themselves primarily as American, as a member of a particular ethnic group, or as both. As Citrin and colleagues (Citrin et al., 2001; Pearson & Citrin, 2006) have found, most Whites identify primarily as American. When given the option, most non-Whites consistently adopt an American identity *and* some other identity. In other words, non-Whites are sometimes reluctant to say they are only American, but are quite willing to say they are American and something else, exhibiting a degree of biculturalism (see also Huynh et al., Chapter 35, this volume). In the 2001 Pilot National Asian American Political Survey (PNAAPS), 61% of respondents said they identify either as American (12%), Asian American (15%), or ethnic American – i.e., Chinese American, Vietnamese American, etc., – (34%) (Lien, Conway, & Wong, 2004). Additionally, in laboratory studies, Devos and Banaji (2005) found no differences between White and Asian American participants in the extent to which they considered themselves part of the American in-group. Devos and Banaji used implicit tests in this study, which means that their findings were not a product of self-presentation motives on the part of Asian participants.[7]

My own research (Schildkraut, 2011) suggests that concerns about the rejection of an American self-identification among today's newcomers and their descendants are exaggerated. In that work, I employ the Twenty-First Century Americanism Survey (21-CAS), a national survey I conducted in 2004 with oversamples of Blacks, Latinos, and Asians. Any resident of the United States over 18 years old and living in a household with a telephone was eligible for inclusion in the sample. Participants were selected through random digit dialing (RDD). Counties with higher percentages of Black, Latino, and Asian residents were targeted more heavily with RDD in order to create the oversamples. Such targeting is a common technique for including larger numbers of people from groups that are traditionally underrepresented when RDD is used alone. The average interview length was 26 min. A Spanish version of the survey was available and was used by 137 respondents.[8]

The survey investigated three types of identities: one's national origin identity (i.e., Dominican, Polish, Japanese), one's pan-ethnic or racial identity (i.e., White, Black, Latino, Asian), and one's identity as American. To establish national origin, respondents were asked, "What countries did your ancestors come from?" Each participant was allowed three responses. If they mentioned more than one, they were then asked, "Which of those countries do you identify with most?" Their answer to that question was used in all subsequent questions that refer to their national origin. To gauge self-identification, respondents were asked three yes/no questions to see whether they ever describe themselves in terms of (a) their national origin, (b) their pan-ethnic group, and (c) being American. They were asked, "Do you ever describe yourself as _____?" The blank was first filled with the respondent's national origin,[9] then with her racial or pan-ethnic group (e.g., White, Black, Latino, Asian), and finally with "American." If a respondent said "yes" to more than one of these three questions (as 90% of respondents did), she was then asked, "Which one of those best describes how you think of yourself most of the time?" The response to this question was used to measure a respondent's primary identity.

Thirty-six percent of respondents said they describe themselves in all three terms, 47% said they use two of the three, and 10% said they use only one.[10] Overall, 78% chose American as their primary identity, 14% chose their racial or pan-ethnic group, and 8% chose their national origin group. Of the 22% of respondents who did not choose "American" as their primary identity (74% of which were non-White), 73% still sometimes describe themselves as American, leaving 6% of the total sample that does not use "American" at all.

Table 36.1 illustrates identity prioritization patterns based on particular variables of interest. Whites, American citizens, people whose families have been in the United States for many generations, and people who primarily speak English at home were quite likely to identify primarily as American. Yet in no case does a pan-ethnic identification outweigh a national-origin or American identity. Additionally, a majority of Latinos, and a plurality of Asians and first-generation respondents, chose "American" as their primary identity. All respondents were

asked how important their chosen identity was to them, and across ethnicity, over 80% of all respondents who chose "American" said this identity was very important. The degree of importance among national origin and pan-ethnic identifiers was substantially weaker. For instance, only 55% of Latinos who chose "Latino" as their primary identity said that being Latino was very important to them, in contrast to the 82% of Latinos who chose "American" and thought that being American was very important to them.

The only groups who were unlikely to see themselves primarily as American were people who speak a language other than English at home and people who are not US citizens. In both of those cases, a national-origin identification predominated. These findings, along with those from the studies discussed above, appear to portray a consistent picture: most people in the United States describe themselves as American in some form most of the time. Moreover, immigrants and their descendants are also increasingly likely to do so (see also Stepick, Dutton Stepick, & Vanderkooy, Chapter 37, this volume).[11]

Table 36.1 Identity prioritization: "Which one best describes how you think of yourself most of the time?"

	Panethnic	National origin	American	n (Raw)
White	7.8	2.8	89.4	1,589
Black	41.6	6.1	52.3	281
Asian	16.7	36.0	47.3	276
Latino	18.2	28.2	53.6	422
	Chi-sq: 739.476, $p < 0.001$			
US citizen	13.1	4.6	82.4	2,435
Not US citizen	26.2	56.1	17.8	249
	Chi-sq: 701.728, $p < 0.001$			
1st generation	20.2	38.0	41.8	530
2nd generation	11.6	11.8	76.6	166
3rd generation	5.9	2.6	91.5	175
4th generation or more	13.6	2.2	84.2	1,765
	Chi-sq: 728.062, $p < 0.001$			
Speaks primarily English at home	12.8	3.7	83.6	2,281
Speaks another language at home	23.6	43.9	32.5	404
	Chi-sq: 721.906, $p < 0.001$			

Note: n = unweighted.
Source: 21st Century Americanism Survey, 2004.

The Political Consequences of Self-Identification

Despite a strong identification with America, enough people prioritize a racial or national-origin identity (alone or in conjunction with an American identity) that it is worth investigating whether there are any politically significant differences that derive from those choices. It is generally believed that the identity choices one makes affect thoughts and behaviors toward many aspects of American society, including patriotism, trust in American political institutions, beliefs about obligations to the national community, and voting behaviors. Group consciousness theory (GCT) is one approach that helps us understand how. This theory posits that objective group membership must be paired with both a psychological attachment to – or self-identification with – the group *and* a sense that the group membership is politicized before the identity itself will affect political attitudes and behavior (Conover, 1988; Conover & Sapiro, 1993; McClain, Johnson Carew, Walton, & Watts, 2009; Miller, Gurin, Gurin, & Malanchuk, 1981). Politicization can involve the perception of discrimination against one's group and against oneself individually, feelings of linked fate, a sense that the group is worth fighting for, perceptions of deprivation relative to other groups in society, and a belief that the political system – and not individual attributes – is to blame for such deprivation (Dawson, 1994; García Bedolla, 2005; Miller et al., 1981; Schildkraut, 2005b).

Proponents of group consciousness theory maintain that such politicized identities mobilize people to become involved in the political process and can inoculate them against the otherwise damaging effects of perceptions of discrimination by providing a psychological resource – or psychological capital (García Bedolla, 2005) – that facilitates engagement with the political system (see also Umaña-Taylor, Chapter 33, this volume). In other words, whereas a person who identifies primarily as American and perceives ethnicity-based discrimination might become withdrawn and alienated from the political community, a person who identifies with the aggrieved group might be more likely to participate and have a belief that political realities can change which, in turn, can even bolster faith in political institutions.

Social identity theory (SIT) is another useful approach for thinking about the potential political consequences of identity choices. SIT posits that people are driven to maintain positive group identities (Tajfel & Turner, 1986; see also Spears, Chapter 9, this volume). The need to maintain a positive group image is so powerful that group identification can promote in-group bias and/or out-group derogation (Theiss-Morse, 2003). Moreover, the perception of external threat to the group heightens the need to see one's group positively and can exacerbate these tendencies. Social identity research has demonstrated that "the mere perception of belonging to a social category is sufficient for group behavior," as measured by "intergroup discrimination in social perception and behavior or intragroup altruism" (Turner, 1982, p. 23). Studies have documented in-group bias with respect to helping behavior and that this bias is *enhanced* by the perception of threat to the in-group (Dovidio & Morris, 1975; Flippen, Hornstein, Siegal, & Weitzman, 1996; Hayden, Jackson, & Guydish, 1984; Hornstein, 1976). As Branscombe, Ellemers, Spears, and Doosje (1999, p. 47) explain, "when outgroup based threats to the ingroup's value in the form of discrimination and devaluation are severe enough... we would expect that most ingroup members would behave in [a] defensive fashion; closing ranks following explicit group-based exclusion allows devalued group members to protect their well being." Thus, whereas GCT predicts little power for group identification without the presence of a politicizing agent, SIT contends that a psychological identification with a group can sometimes be enough to lead people to close ranks around the in-group. Both theories are in agreement, however, in noting that attachments to group identities are especially powerful when politicized by a perception of threat.

The question is whether the power of such politicized identities will lead to more or less engagement with the broader national political community. Here, the two theories generally provide complementary expectations. Much like the group consciousness literature, some social identity scholarship has been concerned with understanding when people in disadvantaged groups will become more likely to engage in actions aimed at improving their status. Such scholarship argues that collective action is more likely when a person identifies with the disadvantaged group, when she/he perceives that the group is disadvantaged, when group boundaries are seen as impermeable (as is typically the case with race and ethnicity), when "cognitive alternatives to the status quo" can be imagined, and when the group's lower status is perceived as illegitimate (Ellemers & Barreto, 2001; Tajfel & Turner, 1986; Wright, 2001; see also Spears, Chapter 9, this volume). These conditions set the stage for the emergence of the psychological capital that the group consciousness literature describes. They create conditions in which people become empowered, confident in their own abilities, and motivated by a feeling of common cause shared with other group members. In SIT terminology, such people would be engaging in a management strategy of *social competition*, in which the subordinate group competes with the dominant group in an attempt to change the existing social structure (Tajfel & Turner, 1986; see also Spears, Chapter 9, this volume). Both theories, therefore, would predict higher rates of political participation among ethnic minorities in the presence of a politicized identity. Moreover, we might expect that politicized identities can inoculate people against the loss of trust in the political system and against the loss in patriotism that can result from the belief that one's group is disadvantaged.

When it comes to a sense of obligation to the American political system and to the people who make up the American national community, however, engagement is predicted to decline among those with politicized identities, at least according to SIT. SIT scholarship has demonstrated that an attachment to a particular group identity paired with the perception that the group identity is threatened leads to withdrawal from prosocial interactions with the out-group (also see Gaertner & Dovidio, 2000). In SIT terminology, this process is a product of the *social creativity* management strategy, in which subordinate group members seek to redefine the domains of comparison with the dominant group and in doing so, often direct positive attention inward (Tajfel & Turner, 1986; see also Spears, Chapter 9, this volume). Thus, when it comes to cooperation, altruism, and a sense of obligation to the *national* community, SIT suggests that identifying with a narrower group such as Latinos or Mexicans could lead to disengagement when that identity is paired with a perception of discrimination. In contrast to social identity research, research on group consciousness has typically only focused on collective action outcomes as the dependent variable and not on prosocial behavior, leaving us with little in the way of expectations regarding how a politicized identity might affect one's sense of obligation to the national community.

With these two theoretical perspectives in mind, the remainder of this section addresses the following questions: Is mere self-identification with a pan-ethnic or national-origin identity enough to reduce patriotism, trust in institutions, a sense of obligation to the United States, and electoral participation? Or does a person need to feel that American society is a threat to that identity before it becomes consequential? How much should Americans worry about people who do not identify primarily as American? More specifically, under what conditions should they worry?

Patriotism. In light of the previous section of this chapter, the first issue to examine is patriotism. Using the 1989 Latino National Political Survey, de la Garza, Falcon, and Garcia (1996) found Mexican Americans to be *more* patriotic than Whites, and that the extent to which one consciously thought of oneself as Latino (instead of as White) did not matter. These authors further found that the least acculturated respondents, in terms of language use and nativity, were more patriotic than the most acculturated. With more recent data, Citrin, Lerman, Murakami, and

Pearson (2007) found that US-born Hispanics had higher levels of patriotism than Whites. And using Citrin et al.,'s measure of identity choice that allows respondents to identify as American, as a member of an ethnic group, or as both, they found that levels of pride in being American were high across all three types of identifiers.[12]

In the twenty-first Century Americanism Survey (Schildkraut, 2011), all respondents who were American citizens were asked if they strongly agree, somewhat agree, somewhat disagree, or strongly disagree with the statement: "I am proud to be an American" (where "strongly agree" was coded as 1 and "strongly disagree" was coded as 0).[13] Overall, 84% of respondents said they strongly agree, and only 1% said they strongly disagree. Relevant bivariate comparisons are presented in Table 36.2, with each cell containing the mean level of patriotism on the 0–1 measure. As the table shows, there is virtually no variation in patriotism levels by identity prioritization, ethnicity, nativity, or language use. The differences displayed in Table 36.2 are statistically significant, but that is because of the large

sample size in the 21-CAS. There may be *statistically* significant differences in Table 36.2, but not *substantive* ones. That the patriotism levels of English speakers and non-English speakers, for example, differ by only 3% points and that both are above 90% portrays more of a picture of similarity than of difference. The high level of patriotism among pan-ethnic and national-origin identifiers remains striking.

SIT might lead us to expect higher levels of patriotism among those who identify primarily as American, especially if the identity is salient and/or threatened, which it might be given how important American identifiers say their identity is to them and given the state of international politics when the 21-CAS was conducted. Yet that turns out not to be the case. Multivariate analyses of the 21-CAS (not shown here) suggest that what matters most in shaping levels of patriotism is whether or not people feel that their racial or ethnic group is discriminated against in the United States, as measured by the sense that one's group is discriminated against in schools and the workplace, and is generally prevented from

Table 36.2 Pride in being American

	Mean level of pride (0–1)	n (Raw)
Panethnic identity	0.87	149
National Origin identity	0.88	319
American identity	0.95	1,959
	$F(2,2424)=30.60$, $p<0.001$, $R^2=0.025$	
White	0.94	1,604
Black	0.93	287
Asian	0.88	212
Latino	0.93	298
	$F(3, 2397)=6.64$, $p<0.001$, $R^2=0.008$	
1st generation	0.92	308
2nd generation	0.91	173
3rd generation	0.91	184
4th generation or more	0.94	1,804
	$F(3, 2522)=3.22$, $p=0.022$, $R^2=0.004$	
Speaks primarily English at home	0.93	2,309
Speaks another language at home	0.90	215
	$F(1, 2522)=11.22$, $p<0.001$, $R^2=0.004$	

Note: n = unweighted.
Source: 21st Century Americanism Survey, 2004.

achieving success. Those who perceived such discrimination had lower levels of patriotism than those who did not. One's primary identity attachment had no effect. SIT and GCT, however, also suggest that a group attachment *in conjunction with* a perception of threat (such as the perception that the group is a target of discrimination) might condition the direct effect of perceptions of threat. Yet that also turns out not to be the case. The interaction of perceptions of discrimination with one's identity choice does not alter the direct effect of perceptions of discrimination on patriotism. In other words, a "politicized" identity (one that contains both a psychological attachment to one's group membership and a perception of discrimination) does not influence levels of patriotism. It is a perception that one's ethnic group is discriminated against, regardless of one's primary identification, which harms levels of patriotism.

Trust in institutions. Trust in American institutions, such as government and law enforcement, is an important factor to consider with respect to identity choices. Previous research has shown that trust affects compliance with political and legal processes, particularly in cases where people dislike the outcomes of those processes (Tyler, 2006; Tyler & Huo, 2002). Trust affects whether people support policies aimed at reducing inequality (Hetherington, 2005). Additionally, it is argued that trust generates a willingness to take risks on behalf of the community (Smith, 2003). It is therefore important to determine whether levels of trust are affected by prioritizing one's ethnic or national-origin group.

Studies have shown that Mexican Americans have more confidence in the executive branch and Congress compared to non-Hispanic Whites (Weaver, 2003), and that Latinos trust the federal government more than other ethnic groups (Pearson & Citrin, 2006). As with patriotism, what seems to matter more are perceptions of discrimination. Using the 1989 Latino National Political Survey, Michelson (2003) found that perceptions of discrimination reduce trust in the federal government. Likewise, Lien and colleagues (2004) found that personal experiences with discrimination led to diminished

trust in local government among Asian Americans.

In the twenty-first Century Americanism Survey (Schildkraut, 2011), trust in government and law enforcement was gauged by asking respondents, "How much of the time do you think you can trust [the government in Washington/law enforcement] to do what is right... just about always, most of the time, some of the time, or never?" "Just about always" is coded as 1, "never" as 0.[14] Most respondents said they trust the government only some of the time (57%) and that they trust law enforcement most of the time (53%). Table 36.3 depicts the mean levels of trust according to particular variables of interest. Table 36.3 suggests that prioritizing an American identity affects trust in law enforcement more than it affects trust in government. Though both results show a significant impact for identity choice, the effect on trust in law enforcement is greater, both statistically and substantively. As with patriotism, however, the *similarities* in levels of trust across identity types are striking. Table 36.3 also depicts Latinos as most trusting of government, Whites as most trusting of law enforcement, and Blacks as least trusting of both. Consistent with earlier research (Michelson, 2003), all three measures of acculturation (citizenship, generation, and language use) appear to reduce both types of trust.

Multivariate analyses (not shown here), however, suggest that the differences in levels of trust in law enforcement by self-identification are statistically nonsignificant once we control for other factors, including variables in Table 36.3 (race/ethnicity, nativity, generation, and primary language spoken at home) as well as other factors such as political party affiliation. Moreover, perceptions of discrimination appear to *reduce* levels of trust among minorities who identify as American, whereas perceptions of discrimination *increase* levels of trust in government among minorities who identify with their ethnic group, as GCT and SIT would predict. With respect to trust in law enforcement, neither GCT nor SIT seems to explain the data: as with patriotism, trust is reduced by perceptions

Table 36.3 Levels of trust

	Trust in:		
	Gov't	Law	n (Raw)
Panethnic identity	0.42	0.55	384
National origin identity	0.46	0.59	295
American identity	0.42	0.63	2,007
	$F_{(2, 2638)}=5.21$, $p=0.006$, $R^2=0.004$	$F_{(2, 2671)}=19.49$, $p<0.001$, $R^2=0.014$	
White	0.46	0.65	1,589
Black	0.35	0.45	281
Asian	0.45	0.59	276
Latino	0.51	0.61	422
	$F_{(3, 2615)}=27.29$, $p<0.001$, $R^2=0.030$	$F_{(3, 2654)}=60.52$, $p<0.001$, $R^2=0.064$	
US citizen	0.44	0.61	2,435
Not US citizen	0.55	0.66	249
	$F_{(1, 2740)}=36.79$, $p<0.001$, $R^2=0.013$	$F_{(1, 2780)}=10.89$, $p=0.001$, $R^2=0.004$	
1st generation	0.50	0.63	530
2nd generation	0.42	0.58	166
3rd generation	0.44	0.61	175
4th generation or more	0.44	0.58	1,765
	$F_{(3, 2687)}=9.92$, $p<0.001$, $R^2=0.011$	$F_{(3, 2724)}=1.95$, $p=0.119$, $R^2=0.002$	
Speaks primarily English at home	0.44	0.61	2,281
Speaks another language at home	0.51	0.63	404
	$F_{(1, 2741)}=24.23$, $p<0.001$, $R^2=0.009$	$F_{(1, 2781)}=2.69$, $p=0.101$, $R^2=0.001$	

Note: n = unweighted; cell entries = mean on zero to one scale.
Source: 21st Century Americanism Survey, 2004.

of discrimination regardless of whether a person identifies primarily as American or as a member of a pan-ethnic or national origin group.

In sum, when minorities prioritize an American identification, it is only beneficial with respect to trust if perceptions of discrimination are absent. However, perceptions of discrimination are rarely absent. In the 21-CAS, nearly one-quarter of the respondents would have likely raised their level of trust in the government had they identified primarily with their pan-ethnic group instead of as American (Schildkraut, 2011). The joint presence of identifying primarily as American and perceptions of discrimination has also been shown to affect

voting behavior (Schildkraut, 2005b). This research suggests that roughly 8% of Latinos would have been more likely to vote in national elections had they identified as something other than American. The probability that an American identifier (as opposed to a pan-ethnic or national-origin identifier) will vote drops *over 50 percentage points* as perceptions of discrimination increase from the lowest to the highest value (Schildkraut, 2005b).

National obligations. Obligation refers to the duties of citizenship, what we "owe" to our compatriots and to our political institutions in exchange for the privileges and rights conferred by membership in the political community. In the United States, there is general consensus that our main obligation is to obey the laws of the land, though many Americans also feel that we have a duty to devote some of our time and resources to the common good. Therefore, as with trust, it is important for us to determine whether (or under what conditions) identity choices influence one's sense of obligation.

Unlike the other areas of inquiry discussed in this chapter, there is very little research on people's thoughts about their national obligations, let alone on whether such thoughts are affected by one's race, ethnicity, or sense of American identity. In the 21-CAS, obligation is measured by offering respondents a list of possible obligations and asking them to indicate whether they think each one is an obligation they owe to other Americans. "Yes" (1), "no" (0), and "it depends" (0.5) were accepted responses. The obligations were giving money to charities, volunteering

in your local community, and serving in the military.[15] Though serving in the military is the only obligation here that applies directly to institutions of the state, the other two explicitly refer to obligations toward Americans in general, and not toward any particular subgroup or community. Overall, it appears that Americans feel that they have all three obligations: charity = 57%; volunteer = 72%; military service = 45% (a plurality). Table 36.4 shows people's sense of obligation broken down by variables relevant to this inquiry. Table 36.4 suggests that people who prioritize an American identity are more likely to say they have an obligation to volunteer and serve in the military compared to people who do not prioritize an American identity. Blacks appeared most likely to say they have an obligation to donate and volunteer, whereas Latinos appeared most likely to say they have an obligation to

Table 36.4 Levels of obligation

	Obligation to:			
	Donate	Volunteer	Serve in military	n (Raw)
Panethnic identity	56	69	33	384
National origin identity	52	69	44	295
American identity	57	74	48	2,007
Chi-sq, p	4.671, 0.323	12.825, 0.012	38.683, 0.000	
White	56	72	46	1,589
Black	65	78	39	281
Asian	54	75	45	276
Latino	49	68	48	422
Chi-sq, p	19.888, 0.003	14.837, 0.022	9.052, 0.171	
US citizen	57	73	45	2,435
Not US citizen	51	65	47	249
Chi-sq, p	2.43, 0.296	9.562, 0.008	6.754, 0.034	
1st generation	54	71	52	530
2nd generation	56	72	72	166
3rd generation	56	71	48	175
4th generation or more	57	73	43	1,765
Chi-sq, p	1.725, 0.943	3.849, 0.697	23.258, .0001	
Speaks primarily English at home	57	73	44	2,281
Speaks another language at home	54	71	50	404
Chi-sq, p	2.887, 0.236	2.263, 0.322	9.182, 0.010	

Note: n = unweighted; cell entries for trust = mean (0–1), cell entries for obligation = % saying yes.
Source: 21st Century Americanism Survey, 2004.

serve in the military. Conversely, Latinos were shown as least likely to say they have an obligation to donate and volunteer, whereas Blacks were shown as least likely to say they have an obligation to serve in the military (though this last result was not statistically significant). Finally, acculturation sometimes matters as well, and in ways contrary to the concerns of immigration critics (Huntington, 2004). The foreign-born, for instance, display a greater sense of obligation to serve in the military, though a lesser sense of obligation to volunteer. Non-English speakers also exhibit a greater sense of obligation to serve in the military than English speakers. It is noteworthy that the question about serving in the military applies most directly to institutions of the state *and* is the item on which we see the newcomers professing more commitment than the "natives."

Multivariate analyses (not shown here) indicate that, contrary to the positive impact that politicized identities have on trust, the joint presence of discrimination and a non-American identity *reduces* one's sense of connection to the American in-group, consistent with social identity theory. For example, Latinos who identify as Latino *and* who think that their pan-ethnic group is discriminated against are less likely than other Latinos to say they have an obligation to donate to charity (Schildkraut, 2011). Likewise, Asian Americans who identify with their national-origin group *and* who think that their national-origin group is mistreated are less likely than other Asians to say they have an obligation to volunteer in their communities. The results, in short, show that the social creativity strategy posited by SIT comes into play when examining how identity choices affect one's sense of obligation to the national community.

Identity Content: How Is American Identity Defined?

Earlier in the chapter, I presented evidence that Americans of all backgrounds are highly patriotic. A question to ask in light of such high levels of patriotism is: what are Americans so proud of?

What kind of statement are people making when they say that they think of themselves primarily as American and that being American is the most important thing in their lives? In light of contemporary concerns about the impact of immigration and ethnic diversity on American national identity, it is also important to wonder whether Americans of different backgrounds even have the same things in mind whey they think about what being "American" means. Many people share Samuel Huntington's concerns when he argues that a multicultural America will become a multicreedal America, and that a multicreedal America cannot survive because a common creed has historically been essential in holding the country together (Huntington, 2004).

The concept of liberalism may be the starting point for any investigation into how Americans define what being American means. As noted earlier, the tenets of liberalism are at the heart of the American Creed, which is widely considered to be the central (if not the only) set of ideals that defines American identity. Liberalism is based on the principles of freedom, equality, opportunity, rule of law, and minimal government intervention into the private lives of citizens.[16] Although most scholars agree on the centrality of liberalism to the notion of American identity, they have disagreed over the extent to which additional ideological traditions are also involved (Banning, 1986; Mills, 1997; Rodgers, 1992; Schildkraut, 2005a; Smith, 1993; 1997; Sullivan, 1982). Recently, however, there has been increasing acknowledgment and evidence that additional traditions also represent key elements of American identity. These traditions include civic republicanism, ethnoculturalism, and incorporationism.

Whereas liberalism emphasizes the rights that come with membership in the American political community, civic republicanism emphasizes the responsibilities. As a political tradition, civic republicanism advances the notion that a self-governing society can only sustain itself if its people do their part to work toward the public good rather than simply work to pursue their own individual interests (Banning, 1986; Held, 1996). A civic republican conception defines American identity in terms of active citizenship, being an informed citizen, and volunteering to do one's part for the greater good. This conception also involves the belief that it is important for Americans to think of themselves first and foremost as Americans. Note, however, that civic republican philosophy is not to be confused with the contemporary Republican Party, which focuses on minimally regulated economic activity and social conservatism.

Ethnoculturalism is an ascriptivist tradition that maintains that American identity is defined by cultural ancestry. Specifically, ethnoculturalism posits that true Americans are White, English-speaking Protestants of Northern European ancestry. For a significant portion of American history, ascriptivist tendencies (such as slavery and the denial of naturalization to Asians) were treated as an aberration from America's true nature (e.g., Hartz, 1955; Huntington, 1981; Lipset, 1963). But increasingly, scholars have argued that ethnoculturalism constitutes a central element of American identity in its own right (Gerstle, 2001; Mills, 1997; Schildkraut, 2005a; Smith, 1997), and even though it has been discredited over time, it continues to be endorsed by a non-trivial segment of the American population (see below).

Finally, incorporationism is the notion that the United States is a "nation of immigrants," and that American identity is uniquely defined by its immigrant tradition (Glazer, 1997; Higham, 1993; Tichenor, 2002). According to incorporationism, to be American means to celebrate one's ethnic heritage while *also* assimilating into the country's dominant culture. Although finding a balance between ethnic diversity and assimilation can be difficult to achieve in practice, doing so constitutes the incorporationist ideal within the American imagination (Tyack, 1999; Walzer, 1996; Zolberg & Woon, 1999). In this sense, incorporationism reflects the bidimensional model of acculturation psychology, where one dimension represents the acquisition of the new culture in the host country and a second dimension represents the maintenance of the original culture. According to this model, people can move along each dimension separately. As

David Sam (2006, p. 17) wrote, this bidimensional model illustrates that "it is possible to identify with or acquire the new culture independently, without necessarily losing the original culture." In the present analysis, we can assume that this bidimensional incorporationist model characterizes what it means for America to be a "nation of immigrants" to the extent to which respondents agree that it is important for Americans *both* to blend into the larger society *and* to maintain traditions from their minority or heritage culture.

The notion of cultural pluralism was first introduced into American political discourse in the 1920s by Horace Kallen (1924), and the concept of the "melting pot" was introduced in 1909 by playwright Israel Zangwill. But the idea of incorporationism as a key component of American identity did not take root until the rights revolutions of the 1960s and 1970s. As David Hollinger (1995, p. 101) noted, it was not until the end of the twentieth century that the nation saw the "sheer triumph" of "the doctrine that the United States ought to sustain rather than diminish a great variety of distinctive cultures carried by ethno-racial groups." This triumph can be seen in the rise and use of alternative metaphors to the melting pot, including the salad bowl and the mosaic, where the individual parts retain their integrity while still combining to create a product that is greater than the sum of its parts (see Licata, Sanchez-Mazas, & Green, Chapter 38, this volume, for a discussion of this pluralist trajectory in Europe).

These four notions of what being American means – liberalism, civic republicanism, ethnoculturalism, and incorporationism – provide the American people with insight regarding appropriate state action in response to political conflicts. Additionally, these notions provide expectations about the political, civic, and cultural beliefs and practices of one's compatriots. For these reasons, political scientists are interested in studying the extent to which the American public agrees that each notion constitutes a central element of American identity. Yet only recently has public opinion analysis begun to incorporate

measures of civic republicanism, ethnoculturalism, and incoporationism into their investigations of how people define American identity (Citrin et al., 2001; Conover, Crewe, &
Searing, 1991; McDaniel & Nooruddin, 2008;
Paxton & Mughan, 2006; Schildkraut, 2005a;
Theiss-Morse, 2004).

The 21-CAS (Schildkraut, 2011) was
designed, in part, to provide a comprehensive
examination of public opinion about what it
means to be American. In the survey, the definitions of American identity described above were
measured by asking respondents this question:

"I'm going to read a list of things that some
people say are important in making someone
a true American. The first one is _____.
Would you say that it should be very important,
somewhat important, somewhat unimportant,
or very unimportant in making someone a true
American?" The items inserted into the blank
were designed to capture liberalism, civic republicanism, ethnoculturalism, or incorporationism.
Table 36.5 lists each item, the tradition it was
intended to measure, and the percentage of
respondents that says the item is either very or
somewhat important.[17]

Table 36.5 American identity items

Intended tradition	Question	% very important	% somewhat important	N
Liberalism	Respecting America's political institutions and laws	80.9	15.9	2,764
	Pursuing economic success through hard work	69.0	21.7	2,760
	Letting other people say what they want, no matter how much you disagree with them	65.9	21.9	2,698
Civic republicanism	Doing volunteer work in one's community	44.3	41.9	2,773
	Thinking of oneself as American	68.9	24.3	2,763
	Feeling American	62.1	28.0	2,678
	Being informed about local and national politics	65.3	29.7	2,770
	Being involved in local and national politics	37.1	43.8	2,761
Ethnoculturalism	Being born in America	24.2	27.1	2,768
	Being a Christian	19.3	15.6	2,745
	Having European ancestors	7.0	10.4	2,707
	Being white	3.8	6.1	2,747
Incorporationism	Carrying on the cultural traditions of one's ancestors, such as the language and food	35.7	37	2,751
	Respecting other people's cultural differences	80.1	16.8	2,773
	Blending into the larger society	36.9	36.5	2,683
	Seeing people of all backgrounds as American	73.1	19.6	2,717
Contested/multiple	Being able to speak English	71.0	23.1	2,787
	Having American citizenship	76.0	17.7	2,773

Note: Weighted results. "Don't know" and "no answer" excluded.
Source: 21st Century Americanism Survey, 2004.

Regarding liberalism, Table 36.5 shows that all liberal measures (respecting political institutions and laws, working hard to achieve success, and permitting free speech) are endorsed by strong majorities as elements of American identity. Although there is more variation on the measures of civic republicanism (feeling and thinking of oneself as American, being informed about and involved in politics, and volunteering), we still find that over 80% say that each item is very or somewhat important in making someone a true American. The measures of ethnoculturalism (being born in America, being a Christian, being White, and having European ancestors) are much less likely to be endorsed as contemporary components of American identity (see also Schildkraut, 2007). However, endorsement of ethnoculturalism is still at a notable level, with over half of the respondents saying that it is very or somewhat important for Americans to be born in America, 35% saying the same about being a Christian, and 10% saying the same about being White.[18] Turning finally to incorporationism, items that refer to more of a "hands-off" approach to the relationship between immigration and American identity (respecting other people's cultural traditions and seeing people of all backgrounds as American) garner much more support than the measures that highlight an active management of cultural differences (carrying on the traditions of one's ancestors and blending into the larger society). That said, however, even those latter items assessing carrying on traditions and blending in achieve majority support when "somewhat" and "very important" are combined.[19]

Multivariate analyses (not shown here) indicate few differences in the extent to which one's ethnic or immigrant background shape how the content of American identity is defined (Schildkraut, 2007; see also Devos & Banaji, 2005).[20] In other words, mistaken are those who fear that the foreign born, Latinos, or Asians define what being American means differently from native-born Whites. Any statistically significant differences were small in magnitude and were outweighed by differences caused by other factors including age, education, political party affiliation, and political ideology (liberal versus conservative). And in some cases, being non-White or of foreign origin led to a *greater* likelihood of endorsing particular conceptions of American identity. For example, foreign-born respondents were more likely than native-born respondents to endorse being informed and involved in politics as central components of American identity. Additionally, the foreign born, Blacks, and Asians were more likely than the US-born and Whites to say that pursuing economic success through hard work denotes true Americanness.

With respect to incorporationism, I do find ethnic differences in the extent to which people think we can "have it all" in terms of cultural diversity and assimilation (Schildkraut, 2007), or rather, in the extent to which they believe that American society is and should be characterized by a bidimensional acculturation process. In particular, Blacks and Latinos were more likely than others to think that the incorporationist ideal is an achievable part of American identity, as evidenced by expressing high levels of support for *both* the item that refers to maintaining cultural difference *and* the item that refers to assimilation. It is important, however, to point out that I do not find any ethnicity-related instances in which one group supports the maintenance of cultural differences whereas the other supports assimilation (e.g., that the foreign born support only the maintenance of difference while the native born only support blending into the larger society). In other words, whereas some groups are more optimistic about the incorporationist ideal, I do not find an ethnic or immigrant divide.

Conclusion

In the past 20 years, public opinion scholars have made great gains in providing empirical data to accompany the centuries-old question of what it means to be American. These data have enabled us to examine whether the ways in which ordinary Americans answer that question matches the answers provided by political philosophers and historians. The data have also allowed us to address normative concerns about whether – or when – ideas such as patriotism or national identity should be encouraged or discouraged among the populace.

The desire to produce empirical insights into public opinion about American identity has taken on new urgency in the past decade as the demographic consequences of mass immigration are being realized in cities and towns in all corners of the nation. At present, politicians, commentators, activists, and scholars in the United States are not only concerned with whether patriotism promotes civic engagement and/or xenophobia, but also with whether levels of patriotism vary systematically across ethnic groups and across immigrant generations. Likewise, they seek answers on whether immigrants and their descendents come to think of themselves as American, and if not, whether anyone should care. The early results suggest that American identity is doing just fine. Levels of patriotism are high and vary little across ethnic or immigrant background. Most Americans of all backgrounds think of themselves as American as opposed to thinking of themselves as members of an ethnic or national-origin group. And for those who prioritize a non-American identity, the level of trust in American institutions, political participation, and sense of obligation to the national community are largely unaffected. The emerging consensus in this research agenda is that interested parties should orient their concerns toward the extent to which non-Whites, immigrants, and their descendents feel that their ethnic group is discriminated against in American society. Such perceptions are far more consequential than whether a person thinks of himself as American or as Dominican.

Much progress remains to be made in addressing these questions. After all, today's third- and fourth-generation Latinos and Asians are from families that immigrated to the United States decades ago. Whether findings about today's third and fourth generation will also characterize tomorrow's third and fourth generation is something that can only be answered with time. Existing research on American patriotism, attachment to American identity, and defining American identity has thus far provided a valuable snapshot of public opinion on these topics at the dawn of the twenty-first century. But the questions that this line of research investigates are not going away any time soon, and the relationships discussed here might change with time. It seems that Americans may be asking, "What does it mean to be American?" for years to come.

Notes

1. Data on demographics were found at the Migration Policy Institute: http://www.migrationinformation.org/datahub/charts/final.fb.shtml, accessed June 19, 2008.
2. One argument against the claim that former communist countries serve as a negative example for the United States is that communist ideals were often imposed on the people through coercive means whereas the set of political ideals that unite Americans and are embodied in political institutions are widely endorsed among the public.
3. Data on demographics were found at the Migration Policy Institute: http://www.migrationinformation.org/datahub/acscensus.cfm, accessed on May 6, 2009.
4. Online data analysis of the General Social Survey is available at http://sda.berkeley.edu/archive.htm, accessed October 26, 2008.
5. A poll conducted by Quinnipiac University in August of 2006 found 53% of respondents opposing the war. Other surveys throughout 2006 also show over 50% of the public in opposition (Roper Center for Public Opinion Research).
6. Note that Citrin et al. (2001) use the term "chauvinism" instead of "nationalism."
7. This same study, however, also showed that Asian Americans often associated Americanness with Whiteness.
8. Data collection was funded by the Russell Sage Foundation, and was conducted from July 12, 2004 – October 8, 2004 by the Social and Economic Sciences and Research Center

(SESRC) at Washington State University (WSU). The final sample has 2,800 respondents (1,633 White, non-Hispanic; 300 Black; 441 Latino; 299 Asian). Households with only cell phones were not a part of the sampling procedure.

9. For a respondent who only named one country of origin, that ancestry was used to fill in the blank.

10. Unless otherwise noted, all figures refer to weighted results, using population weights provided by the SESRC.

11. It is also worth noting that Latinos were the pan-ethnic group most likely to choose *only* an American identity (17%, vs. 8% for Whites, 4% for Blacks, and 6% for Asians).

12. It should be noted that some studies have found that African Americans tend not to be as proud as Whites (D. Davis, 2007; Huddy & Khatib, 2007; Sidanius, Feshback, Levin, & Pratto, 1997).

13. "Somewhat agree" was coded as 0.67 and "somewhat disagree" was coded as 0.33.

14. "Most of the time" was coded as 0.67 and "some of the time" was coded as 0.33.

15. These questions were adopted from Elizabeth Theiss-Morse's Perceptions of the American People Survey, 2002.

16. The term "liberalism" here refers to classical liberalism in political philosophy; it does not refer to the current ideological stances of "liberals" and "conservatives" in American politics.

17. To minimize respondent fatigue, the American identity series was randomly divided into two halves. The first half was asked early in the survey; the second half was asked later. The items within each half were rotated randomly.

18. In multivariate analyses, Blacks and Latinos are often more likely than Whites to endorse ethnoculturalism. It has been suggested that this pattern results from the degree of religiosity in Black and Latino communities (Citrin, Haas, Muste, & Reingold, 1994; Citrin, Reingold, & Green, 1990; Schildkraut, 2005a; 2007; Theiss-Morse, 2005).

19. See Schildkraut (2007) for diagnostic tests on these measures, including scale construction and factor analysis.

20. These multivariate analyses can be found in Schildkraut (2007).

References

Banning, L. (1986). Jeffersonian ideology revisited: Liberal and classical ideas in the new American republic. *William and Mary Quarterly 43*(1), 3–19.

Branscombe, N. R., Ellemers, N., Spears, R., & Doosje, B. (1999). The context and content of social identity threat. In N. Ellemers, R. Spears, B. Doosje (Eds.), *Social identity* (pp. 35–58). Oxford, UK: Blackwell.

Buchanan, P. J. (2006). *State of emergency: The third world invasion and conquest of America* (1st ed.), New York: Thomas Dunne Books/St. Martin's Press.

Citrin, J., Haas, E. B., Muste, C., & Reingold, B. (1994). Is American nationalism changing? Implications for foreign policy. *International Studies Quarterly 38*(1), 1–31.

Citrin, J., Lerman, A., Murakami, M., & Pearson, K. (2007). Testing Huntington: Is Hispanic immigration a threat to American identity?. *Perspectives on Politics 5*(1), 31–48.

Citrin, J., Reingold, B., & Green, D. P. (1990). American identity and the politics of ethnic change. *Journal of Politics 52*, 1124–1154.

Citrin, J., & Sides, J. (2008). Immigration and the imagined community in Europe and the United States. *Political Studies 56*, 33–56.

Citrin, J., Wong, C., & Duff, B. (2001). The meaning of American national identity. In R. Ashmore, L. Jussim, D. Wilder (Eds.), *Social identity, intergroup conflict, and conflict resolution* (pp. 71–100). New York: Oxford University Press.

Conover, P. J. (1988). Feminists and the gender gap. *Journal of Politics 50*, 985–1010.

Conover, P. J., Crewe, I. M., & Searing, D. D. (1991). The nature of citizenship in the United States and Great Britain: Empirical comments on theoretical themes. *Journal of Politics 53*, 800–832.

Conover, P. J., & Sapiro, V. (1993). Gender, feminist consciousness, and war. *American Journal of Political Science 37*, 1079–1099.

Davis, D. (2007). *Negative liberty: Public opinion and the terrorist attacks on America*. New York: Russell Sage Foundation.

Davis, J. A., & Smith, T. W. (1996). *General social surveys, 1996*. Chicago: National Opinion Research Center.

Dawson, M. C. (1994). *Behind the mule: Race and class in African-American politics*. Princeton, NJ: Princeton University Press.

de Figueiredo, R., Jr., & Elkins, Z. (2003). Are patriots bigots? An inquiry into the vices of in-group pride. *American Journal of Political Science 47*, 171–188.

de la Garza, R. O., Falcon, A., & Garcia, F. C. (1996). Will the real Americans please stand up: Anglo and Mexican-American support of core American political values. *American Journal of Political Science 40*, 335–351.

Department of Homeland Security. (2008). *2007 yearbook of immigration statistics*. Retrieved October 26, 2008, from http://www.dhs.gov/ximgtn/statistics/publications/yearbook.shtm.

Devos, T., & Banaji, M. R. (2005). American = White?. *Journal of Personality and Social Psychology 88*, 447–466.

Dovidio, J., & Morris, W. (1975). Effects of stress and commonality of fate on helping behavior. *Journal of Personality and Social Psychology 31*, 145–149.

Ellemers, N., & Barreto, M. (2001). The impact of relative group status: Affective, perceptual, and behavioral consequences. In R. Brown, S. Gaertner (Eds.), *Blackwell handbook of social psychology: Intergroup processes* (pp. 324–343). Malden, MA: Blackwell.

Fetzer, J. S. (2000). *Public attitudes toward immigration in the United States, France, and Germany*. Cambridge, UK: Cambridge University Press.

Flippen, A. R., Hornstein, H. A., Siegal, W. E., & Weitzman, E. A. (1996). A comparison of similarity and interdependence as triggers for in-group formation. *Personality and Social Psychology Bulletin 22*, 882–893.

Gaertner, S., & Dovidio, J. (2000). *Reducing intergroup bias: The common ingroup identity model*. Philadelphia, PA: Psychology Press.

García Bedolla, L. (2005). *Fluid borders: Latino power, identity, and politics in Los Angeles*. Berkeley, CA: University of California Press.

Gerstle, G. (2001). *American crucible: Race and nation in the twentieth century*. Princeton, NJ: Princeton University Press.

Glazer, N. (1997). *We are all multiculturalists now*. Cambridge, MA: Harvard University Press.

Hackney, S. (1997). *One America, indivisible: A national conversation on American pluralism and identity*. Washington, DC: National Endowment for the Humanities.

Hartz, L. (1955). *The liberal tradition in America: An interpretation of American political thought since the Revolution* (1st ed.), New York: Harcourt.

Hayden, S., Jackson, T., & Guydish, J. (1984). Helping behavior of females: Effects of stress and commonality of fate. *Journal of Psychology 117*, 233–237.

Held, D. (1996). *Models of democracy* (2nd ed.), Stanford, CA: Stanford University Press.

Hetherington, M. J. (2005). *Why trust matters: Declining political trust and the demise of American liberalism*. Princeton, NJ: Princeton University Press.

Higham, J. (1993). Multiculturalism and universalism: A history and critique. *American Quarterly 45*(2), 195–219.

Hollinger, D. A. (1995). *Post-ethnic America: Beyond multiculturalism*. New York: Basic Books.

Hornstein, H. A. (1976). *Cruelty and kindness: A new look at aggression and altruism*. Englewood Cliffs, NJ: Prentice-Hall.

Huddy, L., & Khatib, N. (2007). American patriotism, national identity, and political involvement. *American Journal of Political Science 51*, 63–77.

Huntington, S. P. (1981). *American politics: The promise of disharmony*. Cambridge, MA: Belknap Press.

Huntington, S. P. (2004). *Who are we? The challenges to America's identity*. New York: Simon & Schuster.

Kallen, H. (1924). *Culture and democracy in the United States*. New Brunswick, NJ: Transaction Publishers.

Kosterman, R., & Feshbach, S. (1989). Toward a measure of patriotic and nationalistic attitudes. *Political Psychology 10*, 257–274.

Lien, P., Conway, M. M., & Wong, J. (2004). *The politics of Asian Americans: Diversity and community*. New York: Routledge.

Lipset, S. M. (1963). *The first new nation: The United States in historical and comparative perspective*. New York: Basic Books.

McClain, P., Johnson Carew, J., Walton, E., & Watts, C. (2009). Group membership, group identity, and group consciousness: Measures of racial identity in American politics. *Annual Review of Political Science 12*, 471–485.

McDaniel, E., & Nooruddin, I. (2008). *Proud to be an American: How national pride affects visions of national identity*. Unpublished manuscript.

Michelson, M. R. (2003). The corrosive effect of acculturation: How Mexican Americans lose political trust. *Social Science Quarterly 84*(4), 918–933.

Miller, A. H., Gurin, P., Gurin, G., & Malanchuk, O. (1981). Group consciousness and political participation. *American Journal of Political Science 25*(3), 494–511.

Mills, C. W. (1997). *The racial contract*. Ithaca, NY: Cornell University Press.

Myrdal, G. (1944). *An American dilemma*. New York: McGraw-Hill.

Passel, J. (2006). *The size and characteristics of the unauthorized migrant population in the U.S.* Washington, DC: Pew Hispanic Center.

Paxton, P., & Mughan, A. (2006). What's to fear from immigrants? Creating an assimilationist threat scale. *Political Psychology 27*, 549–568.

Pearson, K., & Citrin, J. (2006). The political assimilation of the fourth wave. In T. Lee, S. K. Ramakrishnan, R. Ramirez (Eds.), *Transforming politics, transforming America* (pp. 217–242). Charlottesville: University of Virginia Press.

Rodgers, D. (1992). Republicanism: The career of a concept. *Journal of American History 79*(1), 11–37.

Roper Center for Public Opinion Research. *iPoll Databank*. Retrieved May 6, 2009, from http://www.ropercenter.uconn.edu.ezproxy.library.tufts.edu/ipoll.html

Sam, D. (2006). Acculturation: Conceptual background. In D. Sam, J. Berry (Eds.), *The Cambridge handbook of acculturation psychology* (pp. 11–26). Cambridge, UK: Cambridge University Press.

Schatz, R., Staub, E., & Lavine, H. (1999). On the varieties of national attachment: Blind versus constructive patriotism. *Political Psychology 20*(1), 151–174.

Schildkraut, D. J. (2005a). *Press one for English: Language policy, public opinion, and American identity*. Princeton, NJ: Princeton University Press.

Schildkraut, D. J. (2005b). The rise and fall of political engagement among Latinos: The role of identity and perceptions of discrimination. *Political Behavior 27*, 285–312.

Schildkraut, D. J. (2007). Defining American identity in the 21st century: How much "there" is there?. *Journal of Politics 69*, 597–615.

Schildkraut, D. J. (2011). *Americanism in the twenty-first century: Public opinion in the age of immigration*. New York: Cambridge University Press.

Schlesinger, A. M. (1998). *The disuniting of America: Reflections on a multicultural society.* (Rev. and enlarged.). New York: W.W. Norton.

Sidanius, J., Feshback, S., Levin, S., & Pratto, F. (1997). The interface between ethnic and national attachment: Ethnic pluralism or ethnic dominance?. *Public Opinion Quarterly 61*, 102–133.

Smith, R. M. (1993). Beyond Tocqueville, Myrdal, and Hartz: The multiple traditions in America. *American Political Science Review 87*(3), 549–566.

Smith, R. M. (1997). *Civic ideals: Conflicting visions of citizenship in US history*. New Haven, CT: Yale University Press.

Smith, R. M. (2003). *Stories of peoplehood: The politics and morals of political membership*. Cambridge, UK: Cambridge University Press.

Sullivan, W. (1982). *Reconstructing public philosophy*. Berkeley, CA: University of California Press.

Tajfel, H., & Turner, J. (1986). The social identity theory of intergroup behavior. In W. Austin, S. Worchel (Eds.), *Psychology of intergroup relations* (pp. 7–24). Chicago: Nelson-Hall.

The National Election Studies. (2004). *The 2004 National Election Study*.www.electionstudies.org

Theiss-Morse, E. (2003). *Identification and disidentification: Americans' commitment to the national collective and its consequences*. Paper presented at the annual meeting of the American Political Science Association. Philadelphia, PA.

Theiss-Morse, E. (2004). *Who's in and who's out: American national identity and the setting of boundaries*. Paper presented at the annual meeting

of the Midwest Political Science Association. Chicago, IL.

Theiss-Morse, E. (2005). *Benefitting the national group – at least some of it: The consequences of limiting who counts as an American*. Paper presented at the annual meeting of the Midwest Political Science Association. Chicago, IL.

Theiss-Morse, E. (2006). *The obligations of national identity: Charity, welfare, and the boundaries of the national group*. Paper presented at the annual meeting of the Midwest Political Science Association. Chicago, IL.

Tichenor, D. J. (2002). *Dividing Lines: The politics of immigration control in America*. Princeton, NJ: Princeton University Press.

Tocqueville, Ad. (1835/1990). *Democracy in America*. New York: Vintage Books.

Turner, J. (1982). Towards a Cognitive Redefinition of the Social Group. In H. Tajfel, (Ed.), *Social identity and intergroup relations* (pp. 15–40). Cambridge, UK: Cambridge University Press.

Tyack, D. (1999). Preserving the republic by educating republicans. In N. Smelsner, J. Alexander (Eds.), *Diversity and its discontents: Cultural conflict and common ground in contemporary American society* (pp. 63–83). Princeton, NJ: Princeton University Press.

Tyler, T. (2006). *Why people obey the law*. Princeton, N.J: Princeton University Press.

Tyler, T., & Huo, Y. (2002). *Trust in the law: Encouraging public cooperation with the police and courts*. New York: Russell Sage Foundation.

U.S. Census Bureau. (2008). *Statistical Abstract of the United States*. Retrieved October 26, 2008, from http://www.census.gov/compendia/statab/

Walzer, M. (1996). *What it means to be an American: Essays on the American experience*. New York: Marsilio.

Weaver, C. (2003). Confidence of Mexican Americans in major institutions in the United States. *Hispanic Journal of Behavioral Sciences 25*, 501–512.

World Values Survey. (2004). *World Values Survey, Online Data Analysis*. Retrieved May 6, 2009, from www.worldvaluessurvey.org

Wright, S. (2001). Strategic Collective Action: Social Psychology and Social Change. In R. Brown, S. Gaertner (Eds.), *Blackwell handbook of social psychology: Intergroup processes* (pp. 409–430). Malden, MA: Blackwell.

Zolberg, A. R., & Woon, L. L. (1999). Why Islam is like Spanish: Cultural Incorporation in Europe and the United States. *Politics and Society 27*, 5–38.

Becoming American

Alex Stepick, Carol Dutton Stepick,
and Patricia Vanderkooy

Abstract

The American people, and most of the world, think of the United States as a nation that has welcomed and assimilated immigrants. That image is only partially supported by facts. Until at least the 1960s, the melting pot was really a mold of conformity to the norms established by White Anglo Saxon Protestant (WASP) culture. Immigrants from England nearly instantly became American. Those from continental Europe found their labor welcome, but otherwise often initially encountered resistance to everything else about them. Yet, as "free White people," the possibility of becoming American often became a reality. For people who were non-White, the barriers were far more substantial, and even many Europeans, especially southern and eastern Europeans, were largely excluded from completely becoming American until after World War II, when the United States began to allow more immigrants to enter the country, and when once again their labor became highly valued. Beginning in the 1960s, to a degree never previously encountered in US history, some in the United States celebrated the diversity that immigrants brought with them and encouraged immigrants to become American without surrendering selective aspects of their homeland heritage. At the same time, others continued the nativist, anti-immigrant ways that have deep roots in American history and expressed concerns that these new immigrants did not want to, and could not truly, become American. America is at a crossroads now where the second generation of the latest wave of primarily non-Europeans is attaining adulthood. For those immigrants from non-White backgrounds, such as Black and Latino/Hispanic immigrants, it is unclear if they can ever be accepted or seen as simply "American" or whether they will become African American or Latino American, as posited by segmented assimilation theory. The emerging ethnographic realities indicate that they are becoming American in complex ways that

A. Stepick (✉)
Department of Global and Sociocultural Studies, Florida
International University, Miami, FL, USA
e-mail: stepick@fiu.edu

S.J. Schwartz et al. (eds.), *Handbook of Identity Theory and Research*,
DOI 10.1007/978-1-4419-7988-9_37, © Springer Science+Business Media, LLC 2011

can be conceptualized as multiple identities, rather than the simple divisions among assimilation, biculturalism, and cultural maintenance. What identities immigrants and their offspring adopt reflect how America has treated them, their parents' efforts to maintain some of their heritage, and increased opportunities to live at least part of their lives transnationally across borders.

Globalization is transforming the world with unprecedented numbers of people migrating among countries (see Jensen, Arnett, & McKenzie, Chapter 13, this volume). How people form themselves into societies, and the identities they develop as a result of these groupings, are deeply affected by this profound exposure to and associated mixing of cultures. Calling a country multicultural is insufficient to help us understand the specific dynamics of interpersonal and intergroup ways of relating, which we minimally need to know to understand what it means for immigrants and their children to become American. Because the United States is "a nation of immigrants," its past and present offer lessons about the confluence of many identities. Few of the millions of current inhabitants of the United States are descendants of Native Americans; rather, global immigration was and remains pivotal in establishing the nation and the identity of "American."[1] Nevertheless, there has been, and continues to be, dispute over who is or can become American. On the one hand is the image of America as a melting pot where anyone, regardless of their background, can become American. On the other hand is the extensive history of exclusion, a process generally referred to as nativism, in which Protestants of English descent viewed themselves as the real Americans. Psychologists have found considerable evidence that this attitude continues. DeVos and Banaji (2005), for example, found that both Whites and Asians tended to associate being American with being White.

The authors of this chapter come from sociology and anthropology disciplines, and some key concepts are defined fundamentally differently from those used in psychology. Acculturation and identity are key concepts in sociology and anthropology, but equally important is the concept of social relations between immigrants and natives. Sociologists especially consider as indicators of assimilation the social relationships that immigrants have with their neighbors, coworkers, friends, and romantic and marriage partners. The more that immigrants have social relationships of these types with natives, the more assimilated they are considered to be. Sociologists and anthropologists also consider immigrants' success in education and the labor market, i.e., to what degree immigrants' accomplishments in these areas match those of natives, as important markers of assimilation.

The prevalence and acceptance of the word "assimilation" has changed over time, with most contemporary sociologists and anthropologists now preferring "integration" or "incorporation" – as these terms do not so strongly imply the loss of behaviors or expressions of immigrants' cultural heritage as is often assumed with "assimilation." The scope of this chapter unfortunately is not large enough to incorporate in-depth discussion of the differences in sociological and anthropological disciplinary perspectives versus those from psychology. We hope, however, that this chapter will help bridge some of the disciplinary gap to contribute to an overall better understanding of the enormously complex process of becoming American.

In contemporary sociology and anthropology, the process of becoming American is viewed as a dialectic between the immigrants themselves as they strive to adapt to living in their new environment, and the established residents of the United States (i.e., native-born and not of immediate immigrant descent), who have the power to include or exclude newcomers. Similar to Berry (2005), immigrant identity, and whether and how immigrants become American, emerges through a contestation of the immigrants' own self-attribution (i.e., internal self-categorization) and socially defined or ascriptive conditions specific to the social worlds in which they are embedded (Vertovec, 2001; Wimmer & Glick Schiller, 2003). Moreover, we argue that this dialectic is embedded within power relations in which the locally most powerful group, usually but not always White Americans, has the power to determine the terms of becoming American (Castells, 1997). This power includes obviously the power to determine who is legally admitted to the United States, but it also includes the power to establish informal norms of socially acceptable behavior such as, for example, when it is acceptable to speak a language other than English or where and when women may wear a headscarf. Psychological approaches, such as Licata, Sanchez-Mazas, and Green (Chapter 38, this volume), share much of this perspective.

This chapter addresses the evolution of this dialectic, describing the contradictory trends that exist simultaneously, as well as the social forces that transform some immigrants from excluded to accepted as Americans and to assuming an American identity. We begin with a summary of what immigration scholars mean by "identity." We then describe the processes of becoming American as these processes occurred from the founding of what became the United States through the Great Wave of immigration that occurred at the end of the nineteenth through the beginning of the twentieth century. Out of this Great Wave, immigration scholars developed the core concept of assimilation, which established the starting point for analyses of what it means to become American and how one does so. We then analyze how the most recent wave of immigration, from 1965 to the present, has challenged and modified our understanding of assimilation and of becoming American.

Immigration and Defining Identity

An examination of "becoming American" raises the question of what constitutes American national identity and its relationship to other ethnic and cultural identities (Schildkraut, Chapter 36, this volume). The notion that American identity is and should be a singular, exclusive identity reflects much of the popular political discourse that erupts in response to immigrants, i.e., whether immigrants are fundamentally different from native-born Americans because they come from a different place (Huntington, 2004a, 2004b). Although individuals may adopt hyphenated identities, such as Mexican-American, the essential concern for both the newcomer and the established resident remains with an individual's identification or identifications linked to a geographic place or places of origin, or their sense of belonging to a particular nation. For the United States, the impact of immigration on national identity always has been, and remains, critical since the United States emerged out of colonization that involved people from diverse national origins. Debates surrounding immigrant incorporation, both historically and currently, highlight the political, economic, and social ramifications of immigration in relation to national identity (Brooks, 2007; Higham, 1988; Preston, 2007).

As happens in any field of study, scholars have difficulty agreeing on the precise definition of core concepts. Sociologists and anthropologists have not reached a consensus on precisely what identity is and how it relates to the processes of migration. Hale (2004, p. 34), for example, considers identity as reference points which people use within the social contexts they inhabit. These reference points allow them to comprehend diverse social relationships and to situate themselves and their choices within these contexts. Hale's definition emphasizes that identity is a broad term referring to a wide variety of reference points to which individuals attach themselves. Within a diverse social landscape, individuals root themselves in particular groups or affiliations. These attachments or groupings are what we refer to as "identity." Rahier (1999, p. xxiv) describes identities as descriptors that are both stated and unstated and continually changing within fluid contexts. Thus, identity refers to multiple axes of identification, including gender, age, nationality, class, race, and ethnicity. Although national identity is the form of identity that most often concerns immigration scholars, other dimensions of identity, such as race, intertwine. For example, immigrants and their children who are perceived as White may be more accepted by the established resident White population, and thus may find it easier to claim an unmodified American identity than immigrants of color, i.e., Black, Latino, or Asian immigrants. Immigrants of color, however, may be perceived as having and may claim to have an ethnic minority identity, e.g., African American, and thus have a different sense of what it means to be American.

Our understanding of identity highlights its fluidity. Although identity implies a sense of immobility and constancy, it is perhaps the opposite. This perspective highlights the multiple points of reference that individuals employ, often related to specific contexts and circumstances. For example, Waters (1990) describes the selective use of ancestral identities among White ethnics, noting variability in terms of knowledge of one's ancestors, ancestral surnames, and the social stature of the ancestral group(s).[2] Nederveen Pieterse (2007) also raises concern with the term "*identity*" as overly static – he advocates using the more fluid "*identification*" to highlight individual actors' agency. In addition to fluidity and agency, this semantic shift from "identity" to "identification" highlights the labels which are ascribed to individuals; a pigmentocracy, i.e., a society such as the United States where skin color plays a critical role that limits the available options for minority individuals' identifications (Gans, 2007). For example, someone with dark skin is a "visible minority" and may have to incorporate "non-Whiteness" into her/his identity. Within this constrained context, the individual might choose specific labels related to this marginalization (e.g., Black, African-American).

We focus particularly on first-generation immigrants and their children (frequently referred to as second-generation immigrants). The definition of identity we use evolved from a conception of national identity as essentialized race, i.e., one in which only White Americans were really Americans, to a view of national identity as a socially constructed self-identification that not only develops through

an individual's life, but also varies by context – from public places such as workplace, to private contexts such as home and family. This approach is consistent with Anderson's (1999) understanding of the creation of nations, along with more recent work in social psychology, e.g., Billig (1995). Alternative and contextually emergent identifications include race and pan-ethnic identities (such as "Latino" or "Hispanic"), which both enfold people from diverse nations along with emerging notions of transnationalism, in which identities span nation states (see especially, Glick Schiller & Fouron, 1998; Kilic, 2007; Morawska, 2001). Compared to the immigration of 100 years ago, decreasing travel costs and technological advances in communication allow migrants to maintain ties with their homeland after migration, enabling transnational lives in which identities are not wedded to borders and nation states. In the next section, we review the historical roots of the processes of immigrants becoming American, and then we address how the contemporary immigrants are becoming American.

The Foundation of an Immigrant Nation

Since the beginning of European settlement in what was to become the United States, immigration has been the primary force that has provoked debates over who can, and how to, become American. Most stories of immigration ignore the presence of native indigenous peoples, i.e., American Indians. The early European immigrants, who were primarily English, generally pushed the native peoples aside, notwithstanding the myth of European immigrant-Native American cooperation embodied by Thanksgiving. Although the British governed the American colony, they encouraged immigration, not only of slaves and indentured laborers, but also of other free Europeans including the Dutch who originally settled in what became New York City, as well as Irish, Scots, and the most numerous group, German-speaking immigrants from what later became Germany.

With the exception of Quakers and Jews, if an immigrant wanted to "naturalize," i.e., enjoy the rights of citizenship in the British American colonies, she/he had to be a member of a Protestant church.

Early English colonists disparaged Huguenots for being French and the Scottish and Irish for not being true English (Jones, 1960). German immigrants to England's American colony caused particularly passionate phobias. Belonging to pacifist sects, such as the Amish and Quakers, many German immigrants sought seclusion from rather than assimilation to Anglo American ways. They prompted Benjamin Franklin to challenge, "Why should Pennsylvania, founded by the *English*, become a Colony of *Aliens*, who will shortly be so numerous as to Germanize us instead of Anglifying them?" (Weaver, 1970, p. 50).

On the other hand, some observers viewed America as capable of incorporating everyone, at least everyone who was a free White, and the Naturalization Act of 1790 specifically limited naturalization to those who were "free white persons" ("Naturalization Act," 1790, Chapter 103). Soon after the founding of the United States as a nation, de Crèvecoeur (1782) referred to America as melting individuals into a "new race of men." A half century later, Ralph Waldo Emerson wrote that America was a culturally and racially mixed "smelting pot," although he added that Chinese were fundamentally different (Quoted in Gordon, 1964, p. 117). The historian Frederick Jackson Turner argued that "immigrants were Americanized, liberated and fused into a mixed race," but again he was referring only to those of European descent (see Spickard, 2007, p. xvii). Henry James referred specifically to New York City in 1905 as a "fusion, as of elements in solution in a vast hot pot." The specific phrase, "melting pot" came from Israel Zangwill's 1908 play of that name. Thus, since the country's founding, race has been a critical determinant of who has the opportunity to become American, and allowed the potential inclusion of Whites from different cultural backgrounds, but the exclusion of those defined as non-White.

The early immigration of people primarily from England founded what became the United States, but this first migratory wave was relatively small compared to later immigration. Between the 1880s and the mid-1920s, 23.5 million immigrants came to the United States. Streams of people from England, Ireland, and Germany continued to arrive in this Great Wave. Although those from England were considerable in number, they were never the subject of derision or exclusion. English Americans and their descendants, often referred to as WASPS (White Anglo Saxon Protestants), were generally not even thought of as immigrants. Rather, they were perceived as adding to the core of American society and culture, the standard by which others were judged, and the ideal newcomer to the growing nation (see Spickard, 2007, p. xvii).

The Great Wave also contained many who were not Protestants and some who appeared to be different. Among those settling in the eastern United States, the largest groups of non-WASPs were Catholics and Jews, and darker-skinned people from southern Europe. Fewer numbers of European immigrants in the Great Wave settled directly in the western United States. Instead, many who arrived there were immigrants from Asia; and following the US annexation of Texas, and later what became the southwestern states, many who had been Mexican became part of the United States without moving (Hing, 2004).

Many of the immigrants from the Great Wave reproduced some significant aspects of their native cultures in the United States. German immigrants, particularly those who settled in Midwestern agricultural areas, operated bilingual and monolingual schools and churches, as did Norwegian and other Scandinavian groups. Schools in non-English languages were indeed widespread as were newspapers. In the cities, Irish and German Catholics established Catholic parochial schools and suggested that the public help fund those schools just as it funded schools with Protestant leanings (Spickard, 2007).

These non-WASP newcomers were generally welcomed or at least tolerated because of their role in the economy. The Great Wave coincided with and was closely tied to America's rapid industrialization, which was built upon unskilled and semi-skilled labor. Immigrants were sometimes employed specifically to undermine unionization efforts, but beyond that, industrialization demanded more labor than was otherwise available. The demand for labor extended also to immigrant women, particularly in the garment industry and food production (Butler, 1909). Immigrants filled the jobs generated by industrialization, just as undocumented or illegal immigrants now fill jobs that most Americans are not willing to do – at least not for the wages that are being offered. America could not have become an industrial giant without immigrants, and accordingly, their labor was welcomed.

Other characteristics of the Great Wave immigrants, such as their religion, were not as positively assessed as their ability to perform labor. At the end of the nineteenth century and the beginning of the twentieth century, Jews and Catholics from eastern and southern Europe were viewed as fundamentally distinct from the earlier, mostly Protestant immigrants from western and northern Europe (see, for example, Higham, 1988). These Jewish and Catholic immigrants were generally regarded as not only culturally, but also "racially," distinct from and inferior to Anglo-Saxon and other Northern European, Protestant Americans. Fears abounded that immigrants were not doing what immigrants *should* do, i.e., abandoning the customs of their homeland and becoming American. Non-Protestant European immigrant groups, such as Catholic Irish and Italians, and Jewish Germans and Russians suffered from discrimination. Early in the nineteenth century, three states put limits on voting by Jews. After the civil war of the 1860s, Jews became secondary targets of the Ku Klux Klan. Later, Ivy League universities placed quotas on the maximum number of Jewish students admitted, and private clubs often excluded Jews. In the nineteenth century, a widespread stereotype of Irish, and subsequently of Italians, alleged that they were more loyal to the Pope than to their new homeland (Franchot, 1994).

The welcome accorded to immigrant labor, and the rejection of immigrants' real and alleged social and cultural characteristics, reflected the underlying dialectic between the melting pot ideal and the inclinations toward exclusion. Yet, in spite of prejudice and discrimination, eastern and southern European and non-Protestant immigrants of the Great Wave of immigration were, with time, allowed to become American in some fundamental ways that were denied to non-White immigrants. Unlike peoples who entered the United States from somewhere outside of Europe, every European immigrant, regardless of what part of Europe and regardless of what religion he or she practiced, entered the United States as a "free white person" eligible for future citizenship. This categorization and associated opportunity to become citizens helped European immigrants become an important political force in every industrial city where labor organizers reached out to them. Gradually, beginning with World War I but especially during and after World War II, these European-origin groups became accepted as fellow "white" Americans and eventually intermarried into the White majority. Although negative stereotypes and some discrimination persisted, particularly against Jews, the Europeans of the Great Wave of immigration – and even more so their US-born children – were generally accepted as Americans by the descendents of English-speaking Protestants who had originally demeaned them as inferior.

In the United States, there is a significant historical exception to the general acceptance of and willingness to include European immigrants. World War I fostered a profound emphasis on American nationalism, and US entry into the war transformed ethnic Germans from acceptable White immigrants into enemies who had not become sufficiently American. German-language schools, along with other non-English-language schools, were quickly treated with suspicion, and many states passed laws prohibiting the use of the German language. Germans and other immigrants, particularly Jews who were leaders in organized labor, were seen as potential radicals with ongoing ties and affiliations to socialist revolutions abroad. Prominent German immigrants, including intellectuals, artists, and community leaders who had not acquired citizenship, were incarcerated, an act that foreshadowed the internment camps for Japanese Americans in World War II. Many Germans were also physically assaulted, including at least one who was lynched (Spickard, 2007, p. 181). A consequent widespread push emerged for an "American" identity which emphasized loyalty to America. Many immigrants responded by abandoning or at least hiding their "foreign" heritage. By the end of World War I, "German immigrants" and their descendants had become "White Americans."

By contrast, non-White immigrants received a lesser degree of acceptance in the nineteenth and the first half of the twentieth century. At the advent of European settlement and continuing at least into the eighteenth century in what is now the United States, people of color were presumed to be biologically incapable of becoming American. Colonial America believed that pre-modern societies, as represented by the indigenous Americans, as well as individuals from Africa and Asia, were innately inferior. As mentioned previously, the Naturalization Act of 1790 restricted citizenship to "free white persons" ("Naturalization Act," 1790). Indigenous Native Americans, i.e., American Indians, were not even considered citizens of the United States until 1924. Those of African descent could become citizens only after the Civil War when the 1870 Naturalization Act extended citizenship to not only "white persons," but also "persons of African descent" ("Naturalization Act " 1870, Chapter CCLIV, Section 7). Nevertheless, those of African descent still faced legally sanctioned segregation and tremendous informal prejudice, most dramatically manifested in the lynchings of Blacks after the Civil War and into the twentieth century.

Asian immigrants, such as Chinese, Japanese, Koreans, and Filipinos, arrived in much smaller numbers than migrants from Europe, yet they generated more controversy and opposition than their European counterparts. They were legally ruled to be non-White and banned from marrying Whites in several states. Accordingly, they did not fit into melting-pot discourses at all. The 1870 Naturalization Act, for example, that extended citizenship to those of African descent

specifically barred Asians from becoming US citizens (Gettys, 1934, p. 70). Moreover, the Chinese Exclusion Act of 1882 was the first significant restriction on free immigration into the United States. It was not repealed until 1943. Bias against women was reflected in the 1907 Expatriation Act that declared that an American woman who married a foreign national lost her US citizenship. American men who married foreign women did not lose their citizenship (Nicolosi, 2001). In 1913, California passed a law that effectively barred Chinese and Japanese from owning property in the state, a law which was subsequently passed in other states (Gaines & Cho, 2004). By 1922, a woman who married a foreigner was allowed to retain her US citizenship, unless her husband was Asian – which would result in the loss of her citizenship (Nicolosi, 2001). In 1923 the US Supreme Court ruled that Indians from the Asian subcontinent could not become US citizens, and shortly after in 1924, the Oriental Exclusion Act not only prohibited most immigration from Asia, but also barred from entry the foreign-born wives and children of US citizens of Chinese ancestry (Haney-Lopez, 2006).

People of Mexican descent also confronted barriers to becoming Americans. The 1848 Treaty of Guadalupe Hidalgo, which incorporated the northwestern territories of Mexico into the United States, also granted formal US citizenship to those Mexicans living in those territories who did not choose to become Mexican citizens (Griswold del Castillo, 1992). Nevertheless, people of Mexican descent were not popularly considered to be "real" Americans. In most cases, land ownership rights of those living in the conquered territories were not recognized (Haynes, 2001). Most Western states prohibited marriages between whites and people of color, which was defined as including Mexicans. To escape this discrimination, many of those of Mexican descent in New Mexico referred to themselves as "Spanish-Americans" rather than Mexicans, a label that drew upon Latin America's distinction between indigenous "indios" and "españoles," i.e., Spaniards (Gonzalez, 1969). Being labeled as something other than Mexican could, for example, provide their children with access to the segregated schools reserved for Whites (Menchaca, 2008).

Through the first half of the twentieth century, the forces of inclusion into the melting pot and exclusion of the supposedly racially distinct "others" created a generally informal, but occasionally legally sanctioned, ethnic and racial hierarchy of Americans. People of color faced far more restrictions and obstacles to becoming American. Although the large-scale historic European migrations to the United States are now romanticized and idealized, they were also tinged with racism and discrimination toward immigrants who did not fit the English Protestant ideal.

Theoretical Evolution: From Essentialized Racism to Socially Constructed Identifications

As the social sciences in Europe and the United States developed through the nineteenth and into the early twentieth centuries, they accepted the biological and racist premises of the broader society and sought to apply them. In the United States, anthropology and sociology were used to buttress arguments and policies that favored European immigrants over others, and that favored western European immigrants over those from eastern and southern Europe (Gould, 1981). Race was broadly conceived as what today we would call nationality or ethnicity. People from different nations and even regions were presumed to belong to different races, i.e., they were considered to be biologically and, therefore, socially and psychologically, fundamentally different.

This biological and racial conception was based in a broader framework that has been labeled as "modernism." Modernism is marked by a profound belief in progress, that human societies move forward in a linear progression toward a condition which is considered "better" in some comparative format (Cowen & Shenton, 1995; Giddens, 1990). Western European societies, especially England, as well as North America were judged to be those that were moving

forward, at least by intellectuals and leaders from those societies. Other societies were labeled traditional, and their development was believed to be held back because their citizens were from inferior races. This hierarchy of societies was based upon supposedly innate characteristics and abilities accorded to the different races, which is known as "eugenics." Accordingly, in the United States, the prevailing assumption was that people from the allegedly superior race had a right to push aside and even exterminate (such as occurred with the Native American Indians), enslave (as in the case of Africans), or bar from entry (as with Asians) inferior races (Cowen & Shenton, 1995; Nederveen Pieterse, 2007).

In 1911, in the midst of the Great Wave of immigration, the United States Immigration Commission, better known as the Dillingham Commission, issued a 42-volume report with extensive social and economic data. Considered moderate at the time, the commission invidiously claimed that northern European immigrants were superior to those from eastern and southern Europe. Eugenicists, who prominently contributed to the Dillingham Commission – including Madison Grant in his *The Passing of the Great Race* (1916) – argued that Anglo Saxons, Nordics, and Teutonics (i.e., Germans) should not contaminate their "racial purity" by marrying the "lower types" such as Poles, Italians, and Greeks. These ideas buttressed the nativist movement that sought to curb immigration to the United States, particularly that of the allegedly inferior peoples from anywhere other than western and northern Europe. A series of immigration laws were passed in the early 1920s that severely limited immigration from eastern and southern Europe and reconfirmed the exclusion of the Chinese. These legal restrictions combined with the Great Depression and then World War II to severely restrict immigration to the United States until the late 1940s. In this same era, the 1934 Tydings-McDuffie Act promised Philippine independence from the United States by 1944, but immediately stripped Filipinos of their status as US nationals.

Following World War II, and in response to the racist policies that Hitler's Germany had implemented, US immigration restrictionist policies began to shift toward more humanitarian principles. For example, the War Brides Act in 1945 allowed the foreign war brides of citizen members of the US armed forces to immigrate to the United States. In addition, the Luce-Cellar Act in 1946 extended the right to become naturalized citizens to newly freed Filipinos and Asian Indians, and the Displaced Persons Act of 1948 allowed some of those displaced by World War II to immigrate to the United States.

A scientifically based antiracist movement had begun to emerge in the early twentieth century, when Franz Boas, a pioneering anthropologist, countered the argument that immigrants were biologically different by examining the environmental factors that produced biological variations. He argued that immigrants were not an inferior genetic type, but simply people who had different life experiences, diets and opportunities. He demonstrated that in the second and third generations, the children and grandchildren of immigrants came to resemble native-born youth (Stocking, 1968).

Consequently, anthropology and sociology shifted toward an understanding of identity as emerging from social, rather than biological, processes. Research also became much more ethnographic, based upon direct observation of immigrants in their daily lives. Research on immigrants to the United States began in the early 1900s as the racist anti-immigrant climate was beginning to climax. The nascent Russell Sage Foundation initiated a research project on immigrant laborers throughout Pittsburgh's industries (Butler, 1909). With the publication of Thomas and Znaniecki's *The Polish Peasant in Europe and America* (1918), the University of Chicago became the center of immigration research and established the framework that has influenced immigration studies to this day. Robert E. Park, Ernest Burgess, and W.I. Thomas systematically documented the conditions and attributes of immigrant groups, their occupations, and households. They described immigrant adaptation as a series of stages, in which "persons and groups acquire the memories, sentiments, and attitudes of other persons and groups and, by sharing their experience and history, are incorporated with them in a common cultural life" (Park & Burgess, 1921, p. 735). Park and Burgess articulated what became the key theoretical concept in immigration studies in the United States, assimilation, which described the process by which immigrants became American.

Assimilation Theory and Melting Pots

Park and Burgess's early definitions of assimilation emphasized the cultural and social dimensions of immigrants adapting and fitting into American culture and society. In 1921, for example, they referred to incorporation into a "common cultural life" (1921, p. 735), and a few years later Park (1930, p. 281) defined "social assimilation" as the achievement of "cultural solidarity sufficient at least to sustain a national existence." Influenced by these sociologists, thinking about the process of becoming American moved from its former biological presumptions to a concentration on social and cultural dimensions.

The intellectual trajectory established by Park and Burgess culminated in Milton Gordon's *Assimilation in American Life* (1964). Gordon delineated a number of different dimensions of assimilation. For Gordon and other sociologists, acculturation was often considered the first step in assimilation, and the most noted part of acculturation was almost always language. Someone who preferred to use English over a non-English native language was considered acculturated and becoming more American. Language and other cultural traits, however, were not the only dimensions of assimilation. Sociologists were particularly likely to focus on social relations, i.e., who one's coworkers were, who one's neighbors were, with whom one spent free time (see, among others, Alba & Nee, 2003; Bean & Stevens, 2003; Portes & Rumbaut, 2001). In each case, individuals were considered more socially assimilated when their social relations were more with established residents, i.e., native-born Americans of non-immigrant descent, which was generally interpreted as meaning one's ancestors had been in the United States at least three generations.

For many sociologists, the ultimate attainment of assimilation was marrying an established resident of non-immigrant background. Gordon (1964) also distinguished attitudes toward other groups and civic participation as critical dimensions of assimilation. Following Park and Burgess and their successors, assimilation was the expected outcome, a natural consequence of the immigrant experience in America, at least for immigrants of European descent (Gordon, 1964).

Gordon highlighted generational change as the yardstick to measure changes in immigrant groups. In this straight-line characterization of the assimilation process, the first generation (the foreign-born) were less assimilated and less exposed to American life than were their American-born children (the second generation); and their grandchildren (the third generation) were, in turn, more like the core American mainstream than their parents.

Gordon's analysis conformed well with the experiences of the immigrant flows from Europe in the late nineteenth and early twentieth centuries, whose second- and third-generation offspring had apparently assimilated by the late 1950s and early 1960s when Gordon's research appeared. At the middle of the twentieth century, there were also some social scientists who argued that assimilation was not the same for everyone. Some argued that, rather than a single melting pot, there was instead a triple melting pot, and that immigrants assimilated into more culturally defined subcategories of US society. For example, Protestant, Jewish, and Catholic religious identities were interpreted as culturally defined ethnic identities because of their historical association with particular immigrant flows (Herberg, 1960; Kennedy, 1944).

Led by Robert Park (1930) as early as the 1930s, sociologists never completely accepted the melting pot. Park noted that "where peoples who come together are of divergent cultures and widely different racial stocks, assimilation and amalgamation do not take place so rapidly as they do in other cases" (cited in Gratton, 2002). Moreover, Gordon referred to assimilation not as a melting pot, but as Anglo conformity. Although small elements of foreign cuisine

had become incorporated into American culture, Gordon argued that the norms and ideas of Anglo Americans dominated. Not only was English overwhelmingly the language of the United States, but those in positions of power were disproportionately White Protestants, and if they were not Protestant, they were still most likely to be white and most certainly male.

The reality of the melting pot and the associated notion of assimilation were also challenged by the 1960s white ethnic resurgence, which followed closely on the heels of the Civil Rights Movement. The hyphenated identifications (e.g., Italian-American) that had been vigorously erased by the nationalistic American fervor engendered by the two world wars resurfaced. The phrase "White ethnic" is used to indicate that people who are white also have an ethnicity, as much as people who are Black or Latino. Since throughout the United States people who are white are both numerically and socially dominant, they often perceive themselves to be without ethnicity, to be simply Americans without an ethnic adjective. However, they are generally perceived by Blacks and Latinos as being different from Black Americans or Latino Americans. They are specifically and culturally White Americans. The term "White ethnic" was used as early as 1954 in the sociological literature (McKeown & Chyatte, 1954). Glazer's and Moynihan's (1970) discussion of the Irish and Italians in New York City made the term a central component of any sociological analysis of US ethnic categories. White ethnics were referred to as the "unmeltable ethnics," and included Italians in New York who maintained their ethnic distinctiveness and separation (Glazer & Moynihan, 1970). [See, inter alia, Greeley (1971), Waters (1996) and Doane (1997)].

Sociological and anthropological research on the ethnicity of white ethnics (Alba & Nee, 1997) added nuance to Glazer and Moynihan's notion that white ethnics were "unmeltable." Although white ethnics had not completely assimilated and lost their ethnic heritage, their expressions of ethnicity were typically more symbolic than fundamental. White ethnics did recognize their foreign roots and ate distinctive national foods, but usually ethnic expressions were limited to special occasions and to foods that had been absorbed into American cuisine (Alba & Nee, 1997; Waters, 1990).

By the mid-1960s, sociological assimilation theory had reached its peak and had evolved from a simple assertion that all immigrants become Americans in a similar process to a recognition that, not only did at least some immigrants retain elements of their ancestors' distinct cultural heritage, but also that whites assimilated more easily than others. The Second Great Wave of US immigration that began in 1965 and that consisted of a majority from Latin America and Asia, had even more fundamentally challenged the notions of assimilation and becoming American. This substantial change in immigration policy and immigrants' origins has required further elaborations of assimilation and what it means to become American.

The Second Great Wave of US Immigration: 1965 and Onward

In the wake of World War II, US immigration law gradually loosened most of its restrictions. World War II veterans were permitted to bring home their brides from abroad. The United States accepted some of the European refugees displaced by the war, and it subsequently also accepted some refugees from the aborted Hungarian revolution against Communism in 1955. Indeed, while international law defined refugees as anyone fleeing persecution, the United States consistently favored those fleeing Communist or left-leaning regimes. Following Castro's revolution in Cuba and that country's ensuing conversion to Communism, the United States completely opened its doors to Cubans. In later years, US refugee law was brought in accordance with the broader international definition of refugees (through The Refugee Act of 1980), but frequently the law was still implemented to favor those fleeing Communism and to discriminate against others (see, for example, Teitelbaum, 1983; Zucker & Zucker, 1987). As the Civil Rights Movement progressed, the

United States became increasingly concerned about legally enforced racism. The severe restrictions on immigrants from particular countries embodied in the immigration laws of the 1920s were eliminated in 1965. Immigrants again began streaming into the United States, and many were from Latin America and Asia.

By the end of the twentieth century, the United States had more immigrants, specifically more people born outside the United States, than at the peak of the previous Great Wave at the beginning of the twentieth century. Although the percentage of the total population that was foreign-born (12.6% in 2007) was still less than it had been 100 years earlier when it peaked at 14.7%, the presence of new immigrants again raised questions of assimilation and the prospects for immigrants to become American. The new immigrants also appeared to be different from the previous waves. Although Europeans were among the new immigrants, many more were from Latin America and Asia. As late as 1960, over 70% of US immigrants were from Europe. By 2000, over 50% were from Latin America and over 25% from Asia (Migration Policy Institute, 2010a). Soon, Mexico, which contributed over 30%, was the single largest source of immigrants, followed by China, the Philippines, and India (Migration Policy Institute, 2010b). Although descendants of people from these places were already in the United States in significant numbers, especially in the western United States, the new immigrants were perceived as different and, for some, a challenge to America's identity (Huntington, 2004a, 2004b; Schlesinger, 1992).

The new post-1965 immigration from Latin America and Asia raised questions about the new immigrants' ability to become American, echoing the public debates from the first Great Wave approximately 100 years earlier concerning the supposedly biological racial differences of the Jewish and Catholic eastern and southern Europeans. Arthur Schlesinger (1992), for example, argued that America had become too tolerant of cultural diversity and that the emphasis on multiculturalism in US schools and other institutions would encourage and even assure that immigrants would maintain their homeland cultures and not become American. Borjas (1990, 2006) stressed the characteristics of the immigrants themselves, asserting that they were of a "lower quality," particularly in terms of educational achievement, and thus would not be able to advance economically. Still others emphasized social and economic barriers that might deter immigrants from truly integrating. Gans (1992) observed that the children of immigrants from "less fortunate" socioeconomic circumstances, especially dark-skinned immigrants, faced the risk of being trapped in permanent poverty because these children would lack job opportunities and would be confronted with high rates of unemployment, crime, alcoholism, drug use, and other traits associated with poverty and the frustration of unfulfilled expectations.

At the same time, and as with the Great Wave 100 years earlier, some Americans welcomed the new immigrants. Although manufacturing no longer needed massive supplies of workers, immigrant workers were and still are desired by various sectors of the economy. Since the shortage of labor caused by World War II, immigrants have had a primary presence in agriculture. From the 1980s onwards, immigrants became important components of labor in construction and the broad service industry. Moreover, they became central in one industrial sector: computers and information technology. Over 50% of the PhD-level engineers working in Silicon Valley, for example, are immigrants (Wong, 2005). All of these industries welcome immigrants and their labor.

In the wake of the Civil Rights movement and the associated positive acknowledgment of the contributions of non-Whites to America in the last half of the 1960s, there is a correspondingly greater acceptance and occasionally even celebration of immigrants. Athletes, artists, and scientists usually are welcomed eagerly into the United States, and significant numbers of immigrants hold university positions. Perhaps more significantly, all legal permanent immigrants can become citizens and exercise political power and influence. Immigrants without legal status, however, since they are not in the United States under cover of law, cannot become citizens and are always subject to deportation, except when the US Congress passes special amnesty legislation to allow them to obtain a legal status, as it did in 1986 and has debated doing again. Advocacy groups for immigrants, such as the Hebrew Immigrant Aid Society, the National Asian Pacific American Legal Consortium, and the National Council of La Raza, exist wherever significant numbers of immigrants have settled and in Washington, D.C. Increasingly, immigrant advocacy groups are emerging in states with a relatively recent history of immigration, including One America in the Pacific Northwest and the Mississippi Immigrant Rights Alliance in the heart of the US South. All of these organizations that advocate for immigrants are facilitating increased civic participation by immigrants and seeking to make it easier for immigrants to become American.

Becoming American for the New Second Generation

Until the 1990s, it was difficult to assess empirically in what ways the new immigrants were or were not becoming American, because they had not been in the United States for very long. A consensus gradually developed that the second generation, the children of those who immigrated, represented a more critical test of the opportunities and possibilities of becoming American. The first generation, which generally immigrates as adults, pragmatically has difficulty assimilating. Individuals who immigrate as adults almost always have a foreign accent when speaking English that identifies them as "not American." Generally, it is more difficult to change one's ways after reaching adulthood, and adult immigrants usually devote their energies to the immediate task of earning a living. The children of these immigrants, however, are more deeply affected by US culture. They go through the US school system; they have more free time than working adults; and they are more thoroughly exposed to American society and culture than are their parents.

In the United States, in the first decade of the twenty-first century, over 30 million young people are the children of immigrants (Portes & Rumbaut, 2006). In places of high immigrant concentrations, such as the Miami urban area, 30% of the population is composed of second-generation immigrants. The children of immigrants are still primarily young, with a median age in the early twenties. Accordingly, for many we still do not know in what ways and to what degree they will eventually become American in terms of behavioral acculturation and identification. Nevertheless, they have been the subject of considerable research, and some patterns are emerging along with some new theories to explain these patterns (see, for example, Bean, Brown, & Rumbaut, 2004; Harris, Jamison, & Trujillo, 2008; Hirschman, 1994, 2001; Kasinitz, Mollenkopf, Waters, & Holdaway, 2008; Kroneberg, 2008; Portes, Fernández-Kelly, & Haller, 2005; Rumbaut, 2008; Stepick, Dutton Stepick, Eugene, Teed, & Labissiere, 2001; Stepick, Dutton Stepick, & Labissiere, 2008; Suárez-Orozco, Suárez-Orozco, & Todorova, 2008).

In terms of behavioral acculturation, the children of immigrants are rapidly becoming American. They overwhelmingly prefer to speak English over their parents' heritage language (Portes & Schauffler, 1996). Schildkraut (Chapter 36, this volume) finds much the same thing regarding identification as American. The trend toward preferring English is especially evident over generations. By the third-plus generations (i.e., those whose grandparents or great-grandparents were immigrants), only 14% speak a language other than English at home (Rumbaut, 2004). At the same time, preferring English does not mean that immigrant youth are truly fluent.

For first-generation immigrant youth, there often remains a gap between conversational English and true literacy. While conversational verbal proficiency can be developed within a couple of years, it takes, for most non-native English speakers, 5–7 years under optimal conditions to achieve the level of academic language skills necessary to compete academically with native-born peers.

The preference among second-generation immigrants to speak English holds true regardless of their environment, even if they live in heavily immigrant areas where the majority around them speak a language other than English. They also adopt styles of a presentation of self that allow them to "fit in" with established residents, i.e., with those who were born in the United States to non-immigrant parents (see, for example, Olsen, 1997; Stepick, 1998; Suárez-Orozco, 1989; Suárez-Orozco et al., 2008). The children of immigrants listen to American popular music, dress according to current American youth styles, speak slang, and eat American fast food. By appearances and associated public behaviors, they have assuredly assumed an American identification.

Identity Labels versus Behavioral Acculturation

Paradoxically, at the same time as children of immigrants come to prefer English, American music, and American clothing, the labels they use to describe their identity become more focused on national origin and less on being American. As the children of immigrants go through high school, they generally and gradually come to recognize that, although they may act American, they are reminded by others that they are not solely or thoroughly American. When they are just entering high school, some children of immigrants use the simple label, "American," to identify themselves, and some others use peculiarly American pan-ethnic labels such as African American or Latino. We say peculiarly American because these pan-ethnic labels are generally unknown, or at least not used, in the home countries of these children's parents. As they move through adolescence, many choose a hyphenated label, such as Mexican-American or Chinese-American. However, by the time the same youth are graduating from high school, very few choose an identity label of simply American, and fewer also identify with the pan-ethnic labels. Most still choose a hyphenated label, but many more claim their parents' national-origin labels, such as

Mexican or Haitian, without the hyphen (Portes & Rumbaut, 2001). Thus, in terms of ethnic self-identity labels, there is a movement away from American and toward national origins. Children of immigrants have learned to see themselves within an America that is not a melting pot but instead is composed of peoples of diverse origins.

Not only do the children of immigrants perceive America as multiethnic, but there is also a growing recognition that the processes involved in becoming American are diverse. Immigrant parents generally encourage their children to retain at least some aspects of their homeland culture – and these efforts generally produce mixed results. Many children of immigrants retain and emphasize some of their parents' cultural heritage, but how much and which parts vary considerably. In general, for example, those whose parents are native Spanish speakers are more likely to retain knowledge of Spanish, even if they do prefer to speak in English (Kasinitz et al., 2008; Portes & Rumbaut, 2006). On the other hand, children of Chinese immigrants are especially unlikely to speak their parents' language (Kasinitz et al., 2008). No matter what language their parents speak, the children of immigrants are unlikely to be literate in their parents' language even when they do understand and speak it (Portes, & Rumbaut, 2006; C. Suárez-Orozco et al., 2008).

Selective Acculturation

Many immigrant parents view at least some aspects of American culture as undesirable, even dangerous. Immigrant parents, for example, often are uncomfortable with public displays of sexuality common in US mass media and often embodied in young women's dress. Immigrant parents fear that such displays may produce premature sex and unwanted pregnancies and thus derail their hopes for their children's education (Stepick, 1998; Warikoo, 2005). Immigrant parents also often fear that American youth do not value and put enough effort into their education. Accordingly, many immigrant parents do not want their children interested in sexuality and peer social life instead of studying and do not want their children to Americanize in this fashion (Lopez, 2003; Stepick, 1998). Children of Asian immigrants, particularly those from China, Korea, Vietnam, and India, largely resist these aspects of Americanization and maintain a strong focus on education (Gibson, 1989; Louie, 2004, 2006; Zhou, 2007). Zhou and Bankston (1994, 1996), for example, observed that Vietnamese adolescents were constantly reminded by parents of their duty to show respect for their elders, to take care of younger siblings, to work hard, and to base decisions upon approval of parents, a trait generally referred to as filial piety.

To account for the differential retention of their parents' cultural heritage among Sikhs living in northern California, Gibson (1989) created the concept of selective acculturation. Within this concept, the aspects of immigrant culture that young people retain most notably include respect for education and respect for authority. At the same time, many children of immigrants from Asia selectively Americanize as their parents expect them to learn English and succeed in American schools. Children of immigrants also often incorporate selected aspects of expressive culture from their parents' homeland into their day-to-day lives in the United States. Heritage music from their parents' homeland culture is especially likely to be incorporated into the second generation's repertoire of cultural expressions (see McCann, 2004 on Brazil; Simonett, 2001 on Mexico; Wong, 2004 on Asian Americans). Music is perhaps the element of foreign cultures that Americans most readily accept and integrate, thereby producing musical genres of various origins, yet which are part of the American arts. Immigrants take advantage of America's interest in and ability to absorb different musical styles and use music to imagine their family homeland and assert their place in it as well as in the host society (Flores, 2005; Pacini-Hernandez & Garofalo, 2004). As detailed in the section on conceptualizing multiple identities, selective acculturation can be empirically complex.

Transnational Identities

One aspect of identity was not emphasized in studies of earlier waves of immigrants: transnationalism, that is lives and identities that span national borders. Piore (1979) demonstrated that as much as one-fourth of Italian migrants during the late nineteenth and early twentieth centuries to the United States returned home after a brief stay in the United States and many of those later returned again to the United States, engaging in circular migration back and forth between Italy and the United States. Nevertheless, the focus of research on Italian and other European flows to the United States 100 years ago was on those who settled. With the wave of immigration that began in 1965, studies have focused not only on settlers, but also those who move back and forth, i.e., transnational migrants. The most obvious transnational actors are perhaps merchants who buy goods in their homelands, transport them to the United States for sale, and then take US goods back to their homeland for sale there. Many other migrants also structure their lives across borders, some for religious reasons, some for family or for political reasons. Logically, others could be considered transnational actors, such as seasonal migrant workers, international businesspeople, and international students. These groups are usually not included as immigrants, however, because the emphasis in transnational studies is on people who have demonstrated some form of commitment to settlement, even if settlement is split between two locations. These other groups are considered to be temporary visitors to the United States rather than permanent migrants. Transnationalism has become the focus of considerable research (see, for example, Basch, Glick-Schiller, & Blanc-Szanton, 1994; Glick-Schiller & Fouron, 2001; Kearney, 1995; Levitt & Jaworsky, 2007; Mahler, 1995).

Most migrants living some form of transnational existence are first-generation immigrants, as they are likely to have deeper ties to their homeland than their second-generation children who, by definition, have been socialized primarily in the United States. Nevertheless, the extent and ease of ties to the homeland in a globalized world linked by cell phones, the Internet, and relatively inexpensive air travel affect everyone. And, although most children of immigrants do not maintain significant actual transnational lives, some do this. Many experience significant sentimental ties that affect their sense of identity (Levitt & Waters, 2003).

Even those who never go back to their ancestral homes are frequently raised in households where people, values, goods, and claims from somewhere else are present on a daily basis (Fouron & Glick-Schiller, 2002; Pries, 2004). They may develop the skills and social connections to become transnational activists if and when they choose to do so during a particular life-cycle stage. In the meantime, they participate in at least some activities that emphasize their homeland, such as family celebrations or simply receiving visits of family and friends from the homeland.

In South Florida, children of West Indian immigrants are likely to feel "at home in both cultures," and West Indians and Colombians in particular have been found to most frequently visit their parents' homeland (Haller & Landolt, 2005). Although there has not been much research on the relationship between transnational activities and identity among the children of immigrants, for the first generation, transnational activities and immigrant political integration have been found to complement each other rather than conflict with one another. Some studies have found that transnational and US-focused political activities often appear together and even reinforce each other (DeSipio, 2006; Portes, Escobar, & Arana, 2009). Thus, transnational actors express an attachment and identity that is both American and supportive of their homeland. To draw an analogy from the descendents of the first Great Wave of immigrants, American Jews can easily be both American and supportive of Israel. Similarly, first- and second-generation immigrants can be involved in political activities in their homeland, yet still be engaged in US politics.

Conceptualizing Multiple Identities

For some immigrant youth, the multiple forces of Americanization, selective acculturation, and transnational ties can be confusing and troubling. How can and how should we represent these multiple dimensions of identity? In popular culture, it is often presumed that an individual can only maintain a singular national identity, as evidenced after the United States entered World War I when German Americans were forced to become 100% American, and quickly complied with demands to abandon their German schools, German associations, and other obvious aspects of their German cultural roots. Similar fears about loyalty resulted in the internment of Japanese Americans during World War II. After the Civil Rights struggle of the 1960s and the resulting rise in tolerance and even celebration of multiculturalism, some parts of American society encourage complex identities, whereas others still expect individuals to have a simple, singular identity.

Sociologists and anthropologists agree that identities are complex, but they have not reached a consensus on how to represent the complexity. Many have used the term "hybrid" to reflect the combination of elements from different sources. Close ethnographic observation reveals that many children of immigrants report some blending or hyphenated identities, or embrace a pan-ethnic identity rather than one tied to a specific nationality (Espiritu, 2003; Lopez, 2003; Perez, 2001). Hybridity does indeed capture a significant component of the empirical observations of immigrant identity described above. The children of immigrants, for example, learn to speak English and express an appreciation for American institutions such as education and politics, while simultaneously often practising the same religion and forms of worship that their parents did in their homeland, understanding their parents' native language, and eating their homeland cuisine. Hybrid, however, seems to imply that identity may be fixed, singular, and coherently integrated. The empirical research reveals that identity may vary according to context (cf. Huynh, Nguyen, & Benet-Martínez, Chapter 35,

this volume) and becomes transformed as part of the adolescent psychological development process. How this occurs is described in the next section.

Although the concept of selective acculturation may help explain why some immigrant youth do exceptionally well educationally, taken as a sole explanation it also tends to simplify the complexity of the process of becoming American. New York immigrant youth, for example, report they do not feel fully a part of their immigrant parents' homeland or US ethnic communities, nor do they see themselves as fully "American" – by which they mean established resident Whites whom they know primarily through television. Nevertheless, they do not fret over living between different worlds. They believe they can pick and choose which cultural elements best work in particular situations (Kasinitz et al., 2004, 2008). In the process, in terms of behavioral acculturation, it may be said they have become American.

One limit inherent in believing that children of immigrants can pick and choose cultural elements in their lives is that it tends to overemphasize the choice the children of immigrants have in adopting an identity. Although children of immigrants may choose what music to listen to or what food to eat, they cannot choose the color of their skin. Whereas children of West Indians may elect to maintain their parents' British-inflected accent, they may still be perceived and treated by others as no different from African Americans (Waters, 1999a). Although South Americans may know nothing about Mexico, they may still be treated as no different from Mexicans. In short, wherever prejudice and discrimination exists toward native minorities or particular immigrant groups, children of immigrants who are similar to, or mistaken for, the native minorities or the particular immigrant groups remain subject to the same discrimination.

Another way in which selective acculturation and hybridization approaches tend to oversimplify the understanding of the identities and behaviors of immigrants and their children is by overlooking the reciprocal impact of immigrants and their children on American society and culture. It is important to recognize that, because second-generation immigrants are American by birth, they are also helping to remake what it means to be American (Alba & Nee, 2003; Warikoo, 2005). Just as pizza and wonton soup have become part of American cuisine, contemporary children of immigrants are contributing their own particular flavors to the range of what it means to be American. Their contributions are evident in popular music through such musicians as Carlos Santana (Mexico), Gene Simmons (Israel), Gloria Estefan (Cuba), and Wyclef Jean (Haiti). In the everyday lives of second-generation immigrant adolescents, ethnic displays of identity contribute to always-fluid dimensions of social status, including, for example, sari-themed clothing or henna dyes on skin, which are approximated into an American style termed Indo-chic (Warikoo, 2005).

Field research reveals that, regardless of what ethnic self-identity label a child of immigrants may choose, he or she actually performs different identities in different contexts (see Huynh et al., Chapter 35, this volume). In school, a child of immigrants may enact an American identity and, indeed, after a youth has been in the United States for sometime between 6 months and a year, it is often impossible for outsiders (and occasionally even insiders, such as teachers and principals) to know from outward appearances which children are immigrants and which are natives (See Stepick et al., 2001). But outside of school, a youth often performs a different identity. On Sundays, which are generally focused on family activities, the children of immigrants typically reveal their immigrant origins. They often attend church with their parents, speak their parents' language with adult, first-generation immigrants, eat traditional foods, and listen to music from their parents' homeland. Much like the "unmeltable" White ethnics described by Moynihan and Glazer (1970), in particular contexts these second-generation immigrants display their ethnic origins. Yet, in other contexts, they display or perform their American identity. For this reason, we prefer the phrase multiple identities or what others have called identifications to conceptualize the multiple dimensions of identity for immigrants and their children.

Causes of Assuming and Performing Particular Identities

What are the forces that produce particular conceptions and performances of identity in particular contexts? At a general level, the performance of different aspects and dimensions of identity reflects the dialectic between immigrants' own self-attribution (i.e., internal self-categorization) and socially defined or ascriptive conditions specific to the social worlds in which they are embedded (in psychology, Berry, 2005; and in sociology and anthropology, Vertovec, 2001; Wimmer, 2004). More particularly, behavioral expressions of identity further reflect what forces are the most powerful in an individual's immediate, local lived context. Immigration studies conceptualize this context as the context of reception, i.e., the opportunities available to immigrants and how immigrants are treated by members of the host society (Portes & Böröcz, 1989; Portes & Rumbaut, 2006). If immigrants are welcomed, and if they are treated with respect, then they are more likely to identify with the host population. If on the other hand, they encounter prejudice and discrimination, they are likely to respond with reactive ethnicity, i.e., the development of defensive identities that highlight the positive aspects of their differences. When immigrants confront discrimination, there is a tendency to reaffirm the collective worth of the in-group by drawing an even stronger protective boundary around it, that is, by identifying even more strongly with ethnic traditions and maintaining boundaries from the host society [Rumbaut & Portes, 2001, also see Spears (Chapter 9, this volume) on social identity processes and Licata et al. (Chapter 38, this volume) on similar processes within European contexts].

The context of reception varies significantly by geographic level: from the national level attitudes and policies toward immigrants in general and toward specific national-origin groups down to the regional and local levels of an immigrant's face-to-face relationships in places such as neighborhoods and schools. Immigrants may confront prejudice at the national level yet be welcomed and accommodated locally. Immigrants may also be initially welcomed but subsequently encounter negative policy shifts or new social stereotypes that are rejecting.

Current anti-immigrant attitudes and fervor have been a dominant political theme in the United States since at least the mid-1990s when the state of California passed several referenda that attempted to discriminate against immigrants, with one specifically focused on denying educational, welfare, and health services to undocumented immigrants. California's Proposition 187, which was passed in 1994, mandated that teachers, doctors, social workers, and police check the immigration status of all persons seeking access to public education and health services from publicly funded agencies, and deny services to those in the United States illegally (Alvarez & Butterfield, 2000). Also in California, Proposition 209, passed in 1996, prohibits public institutions from considering race, sex, or ethnicity in, for example, hiring employees or admission to state universities. Although supporters labeled Proposition 209 the "California Civil Rights Initiative," its goal was to eliminate affirmative action (Myers, 2007). Proposition 227, passed in 1998, requires that those California public school students in English as a Second Language (ESL) classes be placed in structured English immersion for a period "not normally to exceed 1 year," then be transferred to mainstream classrooms taught "overwhelmingly in English." This proposition also gave parents the possibility to request alternative programs to ESL for their children, however, the availability of waivers and information to parents has been a challenge in the implementation of this proposition (Crawford, 1997; Johnson & Martinez, 2000).

In the midst of these state legislative actions against immigrants, the federal government also boosted efforts to intercept illegal immigrants along the United States-Mexico border. In spite of the increased federal resources on the border, a vigilante group, the Minutemen, emerged and claimed that they would patrol the border because the US federal forces were too ineffective in their estimation. Bedolla (2000, 2005) indicates that anti-immigrant movements produced an ethnic

reaction among not only immigrants, but also native minorities, particularly those of Latino descent who shared a similar ethnic and working-class background with the targeted immigrants. In the first few years of the 2000s, similar reactive ethnicity was evidenced in massive demonstrations by immigrants throughout the United States as the US Congress considered immigration reform in which some proposals would restrict immigration and deny federal benefits to immigrants already in the United States.

Not all immigrants responded with such forceful reactive ethnicity. Demonstrations in Miami were proportionally much smaller than in New York, Chicago, or Los Angeles, in spite of the fact that Miami proportionally has more immigrants. The reason is that the national and local reception proffered to Miami's primary immigrant group, Cubans, has always been much more open and "welcoming" than that offered to other immigrants in the United States. The organizers of the demonstrations in Miami struggled to unify the longstanding cleavages between Miami's immigrant communities (Vanderkooy & Nawyn, 2011, forthcoming). Early waves of Cuban refugees received unparalleled federal benefits that underwrote the transformation of Miami into one of the focal economic and urban centers of the Caribbean and even all of Latin America (Pedraza-Bailey, 1985; Stepick & Grenier, 1993). Locally, Cuban immigrants and their children have become the most powerful group, superseding the previous White American oligarchy (Portes & Stepick, 1993). Cubans have been able to create a local context in which speaking Spanish is not a negative attribute but is, in fact, an advantage: and where being an immigrant or the child of an immigrant is not demeaned, but rather is accepted as a point of pride. Within Miami, Cuban immigrants and their children experience inclusion, not exclusion. As a result, the children of Cuban immigrants express their sense of belonging in much the same ways that White American youth do throughout the rest of the United States. The children of Cuban immigrants in Miami proprietarily take their central place in society for granted. Only when an event or travel moves them out of the comfort of their region where their community is dominant are they forced to reflect on their sense of belonging or identity.

The first dramatic event that caused Cuban immigrants to recognize that they were not fully American was the Mariel boatlift that, within a few months in 1980, brought over 125,000 refugees from Cuba to South Florida, including some released from Cuba's prisons. The overwhelming influx produced a backlash against all Cubans in the United States, including the creation of the US English Only movement which began in Miami-Dade County. In turn, this backlash prompted strong reactive ethnicity among Miami's Cuban immigrants that had a tremendous local political impact. Within less than a decade, the Cuban community mobilized to elect first- or second-generation Cubans to every significant local political position including mayors, city and county commissions, local school boards, state legislature, and the US House of Representatives. By the early 1990s, Cubans had thoroughly established themselves as the most powerful local group (Stepick & Dutton Stepick, 2001). This created a context of reception for becoming American unlike anywhere else in the United States.

Miami Cubans so thoroughly dominate the local scene in Miami-Dade County that the children of Cuban immigrants often do not realize that they may hold views and values different from the rest of America. They often presume everyone outside of Miami is not so different from them, at least until they are forced to confront "mainstream American" perspectives and opinions about events and issues close to home. The case of Elián Gonzalez, the Cuban rafter boy who became the focus of national attention in 2000–2001, jolted Miami Cuban youth into the realization of how much they may have been taking for granted (Stepick, Grenier, Castro, & Dunn, 2003). Elián Gonzalez was a 6-year-old Cuban boy who survived a raft trip to Miami while his mother drowned and his father remained in Cuba. His father and the Cuban government demanded the return of the child to Cuba, with which the US government eventually complied. In the meantime, the Miami

Cuban community insisted that Elián remain in Miami rather than return to Cuba (Acosta, 2001; De La Torre, 2003; Stepick et al., 2003). Many Miami Cuban youth, who had not been previously politically engaged and who had conceived of themselves as American, suddenly participated in demonstrations and emphasized their Cuban roots. After Elián was returned to Cuba, Vivian, a Cuban teen, concluded "The Americans [meaning non-Hispanic Whites], it's like this is their country and we're not part of this. We are visitors. Just that we're not Americans. We're from other places. We don't belong here."[3] Miguel, a Nicaraguan, added, "I think what she's trying to say is no matter how hard you try, you're always going to be from another country. We're not going to be American. We're going to be Latin."

The Elián case shocked the children of Cuban immigrants in Miami into an awareness of their "otherness" vis-à-vis the national social and political landscape. This event also affected their Nicaraguan peers, who similarly had been largely politically unengaged. The Nicaraguan youth were forced into acknowledging the uniqueness of the region where they lived and their differentness from non-Hispanic Whites. Above all, they were shocked into a new awareness that others in the broader US society beyond Miami might hold different views of the world and of them. They were forced to reflect upon their sense of belonging to their local place as well as their place in the broader US society. The Elián event highlighted how the local context of reception is critical in developing a sense of what it is to be both an American and a child of immigrants, and it also indicated how dramatic events can challenge and change one's sense of identity and self. This event also revealed the limits of Cuban local power. Although, generally, Cubans and other local Latinos could become American on their own terms, the broader society and particularly the national government could enforce its terms when it so decided.

Cubans in Miami represent a case of an extremely positive context of reception. Cuban immigrants automatically receive permanent residency in the United States one year after they set foot on American soil. Although occasionally other Latino adults in Miami complain that Cubans have all the power, at the same time, Latinos from South America and much of the rest of the Americas recognize that in Miami, they can become part of the United States without having to adapt to White American culture. In particular, they do not have to learn English in order to succeed or simply to get by with daily living. In contrast to much of the United States where Latino students report frequent discrimination (Lopez, 2003; Olsen, 1997; Suárez-Orozco, 1989; Valenzuela, 1999), Nicaraguan students, for example, in a local high school maintained that teachers did not discriminate against them, "because they (the teachers) are Hispanic, too, or they're of Hispanic descent" (Konczal, 2002).

However, non-Latino immigrants in Miami, such as Haitians, must contend with a very different context of reception that discriminates and expresses prejudices toward their language, culture, and often their skin color. In spite of a generally pro-immigrant sentiment at the local county level in Miami, Haitian youth have endured extreme and sometimes violent social and cultural discrimination. The US government has routinely sought to discourage Haitians from coming to the United States by using the US Coast Guard to intercept boats off the shores of Haiti that may be headed for the United States. These efforts to intercept Haitians date back to 1981. In 1994, it was extended to interdict Cubans, too. However, for those not interdicted at sea and who make it to US shores, Cubans are allowed to stay and almost all Haitians are incarcerated or sent back to Haiti. Individual Haitians are almost never granted asylum or refugee status regardless of either general political chaos or evidence of individual persecution back in Haiti (Stepick, 1998). Instead, the government jails without parole Haitians who do make it to the United States without a visa and claim that they want to stay. Negative treatment of Haitians by the US Government predates this internment policy; during the 1980s, the US government also mistakenly branded Haitians as public health risks. First, the government claimed that Haitians were bringing tuberculosis into the United States, and then it claimed that Haitians

were one of the sources of the HIV/AIDS virus (George, 1978; Mohl, 1987; Stepick, 1998).

At the more local level, Haitians confront further prejudice and discrimination from the general population, who commonly identifies them as poor and without skills, and undeserving of residence in the United States (Stepick, 1998). The result has been a delayed reactive ethnicity. Younger second-generation Haitian children often feel so stigmatized that they actually hide their Haitian heritage, attempting to pass as Bahamian or African American in order to escape discrimination. Older adolescents, once they have learned how to perform an American identity, such as playing US sports or performing well in school, often re-discover their Haitian heritage and display it proudly (Stepick, 1998; Stepick et al., 2001).

Proximal Hosts and Native Minorities

The particular English accent and vocabulary that the children of immigrants develop, their specific clothing styles, the precise music they prefer, and identity label they adapt depends on where they are in America, who lives in their neighborhood, who attends their schools, and what kind of Americans they interact with most frequently and intensely. Although general American culture, through such media as movies and television, influences immigrants, even more important are face-to-face interactions in one's immediate social environment. Waters (1994, 1999a) has labeled this the "proximal host," i.e., those native-born individuals and earlier immigrants who constitute the social environment that surrounds and most affects immigrants and their children.

Because many immigrants reside in urban areas, often the proximal hosts for the children of immigrants are American minorities – such as African Americans, Latinos, and Asian Americans. There is frequently a difference between the way the immigrant parents and their children perceive and relate to American minorities. Immigrant parents are keenly aware of the stigmatized status of poor, particularly inner-city

African Americans, and they accordingly often distance themselves from them. First-generation immigrant West Indians and Haitians, for example, often prefer to distinguish themselves from African Americans by proclaiming a national identity, such as Jamaican or Haitian (Rogers, 2006; Stepick, 1998; Vickerman, 1998; Waters, 1994, 1999b). This positional identity has also been observed in the case of Dominican immigrants who are generally black by US standards, but who also speak Spanish. They frequently choose to emphasize their Hispanic/Latino identity over a black identity, also as a means to avoid the prejudice and discrimination directed toward poor African Americans (Bailey, 2001, 2007).

Many children of immigrants, however, come to know American minorities far more closely than White Americans, because they attend school with them and grow up with them. Although they occasionally exhibit their parents' fears and negative stereotypes, children of immigrants are much more likely to identify with their American minority peers. Both Haitians and African Americans, for example, acutely experience and astutely assess racism in the United States. The struggle against racism allies African Americans with Haitians. Whenever the US government jails newly arrived Haitians, refusing them the legal immigration status that the US government extends to Cubans, both African Americans and Haitians interpret the actions as based upon racism. Similarly, both African Americans and Haitians in Miami celebrated the 2008 election of Barack Obama as a victory against racism (Castillo et al., 2008). One way in which Haitians and African Americans express their solidarity is through an assertion of a common African history. As a 15-year-old Haitian young man, also in Miami, suggested, "You should tell them we are African 'cause all-a-us came on the slave ships from Africa. Some got off here and some got off there. We're all African." The high school class he was addressing spontaneously erupted in applause (Stepick, 1998, p. 87).

This identification with native minorities among children of immigrants has been termed segmented assimilation (Portes & Zhou, 1993).

In a general sense, segmented assimilation refers to first- and second-generation immigrants of color and means they may assimilate into the segments of US society that they most physically resemble. Thus, Asian immigrant children may assimilate into the Asian American segment of American society; children of Black immigrants, on the other hand, assimilate into the African American segment, whereas children of immigrants from Spanish-speaking countries assimilate into Latino/Hispanic segments.

Some have further argued that some of the children of immigrants identify with and adopt the stereotypical values associated with some poor inner-city youth involved in oppositional values and behaviors, such as demeaning education, being rebellious or self-destructive, and valuing gang life and violent and often illegal activities (Portes & Zhou, 1993). The statistics on incarceration for the children of immigrants indicate that a small proportion of the children of immigrants do indeed drop out of school, and that some do become involved in illegal activities similar (and sometimes identical) to that of some American minority youth. The data also clearly indicate that the majority of the children of immigrants are certainly not involved in such behaviors, even in poor neighborhoods with poor schools (Kasinitz et al., 2008; Rumbaut, 2008). Thus, most children of immigrants do assimilate to a specific segment of American culture, but they do so selectively – generally choosing those elements that allow them to be accepted by their peers but that do not put them in danger.

Immigrant parents, unfortunately, are not always so discerning. They see the clothes that emphasize sexuality, hear the music that may glorify violence, and confront attitudes that defy authority. They often interpret this performance of one aspect of American identity as a rejection of parental values and goals for their children to obtain an education and to find a secure place in American society. The great majority of children of immigrants are more likely, however, to see these American styles as only one aspect of their identity (Kasinitz et al., 2008), one that allows them to be accepted by their peers, but one that does not necessarily compromise their commitment to education and to taking advantage of the opportunities that drew their parents to the United States in the first place.

Conclusion

The American people, and most of the world, think of the United States as a nation that has welcomed immigrants and has made it easy for them to become American. That image is only partially supported by the facts. Until at least the 1960s, the melting pot was really a mold of conformity to the norms established by WASP culture. Immigrants from England nearly instantly became American. Those from continental Europe found their labor welcome, but otherwise often initially encountered resistance to everything else about them. Yet, as "free white people," the possibility of becoming American often became a reality. For people who were non-White, the barriers were far more substantial, and even many Europeans, especially southern and eastern Europeans, were largely excluded from completely becoming American until after World War II, when the United States began to allow more immigrants to enter the country and when once again their labor became highly valued.

Beginning in the 1960s, to a degree never previously encountered in US history, some in the United States celebrated the diversity that immigrants brought with them and encouraged immigrants to become American without surrendering selective aspects of their homeland heritage [what has been called "biculturalism" (Berry, 2005, see also Huynh et al., Chapter 35, this volume)]. At the same time, others continued the nativist, anti-immigrant ways that have deep roots in American history and expressed concerns that these new immigrants did not want to, and could not truly, become American.

America is at a crossroads now where the second generation of the latest wave of primarily non-Europeans is attaining adulthood.

For those immigrants from non-White backgrounds, such as Black and Latino/Hispanic immigrants, it is unclear if they can ever be accepted or seen as simply "American" or whether they will become African American or Latino American. The emerging ethnographic realities indicate that they are becoming American in complex ways that reflect how America has treated them, their parents' efforts to maintain some of their heritage, and increased opportunities to live at least part of their lives transnationally across borders. They are joining the American workforce; they are raising children who speak English; and they are taking part in the American political process. They know that they are American in ways far more fundamental than their parents who were born in another country. At the same time, they are holding onto selected aspects of their parents' culture and identity, and they recognize that they are not American in the same way as White Americans whose families have been in the United States for generations. This generation of immigrants' offspring are finding their place in American society. In the process, they are finding and asserting identities that are outside of the WASP ideal from which social norms have historically flowed in the United States. Through these multiple identities, whether they are reactive or not, this new cohort of immigrant Americans finds pride in difference and is assuredly changing what it means to become American.

Notes

1. We acknowledge that "American" should refer to all of the Americas from Canada to Argentina and Chile. Nevertheless, the most common usage is for it to refer more narrowly to the United States of America, a usage we adopt in this chapter with apologies to those from other nations in the Americas.

2. The phrase "White ethnic" is discussed more thoroughly later in this chapter.

3. All of these quotes come from focus groups with Nicaraguan and Cuban high school students in Miami. The broader project was part of an examination of the academic orientation of immigrant and native minority adolescents. For a description of the methodology, see Stepick (1995).

References

Acosta, I. (2001). *Boy exile turned saint: Elián Gonzalez as a contested religio-ideological symbol among Cuban-American Catholics.* Unpublished master's thesis, Miami: Florida International University.

Alba, R. D., & Nee, V. (1997). Rethinking assimilation theory for a new era of immigration. *International Migration Review, 31*, 826–874.

Alba, R. D., & Nee, V. (2003). *Remaking the American mainstream: Assimilation and contemporary immigration.* Cambridge, MA: Harvard University Press.

Alvarez, R. M., & Butterfield, T. L. (2000). The resurgence of nativism in California? The case of proposition 187 and illegal immigration. *Social Science Quarterly, 81*, 167–179.

Anderson, B. (1999). *Imagined communities: Reflections on the origin and spread of nationalism* (2nd ed.). London: Verso.

Bailey, B. (2001). Dominican-American ethnic/racial identities and United States social categories. *International Migration Review, 35*, 677–708.

Bailey, B. (2007). Shifting negotiations of identity in a Dominican American community. *Latino Studies, 5*(2), 157–181.

Basch, L., Glick-Schiller, N., & Blanc-Szanton, C. (1994). *Nations unbound: Transnational projects, postcolonial predicaments and deterritorialized nation-states.* Amsterdam: Gordon and Breach Science Publishers.

Bean, F. D., Brown, S. K., & Rumbaut, R. (2004). Mexican immigrant political and economic incorporation – *Working Paper 13.* San Diego, CA: The Center for Comparative Immigration Studies, University of California, San Diego.

Bean, F. D., & Stevens, G. (2003). *America's newcomers and the dynamics of diversity.* New York: Russell Sage Foundation.

Bedolla, L. G. (2000). They and we: Identity, gender and politics among Latino youth in Los Angeles. *Social Science Quarterly, 81*, 106–122.

Bedolla, L. G. (2005). *Fluid borders: Latino power, identity, and politics in Los Angeles.* Berkeley and Los Angeles, CA: University of California Press.

Berry, J. W. (2005). Acculturation: Living successfully in two cultures. *International Journal of Intercultural Relations, 29*, 697–712.

Billig, M. (1995). *Banal nationalism.* London: Sage.

Borjas, G. (1990). *Friends or strangers: The impact of immigrants on the U.S. economy.* New York: Basic Books.

Borjas, G. J. (2006). Making it in America: Social mobility in the immigrant population. *The Future of Children, 16*(2), 55–71.

Brooks, D. (2007, July 6). The end of integration, *The New York Times.*

Butler, E. B. (1909). *Women and the trades: Pittsburgh, 1907–1908.* New York: Russell Sage Foundation.

Castells, M. (1997). *The power of identity.* Oxford: Blackwell.

Castillo, A., Duran, J. D., Elfrink, T., Garcia-Roberts, G., O'Neill, N., & Strouse, C. (2008, November 6). Miami loses; of course, Tuesday's presidential result made history. And we celebrated. But all is not well, *Miami New Times.*

Cowen, M., & Shenton, R. (1995). The invention of development. In J. Crush (Ed.), *The power of development* (pp. 27–43). London: Routledge.

Crawford, J. (1997). The campaign against Proposition 227: A post mortem. *Bilingual Research Journal, 21*(1), 1029.

de Crèvecoeur, M. G. J. (1782). *Letters from an American farmer* (reprint 1925 ed.). New York: Albert and Charles Boni.

De La Torre, M. A. (2003). *La lucha for Cuba: Religion and politics on the streets of Miami* Berkeley, CA: University of California Press.

DeSipio, L. (2006). Do home-country political ties limit Latino immigrant pursuit of US Civic engagement and citizenship?. In T. Lee, S. K. Ramakrishnan, R. Ramírez (Eds.), *Transforming politics, transforming America: The political and civic incorporation of immigrants in the United States* (pp. 106–126). Charlottesville, VA: University of Virginia Press.

Devos, T., & Banaji, M. R. (2005). American=white?. *Journal of Personality and Social Psychology, 88*, 447–466.

Doane, A. W., Jr. (1997). Dominant group ethnic identity in the United States: The role of hidden ethnicity in intergroup relations. *The Sociological Quarterly, 38*, 375–397.

Espiritu, Y. L. (2003). *Home bound: Filipino American lives across cultures, communities, and countries.* Berkeley, CA: University of California Press.

Flores, J. (2005). The Diaspora strikes back: Reflections on cultural remittances. *NACLA, 39*, 21–26.

Fouron, G. E., & Glick-Schiller, N. (2002). The generation of identity: Redefining the second generation within a transnational social field. In P. Levitt, M. Waters (Eds.), *The changing face of home: The transnational lives of the second generation* (pp. 168–208). New York: Russell Sage Foundation.

Franchot, J. (1994). *Roads to Rome: The antebellum protestant encounter with Catholicism.* Berkeley, CA: University of California Press.

Gaines, B. J., & Cho, W. K. T. (2004). On California's 1920 alien land law: The psychology and economics of racial discrimination. *State Politics and Policy Quarterly, 4*(3), 271–293.

Gans, H. J. (1992). Second-generation decline: Scenarios for the economic and ethnic futures of the post-1965 American immigrants. *Ethnic and Racial Studies, 15,* 173–192.

Gans, H. J. (2007). Ethnic and racial identity. In M. C. Waters, R. Ueda (Eds.), *The new Americans: A guide to immigration since 1965.* (pp. 98–109). Cambridge: Harvard University Press.

George, P. S. (1978). Colored town: Miami's black community, 1896–1930. *Florida Historical Quarterly, 56*(April), 432–447.

Gettys, L. (1934). *The law of citizenship in the United States.* Chicago: The University of Chicago Press.

Gibson, M. A. (1989). *Accommodation without assimilation: Sikh immigrants in an American high school.* Ithaca, NY: Cornell University Press.

Giddens, A. (1990). *The consequences of modernity.* Stanford, CA: Stanford University Press.

Glazer, N., & Moynihan, D. P. (1970). *Beyond the melting pot: The Negroes, Puerto Ricans, Jews, Italians, and Irish of New York City* (2nd ed.). Cambridge, MA: The MIT Press.

Glick Schiller, N., & Fouron, G. E. (1998). Transnational lives and national identities: The identity politics of Haitian immigrants. *Comparative Urban and Community Research, 6*(1), 130–161.

Glick-Schiller, N., & Fouron, G. (2001). *Georges woke up laughing: Long-distance nationalism and the search for home.* Durham: Duke University Press.

Gonzalez, N. L. (1969). *The Spanish-Americans of New Mexico: A heritage of pride.* Albuquerque, NM: University of New Mexico Press.

Gordon, M. M. (1964). *Assimilation in American life: The role of race, religion, and national origins.* New York: Oxford University Press.

Gould, S. J. (1981). *The mismeasure of man.* New York: W.W. Norton & Company.

Grant, M. (1916). *The passing of the great race* (reprint 1970 ed.). New York: Arnot Press and the New York Times.

Gratton, B. (2002). Race, the children of immigrants, and social science theory. *Journal of American Ethnic History, 21*(4), 74–84.

Greeley, A. M. (1971). *Why can't they be like us? America's white ethnic groups.* New York: E. P. Dutton.

Griswold del Castillo, R. (1992). *The treaty of Guadalupe Hidalgo: A legacy of conflict.* Oklahoma City: University of Oklahoma Press.

Hale, H. E. (2004). Explaining ethnicity. *Comparative Political Studies, 37*(4), 258–485.

Haller, W., & Landolt, P. (2005). The transnational dimensions of identity formation: Adult children of immigrants in Miami. *Ethnic and Racial Studies, 28,* 1182–1214.

Haney-Lopez, I. F. (2006). *White by law: The legal construction of race* (2nd ed.). New York: New York University Press.

Harris, A. L., Jamison, K. M., & Trujillo, M. H. (2008). Disparities in the educational success of immigrants: An assessment of the immigrant effect for Asians and Latinos. *The Annals of the American Academy of Political and Social Science, 620,* 90–114.

Haynes, J. M. (2001). Saying we're sorry? New federal legislation and the forgotten promises of the treaty of Guadalupe Hidalgo. *The Scholar: St. Mary's Law Review on Minority Issues, 3,* 2.

Herberg, W. (1960). *Protestant–Catholic–Jew: An essay in American religious sociology.* Garden City, NY: Anchor Books.

Higham, J. (1988). *Strangers in the land: Patterns of American nativism 1860–1925* (2nd ed.). New Brunswick, N.J: Rutgers University Press.

Hing, B. O. (2004). *Defining America through immigration policy.* Philadelphia: Temple University Press.

Hirschman, C. (1994). Problems and prospects of studying immigrant adaptation from the 1990 population census: From generational comparisons to the process of "Becoming American". *International Migration Review, 28,* 690–713.

Hirschman, C. (2001). The educational enrollment of immigrant youth: A test of the segmented-assimilation hypothesis. *Demography, 38*(3), 317–336.

Huntington, S. P. (2004a). The Hispanic challenge. *Foreign Policy, 141*(March/April), 30–45.

Huntington, S. P. (2004b). *Who are we?: The challenges to America's national identity.* New York: Simon & Schuster.

Johnson, K. R., & Martinez, G. A. (2000). Discrimination by proxy: The case of proposition 227 and the ban on bilingual education. *University of California Davis Law Review, 33*(Summer), 1227–1273.

Jones, M. A. (1960). *American immigration.* Chicago: University of Chicago Press.

Kasinitz, P., Mollenkopf, J., & Waters, M. (Eds.). (2004). *Becoming New Yorkers: Ethnographies of the new second generation.* New York: Russell Sage Foundation.

Kasinitz, P., Mollenkopf, J. H., Waters, M. C., & Holdaway, J. (2008). *Inheriting the city: The children of immigrants come of age.* New York: Russell Sage Foundation.

Kearney, M. (1995). The local and the global: The anthropology of globalization and transnationalism. *Annual Review of Anthropology, 24,* 547–565.

Kennedy, R. J. R. (1944). Single or triple melting-pot? Intermarriage trends in New Haven, 1870–1940. *The American Journal of Sociology, 49*(4), 331–339.

Kilic, Z. (2007). Reluctant citizens? Belonging and immigrant identification in the era of transnationalism. *Dissertation Abstracts International, A: The Humanities and Social Sciences, 67*(11), 4347–4347.

Konczal, L. N. (2002). *The academic orientation of first and second generation Nicaraguan immigrant adolescents.* Unpublished doctoral dissertation, Florida International University, Miami, FL.

Kroneberg, C. (2008). Ethnic communities and school performance among the new second generation in the United States: Testing the theory of segmented assimilation. *Annals of the American Academy of Political and Social Science*, *620*, 138–160.

Levitt, P., & Jaworsky, N. (2007). Transnational migration and beyond. *Annual Review of Sociology*, *33*, 129–156.

Levitt, P., & Waters, M. (Eds.). (2003). *Salsa and ketchup: The transnational lives of the second generation*. New York: Russell Sage Publications.

Lopez, N. (2003). *Hopeful girls, troubled boys*. New York: Routledge.

Louie, V. (2004). *Compelled to excel: Immigration, education, and opportunity among Chinese Americans*. Stanford, CA: Stanford University Press.

Louie, V. (2006). Second-generation pessimism and optimism: How Chinese and Dominicans understand education and mobility through ethnic and transnational orientations. *International Migration Review*, *40*, 537–572.

Mahler, S. J. (1995). *The dysfunctions of transnationalism*. Working Paper #73. New York: Russell Sage Foundation.

McCann, B. (2004). *Hello, hello Brazil: Popular music in the making of modern Brazil*. Durham, N.C: Duke University Press.

McKeown, J. E., & Chyatte, C. (1954). The behavior of fathers as reported by normals, neurotics, and schizophrenics. *American Catholic Sociological Review*, *15*(4), 332–340.

Menchaca, M. (2008). The anti-miscegenation history of the American southwest, 1837–1970. *Cultural Dynamics*, *20*(3), 279–318.

Migration Policy Institute. (2010a). Foreign-born population by region of birth as a percentage of the total foreign-born population, for the United States: 1960 to 2008. Retrieved May 25, 2010, from http://www.migrationinformation.org/datahub/charts/fb.2.shtml

Migration Policy Institute. (2010b). Frequently requested statistics on immigrants and immigration in the United States. Retrieved May 25, 2010, from http://www.migrationinformation.org/USfocus/display.cfm?id=714

Mohl, R. A. (1987). Black immigrants: Bahamians in early twentieth-century Miami. *Florida Historical Quarterly*, *65*(January), 271–297.

Morawska, E. (2001). Immigrants, transnationalism, and ethnicization: A comparison of this wave and the last. In G. Gerstle, J. Mollenkopf (Eds.), *E pluribus unum? Immigrants, civic life, and political incorporation* (pp. 175–212). New York: Russell Sage Foundation.

Myers, C. K. (2007). A cure for discrimination? Affirmative action and the case of California's proposition. *Industrial and Labor Relations Review*, *60*(3), 379–396.

Naturalization Act (1790) § 103.

Naturalization Act (1870) § CCLIV § 7.

Nederveen Pieterse, J. (2007). *Ethnicities and global multiculture: Pants for an octopus*. Lanham, MD: Rowman & Littlefield.

Nicolosi, A. M. (2001). "We do not want our girls to marry foreigners": Gender, race, and American citizenship. *NWSA Journal (National Women's Studies Association Journal)*, *13*(3), 1–21. Retrieved from http://www.iupress.indiana.edu/journals/nwsa/nws13-3.html.

Olsen, L. (1997). *Made in America: Immigrant students in our public schools*. New York: New Press.

Pacini-Hernandez, D., & Garofalo, R. (2004). The emergence of rap Cubano: An historical perspective. In S. Whitely, A. Bennett, S. Hawkins (Eds.), *Music, space, and place: Popular music and cultural identity* (pp. 89–107). Burlington, V.T: Ashgate.

Park, R. E. (1930). Social assimilation. In E. Seligman, A. Johnson (Eds.), *Encyclopedia of the social sciences*. New York: MacMillan.

Park, R. E., & Burgess, E. (1921). *Introduction to the science of sociology*. Chicago: University of Chicago Press.

Pedraza-Bailey, S. (1985). *Political and economic migrants in America: Cubans and Mexicans*. Austin, TX: University of Texas Press.

Perez, L. (2001). *Growing up in Cuban Miami: Immigration, the enclave, and new generations*. New York: Russell Sage Foundation.

Piore, M. J. (1979). *Birds of passage: Migrant labor ad industrial societies*. Cambridge: Cambridge University Press.

Portes, A., & Böröcz, J. (1989). Contemporary immigration: Theoretical perspectives on its determinants and modes of incorporation. *International Migration Review*, *23*, 606–630.

Portes, A., Escobar, C., & Arana, R. (2009). Divided or convergent loyalties?: The political incorporation process of Latin American immigrants in the United States. *International Journal of Comparative Sociology*, *50*(2), 103–136.

Portes, A., Fernández-Kelly, P., & Haller, W. J. (2005). Segmented assimilation on the ground: The new second generation in early adulthood. *Ethnic and Racial Studies*, *28*, 1000–1040.

Portes, A., & Rumbaut, R. G. (2001). *Legacies: The story of the immigrant second generation*. Berkeley, CA: University of California Press.

Portes, A., & Rumbaut, R. G. (2006). *Immigrant America: A portrait* (3rd ed.). Berkeley, CA: University of California Press.

Portes, A., & Schauffler, R. (1996). *Language and the second generation: Bilingualism yesterday and today*. New York: Russell Sage Foundation.

Portes, A., & Stepick, A. (1993). *City on the edge: The transformation of Miami*. Berkeley, CA: University of California Press.

Portes, A., & Zhou, M. (1993). The new second generation: Segmented assimilation and its variants. *The Annals of the American Academy of Political and Social Science*, *530*, 74–96.

Preston, J. (2007, May 22). With an immigration compromise committed to paper, the time for scrutiny begins. *The New York Times*.

Pries, L. (2004). Determining the causes and durability of transnational labour migration between Mexico and the United States: Some empirical findings. *International Migration Review, 42*(2), 3–39.

Rahier, J. M. (Ed.). (1999). *Representations of blackness and the performance of identities.* Westport, CT: Bergin & Garvey.

Rogers, R. R. (2006). *Afro Caribbean immigrants and the politics of incorporation: Ethnicity, exception, or exit.* New York: Cambridge University Press.

Rumbaut, R. G. (2004). Ages, life stages, and generational cohorts: Decomposing the immigrant first and second generations in the United States. *International Migration Review, 38*, 1160–1205.

Rumbaut, R. G. (2008). The coming of the second generation: Immigration and ethnic mobility in southern California. *Annals of the American Academy of Political and Social Science, 620*, 196–236.

Rumbaut, R. G., & Portes, A. (Eds.). (2001). *Ethnicities: Children of immigrants in America.* New York: Russell Sage Foundation.

Schlesinger, A. M., Jr. (1992). *The disuniting of America: Reflections on a multicultural society.* New York: W.W. Norton & Company.

Simonett, H. (2001). *Banda: Mexican musical life across borders.* Middletown, CT: Wesleyan University Press.

Spickard, P. (2007). *Almost all aliens: Immigration, race, and colonialism in American history and identity.* New York: Routledge.

Stepick, A. (1995). Academic orientation of immigrant and native-born minority adolescents: Research Proposal to the National Science Foundation.

Stepick, A. (1998). *Pride against prejudice: Haitians in the United States.* Boston: Allyn and Bacon.

Stepick, A., & Dutton Stepick, C. (2001). Power and identity: Miami Cubans. In M. Suárez-Orozco, C. Suárez-Orozco (Eds.), *Latinos: The research agenda* (pp. 75–92). Berkeley, CA: University of California Press.

Stepick, A., Dutton Stepick, C., Eugene, E., Teed, D., & Labissiere, Y. (2001). Shifting identities and intergenerational conflict: Growing up Haitian in Miami. In R. Rumbaut, A. Portes (Eds.), *Ethnicities: Children of immigrants in America* (pp. 229–266). Berkeley, CA: University of California Press.

Stepick, A., Dutton Stepick, C., & Labissiere, Y. (2008). South Florida's immigrant youth and civic engagement: Major engagement, minor differences. *Applied Developmental Science, 12*(2), 1–9.

Stepick, A., & Grenier, G. (1993). Cubans in Miami. In J. Moore, R. Rivera (Eds.), *In the barrios: Latinos and the underclass debate* (pp. 79–100). New York: Russell Sage Foundation.

Stepick, A., Grenier, G., Castro, M., & Dunn, M. (2003). *This land is our land: Immigrants and power in Miami.* Berkeley, CA: University of California Press.

Stocking, G. W. J. (1968). The critique of racial formalism in historical perspective. In G. W. Stocking (Ed.), *Race, culture and evolution: Essays in the history of anthropology* (pp. 161–196). New York: The Free Press.

Suárez-Orozco, C., Suárez-Orozco, M., & Todorova, I. (2008). *Learning a new land: Immigrant students in American society.* Cambridge, MA: Harvard University Press.

Suárez-Orozco, M. M. (1989). *Central American refugees and U.S. high schools: A psychosocial study of motivation and achievement.* Stanford, CA: Stanford University Press.

Teitelbaum, M. S. (1983). Immigration, refugees and foreign policy. *International Organization, 38*, 3.

Thomas, W. I., & Znaniecki, F. (1918). *The polish peasant in Europe and America; Monograph of an immigrant group.* Chicago: Gorham Press.

Valenzuela, A. (1999). *Subtractive schooling: U.S. Mexican youth and the politics of caring.* Ithaca, NY: State University of New York Press.

Vanderkooy, P., & Nawyn, S. (2011, forthcoming). Identifying the battle lines: Local-national tensions in organizing for comprehensive immigration reform. *American Behavioral Scientist.*

Vertovec, S. (2001). Transnationalism and identity. *Journal of Ethnic and Migration Studies, 27*, 573–582.

Vickerman, M. (1998). *West Indian immigrants and race.* Oxford, UK: Oxford University Press.

Warikoo, N. (2005). Gender and ethnic identity among second-generation Indo-Caribbeans. *Ethnic and Racial Studies, 28*, 803–831.

Waters, M. C. (1990). *Ethnic options: Choosing identities in America.* Berkeley, CA: University of California Press.

Waters, M. C. (1994). Ethnic and racial identities of second-generation black immigrants in New York City. *International Migration Review, 28*, 795–795.

Waters, M. C. (1996). Optional ethnicities: For whites only?. In S. Pedraza, R. Rumbaut (Eds.), *Origins and destinies: Immigration, race, and ethnicity in America* (pp. 444–454). Belmont, CA: Wadsworth Publishing Company.

Waters, M. C. (1999a). *Black identities: West Indian immigrant dreams and American realities.* New York: Russell Sage Foundation.

Waters, M. C. (1999b). Immigrant dreams and American realities: The causes and consequences of the ethnic labor market in American cities. *Work and Occupations, 26*(3), 352–364.

Weaver, G. (1970). Benjamin Franklin and the Pennsylvania Germans. In L. Dinnerstein, F. C. Jaher (Eds.), *The aliens: A history of ethnic minorities in America.* New York: Appleton-Century-Crofts.

Wimmer, A. (2004). Does ethnicity matter? Everyday group formation in three Swiss immigrant neighborhoods. *Ethnic and Racial Studies, 27*, 1–36.

Wimmer, A., & Glick Schiller, N. (2003). Methodological nationalism, the social sciences, and the study of migration: An essay in historical epistemology. *International Migration Review, 37*, 576–610.

Wong, B. P. (2005). *The Chinese in Silicon Valley: Globalization, social networks, and ethnic identity.* Lanham, MD: Rowman and Littlefield.

Wong, D. A. (2004). *Speak it louder: Asian Americans making music*. New York: Routledge.

Zhou, M. (2007). *Divergent origins and destinies: Children of Asian immigrants*. New York: Springer.

Zhou, M., & Bankston, C. (1994). Social capital and the adaptation of the second generation: The case of Vietnamese youth in New Orleans. *International Migration Review, 28*, 821–845.

Zhou, M., & Bankston, C. L., III. (1996). Social capital and the adaptation of the second generation: The case of Vietnamese youth in New Orleans. In A. Portes (Ed.), *The new second generation*. New York: Russell Sage Foundation.

Zucker, N. L., & Zucker, N. F. (1987). *The guarded gate: The reality of American refugee policy*. San Diego, CA: Harcourt Brace Jovanavich.

Identity, Immigration, and Prejudice in Europe: A Recognition Approach

38

Laurent Licata, Margarita Sanchez-Mazas, and Eva G.T. Green

Abstract

Social identity is a double-edged sword. On the one hand, identifying with a social group is a prerequisite for the sharing of common norms and values, solidarity, and collective action. On the other hand, in-group identification often goes together with prejudice and discrimination. Today, these two sides of social identification underlie contradictory trends in the way European nations and European nationals relate to immigrants and immigration. Most European countries are becoming increasingly multicultural, and anti-discrimination laws have been adopted throughout the European Union, demonstrating a normative shift towards more social inclusion and tolerance. At the same time, racist and xenophobic attitudes still shape social relations, individual as well as collective behaviour (both informal and institutional), and political positions throughout Europe. The starting point for this chapter is Sanchez-Mazas' (2004) interactionist approach to the study of racism and xenophobia, which in turn builds on Axel Honneth's (1996) philosophical theory of recognition. In this view, the origin of attitudes towards immigrants cannot be located in one or the other group, but in a dynamic of mutual influence. Sanchez-Mazas' approach is used as a general framework into which we integrate social psychological approaches of prejudice and recent empirical findings examining minority-majority relations. We particularly focus on the role of national and European identities as antecedents of anti-immigrant attitudes held by national majorities. Minorities' reactions to denials of recognition are also examined. We conclude by delineating possible social and political responses to prejudice towards immigrants.

At the very moment we are writing this chapter, about 200 undocumented immigrants – among them children – occupy a large sports hall at the Free University of Brussels in Belgium, where they took shelter after being expelled from a squat (i.e., illegally occupied dwelling) by the police

L. Licata (✉)
Social Psychology Unit, UniversitéLibre de Bruxelles, Bruxelles, Belgium
e-mail: licata@ulb.ac.be

S.J. Schwartz et al. (eds.), *Handbook of Identity Theory and Research*,
DOI 10.1007/978-1-4419-7988-9_38, © Springer Science+Business Media, LLC 2011

more than 3 months ago. These immigrants, like many others, are requesting the abolition of the barriers with which undocumented immigrants are confronted. They are supported by a committee of Belgian volunteers. Similar instances of collective claims from undocumented immigrants have been witnessed throughout Europe during the past two decades (see Düvell, 2008). Reactions from national majorities range from strong xenophobic reactions, where illegal immigrants are portrayed as a threat, to social support and political mobilization for their cause.

Originating from diverse parts of the world (especially from North and Central Africa, Latin America, the Middle East, and Eastern Europe), undocumented immigrants seek shelter in Western Europe for either political or economic reasons, or a combination of both. Some of them are fighting for basic rights: to obtain legal status that would give them the right to live in their new homelands, to have access to decent housing, to get a legal job, or to send their children to school. Whereas some members of the receiving societies contend that illegal immigrants have no right to enter the country's territory and should not be granted any rights, others support their claims on the basis of universal human rights (Steiner, 2009). In contrast, legal immigrants usually benefit from these basic rights, as well as from most civic rights. However, in most European countries, political rights such as voting at local, regional, national, or European elections are still restricted to nationals.[1] In turn, these rights are fully granted to naturalised immigrants, that is, immigrants or people of immigrant descent who are granted citizenship in the country to which they (or their parents) have immigrated. Nevertheless, even some of the cultural, ethnic, or religious practices of naturalised immigrants – such as the right to wear the Muslim headscarf in schools – are often considered by national majorities as lying outside the range of acceptable behaviour. In addition, despite their formal rights being recognised, both legal immigrants and nationals of immigrant descent still suffer from informal rejection from majority members, especially when their physical appearance or style of dress differentiates them from majority members. They still often face negative stereotypes, prejudice, and acts of discrimination.

In this chapter, drawing on Axel Honneth's (1996) philosophical theory of recognition, we present an interactionist approach to prejudice. This approach will be used as a general framework into which we will integrate social psychological approaches to prejudice and recent empirical findings. We particularly focus on the role of national and European identities as antecedents of anti-immigrant attitudes (see Schildkraut, Chapter 36, this volume, for an analysis of similar issues in the US context).

The Denial of, and Struggle for Recognition

To reach a better understanding of contemporary forms of prejudice, it is essential to define the broader societal context in which prejudice is embedded. First, expressing prejudice is but one of the numerous outcomes of the relationships between national majorities and immigrants. Some majority members support restrictive immigration and integration policies, express anti-immigrant prejudice, vote for xenophobic political parties, discriminate against immigrants, or even use violence against them. In contrast, other members of the same societies establish strong affective links (including marriage) with immigrants, donate their time and money to help them, or become involved in collective actions to support them. Second, there are different ways of expressing a negative attitude towards immigrants (Brown, 1995), and ascribing negative stereotypical traits to them is only one of these. For example, one can express a negative attitude towards an asylum seeker by supporting restrictive immigration criteria, and one can derogate a legal immigrant by supporting assimilationist integration policies. The recent vote of a majority of Swiss citizens in support of a law prohibiting the building of minarets (the towers of Mosques) is a case in point. Third, immigrant minorities also have claims related to culture, ethnicity, or religion — such as wearing headscarves in schools, funding religious schools, or being politically represented at local or national levels — that sometimes trigger individual or collective behaviour on the part of both the immigrant and majority groups. Whereas some immigrants remain silent, others engage in collective actions to obtain rights, fight against prejudice and discrimination, or participate in politics. These actions can then trigger prejudice towards or support for immigrants among national majority members. Thus, prejudice should also be conceived as a *reaction* to the actions of minorities and not only as *judgements* about the minority members' "essence". It is necessary to take the back-and-forth interactions between majorities and minorities into account in order to grasp some of the specificities of modern prejudice.

German philosopher Axel Honneth's (1996) theory of "The struggle for recognition", which Sanchez-Mazas (2004, 2007) has applied to the study of racism and xenophobia, provides such an interactionist view of majority-minority relationships. The main tenets of this theory connect majority and minority perspectives and provide a general framework in which social psychological theories of prejudice, as well as recent empirical findings, can be situated. Within this integrative framework, we posit that holding prejudiced attitudes towards immigrants is one of various ways of denying them recognition. Moreover, we regard minorities' reactions to these denials of recognition as fuelled by people's motivation to be symbolically recognised by others. This is similar to the goals of other modern social movements. Indeed, Honneth's (1996) theoretical framework was developed to understand the relationship between majorities and minorities in "modern societies" that is, societies based on the equality of rights, individual freedom, and democracy. We apply it here mainly to the context of the European Union. Nevertheless, the basic principles of this framework also apply to other contexts, such as the United States.

Honneth's (1996) interactionist view of social relationships traces back to George H. Mead's model of identity (Mead, 1934/1967; Serpe & Stryker, Chapter 10, this volume). Starting from the idea that humans are relational animals, Honneth contends that the individual's integrity and identity are shaped by recognition from similar others (Markovà, 1987). In line with this view, we propose a normative and sociopolitical framework that can be drawn upon for examining relations between national majorities and immigrants in contemporary societies, and for understanding prejudice against immigrants as an instance of denying recognition. By denying recognition in various forms, majorities exclude immigrants and people of immigrant descent from the rights and esteem that are granted by default to majority members.

According to Honneth (1996), normative integration in modern societies takes place in three distinct spheres of recognition, corresponding to three ways of relating to oneself and constructing one's personal and social identity. The *private sphere of love and friendship* refers to interpersonal relations such as friendship, romantic relationships, or family ties, and implies strong affective links among a limited number of persons. In democratic societies, the *legal sphere* is the domain where individuals are granted equal rights and moral obligations. To be granted these individual rights demonstrates to the individual that she/he is recognised by others as a morally responsible person. Finally, the *sphere of social esteem* refers to the mutual appreciation of subjects. Individuals judge each other as a function of the values, practices, and cultural identities represented in the surrounding society. People are evaluated positively to the extent that they are perceived as possessing the qualities and abilities that are required to contribute positively to the common practices valued in the group.

Whereas the sphere of love and friendship mainly relates to interpersonal relationships within social groups,[2] the two latter spheres – the legal sphere and the sphere of social esteem – are of particular interest for addressing intergroup relationships between immigrants and majority members, and accordingly we focus on these spheres here. Within these two spheres, individuals are recognised respectively as entitled to rights and as endowed with specific qualities and cultural identities. These spheres represent areas of dispute where minorities formulate demands aiming to satisfy their aspirations for integrity, autonomy, and agency, and where majorities can either grant or deny them recognition. For example, the history of race relations in the USA illustrates that Black people's access to equal rights gradually moved denial of recognition from the legal sphere to that of social esteem: having become full citizens, the Blacks were formally equal to Whites but were still denied social esteem during the Southern "Jim Crow" system of official discrimination. Moreover, the denial of social esteem in the form of racist prejudice did not fade out as a result of the removal of segregationist barriers after the Civil Rights Act of 1964.

The dynamics of claiming recognition, or responding to claims for recognition, may differ as a function of the sphere in which the struggle takes place. Given that struggles for legal recognition are often undertaken in the name of principles of justice acknowledged by the majority (i.e., equal rights), minority members may convince majority members to extend legal recognition to them. Struggles for recognition in the legal sphere are likely to mobilise majority members by highlighting the contradiction between egalitarian principles and discriminatory practices occurring in democratic societies (Katz & Hass, 1988; Myrdal, 1969; Sanchez-Mazas, 1996). In some cases, these struggles induce majority members to support the denied minority's cause, to regret the difficulties faced by minorities, and to act in the name of justice.

However, the transformations occurring in today's world – the importance of identities, political disengagement, the emerging notion of "clash of civilizations" between modern and traditional cultures (Huntington, 1996), and the development of multicultural societies – afford increasing importance to the sphere of social esteem. Whether or not individuals are granted rights, their social value is at stake. However, the informal denial of social esteem is even more salient when the targets of stigmatization benefit from equal formal rights. In modern societies, denials of recognition mostly take place in the sphere of social esteem, that is, in terms of individuals' social value, and in

informal relationships. This is why Honneth (2007) has labelled contemporary society as "The contempt society" – in which minorities struggle against denial of their dignity, of their contribution in society, and of their cultural identities – as opposed to the moral ideal of "The decent society" (Margalit, 1996) where majorities and minorities are recognised similarly. Unlike legal recognition, where people are granted rights regardless of their qualities (either as individuals or as members of social groups), recognition in the sphere of social esteem depends on informal social judgements. According to the dominant cultural frame of reference that prevails in modern societies, it is deemed legitimate to judge people according to their unique qualities, aptitudes, and contributions, rather than according to their belonging to social categories. Accordingly, prejudice towards members of social categories is expressed through the ascription of negative individual traits, in addition to the derogation of the group as a whole. Because individual qualities are at stake, prejudice is less likely to be recognised by the members of minority groups as *group-specific injustice*, compared to the case of deprivation of rights. As a result, group-based collective struggle for recognition is less likely to appear (Ellemers & Barreto, 2009).

The application of the recognition approach to racism and xenophobia has led Sanchez-Mazas (2004) to suggest that, in the case of immigration, a shift in recognition may take place through the transition from the legal barrier separating former immigrants from the receiving society to the citizenship obtained by people of immigrant descent. For example, in France, second/third-generation immigrants are often not recognised as true citizens, despite their access to formal citizenship, as they do not respond to the "cultural obligations" that the French model of integration prescribes in order to become a "true" French citizen (Koopmans & Kriesi, 1997). Such a shift suggests that majorities strive to maintain a social or symbolic distance from minorities even after the formal barriers have been removed, and it accounts for the expression of prejudice in terms of "cultural difference" or "cultural incompatibility".

Our approach can thus account for the changing nature of prejudice according to the cultural and historical context. It therefore complements theoretical contributions in the field of social psychology. Such theories provide keys for understanding general psychological processes that are pervasive across these contexts. We turn first to relevant theoretical contributions defining the basic processes that lie at the root of prejudice towards immigrants among majority group members. We broadly describe the historical and sociopolitical context (i.e., immigration and integration policies) in which the struggle for recognition between majority members and immigrants takes place in European societies, and we report relevant empirical results. Next, we address the immigrants' perspective in an attempt to identify some of the likely reactions to prejudice, and we report corresponding research results. We also discuss how the perspectives of majorities and minorities relate to each other.

Recognition from the Majority/Receiving Country Perspective: Social Psychological Roots of Prejudice

Several major social psychological theories have been drawn upon to understand the psychological roots of prejudice. We review theories of prejudice that focus on characteristics of intergroup relations, such as competition for scarce resources, or on groups' efforts to reach or maintain a positive social identity.

Structural Approaches

Structural approaches locate the causes of prejudice in the structure of intergroup relationships, which can be defined in terms of economic or power inequalities between groups, or in terms of the nature of their interactions (cooperation or competition).

Realistic conflict theory assumes that intergroup attitudes reflect the relationship (or conflict) between groups' material interests (Sherif, 1967). Competition between social groups over limited resources and opportunities has been shown to lead to intergroup conflict. From this perspective, it may be surmised that receiving country members' negative attitudes and discrimination towards immigrants are driven by zero-sum competition over housing, jobs, or other goods, such that the national in-group's gains are proportionate to the immigrant groups' losses – and vice versa. Thus, anti-immigration stances or opposition to policies improving immigrant rights are driven by the objective threat which immigrants pose to the receiving population.

Relative deprivation theory also predicts higher levels of prejudice among people who see themselves and their in-group as relatively disadvantaged in comparison with out-group members (relative group deprivation). This perspective differs from realistic conflict theory because it emphasises the subjective evaluation of this disadvantaged comparison (Pettigrew, Christ, Wagner, Meertens, van Dick, & Zick, 2008). That is, the evaluation does not necessarily reflect objective circumstances, but rather the perceived disadvantage compared to the target of comparison.

Social dominance theory (Sidanius & Pratto, 1999) begins with the assumption that societies are structured as group-based hierarchies that distinguish between dominant and subordinate groups. Individual-level, ideological, and institutional mechanisms, mutually reinforcing each other, produce and sustain group-based social hierarchies. Because supporting group-based inequality serves the group interests of dominants more than that of subordinates, this theory emphasises the dominant group's need to legitimise its power and to maintain group-based systems of social hierarchy. Indeed, the ideological attitudes of dominants will be more strongly driven by desire for dominance than will those of subordinates. Therefore, asymmetrical effects are found in support for specific social ideologies. However, social psychological studies have often indicated the existence of a widespread motivation among members of the subordinate group to support and justify existing social relations (this phenomenon has been labelled "system justification"; Jost & Major, 2001). Such findings may help us to understand the negative reactions of disadvantaged nationals to immigrants and immigration policies, in particular when competition for scarce resources is at stake.

Referring to these structural approaches leads to a framing of immigrant–majority group relationships in terms of unequal distribution of concrete resources, and this therefore raises the question of redistribution of resources rather than that of recognition of identities (see Fraser & Honneth, 2003). Redistribution issues have been central in classic social movements' analyses, such as the Marxist theory of class struggle. Structural approaches are still relevant for understanding some instances of prejudice towards immigrants, as some empirical findings presented below illustrate, although majority-minority relationships in modern societies are often related to symbolic issues of identity and cultural recognition.

Social Identity Theory

Social psychological theories focusing on symbolic motives fit best with Honneth's notion of struggle for recognition. Henri Tajfel's (Tajfel & Turner, 1986; see also Spears, Chapter 9, this volume) social identity theory is one of the most systematic and influential attempts at explaining intergroup relationships by relating them to group members' sense of identity. As such, it appears as a useful complement to the general theoretical framework examining struggle for recognition.

Social identity theory has often been referred to in social psychological approaches to prejudice, including prejudice towards immigrants (Esses, Dovidio, Jackson, & Armstrong, 2001; Huddy, 2001; Nesdale, 2004). Social identity theory is based on the assumption that the self-concept comprises both personal and social elements: one can view herself or himself as an individual in one social context and as a member of a particular group in another context. Two basic motivations, tied to social identities, drive people's attitudes, behaviour, and

perception of the social world: a motivation to obtain a clear picture of one's position in the social structure; and a motivation to obtain or maintain a positive sense of self-esteem (Abrams & Hogg, 1990). A clear representation of the social world is obtained through the cognitive process of categorisation. Positive self-esteem, in turn, is achieved through intergroup comparisons, so that people compare their in-group to out-groups on dimensions that they judge relevant, in order to obtain positive distinctiveness, and thus positive collective self-esteem. This theory is equally useful for understanding majorities' attitudes towards immigrants and for understanding minorities' collective mobilisation (e.g., social movement participation and collective protests) in reaction to discrimination (Simon, 2004).

From the majority perspective, derogating an out-group is only one of many ways through which group members can choose to maintain positive distinctiveness. Although a positive relationship between individuals' levels of in-group identification and out-group derogation has sometimes been suggested, this relationship is often not demonstrated empirically (see, for example, Hinkle & Brown, 1990; Mummendey, Klink, & Brown, 2001). Indeed, according to the social identity perspective, identification should lead to out-group derogation only in specific circumstances (Reicher, 2004; Turner, 1999). Turner (1999) emphasises that people's pursuit of positive distinctiveness *may* lead them to derogate out-group members, depending on several factors: the level of in-group identification; the salience of the relevant social identity; the perceived social structure of intergroup relationships; the relevance of the comparative dimension to the intergroup status relationship (for example, groups with different socioeconomic statuses are often compared on the dimension of competence); and the relevance of the out-group to the particular comparative judgement being made. When these conditions are met, social identity theory predicts that symbolic social identity concerns – that is, the motivation to have a clear and positive representation of one's membership in social groups – may lead to prejudice towards out-group members. Prejudice against immigrants among majority-group members could also arise when they perceive that their social identity – most likely their national identity, but also sub-national (e.g., Flemish or Walloon within Belgium) or supranational (e.g., European) levels of identity – is being symbolically threatened (Branscombe, Ellemers, Spears, & Doosje, 1999) by the divergent values, cultural and religious habits of immigrants, or by their political claims (Simon, 2010).

Social identity theory is thus highly compatible with Honneth's political philosophical theory of recognition. On the one hand, social identity theory provides a social psychological foundation (theoretical and empirical) to Honneth's model, as it demonstrates the importance of identity motives (see Gregg, Sedikides, & Gebauer, Chapter 14, this volume; Vignoles, Chapter 18, this volume) in shaping majority attitudes and behaviour towards minorities as well as minority members' individual or collective actions. On the other hand, Honneth's theory of the struggle for recognition complements social identity theory by situating social identity dynamics within the normative frameworks of contemporary societies, by stressing the interdependence of majorities and minorities, and by distinguishing different types of denials of recognition occurring in different spheres of modern societies and at different moments in the immigration history of each society.

Before turning to more specific instances of denials of recognition to immigrants in European societies, it is worth noting that identity and structural approaches are not mutually exclusive. Hence, they are combined, for example when examining the simultaneous effects of perceived realistic and symbolic threats on immigration attitudes (Stephan & Renfro, 2003). Moreover, Tajfel and Turner (1986) clearly stated from the start that their theory was meant to complement realistic conflict approaches by adding a symbolic dimension. This symbolic dimension consists of people's social identities and belief systems. These belief systems are related to the objective structure of group relations, but only indirectly, such that there is not a "one-to-one relationship" between the objective stratification of a social system and the belief system that represents it. This way of conceiving the relationship between a structural and a symbolic level to account for people's intergroup behaviour is germane to Honneth's (2003) contention that redistribution *is* recognition. That is, unequal distribution of resources is not only unjust *per se*; it also expresses a lack of symbolic recognition from dominant to subordinate groups in society.

Instances of Majorities Denying Recognition to Immigrants

We examine here how majority identity concerns, at the national and at the European Union level, can lead to the denial of recognition of immigrants. We distinguish two broad ways of denying recognition. Focusing on immigrants or potential immigrants who are not yet legally established on the receiving country's territory – candidates for immigration, asylum seekers, or undocumented immigrants – we first examine immigration policies and people's support for these policies. Then we address the situation of established immigrants and their descendents, who are the target of integration policies, and we investigate majority members' attitudes towards such policies. Finally, we examine how national and European identifications relate to these forms of denial of recognition.

Immigration Policies in Europe: Granting or Denying Recognition to Candidates for Immigration

National immigration policies are one expression of recognition. These policies can recognise, as well as deny, immigrants in the process of determining which out-group members are accepted within the boundaries of the national ingroup. In addition to entering the national territory, immigrants also enter a "moral" community with rights and obligations (see Anderson, 1983). Insofar as the definition and implementation of immigration policies take place at an institutional level, these policies relate to the legal sphere of recognition.

The "classic" work-related immigration has been stopped in most European countries since the oil crisis of the 1970s, so that legal ways of immigrating are now generally limited to family reunion, seeking political asylum (following the criteria of the 1951 United Nations *Geneva Convention* on the Status of Refugees), and restricted work-related access. However, the development of the European Union (EU) has facilitated mobility – permanent or temporary – across member states for European citizens. The difference in rights to settle in EU countries between nationals and citizens of other member states has been constantly decreasing since the Rome treaty in 1954 (Groenendijk, 2006). For example, an Italian citizen can settle in a Belgian town nearly as easily as would a Belgian citizen. However, this European citizenship has not been extended to immigrants from outside Europe, so that the access of people emigrating from countries outside of the European Union to European countries has not been facilitated. On the contrary, some commentators have noted the increasing closure of the EU borders, leading to the construction of a "fortress Europe" (Geddes, 2000). The opening of internal borders was actually accompanied by a strengthening of immigration control at the EU external boundaries (Cholewinski, 2002). Moreover, freedom of movement remains restricted for people coming from new EU member-states of Central and Eastern Europe.

Citizens of receiving countries vary in their support for immigration policies when they agree or disagree, for example, with certain entry criteria set for immigrants. When examining the attitudes of the receiving country's citizens towards immigration, we shift from the legal sphere of recognition to the sphere of social esteem, even though supporting restrictive immigration policies does not necessarily imply holding prejudice. In this sphere of recognition, receiving country citizens assign importance to certain characteristics defining who should be allowed to enter and live in the in-group territory. These attitudes, in turn, influence political decision making and can

thus be considered as implicit or indirect forms of immigration control (Brochmann, 1999).

Based on immigration policy debates, one can distinguish between *ascribed* and *acquired* immigration criteria (Green, 2007, 2009), according to a *categorical* or *individual* perception of persons. Ascribed immigration criteria are inherent and collective, and relate to immigrants' membership in social categories such as ethnic or national origin. Endorsement of ascribed criteria is likely to represent an explicitly xenophobic stance, in that this argument dictates that people must be excluded from the possibility of immigration exclusively on the basis of category membership. In contrast, acquired criteria, such as educational qualifications, working skills, or adopting the way of life of the country of immigration are, at least in principle, within individual control. Support for these criteria implies restricting entry to admit only those desirable immigration candidates who have the potential to conform to the way of life by endorsing the receiving country's values and practices (Bourhis, Moïse, Perreault, & Senécal, 1997). A strong expectation of assimilation favours westernised, well-educated, high-status immigrants, and this can be viewed as a form of prejudice if immigrants simultaneously are expected to abandon their cultural heritage. Nevertheless, support for acquired criteria can also express a genuine concern for social integration, provided that the maintenance of cultural minorities' distinctiveness is also recognised.

Social psychological threat theories can be drawn upon to understand why receiving country citizens deny recognition of immigrants by supporting certain strict immigration criteria (Riek, Mania, & Gaertner, 2006; Stephan & Renfro, 2003). Support for ascribed or acquired immigration criteria can reflect perceptions of realistic, material threat: immigrant and national minority out-groups are perceived as competitors (e.g., for jobs or housing), which leads to support for restrictions, regardless of whether or not an objective threat exists (Esses et al., 2001; Pratto & Lemieux, 2001). Symbolic threat reflects a concern for the identity of the national majority (e.g., maintenance of language and culture) instead of its material interests, but this also heightens support for restrictive immigration criteria. For example, immigrants' potentially differing values and belief systems might evoke a perception of threatened national unity (Azzi, 1998), so that prejudice tends to increase as a function of perception of cultural dissimilarity (Zárate, Garcia, Garza, & Hitlan, 2004). Consequently, values of the national majority group serve as the frame of reference for judging national minorities, including immigrants. Support for restrictive immigration criteria thus asserts and bolsters common values within a country (e.g., Sears & Henry, 2005) by regulating entry of immigrants who diverge from majority values and established norms. Both types of threat underlie the denial of recognition of immigrants by increasing support for strict entry criteria. However, symbolic threat underlies more clearly the denial of the social value of traditions, values, and practices of individuals from different national or ethnic origins. From a recognition perspective, immigrant exclusion is thus constructed in parallel to the bolstering of the in-group. Whereas positive value is associated with practices and traditions of the national in-group, negative value is associated with those of the out-group (Jodelet, 2005; Staerklé, 2005).

The ways in which receiving country citizens assign social value to immigrants also depend on the situation prevailing in the receiving country. Recent social-psychological research has shown that support for immigration criteria is affected by national level factors. Green (2009) demonstrated, across 20 European countries, that a poor economic situation (indexed with low gross domestic product), akin to realistic threat on the national level, predicted support for the use of ascribed criteria. Moreover, the positive link between perceived threat and approval of acquired entry criteria was stronger in wealthy than in poorer national contexts. In a study comparing 15 European countries, Scheepers, Gijsberts, and Coenders (2002) showed that a high proportion of non-EU citizens within a country was related to ethnic exclusionism. Semoynov, Raijman, Yom Tov, and Schmidt (2004), in turn, compared attitudes towards foreigners in different regions of Germany: whereas

the actual proportion of the immigrant population in a region did not have effects on attitudes, a high perceived size of the foreign population in the region was associated with perceived threat and discriminatory attitudes towards foreigners. These results indicate the importance of acknowledging the interplay between the collective context and individual-level recognition.

Integration Policies in Europe: Granting or Denying Recognition to Legal Immigrants

Whereas immigration policies regulate the settlement of foreigners to national territories, integration policies address the situation of people who are already legally settled in a country.[3] Further, whereas receiving country members' support for strict immigration criteria can serve as a means for denying entry to immigrants, the denial of recognition often continues once immigrants move and settle in the receiving country. Though integration policies differ from one European country to another, some common policies have been adopted at the EU level (see below) and therefore influence member states' policies (Geddes & Guiraudon, 2004). In addition, national policies are heading in convergent directions, even in domains that are not covered by European conventions.

International comparisons of integration policies reveal different national models of integration. Three ideal types of integration are usually referred to (e.g., Koopmans, Statham, Giugni, & Passy, 2005). The British model is traditionally described as "multicultural" – viewing immigrant minorities as ethnic groups. France is said to be "assimilationist" – expecting immigrants to adopt French culture and thus integrate as individuals. And the German model is often viewed as "segregationist" – with immigrant minorities being excluded from the nation. Countries' integration policies are generally classified as a function of their resemblance with one of these three models. Nevertheless, Joppke (2007) argues that contemporary policy solutions to integration issues converge to such an extent that referring to different national models no longer makes sense. For example, he observes that France, Germany, and the Netherlands (usually seen as multicultural), as well as other European countries, have all introduced compulsory "citizenship trajectories", including courses on the national language, practices, and institutions. In the Netherlands, passing a Dutch citizenship test in one's country of origin is a necessary condition for allowing immigration, even when based on family reunion. However, Jacobs and Rea (2007) contend that national differences persist beyond this apparent convergence towards assimilation.

Kymlicka (2007) observes that this backlash against multiculturalism is in fact restricted to the immigration domain, and specifically targets Muslim immigrants. Other cultural minorities, such as indigenous people (Frisians in the Netherlands, Welsh in Great Britain, or Basques in Spain), are usually not targeted. The 9/11 attacks and the London and Madrid train bombings – as well as other debates following the Danish cartoon affair, or the assassination of filmmaker Theo Van Gogh in the Netherlands – have increased the salience of security issues in the relationship between Muslim communities and European states (Strabac & Listhaug, 2008). According to Richardson (2004), four main themes emerge in public discussions about Islam: the military threat of Muslim countries, the threat of political violence and extremism, the (internal) threat to democracy posed by authoritarian Muslim political leaders and parties, and the social threat of Muslim gender inequality (see also Gianettoni & Roux, 2010).

To sum up, though integration policies are still diverse, they tend to converge, and they sometimes target particular categories of immigrants, who are therefore at risk of being denied recognition in the legal sphere.

National Identification, Multiculturalism, and Denial of Recognition

In the sphere of social esteem, denying recognition to immigrants on the basis of their belonging to a devalued social category equates with holding prejudice against them. National identification has been associated with such denial of recognition. However, the pattern is very variable across societies. Indeed, analysing data from the International Social Survey Programme (ISSP) 2003 module on national identity, Pehrson, Vignoles, and Brown (2009) calculated correlations between national identification and anti-immigrant prejudice within 31 representative national samples (including 21 European countries). These correlations ranged from weakly negative to moderately positive, with significantly positive correlations found in only 18 countries. So, although the relationship between national identification and prejudice towards immigrants clearly exists, it is far from being as strong and universal a phenomenon as one might have expected. It is worth noting, however, that an absence of significant positive correlation was observed only in four European countries (Russia, Portugal, Czech Republic, and Ireland).

Some authors (Condor, 2001; Reicher & Hopkins, 2001) have criticised a widespread tendency to see nations as univocal entities and have argued that there are variations in the way nations are defined. As Billig (1995) has proposed, nations are not concrete realities, but rather ideological constructions that are constantly being reaffirmed through the routine use of national symbols and events like national commemorations or national celebrations. Socially shared definitions of the national group – as homogeneous or diverse – are particularly relevant (Licata, 2003), as are the norms and ideologies that are available in the national contexts, because they can affect the relationship between national identification and attitudes towards immigrants.

Hence, several scholars have argued that the ideological construal of national identity determines whether national identification is related to anti-immigration attitudes (Billiet, Maddens, & Beerten, 2003; Reicher & Hopkins, 2001; Schildkraut, Chapter 36, this volume). For example, in describing the content of national identities, a distinction can be made between ethnic and civic national identity (Smith, 2001; see also Hart, Richardson, & Wilkenfeld,

Chapter 32, this volume). Ethnic national identification involves defining the national group in terms of ethnicity, such as shared ancestral origin, language, and culture, whereas civic national identification is based on citizenship and on common institutional and political allegiance. The relationship between national identification and anti-immigration stances should emerge when immigration is construed as harming and violating the national identity. This is the case for ethnic national identification, because immigrants do not usually share the ancestral origins of receiving country members, nor their language or culture. Hence, research has repeatedly found that perceived cultural dissimilarity (Pettigrew et al., 2008), or perception of cultural threat (Curseu, Stoop, & Schalk, 2007), is a good predictor of prejudice towards immigrants.

Pehrson et al. (2009) showed that the collectively shared definition of nationality at the country level influenced the relationship between individuals' national identification and their prejudice towards immigrants. National identification predicted prejudice most positively in those countries where speaking the national language was considered more important, and in those countries where being a citizen was considered less important, as a criterion for national membership. Also using cross-national ISSP data, Staerklé, Sidanius, Green, and Molina (2005) demonstrated that, among national majority populations, the relationship between national identification and xenophobic attitudes was mediated by ethnic identification: nationals who felt more identified with their country were more hostile towards immigrants because they identified more strongly with the dominant ethnic group (see also Sanchez-Mazas, Van Humskerken, & Casini, 2003; Staerklé, Sidanius, Green, & Molina, 2010). Similarly, Pehrson, Brown, and Zagefka (2009) found that national identification was associated with negative attitudes towards asylum seekers and willingness to support an anti-asylum-seeker group only among individuals endorsing an essentialist ethnic definition of the national in-group. Meeus, Duriez, Vanbeselaere, and Boen (2010) also found that this relationship

was mediated by ethnic definitions of the in-group among Flemish participants in Belgium.[4] Moreover, with longitudinal data, they showed that Flemish identification predicted an increasing tendency to view Flanders as an ethnic rather than civic group 1 year later, which was further associated with increased adoption of anti-immigrant prejudice. These results suggest that people who identify with a national group mostly in ethnic terms tend to internalise a representation of national culture that triggers negative attitudes towards out-group members (including immigrants). These attitudes therefore arise from an interaction between individual-level and group-level influences.

The endorsement or rejection of multiculturalism, as an ideology, has also been related with different levels of anti-immigrant prejudice. According to Berry's (1984) model of acculturation strategies, societies adopting a cultural pluralism or multiculturalism model favour integrationist policies (see also Bourhis et al., 1997). These policies – which should be regarded as a specific form of more general integration policies – allow ethnic minorities to maintain their culture and to engage in intercultural contact with other cultural groups (including the dominant national group). In contrast, assimilationist policies implicitly or explicitly press ethnic minorities to abandon their culture of origin in favour of the dominant culture. Verkuyten and colleagues conducted several studies on the impact of the multicultural "ideology" on intergroup relations in the Netherlands (see Verkuyten, 2006, for a review). First, they consistently found that minority group members (mostly Turkish-Dutch) generally express more support for multiculturalism than Dutch majority members, as this policy is often perceived as favouring minorities. Moreover, experimental studies have demonstrated that, compared to multiculturalism, assimilationism leads to greater levels of in-group identification among majority-group members. Among minority members, however, multiculturalism leads to greater levels of in-group identification. Coenders, Lubbers, Scheepers, and Verkuyten (2008) also showed that the shift from multiculturalism towards assimilationism that took place during the last decade in the Netherlands, regarding both integration policies and public opinion, was accompanied by an increase in negative attitudes towards immigrants and their descendants, especially towards Muslims. They also showed experimentally that rendering an assimilationist (versus multicultural) ideology salient led to more negative attitudes towards immigrants.

In sum, there is evidence that national identification leads to anti-immigrant prejudice only when the nation is defined in ethnic terms and seen as a culturally homogeneous whole. Construing one's nation as plural, where minority groups are recognised and valued, tends to weaken or eliminate this link. Identifying with one's nation can lead to denying recognition to immigrants to the extent that the nation is represented as a monocultural entity, which therefore would be threatened by the presence of immigrants holding different values and cultural references (see Schildkraut, Chapter 36, this volume, for similar findings in the USA).

European Identification and Denial of Recognition

The European integration process has had several important implications for both immigration and integration policies. One of the most important advances towards increased protection of immigrant minorities' rights has been the adoption by EU member states of the anti-discrimination directives based on Article 13 of the Amsterdam Treaty in June 2000. These directives represented a clear shift from local policies based on diverse national models to a common set of rules that covers instances of both direct and indirect discrimination, as well as positive action towards immigrants (Geddes & Guiraudon, 2004).

But the European integration process has also had negative consequences for non-EU nationals. On the one hand, the official introduction of EU citizenship in 1992 favoured a new superordinate level of identification including nationals of all EU countries, and extended some of their rights (e.g., free movement and residence throughout

the Union, the right to vote and stand in local and European elections in any member state, the right to protection by the diplomatic or consular authorities of other member states when in a non-EU member state). On the other hand, this new status has only been granted to nationals of EU member states, which implies that non-EU nationals have since been doubly excluded – from both national and European citizenships. Therefore, one might fear that the European level of identification facilitates out-group rejection at the corresponding level, that is, towards immigrants or people of immigrant descent originating from non-European countries. Indeed, Licata and Klein (2002) found, through a survey among French-speaking Belgian students, that European identification predicted higher levels of xenophobia, independently of national identification and of political orientation. Moreover, they showed that this trend occurred despite the fact that participants widely associated Europe with values of tolerance and fraternity, and with a positive view of intercultural contact. Although these results, based on a non-representative sample, cannot be generalised either to Belgium (Quintelier & Dejaeghere, 2008) or to other European countries, they suggest the very possibility that developing a superordinate European level of identity might also have its pitfalls. Again, this might depend on the way European identity is represented (Chryssochoou, 2000).

Sanchez-Mazas, Van Humskerken, and Gély (2005) found that representing European identity in terms of a shared culture, history, and values was associated with more rejection of non-EU foreigners, whereas a more civic representation of Europe was associated with more favourable attitudes towards them. This raises the question of the way European identity is conceived and how it is promoted as a particular political project (Stråth, 2000). This project is either framed as the development of a new superordinate level of identity that should progressively replace national identities, or as a supplementary level that is meant to coexist with national identities. The first solution would require that national identities progressively fade away and be replaced by a common European identity.

Research by Castano and colleagues (Castano, Yzerbyt, & Bourguignon, 2003) suggested that perceiving the European Union as a real entity – in particular seeing European countries as similar – was associated with favouring European identification. However, Licata (2003) showed that envisioning the European integration process as threatening national identity tended to impede European identification. Moreover, another study (Licata, Klein, Casini, Coscenza, & Azzi, 2003) suggested that perceiving European countries as culturally similar was positively correlated with European identification only when cultural similarity had been presented as normatively desirable, showing that perception of similarity is not a necessary condition for feeling European. These last findings clearly tend to favour the second solution for the European project, which would not seek to reproduce the national ideal – based on a close correspondence between a community of people, a culture, and a state (Gellner, 1983) – at the European level (Habermas, 2001).

Conceptions of Europe and of nations are crucial because they clearly condition the way in which the presence of immigrant communities is perceived within European societies. Again, norms and representations associated with European identity serve to condition majority members' readiness to grant or to deny recognition to immigrants. As we have seen, contradictory tendencies occur simultaneously. On the one hand, integration policies tend to favour cultural diversity and the protection of immigrant rights (at least for some immigrant groups). On the other hand, immigration policies at the European level are becoming increasingly restrictive. This divergence between immigration and integration policies creates a normatively ambiguous situation. Attitudes towards immigration and integration policies are also affected by the way European identity is represented. The supranational model (i.e., pan-European identity) may lead to the rejection of what is perceived to be non-European, whereas envisioning the EU as a supplementary level designed to coexist with national identities should induce a more positive view of cultural diversity and should therefore favour immigrants' recognition.

So far, we have examined theoretical and empirical contributions in the field of social psychology that help explain prejudice against immigrants, and we have addressed them as forms of denials of recognition. As we have argued, these denials may take various forms, such as denial of rights (e.g., settlement, citizenship, social rights, freedom of movement) and denial of social esteem in the form of prejudice or negative opinions of the culture and/or religion of the outgroup. Moreover, different forms of denial of recognition are likely to occur simultaneously. The ways in which minorities react to denials of recognition also take different forms.

Minorities' Reactions to Denials of Recognition

According to Honneth (1996), experiencing denials of recognition has a profound emotional impact on minority members, as recognition is a fundamental symbolic resource needed for the development of positive self-regard. Both legal and informal discrimination are regarded as unjust because, beyond restricting freedom or depriving people of material resources, they harm minority group members with regard to their expectations of equality and respect. This feeling of injustice can lead minority members to react and claim recognition of their rights and social value. However, merely experiencing injustice does not automatically lead to action (Simon, 2010). For example, an immigrant who is unfairly rejected when applying for a job could attribute it to his lack of competence rather than to group discrimination. Hence, Honneth specifies that being the target of denials of recognition leads to collective mobilisation of minority members only to the extent that this denial is viewed as *group-specific*. This is consistent with research on relative deprivation showing that perceptions of the relative positions of groups, and feelings of collective deprivation, leads to a sense of discontent among minorities and is a better predictor of collective action than is personal deprivation (Guimond & Dubé-Simard, 1983). This is also consistent with studies showing that collective reactions to discrimination are only instigated by overt discrimination and not by covert forms of prejudice (Ellemers & Barreto, 2009; Wright & Taylor, 1998).

However, social-psychological approaches to collective movements and protests (Klandermans, 1997; Simon, 2004) suggest that the causal chain linking discontent with collective action is more complex than is envisioned by Honneth's theory, as this causal sequence includes psychological, situational, and structural causes. This causal chain is moderated by many factors, suggesting that immigrant minorities initiate collective action to claim recognition only in a limited range of situations. Hence, victims of discrimination may engage in proactive behaviours motivated by claims of injustice – "voice" strategies. But they can also opt for reactions involving retreat – "exit" strategies, that is, not initiating any collective action; or for submission to authority – "loyalty" strategies (Hirschman, 1970; see also Sanchez-Mazas, Maggi, & Roca i Escoda, 2010). Here, we briefly focus on factors linked with minority group members' identity concerns and with their appraisal of the intergroup situation (discrimination).

Social identity theory's view of the minority perspective also stems from the assumption that serving as the target of negative stereotypes, prejudice, and discriminatory behaviour from dominant groups leads minority members to suffer from a negative social identity (Tajfel & Turner, 1986). But, according to this theory, this suffering leads to collective mobilisation of minorities only in specific circumstances. Responses to inequality, social exclusion, and unsatisfactory social identity differ depending on whether minority group members are concerned with improving the position of one's group as a whole or with improving their own personal status. These two strategies, called social change and social mobility, are chosen according to the way the individual views certain sociostructural characteristics of the social system. Thus, if the boundaries between groups are perceived as permeable, and the system appears stable and legitimate, individual mobility will be preferred

over social change. On the other hand, social change will be more likely to occur if group boundaries are perceived as solid, status differences between the groups are seen as unstable, and social inequality is considered illegitimate. Reicher (2004) adds two other contextual factors: the responses of the dominant group and the relative power of the minority group. Strategies employed by the minority group – especially symbolic ones defining new dimensions of comparison or reinterpreting existing ones – are best achieved if the dominant group accepts the minority group's influence and re-evaluates the dimensions of comparison. Intergroup competition strategies can be adopted, but their success also depends on the dominant group's resistance and will to reassert its domination, and on the power difference between the two groups (Simon, 2004). The Congolese decolonization process is a case in point. Until the late 1950s, most of those who later became independentist leaders, such as Patrice Lumumba, supported the colonial system. Lumumba adhered to the policy of individual mobility implemented by the Belgians (Klein & Licata, 2003), which granted some privileges to the most Europeanized Congolese. From 1957 on, members of the Congolese elite realized that, despite their efforts to reach a better status, they remained "Blacks" in the eyes of the Belgians and were denied access to high-status positions in the colonial administration or private companies. In the absence of opportunities for individual social mobility, they sought social change. In order to mobilize large numbers of Congolese, they had to convince them that the colonial system was illegitimate, that the intergroup boundaries were impermeable, and that, given their numerical majority over the Belgians, the system could be changed. This mobilization process led to protests and riots in 1959, and independence was obtained in 1960 after peaceful negotiations with the Belgian government.

Returning to the distinction between spheres of recognition proposed by Honneth, it is suggested, as far as immigrants are concerned, that a denial of recognition in the form of withholding rights – political, civic, or social – is likely to be interpreted as injustice towards the entire group and to reinforce intergroup boundaries. This is likely what happens when undocumented immigrants are deprived of basic – and in principle universal – rights. In contrast, the perception of being treated unfairly is not straightforward as far as legal immigrants are concerned because citizenship still represents a major basis for legitimising unequal rights between nationals and foreigners. Moreover, the struggle for recognition by claiming equal rights is difficult in the context of indirect and subtle instances of discrimination, which, as argued previously, are the form of denial most encountered in the present moment of the history of immigration. Finally, denials of recognition in the sphere of social esteem – that is, in informal social relationships – which threaten minority group-members' self-esteem, are more likely to be experienced as targeting individuals rather than the whole social category, therefore impeding collective mobilisation.

Social-psychological research on individuals' reactions to stigmatisation (Heatherton, Kleck, Hebl, & Hull, 2000; Swim & Stangor, 1998) has produced contrasting findings: stigmatised persons sometimes adopt behavioural strategies that lead to stereotype confirmation (for a review, see Klein & Snyder, 2003), therefore legitimising the existing social order (Jost & Major, 2001). For example, when the stereotype of incompetence is made salient, African American students may be more likely to confirm this stereotype while performing a task, thus resulting in poorer performance compared to a condition where the stereotype is not made salient (Steele & Aronson, 1995). But they might also actively seek proof that their in-group is subject to discrimination, and thus protect their personal self-esteem by making external attributions for discrimination (Major & O'Brien, 2005). That is, people often do not feel personally responsible when their group is subjected to discrimination because they attribute it to the whole group rather than to their own features. Thus, contrary to Honneth or Tajfel's contention, being the target of denial of recognition should not necessarily engender suffering among minority members. In contrast, the Rejection-Identification Model (Schmitt & Branscombe, 2002) is based on the assumption that targets of discrimination attribute this to internal, stable, and uncontrollable causes (some personal characteristics that they cannot control and which they believe will persist), which damages their psychological well-being. In order to alleviate these negative effects of discrimination on their self-esteem, such individuals increasingly identify with the disadvantaged group, which in turn improves well-being (see also Stepick, Dutton Stepick, & Vanderkooy, Chapter 37, this volume). The psychological benefits of identification (even to a stigmatised group) thus buffer the negative effects of discrimination. Verkuyten and Yildiz (2007) found that, among Turkish immigrants in the Netherlands, perceiving their in-group as being rejected by the majority increased ethnic and religious identification, and decreased national Dutch identification.

Perceived rejection then tends to favour what Simon and Ruhs (2008) labelled "separatist identification" among the immigrants, at the expense of dual identification (a simultaneous identification with the minority group and with the receiving nation; Berry, 1984; see Arnett Jensen, Jensen Arnett, & McKenzie, Chapter 13, this volume). In the case of separatist identification, immigrants' claims for recognition might be shaped exclusively in ethnocultural terms, and eventually lead to non-normative political action (e.g., violent action), whereas dual identification should facilitate immigrants' normative political participation in the receiving society. Indeed, Simon and Ruhs (2008) found that dual identification with both the minority group (German Turks) and with the receiving society (Germany) predicted higher levels of normative political participation as well as support for moderate ethnic and religious organisations, whereas separatist identification was correlated with higher support for radical organisations (albeit not with political violence).

Majority–Minority Interactions and the Normative Framework of Modern Societies

According to Honneth (1996), social change is triggered by struggles for recognition originating from unsatisfied normative expectations.

Thus the dynamics of majority–minority inter-actions can gradually improve the normative framework of contemporary societies. This idea is in line with Kymlicka's (2007) observation that the liberal multicultural ideology emerged in Western European societies not because the cultural majorities were culturally receptive to it, but because minorities have had the opportunity to express their claims publicly. They therefore were able to influence the majority group (Moscovici & Mugny, 1985) and have progressively changed the dominant norms towards more recognition of cultural minorities (although this shift is only partial and does not seem to apply equally to all minorities). Similarly, by asserting their presence in and contribution to receiving societies, and therefore by questioning the legitimacy of legal boundaries, undocumented immigrants contribute to the strengthening of democracy, at great personal costs (Balibar, 2000).

However, the existence of shared normative principles is a prerequisite for majority receptiveness to minorities' claims. The idea of interdependence of majority and minority implies a space of shared communication allowing a process of mutual influence (Doise, 2002). Granting voice to minorities of immigrant origin is a major challenge for contemporary societies. Being fully recognised as participants in the functioning of democratic societies should favour the development of dual identification or integration strategies (Berry, 1984) among minority members. Conversely, being denied recognition in the public space is likely to bolster ethnic "separatist" identities (Azzi, 2010), therefore impeding social integration and potentially leading to politically motivated violence (Moghaddam, 2006). From the majority point of view, immigrants' participation in public democratic debates should lead to a less homogeneous perception of immigrant communities, to the extent that their members will take diverse positions within these debates. This heterogeneous perception is then likely to alleviate stereotyping and prejudice.

Conclusion

The aim of the current chapter was to discuss the social-psychological underpinnings of Honneth's model of recognition and apply it to examining relations between receiving-country majority and immigrant groups in Europe. We drew on social identity theory, as well as on structural approaches of prejudice, and presented empirical research that fits Honneth's framework, which was initially developed in the field of political philosophy. We have proposed that prejudice against immigrants is a particular instance of majority members' denials of recognition, namely a denial of recognition in the sphere of social esteem. We do not advocate giving up the notion of prejudice. Rather, we believe that identifying prejudice as a form of interaction through which one group denies recognition to another group may represent a conceptual expansion of the construct of prejudice. On the one hand, our approach stresses the interactive nature of these processes, and therefore calls for an analysis of these interactions as situated in time. Such a temporal dimension involves both short-term, dynamic relations between majorities and majorities and a long-term, historical contextualisation of these relations. On the other hand, our approach situates prejudice among other forms of denials of recognition, which sometimes precede or coexist with prejudice. Indeed, recognition can also be denied in the legal sphere, when immigrants – particularly illegal immigrants, regardless of the number of years they live in the receiving country – do not benefit from the same rights as majority members, or in the public space, when they are not allowed to participate in public debates. Finally, the recognition approach provides a way to address theoretically the interplay between sociopolitical contexts and social-psychological processes.

The reasons why majority members deny recognition to immigrants are manifold. High levels of prejudice, as well as support for restrictive immigration criteria or assimilationist social policies, have been observed when immigrants and majority members compete, or are perceived as competing, for rare and valuable resources, or when immigration is seen as challenging the dominant hierarchical structure of a society. National identification, as well as European identification, also in some cases predicts higher levels of prejudice towards immigrants. However, in-group identification does not automatically lead to out-group rejection: it does so when the nation is represented in ethnic terms, as a culturally homogeneous group, and when it is associated with norms facilitating discrimination. Representing the European Union as a homogeneous cultural entity with clear group boundaries could thus facilitate prejudice towards immigrants from outside Europe.

Conversely, being the target of denials of recognition has profound consequences for immigrants to the extent that it threatens their social identity. Immigrants can tackle these threats in different ways – choosing voice, exit, or loyalty strategies – as a function of the way they perceive the intergroup situation and depending on the nature of the denial they are facing. Some immigrants choose individual strategies of social mobility or resort to psychological defences to protect their identity, whereas others interpret the denial of recognition as group-specific and eventually initiate strategies of collective mobilisation. In this last case, claims for recognition are formulated. In turn, these claims expressed by immigrant minorities elicit responses from the dominant cultural group in the receiving society, which may grant or deny recognition to the immigrants. Failing to be recognised can then trigger and fuel minority members' collective or individual strategies to satisfy identity needs. From the recognition perspective, then, attitudes of majorities and minorities are formed, and take place, in a dynamic of mutual influence.

Obtaining recognition in the legal sphere typically leads to a shift of demands of the minority group members towards the sphere of social esteem. Obtaining recognition in that sphere then tends to lead immigrant minorities to seek participation in public debates (Sanchez-Mazas, 2004, 2007). This historical sequence is at the heart of the recognition model and allows for delineating different moments in the national or international *history* of majority-immigrant relationships, and for identifying the stakes of *currently* occurring relationships. For example, undocumented immigrants are struggling for the recognition of basic rights, whereas legal immigrants and citizens of immigrant descent are struggling for social esteem or access to the public space. These differing dynamics give rise to different reactions among majorities.

We have applied the recognition approach to the situation of immigrants in contemporary European societies and have highlighted the convergences in immigration and integration policies across Europe. However, one must keep in mind that European countries differ in many ways: immigration history and having a colonial past (Volpato & Licata, 2010), origin of immigrants, geographical distance from the "borders" of Europe, wealth, development of a welfare state, and so forth (Phalet & Kosic, 2006). Moreover, this approach applies to the context of other countries as well. For example, consider the situation of African Americans and Mexicans in the United States (see Stepick et al., Chapter 37, this volume). Mexican immigrants are often perceived as a material threat because they supposedly take majority members' jobs and send their money back to Mexico. This threat translates into a denial of recognition in the sphere of social esteem by way of negative perceptions of this group. Moreover, the absence of a legal obligation to provide bilingual education for Latinos in the United States can be considered a denial in the legal sphere. Affirmative actions to promote diversity at the work place or in higher education are examples of recognition of minorities in the legal sphere. The interactive nature of recognition is also present in Sears's concept of symbolic racism (Sears & Henry, 2005), which taps modern, subtler forms of racial prejudice towards African-Americans, and relates in part to majority members' reactions to minority claims. The perception that the demands of Black leaders are excessive or the interpretation of affirmative action as unjustified favouring of minorities are examples of such reactions.

Finally, we have emphasised the normative benefits that modern societies can draw from implementing policies of recognition for minorities. Whereas denying recognition to immigrants runs the risk of eliciting separatist strategies, or even triggering non-normative action, granting them recognition facilitates their positive participation in democratic processes. Dialogue between majorities and minorities about common principles could then contribute to change the normative frameworks of democratic societies towards more respect for diversity. Granting recognition in the public space does not equate with blindly accepting any claim expressed by any minority; but it implies initiating a process of mutual influence with people of immigrant origin, even though this process can be conflictual. This process entails considering immigrants as a valuable party, and debating with them rather than ignoring their demands or deeming them as irrelevant. If receiving societies prove unable to respond positively to immigrants' claims for recognition, the immigrants will likely seek recognition elsewhere – either within immigrant communities or from their countries of origin – which will seriously impede the development of multicultural, peaceful, and decent societies.

Notes

1. See the Migrant Integration Policy Index for a description of 28 European countries' immigration policies: http://www.integrationindex.eu/
2. However, friendships across intergroup borders can prove efficient in reducing intergroup prejudice (e. g., Turner & Brown, 2008).
3. Here "integration" is used broadly to refer to allowing and promoting immigrants' active participation in society. When discussing the work of Berry (1984) and Bourhis et al. (1994), more fine-grained dimensions of integration will be distinguished.

4. In multiethnic states such as Belgium, Switzerland, or Canada, the basis for prejudiced attitudes towards immigrants may be the ethnic or linguistic group rather than the whole country.

References

Abrams, D., & Hogg, M. A. (1990). *Social identity theory: Constructive and critical advances* London: Harvester-Wheatsheaf.

Anderson, B. (1983). *Imagined communities: Reflection on the origin and spread of nationalism* London: Verso.

Azzi, A. E. (1998). From competitive interests, perceived justice, and identity needs to collective action: Psychological mechanisms in ethnic nationalism. In C. Dandeker, (Ed.), *Nationalism and violence.* (pp. 73–138). New Brunswick, NJ: Transaction Publishers.

Azzi, A. E. (2010). From identity and participation to integration or radicalization: A critical appraisal. In A. E. Azzi, X. Chryssochoou, B. Klandermans, & B. Simon (Eds.), *Identity and participation in culturally diverse societies: A multidisciplinary perspective* (pp.359–367). Oxford, UK: Wiley-Blackwell.

Balibar, E. (2000). What we owe to the Sans-Papiers. In L. Guenther & C. Heesters (Eds.), *Social insecurity.* (pp. 42–43). Toronto: Anansi.

Berry, J. W. (1984). Cultural relations in plural societies: Alternatives to segregation and their sociopsychological implications. In N. Miller & M. B. Brewer (Eds.), *Groups in contact: The psychology of desegregation.* (pp. 11–27). New York: Academic Press.

Billiet, J., Maddens, B., & Beerten, R. (2003). National identity and attitude toward foreigners in a multinational state: A replication. *Political Psychology, 24,* 241–257.

Billig, M. (1995). *Banal nationalism* London: Sage.

Bourhis, R. -Y., Moïse, L. -C., Perreault, S., & Senécal, S. (1997). Towards an interactive acculturation model: A social psychological approach. *International Journal of Psychology, 32,* 369–386.

Branscombe, N. R., Ellemers, N., Spears, R., & Doosje, B. (1999). The context and content of social identity threat. In N. Ellemers, R. Spears, B. Doosje, (Ed.), *Social identity: Context, commitment, content.* (pp. 35–58). Oxford: Blackwell.

Brochmann, G. (1999). Mechanism of control. In G. Brochmann & T. Hammar (Eds.), *Mechanisms of immigration control.* (pp. 1–28). Oxford: Berg.

Brown, R. (1995). *Prejudice: Its social psychology* Oxford: Blackwell.

Castano, E., Yzerbyt, V., & Bourguignon, D. (2003). We are one and I like it: The impact of ingroup entitativity on ingroup identification. *European Journal of Social Psychology, 33,* 735–754.

Cholewinski, R. (2002). Borders and discrimination in the European Union. In M. Anderson, (Ed.), *Police and justice co-operation and the new European borders.* (pp. 81–102). The Hague, London, New York: Kluwer Law International.

Chryssochoou, X. (2000). Memberships in a superordinate level: Re-thinking European union as a multi-national society. *Journal of Community and Applied Social Psychology, 10,* 403–420.

Coenders, M., Lubbers, M., Scheepers, P., & Verkuyten, M. (2008). More than two decades of changing ethnic attitudes in the Netherlands. *Journal of Social Issues, 64,* 269–285.

Condor, S. (2001). Nations and nationalisms: Particular cases and impossible myths. *British Journal of Social Psychology, 40,* 177–182.

Curseu, P. L., Stoop, R., & Schalk, R. (2007). Prejudice toward immigrant workers among Dutch employees: Integrated threat theory revisited. *European Journal of Social Psychology, 37,* 125–140.

Doise, W. (2002). *Human rights as social representations* London, New York: Routledge.

Düvell, F. (2008). Clandestine migration in Europe. *Social Science Information, 47,* 479–497.

Ellemers, N., & Barreto, M. (2009). Collective action in modern times: How modern expressions of prejudice prevent collective action. *Journal of Social Issues, 65,* 749–768.

Esses, V. M., Dovidio, J. F., Jackson, L. M., & Armstrong, T. L. (2001). The immigration dilemma: The role of perceived group competition, ethnic prejudice, and national identity. *Journal of Social Issues, 57,* 389–412.

Fraser, N., & Honneth, A. (2003). *Redistribution or recognition?: A political-philosophical exchange* New York: Verso.

Geddes, A. (2000). *Immigration and European integration: Towards fortress Europe?* Manchester, UK: Manchester University Press.

Geddes, A., & Guiraudon, V. (2004). Britain, France, and EU anti-discrimination policy: The emergence of an EU policy paradigm. *West European Politics, 27,* 334–353.

Gellner, E. (1983). *Nations and nationalism* Ithaca: Cornell University Press.

Gianettoni, L., & Roux, P. (2010). Interconnecting race and gender relations: Racism, sexism and the attribution of sexism to the racialized other. *Sex Roles, 62,* 1–13.

Green, E. G. T. (2007). Guarding the gates of Europe: A typological analysis of immigration attitudes across 21 countries. *International Journal of Psychology, 42,* 365–379.

Green, E. G. T. (2009). Who can enter? A multilevel analysis on public support for immigration criteria across 20 European countries. *Group Processes & Intergroup Relations, 12,* 41–60.

Groenendijk, K. (2006). Citizens and third country nationals: Differential treatment or discrimination? In J. -Y.

Carlier & E. Guild (Eds.), *The future of free movement of persons in the EU.* (pp. 79–101). Bruxelles: Bruylant.

Guimond, S., & Dubé-Simard, L. (1983). Relative deprivation theory and the Quebec nationalist movement: The cognitive-emotion distinction and the person-group deprivation issue. *Journal of Personality and Social Psychology, 44,* 526–535.

Habermas, J. (2001). *The postnational constellation: Political essays* Cambridge, MA: MIT Press.

Heatherton, T. F., Kleck, R. E., Hebl, M. R., & Hull, J. G. (2000). *The social psychology of stigma* New York, NY: Guilford Press.

Hinkle, S., & Brown, R. (1990). Intergroup comparisons and social identity: Some links and lacunae. In D. Abrams & M. A. Hogg (Eds.), *Social identity theory: Constructive and critical advances.* (pp. 48–70). London: Harvester-Wheatsheaf.

Hirschman, A. O. (1970). *Exit, voice, and loyalty; Responses to decline in firms, organizations, and States* Cambridge, MA: Harvard University Press.

Honneth, A. (1996). *The struggle for recognition: The moral grammar of social conflicts* Cambridge, MA: MIT Press.

Honneth, A. (2003). Redistribution as recognition: A response to Nancy Fraser. In N. Fraser & A. Honneth (Eds.), *Redistribution or recognition? A political-philosophical exchange.* (pp. 110–197). New York: Verso.

Honneth, A. (2007). *Disrespect: The normative foundations of critical theory* Cambridge, UK: Polity Press.

Huddy, L. (2001). From social to political identity: A critical examination of social identity theory. *Political Psychology, 22,* 127–156.

Huntington, S. P. (1996). *The clash of civilizations and the remaking of world order* New York: Simon & Schuster.

Jacobs, D., & Rea, A. (2007). The end of national models? Integration courses and citizenship trajectories in Europe. *International Journal on Multicultural Societies, 9,* 264–283.

Jodelet, D. (2005). Formes et figures de l'altérité [Forms and figures of otherness]. In M. Sanchez-Mazas & L. Licata (Eds.), *L'Autre: Regards psychosociaux.* (pp. 23–48). Grenoble: Presses Universitaires de Grenoble.

Joppke, C. (2007). Beyond national models: Civic integration policies for immigrants in Western Europe. *West European Politics, 30,* 1–22.

Jost, J. T., & Major, B. (2001). *The psychology of legitimacy: Emerging perspectives on ideology, justice, and intergroup relations* New York: Cambridge University Press.

Katz, I., & Hass, R. G. (1988). Racial ambivalence and American value conflict – correlational and priming studies of dual cognitive structures. *Journal of Personality and Social Psychology, 55,* 893–905.

Klandermans, B. (1997). *The social psychology of protest* Oxford, UK: Blackwell Publishers.

Klein, O., & Licata, L. (2003). When group representations serve social change: The speeches of

Patrice Lumumba during the Congolese decolonization. *British Journal of Social Psychology*, *42*, 571–593.

Klein, O., & Snyder, M. (2003). Stereotypes and behavioral confirmation: From interpersonal to intergroup perspectives. In M. P. Zanna, (Ed.), *Advances in Experimental Social Psychology*. (Vol. 35., pp. 153–234). San Diego, CA: Academic Press.

Koopmans, R., & Kriesi, H. (1997). Citoyenneté, identité nationale et mobilisation de l'extrême-droite. Une comparaison entre la France, l'Allemagne, les Pays-Bas et la Suisse [Citizenship, national identity, and extreme right mobilisation. A comparison between France, Germany, the Netherlands and Switzerland]. In P. Birnbaum, (Ed.), *Sociologie des nationalismes*. Paris: PUF.

Koopmans, R., Statham, P., Giugni, M., & Passy, F. (2005). *Contested citizenship: Immigration and cultural diversity in Europe* Minneapolis: University of Minnesota Press.

Kymlicka, W. (2007). *Multicultural odysseys Navigating the new international politics of diversity* Oxford, UK: Oxford University Press.

Licata, L. (2003). Representing the future of the European union: Consequences on national and European identifications. *Papers on Social Representations*, *12*, 5.1–5.22.

Licata, L., & Klein, O. (2002). Does European citizenship breed xenophobia?: European identification as a predictor of intolerance towards immigrants. *Journal of Community and Applied Social Psychology*, *12*, 323–337.

Licata, L., Klein, O., Casini, A., Coscenza, A., & Azzi, A. E. (2003). Driving European identification through discourse: Do nationals feel more European when told they are all similar?. *Psychologica Belgica*, *43*, 85–102.

Major, B., & O'Brien, L. T. (2005). The social psychology of stigma. *Annual Review of Psychology*, *56*, 393–421.

Margalit, A. (1996). *The decent society* Cambridge, MA: Harvard University Press.

Marková, I. (1987). Knowledge of the self through interaction. In K. Yardley & T. Honess (Eds.), *Self and identity: Psychosocial perspectives*. (pp. 65–80). New York: Wiley.

Mead, G. H. (1934/1967). *Mind, self, and society from the standpoint of a social behaviorist* (Vol. 1). Chicago: The University of Chicago Press.

Meeus, J., Duriez, B., Vanbeselaere, N., & Boen, F. (2010). The role of national identity representation in the relation between ingroup identification and outgroup derogation: Ethnic versus civic representation. *British Journal of Social Psychology, 49*(2), 305–320.

Moghaddam, F. M. (2006). *From the terrorists' point of view: What they experience and why they come to destroy* Westport, CT: Praeger Security International.

Moscovici, S., & Mugny, G. (1985).*Perspectives on minority influence*. Cambridge University Press.

Mummendey, A., Klink, A., & Brown, R. (2001). Nationalism and patriotism: National identification and out-group rejection. *British Journal of Social Psychology*, *40*, 159–171.

Myrdal, G. (1969). *An American dilemma. The Negro problem and modern democracy* [1944]. New York: Harper & Row.

Nesdale, D. (2004). Social identity processes and children's ethnic prejudice. In M. Bennett & F. Sani (Eds.), *The development of the social self*. (pp. 219–245). Hove: Psychology Press.

Pehrson, S., Brown, R., & Zagefka, H. (2009). When does national identification lead to the rejection of immigrants? Cross-sectional and longitudinal evidence for the role of essentialist in-group definitions. *British Journal of Social Psychology*, *48*, 61–76.

Pehrson, S., Vignoles, V. L., & Brown, R. (2009). National identification and anti-immigrant prejudice: Individual and contextual effects of national definitions. *Social Psychology Quarterly*, *72*, 24–38.

Pettigrew, T. F., Christ, O., Wagner, U., Meertens, R. W., van Dick, R., & Zick, A. (2008). Relative deprivation and intergroup prejudice. *Journal of Social Issues*, *64*, 385–401.

Pettigrew, T. F., Jackson, J. S., Brika, J. B., Lemaine, G., Meertens, R. W., Wagner, U., et al. (1997). Outgroup prejudice in Western Europe. *European Review of Social Psychology*, *8*, 241–273.

Phalet, K., & Kosic, A. (2006). Acculturation in European societies. In D. L. Sam & J. W. Berry (Eds.), *The Cambridge handbook of acculturation psychology*. (pp. 331–348). Cambridge, NY: Cambridge University Press.

Pratto, F., & Lemieux, A. F. (2001). The psychological ambiguity of immigration and its implications for promoting immigration policy. *Journal of Social Issues*, *57*, 413–430.

Quintelier, E., & Dejaeghere, Y. (2008). Does European citizenship increase tolerance in young people?. *European Union Politics*, *9*, 339–362.

Reicher, S. (2004). The context of social identity: Domination, resistance, and change. *Political Psychology*, *25*, 921–945

Reicher, S., & Hopkins, N. (2001). *Self and nation* London: Sage.

Richardson, J. E. (2004). *(Mis) representing Islam: The racism and rhetoric of British broadsheet newspapers* Philadelphia, PA: John Benjamins Publishing Company.

Riek, B. M., Mania, E. W., & Gaertner, S. L. (2006). Intergroup threat and outgroup attitudes: A meta-analytic review. *Personality and Social Psychology Review*, *10*, 336–353.

Sanchez-Mazas, M. (1996). Minority influence under value conflict: The case of human rights and xenophobia. *British Journal of Social Psychology*, *35*, 169–178.

Sanchez-Mazas, M. (2004). *Racisme et xénophobie* [Racism and xenophobia]. Paris: Presses Universitaires de France.

Sanchez-Mazas, M. (2007). Violence or persuasion? Denial of recognition and opportunities for action in contemporary societies. *Diogenes, 217*, 94–106.

Sanchez-Mazas, M., Maggi, J., & Roca i Escoda, M. (2010). De la contrainte à la restitution. En quête de la voix des sans-droits [From constraint to restitution. Searching the voice of the rightless]. In J. -P. Payet, C. Rostaing, &, f Giuliani, (Eds), *La relation d'enquête. La sociologie au défi des acteurs faibles*. Rennes, France: Presses Universitaires de Rennes.

Sanchez-Mazas, M., Van Humskerken, F., & Casini, A. (2003). Towards a social representational approach to citizenship: Political positioning in lay conceptions of the Belgian and of the European citizen. *Psychologica Belgica, 43*, 55–84.

Sanchez-Mazas, M., Van Humskerken, F., & Gély, R. (2005). La citoyenneté européenne et l' "Autre du dedans" [European citizenship and the « Other from the inside »]. In M. Sanchez-Mazas & L. Licata (Eds.), *L'Autre: Regards psychosociaux*. (pp. 309–336). Grenoble, France: Presses Universitaires de Grenoble.

Scheepers, P., Gijsberts, M., & Coenders, M. (2002). Ethnic exclusionism in European countries – Public opposition to civil rights for legal migrants as a response to perceived ethnic threat. *European Sociological Review, 18*, 17–34.

Schmitt, M. T., & Branscombe, N. R. (2002). Meaning and consequences of perceived discrimination in advantaged and privileged social groups. *European Review of Social Psychology, 12*, 167–199.

Sears, D. O., & Henry, P. J. (2005). Over thirty years later: A contemporary look at symbolic racism. *Advances in Experimental Social Psychology, 37*, 95–150.

Semyonov, M., Raijman, R., Yom Tov, A., & Schmidt, P. (2004). Population size, perceived threat, and exclusion: A multiple-indicators analysis of attitudes toward foreigners in Germany. *Social Science Research, 33*, 681–701.

Sherif, M. (1967). *Group conflict and co-operation: Their social psychology* London: Routledge & K. Paul.

Sidanius, J., & Pratto, F. (1999). *Social dominance: An intergroup theory of social hierarchy and oppression* New York, NY: Cambridge University Press.

Simon, B. (2004). *Identity in modern society: A social psychological perspective* Malden, MA: Blackwell.

Simon, B. (2010). Collective identity and political engagement. In A. E. Azzi, X. Chryssochoou, B. Klandermans, B. Simon, (Eds.), *Identity and participation in culturally diverse societies: A multidisciplinary perspective* (pp. 137–157). Oxford, UK: Wiley-Blackwell.

Simon, B., & Ruhs, D. (2008). Identity and politicization among Turkish migrants in Germany: The role of dual identification. *Journal of Personality and Social Psychology, 95*, 1354–1366.

Smith, A. D. (2001). *Nationalism: Theory, ideology, history* Malden, MA: Polity Press.

Staerklé, C. (2005). L'idéal démocratique perverti: Représentations antagonistes dans la mise en altérité du non-Occident [The perverted democratic ideal: Antagonistic representations in the othering of the non-West]. In M. Sanchez-Mazas, L. Licata, (Eds.), *L'Autre: Regards psychosociaux*. (pp. 117–148). Grenoble: Presses Universitaires de Grenoble.

Staerklé, C., Sidanius, J., Green, E. G. T., & Molina, L. (2005). Ethnic minority-majority asymmetry and attitudes towards immigrants across 11 nations. *Psicologia Politica, 30*, 7–26.

Staerklé, C., Sidanius, J., Green, E. G. T., & Molina, L. (2010). Ethnic minority-majority asymmetry in national attitudes around the world: A multilevel analysis. *Political Psychology, 31*, 491–519.

Steele, C., & Aronson, J. (1995). Stereotype threat and the intellectual performance of African Americans. *Journal of Personality and Social Psychology, 69*, 797–811.

Steiner, N. (2009). *International migration and citizenship today* London: Taylor & Francis.

Stephan, W. G., & Renfro, C. L. (2003). The role of threat in intergroup relations. In D. M. Mackie, E. R. Smith, (Eds.), *From prejudice to intergroup emotions: Differentiated reactions to social groups*. (pp. 191–207). New York: Psychology Press.

Strabac, Z., & Listhaug, A. (2008). Anti-Muslim prejudice in Europe: A multilevel analysis of survey data from 30 countries. *Social Science Research, 37*(1), 268–286.

Stråth, B. (2000). *Europe and the other and Europe as the other*. Bruxelles: PIE-Peter Lang.

Swim, J. K., & Stangor, C. (1998). *Prejudice: The target's perspective* San Diego, CA: Academic Press.

Tajfel, H., & Turner, J. C. (1986). The social identity theory of intergroup behavior. In S. Worchel, W. G. Austin, (Eds.), *The psychology of intergroup relations*. (pp. 7–24). Chicago: Nelson-Hall.

Turner, J. C. (1999). Some current issues in research on social identity and self-categorisation theories. In N. Ellemers, R. Spears, B. Doosje, (Eds.), *Social identity: Context, commitment, content*. (pp. 6–34). Oxford: Blackwell.

Turner, R. N., & Brown, R. (2008). Improving children's attitudes toward refugees: An evaluation of a school-based multicultural curriculum and an anti-racist intervention. *Journal of Applied Social Psychology, 38*, 1295–1328.

Verkuyten, M. (2006). Multicultural recognition and ethnic minority rights: A social identity perspective. *European Review of Social Psychology, 17*, 148–184.

Verkuyten, M., & Yildiz, A. A. (2007). National (dis)identification and ethnic and religious identity: A study among Turkish-Dutch Muslims. *Personality and Social Psychology Bulletin, 33*, 1448–1462.

Volpato, C., & Licata, L. (2010). Introduction: Collective memories of colonial violence. *International Journal of Conflict and Violence*, *4*, 4–10.

Wright, S. C., & Taylor, D. M. (1998). Responding to Tokenism: Individual action in the face of collective injustice. *European Journal of Social Psychology*, *28*, 647–667.

Zárate, M. A., Garcia, B., Garza, A. A., & Hitlan, R. T. (2004). Cultural threat and perceived realistic group conflict as dual predictors of prejudice. *Journal of Experimental Social Psychology*, *40*(1), 99–105.

Identity, Genocide, and Group Violence

39

David Moshman

Abstract

Social identity is typically multidimensional, involving connections and commitments to multiple overlapping groups. Because abstract groups such as nations, cultures, or religions have the potential to outlast the individuals who compose them at any given point in time, affiliation with such groups provides a sense of continuity, permanence, and meaning. Thus, we are highly motivated to act on behalf of groups central to our social identities and against other groups that threaten or impede our own. On the basis of these theoretical considerations, the chapter provides a four-phase model of genocide. The first phase involves a dichotomization of identity that divides the social universe into "us" and "them." Phase 2 involves a process of dehumanization that places "them" outside the realm of moral obligation. This enables and justifies violence against the out-group, up to and including genocide (phase 3). Such justification is supplemented, in a final phase, by denial of what really happened, thus enabling the perpetrators to maintain their moral self-conceptions. These phases are illustrated with examples encompassing the Holocaust, the 1994 genocide in Rwanda, the Latin American dirty wars of the 1970s and 1980s, and the European conquest of the Americas since 1492. The analysis is then extended to other cases of group violence, including the 1948 ethnic cleansing of Palestine, the September 11, 2001 attacks on the World Trade Centers and Pentagon, and the atomic bombing of Hiroshima.

Identity is a concept that spans psychology and sociology, or more broadly the behavioral and social sciences. Indeed, much of its theoretical power derives from its potential to connect multiple levels of explanation. Such connection is critical to explaining genocide, an act of group against group that is perpetrated by many individuals against many others. Neither psychology nor sociology can explain genocide alone. Identity, I suggest, is the key concept that enables us to connect these levels of explanation with each other and with the phenomena of genocide.

In this chapter, I consider the relation of identity to genocide and other group violence. After

D. Moshman (✉)
Department of Educational Psychology, University of Nebraska, Lincoln, NE, USA
e-mail: dmoshman1@unl.edu

S.J. Schwartz et al. (eds.), *Handbook of Identity Theory and Research*,
DOI 10.1007/978-1-4419-7988-9_39, © Springer Science+Business Media, LLC 2011

preliminary discussion concerning the nature of identity and of genocide, I suggest four phases of genocide (Moshman, 2007): (1) dichotomization of identities; (2) dehumanization of the other; (3) destruction of the other; and (4) denial, which preserves a subjective moral identity. These phases are illustrated with examples from Rwanda, the Holocaust, the Latin American dirty wars of the 1970s and 1980s, and the European conquest of the Americas. I then conceptualize genocide as the destruction of social identity. Extending the analysis, I consider the roles of dichotomization, dehumanization, and denial in ethnic cleansing, terrorism, and other forms of group violence that also attack social identities. Finally, I provide some suggestions for minimizing group violence.

Identity and Genocide

I begin with definitional and conceptual issues concerning the nature of identity and the nature of genocide.

The Nature of Identity

Consistent with the organization of this volume, I distinguish two aspects of identity: personal and social. By *personal identity,* I mean roughly what is meant by identity in the literature of developmental psychology, extending from the mid-century psychoanalytic conceptualization of ego identity formation in adolescence (Erikson, 1968) through the identity status approach that dominated the 1970s and 1980s (see Kroger & Marcia, Chapter 2, this volume) and the more cognitive and process-oriented approaches of the past several decades (e.g., Berzonsky, Chapter 3, this volume). One's identity, in this view, is personal in that it is one's own theory of who one is. More specifically, I have suggested, *to have an identity is to have an explicit theory of yourself as a person* – that is, as a singular and continuous rational agent, extending from the past through the future, and acting on the basis of

beliefs and values that you see as defining who you are (Moshman, 2011).

Identity in this view is intrinsically subjective but constrained by objective realities. One's various personality traits, for example, constitute aspects of one's (actual) self, not one's identity. If one comes to see being honest as fundamental to who one is, and organizes one's other self-conceptions around this self-conception, then being an honest person is central to one's (subjective) identity. If in fact one cheats and lies to everyone around, this (subjective) self-conception is (objectively) false. It remains nonetheless one's identity, because it is one's theory of oneself, but the discrepancy between identity and behavior, at least to the extent that one comes to recognize it, may pressure one to either modify one's behavior or reconstruct one's identity.

By *social identity,* I mean roughly what is meant by identity in most of the social sciences and the humanities, including social psychology. Social identity refers to those aspects of identity that involve relations to others (e.g., Chen, Boucher, & Kraus, Chapter 7, this volume) and especially to groups (Spears, Chapter 9, this volume). To the extent that such groups are abstract social entities such as nations, cultures, or religions, rather than just collections of people, they have the potential to outlast the individuals who compose them at any given time. Affiliation with such groups thus provides our identities with a deepened sense of continuity, permanence, and meaning. As a result, we are highly motivated to act on behalf of groups central to our social identities.

The concept of social identity helps us steer between the Scylla and Charybdis of psychological and sociological reductionism (Postmes & Jetten, 2006). If we see social identity as simply an aspect of personal identity, we veer toward an overly psychological conception of individual people as pre-existing autonomous agents who create social groups. If instead we see social identity as simply a matter of being part of a group, we veer toward an overly sociological conception of groups as pre-existing entities that mold the identities of their members. The challenge is to maintain a more dialectical conception of social identity that connects the sociological reality of human groups to the psychological reality of personal identities.

The Nature of Genocide

The term *genocide* was introduced by Raphael Lemkin in his 1944 book *Axis Rule in Occupied Europe*. He defined it as "the destruction of a nation or of an ethnic group" (p. 79). This includes, but is not limited to, immediate destruction through mass killings. The term *genocide* signifies

> a coordinated plan of different actions aiming at the destruction of essential foundations of the life of national groups, with the aim of annihilating the groups themselves. The objectives of such a plan would be disintegration of the political and social institutions, of culture, language, national feelings, religion, and the economic existence of national groups, and the destruction of the personal security, liberty, health, dignity, and even the lives of the individuals belonging to such groups. Genocide is directed against the national group as an entity, and the actions involved are directed against individuals, not in their individual capacity, but as members of the national group (Lemkin, 1944, p. 79).

Genocide thus overlaps with mass killing but is not identical to it. Mass killing is the killing of many individuals; genocide is the destruction of a group.

On December 11, 1946, the General Assembly of the United Nations passed the following resolution:

> Genocide is a denial of the right of existence of entire human groups, as homicide is the denial of the right to live of individual human beings; such denial of the right of existence shocks the conscience of mankind, results in great losses to humanity in the form of cultural and other contributions represented by these groups, and is contrary to moral law and to the spirit and aims of the United Nations (United Nations, 1946).

The resolution went on to clarify the application of the term to "racial, religious, political and other groups." It affirmed "that genocide is a crime under international law which the civilized world condemns."

Consistent with Lemkin's conception of genocide as a crime against groups, the General Assembly resolution begins with an explanation that genocide is not mass murder but a crime at a different level of analysis that is analogous to murder. Genocide is to a social group as murder is to an individual. It is the denial of the right to exist. Although the resolution had no legal force, its general approach, rooted in Lemkin's original conception, has much to commend it (Churchill, 1997; Moshman, 2008).

The legal definition of genocide was provided 2 years later in the 1948 United Nations Genocide Convention. An awkward and unprincipled hodgepodge of criteria, this definition is what emerged from political negotiations and compromises among the great powers – all of which were guilty of major atrocities, and none of which wanted to be guilty of genocide (Kuper, 1981). Despite its authoritative status as international law, the Genocide Convention has been rejected by almost all historians and social scientists as unusable for research purposes. There is no consensus, however, about what should replace it (Curthoys & Docker, 2008; Shaw, 2007). Proposed definitions vary with respect to at least eight dimensions (Moshman, 2008).

One of those dimensions, for example, is intent (Browning, 2004; Fein, 1993; Mann, 2005; Shaw, 2007; Straus, 2006, 2008). Even in clear cases of genocide such as Rwanda and the Holocaust, perpetrators do not issue official proclamations of genocide on behalf of their group. Genocides involve multiple agents with multiple perceptions, intentions, and motives. Genocide is typically an evolving process, moreover. At both individual and group levels, intent changes over time in response to changing conditions. This is not to say group intent is a meaningless concept or that it can never be empirically determined. Genocides do not happen by accident. Group intent may be implicit in, and inferred from, a genocidal act or process. But intent is not just something a group has or doesn't have.

Intent is one of many issues about which scholars of genocide continue to debate, and some of those debates go to the heart of what constitutes genocide. For present purposes, following Lemkin and the UN Resolution, I define *genocide* as *an act or process of destruction aimed at an abstractly defined group of people*. There may be many perpetrators, but their actions must be sufficiently coordinated to constitute a singular act or process. The genocidal process may include deliberate acts of mass killing, but it may also consist, entirely or in part, of other actions undermining the biological, social, or cultural integrity of the victim group. The acts of destruction may be aimed at individuals, but the individuals are targeted on the basis of their actual or perceived association with a national, ethnic, racial, religious, political, socioeconomic, or other abstractly defined group. The group must be deliberately targeted, but the process may be deemed genocidal even if the motives of the perpetrators are complex and multifaceted, even if their intentions shift over time, even if their perceptions of the victim group are wildly inaccurate, and even if the extent of destruction is less than total.

Phases of Genocide

Examination of diverse genocides from multiple regions of the world indicates a common pattern of four overlapping phases (Moshman, 2007): First, there is a dichotomization of identities such that everyone is either one of "us" or one of "them." Second, there is a process of dehumanization of the other that serves the purpose of removing them from the universe of moral concern, thus enabling us to act toward them in ways that would be morally unacceptable among people. Next comes destruction of the other. Finally, beginning even before the actual destruction and lasting long after, there is denial, which preserves a subjective moral identity.

In this section, I discuss these four phases of genocide, with examples from Rwanda, the Holocaust, the Latin American dirty wars, and the conquest of the Americas.

Dichotomization of Identities

People generally define themselves on the basis of multiple affiliations and commitments (e.g., ethnic, religious, political, sexual, and vocational; see Kroger & Marcia, Chapter 2, this volume), some more central to identity than others (with their relative centrality varying across persons). Because there are so many potential dimensions of identity, so many options with respect to each, so many possible combinations of those options and dimensions, and so many ways to prioritize and coordinate them, we each form a unique personal identity that is in part our own creation. Any two individuals, however, are likely to have affiliations and commitments in common and thus a shared social identity. More generally, we might say that the typical state of a society involves overlapping social identities such that each individual is both unique and a part of multiple groups. Dichotomized identities, then, are not typical. They often arise, however, due to contact between societies or forces within a society.

When two very different societies come suddenly into contact, potential social identities that cut across them are at least initially inconceivable due to the cultural (as well as geographical) divide between them. In the various first contacts with the indigenous peoples of the Americas beginning in 1492, for example, the women of Spain, France, England, Portugal, and their colonies could not come together in feminist solidarity even with each other, much less with the women of the indigenous societies that their own societies were destroying. Indigenous women were to them, for the most part, female Indians, not fellow women. Similarly, European youth did not join indigenous youth to work against the genocides of the older generations in their various societies. No common generational ground was even conceivable across the cultural divide between Europe (including its colonies) and the Americas, especially at first.

In other cases, dichotomized identities are the outcome of a process of dichotomization within an existing society. This involves the construction of social and cultural understandings that render some potential dimensions of identity so salient that all others become peripheral. People increasingly define themselves, and construe each other, with respect to a small number of dimensions. If the process continues to its end, one dimension is highlighted above all others as what does or should define everyone, and that dimension is reduced to two categories (Brewer, 2001; Kelman, 2001; Maalouf, 2001; Sen, 2006; Stanton, 2004; Weitz, 2003).

An extreme example of deliberate dichotomization is the 1994 genocide in Rwanda (Des Forges, 1999; Gourevitch, 1998; Mamdani, 2001; Mann, 2005; Moshman, 2004b; Stanton, 2004; Straus, 2006, 2008). Unlike most African countries, Rwanda existed as a nation prior to European colonization. There was a longstanding but fluid distinction between Hutu and Tutsi based on a combination of ancestry and socioeconomic status, assessed in part on the basis of owning cattle. Contrary to Western media portrayals, the Hutu and Tutsi were not tribes or ethnic groups. They lived among each other, shared religious beliefs, and intermarried. Rwanda was a single society with a typical pattern of unique personal identities (in which being Hutu or Tutsi might be very important, less important, or irrelevant) and overlapping social identities (such that being Hutu or Tutsi was just one of many ways two Rwandans might share a social identity). The Tutsi (who constituted about 15% of the population) dominated politically and economically, but some Hutu attained a measure of power and economic success, and many Tutsi were as poor and marginalized as the majority of Hutu.

European rule from the 1890s to the early 1960s reinforced Tutsi power as a means of controlling the country. Identity cards that distinguished Hutu from Tutsi became mandatory, thus officially dichotomizing the population. In the early 1960s, Rwanda became independent under the control, for the first time, of its Hutu majority, many of whom saw their attainment of power as a democratic victory after centuries of illegitimate domination by the Tutsi minority. Many Tutsi, in turn, aimed to regain what they saw as their rightful authority. Efforts to eliminate official identity cards were unsuccessful.

By the early 1990s, Rwandans could still have multifaceted identities and many still saw being Rwandan as something different from and more fundamental than being Hutu or Tutsi, but the pressure to be Hutu or Tutsi above all was intensifying. This was due in part to the threat of a Tutsi-dominated army making incursions from Uganda and in part to the rise of a political movement that called itself Hutu Power, which defined Rwanda as a Hutu nation and denounced the Tutsi as aliens descended from Ethiopian immigrants who had taken control of Rwanda long before the European colonizers. Hutu Power had strong governmental connections and made systematic use of radio to spread anti-Tutsi propaganda across Rwanda. Rwandans could see themselves as affiliated with or committed to a variety of religions, professions, activities, ideologies, political parties, and so forth but faced relentless pressure to see themselves as, first and foremost, Hutu or Tutsi.

One common dynamic in situations of group violence is that moderates on each side are undermined by extremists on the other whose ideologies and violence challenge moderate claims about the rationality and humanity of the other side. In Rwanda leading up to 1994, moderate Hutu who advocated among their fellow Hutu a vision of Rwanda for all Rwandans were undermined by Tutsi extremists who advocated a return to Tutsi rule, thus confirming the claims of Hutu extremists about what the Tutsi really wanted. Correspondingly, moderate Tutsi who advocated among their fellow Tutsi an inclusive and democratic conception of Rwanda were undermined by the Hutu Power position that the Hutu were the true Rwandan nation, leaving no place for Tutsi. As the Hutu Power movement turned to deadly violence against moderate Hutu and all Tutsi, the middle ground collapsed entirely, dichotomizing Rwanda into supporters of Hutu Power and everyone else. In the opening days of the 1994 genocide, thousands of moderate Hutu who accepted the Tutsi as part of the Rwandan nation were killed by advocates of Hutu Power for betraying their Hutu identity. By the time the 100-day genocide ended, over half a million Tutsi had been killed, many of them identified, at the point of a machete, on the basis of their identity cards.

Dehumanization of the Other

Having differentiated the other from ourselves, we are now in a position to dehumanize. Dehumanization is an everyday social phenomenon (Haslam, 2006). Dichotomization of identities, however, enables more radical and systematic forms of group dehumanization (Weitz, 2003). Targets of genocide have been variously labeled weeds, rats, vermin, dogs, wolves, cows, monkeys, viruses, maggots, microbes, parasites, plague, pests, snakes, spiders, lice, locusts, cockroaches, cancerous cells, or malignant tumors. Less biologically, they have been portrayed and seen as heretics, heathens, infidels, barbarians, savages, subversives, or terrorists. Whatever we call them, the point is that they are not part of the human universe of persons, not subject to norms of human rights and justice, not among those to whom our moral obligations extend (Fein, 1993). They are not just different from us (dichotomization) but less worthy than us (dehumanization). Our moral obligations to others are obligations to other *people* and to the social identities that define us as people and bind us to each other, not to an undifferentiated mass of weeds, rats, vermin, subversives, or terrorists. Thus, we prepare ourselves psychologically to do things to others that we would never do to (those we see as) people.

The Hutu Power movement, for example, successfully spread a conception of the Tutsi as cockroaches. They were not just a group distinct from the Hutu; they were a group distinct from humanity. They were not just different; they were not human at all, lacking both individual identity and moral status. Cockroaches, from a human point of view, are interchangeable; to kill a cockroach simply means one less cockroach, regardless of which one you kill. Similarly, to kill a Tutsi can be seen simply as decreasing the number of Tutsi, who lack the individuality that might raise questions of individual rights. In the moral worldview of Hutu Power, all Hutu were obligated, first and foremost, to each other

and to the Hutu nation of Rwanda. For any true Hutu, in this view, elimination of the Tutsi threat, and if necessary of the Tutsi themselves, was a moral imperative. And this created a psychological imperative not to see the humanity of the Tutsi. If cockroaches need to be eliminated, it becomes especially important to keep thinking of them as cockroaches.

The path toward the Holocaust within Germany after 1933 involved a dichotomization of Jews from Germans such that Jewish Germans became German Jews and ultimately just Jews. Jewishness became a defining quality regardless of nationality, beliefs, profession, political affiliation, or anything else. The dichotomization led directly to increasingly extreme forms of dehumanization. By the time the Polish death camps were operating at peak capacity in 1942–1943, Franz Stangl, commandant of Treblinka, saw the arriving Jews getting off the trains as "cattle," a mindless herd, making its way toward the slaughterhouse where it would be transformed into "a mass of rotting flesh" that "had nothing to do with humanity." The Jews were "cargo" to be transported and their bodies were garbage to be disposed of. "I rarely saw them as individuals," Stangl explained. "It was always a huge mass" (Sereny, 1983, p. 201).

In Argentina in the late 1970s, some 30,000 individuals, mostly young adults who worked with the poor or expressed commitments to social justice, were kidnapped and tortured to death by the military government. Was it moral to treat them this way? The question need not be asked because, as General Ramon Camps pointed out, "it wasn't people that disappeared, but subversives" (Fisher, 1989, p. 102). Chile and other countries also "disappeared" their subversives. In Guatemala and El Salvador, entire villages were deemed subversive, often because they were in subversive regions, thus justifying genocidal massacres of all their inhabitants (Archdiocese of Guatemala, 1999; Danner, 1994; Manz, 2004; Moshman, 2004a; Sanford, 2003, 2008). Were the children subversive? Again, a question that need not be asked. The children were part of a subversive village, not individuals. In Guatemala, where the death toll of the dirty war reached

200,000, Mayans who survived the destruction of their villages were finished off in coordinated military operations known as "hunting the deer" (Sanford, 2003, p. 160, 2008, p. 563).

But of course, dehumanization of indigenous Americans is nothing new. Rebellious natives in the Americas, reasoned seventeenth-century philosopher John Locke in his *Two Treatises on Civil Government,* had "declared war against all mankind, and therefore may be destroyed as a lion or tiger, one of those wild savage beasts with whom men can have no society or security" (quoted in McDonnell & Moses, 2005, p. 513). No less philosophical, nineteenth-century settlers in the American southwest saw the Apaches as wolves – "the most savage wild beast" – that must be hunted to the point of "extermination" (Jacoby, 2008).

Destruction of the Other

Dichotomization and dehumanization are, I suggest, necessary but not sufficient conditions for genocide. There are both empirical and theoretical bases for this claim.

Empirically, dichotomization and dehumanization do not always progress to the point of genocide but there are no cases, to my knowledge, where genocide was not preceded by radical forms of dichotomization and dehumanization. This is a matter to which I will return in the later discussions of ethnic cleansing, terrorism, and other group violence.

Theoretically, genocide requires (1) a small number of primary groups and (2) a way to rationalize destruction of a disfavored group. Dichotomization replaces the many dimensions along which people vary with a small number of categories, thus replacing networks of relationships with discrete groups. Dehumanization enables us not to recognize another category as consisting of persons entitled to moral treatment. Dichotomization and dehumanization together set the conditions for violence against the dehumanized group, but do not guarantee such violence, much less guarantee that destruction of the other group will be sought or achieved.

Whether a situation turns genocidal is a complex function of many interacting forces – psychological, sociological, economic, political, cultural, historical, and legal – and of the actions and interactions of large numbers of individuals. No existing theory or model successfully predicts whether or when dichotomization and dehumanization will continue to destruction. Some scholars propose that genocide can be explained on the basis of a small number of key causal factors, but there is no consensus on what those are (Shaw, 2007). Regardless, if genocide takes place, the next step is to create a history in which it didn't.

Denial to Preserve Moral Identity

Denial begins even before destruction – that is, before a genocide takes place. Before and during genocide, dehumanization enables us not to see our victims as persons and thus not to see the human consequences and moral significance of our actions. Denial continues, however, long after the period of active destruction is complete, enabling us and our descendants to avoid acknowledging what we have done. Thus, it constitutes genocide's normative final phase (Woolf & Hulsizer, 2005).

In addition to ongoing dehumanization, processes of denial take a variety of forms (Bandura, 1999; Cohen, 2001; Hulsizer, Monro, Fagerlin, & Taylor, 2004; Loewen, 1995; Moshman, 2004a, 2007). Among the most common are the following:

1. We simply refuse to acknowledge or consider the facts.
2. We decline to investigate something we don't want to know more about.
3. We remember facts that reinforce our views and don't remember facts that don't.
4. We manipulate the definition of genocide to exclude our own atrocities and focus instead on the evils of our enemies.
5. We insist that we had no choice under the circumstances, whatever they may have been, and that we did what anyone would have done.
6. We educate our children to understand the rightness of our cause and perspective and the wrongness of theirs.

Underlying all of these processes of denial is a widely shared commitment to preserve and defend, individually and collectively, our identities as moral agents. Some people may have stronger moral identities than do others, in the sense that morality is more central to their self-conceptions (Hardy & Carlo, Chapter 19, this volume), but it seems likely that nearly all people in all cultural contexts see themselves as fundamentally moral, whatever be their flaws, rather than fundamentally evil. We maintain our moral self-conceptions partly by behaving well and partly by denying, even to ourselves, our most egregious moral failures (Bandura, 1999; Moshman, 2004a). We may not be perfect, we gladly grant, but surely we have not committed genocide.

The dirty war in Argentina is known for what came to be called *disappearances*. The disappeared were gone. The military and government claimed to know nothing. Maybe the young men had gone off to join subversive groups, they suggested. Maybe the young women had become prostitutes. The children kidnapped with their parents or born in prison had never existed. There were no disappeared. Perhaps there were some missing individuals, the official doctrine acknowledged, but no social identity had been targeted or destroyed (Arditti, 1999; Bouvard, 1994; Fisher, 1989; Mellibovsky, 1997).

In Central America – especially Guatemala and El Salvador – entire villages were "disappeared," hundreds of them, their inhabitants massacred down to the last child (Archdiocese of Guatemala, 1999; Danner, 1994; Manz, 2004; Moshman, 2004a; Sanford, 2003, 2008). The United States armed and trained the perpetrators, which was a matter of political controversy in the 1980s, but there is no longer any debate in the United States as to whether US involvement in the Central American dirty wars was morally justified. The matter is simply never discussed. At least with respect to the mainstream media, the public educational system, and the major political parties, the denial of these and other such aspects of history is total.

Decades before the dirty wars, Operation Reinhard (Arad, 1987) was deemed by the Nazis, after serious debate, to be a top secret matter that must be hidden from history. Its three death camps – Belzec, Sobibor, and Treblinka – processed and killed more than 1.5 million Jews in 1942–1943. At first, Jewish slave laborers buried the bodies. Then, to maximize future deniability, they were instructed to burn all new bodies and to dig up the hundreds of thousands of buried bodies and burn them. After the transports, gassings, and cremations had ended in Treblinka, the last 30 Jewish slaves – 28 men and 2 women – spent each night in freight cars on the railway spur. In late November 1943, they were shot by three SS men, five at a time, each group cremating the corpses of the prior group, until the final group was cremated by Ukrainian guards. Treblinka was then demolished, as were Belzec and Sobibor. A small farm, with a farmhouse occupied by a former Ukrainian guard and his family, emerged at the site of each of Operation Reinhard's three death camps. Following orders aimed to protect German moral identity, Operation Reinhard ended with a systematic effort to eliminate itself and its victims from history.

Meanwhile, the nations of the Americas remain virtually oblivious to their emergence from a series of genocides that eliminated hundreds of targeted indigenous cultural groups (Barkan, 2003; Cave, 2008; Churchill, 1997; Jacoby, 2008; Kiernan, 2007; Stannard, 1992). No one wants to identify with a nation founded in genocide. Hiding our eyes from what we do not want to see, we fail to observe destruction all around us. More literally, hiding our minds from what we do not want to know, we fail to conceptualize genocide. Instead, in the language of denial, we see "progress" in the replacement of "barbarian" cultures with our own "civilization," the working out of a "manifest destiny."

Genocide as the Destruction of Identity

Genocide is usefully construed as the destruction of social identities (Powell, 2007). In the context of a mass killing, this conceptualization may seem far too subtle, even morally oblivious, but if our intent is to understand genocide, we must distinguish it from mass killing. Mass killing is the killing of many people, but genocide destroys something more than some number of people. The "something more" is a social identity. We can best see this in a case that separates, insofar as this is possible, genocide from mass killing.

From the late nineteenth century to the mid-twentieth century, the governments of the United States and Canada ran boarding schools for indigenous children from dozens of tribes (Adams, 1995; Churchill, 2004). The intent was to eliminate indigenous cultures by severing the link between generations and assimilating the children to American society. No one would be killed, in theory, but the indigenous cultures would disappear with the passing of the present generation.

The students, accordingly, were isolated from their families and communities. They received "white man's" names to replace those by which they had been known. They were issued clothing appropriate for their gender in "civilized" society. Boys, often to their great dismay, had their long hair cut. They were required to learn English and forbidden to speak their native languages. Christian beliefs and middle-class values dominated the curriculum. History was taught as the progress of civilization in the Americas since 1492. Girls were trained in domestic skills and boys in agricultural and industrial skills so that they could function in society.

The motto was "Kill the Indian, save the man." Indian schools proudly illustrated their success with before-and-after photographs that showed young savages transformed into civilized Americans. The children were "saved." What was "killed" was the social identity that would otherwise have linked them to their childhoods and ancestral cultures.

It would be morally blind to see no distinction between the Indian boarding schools and the death camps of Operation Reinhard. But it misses the point of genocide to see no similarity. Once we see genocide as an attack on social identity, moreover, we can better understand its connections to other forms of group violence.

Identity and Group Violence

Genocide is one of many forms of group violence. Thus, the connection of identity to genocide may best be seen as part of a more general connection of identity to group violence. For present purposes, I focus on ethnic cleansing and terrorism, and then touch briefly on torture, disappearances, and mass killing. In each case, it turns out, the same identity processes observed across a range of genocides – dichotomization, dehumanization, and denial – play central roles. This is consistent with the earlier conclusion that dichotomization and dehumanization do not necessarily lead to genocide. It appears instead that dichotomization, dehumanization, and denial are associated generally with attacks on social identity.

Ethnic Cleansing

Ethnic cleansing, like genocide, has a variety of overlapping definitions, none of which can be deemed authoritative. Rather than reviewing and analyzing these, suffice it to say that ethnic cleansing aims to eliminate some group from some place; its extreme form is genocide, which aims to eliminate a group from the world. For present purposes, I focus on a case that qualifies as ethnic cleansing under any definition: the 1948 ethnic cleansing of Palestine (Pappe, 2004, 2006).

Zionist ideology in the late nineteenth and early twentieth centuries portrayed Palestine to European Jews as "a land without a people for a people without a land." In fact, the land was inhabited by hundreds of thousands of people with an emerging national identity as Palestinians (Khalidi, 1997). As European Jews arrived in Palestine in the early twentieth century, it became increasingly clear that the creation of a Jewish state would require removing much of the Palestinian population in order to decrease the proportion of non-Jews to a manageable level. "I am for compulsory transfer," David Ben-Gurion told the Jewish Agency Executive in June 1938,

"I do not see anything immoral in it." (quoted in Pappe, 2006, p. xi)

The next decade saw World War II, the Holocaust, and a postwar influx of European Jewish refugees into Palestine. The new United Nations decided that, under the circumstances, a radical dichotomization was in order. Thus it devised the 1948 partition of Palestine. The indigenous Palestinians at this time still constituted about two-thirds of the population and owned almost all of the cultivated land. Nevertheless, the United Nations designated most of Palestine for the creation of a Jewish state. For the Zionists to realize their dream, however, they needed to get as many of the native Palestinians as possible out of what would become Israel. The Hagana, a Zionist paramilitary force, prepared for transfer (Pappe, 2006).

Plan Dalet, launched in March 1948 by Ben-Gurion and the Hagana, implemented the ethnic cleansing of what was about to become Israel. In the next few months, hundreds of villages were systematically emptied and destroyed. Some 700,000 Palestinians were expelled or fled in terror. Massacres of Palestinians by Jewish forces killed hundreds, including dozens of young children, and encouraged the frantic exodus of others who feared they and their villages would be next. Consistent with the purpose of the ethnic cleansing, virtually none were ever permitted to return. Instead, Palestinian villages were systematically replaced with Jewish settlements or Jewish National Fund forests (Pappe, 2006).

The ethnic cleansing was followed immediately by denial (McGowan & Ellis, 1998). The standard story, now rejected by all serious historians, told of an Israeli David fighting off the mighty Goliath of the invading Arab armies. Palestinians, the story goes, were told by their Arab supporters to get out of the way until they could later return in victory. Israeli history texts taught these founding myths until at least the 1980s (Podeh, 2002). Texts of the 1990s were revised on the basis of new historical evidence (especially Morris, 1987), but the old myths persist.

At an official level, Israel continues to deny the historical reality of the 1948 ethnic cleansing of Palestine and continues to dehumanize Palestinian victims of the ethnic cleansing and their descendants by refusing to recognize their fundamental human right to return to their 1948 homes or be compensated for what is irretrievably lost. The original dichotomization, of course, remains firmly in place. The case of Palestine is consistent with the hypothesis that dichotomization of identities, dehumanization of the other, and denial to maintain moral identity are relevant to group violence generally, not just to acts of genocide.

Terrorism

Terrorism has been seen by many as raising issues of identity (Schwartz, Dunkel, & Waterman, 2009). Perpetrators of terrorism identify strongly with their own group and see themselves as acting on its behalf to achieve its legitimate purposes (Moghaddam, 2006; Pape, 2005). They typically see what they are doing, or have done, as morally acceptable, admirable, or even obligatory under the circumstances. I consider here (1) the best-known example of terrorism and then (2) the deadliest day of terrorism (which was not the same day).

On September 11, 2001, planes flew into both towers of the World Trade Center in New York City and the Pentagon in Washington, DC. A fourth plane was also intended to hit a government building in Washington but crashed in Pennsylvania. About 3,000 people were killed. The plan, it turned out, was devised by an Islamist group known as Al-Qaeda, led by Osama bin Laden.

As is always the case, bin Laden and Al-Qaeda had their reasons (Lawrence, 2005; Moghaddam, 2006). They saw themselves as acting on behalf of Islam and their Muslim brethren against the ongoing violence, encroachments, and humiliations inflicted by America and its allies, including Israel, on the Muslim world. The targets hit by their planes – the Pentagon and World Trade Centers – were centers and symbols of the military and economic might of the United States and were occupied by those serving its purposes. The means used to attack the United States reflected the means available. And very few of the victims were children. Far from being unjustified and immoral, the September 11 attacks were seen by the perpetrators as morally praiseworthy.

But having what one sees as good reasons for acts of violence does not remove such acts from the category of terrorism. Bin Laden and Al-Qaeda engaged in deadly violence against people who had done no particular wrong in order to traumatize and intimidate Americans. By any definition, this was an act of terrorism.

And now: What was the deadliest day of terrorism in the history of the world? The answer, to the best of my knowledge, is August 6, 1945. That was the day the United States dropped an atom bomb on the city of Hiroshima, killing perhaps a hundred thousand people that very day and subjecting many thousands more to horrifying and deadly aftereffects. Given the scale of this mass killing, some scholars have considered it a genocidal act (Kuper, 1981; Markusen & Kopf, 1995). But the bombing of Hiroshima was not intended to destroy the people of Japan. It was intended to terrorize them into submission. Thus, it seems more accurate to call it an act of terrorism than an act of genocide.

No less than Al-Qaeda, the United States had its reasons. The United States was at war with Japan. It had been attacked at Pearl Harbor. It was saving lives by bringing the war to an end. It was doing what had to be done. These justifications are sufficient to convince most Americans that the bombing of Hiroshima was morally justified and did not constitute an act of terrorism.

More objective observers disagree (Grayling, 2006; Markusen & Kopf, 1995). Perpetrators of terrorism always have justifications of this sort that maintain their moral identities. They usually believe – often with good reason – that they were, are, or could soon be under attack. Their deadly violence is typically seen as a necessary part of a larger war. They commonly believe that theirs is the only path to a just peace. They easily convince themselves that whatever they do is saving more lives, in the long run, than it costs. Thus denial operates universally, blinding us all to our responsibility for deadly violence.

Thousands of the victims of Hiroshima were children, the most clearly innocent of all innocent victims. But Americans rarely think about the victims of Hiroshima even *en masse*, and never as individual people. Dichotomization and dehumanization are sufficiently powerful to enable the mass killing of children, and denial is sufficiently powerful to leave it in the past.

Torture, Disappearances, and Mass Killing

I conclude this section on group violence with a few more examples from several additional categories. Systematic programs of torture have been widespread for millennia. In the 1970s and 1980s, torture was central to the Latin American dirty wars. Its best-known site in recent years has been Abu Ghraib in Iraq (Danner, 2004; Gourevitch & Morris, 2008; Zimbardo, 2007), but the United States has also engaged in systematic programs of torture at Bagram Air Force Base in Afghanistan, at Guantanamo Bay Detention Camp in Cuba, and at an unknown number of secret "black sites." The United States has also practiced *extraordinary rendition*, in which prisoners are secretly and illegally transferred to other countries for the purpose of subjecting them to more heinous tortures (Mayer, 2008).

In sites where torture is performed, there is a clear dichotomization between those who can be tortured and those who can torture. Those to be tortured are seen as less than human – subversives, terrorists, extremists, fanatics – and the process of torture relentlessly reduces their humanity to the basics of biology. Torture is usually conducted secretly, often in secret places on secret prisoners. It is denied linguistically by calling it "interrogation" or "enhanced interrogation."

To be disappeared is to be taken, typically by governmental agents, without acknowledgment. The intent may be in part to eliminate political groups and views deemed objectionable, in part to terrorize those actually or potentially associated with such groups or views, and in part to permit denial of responsibility. The disappearances associated with Argentina's dirty war of the late 1970s were of a scale and nature to be deemed genocidal under most definitions.

The major program of disappearances in the first decade of the twenty-first century was the US abduction of an unknown number of people and their transport to secret "black sites" for torture. Because the victims were seen by most Americans as an amorphous and subhuman mass of Islamic terrorists, questions of their individual human rights did not arise. It remains to be seen whether this practice has been genuinely discontinued, whether the full story will ever be told, and whether anyone will be held accountable. Denial is often rooted in nationalist commitments that transcend political parties and changes in administration.

In mass killing, a large number of people are killed, usually because of the group to which they are thought to belong. If the intent is to kill enough individuals to eliminate the group itself, mass killing is genocide. Killings of multiple defenseless people on a smaller scale are usually called massacres. Killings of all people in a village, including children, are often called genocidal massacres.

Mass killings are usually not aimed at particular individuals as individuals, but their targets are not random. Almost always, they are crimes of group violence involving dichotomized social identities. Ongoing dehumanization of those to be killed renders the killing something less than murder. After the killing, powerful social and psychological processes extend the dehumanization of the victims by denying the crime, thus denying that they ever existed (Moshman, 2004a).

Minimizing Group Violence

To review briefly, identity has been defined as an explicit theory of oneself as a person (Moshman, 2011). To see oneself as a person is, in large part, to see oneself in relation to other people and to social groups. Social identity is typically multidimensional, involving connections and commitments to multiple overlapping groups.

On the basis of identity considerations, a four-phase model of genocide (Moshman, 2007) was presented. The first phase involves a dichotomization of identities that divides the social universe into "us" and "them." Phase 2 involves a process of dehumanization that places "them" outside the realm of moral obligation. This enables and justifies violence against the out group, up to and including genocide (phase 3). Such justification is supplemented, in a final phase, by denial of what really happened, thus enabling the perpetrators to maintain their moral self-conceptions.

Examination of other forms of group violence suggested that the three basic identity processes associated with genocide – dichotomization, dehumanization, and denial – may be general to group violence, which comes in many forms, including genocide, ethnic cleansing, terrorism, torture, disappearances, and mass killing. Large-scale acts of violence, moreover, usually fit multiple categories. The Holocaust encompassed all six of those listed above, and it is not unique in cutting across whatever conceptual categories we come up with. With respect to addressing group violence, then, what may be most important is not sharply distinguishing various forms of violence but rather recognizing their common themes of dichotomization, dehumanization, and denial.

Identity always has a strong component of social identity, which always entails some degree of in-group/out-group differentiation. The potential for dichotomization is thus always present (see Spears, Chapter 9, this volume). Resisting dichotomization is not a matter of suggesting that everyone feel equally related to everyone else or that no one ever feel part of a group or opposed to some other group. Rather, it is a matter of maintaining multiple connections, multiple affiliations, and overlapping groups. That is, we must "tame the wild beast of identity" (Maalouf, 2001, p. 157) by encouraging and maintaining multifaceted identities (Maalouf, 2001; Sen, 2006).

As noted earlier in connection with Rwanda, a common dynamic of group violence is that moderate claims about the rationality and humanity of the other are undermined by extremist ideologies and violence from that other side. The history since the 1948 partition of Palestine provides many examples of extremists on each side undermining moderates on the other and thus further dichotomizing the situation. For some this is just one piece, albeit a crucial one, in the broader "war of civilizations" between the "West" and "Islam," dichotomization on a still grander and more dangerous scale. "Moderates," in this context, are those working against dichotomization.

In resisting dichotomization, however, we must be wary of recreating it in the very distinction of extremists from moderates. The label "extremist," moreover, is not just dichotomizing but also dehumanizing in suggesting a group beyond rationality and discourse, hardly even human, and a radical danger to us all. What obligations could we possibly have to extremists? Wouldn't the world be a better place if we could just eliminate them all? Thus, we slip all too readily from dichotomization to dehumanization to utopian dreams of genocide (Weitz, 2003).

Fundamentally, I suggest, the problem is not terminology but conceptualization. Who counts as a person? This is reflected in our language but it is very much a matter of political and religious ideology and identity, with profound consequences for individuals and groups. Those failing to qualify as persons fall outside the universe of moral obligation. Challenging dehumanization requires argumentation and reconceptualization, not just careful language.

As for denial, it is pervasive and invisible, requiring active efforts to identify and overcome it. Even when historians debunk myths of the past, those myths often persist in the present and future. Israel, as discussed above, was born in an ethnic cleansing, with horrific ongoing consequences more than six decades later. Despite the work of Israeli historians such as Morris (1987) and Pappe (2004, 2006), this continues to be denied. Similarly, on a much larger scale, the nations of the Americas remain largely oblivious to the fact that they were born

through processes of ethnic cleansing and genocide directed at hundreds of indigenous cultural groups. And then there is the rest of the world. People everywhere live in denial of their history because the needs of patriotic national identity make the truth unacceptable (Moshman, 2009). Whatever else we do, we should determine and teach the truth.

Ordinary Identities

People typically see genocide as rare and attribute it to evil individuals or fanatical group hatreds. Perhaps the single most important conclusion of research on genocide has been the emerging consensus that genocide and other extreme forms of group violence are, on the contrary, all too common and are for the most part the work of "ordinary men" (and women) playing social roles in groups, institutions, and practices central to their identities (Arendt, 1994; Ashmore, Jussim, Wilder, & Heppen, 2001; Bandura, 1999; Browning, 1998, 2004; Gourevitch & Morris, 2008; Grayling, 2006; Mann, 2005; Markusen & Kopf, 1995; Moshman, 2005, 2007; Sereny, 1983; Shaw, 2007; Staub, 2001; Waller, 2002; Woolf & Hulsizer, 2005; Zimbardo, 2007).

Similarly, the present analysis suggests that genocide is the outcome of ordinary identities and ubiquitous psychological and social processes of dichotomization, dehumanization, and denial. The first challenge in explaining genocide and other group violence is to recognize that what we need to explain is not how "they" (who are evil, hateful, and violent) differ from "us" (who want only peace and justice) but rather why we all turn so often to group violence and support the violence of our own groups. The problem lies not in particular kinds of identity but in its general nature. As long as we have social identities – which is to say as long as we remain human – we will remain prone to group violence.

Genocide and other forms of group violence have played major roles in human history everywhere, and continue to do so. Perhaps they always will, not because we have genes for genocide but because we have social identities. Even if group violence cannot be eliminated, however, we can reduce it substantially and sometimes prevent it from escalating to genocide, by taking into account what we know of our identity processes. Of course, there is more to learn, but we know at least three things: We should be wary of efforts to divide us from others; we should resist dehumanization of others; and we should identify and challenge denials of the truth.

References

Adams, D. W. (1995). *Education for extinction: American Indians and the boarding school experience, 1875–1928*. Lawrence, KS: University of Kansas Press.

Arad, Y. (1987). *Belzec, Sobibor, Treblinka: The Operation Reinhard death camps*. Bloomington, IN: Indiana University Press.

Archdiocese of Guatemala (1999). *Guatemala: Never again!* Maryknoll, NY: Orbis.

Arditti, R. (1999). *Searching for life: The grandmothers of the Plaza de Mayo and the disappeared children of Argentina*. Berkeley, CA: University of California Press.

Arendt, H. (1994). *Eichmann in Jerusalem: A report on the banality of evil*. New York: Penguin. (Original work published in 1963).

Ashmore, R. D., Jussim, L., Wilder, D., & Heppen, J. (2001). Conclusion: Toward a social identity framework for intergroup conflict. In R. D. Ashmore, L. Jussim, & D. Wilder (Eds.), *Social identity, intergroup conflict, and conflict reduction* (pp. 213–249). Oxford: Oxford University Press.

Bandura, A. (1999). Moral disengagement in the perpetration of inhumanities. *Personality and Social Psychology Review, 3*, 193–209.

Barkan, E. (2003). Genocides of indigenous peoples: Rhetoric of human rights. In G. Gellately & B. Kiernan (Eds.), *The specter of genocide: Mass murder in historical perspective* (pp. 117–139). Cambridge, UK: Cambridge University Press.

Bouvard, M. G. (1994). *Revolutionizing motherhood: The mothers of the Plaza de Mayo*. Wilmington, DE: SR Books.

Brewer, M. B. (2001). Ingroup identification and intergroup conflict: When does ingroup love become outgroup hate? In R. D. Ashmore, L. Jussim, & D. Wilder (Eds.), *Social identity, intergroup conflict, and conflict reduction* (pp. 17–41). Oxford: Oxford University Press.

Browning, C. R. (1998). *Ordinary men: Reserve police battalion 101 and the final solution in Poland*. New York: Harper Perennial.

Browning, C. R. (2004). *The origins of the final solution: The evolution of Nazi Jewish policy, September 1939-March 1942*. Lincoln: University of Nebraska Press.

Cave, A. A. (2008). Genocide in the Americas. In D. Stone (Ed.), *The historiography of genocide* (pp. 273–295). Hampshire, UK: Palgrave Macmillan.

Churchill, W. (1997). *A little matter of genocide: Holocaust and denial in the Americas, 1492 to the present*. San Francisco: City Lights Books.

Churchill, W. (2004). *Kill the Indian, save the man: The genocidal impact of American Indian residential schools*. San Francisco: City Lights Books.

Cohen, S. (2001). *States of denial: Knowing about atrocities and suffering*. Cambridge, UK: Polity Press.

Curthoys, A., & Docker, J. (2008). Defining genocide. In D. Stone (Ed.), *The historiography of genocide* (pp. 9–41). Hampshire, UK: Palgrave Macmillan.

Danner, M. (1994). *The massacre at El Mozote*. New York: Vintage.

Danner, M. (2004). *Torture and truth: America, Abu Ghraib, and the war on terror*. New York: New York Review Books.

Des Forges, A. (1999). *Leave none to tell the story: Genocide in Rwanda*. New York: Human Rights Watch.

Erikson, E. H. (1968). *Identity: Youth and crisis*. New York: Norton.

Fein, H. (1993). *Genocide: A sociological perspective*. London: Sage.

Fisher, J. (1989). *Mothers of the disappeared*. Boston: South End Press.

Gourevitch, P. (1998). *We wish to inform you that tomorrow we will be killed with our families: Stories from Rwanda*. New York: Picador.

Gourevitch, P., & Morris, E. (2008). *Standard operating procedure*. New York: Penguin.

Grayling, A. C. (2006). *Among the dead cities: The history and moral legacy of the WWII bombing of civilians in Germany and Japan*. New York: Walker.

Haslam, N. (2006). Dehumanization: An integrative review. *Personality and Social Psychology Review, 10*, 252–264.

Hulsizer, M. R., Monro, G. D., Fagerlin, A., & Taylor, S. P. (2004). Molding the past: Biased assimilation of historical information. *Journal of Applied Social Psychology, 34*, 1048–1074.

Jacoby, K. (2008). "The broad platform of extermination": Nature and violence in the nineteenth century North American borderlands. *Journal of Genocide Research, 10*, 249–267.

Kelman, H. C. (2001). The role of national identity in conflict resolution: Experiences from Israeli–Palestinian problem-solving workshops. In R. D. Ashmore, L. Jussim, & D. Wilder (Eds.), *Social identity, intergroup conflict, and conflict reduction* (pp. 187–212). Oxford: Oxford University Press.

Khalidi, R. (1997). *Palestinian identity: The construction of modern national consciousness*. New York: Columbia University Press.

Kiernan, B. (2007). *Blood and soil: A world history of genocide and extermination from Sparta to Darfur*. New Haven, CT: Yale University Press.

Kuper, L. (1981). *Genocide: Its political use in the twentieth century*. New Haven, CT: Yale University Press.

Lawrence, B. (Ed.) (2005). *Messages to the world: The statements of Osama bin Laden*. London: Verso.

Lemkin, R. (1944). *Axis rule in occupied Europe*. Washington, DC: Carnegie Endowment.

Loewen, J. W. (1995). *Lies my teacher told me: Everything your American history textbook got wrong*. New York: Touchstone.

Maalouf, A. (2001). *In the name of identity: Violence and the need to belong*. New York: Arcade.

Mamdani, M. (2001). *When victims become killers: Colonialism, nativism, and the genocide in Rwanda*. Princeton, NJ: Princeton University Press.

Mann, M. (2005). *The dark side of democracy: Explaining ethnic cleansing*. Cambridge, UK: Cambridge University Press.

Manz, B. (2004). *Paradise in ashes: A Guatemalan journey of courage, terror, and hope*. Berkeley, CA: University of California Press.

Markusen, E., & Kopf, D. (1995). *The Holocaust and strategic bombing: Genocide and total war in the twentieth century*. Boulder, CO: Westview.

Mayer, J. (2008). *The dark side: The inside story of how the war on terror turned into a war on American ideals*. New York: Doubleday.

McDonnell, M. A., & Moses, A. D. (2005). Raphael Lemkin as historian of genocide in the Americas. *Journal of Genocide Research, 7*, 501–529.

McGowan, D., & Ellis, M. H. (Eds.). (1998). *Remembering Deir Yassin: The future of Israel and Palestine*. Brooklyn: Olive Branch Press.

Mellibovsky, M. (1997). *Circle of love over death: Testimonies of the mothers of the Plaza de Mayo*. Willimantic, CT: Curbstone Press.

Moghaddam, F. M. (2006). *From the terrorists' point of view: What they experience and why they come to destroy*. Westport, CT: Praeger Security International.

Morris, B. (1987). *The birth of the Palestinian refugee problem, 1947–1949*. Cambridge, UK: Cambridge University Press.

Moshman, D. (2004a). False moral identity: Self-serving denial in the maintenance of moral self-conceptions. In D. K. Lapsley & D. Narvaez (Eds.), *Moral development, self, and identity* (pp. 83–109). Mahwah, NJ: Erlbaum.

Moshman, D. (2004b). Theories of self and theories as selves: Identity in Rwanda. In C. Lightfoot, C. Lalonde, & M. Chandler (Eds.), *Changing conceptions of psychological life* (pp. 183–206). Mahwah, NJ: Erlbaum.

Moshman, D. (2005). Genocidal hatred: Now you see it, now you don't. In R. J. Sternberg (Ed.), *The psychology of hate* (pp. 185–209). Washington, DC: American Psychological Association.

Moshman, D. (2007). Us and them: Identity and genocide. *Identity, 7*, 115–135.

Moshman, D. (2008). Conceptions of genocide and perceptions of history. In D. Stone (Ed.), *The historiography of genocide* (pp. 71–92). Hampshire, UK: Palgrave Macmillan.

Moshman, D. (2009). *Liberty and learning: Academic freedom for teachers and students*. Portsmouth, NH: Heinemann.

Moshman, D. (2011). *Adolescent rationality and development: Cognition, morality, and identity* (3rd ed.). New York: Psychology Press.

Pape, R. A. (2005). *Dying to win: The strategic logic of suicide terrorism*. New York: Random House.

Pappe, I. (2004). *A history of modern Palestine: One land, two peoples*. Cambridge, UK: Cambridge University Press.

Pappe, I. (2006). *The ethnic cleansing of Palestine*. Oxford: Oneworld Publications.

Podeh, E. (2002). *The Arab–Israeli conflict in Israeli history textbooks, 1948–2000*. Westport, CT: Bergin & Garvey.

Postmes, T., & Jetten, J. (Eds.). (2006). *Individuality and the group: Advances in social identity*. London: Sage.

Powell, C. (2007). What do genocides kill? A relational conception of genocide. *Journal of Genocide Research, 9*, 527–547.

Sanford, V. (2003). *Buried secrets: Truth and human rights in Guatemala*. Hampshire, UK: Palgrave Macmillan.

Sanford, V. (2008). !Si hubo genocidio en Guatemala! Yes! There was genocide in Guatemala. In D. Stone (Ed.), *The historiography of genocide* (pp. 543–576). Hampshire, UK: Palgrave Macmillan.

Schwartz, S. J., Dunkel, C. S., & Waterman, A. S. (2009). Terrorism: An identity theory perspective. *Studies in Conflict & Terrorism, 32*, 1–23.

Sen, A. (2006). *Identity and violence: The illusion of destiny*. New York: Norton.

Sereny, G. (1983). *Into that darkness: An examination of conscience*. New York: Vintage.

Shaw, M. (2007). *What is genocide?* Cambridge, UK: Polity.

Stannard, D. E. (1992). *American holocaust: The conquest of the New World*. Oxford: Oxford University Press.

Stanton, G. H. (2004). Could the Rwandan genocide have been prevented? *Journal of Genocide Research, 6*, 211–228.

Staub, E. (2001). Individual and group identities in genocide and mass killing. In R. D. Ashmore, L. Jussim, & D. Wilder (Eds.), *Social identity, intergroup conflict, and conflict reduction* (pp. 159–184). Oxford: Oxford University Press.

Straus, S. (2006). *The order of genocide: Race, power, and war in Rwanda*. Ithaca, NY: Cornell University Press.

Straus, S. (2008). The historiography of the Rwandan genocide. In D. Stone (Ed.), *The historiography of genocide* (pp. 517–542). Hampshire, UK: Palgrave Macmillan.

United Nations General Assembly Resolution 96 (I), "The Crime of Genocide," Fifty-fifth plenary meeting, 11 December 1946.

Waller, J. (2002). *Becoming evil: How ordinary people commit genocide and mass killing*. Oxford: Oxford University Press.

Weitz, E. D. (2003). *A century of genocide: Utopias of race and nation*. Princeton, NJ: Princeton University Press.

Woolf, L. M., & Hulsizer, M. R. (2005). Psychosocial roots of genocide: Risk, prevention, and intervention. *Journal of Genocide Research, 7,* 101–128.

Zimbardo, P. (2007). *The Lucifer effect: Understanding how good people turn evil*. New York: Random House.

Epilogue: What's Next for Identity Theory and Research?

Seth J. Schwartz, Vivian L. Vignoles, and Koen Luyckx

This handbook has brought together, for the first time, several different lines of identity theory and research. Indeed, as outlined in the introductory chapter, our goal has been to map the landscape of identity studies and to provide expert reviews of various areas of this landscape. In doing so, we have begun to answer some important questions about identity—but we have also raised new ones. Hopefully, we have also created exciting integrative possibilities for the field as it moves forward. Although it is impossible for any edited volume to cover all of the identity-related perspectives that have been advanced, we believe that we have surveyed a wide range of models and have captured much of the diversity within the field of identity studies.

We, the editors, have learned an incredible amount from editing this book. The richness and diversity within the field of identity studies is staggering—which offers both a tremendous challenge and a tremendous opportunity. We continue to believe that integration is both possible and desirable among the many perspectives presented in this book. Yet, it is important to create an integrative framework that can genuinely give space to the insights available from each perspective, rather than forcing diverse perspectives into an overly narrow and restrictive synthesis. With this in mind, in this closing chapter, we revisit some of the key divisions in the literature that we identified at the beginning of the book. We consider how far we have come, as well as what remains to be done in order to facilitate the integration that we have envisioned.

Issue 1: Identity as a Multilevel Construct

Operationalizing "identity" is not an easy task. To truly capture the complexity of this construct, we must move beyond isolated sub-disciplines, put forward integrative theoretical propositions, and design innovative research studies that capture multiple components and processes of identity. For example, Umaña-Taylor (Chapter 33, this volume) illustrates how two prominent and largely separate perspectives on identity—the neo-Eriksonian approach and the social identity approach—actually complement one another well and can be used together to provide a much fuller understanding of the dynamics of ethnic identity than would be possible using either perspective on its own. To illustrate the possibilities for further integration of this kind, one might consider the role of identity in the workplace. On the one hand, Skorikov and Vondracek (Chapter 29, this volume) examine occupational identity at the level of the individual person—who am I as a worker, and where am I going in my working life? On the other hand, Haslam and Ellemers (Chapter 30, this volume) address the domain of work by viewing the workplace as a context

S.J. Schwartz (✉)
Department of Epidemiology and Public Health, Leonard
M. Miller School of Medicine, University of Miami,
Miami, FL, USA
e-mail: sschwartz@med.miami.edu

S.J. Schwartz et al. (eds.), *Handbook of Identity Theory and Research*,
DOI 10.1007/978-1-4419-7988-9, © Springer Science+Business Media, LLC 2011

for group activity. These perspectives highlight differing components of a single domain of life—the workplace—and as such, the potential may exist for integrating them into a larger model of how individuals choose careers and, at the same time, how group dynamics in the work context determine the effectiveness of leadership, feelings of motivation, and perceptions of stress among employees. Both the "inner" (choosing a career) and "outer" (workplace dynamics) worlds of work are important, and integrating them might indeed be important in helping individuals to develop a work identity—both in terms of the type of work one pursues and in terms of the effectiveness with which that work is performed.

The workplace is only one example of how exciting, innovative, and practically useful ideas can be pursued, based on bringing together diverse perspectives on identity. The issue of international migration—which is quite polarizing and divisive in many countries—can also be viewed from both "inner" and "outer" perspectives. That is, the phenomenon that we call "migration" is comprised of the experiences and views of the individual migrant, the "culture" (defined in many different ways) of the migrant group, and the ways in which the migrant group interacts with—and is perceived by—the receiving society. As such, chapters in this volume by Huynh, Nguyen, and Benet-Martínez (Chapter 35: the inner experience of the migrant person), Stepick, Dutton Stepick, and Vanderkooy (Chapter 37: the ways in which the choices available to individual migrants are constrained by the group to which they belong), and both Schildkraut (Chapter 36) and Licata et al. (Chapter 38: ways in which the receiving society views and interacts with migrant groups) suggest exciting directions in which the study of migration can be extended and expanded. How are the migrant's sense of her/himself, group memberships, and relations with other people affected by the interplay among these various identity aspects and processes? These diverse perspectives, and their potential integration, suggest that the study of international migration is far more complex than is often portrayed in both academic and lay discourse.

Issue 2: Interplay of Short- and Long-Term Processes

Another important direction for integration involves exploring the links between short-term (e.g., moment-to-moment, daily variation) and long-term (e.g., across a span of months or years) identity processes (e.g., Klimstra et al., 2010). Short-term approaches, such as analyzing contextual shifts in the salience of personal and social identities (Spears, Chapter 9, this volume), the way individuals position themselves in conversations (Bamberg, De Fina, & Schiffrin, Chapter 8, this volume), or the ways in which people defend against threats to their self-esteem (Gregg, Sedikides, & Gebauer, Chapter 14, this volume), may represent the "building blocks" that comprise longer-term developmental trajectories in the development of self. The minute-by-minute, hour-by-hour, and day-by-day transactions in which one engages may bring about changes in identity exploration or commitment that may "add up" over longer periods of time (e.g., Luyckx, Schwartz, Goossens, Beyers, & Missotten, Chapter 4, this volume). And such changes in identity processes over longer periods of time may, in turn, represent the building blocks from which individuals construct an overall life story (see McAdams, Chapter 5, this volume). So the ways in which time is conceptualized within the study of identity allow for integration of different perspectives that focus on different timescales (Lichtwarck-Aschoff, van Geert, Bosma, & Kunnen, 2008).

Issue 3: Identity Discovery and Identity Construction

In the introductory chapter, we raised the issue of whether identity is discovered, personally constructed, or socially constructed. A number of chapters in this book addressed this issue (e.g., for self-discovery, Soenens & Vansteenkiste, Chapter 17, and Waterman, Chapter 16; for personal construction, Berzonsky, Chapter 3; and for social construction, Bamberg, De Fina, &

Schiffrin, Chapter 8). To address empirically the issue of how identity comes into being, innovative methodologies may need to be developed. A number of issues need to be considered regarding how these methodologies might be created. First, we are somewhat skeptical of the value of relying straightforwardly on individuals' self-reports of the extent to which they have discovered their "true selves" (e.g., Waterman, Chapter 16, this volume). Individuals may not be able to distinguish, or they may even be motivated to avoid considering objectively, whether the "true self" that they are experiencing existed prior to its discovery or whether in reality they are experiencing a sense of fit and authenticity with a sense of self that they have constructed. Experimental methods, such as those used in social psychology, may be useful in determining the extent to which individuals are aware of precisely *what* they are discovering (cf. Schlenker & Weigold, 1990). For example, one might randomly assign participants to conditions where they receive descriptions of themselves that they are encouraged to believe are "true" or "authentic," when actually these are known to be either biased or random. If such an experimental manipulation is successful in prompting individuals to report feelings of self-discovery, then this could suggest that people's experiences of true self are in fact personally or socially constructed—or at least that this can sometimes be the case.

It may also be useful to conduct qualitative (narrative or discursive) studies to understand better how people experience the processes involved in self-construction and self-discovery. Such studies might utilize structured interview measures, similar to those that have been used to assess identity status (e.g., Marcia & Archer, 1993). A set of questions would be devised, such as "How did you come to know who you are?" and "Do you feel that you have discovered who you really are—and if so, how did you do this?" Such questions would allow individuals to describe their experiences of personal self-construction and self-discovery and to answer the question of *how* individuals come to realize, or feel, that they have discovered their "true" selves.

Future research must also explore in greater depth the interplay between personal and social processes of identity construction. This is connected to what Côté and Levine (2002) have labeled the "structure-agency debate" within sociology: how much of individual behavior is the result of free choice versus contextual constraint? As an interesting example of how this might be addressed, consider the construct of "commitment" as defined within the neo-Eriksonian (Kroger & Marcia, Chapter 2, this volume; Luyckx et al., Chapter 4, this volume) and symbolic interactionist (Serpe & Stryker, Chapter 10, this volume) perspectives. Within the neo-Eriksonian approach, commitment is typically taken to imply an individual's conscious decision to adhere to a specific set of goals, values, and beliefs (Bosma & Kunnen, 2001). Seemingly in contrast, within symbolic interactionism, commitment refers to a person's occupying a specific social structural position that will tend to prescribe certain identities and behaviors and proscribe others (Stryker, 2003). At first blush, neo-Eriksonian commitment and symbolic interactionist commitment look like radically different constructs, despite the shared name. Yet, on closer inspection, there may be a lot more commonality between the processes underlying these constructs than at first appears. From a neo-Eriksonian perspective, a person may form a commitment largely based on social contextual influences or even pressures—not so different from the symbolic interactionist concept. Similarly, from a symbolic interactionist perspective, a person may enter willingly into a social structural position of commitment—for example, by starting a new job or getting married—which might be viewed in neo-Eriksonian terms as the behavioral component of a personally endorsed commitment. So agency operates within the constraints of structure while, at least to some extent, agency can help to determine the structural position in which individuals find themselves. Thus, the difference between the two concepts of "commitment" arguably turns out to be a difference of emphasis, rather than a difference of kind.

An important direction for future work, then, is to situate agency-based methodological approaches to identity (e.g., Schwartz, Côté, & Arnett, 2005) within the larger auspices of methodologies drawn from the symbolic interactionist and other role-based perspectives. For example, Bosma and Kunnen (2001) and Phillips and Pittman (2003) have suggested that contextual factors, such as socioeconomic status and cultural expectations, constrain the potential identity alternatives that are available for the person to select (see also Oyserman & James, Chapter 6, this volume). Ethnographic methodologies—as well as multilevel studies that study both individual and contextual variables—should be used to explore the ways in which contextual processes promote or inhibit the range of identity elements and positions from which one can choose (see the next section for an example of this approach). Additionally, the concept of "individuals as producers of their own development" (Lerner & Busch-Rossnagel, 1981) might be invoked, perhaps through narrative or discursive analyses, to examine the ways in which the commitments that individuals intentionally enact may subsequently become structural roles that then constrain the range of identity commitments that can be enacted at a later time. For example, entering into marriage and becoming a parent may contraindicate certain career moves that require a great deal of flexibility and traveling. Interdisciplinary, cross-perspective work is necessary to examine the processes involved in the interplay between explicit and implicit commitments.

Issue 4: Multiple Methodologies

In addressing these complex theoretical issues, much could be gained from the combined use of qualitative and quantitative methods. Of course, this is not a new idea (see, e.g., Bryman, 1988; Denzin, 1978; Flick, 1992; Reicher, 1994). For example, some have suggested a circular movement between the two methodological approaches: qualitative analyses might be used to explore new and complex phenomenon, leading to the generation of more sophisticated hypotheses for subsequent quantitative testing, and then further qualitative analyses might be conducted to explore surprising or unexplained results from the quantitative analysis, etc. But, although many writers have called for mixed-method research on identity processes, such research in the identity studies field remains relatively scarce (for exceptions, see Rodriguez, Schwartz, & Whitbourne, 2010; Verkuyten, 2005). Admittedly, mixed method research is difficult, because each method requires detailed training and experience (e.g., inferential statistics versus grounded-theory methods), and qualitative and quantitative methods require different sets of skills. Nevertheless, a good first step would be for quantitative-based researchers to read and seriously consider what they can learn from qualitative identity research, and vice versa.

As an example of this latter approach, Pehrson, Vignoles, and Brown (2009; see also Licata, Sanchez-Mazas, & Green, Chapter 38, this volume) conducted a quantitative analysis to test a prediction that they had derived originally from critical discourse theory (Parker, 1992; see also Bamberg et al., Chapter 8, this volume). A key theoretical idea underlying their study was that macro-level ideological discourses (in this case, particular social constructions of nationhood) can make certain identity positions easier to occupy and others less so (in this case, how easy it is to be strongly identified with one's nation while simultaneously espousing positive attitudes toward immigrants). In a multilevel analysis of survey data from 31 nations, they found support for this prediction. Specifically, in those nations where national membership was defined to a greater extent in terms of shared language, they found that national identification was correlated with negative attitudes to immigrants (in these nations, either one could identify with the nation, or one could have a positive attitude to immigrants), whereas in those nations where national membership was defined in terms of shared citizenship, no such correlation was found (in these nations, the discursive climate made it easier to identify strongly and yet also express positive attitudes toward immigrants).

This study, along with Verkuyten's (2005) pairing of discursive and experimental approaches, illustrates ways in which qualitative and quantitative approaches can be used together to develop and test broader and more sophisticated theoretical propositions. And, given that methodological approaches are often associated with specific theoretical worldviews and with certain types of research questions, mixed-method studies provide exciting possibilities for integration. Through such combined qualitative–quantitative lines of research, we can achieve the best of both worlds—drawing on the strengths, and compensating for the weaknesses, of both methodological approaches.

Concluding Remarks

In closing, this handbook represents one of the first steps in—and hopefully it will be an important catalyst for—a coming together of the various currents of identity theory and research. Such an integration, extension, and expansion of current work may be the most effective response to critics such as Brubaker and Cooper (2000) and Gergen (1991), who have asserted that identity represents a "catch-all" term for anything related to the self. We hope to have clarified our conceptions of what identity is, and what it is not—as well as delineating the various dimensions of identity and how they fit together to create the whole that is the person, the relationship, the group, and the society. However, much work remains to be done, and it is important for future theoretical and empirical efforts to draw from a variety of fields, disciplines, and perspectives including and even beyond those in this handbook (see also Wetherell & Mohanty, 2010). It is our hope that the collection of chapters in this book inspires a new, integrative, and expansive line of identity theory and research.

References

Bosma, H. A., & Kunnen, E. S. (2001). Determinants and mechanisms in ego identity development: A review and synthesis. *Developmental Review, 21,* 39–66.

Brubaker, R., & Cooper, F. (2000). Beyond "identity". *Theory and Society, 29,* 1–47.

Bryman, A. (1988). *Quantity and quality in social research.* London: Routledge.

Côté, J. E., & Levine, C. G. (2002). *Identity formation, agency, and culture: A social-psychological synthesis.* Mahwah, NJ: Lawrence Erlbaum Associates.

Denzin, N. K. (1978). *The research act: A theoretical introduction to sociological methods* (2nd ed.). New York: McGraw-Hill.

Flick, U. (1992). Triangulation revisited: Strategy of validation or alternative? *Journal for the Theory of Social Behaviour, 22,* 175–197.

Gergen, K. J. (1991). *The saturated self: Dilemmas of identity in contemporary life.* New York: Basic.

Klimstra, T. A., Luyckx, K., Hale, W. W., III, Frijns, T., van Lier, P. A. C., & Meeus, W. H. J. (2010). Short-term fluctuations in identity: Introducing a micro-level approach to identity formation. *Journal of Personality and Social Psychology, 99,* 191–202.

Lerner, R. M., & Busch-Rossnagel, N. A. (1981). Individuals as producers of their development: Conceptual and empirical bases. In R. M. Lerner & N. A. Busch-Rossnagel (Eds.), *Individuals as producers of their development: A life-span perspective* (pp. 1–36). New York: Academic Press.

Lichtwarck-Aschoff, A., van Geert, P., Bosma, H., & Kunnen, S. (2008). Time and identity: A framework for research and theory formation. *Developmental Review, 28,* 370–400.

Marcia, J. E., & Archer, S. L. (1993). Identity status interview: Late adolescent college form. In J. E. Marcia, A. S. Waterman, D. R. Matteson, S. L. Archer, & J. L. Orlofsky (Eds.), *Ego identity: A handbook for psychosocial research* (pp. 303–318). New York: Springer-Verlag.

Parker, I. (1992). *Discourse dynamics: Critical analysis for social and individual psychology.* London: Routledge.

Pehrson, S., Vignoles, V. L., & Brown, R. (2009). National identification and anti-immigrant prejudice: Individual and contextual effects of national definitions. *Social Psychology Quarterly, 72,* 24–38.

Phillips, T. M., & Pittman, J. F. (2003). Identity processes in poor adolescents: Exploring the linkages between economic disadvantage and the primary task of adolescence. *Identity: An International Journal of Theory and Research, 3,* 115–129.

Reicher, S. (1994). Particular methods and general assumptions. *Journal of Community and Applied Social Psychology, 4*(3), 293–303.

Rodriguez, L., Schwartz, S. J., & Whitbourne, S. K. (2010). American identity revisited: The relation between national, ethnic, and personal identity in a multiethnic sample of emerging adults. *Journal of Adolescent Research, 25*, 324–349.

Schlenker, B. R., & Weigold, M. F. (1990). Self-consciousness versus self-presentation: Being autonomous versus appearing autonomous. *Journal of Personality and Social Psychology, 59*, 820–828.

Schwartz, S. J., Côté, J. E., & Arnett, J. J. (2005). Identity and agency in emerging adulthood: Two developmental routes in the individualization process. *Youth and Society, 37*, 201–229.

Stryker, S. (2003). Whither symbolic interactionism? Reflections on a personal odyssey. *Symbolic Interaction, 26*, 95–109.

Verkuyten, M. (2005). Immigration discourses and their impact on multiculturalism: A discursive and experimental study. *British Journal of Social Psychology, 44*, 223–240.

Wetherell, M., & Mohanty, C. T. (Eds.) (2010). *The Sage handbook of identities*. London: Sage.

Author Index

Subject Index

Note: The letters 'f', 't' and 'n' following the locators refer to figures, tables and notes respectively.

Printed by Printforce, the Netherlands